Hillary Cahan
July 1988

# Foundations of Financial Management

# Foundations of Financial Management

**Stanley B. Block**
Texas American Bank/Fort Worth Chair of Finance
Texas Christian University

**Geoffrey A. Hirt**
Chairman of the Department of Finance
DePaul University

1987 Fourth Edition

**IRWIN**
Homewood, Illinois 60430

*Cover photo: Woodfin Camp & Associates,*
*Craig Aurness, Century City, Calif.*



ISBN 0-256-03622-5

Library of Congress Catalog Card No. 86–81794

*Printed in the United States of America*

3 4 5 6 7 8 9 0 K 4 3 2 1 0 9 8 7

# Preface

The fourth edition of *Foundations of Financial Management* provides a number of changes from the third edition while still maintaining the basic strengths. The authors remain strongly committed to presenting the concepts of finance in an enlightening and interesting manner. Because very careful treatment is given to conceptual material related to valuation, capital structure formulation, and risk-return considerations, the student is also given a very sound background in important aspects of the theory of finance.

The authors remain committed to enabling the student to gain a firmer grasp on material previously covered in accounting, but now translated into the financial decision-making process. The special chapter devoted to a review of accounting (Chapter 2) also includes considerations of current versus historical cost issues. Ex-students embarking on a successful career in finance, as well as potential employers, continue to emphasize the need for facility and confidence in the areas of financial analysis and planning. The authors concur.

Among the major changes in the fourth edition is a division of the previous Chapter 10, Valuation and Cost of Capital, into two chapters. The first of the two chapters deals exclusively with valuation and rates of return. The second chapter is centered around cost of capital. By expanding to two chapters, we are able to cover more material relating to valuation concepts. We have taken particular care to write the material on valuation so that it can be understood and easily applied by the student. It is no more or less difficult than other material in the book. The valuation chapter immediately follows time value of money so the student can put present value concepts to immediate application. The cost of capital chapter then follows the valuation material. It is easy to show that the cost of capital to the corporation is directly linked to the valuation and required rates of return of security holders. A number of texts divide up this material throughout different sections of a book: we find this can cause a continuity problem. In general, we feel that some of the most important changes in this fourth edition have come in the valuation/cost of capital section described above. While the presentation level has not changed, it is more complete.

Many readers stress the need to present real-world examples to support textual material. We have taken care to integrate the use of actual examples, particularly in the sections dealing with long-term financing and working capital management.

A number of contemporary factors and issues are also highlighted in the fourth edition. These include corporate restructuring and divestitures, leveraged buy-outs, the changing nature of the financial services industry, new forms of stock issuance (such as General Motors Class E and Class H common stock), the increased importance of corporate stock repurchases, and advances in computerized cash management. Attention is also given to such topics as shelf registration, floating rate and zero-coupon debt issue, and the Euromarket for securities.

The effects of Reagan administration policy are also woven into the coverage of the economic environment, and the authors remain sensitive to the impact of both inflation and disinflation on reported profits, cash flow, and valuation.

In terms of structure, the major parts of the book are the Introduction (goals and functions of financial management), Financial Analysis and Planning, Working Capital Management, The Capital Budgeting Process, Long-Term Financing, and Expanding the Perspective of Corporate Finance (mergers and international financial management). A short introductory essay precedes each section and serves as a guide for the material to follow. For example, in the part on capital budgeting, the interrelationship between the time value of money, valuation, the cost of capital, the decision process, and the goals of the firm are laid out for the reader.

The professor who wishes to revise the order of material coverage can easily accomplish that objective. For example, Part Four of the book (time value of money, valuation, cost of capital, etc.) can be presented toward the beginning of the course and working capital (or other topics) at a later point. The book covers virtually all topics; it is merely a question of the professor's preferred order of topical coverage. As is true of most introductory finance texts, it is almost impossible for the instructor to cover every topic so some early decisions must be made.

The material in the text is supported by an unusually large number of questions and problems, particularly in the financial analysis and capital budgeting areas. The problems begin at a very basic level and increase in complexity, with optional comprehensive problems at the end of many chapters. There are approximately 20 percent more problems in the fourth edition than in the third edition, with well over half the old problems rewritten. Many of the problems better reflect the changing corporate environment. Risk-return considerations also are given increased attention.

There are six other teaching support items in the overall package. The *Instructor's Manual* contains detailed solutions to all the problems at the end of the chapters as well as teaching notes or strategies for each of the 21 chapters. To further aid the professor, we provide a separate test bank of over 1,100 short-answer questions. This test bank is also available in a computerized format on floppy disk called *Computest*. There are a large number of Transparency Masters (listed in the *Instructor's Manual*) that can be used in the classroom. Also, an excellent student *Study Guide* has been developed by Dwight C. Anderson in which he outlines the chapters and presents and solves sample questions and problems.

Finally, there is a computer software package entitled, "A Financial Analyst's Spreadsheet Using Scratch Pad." It is tailor designed for the text with its own manual and disk. Please contact Richard D. Irwin or your representative if you are interested in seeing any of these support items.

We wish to thank those finance professors who have contributed directly to the preparation of the manuscript, particularly Tim Gallagher for his help in problem development and G. N. Naidu for his work in the area of international financial management.

For their valuable reviews and helpful comments, we are grateful to Eric Anderson, Dwight C. Anderson, Brian T. Belt, Joseph Bentley, William J. Bertin, Debela Birru, Rolf Christensen, Allan Conway, Laverne Cox, Fred Ebeid, Jim Gahlon, Tim Gallagher, John R. Hall, Charles Higgins, Stanley Jacobs, Bill Kitrell, Joseph Levitsky, Joe Lipscomb, John P. Listro, Paul Marciano, Michael Matukonis, Wayne E. McWee, Jerry D. Miller, John D. Markese, Joe Massa, John Meador, Harlan Platt, Roger Potter, Franklin Potts, Mark Sunderman, Robert Swanson, Mike Tuberose, Donald E. Vaughn, Gary Wells, Don Wort, and Ergun Yener. We also wish to thank Dimitrios Pachis, Peter R. Kensicki, Bernie J. Grablowsky, John H. Lewis, Heber Maulton, Coleen C. Pantalone, Chris Prestopino, Frederick Rommel, Abu Selimuddin, William Doyle Smith, Ezra Byler, and Joanne Sheridan. We further wish to express our appreciation to Dave Ritzwoller for his help in proofreading the manuscript and to John Bajkowski and Alexandra Vitoulkus for their help in material development. We also express our thanks to our respective institutions for their administrative support.

Finally, we are particularly grateful to our families for their patience and tolerance throughout the development of the fourth edition.

**Stanley B. Block**
**Geoffrey A. Hirt**

# Contents

## PART TWO
## Financial Analysis and Planning

## PART FIVE
## Long-Term Financing

# PART ONE

# Introduction

# 1 The Goals and Functions of Financial Management

The financial manager's contribution to directing the operations of the firm has become increasingly critical in the 1980s. Some have referred to the era we live in as the morning after the biggest credit binge in U.S. history. In a time of unpredictable economic turns, fluctuating interest rates, inflation and disinflation, painful shortages and excesses, and extreme optimism and pessimism, the chief financial officer must maintain the financial viability of the firm. As financial markets become more international, the chief financial officer must also manage the global financial affairs of the firm. The board of directors and the president look to the financial division to provide a precious resource—capital—and to manage it in an efficient and profitable fashion.

## The Field of Finance

The field of finance is closely related to economics and accounting, and financial managers need to have an understanding of the relationships between these fields. Economics provides a structure for decision making in such areas as risk analysis, pricing theory through supply and demand relationships, comparative return analysis, and many other important areas. Economics also provides the broad picture of the economic environment in which corporations are continually making decisions. A financial manager must understand the institutional structure of the Federal Reserve System, the commercial banking system, and the interrelationships between the various sectors of the economy. Economic variables, such as gross national product, industrial production, disposable income, unemployment, inflation, interest rates, and taxes (to name a few), must fit into the financial manager's decision model and be applied correctly. These terms will be presented throughout the text and integrated into the financial process.

Accounting is sometimes said to be the language of finance in that it provides financial data through income statements, balance sheets, and sources and uses of funds statements. The financial manager must know how to interpret and use these statements in the allocation of the firm's financial resources to generate the best return possible in the long run. Finance is the link that integrates economic theory with the numbers of accounting, and all corporate managers—whether in the area of production, sales, research, marketing, management, or long-run strategic planning—must know what it means to assess the financial performance of the firm.

Many students approaching the field of finance for the first time might wonder what career opportunities exist. For those who develop the necessary skills and training, job positions in the field include corporate financial officer, banker, stockbroker, financial analyst, portfolio manager, investment banker, financial consultant, or personal financial planner. As the student progresses through the text, he or she will become increasingly familiar with the important role of the various participants in the financial decision-making process. A financial manager addresses such varied issues as decisions on plant location, the raising of capital, or simply, how to get the highest return on x million dollars between five o'clock this afternoon and eight o'clock tomorrow morning. Training in finance has served as a stepping-stone to a number of the top corporate positions in the country.

## Evolution of Finance as a Field of Study

To appreciate and understand the shifting emphasis in finance as a field of study, some historical perspective is essential. We see a field that has matured with the passage of time.

At the turn of the century, finance emerged as a field separate from economics but still closely linked. The major focus of study reflected the developments of the time, namely the building of giant industrial corporations by Rockefeller, Carnegie, Du Pont, and others. A student of finance would have spent much time learning about the financial instruments that were essential to mergers and acquisitions.

With the development and implementation of antitrust legislation, corporate consolidations became less important, and more normal patterns of growth were emphasized. Attention shifted to stocks and bonds and other securities utilized for raising capital. The role of the investment banker or middleman in a security offering also received much attention. No doubt, the great bull market of the 1920s contributed to the emphasis in raising capital.

In the 1930s the shock of the Depression ushered in an era of conservatism, and attention shifted to such topics as preservation of capital, maintenance of liquidity, reorganization of financially troubled corporations, and the bankruptcy process. The federal government assumed a much larger role in regulating business through the Securities Act of 1933 and the Securities Exchange Act of 1934. A by-product of this regulation was the development of published data related to corporate performance. The groundwork was laid for the sophisticated analysis of corporate information that would take place in later decades.

The 1940s and early 1950s offered little new in the study or practice of corporate finance. However, in the mid-50s a major shift in emphasis took place. Up to that time, the study procedures of finance had been descriptive or definitional in nature. Furthermore, the orientation had been from the viewpoint of a third party or outsider looking in. This all changed in the mid-50s as a more analytical, decision-oriented approach began to evolve.

The first area of study to generate the newfound enthusiasm for decision-related analysis was capital budgeting.[1] The financial manager was presented with analytical techniques for allocating resources among the various assets of the firm. The enthusiasm spread to other decision-making areas of the firm—such as cash and inventory management, capital structure formulation, and dividend policy. The emphasis shifted from that of the outsider looking in to that of the financial manager

---

[1]A starting point was Joel Dean's *Capital Budgeting* (New York: Columbia University Press, 1951).

forced to make tough day-to-day decisions affecting the performance of the firm.

From the late 1960s through today, the emphasis of financial management has also sharply focused on risk–return relationships and the maximization of return for a given level of risk. This risk–return emphasis was accompanied by corporate implementation of portfolio management strategies. In an attempt to reduce risk, companies in the 1960s began to diversify their portfolio of assets into unrelated industries, thus creating conglomerates. High inflation from the 1970s to 1982 created low profitability and caused large increases in debt for many companies. Firms were forced to replace plant and equipment (at inflated prices) with borrowed money since they did not have the benefit of large earnings from operations. By 1981–82, this borrowing binge caught up with many companies, and the increased financial risk showed up in record numbers of corporate bankruptcies. By 1986, firms were emphasizing the return aspect of the risk–return trade-off; they did so by focusing on high-profit products while selling off their marginal and losing divisions. Such restructuring of assets resulted in many firms moving away from a strategy of conglomerate diversification to a more narrow focus on "doing what you do well, profitably." This shift toward the return side of the equation has been partially caused by increased international competition and the use of advanced technology in the production process. Accompanying these developments has been a sharpened focus on the financial objectives of the firm.

## Goals of Financial Management

One may suggest that the most important goal for financial management is to "earn the highest possible profit for the firm." Under this criterion, each decision would be evaluated on the basis of its overall contribution to the firm's earnings. While this seems to be a desirable approach, there are some serious drawbacks to profit maximization as the primary goal of the firm.

First, a change in profit may also represent a change in risk. A conservative firm that earned $1.25 per share may be a less desirable investment if its earnings per share increases to $1.50, but the risk inherent in the operation increases even more.

A second possible drawback to the goal of maximizing profit is that it fails to take into account the timing of the benefits. For example, if we could choose between the following two alternatives, we might be indifferent if our emphasis were solely on maximizing earnings.

| | Earnings per Share | | |
|---|---|---|---|
| | Period One | Period Two | Total |
| Alternative A . . . . . . . | $1.50 | $2.00 | $3.50 |
| Alternative B . . . . . . . | 2.00 | 1.50 | 3.50 |

Both investments would provide $3.50 in total earnings, but Alternative B is clearly superior because the larger benefits occur earlier. We could reinvest the difference in earnings for Alternative B one period sooner.

Finally, the goal of maximizing profit suffers from the almost impossible task of accurately measuring the key variable in this case, namely, "profit." As you will observe throughout the text, there are many different economic and accounting definitions of profit, each open to its own set of interpretations. Furthermore, new problems related to inflation and international currency transactions complicate the issue. Constantly improving methods of financial reporting offer some hope in this regard, but many problems remain.

## A Valuation Approach

While there is no question that profits are important, the key issue is how to use them in setting a goal for the firm. The ultimate measure of performance is not what we earned but how the earnings are *valued* by the investor. In making an analysis of the firm, the investor will also consider the risk inherent in the firm's operation, the time pattern over which the firm's earnings increase or decrease, the quality and reliability of reported earnings, and many other factors. The financial manager, in turn, must be sensitive to all of these considerations. He or she must question the impact of each decision on the firm's overall valuation. If a decision maintains or increases the firm's overall value, it is acceptable from a financial viewpoint; otherwise, it should be rejected. This principle is demonstrated throughout the text.

## Maximizing Stockholder Wealth

The broad goal of the firm can be brought into focus if we say that the financial manager should attempt to *maximize the wealth of the firm's shareholders* through achieving the highest possible value for the firm. This is not a simple task, since the financial manager cannot directly control the firm's stock price, but can only act in a way that is consistent with the desires of the shareholders in general. Since stock prices are affected by expectations of the future as well as by the economic environment, much of what affects stock prices is beyond management's direct control. Even firms with good earnings and favorable financial trends do not always perform well in a declining stock market over the short term.

The concern is not so much with daily fluctuations in stock value as with long-term wealth maximization. This can be a difficult task in light of changing investor expectations. In the 1950s and 1960s the investor emphasis was on maintaining rapid rates of earnings growth. In the 1970s and 1980s, investors have become more conservative, putting a premium on lower risk and, at times, high current dividend payments.

Does modern corporate management actually follow the goal of maximizing shareholder wealth as we have defined it? In many large corporations stock ownership is diffused and fragmented and management, with a relatively small ownership position, often controls policy. Under these circumstances, management may be more interested in maintaining its own tenure and protecting "private spheres of influence" than in maximizing stockholder wealth. For example, suppose the management of a corporation receives a tender offer to merge the corporation into a second firm; while this offer might be attractive to stockholders, it might be quite unpleasant to present management. Management is often more willing to satisfy, while maintaining the status quo, than to maximize.

The answer to this issue is twofold. First, in most cases "enlightened management" is aware that the only way to maintain its position over the long run is to be sensitive to shareholder concerns. Poor stock price performance relative to other companies often leads to undesirable takeovers and proxy fights for control. Second, management often has sufficient stock option incentives that motivate them to achieve market value maximization for their own benefit.

### Social Responsibility

Is our goal of stockholder wealth maximization consistent with a concern for social responsibility for the firm? In most instances the answer is yes. By adopting policies that maximize values in the market, the firm is able to attract capital, provide employment, and offer benefits to its community. This is the basic strength of the private enterprise system.

Nevertheless, certain socially desirable actions such as pollution control, equitable hiring practices, and fair pricing standards may at times be inconsistent with earning the highest possible profit or achieving maximum valuation in the market. For example, pollution control projects frequently offer a very low return. Does this mean that firms should not exercise social responsibility in regard to pollution control? The answer is no—but certain cost-increasing activities may have to be mandatory rather than voluntary, at least initially, to ensure that the burden falls equally over all business firms.

## Functions of Financial Management

Having examined the goals and objectives of financial management, let us turn our attention to the functions that it must perform. It is the responsibility of financial management to allocate funds to current and fixed assets, to obtain the best mix of financing alternatives, and to develop an appropriate dividend policy within the context of the firm's objectives. These functions are performed on a day-to-day basis as well as through infrequent approaches to the capital markets to acquire new funds. The daily activities of financial management include credit management, inventory control, and the receipt and disbursement of funds. Less routine functions encompass the sale of stocks and bonds and the establishment of a capital budgeting and dividend plan.

Figure 1–1
Functions of the financial manager

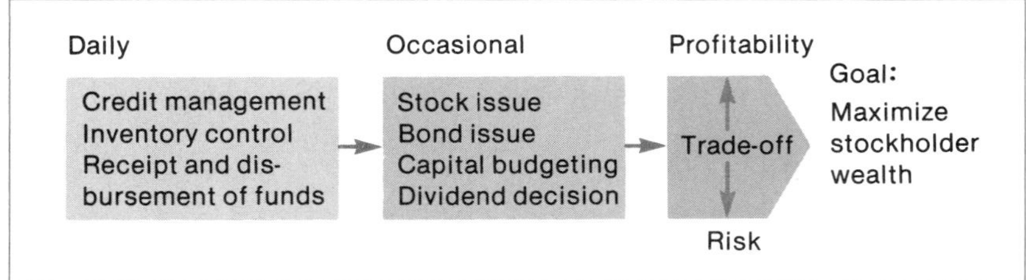


As indicated in Figure 1–1, all these functions are carried out while balancing the profitability and risk components of the firm.

The appropriate risk-return trade-off must be determined in order to maximize the market value of the firm for its shareholders. The risk-return decision will influence not only the operational side of the business (capital versus labor or product A versus product B) but also the financing mix (stocks versus bonds versus retained earnings).

## Forms of Organization

The finance function may be carried out within a number of different forms of organizations. Of primary interest are the sole proprietorship, the partnership, and the corporation.

**Sole proprietorship** This form of organization represents single-person ownership and offers the advantages of simplicity of decision making and low organizational and operating costs. Most small businesses with 1 to 10 employees are sole proprietorships. The major drawback of the sole proprietorship is that there is unlimited liability to the owner. In settlement of the firm's debts, he or she can lose not only the capital that has been invested in the business, but also personal assets. This drawback can be serious, and the student should realize that few lenders are willing to advance funds to a small business without a personal liability commitment.

The profits or losses of a sole proprietorship are taxed as though they belong to the individual owner. Thus, if a sole proprietorship makes $25,000, the owner will claim the profits in his or her tax return. (In the corporate form of organization the corporation first pays a tax on profits, and then the owners of the corporation pay a tax on any distributed profits.) Approximately 75 percent of the 10 million business firms in this country are organized as sole proprietorships, and these produce approximately 10 percent of the total revenue and 25 percent of the total profits of the U.S. economy.

**Partnership** This second form of organization is similar to a sole proprietorship except that there are two or more owners. Mulitiple ownership makes it possible to raise more capital and to share ownership responsibilities. Most partnerships are formed through an agreement between the participants, known as the *articles of partnership*, which specifies the ownership interest, the methods for distributing profits, and the means for withdrawing from the partnership. For taxing purposes, partnership profits or losses are allocated directly to the partners, and there is no double taxation, as there is in the corporate form.

Like the sole proprietorship, the partnership arrangement carries unlimited liability for the owners. While the partnership offers the advantage of *sharing* possible losses, it presents the problem of owners with unequal wealth having to absorb losses. If three people form a partnership with a $10,000 contribution each and the business loses $100,000, one wealthy partner may have to bear a disproportionate share of the losses if the other two partners do not have sufficient personal assets.

To circumvent this shared unlimited liability feature, a special form of partnership, called a *limited partnership*, can be utilized. Under this arrangement, one or more partners are designated general partners and have unlimited liability for the debts of the firm; other partners are designated limited partners and are only liable for their initial contribution. The limited partners are normally prohibited from being active in the management of the firm. You may have heard of limited partnerships in real estate syndications in which a number of limited partners are doctors, lawyers, and CPAs and there is one general partner who is a real estate professional. Not all financial institutions will extend funds to a limited partnership.

**Corporation** In terms of revenue and profits produced, the corporation is by far the most important type of economic unit. While only 17 percent of U.S. business firms are corporations, over 80 percent of sales and over 65 percent of profits can be attributed to the corporate form of organization. The corporation is unique—it is a legal entity unto itself. Thus the corporation may sue or be sued, engage in contracts, and acquire property. A corporation is formed through *articles of incorporation,* which specify the rights and limitations of the entity.

A corporation is owned by stockholders who enjoy the privilege of limited liability, meaning that their liability exposure is generally no greater than their initial investment.[2] A corporation also has a continual life and is not dependent on any one stockholder for maintaining its legal existence.

A key feature of the corporation is the easy divisibility of the ownership interest through the issuance of shares of stock. While it would be nearly impossible to have more than 50 or 100 partners in most businesses, a corporation may have more than a million shareholders. A current example of a firm with over 1 million stockholders is General Motors.

The shareholders' interests are ultimately managed by the corporation's board of directors. The directors, who may include key management personnel of the firm as well as outside directors not permanently employed by it, serve in a stewardship capacity and may be liable for the mismanagement of the firm or for the misappropriation of funds. Outside directors of large public corporations may be paid more than $10,000 a year to attend meetings and share in important decisions. For example, Eastman Kodak pays its outside directors approximately $12,000 per year, while IBM and General Motors pay more than $15,000 annually.[3]

Because the corporation is a separate legal entity, it reports and pays taxes on its *own* income. As previously mentioned, any remaining income that is paid to the stockholders in the form of dividends will require the payment of a second tax by the stockholders. One of the key disadvantages to the corporate form of organization is this potential double taxation of earnings.

There is, however, one way to circumvent the double taxation of a normal corporation and that is through formation of a Subchapter S

---

[2]An exception to this rule is made if they buy their stock at less than par value. Then they would be liable for up to the par value.

[3]"Compensation for Outside Directors," *Harvard Business Review* 57 (November–December 1979), pp. 18–28. Also corporate prospectuses.

corporation. With a Subchapter S corporation, the income is taxed as direct income to the stockholders and thus is taxed only once, as in a partnership. Nevertheless, the stockholders receive all the organizational benefits of a corporation, including limited liability. The Subchapter S designation, as amended by 1982 tax legislation, can apply to corporations with up to 35 stockholders.[4] Thus only relatively small entities can elect Subchapter S status.

Because of the all-pervasive impact of the corporation on our economy and because most growing businesses eventually become corporations, the effects of many decisions in this text are considered from the corporate viewpoint.

## Recent Economic Developments

A number of key issues of the late 1970s and 1980s are given special attention in the text. Even though inflation has been significantly reduced from double digits to the 3–4 percent range during the 1980s, leading economists and financial analysts now accept some degree of inflation as a way of life in the United States and throughout the world. A 3–4 percent inflation rate is still several times the average rate from 1925 to 1965. Inflation-induced profits of the late 1960s and 1970s are somewhat in the past, but the intelligent student should not ignore the lessons of inflated phantom profits and undervalued assets of the past two decades. The student should be equally aware of the benefits, drawbacks, and implications of disinflation (a slowing down of price increases). The problems and opportunities related to inflation and disinflation receive particular attention in the later discussion of financial analysis.

A second aspect of contemporary finance is the extreme reliance that financial managers have placed on the use of debt. Debt-to-asset ratios have moved from 25 percent to approximately 45 percent of assets in the last 20 years, and the typical firm's ability to cover its interest expenses has eroded. This is not a short-term, cyclical phenomenon but rather a slow, steady process that has taken place in good times as well as bad. While many firms that were formerly in financial trouble

[4]The 1982 legislation also eliminated restrictions on the type of income that could be earned by a Subchapter S corporation.

have recovered miraculously (Chrysler, for instance), other firms in industries such as farm equipment, steel, trucks, and oil well drilling equipment are suffering from low profitability, international competition, faltering domestic markets, and high debt.

Third, restructuring of the balance sheet is possibly one of the most important phenomena currently taking place in corporate America, and one of the results is an increase in the use of debt relative to ownership capital. Firms are repurchasing shares of common stock in the open market either because they do not have better investment opportunities (Exxon); because management thinks that the stock is underpriced (Ford, Amoco); or because management is trying to avoid an unfriendly takeover (Phillips Petroleum, Revlon, CBS).[5] The shares may be repurchased with excess cash or through the issuance of new debt. In 1985 Exxon bought back 46.6 million common shares worth $2.3 billion, Ford repurchased 20 million shares for $980 million, and Phillips Petroleum thwarted a takeover by T. Boone Pickens by repurchasing 81.5 million shares of stock valued at $4.1 billion.

Restructuring was not just confined to stock repurchases in the mid-1980s but also included mergers and acquisitions of gigantic proportions unheard of in other decades. Firms were buying or merging with companies in similar and related industries. Rather than just seeking risk reduction through diversification, firms were acquiring greater market share, brand name products, hidden asset values, or technology—or they were simply looking for size to help them "play the game" in an international arena. In the biggest of all combinations, Standard Oil of California acquired Gulf Oil in 1984 for $13.3 billion and, in the process, increased the firm's debt by billions of dollars and changed the company name to Chevron. Phillip Morris, the consumer products company that holds such brand names as Miller Beer and Phillip Morris cigarettes, acquired General Foods for $5.8 billion in a merger that expanded its existing market emphasis. On the other hand, General Motors went after technology by buying Electronic Data Systems (a computer services company, for $2.5 billion) and Hughes Aircraft (a huge defense and electronics company, for $5.8 billion). Many of these stories are covered in more detail in later chapters. You should also be

---

[5] The corporate repurchase of shares may also be viewed as an alternative to paying a cash dividend. This topic is covered more thoroughly in Chapter 18, Dividend Policy and Retained Earnings.

aware that some corporations have restructured their balance sheets by selling off (divesting) unprofitable or unwanted divisions over a period of time.

Finally, extreme volatility of interest rates has been a key factor in the recent economic environment. In 1969 corporations paid over 8 percent for bank funds. In 1972 the prime rate dropped to less than 5 percent—then spiraled to almost 12.5 percent in 1974. To the relief of many, the prime rate eventually fell to 6.25 percent in 1976. However, an upward movement began with the economic recovery of the late 1970s, and by the early 1980s, short-term interest rates were around the 20 percent range before beginning a sharp decline to less than 10 percent in 1986. These rates are portrayed in Figure 1–2 alongside the annual rates of inflation as measured by the consumer price index (CPI). In all years except 1975 the prime rate exceeded inflation. Notice that the difference between the prime rate and the inflation rate was very small from about 1970 to 1980, but when inflation began to subside in 1981 the difference was close to 6 percent. This may indicate that

**Figure 1–2**
**Prime rate* versus percent change in the consumer price index (CPI) (average annual rates)**

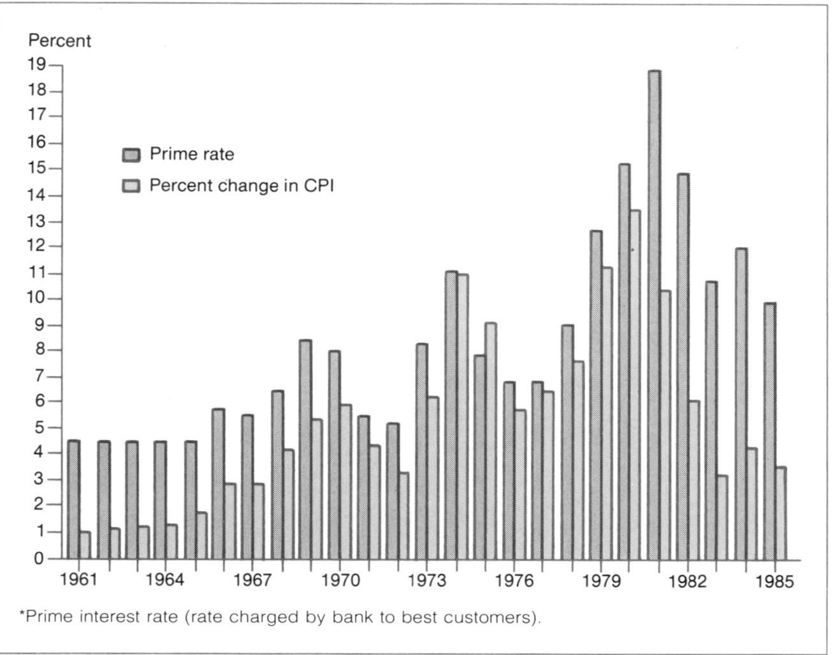


*Prime interest rate (rate charged by bank to best customers).

lenders do not believe inflation will stay at reasonable levels for good. It would be nice to get back to the 1 percent inflation rate of the early 1960s, but it might be prudent to wait awhile longer before we forget the lessons learned in the management of corporate assets under inflation.

## Format of the Text

The material in this text is covered under six major headings. The student progresses from the development of basic analytical skills in accounting and finance to the utilization of decision-making techniques in working capital management, capital budgeting, long-term financing, and other related areas. A total length of 21 chapters should make the text appropriate for one-semester coverage.

The student is given a thorough grounding in financial theory in a highly palatable and comprehensive fashion—with careful attention to definitions, symbols, and formulas. The intent is, above all, that the student develop a thorough understanding of the basic concepts in finance.

Although we prefer to cover the chapters in the order presented, other faculty have moved working capital management so that it follows Part Five. This permits covering the topics of time value of money, valuation, cost of capital, and capital budgeting earlier in the course.

### Parts

**1. Introduction** This section examines the goals and objectives of financial management. The present-day emphasis on decision making and risk management is stressed, with an update of significant events influencing the study of finance.

**2. Financial analysis and planning** The student is first given the opportunity to review the basic principles of accounting as they relate to finance (emphasis is placed on financial statements and funds flow). This review material, in Chapter 2, is optional—and the student may judge whether he or she needs this review before progressing through the section.

Additional material in this part includes a thorough study of ratio analysis, budget construction techniques, and the development of comprehensive pro forma statements. The effect of heavy fixed commitments, in the form of either debt or plant and equipment, is examined in a discussion of leverage.

**3. Working capital management** The techniques for managing the short-term assets of the firm and the associated liabilities are examined. The material is introduced in the context of risk–return analysis. The financial manager must constantly choose between liquid, low-return assets (perhaps marketable securities) and more profitable, less liquid assets (such as inventory). Sources of short-term financing are also considered.

**4. The capital budgeting process** The decision on capital outlays is among the most significant that a firm will have to make. In terms of study procedure, we attempt to carefully lock down "time value of money" calculations, then proceed to the valuation of bonds and stocks, emphasizing present-value techniques. The valuation chapter develops the traditional dividend valuation model and examines bond price sensitivity in response to discount rates and inflation. An appendix presents the supernormal dividend growth model, or what is sometimes called the "two-stage" dividend model. After careful grounding in valuation practice and theory, we move into an examination of the cost of capital and capital structure. The text then moves to the actual capital budgeting decision, making generous use of previously learned material and employing the concept of marginal analysis. The concluding chapter in this part covers risk–return analysis in capital budgeting, with a brief exposure to portfolio theory and a consideration of market value maximization.

**5. Long-term financing** The student is introduced to U.S. financial markets as they relate to corporate financial management. The student considers the sources and uses of funds in the capital markets—with coverage given to warrants and convertibles, as well as the more conventional methods of financing. The guiding role of the investment banker in the distribution of securities is also analyzed. Furthermore, the student is encouraged to think of leasing as a form of debt.

**6. Expanding the perspective of corporate finance** A chapter on corporate mergers considers external growth strategy and serves as an integrative tool to bring together such topics as profit management, capital budgeting, portfolio considerations, and valuation concepts. A second chapter on international financial management describes the growth of the international financial markets, the rise of multinational business, and the effects on corporate financial management. The issues discussed in these two chapters highlight corporate diversification and risk-reduction attempts prevalent in the 1970s and continuing well into the 1980s.

## List of Terms

**stockholder wealth maximization**
**sole proprietorship**
**partnership**
**inflation**
**restructuring**
**disinflation**
**prime rate**
**limited partnership**
**corporation**
**Subchapter S corporation**
**conglomerate**

## Discussion Questions

1. Some of the early concerns of financial management were related to preservation of capital, maintenance of liquidity, and reorganizations. Do you think these topics are still important in our current unpredictable economic environment?
2. How has the finance discipline changed since the 1940s and early 1950s?
3. What is meant by the goal of maximization of stockholder wealth? Why is profit maximization, by itself, an inappropriate goal?
4. Contrast the liability provisions for a sole proprietorship, a partnership, a limited partnership, and a corporation.
5. Why is the corporate form best suited to a large organization?

6. Why does the financial manager need to be concerned with inflation? With disinflation?

7. What are some ways in which corporations are restructuring their balance sheets and other related activities?

## Selected References

Anderson, Leslie P.; Vergil V. Miller; and Donald L. Thompson. *The Finance Function.* Scranton, Pa.: Intext, 1971.

Anthony, Robert N. "The Trouble with Profit Maximization." *Harvard Business Review* 38 (November–December 1960), pp. 126–34.

Branch, Ben. "Corporate Objectives and Market Performance." *Financial Management* 2 (Summer 1973), pp. 24–29.

Brennan, Michael J., and Eduardo S. Schwartz. "Regulation and Corporate Investment Policy." *Journal of Finance* 37 (May 1982), pp. 289–300.

*Business Conditions Digest.* U.S. Department of Commerce, December 1979.

"Compensation for Outside Directors." *Harvard Business Review* 57 (November–December 1979), pp. 18–28.

Davis, Keith. "Social Responsibility Is Inevitable." *California Management Review* 19 (Fall 1976), pp. 14–20.

Dean, Joel. *Capital Budgeting.* New York: Columbia University Press, 1951. "The Debt Economy." *Business Week,* October 12, 1974, p. 45.

Dewing, Arthur S. *The Financial Policy of Corporations,* 5th ed., vol. 1. New York: Ronald, 1953, chap. 1.

Donaldson, Gordon. "Financial Goals: Management vs. stockholders." *Harvard Business Review* 41 (May–June 1963), pp. 16–29.

Hearth, Douglas, and Janis K. Zaima. "Voluntary Corporate Divestiture and Value." *Financial Management* 13 (Spring 1984), pp. 10–16.

Hill, Lawrence W. "The Growth of the Corporate Finance Function." *Financial Executive* 44 (July 1976), pp. 38–43.

*Historical Chart Book.* Board of Governors of the Federal Reserve System, 1979.

Lewellen, Wilbur G. "Management and Ownership in the Large Firm." *Journal of Finance* 24 (May 1969), pp. 299–322.

Seitz, Neil. "Shareholder Goals, Firm Goals and Firm Financing Decisions." *Financial Management* 37 (Autumn 1982), pp. 20–26.

Solomon, Ezra. *The Theory of Financial Management*. New York: Columbia University Press, 1963, pp. 15–26.

Vance, Jack O. "The Changing Role of the Corporate Financial Executive." *Financial Executive* 31 (March 1963), pp. 27–29.

Weston, J. Fred. "Developments in Finance Theory." *Financial Management* 10 (Tenth Anniversary Issue, 1981), pp. 5–22.

# PART TWO

# Financial Analysis and Planning

## Introduction

In this day of ever-increasing pressures to "tell the truth" from the Securities and Exchange Commission, the Federal Trade Commission, and various investor and consumer groups, the presentation and understanding of financial data are critical. Furthermore, increasing complexities in the business environment mean that new methods of reporting the financial condition of the firm are certain to take place. The student must be well positioned to understand the old rules of the game and to appreciate new developments on the horizon.

In Chapter 2, we review some of the basic principles of accounting. The student should have a reasonable understanding of financial statements and related concepts before studying the more analytical material. Students with a strong background in accounting may choose to merely gloss over this material.

We then proceed to a study of company performance through ratio analysis in Chapter 3. The purpose of ratio analysis is to examine financial data on a relative basis. Net profit means very little unless it is compared to some other measure such as sales, total assets, or net worth in an appropriate ratio format. Net income of $100,000 offers little insight, but a ratio of net income to sales of 5 percent may suggest a great deal in comparison to past performance and other companies.

An important dimension in financial analysis is a consideration of the impact of inflation and disinflation on the financial fortunes of the firm. The authors present examples showing how changing prices may distort the normally reported income of the firm.

In Chapter 4, we shift the emphasis from "what was" to "what will be" as we go through the process of financial forecasting. To anticipate future financing requirements, the firm must determine what the income statement, balance sheet, and cash budget will look like for the planning period. In the process of financial forecasting, we are forced to make predictions about future sales, inventory levels, receivables, and other accounts, and then to combine our forecasts into a structured set of financial statements. Upon completion of Chapter 4, the student should have a better understanding not only of forecasting but also of all the elements that make up the financial structure of the firm.

As a last topic of consideration in Part Two, we look at management's use of leverage to magnify the results of the firm. By leverage, we mean the utilization of a high percentage of fixed assets or "fixed cost" debt in the management and operation of the firm. As indicated in Chapter 5, if we are able to achieve a high volume of operation, our fixed costs should allow for strong profitability as our revenues go up while much of our costs remain constant. At a low level of operation, perhaps in a recession, the opposite results will take place, and our heavy fixed costs could force us into bankruptcy. We must learn how to handle this two-edged sword in an effective fashion.

# 2 Review of Accounting

The language of finance flows logically from accounting. In order to ensure that the student is adequately prepared to study important financial concepts, we must lock in the preparatory material from the accounting area. Much of the early frustration suffered by students who have difficulty with finance can be overcome if such concepts as retained earnings, stockholders' equity, depreciation, and historical/replacement cost accounting are brought into focus.

In this chapter, we examine the three basic types of financial statements—the income statement, the balance sheet, and the sources and uses of funds statement—with particular attention paid to the interrelationships among these three measurement devices. As special preparation for the financial manager, we briefly examine income tax considerations affecting financial decisions.

## Income Statement

The income statement is the major device for measuring the profitability of a firm over a period of time. An example of the income statement is presented in Table 2–1 for the Kramer Corporation.

**Table 2–1**

KRAMER CORPORATION
Income Statement
For the Year Ended December 31, 1987

| | | |
|---|---|---|
| 1. | Sales | $2,000,000 |
| 2. | Cost of goods sold | 1,500,000 |
| 3. | Gross profits | 500,000 |
| 4. | Selling and administrative expense | 220,000 |
| 5. | Depreciation expense | 50,000 |
| 6. | Operating profit (EBIT)* | 230,000 |
| 7. | Interest expense | 20,000 |
| 8. | Earnings before taxes (EBT) | 210,000 |
| 9. | Taxes | 99,500 |
| 10. | Earnings after taxes (EAT) | 110,500 |
| 11. | Preferred stock dividends | 10,500 |
| 12. | Earnings available to common stockholders | $ 100,000 |
| 13. | Shares outstanding | 100,000 |
| 14. | Earnings per share | $1.00 |

*Earnings before interest and taxes.

First, note that the income statement covers a defined period of time, whether it be one month, three months, or a year. The statement is presented in a stair-step or progressive fashion so that we can examine the profit or loss after each type of expense item is deducted.

We start with sales and deduct cost of goods sold to arrive at gross profit. The $500,000 thus represents the difference between what we bought or manufactured our goods for and the sales price. We then subtract selling and administrative expense and depreciation from gross profit to determine our profit (or loss) purely from operations of $230,000.[1] It is possible for a company to enjoy a high gross profit margin (25–50 percent) but a relatively low operating profit because of heavy expenses incurred in marketing the product and managing the company.

Having obtained operating profit (essentially a measure of how efficient management is in generating revenues and controlling expenses),

[1] Depreciation was not treated as part of cost of goods sold in this instance, but rather as a separate expense. All or part of depreciation may be treated as part of cost of goods sold, depending on the circumstances.

we now adjust for revenues and expenses not related to operational matters. In this case we pay $20,000 in interest and arrive at earnings before taxes of $210,000. Our tax payments are $99,500, leaving aftertax income of $110,500.

## Return to Capital

Before proceeding further, we should note that there are three primary sources of capital—the bondholders, who received $20,000 in interest (item 7); the preferred stockholders, who will receive $10,500 in dividends (item 11); and the common stockholders. After the $10,500 dividend has been paid to the preferred stockholders, there will be $100,000 in earnings available to the common stockholders (item 12). In computing earnings per share, we must interpret this in terms of the number of shares outstanding. As indicated in item 13, there are 100,000 shares outstanding, so the $100,000 of earnings available to the common stockholders may be translated into earnings per share of $1. Needless to say, common stockholders are sensitive to the number of shares outstanding—the more shares, the lower the earnings per share. A corollary to this is that, before any new shares are issued, the financial manager must be sure they will eventually generate sufficient earnings to avoid reducing earnings per share.

The $100,000 of profit ($1 earnings per share) may be paid out to the common stockholders in the form of dividends or retained in the company for subsequent reinvestment. The reinvested funds theoretically belong to the common stockholders, who hope they will provide future earnings and dividends. In the case of the Kramer Corporation, we assume that $50,000 in dividends will be paid out to the common stockholders, with the balance retained in the corporation for their benefit. A short supplement to the income statement, a statement of retained earnings (see Table 2–2), usually indicates the disposition of earnings.[2]

We see that $50,000 has been added to previously accumulated earnings of $250,000.

---

[2]The statement may also indicate any adjustments to previously reported income as well as any restrictions on cash dividends.

**Table 2–2**

Statement of Retained Earnings
For the Year Ended December 31, 1987

| | |
|---|---|
| Retained earnings, balance, January 1, 1987 | $250,000 |
| Add: Earnings available to common stockholders, 1987 | 100,000 |
| Deduct: Cash dividends declared in 1987 | 50,000 |
| Retained earnings, balance, December 31, 1987 | 300,000 |

## Price–Earnings Ratio Applied to Earnings per Share

A concept utilized throughout the text is the price–earnings ratio. This refers to the multiplier applied to earnings per share to determine current value. In the case of the Kramer Corporation, earnings per share were $1. If the firm enjoyed a price–earnings ratio of 12, the market value of each share would be $12. The price–earnings ratio (or P/E ratio, as it is commonly called) is influenced by the earnings and the sales growth of the firm, the risk (or volatility in performance), the debt–equity structure of the firm, the dividend payment policy, the quality of management, and a number of other factors. Since companies have various levels of earnings per share, price–earnings ratios allow us to compare the relative market value of many companies based on $1 of earnings per share.

**Table 2–3**
**Price–earnings ratios for selected U.S. corporations**

| | | *P/E Ratio* | | | |
|---|---|---|---|---|---|
| *Corporation* | *Industry* | *Jan. 2 1976* | *Jan. 2 1980* | *Jan. 3 1983* | *Jan. 2 1986* |
| Exxon | International oil | 8 | 6 | 10 | 9 |
| Texas Utilities | Public utilities | 9 | 7 | 6 | 7 |
| CBS | Broadcasting | 11 | 7 | 12 | 18 |
| Gillette | Grooming aids | 11 | 6 | 9 | 14 |
| Halliburton | Oil service | 12 | 13 | 7 | 12 |
| Winn-Dixie | Retail | 14 | 8 | 11 | 14 |
| Eckerd Corp. | Drug stores | 15 | 9 | 14 | 14 |
| IBM | Computers | 17 | 12 | 15 | 16 |
| Upjohn | Ethical drugs | 18 | 10 | 10 | 19 |
| Digital Equipment | Computers | 24 | 10 | 20 | 21 |
| McDonald's | Restaurants | 26 | 9 | 10 | 16 |
| Standard & Poor's (500 Stock Index) | | 13 | 7 | 11 | 14 |

The P/E ratio indicates expectations about the future of a company. Firms expected to provide returns greater than those for the market in general with equal or less risk often have P/E ratios higher than the market P/E ratio. Expectations of returns and P/E ratios do change over time, as Table 2–3 illustrates.

Price–earnings ratios can be confusing at times. When a firm's earnings are dropping rapidly or perhaps even approaching zero, its stock price, though declining too, may not match the magnitude of falloff in earnings. This process can give the appearance of an increasing P/E ratio under adversity. This happens from time to time in the auto industry and other cyclical industries. For example, in 1983 General Motors was trading at a P/E of over 20 because of extremely modest earnings. At the time, the average P/E, as measured by the Standard & Poor's 500 Stock Index, was 11.

## Limitations of the Income Statement

The economist defines income as the change in real worth that takes place between the beginning and the end of a specified time period. To the economist, an increase in the value of a firm's land as a result of a new airport being built on adjacent property is an increase in the real worth of the firm and therefore represents income. Similarly, the elimination of a competitor might also increase the firm's real worth and therefore result in income in an economic sense. The accountant does not ordinarily employ such broad definitions. Accounting values are established primarily by actual transactions, and income that is gained or lost during a given period is a function of verifiable transactions. While the potential sales price of your property may go from $100,000 to $200,000 as a result of new developments in your area, your stockholders may only perceive a much smaller gain or loss from operations.

Also, as will be pointed out in Chapter 3, Financial Analysis, there is some flexibility in the reporting of transactions, so that similar events may result in differing measurements of income at the end of a time period. The intent of this section is not to criticize the accounting profession, for it is certainly among the best-organized, trained, and paid professions, but to alert students to imperfections already well recognized within the profession.

## Balance Sheet

The balance sheet indicates what the firm owns and how these assets are financed in the form of liabilities or ownership interest. While the income statement purports to show the profitability of the firm, the balance sheet delineates the firm's holdings and obligations. Together these statements are intended to answer two questions: How much did the firm make or lose, and what is a measure of its worth? A balance sheet for the Kramer Corporation is presented in Table 2–4.

Note that the balance sheet is a picture of the firm at a point in time —in this case December 31, 1987. It does not purport to represent the result of transactions for a specific month, quarter, or year, but rather is a cumulative chronicle of all transactions that have affected the corporation since its inception. In contrast, the income statement measures results only over a short, quantifiable period of time. Generally, balance sheet items are stated on an original cost basis rather than at present worth.

### Interpretation of Balance Sheet Items

Asset accounts are listed in order of liquidity. The first category of current assets covers items that may be converted to cash within one year (or within the normal operating cycle of the firm). A few items are worthy of mention. *Marketable securities* are temporary investments of excess cash. The value shown in the account is the lower of cost or current market value. *Accounts receivable* include an allowance for bad debts (based on historical evidence) to determine their anticipated collection value. *Inventory* may be in the form of raw material, goods in process, or finished goods, while *prepaid expenses* represent future expense items that have already been paid, such as insurance premiums or rent.

*Investments*, unlike marketable securities, represent a longer-term commitment of funds (at least one year). They may include stocks, bonds, or investments in other corporations. Frequently, the account will contain stock in companies that the firm is acquiring.

*Plant and equipment* is carried at original cost minus accumulated depreciation. Accumulated depreciation is not to be confused with the depreciation expense item indicated in the income statement in Table 2–1. Accumulated depreciation is the sum of all past and present

Table 2–4

KRAMER CORPORATION
Statement of Financial Position (Balance Sheet)
December 31, 1987

| *Assets* | | |
|---|---|---|
| Current assets: | | |
| Cash | | $ 40,000 |
| Marketable securities | | 10,000 |
| Accounts receivable | $ 220,000 | |
| Less: Allowance for bad debts | 20,000 | 200,000 |
| Inventory | | 180,000 |
| Prepaid expenses | | 20,000 |
| Total current assets | | 450,000 |
| Other assets: | | |
| Investments | | 50,000 |
| Fixed assets: | | |
| Plant and equipment, original cost | 1,100,000 | |
| Less: Accumulated depreciation | 600,000 | |
| Net plant and equipment | | 500,000 |
| Total assets | | $1,000,000 |
| *Liabilities and Stockholders' Equity* | | |
| Current liabilities: | | |
| Accounts payable | | $ 80,000 |
| Notes payable | | 100,000 |
| Accrued expenses | | 30,000 |
| Total current liabilities | | 210,000 |
| Long-term liabilities: | | |
| Bonds payable, 1995 | | 90,000 |
| Total liabilities | | 300,000 |
| Stockholders' equity: | | |
| Preferred stock, $100 par value, 500 shares | | 50,000 |
| Common stock, $1 par value, 100,000 shares | | 100,000 |
| Capital paid in excess of par (common stock) | | 250,000 |
| Retained earnings | | 300,000 |
| Total stockholders' equity | | 700,000 |
| Total liabilities and stockholders' equity | | $1,000,000 |

depreciation charges on currently owned assets, while depreciation expense is the current year's charge. If we subtract accumulated depreciation from the original value, the balance ($500,000) tells us how much of the original cost has not been expensed in the form of depreciation.

Total assets are financed through either liabilities or stockholders' equity. Liabilities represent financial obligations of the firm and move from current liabilities (due within a year) to longer-term obligations, such as bonds payable in 1995.

Among the short-term obligations, *accounts payable* represent amounts owed on open account to suppliers, while *notes payable* are generally short-term signed obligations to the banker or other creditors. An *accrued expense* is generated when a financial service has been provided or an obligation incurred and payment has not yet taken place. We may owe workers additional wages for services provided or the government taxes on earned income.

In the balance sheet presented in Table 2–4, we see that the $1,000,000 in total assets of the Kramer Corporation was financed by $300,000 in debt and $700,000 in the form of stockholders' equity. Stockholders' equity represents the total contribution and ownership interest of preferred and common stockholders.

The *preferred stock* investment position is $50,000, based on 500 shares at $100 par. In the case of *common stock*, 100,000 shares have been issued at a total par value of $100,000, plus an extra $250,000 in *capital paid in excess of par* for a sum of $350,000. We can assume that the 100,000 shares were originally sold at $3.50 each.

| | | | |
|---|---|---|---|
| 100,000 shares | $1.00 | Par value | $100,000 |
| | 2.50 | Capital paid in excess of par | 250,000 |
| | $3.50 | Price per share | $350,000 |

Finally, there is $300,000 in *retained earnings*. This value, previously determined in the statement of retained earnings (Table 2–2), represents the firm's cumulative earnings since inception minus dividends and any other adjustments.

## Concept of Net Worth

Stockholders' equity minus the preferred stock component represents the *net worth*, or *book value*, of the firm. There is some logic to the approach. If you take everything that the firm owns and subtract the debt and preferred stock obligation,[3] the remainder belongs to the common stockholder and represents net worth. In the case of the Kramer Corporation, we show:

| | |
|---|---|
| Total assets | $1,000,000 |
| Total liabilities | 300,000 |
| Stockholders' equity | 700,000 |
| Preferred stock obligation | 50,000 |
| Net worth assigned to common | $ 650,000 |
| Common shares outstanding | 100,000 |
| Net worth, or book value, per share | $6.50 |

The original cost per share was $3.50; the net worth, or book value, per share is $6.50; and the market value (based on a P/E ratio of 12 and earnings per share of $1) is $12. It is this last value that is of primary concern to the financial manager and the security analyst.

## Limitations of the Balance Sheet

Lest we attribute too much significance to the balance sheet, we need to examine some of the underlying concepts supporting its construction. Most of the values on the balance sheet are stated on a historical or original cost basis. This may be particularly troublesome in the case of plant and equipment and inventory, which may now be worth two or three times the original cost or—from a negative viewpoint—may require many times the original cost for replacement.

The accounting profession has been grappling with this problem for decades, and the discussion becomes particularly intense each time inflation rears it ugly head. In October 1979 the Financial Accounting Standards Board (FASB) issued a ruling that required large companies to disclose inflation-adjusted accounting data in their annual reports. The ruling was extended for five more years in 1984. This information

[3]An additional discussion of preferred stock is presented in Chapter 17, Common and Preferred Stock Financing. Preferred stock represents neither a debt claim nor an ownership interest in the firm. It is a hybrid, or intermediate, type of security.

is disclosed in addition to the traditional historical cost data and can show up in obscure footnotes or in a separate full-fledged financial section with detailed explanations. In any event, it is considered supplemental.

Inflation-adjusted accounting is a relatively new concept in accounting practice, and most likely it will undergo many modifications over time. Initially, the FASB required the use of two separate methods. The first, the *constant-dollar method*, adjusts statements by using the consumer price index. The second, the *current-cost method* (sometimes referred to as replacement cost), requires assets to be revalued at their current cost. It now appears that the second method is the more widely accepted, and in 1984 the FASB dropped the constant-dollar reporting method for companies using current-cost information. Overall, these adjustments will affect inventory and plant and equipment the most, thus affecting overall balance sheet accounts and the total asset value of the firm. The revaluation will also affect inflation-adjusted profits, through adjustments to depreciation expense, and cost of goods sold through higher inventory costs. These expenses will be higher, to reflect inflation, and therefore profits will be smaller than they would be on a historical-cost basis.

Many financial executives think that the new data will simply confuse most investors, but others see benefits. The most important benefit will be the ability to determine if a company is generating enough cash flow from internal operations to replace worn-out equipment and maintain existing levels of production. Another benefit to investors will come from being able to measure dividends, income, and stock prices in dollars adjusted for inflation. What effect this will have on the market price of common stock and on total stockholder wealth is uncertain. Because the concept of net worth (book value) developed in the previous section is based on historical asset costs (Assets − Liabilities − Preferred stock), net worth may bear little relationship to reality. The use of current cost data to determine book value may or may not be better as an approximation of the stock price. In Table 2–5 we look at large disparities between market value per share and historical book value per share for a number of publicly traded companies at the end of 1985. Besides asset valuation, a number of other factors may explain the wide differences between per share values, such as industry outlook, growth prospects, quality of management, and risk–return expectations.

**Table 2–5**
**Comparison of market value to book value per share, December 1985**

| Corporation | Market Value per Share | Book Value per Share | Ratio of Market Value to Book Value |
|---|---|---|---|
| American Home Products | $ 63.75 | $15.55 | 4.10 |
| Analog Devices | 26.25 | 6.50 | 4.04 |
| Merck & Co. | 135.50 | 38.15 | 3.55 |
| Lin Broadcasting | 38.75 | 11.45 | 3.38 |
| Squibb Corp. | 80.75 | 26.60 | 3.04 |
| Fruehauf | 24.25 | 31.45 | 0.77 |
| U.S. Steel | 25.50 | 43.80 | 0.58 |
| Control Data | 20.75 | 36.60 | 0.57 |
| Tesoro Petroleum | 9.75 | 25.90 | 0.38 |
| Long Island Lighting | 8.00 | 25.30 | 0.32 |

## Sources and Uses of Funds Statement

In September 1971, the accounting profession added the sources and uses of funds statement as a third required financial statement along with the balance sheet and the income statement.[4] As indicated in Figure 2–1, the sources and uses of funds statement allows us to measure how changes in the balance sheet were financed over a period of time. While the balance sheet is nothing more than a snapshot of the firm at a point in time, if we put together two such snapshots, we can ascertain significant changes.

By examining the sources and uses of funds statement, analysts can determine the relative buildup in short-term and long-term assets. Furthermore, they can examine the various means of financing that have been utilized to support the firm's growth (if there is, in fact, growth). They can then determine if a proper mix is being utilized and the implications for financing in the future.

### Sources of Funds

In consulting a sources and uses of funds statement, an *increase in stockholders' equity* is considered a source of financing, as indicated in

[4]APB, "Reporting Changes in Financial Position," *APB Opinion No. 19* (New York: AICPA, 1971).

**Figure 2–1**
**Relationship of funds statement to balance sheet**

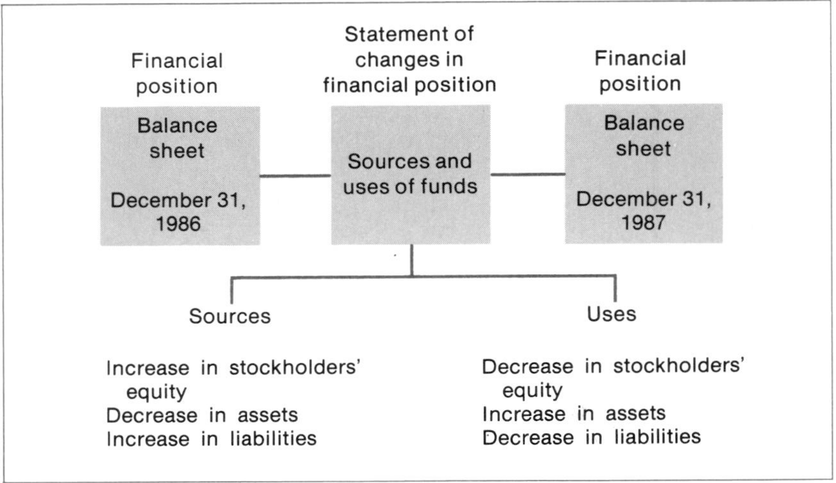


Figure 2–1. This may include additional profit, new preferred or common stock, and other types of capital infusion into the firm. Another source of financing, albeit indirect, is a *reduction in asset holdings*. To the extent we reduce our financial commitment to receivables, inventory, or plant and equipment, we free up funds for use elsewhere—perhaps in new-product development or in other asset accounts. Finally, an *increase in liabilities* represents a flow of new funds into the business. For example, if there is an increase of $50,000 in bank loans (notes payable), these funds can be redeployed to pay salaries, to support our asset base, or for other functions.

## Uses of Funds

We now look at the opposite side of the coin. A *reduction* in stockholders' equity is a use of funds; it may represent losses to the firm or a reduction of outstanding shares. Another use of funds is a *reduction in liability* accounts (a loan balance is reduced as funds are used to retire a debt). An *increase* in the cash account as well as an increase in any asset account, such as inventory or plant and equipment, is a use of funds. For example, as cash is increased it sits idle in a checking account and is used to maintain minimum cash balances. When the cash is spent, this storehouse of cash is a source of funds, and the cash account on the balance sheet will decline.

## Developing a Statement

In order to illustrate the preceding concepts, we will examine data for the Kramer Corporation for year-end 1986 and 1987. The financial information is provided in Table 2–6. We examine the changes in

**Table 2–6**

KRAMER CORPORATION
Comparative Balance Sheets

| | Year-End 1986 | Year-End 1987 | Change | Source (S) or Use (U) |
|---|---|---|---|---|
| *Assets* | | | | |
| Current assets: | | | | |
| Cash | $ 30,000 | $ 40,000 | +$10,000 | U |
| Marketable securities | 10,000 | 10,000 | — | — |
| Accounts receivable (net) | 170,000 | 200,000 | + 30,000 | U |
| Inventory | 130,000 | 180,000 | + 50,000 | U |
| Prepaid expenses | 30,000 | 20,000 | − 10,000 | S |
| Total current assets | 370,000 | 450,000 | — | — |
| Investments | 50,000 | 50,000 | — | — |
| Plant and equipment | 1,000,000 | 1,100,000 | — | — |
| Less: Accumulated depreciation | 550,000 | 600,000 | — | — |
| Net plant and equipment | 450,000 | 500,000 | + 50,000 | U |
| Total assets | $ 870,000 | $1,000,000 | — | — |
| *Liabilities and Stockholders' Equity* | | | | |
| Current liabilities: | | | | |
| Accounts payable | $ 50,000 | $ 80,000 | +$30,000 | S |
| Notes payable | 60,000 | 100,000 | + 40,000 | S |
| Accrued expenses | 40,000 | 30,000 | − 10,000 | U |
| Total current liabilities | 150,000 | 210,000 | — | — |
| Long-term liabilities: | | | | |
| Bonds payable, 1990 | 70,000 | 90,000 | + 20,000 | S |
| Total liabilities | 220,000 | 300,000 | — | — |
| Stockholders' equity: | | | | |
| Preferred stock, $100 par value | 50,000 | 50,000 | — | — |
| Common stock, $1 par value | 100,000 | 100,000 | — | — |
| Capital paid in excess of par | 250,000 | 250,000 | — | — |
| Retained earnings | 250,000 | 300,000 | + 50,000 | S |
| Total stockholders' equity | 650,000 | 700,000 | — | — |
| Total liabilities and stockholders' equity | $ 870,000 | $1,000,000 | — | — |

individual balance sheet accounts and label them as either sources or uses of funds.

We then summarize these worksheet data in the form of a sources and uses of funds statement in Table 2–7. Changes to stockholders' equity are presented first, and then changes in assets and liabilities. The material in Table 2–7 represents a "first run" at a sources and uses of funds statement.

Clearly the sources and uses of funds must balance in Table 2–7. We see how our buildup in assets was financed primarily through an increase in stockholders' equity and liabilities.

**Adjustments** Based on additional data from the income statement, a number of adjustments may be made to the sources and uses of funds statement in Table 2–7. These include a reconciliation of change in retained earnings and a reconciliation of change in net plant and equipment.

*1. Reconciliation of change in retained earnings*—It is helpful to show the net income component of the change in retained earnings as a source of funds and the payment of dividends as a use of funds. By referring to Tables 2–1 and 2–2, we observe that net income for the entire year of 1987 was $100,000 and that cash dividends were $50,000. Together they equal the $50,000 change in retained earnings shown in Table 2–7.

*2. Reconciliation of change in net plant and equipment*—In Table 2–7, we have merely shown a $50,000 change in plant and equipment. It is instructive to break this number down between the actual increase in plant and equipment, a use, and depreciation, a "presumed" source

**Table 2–7**

KRAMER CORPORATION
Sources and Uses of Funds Statement
For the Year Ended December 31, 1987

| *Sources* | | *Uses* | |
|---|---|---|---|
| Increase in retained earnings | $ 50,000 | Increase in cash | $ 10,000 |
| Decrease in prepaid expenses | 10,000 | Increase in accounts receivable | 30,000 |
| Increase in accounts payable | 30,000 | Increase in inventory | 50,000 |
| Increase in notes payable | 40,000 | Increase in net plant and equipment | 50,000 |
| Increase in bonds payable | 20,000 | Decrease in accrued expenses | 10,000 |
| | $150,000 | | $150,000 |

Table 2–8

KRAMER CORPORATION
Revised Sources and Uses of Funds Statement
For the Year Ended December 31, 1987

| Sources | | Uses | |
|---|---|---|---|
| *Net income | $100,000 | *Dividends paid | $ 50,000 |
| †Depreciation (charged without cash outlay) | 50,000 | Increase in cash | 10,000 |
| Decrease in prepaid expenses | 10,000 | Increase in accounts receivable | 30,000 |
| Increase in accounts payable | 30,000 | Increase in inventory | 50,000 |
| Increase in notes payable | 40,000 | †Increase in plant and equipment | 100,000 |
| Increase in bonds payable | 20,000 | Decrease in accrued expenses | 10,000 |
| | $250,000 | | $250,000 |

* and † are explained in the text.

(an item to receive much further attention). Referring back to Table 2–6, we see a $100,000 increase in plant and equipment and a $50,000 increase in accumulated depreciation,[5] thus explaining the $50,000 change in net plant and equipment. Our revised sources and uses of funds statement is shown in Table 2–8.

The changes between Table 2–7 and Table 2–8 are indicated by an asterisk or a dagger. The asterisk refers to the replacement of "increase in retained earnings" of $50,000 with the separate showings of net income and dividends. The dagger indicates that the increase in "*net* plant and equipment" has been replaced by two items, increase in plant and equipment and depreciation.

## Analysis

In analyzing a sources and uses of funds statement, the reader basically goes from the right-hand side to the left-hand side. The uses or buildup in assets should be matched against the sources of financing.

[5]The increase in accumulated depreciation in this case equals the depreciation expense charged in Table 2–1. If they were different values, we would use the depreciation expense item as a source of funds and make further adjustments to change plant and equipment to arrive at the change in the *net* plant and equipment value on the balance sheet. Increases in accumulated depreciation and depreciation expense for the period may differ when old plant and equipment is retired and deductions from accumulated depreciation take place.

For example, are increases in long-term assets being supported by profits and long-term borrowing, or are they being financed by the more dangerous route of short-term borrowings? In Table 2–8, we see a $100,000 increase in plant and equipment that is primarily financed by long-term net income, minus dividends paid, of $50,000 and a $20,000 increase in the long-term liability, bonds payable.[6] The situation is reasonably well in balance. A more dangerous situation occurs if we attempt to finance virtually all long-term needs with short-term funds. If money becomes "tight" and interest rates go up, continued short-term financing may be difficult to find or become prohibitively expensive. A long-term–short-term imbalance can ultimately lead to bankruptcy.

The relationship between accounts receivable and accounts payable should also be examined. If we have to finance our customers in the form of receivables, we would like to have our suppliers finance us. In the present case the increases in accounts receivable and accounts payable are equal, which appears to be a satisfactory circumstance. Nevertheless, in examining the original financial statement in Table 2–6, we observe that accounts receivable in total ($200,000) greatly exceed accounts payable ($80,000).

The analyst should do additional analysis on each side of the sources and uses of funds statement. On the left-hand side, he or she must examine the relative contribution made by the different sources of financing. In this example, profits appear to be significant. On the right-hand side, he or she must examine the relative growth of the asset accounts. For the Kramer Corporation, the growth in receivables and inventory does not appear to be excessive, although an in-depth analysis would be necessary to make a final determination. The relatively large buildup in plant and equipment also calls for further study. (Is the overall liquidity of the firm being diminished?)

### Net Working Capital Approach

In presenting the sources and uses of funds statement in Table 2–8, we have looked at the changes in every account. This is known as the *cash approach*. Some analysts prefer an abbreviated form known as the *net working capital approach*. In order to understand this second ap-

---

[6] In a limited sense, depreciation also adds to cash flow, but this topic is deferred until a later section.

proach, we first define net working capital as the difference between current assets and current liabilities. If a firm has $100,000 in current assets and $40,000 in current liabilities, we speak of its net working capital position as being at $60,000. Under the net working capital approach, all changes in net working capital (changes in cash, accounts receivable, accounts payable, notes payable, etc.) are netted out as one major item with a single entry to the statement. Only the noncurrent changes in the balance sheet are delineated individually.

Since most of the financial management literature is concerned with the more complete cash approach, we merely mention the net working capital approach as a second alternative that carries the approval of the accounting profession.

## Depreciation and Funds Flow

One of the most confusing items to finance students is whether depreciation is a source of funds to the corporation. In Table 2–8, we listed "depreciation charged without cash outlay" as a source of funds. This statement deserves further clarification. The reason we added back depreciation was not that depreciation was a new source of funds, but rather that we subtracted this noncash deduction in arriving at net income and now have to add it back to determine the amount of actual funds on hand.

Depreciation represents an attempt to allocate the initial cost of an asset over its useful life. In essence, we attempt to match the annual expense of plant and equipment ownership against the revenues that are being produced. Nevertheless, the charging of depreciation is purely an accounting entry and does not directly involve the movement of funds. To go from accounting flows to cash flows in Table 2–8, we restored the noncash deduction of $50,000 for depreciation that was subtracted in Table 2–1, the income statement.[7]

Let us examine a very simple case involving depreciation. Assume that we purchase a machine for $500 with a five-year life and that we pay for it in cash. Our depreciation schedule calls for equal annual depreciation charges of $100 per year for five years. Assume further that our firm has $1,000 in earnings before depreciation and taxes and that the tax obligation is $450. Note the difference between accounting flows and cash flows for the first two years in Table 2–9.

---

[7]A number of other adjustments of this nature could be made, but depreciation is the most significant.

**Table 2–9**
**Comparison of accounting and cash flows**

| | Year 1 (1) Accounting Flows | Year 1 (2) Cash Flows |
|---|---|---|
| Earnings before depreciation and taxes (EBDT) | $1,000 | $1,000 |
| Depreciation | 100 | 100 |
| Earnings before taxes (EBT) | 900 | 900 |
| Taxes | 450 | 450 |
| Earnings after taxes (EAT) | $ 450 | 450 |
| Purchase of equipment | | −500 |
| Depreciation charged without cash outlay | | +100 |
| Cash flow | | $ 50 |

| | Year 2 (1) Accounting Flows | Year 2 (2) Cash Flows |
|---|---|---|
| Earnings before depreciation and taxes (EBDT) | $1,000 | $1,000 |
| Depreciation | 100 | 100 |
| Earnings before taxes (EBT) | 900 | 900 |
| Taxes | 450 | 450 |
| Earnings after taxes (EAT) | $ 450 | 450 |
| Depreciation charged without cash outlay | | +100 |
| Cash flow | | $ 550 |

Since we took $500 out of cash flow originally (in column 2), we do not wish to take it out again. Thus, we add back $100 in depreciation each year to "wash out" the subtraction in the income statement.

## Income Tax Considerations

Virtually every financial decision is influenced by federal income tax considerations. Primary examples are the lease versus purchase decision, the issuance of common stock versus debt decision, and the decision to replace an asset. While the intent of this section is not to review the rules, regulations, and nuances of the Federal Income Tax Code, we will examine how tax matters influence corporate financial decisions. The primary orientation will be toward the principles governing "corporate" tax decisions, though many of the same principles apply to a sole proprietorship or a partnership.

## Corporate Tax Rate

The provisions of the tax law in existence in 1986 specify the corporate tax rates shown in Table 2–10.[8]

The average tax rate is 25.75 percent on $100,000 of income. The marginal tax rate is the percentage that applies to each new dollar of taxable income. While the marginal rate gets adjusted in $25,000 increments from 15 percent to 40 percent on the first $100,000 of taxable income, the marginal rate on all amounts greater than $100,000 stays constant at 46 percent. From Table 2–10 we can see that the tax paid on the first $100,000 of income is $25,750; the marginal tax on the next $100,000 of income is $46,000, for a total tax of $71,750 on taxable income of $200,000. This gives us an average tax rate of 35.88 percent.

$$\text{Average tax rate} = \frac{\$71{,}750}{\$200{,}000} = 35.88\%$$

## Cost of a Tax-Deductible Expense

The businessman often states that a tax-deductible item such as interest on loans, travel expenditures, or salaries only costs about half the amount expended, on an aftertax basis. We shall investigate how this process works. Let us examine the tax statements of two corporations—the first pays $100,000 in interest, and the second has no interest expense. An average tax rate of 40 percent is used for each computation.

**Table 2–10**
**Corporate tax schedule: Marginal and average rates**

| *Marginal Tax Rate* | | *Incremental Income* | *Incremental Taxes* | *Cumulative Taxes* | *Average Tax Rate* |
|---|---|---|---|---|---|
| 15% . . . . | on first | $ 25,000 | $ 3,750 | $ 3,750 | 15.00% |
| 18 . . . . . | on second | 25,000 | 4,500 | 8,250 | 16.50 |
| 30 . . . . . | on third | 25,000 | 7,500 | 15,750 | 21.00 |
| 40 . . . . . | on fourth | 25,000 | 10,000 | 25,750 | 25.75 |
| 46 . . . . . | over | 100,000 | — | — | — |

[8]Congress is currently in the process of revising the tax codes as of June, 1986.

| | Corporation A | Corporation B |
|---|---|---|
| Earnings before interest and taxes | $400,000 | $400,000 |
| Interest | 100,000 | 0 |
| Earnings before taxes (taxable income) | 300,000 | 400,000 |
| Taxes (40%) | 120,000 | 160,000 |
| Earnings after taxes | $180,000 | $240,000 |
| Difference in earnings after taxes—$60,000 | | |

Although Corporation A paid out $100,000 more in interest than Corporation B, its earnings after taxes are only $60,000 less than those of Corporation B. Thus, we say that the $100,000 in interest cost it only $60,000 in aftertax earnings. The aftertax cost of a tax-deductible expense can be computed as the actual expense times one minus the tax rate. In this case, we show $100,000 (1 − Tax rate), or $100,000 × 0.60 = $60,000. The reasoning in this instance is that the $100,000 is deducted from earnings before determining taxable income, thus saving us $40,000 in taxes and only costing $60,000 on a net basis.

Because a dividend on common stock is not tax deductible, we say that it cost us 100 percent of the amount paid. From a purely corporate cash flow viewpoint, the firm would be indifferent between paying $100,000 in interest and $60,000 in dividends.

## Depreciation as a Tax Shield

Although depreciation is not a new source of funds, it does provide the important function of shielding part of our income from taxes. Let us examine Corporation A and B again, this time with an eye toward depreciation rather than interest. Corporation A charges off $100,000 in depreciation, while Corporation B charges off none.

| | Corporation A | Corporation B |
|---|---|---|
| Earnings before depreciation and taxes | $400,000 | $400,000 |
| Depreciation | 100,000 | 0 |
| Earnings before taxes | 300,000 | 400,000 |
| Taxes (40%) | 120,000 | 160,000 |
| Earnings after taxes | 180,000 | 240,000 |
| + Depreciation charged without cash outlay | 100,000 | 0 |
| Cash flow | $280,000 | $240,000 |
| Difference—$40,000 | | |

We compute earnings after taxes and then add back depreciation to get cash flow. The difference between $280,000 and $240,000 indicates that Corporation A enjoys $40,000 more in cash flow. The reason is that depreciation shielded $100,000 from taxation in Corporation A and saved $40,000 in taxes, which eventually showed up in cash flow. Though depreciation is not a new source of funds, it does provide tax shield benefits that can be measured as depreciation times the tax rate, or in this case $100,000 × 0.40 = $40,000. A more comprehensive discussion of depreciation's effect on cash flow is presented in Chapter 12, as part of the long-term capital budgeting decision.

## Summary

The financial manager must be thoroughly familiar with the language of accounting in order to administer the financial affairs of the firm. The income statement provides a measure of the firm's profitability over a specified period of time. Earnings per share represents residual income to the common stockholder that may be paid out in the form of dividends or reinvested to generate future profits and dividends. A limitation of the income statement is that it reports income and expense primarily on a transaction basis and thus may not recognize certain major economic events as they occur.

The balance sheet is a snapshot of the financial position of the firm at a point in time, with the stockholders' equity section purporting to represent ownership interest. Because the balance sheet is presented on a historical-cost basis, it may not reflect the true value of the firm. However, beginning with the 1979 corporate annual reports of large companies, the Financial Accounting Standards Board required inflation-adjusted accounting statements.

The sources and uses of funds statement reflects changes in the financial position of the firm between reporting dates. Through the statement, we get a rough picture of the firm's financing characteristics and of its relative reliance on short-term and long-term funding.

Finally, we examine the corporate tax structure and the tax implications of interest, dividends, and depreciation. The aftertax cost and cash flow implications of these items are important throughout the text.

## List of Terms

| | |
|---|---|
| **income statement** | **sources and uses of funds statement** |
| **earnings per share** | **marginal corporate tax rate** |
| **P/E ratio** | **historical-cost accounting** |
| **balance sheet** | **current-cost accounting** |
| **stockholders' equity** | **constant-dollar accounting** |
| **liquidity** | **cash flows** |
| **net worth, or book value** | |

## Discussion Questions

1. Discuss some of the financial variables that have an effect on the price–earnings ratio.
2. What is the difference between book value per share of common stock and market value per share? Why does this disparity occur?
3. Explain how depreciation generates cash flows for the company.
4. What is the difference between accumulated depreciation and depreciation expense? How are they related?
5. How is the income statement related to the balance sheet?
6. Discuss how inflation affects the balance sheet and the income statement. What specific items are most influenced by inflation?
7. What items on the sources and uses of funds statement need to be reconciled with the income statement? Why?
8. How can we use a sources and uses of funds statement to analyze how a firm's assets were financed?
9. Why is interest expense said to cost the firm approximately half of the actual expense, while dividends cost it 100 percent of the outlay?

10. What do inflation-adjusted accounting statements offer to the financial manager and the stockholder?

## Problems

1. Ron's Aerobics, Inc., has the following taxable income for 1985 and 1986.

| | |
|---|---|
| 1985 . . . . | $ 68,000 |
| 1986 . . . . | 142,000 |

*a.* Compute the total tax obligation for Ron's Aerobics each year.
*b.* Compute the average tax for each year.

2. Given the following information, prepare, in good form, an income statement for the Nix Corporation. Use the corporate tax rates in Chapter 2 to calculate taxes.

| | |
|---|---|
| Selling and administrative expense . . . . | $ 90,000 |
| Depreciation expense . . . . . . . . . . | 50,000 |
| Sales. . . . . . . . . . . . . . . . . . | 500,000 |
| Interest expense. . . . . . . . . . . . . | 20,000 |
| Cost of goods sold . . . . . . . . . . . | 220,000 |

3. The Singleday Book Company has sold 1,400 finance textbooks to High Tuition University for $35 each. These books cost Singleday $22 each to produce. In addition, Singleday spent $2,000 in selling expense to convince the university to buy its books. Singleday borrowed $15,000 on January 1, 1986, on which it paid 12 percent interest. Both principal and interest were paid on December 31, 1986. Singleday's tax rate is 30 percent. Depreciation expense for the year was $4,000.

Did Singleday make a profit in 1986? Verify with an income statement presented in good form.

4. Classify the following balance sheet items as current or noncurrent.

| | |
|---|---|
| Inventory | Retained earnings |
| Accounts payable | Marketable securities |
| Preferred stock | Accounts receivable |
| Prepaid expenses | Plant and equipment |
| Bonds payable | Accrued wages payable |

5. Arrange the following income statement items so that they are in the proper order of an income statement.

| | |
|---|---|
| Depreciation expense | Operating profit |
| Gross profit | Selling and administrative expense |
| Interest expense | Sales |
| Taxes | Earnings before taxes |
| Preferred stock dividends | Cost of goods sold |
| Shares outstanding | Earnings available to common stockholders |
| Earnings per share | |
| Earnings after taxes | |

6. Identify the following as a source of funds or a use of funds.

| | |
|---|---|
| Increase in inventory | Dividend payment |
| Decrease in prepaid expenses | Increase in notes payable |
| Decrease in retained earnings | Depreciation expense |
| Increase in cash | Decrease in accounts payable |
| Decrease in inventory | Increase in investments |

7. The Aaron Corporation has an operating profit of $210,000. Interest expense for the year was $15,000; preferred dividends paid were $10,550; and common dividends paid were $37,500. The tax was $69,450. The Aaron Corporation has 25,000 shares of common stock outstanding.

   *a*. Calculate the earnings per share and common dividends per share for the Aaron Corporation.
   *b*. What was the increase in retained earnings for the year?

8. The Elliot Corporation had $450,000 of retained earnings on December 31, 1987. The company paid dividends of $25,000 in 1987 and had retained earnings of $400,000 on December 31, 1986. How much did Elliot earn during 1987, and what would its earnings per share be if 20,000 shares of common stock are outstanding?

9. The Jupiter Corporation has a gross profit of $700,000 and $240,000 in depreciation expense. The Saturn Corporation also has $700,000

in gross profit, with $40,000 in depreciation expense. Selling and administrative expense is $160,000 for each company.

Given that the tax rate is 40 percent, compute the cash flow for both companies. Explain the difference in cash flow between the two firms.

**10.** Fill in the blank spaces with categories 1 through 7 below.

1. Balance sheet (BS).
2. Income statement (IS).
3. Current assets (CA).
4. Fixed assets (FA).
5. Current liabilities (CL).
6. Long-term liabilities (LL).
7. Stockholders' equity (SE).

| *Indicate Whether Item Is on Balance Sheet (BS) or Income Statement (IS)* | *If on Balance Sheet, Designate Which Category* | *Item* |
|---|---|---|
| ______________ | ______________ | Retained earnings |
| ______________ | ______________ | Income tax expense |
| ______________ | ______________ | Accounts receivable |
| ______________ | ______________ | Common stock |
| ______________ | ______________ | Capital in excess of par value |
| ______________ | ______________ | Bonds payable, maturity 1999 |
| ______________ | ______________ | Notes payable (six months) |
| ______________ | ______________ | Net income |
| ______________ | ______________ | Selling and administrative expenses |
| ______________ | ______________ | Inventories |
| ______________ | ______________ | Accrued expenses |
| ______________ | ______________ | Cash |
| ______________ | ______________ | Plant and equipment |
| ______________ | ______________ | Sales |
| ______________ | ______________ | Operating expenses |
| ______________ | ______________ | Marketable securities |
| ______________ | ______________ | Accounts payable |
| ______________ | ______________ | Interest expense |
| ______________ | ______________ | Income tax payable |

**11.** The balance sheet of Neeley Corporation includes the following stockholders' equity section:

*Stockholders' Equity*

| | |
|---|---|
| Common stock, $2 par, 100,000 shares outstanding | $ 200,000 |
| Capital paid in excess of par | 850,000 |
| Retained earnings | 400,000 |
| Total shareholders' equity | $1,450,000 |

Assuming that there has been only one issue of stock, what was the original selling price of Neeley Company's common stock?

**12.** Arrange the following items in proper balance sheet presentation.

| | |
|---|---|
| Accumulated depreciation | $250,000 |
| Retained earnings | 73,000 |
| Cash | 10,000 |
| Bonds payable | 125,000 |
| Accounts receivable | 48,000 |
| Plant and equipment—original cost | 600,000 |
| Accounts payable | 25,000 |
| Allowance for bad debts | 3,000 |
| Common stock, $1 par, 100,000 shares outstanding | 100,000 |
| Inventory | 50,000 |
| Preferred stock, $50 par, 1,000 shares outstanding | 50,000 |
| Marketable securities | 20,000 |
| Investments | 8,000 |
| Notes payable | 30,000 |
| Capital paid in excess of par (common stock) | 80,000 |

**13.** Monique's Boutique has assets of $600,000, current liabilities of $150,000, and long-term liabilities of $120,000. There is $75,000 in preferred stock outstanding. Thirty thousand shares of common stock have been issued.

*a.* Compute book value (net worth) per share.
*b.* If there is $33,600 in earnings available to common stockholders and Monique's stock has a P/E of 12 times earnings per share, what is the current price of the stock?
*c.* What is the ratio of market value per share to book value per share?

**14.** In Problem 13, if the firm sells at two times book value per share, what will the P/E ratio be?

**15.** Following is the December 31, 1986, balance sheet of Hillcrest Corporation:

| *Current Assets* | | *Liabilities* | |
|---|---|---|---|
| Cash | $ 10,000 | Accounts payable | $ 12,000 |
| Accounts receivable | 15,000 | Notes payable | 20,000 |
| Inventory | 25,000 | Bonds payable | 50,000 |
| Miscellaneous | 12,000 | | |
| *Fixed Assets* | | *Stockholders' Equity* | |
| Plant and equipment | $250,000 | Common stock | $ 75,000 |
| Less: Accumulated depreciation | 50,000 | Paid-in capital | 25,000 |
| Net plant and equipment | 200,000 | Retained earnings | 80,000 |
| Total assets | $262,000 | Total liabilities and stockholders' equity | $262,000 |

Sales for 1987 were $220,000, and cost of goods sold was 60 percent of sales. Depreciation expense was 10 percent of the net plant and equipment at the beginning of the year. Interest expense for the bonds payable was 8 percent, while interest on the notes payable was 10 percent. These interest expenses are based on December 31, 1986, balances. Selling and administrative expenses were $22,000, and the tax rate averaged 18 percent.

During the year 1987, accounts receivable and inventory increased by 10 percent, and accounts payable increased by 25 percent. A new machine was purchased on December 30, 1987, at a cost of $35,000. A cash dividend of $12,800 was paid to common stockholders at the end of 1987. Also, notes payable increased by $6,000, and bonds payable decreased by $10,000.

*a.* Prepare an income statement for 1987.
*b.* Prepare a balance sheet as of December 31, 1987.
*c.* Prepare a statement of sources and uses of funds similar to Table 2–8.

**16.** Construct a sources and uses of funds statement similar to Table 2–7 from the following data for the Madison Corporation.

MADISON CORPORATION

| *Assets* | *Year-End 1986* | *Year-End 1987* | *Change* | *Source (S) or Use (U)* |
|---|---|---|---|---|
| Current assets: | | | | |
| Cash | $ 200,000 | $ 220,000 | | |
| Marketable securities | 70,000 | 60,000 | | |
| Accounts receivable | 390,000 | 430,000 | | |
| Inventory | 520,000 | 540,000 | | |
| Prepaid expenses | 20,000 | 25,000 | | |
| Total current assets | 1,200,000 | 1,275,000 | | |

| *Assets* | *Year-End 1986* | *Year-End 1987* | *Change* | *Source (S) or Use (U)* |
|---|---|---|---|---|
| Plant and equipment | 600,000 | 790,000 | | |
| Less: Accumulated depreciation | 160,000 | 200,000 | | |
| Net plant and equipment | 440,000 | 590,000 | | |
| Total assets | $1,640,000 | $1,865,000 | | |
| *Liabilities and Stockholders' Equity* | | | | |
| Current liabilities: | | | | |
| Accounts payable | $ 265,000 | $ 280,000 | | |
| Notes payable | 200,000 | 340,000 | | |
| Accrued expenses | 55,000 | 65,000 | | |
| Total current liabilities | 520,000 | 685,000 | | |
| Long-term liabilities: | | | | |
| Bonds payable, 1994 | 400,000 | 360,000 | | |
| Total liabilities | 920,000 | 1,045,000 | | |
| Stockholders' equity: | | | | |
| Preferred stock, $100 par value | 100,000 | 100,000 | | |
| Common stock, $2 par value | 90,000 | 100,000 | | |
| Capital paid in excess of par | 170,000 | 220,000 | | |
| Retained earnings | 360,000 | 400,000 | | |
| Total stockholders' equity | 720,000 | 820,000 | | |
| Total liabilities and stockholders' equity | $1,640,000 | $1,865,000 | | |

*(The following questions apply to the Madison Corporation as presented in Problem 16)*

**17.** Assume that the Madison Corporation paid out dividends of $15,000 in 1987 and the change in accumulated depreciation is equal to the depreciation expense for the year.

Compute a revised sources and uses of funds statement similar to Table 2–8. (Net income can be defined as change in retained earnings plus dividends paid.)

**18.** Compute the book value per share for each year for the Madison Corporation.

**19.** If the market value of a share of common stock is 1.3 times book value for 1987, what is the firm's P/E ratio for 1987?

**20.** Has the buildup in fixed assets been financed in a satisfactory manner? Briefly discuss.

## Selected References

Arthur Andersen and Co. Study. *Objectives of Financial Statements for Business Enterprises*. Chicago, 1972.

Bierman, Harold, Jr. "Toward a Constant Price-Earnings Ratio." *Financial Analysts Journal* 38 (September–October 1982), pp. 62–65.

"Financial Reporting and Changing Prices; A Guide to Implementing FASB Statement 33." Touche, Ross and Co., 1979.

Helfert, Erich A. *Techniques of Financial Analysis*. 5th ed. Homewood, Ill.: Richard D. Irwin, 1982.

Lambert, S. J., III., and Christine V. Zavgren. "The Objectives of the Statement of Financial Accounting Concepts No. 1." *Financial Executive*, May 1982, pp. 26–30.

Louderback, Joseph G., and Geraldine F. Dominiak. *Managerial Accounting* 3d ed. Boston: Kent Publishing, 1982.

Kroll, Yoman. "On the Differences between Accrual Accounting Figures and Cash Flows: The Case of Working Capital." *Financial Management* 14 (Spring 1985), pp. 75–82.

Norby, William C. "Accounting for Financial Analysis." *Financial Analysts Journal* 38 (July–August 1982), pp. 33–35.

*Opinions and Statements* of the American Institute of Certified Public Accountants (AICPA) and the Financial Accounting Standards Board (FASB).

Welsch, Glenn, A., Charles T. Zlatkovich, and John A. White. *Intermediate Accounting*. 6th ed. Homewood, Ill.: Richard D. Irwin, 1982.

# 3 Financial Analysis

In Chapter 2, Review of Accounting, we examined the basic assumptions of accounting and the various components that make up the financial statements of the firm. We now use this fundamental material as a springboard into financial analysis—to evaluate the financial performance of the firm.

The format for the chapter is twofold. In the first part we will use financial ratios to evaluate the relative success of the firm. Various measures such as net income to sales and current assets to current liabilities will be computed for a hypothetical company and examined in light of industry norms and past trends.

In the second part of the chapter we explore further the impact of inflation and disinflation on financial operations over the last decade. Heretofore given scant coverage in financial textbooks, the material is significant for financial managers of the future. The student begins to appreciate the impact of rising prices (or at times, declining prices) on the various financial ratios. The chapter concludes with a discussion of how other factors—in addition to price changes—may distort the financial statements of the firm. Terms such as net income to sales, return on investment, and inventory turnover take on much greater meaning when they are evaluated through the eyes of a financial manager who does more than merely pick out the top or bottom line of an income statement. The examples in the chapter are designed from the viewpoint of a financial manager (with only minor attention to accounting theory).

## Ratio Analysis

Ratios are used in much of our daily life. We buy cars based on miles per gallon; we evaluate baseball players by earned run averages and batting averages, basketball players by field goal and foul-shooting percentages, and so on. These are all ratios constructed to judge comparative performance. Financial ratios serve a similar purpose, but you must know what is being measured in order to construct a ratio and to understand the significance of the resultant number.

Financial ratios are used to weigh and evaluate the operating performance of the firm. While an absolute value such as earnings of $50,000 or accounts receivable of $100,000 may appear satisfactory, its acceptability can only be measured in relation to other values. For this reason, financial managers place heavy emphasis on ratio analysis.

For example, are earnings of $50,000 actually good? If we earned $50,000 on $500,000 of sales (10 percent "profit margin" ratio), that might be quite satisfactory—whereas earnings of $50,000 on $5,000,000 could be disappointing (a meager 1 percent return). After we have computed the appropriate ratio, we must compare our results to those achieved by similar firms in our industry as well as to our own past record of performance. Even then, this "number crunching" process is not fully adequate, and we are forced to supplement our financial findings with an evaluation of company management, physical facilities, and numerous other factors.

For comparative purposes, a number of organizations provide industry data. For example, Dun & Bradstreet compiles data on 800 different lines of business, while Robert Morris Associates provides ratios on over 150 industry classifications. Quite often the most valuable industry figures come from the various trade organizations to which firms belong (for example, the National Retail Furniture Association or the National Hardware Association).

Many libraries and universities subscribe to financial services such as Standard & Poor's Industry Surveys and Corporate Reports, the Value Line Investment Survey, and Moody's Investment Service. Standard & Poor's also leases a computer data base called Compustat to banks, corporations, investment organizations, and universities. Compustat contains financial statement data on over 3,000 companies for a 20-year period. These data can be used to make countless ratios to measure corporate performance. The ratios classified in this text are a sample of the major ratio categories, but others can also be constructed.

## Classification System

We will separate 13 significant ratios into four primary categories.

A. Profitability ratios.
   1. Profit margin.
   2. Return on assets (investment).
   3. Return on equity.

B. Asset utilization ratios.
   4. Receivable turnover.
   5. Average collection period.
   6. Inventory turnover.
   7. Fixed asset turnover.
   8. Total asset turnover.

C. Liquidity ratios.
   9. Current ratio.
   10. Quick ratio.

D. Debt utilization ratios.
   11. Debt to total assets.
   12. Times interest earned.
   13. Fixed charge coverage.

The first grouping, the profitability ratios, allows us to measure the ability of the firm to earn an adequate return on sales, total assets, and invested capital. Many of the problems related to profitability can be explained, in whole or in part, by the firm's ability to effectively employ its resources. Thus the next category of ratios is asset utilization. Under this heading, we measure the speed at which the firm is turning over accounts receivable, inventory, and longer-term assets. In other words, asset utilization ratios measure how many times per year a company sells its inventory or collects its entire accounts receivable. For long-term assets, the utilization ratio tells us how productive the fixed assets are in terms of sales generation.

In Category C, the liquidity ratios, the primary emphasis moves to the firm's ability to pay off short-term obligations as they come due. In Category D, debt utilization ratios, the overall debt position of the firm is evaluated in light of its asset base and earning power.

The users of financial statements will attach different degrees of importance to the four categories of ratios. To the potential investor or security analyst, the critical consideration is profitability, with secondary consideration given to such matters as liquidity and debt utilization. For the banker or trade creditor, the emphasis shifts to the firm's current ability to meet debt obligations. The bondholder, in turn, may be primarily influenced by debt to total assets—while also eyeing the profitability of the firm in terms of its ability to cover debt obligations. Of course, the shrewd analyst looks at all the ratios, but with different degrees of attention.

## The Analysis

Definitions alone carry little meaning in analyzing or dissecting the financial performance of a company. For this reason, we shall apply our four categories of ratios to a hypothetical firm, the Saxton Company, as presented in Table 3–1. The use of ratio analysis is rather like solving a mystery in which each clue leads to a new area of inquiry.

**A. Profitability ratios** We first look at the profitability ratios. Note that the appropriate ratio is computed for the Saxton Company and is then compared to representative industry data on page 57.

The Saxton Company shows a lower return on the sales dollar (5 percent) than the industry average of 6.5 percent. However, its return on assets (investment) of 12.5 percent exceeds the industry norm of 10 percent. There is only one possible explanation for this occurrence—a more rapid turnover of assets than that generally found within the industry. This is verified in ratio *2b*, in which sales to total assets is 2.5 for the Saxton Company and only 1.5 for the industry. Thus Saxton

**Table 3–1**
**Financial statements for ratio analysis**

SAXTON COMPANY
Income Statement
For the Year 1987

| | |
|---|---|
| Sales (all on credit) | $4,000,000 |
| Cost of goods sold | 3,000,000 |
| Gross profit | 1,000,000 |
| Selling and administrative expense* | 450,000 |
| Operating profit | 550,000 |
| Interest expense | 50,000 |
| Extraordinary loss | 100,000 |
| Net income before taxes | 400,000 |
| Taxes (50%) | 200,000 |
| Net income | $ 200,000 |

*Includes $50,000 in lease payments.

BALANCE SHEET
As of December 31, 1987
*Assets*

| | |
|---|---|
| Cash | $ 30,000 |
| Marketable securities | 50,000 |
| Accounts receivable | 350,000 |
| Inventory | 370,000 |
| Total current assets | 800,000 |
| Net plant and equipment | 800,000 |
| Total assets | $1,600,000 |

*Liabilities and Stockholders' Equity*

| | |
|---|---|
| Accounts payable | $ 50,000 |
| Notes payable | 250,000 |
| Total current liabilities | 300,000 |
| Long-term liabilities | 300,000 |
| Total liabilities | 600,000 |
| Common stock | 400,000 |
| Retained earnings | 600,000 |
| Total liabilities and stockholders' equity | $1,600,000 |

earns less on each sales dollar, but it compensates by turning over its assets more rapidly.

Return on total assets as described through the two components of profit margin and asset turnover is part of the Du Pont system of financial analysis.

Return on assets (investment) = Profit margin × Asset turnover

The Du Pont company was a forerunner in stressing that satisfactory return on assets may be achieved through high profit margins or rapid turnover of assets, or a combination of both. We shall also soon observe that under the Du Pont system of analysis, the use of debt may be important. The Du Pont system causes the analyst to examine the sources of a company's profitability. Since the profit margin is an income statement ratio, a high profit margin indicates good cost control, whereas a high asset turnover ratio demonstrates efficient use of the assets on the balance sheet. Different industries have different operating and financial structures. For example, in the heavy capital goods industry the emphasis is on a high profit margin with a low asset turnover—whereas in food processing, the profit margin is low and the key to satisfactory returns on total assets is a rapid turnover of assets.

### *A. Profitability ratios—*

| | *Saxton Company* | *Industry Average* |
|---|---|---|
| 1. Profit margin = $\frac{\text{Net income}}{\text{Sales}}$ | $\frac{\$200{,}000}{\$4{,}000{,}000} = 5\%$ | 6.5% |
| 2. Return on assets (investment) = | | |
| *a.* $\frac{\text{Net income}}{\text{Total assets}}$ | $\frac{\$200{,}000}{\$1{,}600{,}000} = 12.5\%$ | 10% |
| *b.* $\frac{\text{Net income}}{\text{Sales}} \times \frac{\text{Sales}}{\text{Total assets}}$ | 5% × 2.5 = 12.5% | 6.5% × 1.5 = 10% |
| 3. Return on equity = | | |
| *a.* $\frac{\text{Net income}}{\text{Stockholders' equity}}$ | $\frac{\$200{,}000}{\$1{,}000{,}000} = 20\%$ | 15% |
| *b.* $\frac{\text{Return on assets (investment)}}{(1 - \text{Debt/Assets})}$ | $\frac{0.125}{1 - 0.375} = 20\%$ | $\frac{0.10}{1 - 0.33} = 15\%$ |

Equally important to a firm is its return on equity or ownership capital. For the Saxton Company, return on equity is 20 percent, versus an industry norm of 15 percent. Thus the owners of Saxton Company are more amply rewarded than are other shareholders in the industry. This may be the result of one or two factors: a high return on total assets or a generous utilization of debt or a combination thereof. This can be seen through Equation 3*b*, which represents a modified or second version of the Du Pont formula.

$$\text{Return on equity} = \frac{\text{Return on assets (investment)}}{(1 - \text{Debt/Assets})}$$

Note the numerator, return on assets, is taken from Formula 2, which represents the initial version of the Du Pont formula (Return on assets = Net income/Sales × Sales/Total assets). Return on assets is then divided by [1 − (Debt/Assets)] to account for the amount of debt in the capital structure. In the case of the Saxton Company, the modified version of the Du Pont formula shows:

$$\text{Return on equity} = \frac{\text{Return on assets (investment)}}{(1 - \text{Debt/Assets})}$$

$$= \frac{12.5\%}{1 - 0.375} = 20\%$$

Actually the return on assets of 12.5 percent in the numerator is higher than the industry average of 10 percent, and the ratio of debt to assets in the denominator of 37.5 percent is higher than the industry norm of 33 percent. Both the numerator and denominator contribute to a higher return on equity than the industry average (20 percent versus 15 percent). Note that if the firm had a 50 percent debt-to-assets ratio, return on equity would be up to 25 percent.[1]

$$\text{Return on equity} = \frac{\text{Return on assets (investment)}}{(1 - \text{Debt/Assets})}$$

$$= \frac{12.5\%}{1 - 0.50} = 25\%$$

This does not necessarily mean that debt is a positive influence, only that it can be used to boost return on equity. The ultimate goal for the firm is to achieve maximum valuation for its securities in the marketplace, and this goal may or may not be advanced by using debt to increase return on equity. Because debt represents increased risk, a

[1]The return could be slightly different from 25 percent because of changing financing costs with higher debt.

Figure 3–1
Du Pont analysis

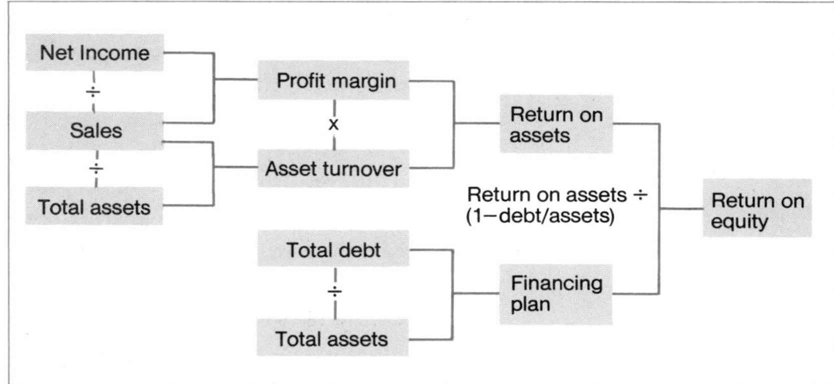


lower valuation of higher earnings is possible.[2] Every situation must be evaluated individually.

The reader may wish to review Figure 3–1, which illustrates the key points in the Du Pont system of analysis.

As an example of the Du Pont analysis, in Table 3–2 we compare Exxon Corporation and Texaco, two well-diversified oil companies, using 1984 year-ending data. It is clear that for the year 1984, Exxon outperformed Texaco in each area. Exxon had a higher profit margin on each dollar of sales and made more efficient use of the firm's assets. Its combined return on assets was over three times those of Texaco's. Exxon used less debt than Texaco (41.4 percent versus 58.4 percent) and still was able to generate a higher return on equity than Texaco.

Finally as a general statement in computing all the profitability ratios, the analyst must be sensitive to the age of the assets. Plant and equip-

Table 3–2
Position of Exxon versus Texaco, using the Du Pont method of analysis

| | Profit Margin | × | Asset Turnover | = | Return on Assets | ÷ | (1 − Debt/Assets) | | Return on Equity |
|---|---|---|---|---|---|---|---|---|---|
| Exxon | 6.08% | × | 1.85 | = | 11.24% | ÷ | (1 − .414) | = | 19.18% |
| Texaco | 2.20 | × | 1.43 | = | 3.15 | ÷ | (1 − .584) | = | 7.57 |

[2]Further discussion of this point is presented in Chapter 5, Operating and Financial Leverage, and Chapter 10, Valuation and Rates of Return.

ment purchased 15 years ago may be carried on the books far below its replacement value in an inflationary economy. A 20 percent return on assets purchased in the late 1950s or early 1960s may be inferior to a 15 percent return on newly purchased assets.

**B. Asset utilization ratios** The second category of ratios relates to asset utilization, and the ratios in this category may well explain why one firm is able to turn over its assets more rapidly than another. Notice that all of these ratios below relate the balance sheet (assets) to the income statement (sales). The Saxton Company's rapid turnover of assets is explained in ratios 4, 5, and 6.

Saxton collects its receivables faster than does the industry. This is shown by receivables turnover of 11.4 times versus 10 times for the industry, and in daily terms by the average collection period of 32 days, which is 4 days faster than that of the industry norm. The average collection period suggests how long, on the average, our customers' accounts stay on our books. The Saxton Company has $350,000 in accounts receivable and $4,000,000 in credit sales, which when divided by 360 days yields average daily credit sales of $11,111. We divide accounts receivable of $350,000 by average daily credit sales of $11,111 to determine how many days that credit sales are on the books (32 days).

*B. Asset utilization ratios—*

| | *Saxton Company* | *Industry Average* |
|---|---|---|
| 4. Receivables turnover = $\frac{\text{Sales (credit)}}{\text{Receivables}}$ | $\frac{\$4{,}000{,}000}{\$350{,}000} = 11.4$ | 10 times |
| 5. Average collection period = $\frac{\text{Accounts receivable}}{\text{Average daily credit sales}}$ | $\frac{\$350{,}000}{\$11{,}111} = 32$ | 36 days |
| 6. Inventory turnover = $\frac{\text{Sales}}{\text{Inventory}}$ | $\frac{\$4{,}000{,}000}{\$370{,}000} = 10.8$ | 7 times |
| 7. Fixed asset turnover = $\frac{\text{Sales}}{\text{Fixed assets}}$ | $\frac{\$4{,}000{,}000}{\$800{,}000} = 5$ | 5.4 times |
| 8. Total asset turnover = $\frac{\text{Sales}}{\text{Total assets}}$ | $\frac{\$4{,}000{,}000}{\$1{,}600{,}000} = 2.5$ | 1.5 times |

In addition, the firm turns over its inventory 10.8 times per year as contrasted with an industry average of 7 times.[3] This tells us that Saxton is able to generate more sales per dollar of inventory than the average company in the industry does, and we can assume that the firm uses very efficient inventory-ordering and cost-control methods.

The firm maintains a slightly lower ratio of sales to fixed assets (plant and equipment) than does the industry (5 versus 5.4). This is a relatively minor consideration in view of the rapid movement of inventory and accounts receivable. Finally, the rapid turnover of total assets is again indicated (2.5 versus 1.5).

**C. Liquidity ratios** After considering profitability and asset utilization, the analyst needs to examine the liquidity of the firm. The Saxton Company's liquidity ratios fare quite well in comparison with the industry. Further analysis might call for a cash budget to determine if we can meet each maturing obligation as it comes due.

*C. Liquidity ratios—*

| | Saxton Company | Industry Average |
|---|---|---|
| 9. Current ratio = $\frac{\text{Current assets}}{\text{Current liabilities}}$ | $\frac{\$800{,}000}{\$300{,}000} = 2.67$ | 2.1 |
| 10. Quick ratio = $\frac{\text{Current assets} - \text{Inventory}}{\text{Current liabilities}}$ | $\frac{\$430{,}000}{\$300{,}000} = 1.43$ | 1.0 |

**D. Debt utilization ratios** The last grouping of ratios, debt utilization, allows the analyst to measure the prudence of the debt management policies of the firm.

Debt to total assets of 37.5 percent is slightly above the industry average of 33 percent, but well within the prudent range of 50 percent or less. One of the ways to benefit from an inflationary economy is

[3]This ratio may also be computed by using "cost of goods sold" in the numerator. While this offers some theoretical advantages in terms of using cost figures in both the numerator and denominator, Dun and Bradstreet and other credit reporting agencies generally show turnover as in ratio 6.

through the utilization of heavy long-term debt, enabling long-standing obligations to be repaid in inflated dollars with the passage of time.

*D. Debt utilization ratios—*

| | Saxton Company | | Industry Average |
|---|---|---|---|
| 11. Debt to total assets = $\frac{\text{Total debt}}{\text{Total assets}}$ | $\frac{\$600{,}000}{\$1{,}600{,}000}$ | = 37.5% | 33% |
| 12. Times interest earned = $\frac{\text{Income before interest and taxes}}{\text{Interest}}$ | $\frac{\$550{,}000}{\$50{,}000}$ | = 11 | 7 times |
| 13. Fixed charge coverage = $\frac{\text{Income before fixed charges and taxes}}{\text{Fixed charges}}$ | $\frac{\$600{,}000}{\$100{,}000}$ | = 6 | 5.5 times |

Ratios for times interest earned and fixed charge coverage show that the Saxton Company debt is being well managed compared to the debt management of other firms in the industry. Times interest earned indicates the number of times that our income before interest and taxes covers the interest obligation (11). The higher the ratio, the stronger is the interest-paying ability of the firm. The figure for income before interest and taxes in the ratio is the equivalent of the operating profit figure presented in Table 3–1.

Fixed charge coverage measures the firm's ability to meet all fixed obligations rather than interest payments alone, on the assumption that failure to meet any financial obligation will endanger the position of the firm. In the present case the Saxton Company has lease obligations of $50,000 as well as the $50,000 in interest expenses. Thus the total fixed charge financial obligation is $100,000. We also need to know the income before all fixed charge obligations. In this case, we take income before interest and taxes (operating profit) and add back the $50,000 in lease payments.

| | |
|---|---|
| Income before interest and taxes . . . . . . | $550,000 |
| Lease payments. . . . . . . . . . . . . . | 50,000 |
| Income before fixed charges and taxes . . . | $600,000 |

The fixed charges are safely covered 6 times, exceeding the industry norm of 5.5 times. The various ratios are summarized in Table 3–3.

**Table 3–3**
**Ratio analysis**

| | Saxton Company | Industry Average | Conclusion |
|---|---|---|---|
| A. Profitability | | | |
| 1. Net income to sales | 5% | 6.5% | Below average |
| 2. Net income to total assets | 12.5% | 10% | Above average due to high turnover |
| 3. Net income to stockholders' equity | 20% | 15% | Good due to ratios 2 and 10 |
| B. Asset Utilization | | | |
| 4. Receivable turnover | 11.4 | 10 | Good |
| 5. Average collection period | 32 | 36 | Good |
| 6. Inventory turnover | 10.8 | 7 | Good |
| 7. Fixed asset turnover | 5 | 5.4 | Below average |
| 8. Total asset turnover | 2.5 | 1.5 | Good |
| C. Liquidity | | | |
| 9. Current ratio | 2.67 | 2.1 | Good |
| 10. Quick ratio | 1.43 | 1.0 | Good |
| D. Debt Utilization | | | |
| 11. Debt to total assets | 37.5% | 33% | Slightly more debt |
| 12. Times interest earned | 11 | 7 | Good |
| 13. Fixed charge coverage | 6 | 5.5 | Good |

The conclusions reached in comparing the Saxton Company to industry averages are generally valid, though exceptions may exist. For example, a high inventory turnover is considered "good" unless it is achieved by maintaining unusually low inventory levels, which may hurt future profitability.

In summary, the Saxton Company more than compensates for a lower return on the sales dollar by a rapid turnover of assets, principally inventory and receivables, and a wise use of debt. The student should be able to use these 13 measures to evaluate the financial performance of any firm.

## Trend Analysis

Over the course of the business cycle, sales and profitability may expand and contract, and ratio analysis for any one year may not present an accurate picture of the firm. Therefore, we look at trend analysis of performance over a number of years. However, without industry

Figure 3–2
Trend analysis

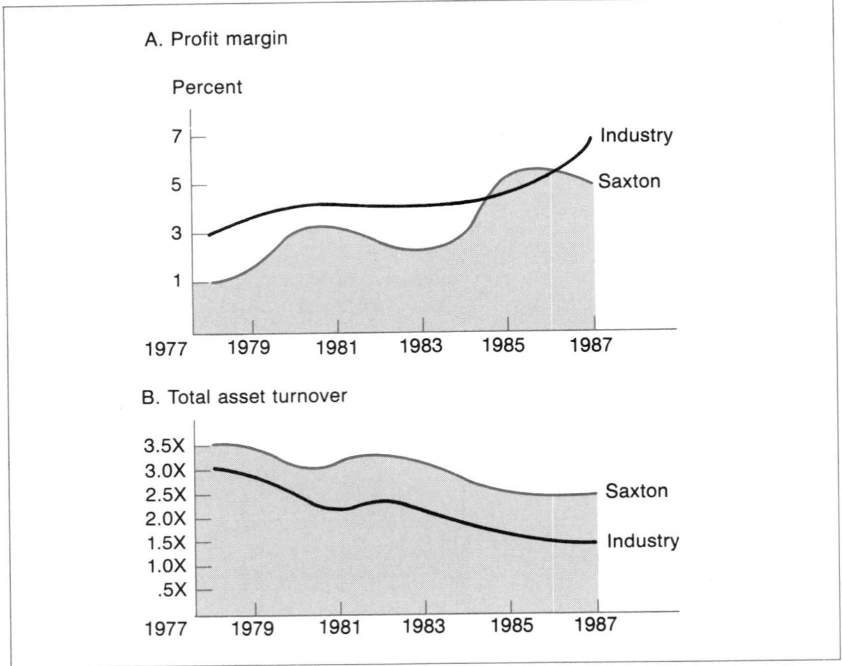


comparisons even trend analysis may not present a complete picture. For example, in Figure 3–2 we see that the profit margin for the Saxton Company has improved, while asset turnover has declined. This by itself may look good for the profit margin and bad for asset turnover. However, when compared to industry trends, we see that the firm's profit margin is still below the industry average. On asset turnover, Saxton has improved in relation to the industry even though it is in a downward trend. Similar data could be generated for the other ratios.

By analyzing companies in the same industry, one company can compare its performance to the industry leader. In the case of the oil industry, Exxon Corporation is the world's largest and most consistent company. If we compare Texaco and Chevron to Exxon, we assume that the goal of management is to become the best, not just match the average performance for the industry. Using the profit margin and

**Table 3–4**
**Trend analysis, using an industry leader**

| | Exxon | | Chevron | | Texaco | |
|---|---|---|---|---|---|---|
| Year | Profit Margin | Return on Equity | Profit Margin | Return on Equity | Profit Margin | Return on Equity |
| 1976 | 5.4% | 14.3% | 4.5% | 12.6% | 3.3% | 9.7% |
| 1977 | 4.5 | 12.4 | 4.9 | 13.3 | 3.3 | 9.9 |
| 1978 | 4.6 | 13.7 | 4.8 | 13.4 | 3.0 | 9.0 |
| 1979 | 5.4 | 19.1 | 6.0 | 19.2 | 4.6 | 16.5 |
| 1980 | 5.5 | 22.2 | 5.9 | 21.7 | 4.4 | 17.9 |
| 1981 | 5.2 | 19.5 | 5.4 | 18.7 | 4.0 | 16.8 |
| 1982 | 4.3 | 14.6 | 4.0 | 10.4 | 3.0 | 10.0 |
| 1983 | 5.6 | 16.9 | 6.4 | 12.5 | 3.1 | 8.4 |
| 1984 | 6.1 | 19.2 | 6.3 | 11.5 | 2.2 | 7.6 |
| 1985 est. | 6.1 | 18.5 | 3.3 | 10.5 | 1.8 | 6.5 |

return on equity as selected ratios, Table 3–4 compares these three companies.

If we look at the overall trend in profitability in Table 3–4, a cyclical pattern seems to exist. Every four or five years the profitability of each company seems to peak. While Chevron has been able to match Exxon on generating profits on sales, its return on equity exceeded Exxon's only in 1977 and 1979. Texaco on the other hand, has less consistency and is less competitive than either firm in generating profits. Since further information indicates that Exxon also has the lowest debt-to-asset ratio of the three companies over this 10-year period, it appears that the *quality* of its return on equity is higher than either Chevron's or Texaco's. In recent years, Chevron and Texaco both seem to be slipping farther behind the industry leader. Of course, Texaco also faces the problem of a large legal obligation in a lawsuit by Pennzoil.

## Impact of Inflation on Financial Analysis

Prior to, coincident with, or following the computation of financial ratios, we should explore the impact of inflation and other sources of distortion on the financial reporting of the firm. As illustrated in this section, inflation causes phantom sources of profit that may mislead even the most alert analyst. Disinflation also causes certain problems and we shall eventually consider these as well.

The major problem during inflationary times is that revenue is almost always stated in current dollars, whereas plant and equipment or inventory may have been purchased at lower price levels. Thus, profit may be more a function of increasing prices than of satisfactory performance.

## An Illustration

The Stein Corporation shows the accompanying income statement for 1986 (Table 3–5). At year-end the firm also has 100 units still in inventory at $1 per unit and $200 worth of plant and equipment with a 20-year life.

Assume that in 1987 the number of units sold remains constant at 100. However, inflation causes a 10 percent increase in price, from $2 to $2.20. Total sales will go up to $220, but with no actual increase in physical volume. Further assume the firm uses FIFO inventory pricing, so that inventory first purchased will be written off against current sales. In this case 1986 inventory will be written off against 1987 sales revenue.

The 1987 income statement of the Stein Corporation is shown in Table 3–6.

The company appears to have increased profit by $11 simply as a result of inflation. But not reflected is the increased cost of replacing

Table 3–5

STEIN CORPORATION
Net Income for 1986

| | | |
|---|---|---|
| Sales | $200 | (100 units at $2) |
| Cost of goods sold | 100 | (100 units at $1) |
| Gross profit | 100 | |
| Selling and administrative expense | 20 | |
| Depreciation | 10 | |
| Operating profit | 70 | |
| Taxes (40%) | 28 | |
| Aftertax income | $ 42 | |

Table 3–6

STEIN CORPORATION
Net Income for 1987

| | | |
|---|---|---|
| Sales | $220 | (100 units at 1987 price of $2.20) |
| Cost of goods sold | 100 | (100 units at $1.00) |
| Gross profit | 120 | |
| Selling and administrative expense | 22 | (10% of sales) |
| Depreciation | 10 | |
| Operating profit | 88 | |
| Taxes (40%) | 35 | |
| Aftertax income | $ 53 | |

plant and equipment. Presumably, its replacement cost has increased in an inflationary environment.

As mentioned in Chapter 2, inflation-related information is now required by the FASB for large companies, but only on a supplemental basis. What are the implications of this adjusted data? From a study[4] of 10 chemical firms and 8 drug companies, using current cost (replacement cost) data found in the financial 10K statements that these companies filed with the Securities and Exchange Commission, it was found that the changes shown in Table 3–7 occurred in their assets, income, and selected ratios.

**Table 3–7**
**Comparison of replacement cost accounting and historical cost accounting**

| | *Ten Chemical Companies* | | *Eight Drug Companies* | |
|---|---|---|---|---|
| | *Replacement Cost* | *Historical Cost* | *Replacement Cost* | *Historical Cost* |
| Increase in assets | 28.4% | — | 15.4% | — |
| Decrease in net income before taxes | (45.8%) | — | (19.3%) | — |
| Return on assets | 2.8% | 6.2% | 8.3% | 11.4% |
| Return on equity | 4.9% | 13.5% | 12.8% | 19.6% |
| Debt-to-assets ratio | 34.3% | 43.8% | 30.3% | 35.2% |
| Interest coverage ratio (times interest earned) | 7.1 × | 8.4 × | 15.4 × | 16.7 × |

[4]Jeff Garnett and Geoffrey A. Hirt, "Replacement Cost Data: A Study of the Chemical and Drug Industry for Years 1976 through 1978." Replacement cost is but one form of current cost. Nevertheless, it is widely used as a measure of current cost.

The comparison of replacement cost and historical cost accounting methods in the table shows that replacement cost reduces income but at the same time increases assets. This increase in assets lowers the debt-to-assets ratio since debt is a monetary asset that is not revalued because it is paid back in nominal dollars. The decreased debt-to-assets ratio would indicate that the financial leverage of the firm is decreased, but a look at the interest coverage ratio tells a different story. Because the interest coverage ratio measures the operating income available to cover interest expense, the declining income penalizes this ratio and the firm has decreased its ability to cover its interest cost.

### Disinflation Effect

As long as prices continue to rise in an inflationary environment, profits appear to feed on themselves. The main objection is that when price increases moderate (disinflation), there will be a rude awakening for management and unsuspecting stockholders as expensive inventory is charged against softening retail prices. A 15 or 20 percent growth rate in earnings may be little more than an "inflationary illusion." Industries most sensitive to inflation-induced profits are those with cyclical products, such as lumber, copper, rubber, and food products, and also those in which inventory is a significant percentage of sales and profits.

A leveling off of prices is, of course, not necessarily bad. Even though inflation-induced corporate profits may be going down, investors may be more willing to place their funds in financial assets such as stocks and bonds. The reason for the shift may be a belief that declining inflationary pressures will no longer seriously impair the purchasing power of the dollar. Lessening inflation means that the required return that investors demand on financial assets will be going down, and with this lower demanded return, future earnings or interest should receive a higher current valuation.

None of the above happens with a high degree of certainty. To the extent that investors question the permanence of disinflation (leveling off of price increases), they may not act according to the script. That is, lower rates of inflation will not necessarily produce high stock and bond prices unless the price pattern appears sustainable over a reasonable period of time.

Whereas financial assets such as stocks and bonds have the potential (whether realized or not) to do well during disinflation, such is not the case for tangible (real) assets. Precious metals, such as gold and silver, gems, and collectibles, that boomed in the highly inflationary environment of the late 1970s fell off sharply in the early 1980s, as softening prices caused less perceived need to hold real assets as a hedge against inflation. The shifting back and forth by investors between financial and real assets may take place many times over a business cycle. Financial assets during 1982–85 have performed extremely well. Will they continue to outperform real assets? What are current expectations?

During the years 1982–85, inflation had been running slightly under 4 percent, which was substantially less than the previous 10-year average. Some economists think that inflation will rapidly increase in the late 1980s because of the large U.S. deficits and rapid increase in the money supply. Others estimate that the U.S. may face more disinflation, even to the point of the deflation (actual declining prices) found during the 1930s depression. While most economists are obviously clustered at the middle of these two extremes, there seems to be more uncertainty about the future of inflation now than in the last 20 years. The knowledgeable student will be aware of the ramifications of both inflation and disinflation in financial decision making.

## Other Elements of Distortion in Reported Income

The effect of changing prices is but one of a number of problems the analyst must cope with in evaluating a company. Other issues, such as the reporting of revenue, the treatment of nonrecurring items, and the tax write-off policy, cause dilemmas for the financial manager or analyst. The point may be illustrated by considering the income statements for two hypothetical companies in the same industry (Table 3–8). Both firms had identical operating performances for 1987—but Company A is very conservative in reporting its results, while Company B has attempted to maximize its reported income.

If both companies had reported income of $200,000 in the prior year of 1986, Company B would be thought to be showing substantial growth in 1987 with net income of $650,000, while Company A is reporting a "flat" or no-growth year of $200,000 in 1987. However,

Table 3–8

Income Statement
For the Year 1987

| | Conservative (A) | High Reported Income (B) |
|---|---|---|
| Sales | $4,000,000 | $4,200,000 |
| Cost of goods sold | 3,000,000 | 2,400,000 |
| Gross profit | 1,000,000 | 1,800,000 |
| Selling and administrative expense | 450,000 | 450,000 |
| Operating profit | 550,000 | 1,350,000 |
| Interest expense | 50,000 | 50,000 |
| Extraordinary loss | 100,000 | |
| Net income before taxes | 400,000 | 1,300,000 |
| Taxes (50%) | 200,000 | 650,000 |
| Net income | 200,000 | 650,000 |
| Extraordinary loss (net of tax) | | 50,000 |
| Net income transferred to retained earnings | $ 200,000 | $ 600,000 |

we have already established the fact that the companies have equal operating performance.

## Explanation of Discrepancies

Let us examine how the inconsistencies in Table 3–8 could take place. Emphasis is given to a number of key elements on the income statement.

**Sales** Company B reported $200,000 more in sales, although actual volume was precisely the same. This may be the result of different concepts of revenue recognition.

For example, certain assets may be sold on an installment basis over a long period of time. A conservative firm may defer recognition of the sales or revenue until each payment is received, while other firms may attempt to recognize a fully effected sale at the earliest possible date. Similarly, firms that lease assets may attempt to consider a long-term lease as the equivalent of a sale, while more conservative firms such as IBM or Digital Equipment only recognize as revenue each lease payment as it comes due. Although the accounting profession attempts to establish appropriate methods of financial reporting through generally accepted accounting principles, there is variation of reporting among firms.

**Cost of goods sold** The conservative firm (Company A) may well be using LIFO accounting in an inflationary environment, thus charging the last-purchased, more expensive items against sales, while Company B uses FIFO accounting—charging off less expensive inventory against sales. The $600,000 difference in cost of goods sold may also be explained by varying treatment of research and development costs.

**Extraordinary gains/losses** Nonrecurring gains or losses may occur from the sale of corporate fixed assets, lawsuits, or similar nonrecurring events. Some analysts argue that such extraordinary events should be included in computing the current income of the firm, while others would leave them off in assessing operating performance. Unfortunately, there is some inconsistency in the manner in which nonrecurring losses are treated in spite of determined attempts by the accounting profession to ensure uniformity of action. The conservative firm A has written off its $100,000 extraordinary loss against normally reported income, while firm B carries a subtraction against net income only after the $650,000 amount has been reported. Both had similar losses of $100,000, but firm B's is shown net of tax implications at $50,000.

Extraordinary gains and losses occur among large companies more often than you might think. In the last few years (1983–85) Chrysler Corporation has been a good example of a firm whose earnings have been affected by tax loss carry-forwards from the accumulated losses of more than $3.5 billion suffered during 1978–82. Chevron, which was previously compared to Exxon, had nonrecurring per-share losses of 24¢ in 1982, 50¢ in 1983, and 46¢ in 1984. These losses arose from its consolidation and disposition of assets when it acquired the Gulf Oil Corporation. In this age of mergers, tender offers, and buy-outs, understanding the finer points of financial statements becomes even more important.

### Net Income

Firm A has reported net income of $200,000, while Firm B claims $650,000 before subtraction of extraordinary losses. The $450,000 difference is attributed to different methods of financial reporting, and it should be recognized as such by the analyst. No superior performance has actually taken place. The analyst must remain ever alert in examining each item in the financial statements, rather than accepting bottom-line figures.

## Summary

The subject of financial analysis was divided into two categories: an examination of ratio analysis and a study of the shortcomings in reported financial data from the viewpoint of a financial manager. Under ratio analysis, we developed four categories of ratios: profitability, asset utilization, liquidity, and debt utilization. Each ratio for the firm should be compared to industry measures and analyzed in light of past trends. The use of ratio analysis is rather like the solving of a mystery in which each clue leads to a new area of inquiry.

Financial analysis in the 1980s also calls for an awareness of the impact of inflation and disinflation on the reported income of the firm. Inflation leads to phantom profits which are created as a result of buying goods and reselling them at inflation-induced higher prices. The process is further magnified by the use of FIFO accounting, in which older inventory items are costed against current prices. Alternate methods of financial reporting may allow firms with equal performance to report different results.

## List of Terms

**FIFO**
**LIFO**
**replacement cost**
**inventory profits**
**Du Pont system of ratio analysis**
**disinflation**
**trend analysis**
**Dun & Bradstreet**
**profitability ratios**
**asset utilization ratios**
**liquidity ratios**
**debt utilization ratios**

## Discussion Questions

1. If we divide users of ratios into short-term lenders, long-term lenders, and stockholders, which ratios would each group be *most* interested in, and for what reasons?

2. Inflation can have significant effects on income statements and balance sheets, and therefore on the calculation of ratios. Discuss the possible impact of inflation on the following ratios, and explain the direction of the impact based on your assumptions.

   *a*. Return on investment.
   *b*. Inventory turnover.
   *c*. Fixed asset turnover.
   *d*. Debt-to-assets ratio.

3. Explain how the Du Pont system of analysis breaks down return on assets. Also explain how it breaks down return on stockholders' equity.

4. How would our analysis of profitability ratios be distorted if we used income before taxes? Income before interest and taxes?

5. Is there any validity in rule-of-thumb ratios for all corporations, for example, a current ratio of 2 to 1 or debt to assets of 50 percent?

6. Why is trend analysis helpful in analyzing ratios?

7. What effect will disinflation following a highly inflationary period have on the reported income of the firm?

8. Why might disinflation prove to be favorable to financial assets?

9. Comparisons of income can be very difficult for two companies even though they sell the same products in equal volume. Why?

## Problems

1. Watson Data Systems is considering expansion into a new word processing product line. New assets to support expansion will cost $500,000. It is estimated that Watson can generate $1,200,000 in annual sales, with a 6 percent profit margin.

What would net income and return on assets (investment) be for the year?

2. Using the Du Pont method, evaluate the effects of the following relationships for the Lollar Corporation.

   *a.* Lollar Corporation has a profit margin of 5 percent and its return on assets (investment) is 13.5 percent. What is its assets turnover?
   *b.* If the Lollar Corporation has a debt-to-total-assets ratio of 60 percent, what will the firm's return on equity be?
   *c.* What would happen to return on equity if the debt-to-total-assets ratio decreased to 40 percent?

3. *a.* Trace Manufacturing had an asset turnover of 1.2 times per year. If the return on total assets (investment) was 7.2 percent, what was Trace's profit margin?
   *b.* The following year, on the same level of assets, Trace's asset turnover declined to 1.0 times and its profit margin was 7.2 percent. How did the return on total assets change from that of the previous year?

4. A firm has sales of $1.2 million, and 10 percent of the sales are for cash. The year-end accounts receivable balance is $360,000. What is the average collection period? (Use a 360-day year.)

5. The balance sheet for the Bryan Corporation is given below. Sales for the year were $3,040,000, with 75 percent of sales on credit.

BRYAN CORPORATION
Balance Sheet 198X

| *Assets* | | *Liabilities and Stockholders' Equity* | |
|---|---|---|---|
| Cash | $ 50,000 | Accounts payable | $220,000 |
| Accounts receivable | 280,000 | Accrued taxes | 80,000 |
| Inventory | 240,000 | Bonds payable (long-term) | 118,000 |
| Plant and equipment | 380,000 | Common stock | 100,000 |
| | | Paid-in capital | 150,000 |
| | | Retained earnings | 282,000 |
| Total assets | $950,000 | Total liabilities and stockholders' equity | $950,000 |

Compute the following ratios:

*a.* Current ratio.
*b.* Quick ratio.

*c*. Debt to total assets.
*d*. Asset turnover.
*e*. Average collection period.

6. The Meredith Corporation's income statement is given below.

   *a*. What is the times-interest-earned ratio?
   *b*. What would be the fixed-charge-coverage ratio?

MEREDITH CORPORATION

| | |
|---|---|
| Sales | $200,000 |
| Cost of goods sold | 116,000 |
| Gross profit | 84,000 |
| Fixed charges (other than interest) | 24,000 |
| Income before interest and taxes | 60,000 |
| Interest | 12,000 |
| Income before taxes | 48,000 |
| Taxes (50%) | 24,000 |
| Income after taxes | $ 24,000 |

7. Using the income statement for the Sports Car Tire Company, compute the following ratios:

   *a*. The interest coverage.
   *b*. The fixed charge coverage.

   The total assets for this company equal $40,000. Set up the equation for the Du Pont system of ratio analysis, and compute *c*, *d*, and *e*.

   *c*. Return on investment (assets).
   *d*. Profit margin.
   *e*. Total asset turnover.

THE SPORTS CAR TIRE COMPANY

| | |
|---|---|
| Sales | $20,000 |
| Less: Cost of goods sold | 9,000 |
| Gross profit | $11,000 |
| Less: Selling and administrative expense | 4,000 |
| Less: Lease expense | 1,000 |
| Operating profit* | $ 6,000 |
| Less: Interest expense | 500 |
| Earnings before taxes | $ 5,500 |
| Less: Taxes (40%) | 2,200 |
| Earnings after taxes | $ 3,300 |

*Equals income before interest and taxes

8. A firm has net income before taxes of $120,000 and interest expense of $24,000.

   *a.* What is the times-interest-earned ratio?
   *b.* If the firm's lease payments are $40,000, what is the fixed charge coverage?

9. In January 1977 the Status Quo Company was formed. Total assets were $500,000, of which $300,000 consisted of depreciable fixed assets. Status Quo uses straight-line depreciation, and in 1977 it estimated its fixed assets to have useful lives of 10 years. Aftertax income has been $26,000 per year each of the last 10 years. Other assets have not changed since 1977.

   *a.* Compute return on assets at year-end for 1977, 1979, 1982, 1984, and 1986. (Use $26,000 in the numerator for each year.)
   *b.* To what do you attribute the phenomenon shown in part *a*?
   *c.* Now assume that income increased by 10 percent each year. What effect would this have on your above answers? Comment.

10. The Lawton Corporation has the following information on net income and sales. Industry information is also shown.

| *Year* | *Net Income* | *Sales* | *Industry Data on Profit Margin* |
|---|---|---|---|
| 1985 . . . . | $160,000 | $2,500,000 | 6.0% |
| 1986 . . . . | 180,000 | 3,200,000 | 4.9 |
| 1987 . . . . | 180,000 | 3,600,000 | 3.8 |

As an industry analyst examining the profit margin, are you likely to offer praise or criticism for the firm?

11. The Hobart Corporation shows the following income statement. The firm uses FIFO inventory accounting.

HOBART CORPORATION
Income Statement for 1986

| | | |
|---|---|---|
| Sales . . . . . . . . . . . . | $100,000 | (10,000 units at $10) |
| Cost of goods sold . . . . . . | 50,000 | (10,000 units at $5) |
| Gross profit . . . . . . . . . | 50,000 | |
| Selling and administrative expense . . . . . . . . . . | 5,000 | |
| Depreciation . . . . . . . . . | 10,000 | |
| Operating profit . . . . . . . | 35,000 | |
| Taxes (40%) . . . . . . . . . | 14,000 | |
| Aftertax income . . . . . . . . | $ 21,000 | |

*a.* Assume in 1987 the same 10,000 unit volume is maintained, but that the sales price increases by 10 percent. Because of FIFO inventory policy, old inventory will still be charged off at $5 per unit. Also assume that selling and administrative expense will be 5 percent of sales and depreciation will be unchanged. The tax rate is 40 percent. Compute aftertax income for 1987.

*b.* In part *a*, by what percent did aftertax income increase as a result of a 10 percent increase in the sales price? Explain why this impact took place.

*c.* Now assume in 1988 the volume remains constant at 10,000 units, but that the sales price decreases by 15 percent from its 1987 level. Also because of FIFO inventory policy, cost of goods sold reflects the inflationary conditions of the prior year and are $5.50 per unit. Further assume that selling and administrative expense will be 5 percent of sales and depreciation will be unchanged. The tax rate is 40 percent. Compute aftertax income.

**12.** The Diverse Corporation has three subsidiaries:

| | *Housing* | *Shoes* | *Movies* |
|---|---|---|---|
| Sales | $12,000,000 | $2,000,000 | $6,000,000 |
| Net income (after taxes) | 900,000 | 100,000 | 500,000 |
| Assets | 6,000,000 | 1,600,000 | 5,000,000 |

*a.* Which division has the lowest return on sales?

*b.* Which division has the highest return on assets?

*c.* Compute return on assets for the entire corporation.

*d.* If the $5,000,000 investment in the movie division is sold off and redeployed in the housing subsidiary at the same rate of return on assets currently achieved in the housing division, what will be the new return on assets for the entire corporation?

**13.** Construct the current assets section of the balance sheet shown here from the following data:

| | |
|---|---|
| Yearly sales (credit) | $420,000 |
| Inventory turnover | 7 times |
| Current liabilities | $ 80,000 |
| Current ratio | 2 |
| Quick ratio | 1.25 |
| Average collection period | 36 days |

| | |
|---|---|
| Current assets: | $ |
| Cash | ______ |
| Accounts receivable | ______ |
| Inventory | ______ |
| Total current assets | ______ |

**14.** The Shannon Corporation has sales of $750,000. Given the following ratios, fill in the balance sheet below.

| | |
|---|---|
| Total assets turnover | 2.5 times |
| Cash to total assets | 2.0 percent |
| Accounts receivable turnover | 10.0 times |
| Inventory turnover | 15.0 times |
| Current ratio | 2.0 times |
| Debt to total assets | 45.0 percent |

SHANNON CORPORATION
Balance Sheet, 198X

| Assets | | Liabilities and Stockholders' Equity | |
|---|---|---|---|
| Cash | ______ | Current debt | ______ |
| Accounts receivable | ______ | Long-term debt | ______ |
| Inventory | ______ | Total debt | ______ |
| Total current assets | ______ | Net worth | ______ |
| Fixed assets | ______ | Total liabilities and stockholders' | |
| Total assets | ______ | equity | ______ |

**15.** We are given the following information for the Pettit Corporation.

| | |
|---|---|
| Sales (credit) | $3,000,000 |
| Cash | 150,000 |
| Inventory | 850,000 |
| Current liabilities | 700,000 |
| Asset turnover | 1.25 times |
| Current ratio | 2.50 times |
| Debt-to-assets ratio | 40% |
| Receivables turnover | 6 times |

Current assets are composed of cash, marketable securities, accounts receivable and inventory. Calculate the following balance sheet items.

*a.* Accounts receivable.
*b.* Marketable securities.
*c.* Fixed assets.
*d.* Long-term debt.

**16.** The following data are from U Guessed It Company's financial statements. U Guessed It is a manufacturer of board games for young adults, and it competes with Marker Brothers and Bilton Radley. Sales (all credit) were $20 million for 1983.

| | |
|---|---|
| Sales to total assets | 2 times |
| Total debt to assets | 40% |
| Current ratio | 3.0 times |

| | |
|---|---|
| Inventory turnover | 5.0 times |
| Average collection period | 18 days |
| Fixed asset turnover | 5.0 times |

**Fill in the brief balance sheet:**

| | | | |
|---|---|---|---|
| Cash | ______ | Current debt | ______ |
| Accounts receivable | ______ | Long-term debt | ______ |
| Inventory | ______ | Total debt | ______ |
| Total current assets | ______ | Net worth | ______ |
| Fixed assets | ______ | Total liabilities | |
| Total assets | ______ | and equity | ______ |

**17. Using the financial statements for the Hobart Corporation, calculate the 13 basic ratios found in the chapter.**

HOBART CORPORATION
Balance Sheet
December 31, 1986

*Assets*

| | |
|---|---|
| Current assets: | |
| Cash | $ 50,000 |
| Marketable securities | 20,000 |
| Accounts receivable (net) | 160,000 |
| Inventory | 200,000 |
| Total current assets | $430,000 |
| Investments | 60,000 |
| Plant and equipment | 600,000 |
| Less: Accumulated depreciation | (190,000) |
| Net plant and equipment | 410,000 |
| Total assets | $900,000 |

*Liabilities and Stockholders' Equity*

| | |
|---|---|
| Current liabilities: | |
| Accounts payable | $ 90,000 |
| Notes payable | 70,000 |
| Accrued taxes | 10,000 |
| Total current liabilities | $170,000 |
| Long-term liabilities: | |
| Bonds payable | 150,000 |
| Total Liabilities | $320,000 |
| Stockholders' equity: | |
| Preferred stock, $50 par value | 100,000 |
| Common stock, $1 par value | 80,000 |
| Capital paid in excess of par | 190,000 |
| Retained earnings | 210,000 |
| Total stockholders' equity | $580,000 |
| Total liabilities and stockholders' equity | $900,000 |

HOBART CORPORATION
Income Statement
For the Year Ending December 31, 1986

| | |
|---|---|
| Sales (on credit) | $1,980,000 |
| Less: Cost of goods sold | 1,280,000 |
| Gross profit | 700,000 |
| Less: Selling and administrative expenses | 475,000* |
| Operating profit (EBIT) | 225,000 |
| Less: Interest expense | 25,000 |
| Earnings before taxes (EBT) | 200,000 |
| Less: Taxes of 40% | 80,000 |
| Earnings after taxes (EAT) | $ 120,000 |

*Includes $35,000 in lease payments.

**18.** *(Comprehensive problem)*
Given the financial statements for Jones Corporation and Smith Corporation shown here:

*a.* To which one would you, as credit manager for a supplier, approve the extension of (short-term) trade credit? Why? Compute all ratios before answering.
*b.* In which one would you buy stock? Why?

JONES CORPORATION

| *Current Assets* | | *Liabilities* | |
|---|---|---|---|
| Cash | $ 20,000 | Accounts payable | $100,000 |
| Accounts receivable | 80,000 | Bonds payable—10% | 80,000 |
| Inventory | 50,000 | | |
| *Long-Term Assets* | | *Stockholders' Equity* | |
| Fixed assets | $500,000 | Common stock | $150,000 |
| Less: Accum. dep. | (150,000) | Paid-in capital | 70,000 |
| Net fixed assets | 350,000 | Retained earnings | 100,000 |
| | $500,000 | | $500,000 |

| | |
|---|---|
| Sales (on credit) | $1,250,000 |
| Cost of goods sold | 750,000 |
| Gross profit | 500,000 |
| Selling and administrative expense | 257,000* |
| Less: Depreciation expense | 50,000 |
| Operating profit | 193,000 |
| Interest expense | 8,000 |
| Earnings before taxes | 185,000 |
| Tax expense (50%) | 92,500 |
| Net income | $ 92,500 |

*Includes $7,000 in lease payments.

Jones Corporation has 75,000 shares outstanding.

SMITH CORPORATION

| *Current Assets* | | *Liabilities* | |
|---|---|---|---|
| Cash | $ 35,000 | Accounts payable | $ 75,00 |
| Marketable securities | 7,500 | Bonds payable—10% | 210,000 |
| Accounts receivable | 70,000 | | |
| Inventory | 75,000 | | |
| *Long-Term Assets* | | *Stockholders' Equity* | |
| Fixed assets | $500,000 | Common stock | $ 75,000 |
| Less: Accum. dep. | (250,000) | Paid-in capital | 30,000 |
| Net fixed assets | 250,000 | Retained earnings | 47,500 |
| | $437,500 | | $437,500 |

| | |
|---|---|
| Sales (on credit) | $1.000.000 |
| Cost of goods sold | 600.000 |
| Gross profit | 400.000 |
| Selling and administrative expense | 224.000* |
| Depreciation expense | 50.000 |
| Operating profit | 126.000 |
| Interest expense | 21.000 |
| Earnings before taxes | 105.000 |
| Tax expense | 52.500 |
| Net income | $ 52.500 |

*Includes $7.000 in lease payments.

Smith corporation has 75.000 shares outstanding.

**19.** (*Comprehensive problem on trend analysis and industry comparisons.*) Bob Adkins has recently been approached by his first cousin, Ed Lamar, with a proposal to buy a 15 percent interest in Lamar Swimwear. The firm manufactures stylish bathing suits and sun-screen products.

Mr. Lamar is quick to point out the increase in sales that has taken place over the last three years as indicated in the income statement, Exhibit 1. The annual growth rate is 25 percent. A balance sheet for a similar time period is shown in Exhibit 2, and selected industry ratios are presented in Exhibit 3. Note the industry growth rate in sales is only 10–12 percent per year.

There was a steady real growth of 3–4 percent in gross national product during the period under study. The rate of inflation was in the 5–6 percent range.

The stock in the corporation has become available due to the ill health of a current stockholder, who is in need of cash. The issue here is not to determine the exact price for the stock, but rather whether Lamar Swimwear represents an attractive investment situation. Although Mr. Adkins has a primary interest in the profitability ratios, he will take a close look at all the ratios. He has no fast and firm rules about required return on investment, but rather wishes to analyze the overall condition of the firm. The firm does not currently pay a cash dividend, and return to the investor must come from selling the stock in the future. After doing a thorough analysis (including ratios for each year and comparisons to the industry), what comments and recommendations can you offer to Mr. Adkins.

Exhibit 1

LAMAR SWIMWEAR
Income Statement

| | 198X | 198Y | 198Z |
|---|---|---|---|
| Sales (all on credit) | $1.200.000 | $1.500.000 | $1.875.000 |
| Cost of goods sold | 800.000 | 1.040.000 | 1.310.000 |
| Gross profit | $ 400.000 | $ 460.000 | $ 565.000 |
| Selling and administrative expense* | 239.900 | 274.000 | 304.700 |
| Operating profit (EBIT) | $ 160.100 | $ 186.000 | $ 260.300 |
| Interest expense | 35.000 | 45.000 | 85.000 |
| Net income before taxes | $ 125.100 | $ 141.000 | $ 175.300 |
| Taxes | 36.900 | 49.200 | 55.600 |
| Net income | $ 88.200 | $ 91.800 | $ 119.700 |
| Shares | 30.000 | 30.000 | 38.000 |
| Earnings per share | $2.94 | $3.06 | $3.15 |

*Includes $15.000 in lease payments for each year.

Exhibit 2

LAMAR SWIMWEAR
Balance Sheet

| Assets | 198X | 198Y | 198Z |
|---|---|---|---|
| Cash | $ 30.000 | $ 40.000 | $ 30.000 |
| Marketable securities | 20.000 | 25.000 | 30.000 |
| Accounts receivable | 170.000 | 259.000 | 360.000 |
| Inventory | 230.000 | 261.000 | 290.000 |
| Total current assets | $ 450.000 | $ 585.000 | $ 710.000 |
| Net plant and equipment | 650.000 | 765.000 | 1.390.000 |
| Total assets | $1.100.000 | $1.350.000 | $2.100.000 |

| *Liabilities and Stockholders' Equity* | *198X* | *198Y* | *198Z* |
|---|---|---|---|
| Accounts payable | $ 200,000 | $ 310,000 | $ 505,000 |
| Accrued expenses | 20,400 | 30,000 | 35,000 |
| Total current liabilities | $ 220,400 | $ 340,000 | $ 540,000 |
| Long-term liabilities | 325,000 | 363,600 | 703,900 |
| Total liabilities | $ 545,400 | $ 703,600 | $1,243,900 |
| Common stock ($2 par) | 60,000 | 60,000 | 76,000 |
| Capital paid in excess of par | 190,000 | 190,000 | 264,000 |
| Retained earnings | 304,600 | 396,400 | 516,100 |
| Total stockholders' equity | $ 554,600 | $ 646,400 | $ 856,100 |
| Total liabilities and stockholders' equity | $1,100,000 | $1,350,000 | $2,100,000 |

Exhibit 3

Selected Industry Ratios

| | *198X* | *198Y* | *198Z* |
|---|---|---|---|
| Growth in sales | | 10.00% | 12.00% |
| Profit margin | 7.71% | 7.82% | 7.96% |
| Return on assets (investment) | 8.09% | 8.68% | 8.95% |
| Return on equity | 14.31% | 15.26% | 16.01% |
| Receivables turnover | 9.02 × | 8.86 × | 9.31 × |
| Average collection period | 39.9 days | 40.6 days | 38.7 days |
| Inventory turnover | 4.24 × | 5.10 × | 5.11 × |
| Fixed asset turnover | 1.60 × | 1.64 × | 1.75 × |
| Total asset turnover | 1.05 × | 1.10 × | 1.12 × |
| Current ratio | 1.96 × | 2.25 × | 2.40 × |
| Quick ratio | 1.37 × | 1.41 × | 1.38 × |
| Debt to total assets | 43.47% | 43.11% | 44.10% |
| Times interest earned | 6.50 × | 5.99 × | 6.61 × |
| Fixed charge coverage | 4.70 × | 4.69 × | 4.73 × |
| Growth in earnings per share | | 10.10% | 13.30% |

## Selected References

Altman, Edward I. "Financial Ratios, Discriminant Analysis, and the Prediction of Corporate Bankruptcy." *Journal of Finance* 23 (September 1968), pp. 589–609.

Benishay, Haskell. "Economic Information in Financial Ratio Analysis." *Accounting and Business Research* 2 (Spring 1971), pp. 174–79.

Callard, Charles G., and David C. Kleinman. "Inflation-Adjusted Accounting: Does it Matter?" *Financial Analysts Journal* 41 (May–June 1985), pp. 51–59.

Chen, Kung H., and Thomas A. Shimerda. "An Empirical Analysis of Useful Financial Ratios." *Financial Management* 10 (Spring 1981), pp. 51–60.

Copeland, Ronald M.; Joseph F. Wojdak; and John K. Shank. "The Use of LIFO to Offset Inflation." *Harvard Business Review* 49 (May–June 1971), pp. 91–100.

D'Ambrosio, Charles A. "Truth Reality and Financial Analysis." *Financial Analysts Journal* 38 (July–August 1982), pp. 24–25.

Davidson, S., and R. L. Weil. "Inflation Accounting." *Financial Analysts Journal* 31 (January–February), pp. 27–31, 70–84.

Friedman, Milton. "Economic Miracles." *Newsweek* 8 (January 21, 1974), p. 80.

Gandolfi, Arthur E. "Inflation, Taxation, and Interest Rates." *Journal of Finance* 37 (June 1982), 797–807.

Garnett, Jeff, and Geoffrey A. Hirt. "Replacement Cost Data: A Study of the Chemical and Drug Industry for Years 1976 through 1978." An unpublished study at Illinois State University, January 1980.

Helfert, Erich A. *Techniques of Financial Analysis*. 5th ed. Homewood, Ill.: Richard D. Irwin, 1982, chap. 2.

Jaedicke, Robert K., and Robert T. Sprouse. *Accounting Flows, Income, Funds, and Cash*. Englewood Cliffs, N.J.: Prentice-Hall, 1965, chap. 7.

Lev, Baruch. *Financial Statement Analysis: A New Approach*. Englewood Cliffs, N.J.: Prentice-Hall, 1974, chaps. 2–5.

Modigliani, Franco, and Richard A. Cohn. "Inflation Rational Valuation and the Market." *Financial Analysts Journal* 35 (March–April 1979), pp. 24–44.

Shank, John K. *Price-Level Adjusted Statements and Management Decisions*. New York: Financial Executives Research Foundations, 1975.

Siegel, Joel G. "The 'Quality of Earnings' Concept—A Survey." *Financial Analysts Journal* 38 (March–April 1982), 60–68.

Terborgh, George. "Inflation and Corporate Profits." *Readings in Financial Analysis*. Institute of Charters Financial Analysts. Homewood, Ill.: Richard D. Irwin, 1973, pp. 153–65.

Von Furstenberg, George M., and Burton G. Malkiel. "Financial Analysis in an Inflationary Environment." *Journal of Finance* 32 (May 1977), pp. 575–88.

Wallich, Henry C. "Investment Income during Inflation." *Financial Analysts Journal* 34 (March–April 1978), pp. 34–37.

Weston, J. Fred. "Financial Analysis: Planning and Control." *Financial Executive* 33 (July 1965), pp. 40–48.

Young, Allen H. "Alternative Estimates of Corporate Depreciation and Profits." *Survey of Current Business* 48 (April and May 1968), pp. 17–28, 16–28.

# 4 Financial Forecasting

The old notion of the corporate treasurer burning the midnight oil in order to find new avenues of financing before dawn is no longer in vogue. If there is one talent that is essential to the financial manager, it is the ability to plan ahead and to make necessary adjustments before actual events occur. Quite likely, we could construct the same set of external events for two corporations (inflation, recession, severe new competition, etc.), and one would survive, while the other would not. The outcome might be a function not only of their risk-taking desires, but also of their ability to hedge against risk with careful planning.

While we may assume that no growth or a decline in volume is the primary cause for a shortage of funds, this is not necessarily the case. A rapidly growing firm may witness a significant increase in accounts receivable, inventory, and plant and equipment that cannot be financed in the normal course of business. Assume that sales go from \$100,000 to \$200,000 in one year for a firm that has a 5 percent profit margin on sales. At the same time, assume that assets represent 50 percent of sales and go from \$50,000 to \$100,000 as sales double. The \$10,000 of profit (5 percent × \$200,000) will hardly be adequate to finance the

$50,000 asset growth. The remaining $40,000 must come from suppliers, the bank, and perhaps stockholders. The student should recognize that profit alone is generally inadequate to finance significant growth and that a comprehensive financing plan must be developed. All too often, the small businessman (and sometimes the big one as well) is mystified by an increase in sales and profits but less cash in the till.

## Constructing Pro Forma Statements

The most comprehensive means of financial forecasting is to go through the process of developing a series of pro forma, or projected, financial statements. We will give particular attention to the *pro forma income statement*, the *cash budget*, and the *pro forma balance sheet*. Based on the projected statements, the firm is able to judge its future level of receivables, inventory, payables, and other corporate accounts as well as its anticipated profits and borrowing requirements. The financial officer can then carefully track actual events against the plan and make necessary adjustments. Furthermore, the statements are often required by bankers and other lenders as a guide for the future.

A systems approach is necessary for the development of pro forma statements. We first construct a pro forma income statement based on sales projections and the production plan, then translate this material into a cash budget, and finally assimilate all previously developed material into a pro forma balance sheet. The process of developing pro forma financial statements is depicted in Figure 4–1. We will use a six-month time frame to facilitate the analysis, though the same procedures could be extended to one year or longer.

## Pro Forma Income Statement

Assume that the Goldman Corporation has been requested by its bank to provide pro forma financial statements for midyear 1987. The pro forma income statement will provide a projection of how much profit the firm anticipates making over the ensuing time period. In developing the pro forma income statement, we will follow four important steps.

Figure 4–1
Development of pro forma statements

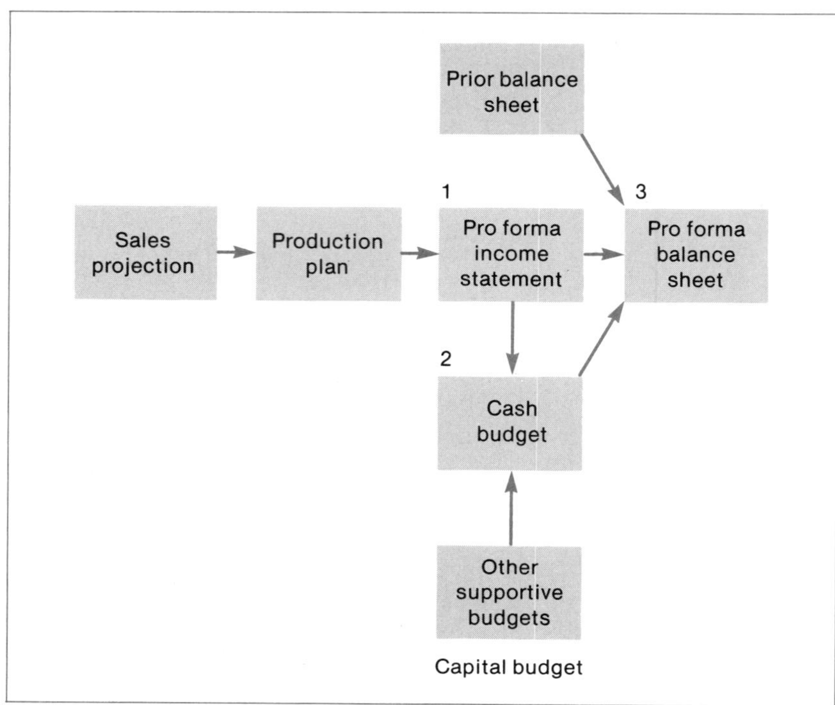


1. Establish a sales projection.
2. Determine a production schedule and the associated use of new material, direct labor, and overhead, to arrive at gross profit.
3. Compute other expenses.
4. Determine profit by completing the actual pro forma statement.

## Establish a Sales Projection

For purposes of analysis, we shall assume that the Goldman Corporation has two primary products: wheels and casters. Our sales projection calls for the sale of 1,000 wheels and 2,000 casters at prices of $30 and $35, respectively. As indicated in Table 4–1, we anticipate total sales of $100,000.

It is assumed that the sales projections were derived from both an external and internal viewpoint. Using the former, we analyze our

**Table 4–1**
**Projected wheel and caster sales (first six months, 1987)**

| | *Wheels* | *Casters* | |
|---|---|---|---|
| Quantity | 1,000 | 2,000 | |
| Sales price | $30 | $35 | |
| Sales revenue | $30,000 | $70,000 | |
| Total | | | $100,000 |

prospective sales in light of economic conditions affecting our industry and our company. Statistical techniques such as regression and time series analysis may be employed in the process. Internal analysis calls for surveying our own salespeople within their territories. Ideally, we would proceed along each of those paths in isolation of the other and then assimilate the results into one meaningful projection.

### Determine a Production Schedule and the Gross Profit

Based on anticipated sales, we determine the necessary production plan for the six-month period. The number of units produced will depend on the beginning inventory of wheels and casters, our sales projection, and the desired level of ending inventory. Assume that on January 1, 1987, the Goldman Corporation has in stock the items shown in Table 4–2.

We will add the projected quantity of unit sales for the next six months to our desired ending inventory and subtract our stock of beginning inventory (in units) to determine our production requirements.

*Units*

\+ Projected sales
\+ Desired ending inventory
− *Beginning* inventory
= Production requirements

**Table 4–2**
**Stock of beginning inventory**

| | *Wheels* | *Casters* | |
|---|---|---|---|
| Quantity | 85 | 180 | |
| Cost | $16 | $20 | |
| Total value | $1,360 | $3,600 | |
| Total | | | $4,960 |

In Table 4–3, we see a required production level of 1,015 wheels and 2,020 casters.

**Table 4–3**
**Production requirements for six months**

| | Wheels | Casters |
|---|---|---|
| Projected unit sales (Table 4–1) | +1,000 | +2,000 |
| Desired ending inventory (assumed to represent 10% of unit sales for the time period) | +100 | +200 |
| Beginning inventory (Table 4–2) | −85 | −180 |
| Units to be produced | 1,015 | 2,020 |

We must now determine the cost to produce these units. In Table 4–2 we saw that the cost of units in stock was $16 for wheels and $20 for casters. However, we shall assume that the price of materials, labor, and overhead going into the products is now $18 for wheels and $22 for casters, as indicated in Table 4–4.

**Table 4–4**
**Unit costs**

| | Wheels | Casters |
|---|---|---|
| Materials | $10 | $12 |
| Labor | 5 | 6 |
| Overhead | 3 | 4 |
| Total | $18 | $22 |

The *total* cost to produce the required items for the next six months is shown in Table 4–5.

**Table 4–5**
**Total production costs**

| | Wheels | Casters | |
|---|---|---|---|
| Units to be produced (Table 4–3) | 1,015 | 2,020 | |
| Cost per unit (Table 4–4) | $18 | $22 | |
| Total cost | $18,270 | $44,440 | $62,710 |

**Cost of goods sold** The main consideration in constructing a pro forma income statement is the costs specifically associated with units sold during the time period. Note that in the case of wheels we anticipate sales of 1,000 units, as indicated in Table 4–1 but are producing 1,015, as indicated in Table 4–5, to increase our inventory level by 15 units. For profit measurement purposes, we will *not* charge these extra 15 units against current sales.[1] Furthermore, in determining the cost of the 1,000 units sold during the current time period, we will *not* assume that all of the items sold represent inventory manufactured in this period. In the case of the Goldman Corporation, we shall assume that it uses FIFO (first-in, first-out) accounting and that it will first allocate the cost of current sales to beginning inventory and then to goods manufactured during the period.

In Table 4–6, we look at the revenue, associated cost of goods sold, and gross profit for both products. For example, 1,000 units of wheels are to be sold at a total revenue of $30,000. Of the 1,000 units, 85 units are from beginning inventory at a $16 cost (Table 4–2) and the balance of 915 units are from current production at an $18 cost. The total cost of goods sold for wheels is $17,830, yielding a gross profit of $12,170. The pattern is the same for casters, with sales of $70,000, cost of goods sold of $43,640, and gross profit of $26,360. The combined sales for the two products are $100,000, with cost of goods sold of $61,470 and gross profit of $38,530.

**Table 4–6**
**Allocation of manufacturing cost and determination of gross profits**

| | | *Wheels* | | *Casters* | *Combined* |
|---|---|---|---|---|---|
| Quantity sold (Table 4–1) | | 1,000 | | 2,000 | 3,000 |
| Sales price | | $30 | | $35 | |
| Sales revenue | | $30,000 | | $70,000 | $100,000 |
| Cost of goods sold: | | | | | |
| Old inventory (Table 4–2) | | | | | |
| Quantity (units) | 85 | | 180 | | |
| Cost per unit | $16 | | $20 | | |
| Total | | $ 1,360 | | $ 3,600 | |
| New inventory (the remainder) | | | | | |
| Quantity (units) | 915 | | 1,820 | | |
| Cost per unit (Table 4–4) | $18 | | $22 | | |
| Total | | 16,470 | | 40,040 | |
| Total cost of goods sold | | 17,830 | | 43,640 | $ 61,470 |
| Gross profit | | $12,170 | | $26,360 | $ 38,530 |

[1] Later on in the analysis we will show the effect that these extra units have on the cash budget and the balance sheet.

At this point, we also compute the value of ending inventory for later use in constructing financial statements. As indicated in Table 4–7, the value of ending inventory will be $6,200.

Table 4–7
Value of ending inventory

| | |
|---|---|
| + Beginning inventory (Table 4–2) | $ 4,960 |
| + Total production costs (Table 4–5) | 62,710 |
| Total inventory available for sales | 67,670 |
| − Cost of goods sold (Table 4–6) | 61,470 |
| Ending inventory | $ 6,200 |

### Other Expense Items

Having computed total revenue, cost of goods sold, and gross profits, we must now subtract other expense items to arrive at a net profit figure. We deduct general and administrative expenses as well as interest expenses from gross profit to arrive at earnings before taxes, then subtract taxes to determine aftertax income, and finally deduct dividends to ascertain the contribution to retained earnings. For the Goldman Corporation, we shall assume that general and administrative expenses are $12,000, interest expense is $1,500, and dividends are $1,500.

### Actual Pro Forma Income Statement

Combining the gross profit in Table 4–6 with our assumptions on other expense items we arrive at the pro forma income statement presented in Table 4–8. We anticipate earnings after taxes of $20,024, dividends of $1,500, and an increase in retained earnings of $18,524.

## Cash Budget

As previously indicated, the generation of sales and profits does not necessarily ensure that there will be adequate cash on hand to meet financial obligations as they come due. A profitable sale may generate accounts receivables in the short run, but no immediate cash to meet maturing obligations. For this reason, we must translate the pro forma

Table 4–8

Pro Forma Income Statement
June 30, 1987

| | |
|---|---|
| Sales revenue | $100,000 |
| Cost of goods sold | 61,470 |
| Gross profit | 38,530 |
| General and administrative expense | 12,000 |
| Operating profit (EBIT) | 26,530 |
| Interest expense | 1,500 |
| Earnings before taxes (EBT) | 25,030 |
| Taxes (20%)* | 5,006 |
| Earnings after taxes (EAT) | 20,024 |
| Common stock dividends | 1,500 |
| Increase in retained earnings | $ 18,524 |

*Though profit before taxes is slightly over $25,000, a convenient rate of 20 percent is applied to the full amount. The corporate rate is currently slightly different from the rate that is applied in the table.

income statement into cash flows. In this process we divide the longer-term pro forma income statement into smaller and more precise time frames in order to appreciate the seasonal and monthly patterns of cash inflows and outflows. Some months may represent particularly high or low sales volume or may require dividends, taxes, or capital expenditures.

## Cash Receipts

In the case of the Goldman Corporation, we break down the pro forma income statement for the first half of 1987 into a series of monthly cash budgets. In Table 4–1 we showed anticipated sales of $100,000 over this time period; we shall now assume that these sales can be divided into monthly projections, as indicated in Table 4–9.

A careful analysis of past sales and collection records indicates that 20 percent of sales are collected in the month of sales and 80 percent

Table 4–9
Monthly sales pattern

| *January* | *February* | *March* | *April* | *May* | *June* |
|---|---|---|---|---|---|
| $15,000 | $10,000 | $15,000 | $25,000 | $15,000 | $20,000 |

**Table 4–10**
**Monthly cash receipts**

| | Dec. | Jan. | Feb. | March | April | May | June |
|---|---|---|---|---|---|---|---|
| Sales | $12,000 | $15,000 | $10,000 | $15,000 | $25,000 | $15,000 | $20,000 |
| Collections (20% of current sales) | | $ 3,000 | $ 2,000 | $ 3,000 | $ 5,000 | $ 3,000 | $ 4,000 |
| Collections (80% of previous month's sales) | | 9,600 | 12,000 | 8,000 | 12,000 | 20,000 | 12,000 |
| Total cash receipts | | $12,600 | $14,000 | $11,000 | $17,000 | $23,000 | $16,000 |

in the following month. The cash receipt pattern related to monthly sales is shown in Table 4–10. It is assumed that sales for December 1986 were $12,000.

The cash inflows will vary between $11,000 and $23,000, with the high point in receipts coming in May.

We now examine the monthly outflows.

## Cash Payments

The primary considerations for cash payments are monthly costs associated with inventory manufactured during the period (material, labor, and overhead) and disbursements for general and administrative expenses, interest payments, taxes, and dividends. We must also consider cash payments for any new plant and equipment, an item that does not show up on our pro forma income statement.

Costs associated with units manufactured during the period may be taken from the data provided in Table 4–5, Total Production Costs. In Table 4–11, we simply recast these data in terms of materials, labor, and overhead.

**Table 4–11**
**Component costs of manufactured goods**

| | Wheels | | | Casters | | | |
|---|---|---|---|---|---|---|---|
| | Units Produced | Cost per Unit | Total Cost | Units Produced | Cost per Unit | Total Cost | Combined Cost |
| Materials | 1,015 | $10 | $10,150 | 2,020 | $12 | $24,240 | $34,390 |
| Labor | 1,015 | 5 | 5,075 | 2,020 | 6 | 12,120 | 17,195 |
| Overhead | 1,015 | 3 | 3,045 | 2,020 | 4 | 8,080 | 11,125 |
| | | | | | | | $62,710 |

We see that the total costs for components in the two products are material $34,390, labor $17,195, and overhead $11,125. We shall assume that all of these costs are incurred on an equal monthly basis over the six-month period. Even though the sales volume varies from month to month, we assume that we are employing level monthly production to ensure maximum efficiency in the use of various productive resources. Average monthly costs for materials, labor, and overhead are as shown in Table 4–12.

We shall pay for materials one month after the purchase has been made. Labor and overhead represent direct monthly cash outlays, as is true of interest, taxes, dividends, and assumed purchases of $8,000 in new equipment in February and $10,000 in June. We summarize all of our cash payments in Table 4–13. Past records indicate that $4,500 in materials was purchased in December.

**Table 4–12**
**Average monthly manufacturing costs**

| | *Total Costs* | *Time Frame* | *Average Monthly Cost* |
|---|---|---|---|
| Materials | $34,390 | 6 months | $5,732 |
| Labor | 17,195 | 6 months | 2,866 |
| Overhead | 11,125 | 6 months | 1,854 |

**Table 4–13**
**Summary of all monthly cash payments**

| | *Dec.* | *Jan.* | *Feb.* | *March* | *April* | *May* | *June* |
|---|---|---|---|---|---|---|---|
| *From Table 4–12:* | | | | | | | |
| Monthly material purchase | $4,500 | $ 5,732 | $ 5,732 | $ 5,732 | $ 5,732 | $ 5,732 | $ 5,732 |
| Payment for material (prior month's purchase) | | $ 4,500 | $ 5,732 | $ 5,732 | $ 5,732 | $ 5,732 | $ 5,732 |
| Monthly labor cost | | 2,866 | 2,866 | 2,866 | 2,866 | 2,866 | 2,866 |
| Monthly overhead | | 1,854 | 1,854 | 1,854 | 1,854 | 1,854 | 1,854 |
| *From Table 4–8:* | | | | | | | |
| General and administrative expense ($12,000 over 6 months) | | 2,000 | 2,000 | 2,000 | 2,000 | 2,000 | 2,000 |
| Interest expense | | | | | | | 1,500 |
| Taxes (two equal payments) | | | | 2,503 | | | 2,503 |
| Cash dividend | | | | | | | 1,500 |
| *Also:* | | | | | | | |
| New equipment purchases | | | 8,000 | | | | 10,000 |
| Total payments | | $11,220 | $20,452 | $14,955 | $12,452 | $12,452 | $27,953 |

## Actual Budget

We are now in a position to bring together our monthly cash receipts and payments into a cash flow statement, illustrated in Table 4–14. The difference between monthly receipts and payments is net cash flow for the month.

**Table 4–14**
**Monthly cash flow**

| | Jan. | Feb. | March | April | May | June |
|---|---|---|---|---|---|---|
| Total receipts (Table 4–10) | $12,600 | $14,000 | $11,000 | $17,000 | $23,000 | $16,000 |
| Total payments (Table 4–13) | 11,220 | 20,452 | 14,955 | 12,452 | 12,452 | 27,953 |
| Net cash flow | $ 1,380 | ($ 6,452) | ($ 3,955) | $ 4,548 | $10,548 | ($11,953) |

The primary purpose of the cash budget is to allow the firm to anticipate the need for outside funding at the end of each month. In the present case, we shall assume that the Goldman Corporation wishes to have a minimum cash balance of $5,000 at all times. If it goes below this amount, the firm will borrow funds from the bank. If it goes above $5,000 and the firm has a loan outstanding, it will use the excess funds to reduce the loan. This pattern of financing is demonstrated in Table 4–15—a fully developed cash budget with borrowing and repayment provisions.

The first line in Table 4–15 shows our net cash flow, which is added to the beginning cash balance to arrive at the cumulative cash balance. The fourth entry is the additional monthly loan or loan repayment, if any, required to maintain a minimum cash balance of $5,000. In order to keep track of our loan balance, the fifth entry presents cumulative loans outstanding for all months. Finally, we show the cash balance at

**Table 4–15** **Cash budget with borrowing and repayment**

| | Jan. | Feb. | March | April | May | June |
|---|---|---|---|---|---|---|
| 1. Net cash flow | $1,380 | ($6,452) | ($3,955) | $4,548 | $10,548 | ($11,953) |
| 2. Beginning cash balance | 5,000* | 6,380 | 5,000 | 5,000 | 5,000 | 11,069 |
| 3. Cumulative cash balance | 6,380 | (72) | 1,045 | 9,548 | 15,548 | (884) |
| 4. Monthly loan or (repayment) | — | 5,072 | 3,955 | (4,548) | (4,479) | 5,884 |
| 5. Cumulative loan balance | — | 5,072 | 9,027 | 4,479 | — | 5,884 |
| 6. Ending cash balance | 6,380 | 5,000 | 5,000 | 5,000 | 11,069 | 5,000 |

*We assume that the Goldman Corporation has a beginning cash balance of $5,000 on January 1, 1987, and that it desires a minimum monthly ending cash balance of $5,000.

the end of the month, which becomes the beginning cash balance for the next month.

At the end of January the firm has $6,380 in cash, but by the end of February the cumulative cash position of the firm is negative, necessitating a loan of $5,072 to maintain a $5,000 cash balance. The firm has a loan on the books until May, at which time there is an ending cash balance of $11,069. During the months of April and May the cumulative cash balance is greater than the required minimum cash balance of $5,000, so loan repayments of $4,548 and $4,479 are made to retire the loans completely in May. In June, the firm is once again required to borrow $5,884 in order to maintain a $5,000 cash balance.

## Pro Forma Balance Sheet

Now that we have developed a pro forma income statement and a cash budget, it is relatively simple to integrate all of these items into a pro forma balance sheet. Because the balance sheet represents cumulative changes in the corporation over time, we first examine the *prior* period's balance sheet and then translate these items through time to represent June 30, 1987. The last balance sheet, dated December 31, 1986, is shown in Table 4–16.

Table 4–16

Balance Sheet
December 31, 1986

| *Assets* | |
|---|---|
| Current assets: | |
| Cash | $ 5,000 |
| Marketable securities | 3,200 |
| Accounts receivable | 9,600 |
| Inventory | 4,960 |
| Total current assets | 22,760 |
| Plant and equipment | 27,740 |
| Total assets | $50,500 |
| *Liabilities and Stockholders' Equity* | |
| Accounts payable | $ 4,500 |
| Notes payable | 0 |
| Long-term debt | 15,000 |
| Common stock | 10,500 |
| Retained earnings | 20,500 |
| Total liabilities and stockholder's equity | $50,500 |

Figure 4–2
Development of a pro forma balance sheet

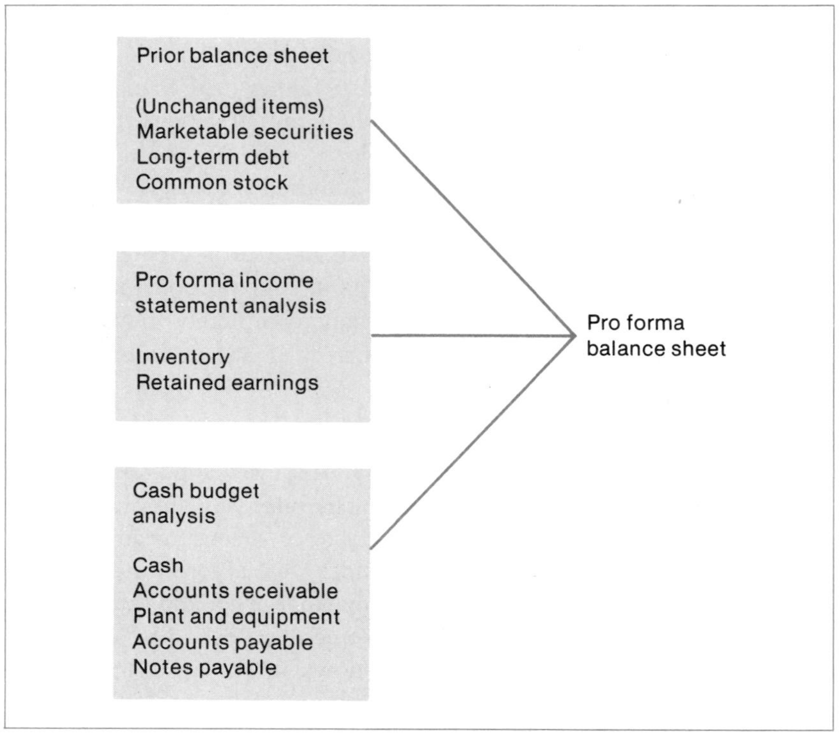


In constructing our pro forma balance sheet for June 30, 1987, some of the accounts from the old balance sheet will remain unchanged, while others will take on new values, as indicated by the pro forma income statement and cash budget. The process is depicted in Figure 4–2.

We present the new pro forma balance sheet as of June 30, 1987, in Table 4–17.

**Explanation of pro forma balance sheets** Each item in Table 4–17 can be explained on the basis of a prior calculation or assumption.

1. Cash ($5,000)—minimum cash balance as shown in Table 4–15.
2. Marketable securities ($3,200)—remains unchanged from prior period's value in Table 4–16.

**Table 4–17**

Pro Forma Balance Sheet
June 30, 1987

| *Assets* | |
|---|---|
| Current assets: | |
| 1. Cash | $ 5,000 |
| 2. Marketable securities | 3,200 |
| 3. Accounts receivable | 16,000 |
| 4. Inventory | 6,200 |
| Total current assets | 30,400 |
| 5. Plant and equipment | 45,740 |
| Total assets | $76,140 |
| *Liabilities and Stockholders' Equity* | |
| 6. Accounts payable | $ 5,732 |
| 7. Notes payable | 5,884 |
| 8. Long-term debt | 15,000 |
| 9. Common stock | 10,500 |
| 10. Retained earnings | 39,024 |
| Total liabilities and stockholders' equity | $76,140 |

3. Accounts receivable ($16,000)—based on June sales of $20,000 in Table 4–10. Twenty percent will be collected that month, while 80 percent will become accounts receivable at the end of the month.

$20,000 sales
× 80% receivables
$16,000

4. Inventory ($6,200)—ending inventory as shown in Table 4–7.
5. Plant and equipment ($45,740).

| | |
|---|---|
| Initial value (Table 4–16) | $27,740 |
| Purchases* (Table 4–13) | 18,000 |
| Plant and equipment | $45,740 |

*For simplicity, depreciation is not explicitly considered.

6. Accounts payable ($5,732)—based on June purchases in Table 4–13. They will not be paid until July, and thus are accounts payable.

7. Notes payable ($5,884)—the amount we must borrow to maintain our cash balance of $5,000, as shown in Table 4–15.
8. Long-term debt ($15,000)—remains unchanged from prior period's value in Table 4–16.
9. Common stock ($10,500)—remains unchanged from prior period's value in Table 4–16.
10. Retained earnings ($39,024)

| | |
|---|---|
| Initial value (Table 4–16) | $20,500 |
| Transfer of pro forma income to retained earnings (Table 4–8) | 18,524 |
| Retained earnings | $39,024 |

### Analysis of Pro Forma Statement

In comparing the pro forma balance sheet (Table 4–17) to the prior balance sheet (Table 4–16), we note that assets are up by $25,640.

| | |
|---|---|
| Total assets (June 30, 1987) | $76,140 |
| Total assets (Dec. 31, 1986) | 50,500 |
| Increase | $25,640 |

The growth must be financed by accounts payable, notes payable, and profit (as reflected by the increase in retained earnings). Though the company will enjoy a high degree of profitability, it must still look to bank financing of $5,884 to support the increase in assets. This represents the difference between the $25,640 buildup in assets, and the $1,232 increase in accounts payable as well as the $18,524 buildup in retained earnings.

## Percent-of-Sales Method

An alternative to going through the process of tracing cash and accounting flows to determine financial needs is to assume that accounts on the balance sheet will maintain a given percentage relationship to sales. We then indicate a change in the sales level and ascertain our related financing needs. This is known as the *percent-of-sales method*. For example, for the Howard Corporation, introduced in Table 4–18,

Table 4–18

HOWARD CORPORATION
Balance Sheet and Percent-of-Sales Table

| *Assets* | | *Liabilities and Stockholders' Equity* | |
|---|---|---|---|
| Cash | $ 5,000 | Accounts payable | $ 40,000 |
| Accounts receivable | 40,000 | Accrued expenses | 10,000 |
| Inventory | 25,000 | Notes payable | 15,000 |
| Total current assets | $ 70,000 | Common stock | 10,000 |
| Equipment | 50,000 | Retained earnings | 45,000 |
| Total assets | $120,000 | Total liabilities and stockholders' equity | $120,000 |

$200,000 sales
*Percent of Sales*

| | | | |
|---|---|---|---|
| Cash | 2.5% | Accounts payable | 20.0% |
| Accounts receivable | 20.0 | Accrued expenses | 5.0 |
| Inventory | 12.5 | | 25.0% |
| Total current assets | 35.0 | | |
| Equipment | 25.0 | | |
| | 60.0% | | |

we show the following balance sheet accounts in dollars and their percent of sales, based on a sales volume of $200,000.

We observe that cash of $5,000 represents 2.5 percent of sales of $200,000; receivables of $40,000 is 20 percent of sales; and so on. No percentages are computed for notes payable, common stock, and retained earnings because they are not assumed to maintain a direct relationship with sales volume. Note that any dollar increase in sales will necessitate a 60 percent increase in assets,[2] of which 25 percent will be spontaneously or automatically financed through accounts payable and accrued expenses, leaving 35 percent to be financed by profit or additional outside sources of financing. We will assume that the Howard Corporation has an aftertax return of 6 percent on the sales dollar and that 50 percent of profits are paid out as dividends.[3]

[2]We are assuming equipment increases in proportion to sales. In certain cases, there may be excess capacity, and equipment (or plant and equipment) will not increase.

[3]Some may wish to add back depreciation under the percent-of-sales method. Most, however, choose the assumption that funds generated through depreciation (in the sources and uses of funds sense) must be used to replace the fixed assets to which depreciation is applied.

If sales increase from \$200,000 to \$300,000, the \$100,000 increase in sales will necessitate \$35,000 (35 percent) in additional financing. Since we will earn 6 percent on total sales of \$300,000, we will show a profit of \$18,000. With a 50 percent dividend payout, \$9,000 will remain for internal financing. This means that \$26,000 out of the \$35,000 must be financed from outside sources. Our formula to determine the need for new funds is:

Required new funds

$$\text{(RNF)} = \frac{A}{S}(\Delta S) - \frac{L}{S}(\Delta S) - PS_2(1 - D) \qquad (4\text{–}1)$$

where

$\frac{A}{S}$ = Percentage relationship of variable assets to sales [60%]
$\Delta S$ = Change in sales [\$100,000]
$\frac{L}{S}$ = Percentage relationship of variable liabilities to sales [25%]
$P$ = Profit margin [6%]
$S_2$ = New sales level [\$300,000]
$D$ = Dividend payout ratio

Plugging in the values we show:

60% (\$100,000) − 25% (\$100,000) − 6% (\$300,000) (1 − 0.5) =
\$60,000 − \$25,000 − \$18,000 (0.5) =
\$35,000 − \$9,000 =
\$26,000 required sources of new funds

Presumably the \$26,000 can be financed at the bank or through some other appropriate source.

The student will observe that using the percent-of-sales method is a much easier task than tracing through the various cash flows to arrive at the pro forma statements. Nevertheless, the output is much less meaningful and we do not get a month-to-month breakdown of the data. The percent-of-sales method is a "broad brush" approach, while the development of pro forma statements is more exacting. Of course, whatever method we use, the results are only as meaningful or reliable as the assumptions about sales and production that went into the numbers.

## Summary

The process of financial forecasting allows the financial manager to anticipate events before they occur, particularly the need for raising funds externally. An important consideration is that growth itself may call for additional sources of financing because profit is often inadequate to cover the net buildup in receivables, inventory, and other asset accounts.

We develop pro forma financial statements from an overall corporate systems viewpoint. The time perspective is usually six months to a year in the future. In developing a pro forma income statement, we begin by making sales projections, then we construct a production plan, and finally we consider all other expenses. From the pro forma income statement we proceed to a cash budget, in which the monthly or quarterly cash inflows and outflows related to sales, expenditures, and capital outlays are portrayed. All of this information can be assimilated into a pro forma balance sheet in which asset, liability, and stockholders' equity accounts are shown. Any shortage of funds is assumed to be financed through notes payable (bank loans).

We may take a shortcut to financial forecasting through the use of the percent-of-sales method. Under this approach, selected balance sheet accounts are assumed to maintain a constant percentage relationship to sales, and thus for any given sales amount we can ascertain balance sheet values. Once again a shortage of funds is assumed to be financed through notes payable.

## List of Terms

**pro forma balance sheet**
**pro forma income statement**
**cash budget**
**cost of goods sold**
**percent-of-sales method**

## Discussion Questions

1. What are the basic benefits and purposes of developing pro forma statements and a cash budget?

2. Explain how the collections and purchases schedules are related to the borrowing needs of the corporation.

3. With inflation what are the implications of using LIFO and FIFO inventory methods? How do they affect the cost of goods sold?

4. Explain the relationship between inventory turnover and purchase needs.

5. Rapid corporate growth in sales and profits can cause financing problems. Elaborate on this statement.

6. Discuss the advantage and disadvantage of level production schedules in firms whose sales are cyclical.

7. What conditions would help make a percent-of-sales forecast as accurate as pro forma financial statements and cash budgets?

## Problems

1. Sales for Southwest Sales Company are expected to be 3,000 units for the coming month. The company likes to maintain 15 percent of unit sales for each month in ending inventory. Beginning inventory is 600 units.

   How many units should Southwest Sales produce for the coming month?

2. On December 31 of last year, Wolfson Corporation had in inventory 400 units of its product which cost $21 per unit to produce. During January, the company produced 800 units at a cost of $24 per unit.

   Assuming that Wolfson Corporation sold 700 units in January, what was cost of goods sold (assume FIFO inventory method)?

3. At the end of January, Dexter Corporation had an inventory of 500 units which cost $15 per unit to produce. During February the company produced 650 units at a cost of $17 per unit.

   If Dexter Corporation sold 900 units in February, what was its cost of goods sold (assume LIFO inventory accounting)?

4. Cox Corporation produces a product with the following costs as of July 1, 1986:

| | |
|---|---|
| Material . . . . . | $2 per unit |
| Labor . . . . . . | 4 per unit |
| Overhead . . . . | 2 per unit |

Beginning inventory on July 1 was 3,000 units. From July 1 to December 31, 1986, Cox produced 12,000 units. These units had a material cost of $3 per unit. Other costs were the same. Cox uses FIFO inventory accounting.

Assuming that Cox sold 13,000 units during the last six months of the year at $16 each, what will gross profit be? What is the value of ending inventory?

5. Blue Ridge Corporation has forecast credit sales for the fourth quarter of the year:

| | |
|---|---|
| September (actual) | $50,000 |
| *Fourth quarter* | |
| October . . . . . . . | 40,000 |
| November . . . . . . | 35,000 |
| December . . . . . . | 60,000 |

Experience has shown that 20 percent of sales are collected in the month of sales, 70 percent in the following month, and 10 percent are never collected.

Prepare a schedule of cash receipts for the Blue Ridge Corporation covering the fourth quarter (October through December).

6. The Denver Corporation has forecast the following sales for the first seven months of the year:

| | | | |
|---|---|---|---|
| January . . . . | $10,000 | May . . . . | $10,000 |
| February . . . . | 12,000 | June . . . . | 16,000 |
| March . . . . . | 14,000 | July . . . . | 18,000 |
| April . . . . . . | 20,000 | | |

Monthly material purchases are set equal to 30 percent of forecasted sales for the next month. Of the total material costs, 40 percent are paid in the month of purchase and 60 percent in the following month. Labor costs will run $4,000 per month, and fixed overhead is $2,000 per month. Interest payments on the debt will be $3,000 for both March and June. Finally, the Denver salesmen will receive a 1.5 percent commission on total sales for the first six months of the year, to be paid on June 30.

Prepare a monthly summary of cash payments for the six-month period from January through June. (Note: Compute prior December purchases to help get total material payments for January.)

**7.** The Boswell Corporation forecasts its sales in units for the next four months as follows:

| | |
|---|---|
| March . . . . | 6,000 |
| April . . . . . | 8,000 |
| May . . . . . | 5,500 |
| June . . . . . | 4,000 |

Boswell maintains an ending inventory for each month in the amount of one and one half times the expected sales in the following month. The ending inventory for February (March's beginning inventory) reflects this policy. Materials cost $5 per unit and are paid in the month after production. Labor cost is $10 per unit and is paid for in the month incurred. Fixed overhead is $12,000 per month. Dividends of $20,000 are to be paid in May. Five thousand units were produced in February.

Complete a production schedule and a summary of cash payments for March, April, and May. Remember that production in any one month is equal to sales plus desired ending inventory minus beginning inventory.

**8.** The Ace Battery Company has forecast its sales in units as follows:

| | | | |
|---|---|---|---|
| January . . . . | 800 | May . . . . | 1,350 |
| February . . . . | 650 | June . . . . | 1,500 |
| March . . . . . | 600 | July . . . . | 1,200 |
| April . . . . . . | 1,100 | | |

Ace always keeps an ending inventory equal to 120 percent of the next month's expected sales. The ending inventory for December (January's beginning inventory) is 960 units, which is consistent with this policy. Materials cost $12 per unit and are paid for in the month after purchase. Labor cost is $5 per unit and is paid in the month the cost is incurred. Overhead costs are $6,000 per month. Interest of $8,000 is scheduled to be paid in March, and employee bonuses of $13,200 will be paid in June.

Prepare a monthly production schedule and a monthly summary of cash payments for the period of January through June. Ace produced 600 units in December.

**9.** Ed's Waterbeds has made the following sales projections for the next six months. All sales are credit sales.

| | | | |
|---|---|---|---|
| March . . . . | $12,000 | June . . . . . | $14,000 |
| April . . . . . | 16,000 | July . . . . . | 17,000 |
| May . . . . . | 10,000 | August . . . . | 18,000 |

Sales in January and February were $13,500 and $13,000, respectively. Experience has shown that of total sales, 10 percent are uncollectible, 30 percent are collected in the month of sale, 40 percent are collected in the following month, and 20 percent are collected two months after sale.

Prepare a monthly cash receipts schedule for the firm for March through August.

Of the sales expected to be made during the six months from March through August, how much will still be uncollected at the end of August? How much of this is expected to be collected?

**10.** Warren's Auto Parts has expected sales of $20,000 in September, $25,000 in October, $35,000 in November, and $30,000 in December. Of the company's sales, 20 percent are for cash and 80 percent are on credit. Experience shows that 40 percent of accounts receivable are paid in the month after sale, while the remaining 60 percent is paid two months after. Determine collections for November and December.

Also assume the company's cash payments for November and December are $28,000 and $25,000, respectively. The beginning cash balance in November is $6,000, which is the desired minimum balance.

Prepare a cash budget with borrowing needed or repayments for November and December.

**11.** Jim Daniels Health Products has eight stores. The firm wishes to expand by two more stores and needs a bank loan to do this. Mr. Hewitt, the banker, will finance construction if the firm can present an acceptable three-month financial plan for January through March. The following are actual and forecasted sales figures:

| *Actual* | | *Forecast* | | *Additional Information* | |
|---|---|---|---|---|---|
| November . . . . | $200,000 | January . . . . | $280,000 | April forecast . . . . | $330,000 |
| December . . . . | 220,000 | February . . . . | 320,000 | | |
| | | March . . . . . | 340,000 | | |

Of the firm's sales, 40 percent are for cash and the remaining 60 percent are on credit. Of credit sales, 30 percent are paid in the month after sale and 70 percent are paid in the second month after sale. Materials cost 30 percent of sales and are purchased and received each month in amounts sufficient to cover the following month's expected sales. Materials are paid for in the month after they are received. Labor expense is 40 percent of sales and is paid in the month of sales. Selling and administrative expense is 5 percent of sales and is also paid in the month of sales. Overhead expense is $28,000 in cash per month. Depreciation expense is $10,000 per month. Taxes of $8,000 will be paid in January, and dividends of $2,000 will be paid in March. Cash at the beginning of January is $80,000 and the desired minimum cash balance is $75,000.

For January, February, and March, prepare a schedule of monthly cash receipts, monthly cash payments, and a complete monthly cash budget with borrowing and repayment.

**12.** Ellis Electronics Company's actual sales and purchases for April and May are shown here along with forecasted sales and purchases for June through September.

| | *Sales* | *Purchases* |
|---|---|---|
| April (actual) | $320.000 | $130.000 |
| May (actual) | 300.000 | 120.000 |
| June (forecast) | 275.000 | 120.000 |
| July (forecast) | 275.000 | 180.000 |
| August (forecast) | 290.000 | 200.000 |
| September (forecast) | 330.000 | 170.000 |

The company makes 10 percent of its sales for cash and 90 percent on credit. Of the credit sales, 20 percent are collected in the month after the sale and 80 percent are collected two months after. Ellis pays for 40 percent of its purchases in the month after purchase and 60 percent two months after.

Labor expense equals 10 percent of the current month's sales. Overhead expense equals $12,000 per month. Interest payments of $30,000 are due in June and September. A cash dividend of $50,000 is scheduled to be paid in June. Taxes of $25,000 are due in June and September. There is a scheduled capital outlay of $300,000 in September.

Ellis Electronics' ending cash balance in May is $20,000. The minimum desired cash balance is $15,000. Prepare a schedule of monthly cash receipts, monthly cash payments, and a complete monthly cash budget with borrowing and repayments for June through September. The maximum desired cash balance is $50,000. Excess cash (above $50,000) is used to buy marketable securities. Marketable securities are sold before borrowing funds in case of a cash shortfall (less than $15,000).

**13.** The Meadow Milk Company has plants in five states and operates a very large home delivery service. Sales for last year were $100 million, and the balance sheet at year-end is similar in percentage of sales to that of previous years (and this will continue in the future). All assets and current liabilities will vary directly with sales.

Balance Sheet
(in $ millions)

| *Assets* | | *Liabilities and Stockholders' Equity* | |
|---|---|---|---|
| Cash | $ 5 | Accounts payable | $ 5 |
| Accounts receivable | 15 | Accrued wages | 6 |
| Inventory | 30 | Accrued taxes | 4 |
| Current assets | $50 | Current liabilities | $15 |
| Fixed assets | 40 | Notes payable | 30 |
| | | Common stock | 25 |
| | | Retained earnings | 20 |
| Total assets | $90 | Total liabilities and stockholders' equity | $90 |

Meadow Milk has an aftertax profit margin of 7 percent and a dividend payout ratio of 30 percent.

If sales grow by 10 percent next year, determine how many dollars are needed to finance the expansion. How many dollars will be financed externally, and how many internally? (Assume that Meadow Milk is already using assets at full capacity and that plant must be added.)

**14.** The Longbranch Western Wear Co. has the following financial statements, which are representative of the company's historical average.

Income Statement

| | |
|---|---|
| Sales | $200.000 |
| Expenses | 158.000 |
| Earnings before interest and taxes | $ 42.000 |
| Interest | 2.000 |
| Earnings before taxes | $ 40.000 |
| Taxes | 20.000 |
| Earnings after taxes | $ 20.000 |
| Dividends | 10.000 |

Balance Sheet

| *Assets* | | *Liabilities and Stockholders' Equity* | |
|---|---|---|---|
| Cash | $ 5.000 | Accounts payable | $ 5.000 |
| Accounts Receivable | 10.000 | Accrued wages | 1.000 |
| Inventory | 15.000 | Accrued taxes | 2.000 |
| Current assets | $ 30.000 | Current liabilities | $ 8.000 |
| Fixed assets | 70.000 | Notes payable | 7.000 |
| | | Long-term debt | 15.000 |
| | | Common stock | 20.000 |
| | | Retained earnings | 50.000 |
| Total assets | $100.000 | Total liabilities and stockholders' equity | $100.000 |

Longbranch is expecting a 20 percent increase in sales next year, and management is concerned about the company's need for external funds. The increase in sales is expected to be carried out without any expansion of fixed assets, but rather through more efficient asset utilization in the existing store. Only current liabilities vary directly with sales.

Using a percent-of-sales method, determine whether Longbranch Western Wear has external financing needs. (Hint: A profit margin and payout ratio must be found from the income statement.)

15. Harvard Prep Shops, a clothing chain, had sales of $300 million last year. The business has a steady net profit margin of 15 percent and a dividend payout ratio of 30 percent. The balance sheet for the end of last year is shown on page 111.

Balance Sheet
End of Year
($ millions)

| *Assets* | | *Liabilities and Stockholders' Equity* | |
|---|---|---|---|
| Cash | $ 7 | Accounts payable | $ 55 |
| Accounts receivable | 28 | Accrued expenses | 15 |
| Inventory | 60 | Other payables | 20 |
| Plant and equipment | 115 | Common stock | 30 |
| | | Retained earnings | 90 |
| Total assets | $210 | Total liabilities and stockholders' equity | $210 |

The firm anticipates there will be a large increase in the demand for tweed sportcoats and deck shoes. An overall sales increase of 25 percent is forecast. All balance sheet accounts are expected to maintain the same percent-of-sales relationships as last year except for common stock and retained earnings. No change in the number of common stock shares is scheduled and retained earnings will change as dictated by the profits and dividend policy (remember the net profit margin is 15 percent).

*a.* Will any external financing be required for the firm during the coming year?

*b.* What would the need for external financing be if the net profit margin increased to 20 percent and the dividend payout ratio was increased to 65 percent?

**16.** (*Comprehensive problem—external funds*)
The Mansfield Corporation had 1986 sales of $100 million. The balance sheet items that vary directly with sales and the profit margin are as follows:

| | *Percent* |
|---|---|
| Cash | 5% |
| Accounts receivable | 15 |
| Inventory | 20 |
| Net fixed assets | 40 |
| Accounts payable | 15 |
| Accruals | 10 |
| Profit margin after taxes | 10 |

The dividend payout rate is 50 percent of earnings, and the balance in retained earnings at the beginning of 1986 was $33 million.

Common stock and the company's long-term bonds are constant at $10 million and $5 million, respectively. Notes payable are currently $7 million.

*a.* How much additional external capital will be required for next year if sales increase 15 percent? (Assume that the company is already operating at full capacity.)
*b.* What will happen to external fund requirements if Mansfield Corporation reduces the payout ratio, grows at a slower rate, or suffers a decline in its profit margin? Discuss each of these separately.
*c.* Prepare a pro forma balance sheet for 1987 assuming that any external funds being acquired will be in the form of notes payable. Disregard the information in part *b* in answering this question (that is, use the original information and part *a* in constructing your pro forma balance sheet).

**17.** (*Comprehensive financial forecasting problem—seasonal production*) The difficult part of solving a problem of this nature is to know what to do with the information contained within a story problem. Therefore, this problem will be easier to complete if you rely on Chapter 4 for the format of all required schedules.

The Adams Corporation makes standard-size 2-inch fasteners which it sells for $155 per thousand. Mr. Adams is the majority owner and manages the inventory and finances of the company. He estimates sales for the following months to be:

| | |
|---|---|
| January . . . . | $263,500 (1,700,000 fasteners) |
| February . . . . | $186,000 (1,200,000 fasteners) |
| March . . . . . | $217,000 (1,400,000 fasteners) |
| April . . . . . . | $310,000 (2,000,000 fasteners) |
| May . . . . . . | $387,500 (2,500,000 fasteners) |

Last year Adams Corporation's sales were $175,000 in November and $232,500 in December (1,500,000 fasteners).

Mr. Adams is preparing for a meeting with his banker to arrange the financing for the first quarter. Based on his sales forecast and the following information provided by him, your job as his new financial analyst is to prepare a monthly cash budget, a monthly and quarterly pro forma income statement, a pro forma quarterly balance sheet, and all necessary supporting schedules for the first quarter.

Past history shows that the Adams Corporation collects 50 percent of its accounts receivable in the normal 30-day credit period (the month after the sale) and the other 50 percent in 60 days (two months after the sale). It pays for its materials 30 days after receipt. In general, Mr. Adams likes to keep a two-month supply of inventory on hand in anticipation of sales. Inventory at the beginning of December was 2,600,000 units. (This was not equal to his desired two-month supply.)

The major cost of production is the purchase of raw materials in the form of steel rods which are cut, threaded, and finished. Last year raw material costs were $52 per 1,000 fasteners, but Mr. Adams has just been notified that material costs have risen, effective January 1, to $60 per 1,000 fasteners. The Adams Corporation uses FIFO inventory accounting. Labor costs are relatively constant at $20 per thousand fasteners since workers are paid on a piecework basis. Overhead is allocated at $10 per thousand units, and selling and administrative expense is 20 percent of sales. Labor expense and overhead are direct cash outflows paid in the month incurred, while interest and taxes are paid quarterly.

The corporation usually maintains a minimum cash balance of $25,000, and it puts its excess cash into marketable securities. The average tax rate is 40 percent, and Mr. Adams usually pays out 50 percent of net income in dividends to stockholders. Marketable securities are sold before funds are borrowed when a cash shortage is faced. Ignore the interest on any short-term borrowings. Interest on the long-term debt is paid in March, as are taxes and dividends.

As of year-end, the Adams Corporation balance sheet was as follows:

ADAMS CORPORATION
Balance Sheet
December 31, 198X

*Assets*

| | | |
|---|---|---|
| Current assets: | | |
| Cash | $ 30,000 | |
| Accounts receivable | 320,000 | |
| Inventory | 237,800 | |
| Total current assets | | $ 587,800 |
| Fixed assets: | | |
| Plant and equipment | 1,000,000 | |
| Less: Accumulated depreciation | 200,000 | 800,000 |
| Total assets | | $1,387,800 |

*Liabilities and Stockholders' Equity*

| | | |
|---|---|---|
| Accounts payable | $ 93,600 | |
| Notes payable | 0 | |
| Long-term debt, 8 percent | 400,000 | |
| Common stock | 504,200 | |
| Retained earnings | 390,000 | |
| Total liabilities and stockholders' equity | | $1,387,800 |

## Selected References


Ansoff, H. Igor. "Planning as a Practical Management Tool." *Financial Executive* 32 (June 1964), pp. 34–37.

Chambers, John C.; Satinder K. Mullick; and Donald D. Smith. "How to Choose the Right Forecasting Technique." *Harvard Business Review* 49 (July-August 1971), pp. 45–74.

Chisholm, R. K., and G. R. Whitaker, Jr. *Forecasting Methods*. Homewood, Ill.: Richard D. Irwin, 1971.

Donaldson, Gordon. "Strategy for Financial Emergencies." *Harvard Business Review* 47 (November-December 1969), pp. 67–79.

Francis, Jack Clark, and Dexter R. Rowell. "A Simultaneous Equation Model of the Firm for Financial Analysis and Planning." *Financial Management* 7 (Spring 1978), pp. 29–44.

Higgins, Robert C. "How Much Growth Can a Firm Afford?" *Financial Management* 6 (Fall 1977), pp. 7–16.

Jaedicke, Robert K., and Robert T. Sprouse. *Accounting Flows: Income, Funds, and Cash*. Englewood Cliffs, N.J.: Prentice-Hall, 1965, chaps. 5 and 6.

Lerner, Eugene M. "Simulating a Cash Budget." *California Management Review* 11 (Winter 1968), pp. 79–86.

Lynch, Richard M. *Accounting for Management Planning and Control*. New York: McGraw-Hill, 1967, chap. 6.

Lyneis, James M. "Designing Financial Policies to Deal with Limited Financial Resources." *Financial Management* 4 (Spring 1975), pp. 13–24.

Maier, Steven F.; David W. Robinson; and James H. Vander Weide. "A Short-Term Disbursement Forecasting Model." *Financial Management* 10 (Spring 1981), pp. 9–19.

Parker, George G. C., and Edilberto L. Segura. "How to Get a Better Forecast." *Harvard Business Review* 49 (March-April 1971), pp. 99–109.

Preston, Gerald R. "Considerations in Long-Range Planning." *Financial Executive* (May 1968), pp. 44–49.

Rappaport, Louis H. *SEC Accounting Practice and Procedures*. 3d ed. New York: Ronald, 1972, chap. 21.

Welsch, Glenn A. *Budgeting: Profit Planning and Control*. 2d ed. Englewood Cliffs, N.J.: Prentice-Hall, 1964, chaps. 2 and 11.

Weston, J. Fred. "Forecasting Financial Requirements." *Accounting Review* 33 (July 1958), pp. 427–40.

Wright, Leonard T. *Financial Management: Analytical Techniques*. Columbus, Ohio: Grid, 1974, chap. 4.

# 5 Operating and Financial Leverage

In the physical sciences as well as in politics, the term *leverage* has been popularized to mean the use of special force and effects to produce more than normal results from a given course of action. In business, the same concept is applied, with the emphasis on the employment of "fixed cost" items in anticipation of magnifying returns at high levels of operation. The student should recognize that leverage is a two-edged sword—producing highly favorable results when things go well, and quite the opposite under negative conditions.

## Leverage in a Business

Assume that you are approached with an opportunity to start your own business. You are to manufacture and market industrial parts, such as ball bearings, wheels, and casters. You are faced with two primary decisions.

First, you must determine the amount of fixed-cost plant and equipment that you wish to use in the production process. By installing modern, sophisticated equipment, you can virtually eliminate labor in the production of inventory. At high volume, you will do quite well, as most of your costs are fixed. At low volume, however, you could face difficulty in making your fixed payments for plant and equipment. If you decide to use expensive labor rather than machinery, you will lessen your opportunity for profit, but at the same time you will lower your exposure to risk (you can lay off part of the work force).

Second, you must determine how you will finance the business. If you rely on debt financing and the business is successful, you will generate substantial profits as an owner, paying only the fixed costs of debt. Of course, if the business starts off poorly, the contractual obligations related to debt could mean bankruptcy. As an alternative, you might decide to sell equity rather than borrow, a step that will lower your own profit potential (you must share with others) but minimize your risk exposure.

In both decisions, you are making very explicit decisions about the use of leverage. To the extent that you go with a heavy commitment to fixed costs in the operation of the firm, you are employing operating leverage. To the extent that you utilize debt in the financing of the firm, you are engaging in financial leverage. We shall carefully examine each type of leverage and then show the combined effect of both.

## Operating Leverage

Operating leverage reflects the extent to which fixed assets and associated fixed costs are utilized in the business firm. As indicated in Table 5–1, a firm's operational costs may be classified as fixed, variable, or semivariable.

For purposes of analysis, variable and semivariable costs will be combined. In order to evaluate the implications of heavy fixed asset use, we employ the technique of break-even analysis.

Table 5–1
Classification of costs

| *Fixed* | *Variable* | *Semivariable* |
|---|---|---|
| Rental | Raw material | Utilities |
| Depreciation | Factory labor | Repairs and maintenance |
| Executive salaries | Sales commissions | |
| Property taxes | | |

## Break-Even Analysis

How much will changes in volume affect cost and profit? At what point does the firm break even? What is the most efficient level of fixed assets to employ in the firm? A break-even chart is presented in Figure 5–1 to answer some of these questions. The number of units produced and sold are shown along the horizontal axis, and revenue and costs are shown along the vertical axis.

**Figure 5–1**
**Break-even chart: Leveraged firm**

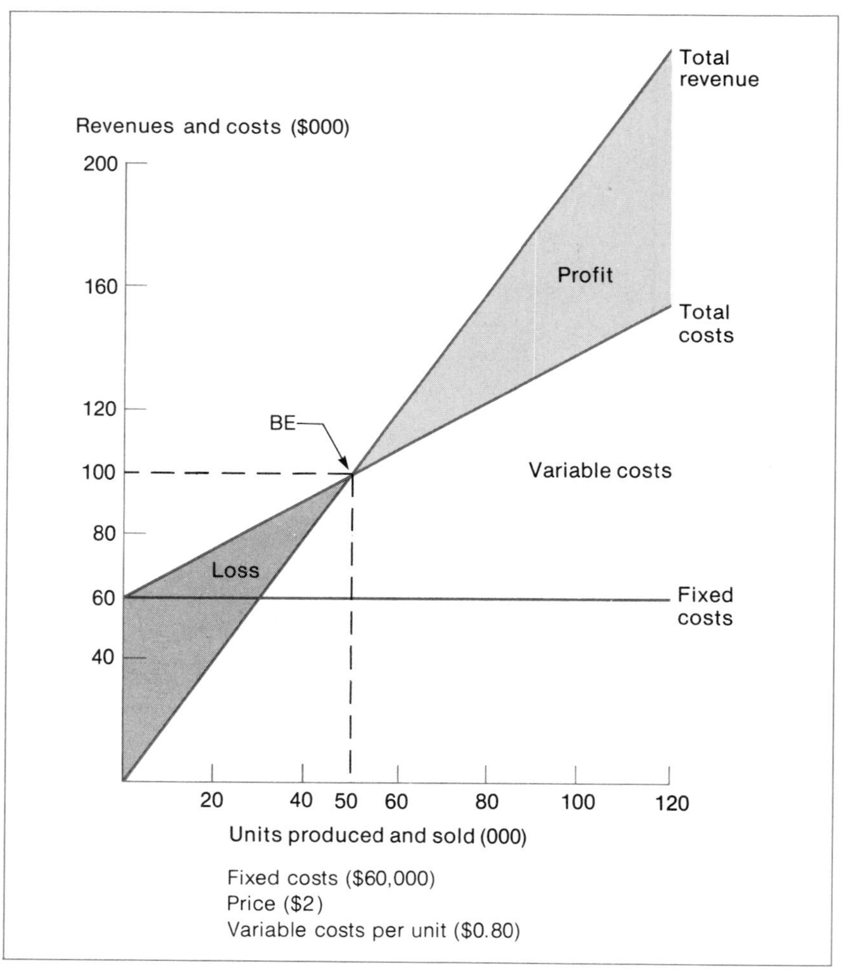

Note, first of all, that our fixed costs are \$60,000, regardless of volume, and that our variable costs (at \$0.80 per unit) are added to fixed costs to determine total costs at any point. The total revenue line is determined by multiplying price (\$2) times volume.

Of particular interest is the break-even (*BE*) point at 50,000 units, where the total costs and total revenue lines intersect. The numbers are as follows:

| Units = 50,000 | | | | |
|---|---|---|---|---|
| *Total variable costs (TVC)* | *Fixed costs (FC)* | *Total costs (TC)* | *Total revenue (TR)* | *Operating income (loss)* |
| (50,000 × \$0.80) \$40,000 | \$60,000 | \$100,000 | (50,000 × \$2) \$100,000 | 0 |

The break-even point for the company may also be determined by use of a simple formula—in which we divide fixed costs by the contribution margin on each unit sold, with the contribution margin defined as price minus variable cost per unit.

$$BE = \frac{\text{Fixed costs}}{\text{Contribution margin}} = \frac{\text{Fixed costs}}{\text{Price} - \text{variable costs per unit}} = \frac{FC}{P - VC} \quad (5\text{–}1)$$

$$\frac{\$60{,}000}{\$2.00 - \$0.80} = \frac{\$60{,}000}{\$1.20} = 50{,}000 \text{ units}$$

Since we are getting a \$1.20 contribution toward covering fixed costs from each unit sold, minimum sales of 50,000 units will allow us to cover our fixed costs (50,000 units × \$1.20 = \$60,000 fixed costs). Beyond this point, we move into a highly profitable range in which each unit of sales brings a profit of \$1.20 to the company. As sales increase from 50,000 to 60,000 units, operating profits increase by \$12,000 as indicated in Table 5–2; as sales increase from 60,000 to 80,000 units, profits increase by another \$24,000; and so on. As further indicated in Table 5–2, at low volumes such as 40,000 or 20,000 units our losses are substantial (\$12,000 and \$36,000 in the red).

It is assumed that the firm depicted in Figure 5–1 is operating with a high degree of leverage. The situation is analogous to that of an airline

**Table 5–2**
**Volume-cost-profit analysis: Leveraged firm**

| Units Sold | Total Variable Costs | Fixed Costs | Total Costs | Total Revenue | Operating Income (loss) |
|---|---|---|---|---|---|
| 0 | 0 | $60,000 | $ 60,000 | 0 | $(60,000) |
| 20,000 | $16,000 | 60,000 | 76,000 | $ 40,000 | (36,000) |
| 40,000 | 32,000 | 60,000 | 92,000 | 80,000 | (12,000) |
| 50,000 | 40,000 | 60,000 | 100,000 | 100,000 | 0 |
| 60,000 | 48,000 | 60,000 | 108,000 | 120,000 | 12,000 |
| 80,000 | 64,000 | 60,000 | 124,000 | 160,000 | 36,000 |
| 100,000 | 80,000 | 60,000 | 140,000 | 200,000 | 60,000 |

which must carry a certain number of people on board to break even, but beyond that point is in a very profitable range.

## A More Conservative Approach

Not all firms would choose to operate at the high degree of operating leverage exhibited in Figure 5–1. Fear of not reaching the 50,000-unit break-even level may discourage some companies from heavy utilization of fixed assets. More expensive variable costs may be substituted for automated plant and equipment. Assume that fixed costs for a more conservative firm can be reduced to $12,000—but that variable costs will go from $0.80 to $1.60. If the same price assumption of $2 per unit is employed, the break-even level is 30,000 units.

$$BE = \frac{\text{Fixed costs}}{\text{Price} - \text{variable cost per unit}} = \frac{FC}{P - VC} = \frac{\$12{,}000}{\$2 - \$1.60} = \frac{\$12{,}000}{\$0.40} = 30{,}000 \text{ units}$$

With fixed costs reduced from $60,000 to $12,000, the loss potential is small. Furthermore, the break-even level of operations is a comparatively low 30,000 units. Nevertheless, the use of a virtually unleveraged approach has cut into the potential profitability of the more conservative firm, as indicated in Figure 5–2.

Even at high levels of operation, the potential profit is rather small. As indicated in Table 5–3, at a 100,000-unit volume, operating income is only $28,000—some $32,000 less than that for the "leveraged" firm previously analyzed in Table 5–2.

Figure 5–2
Break-even chart:
Conservative firm

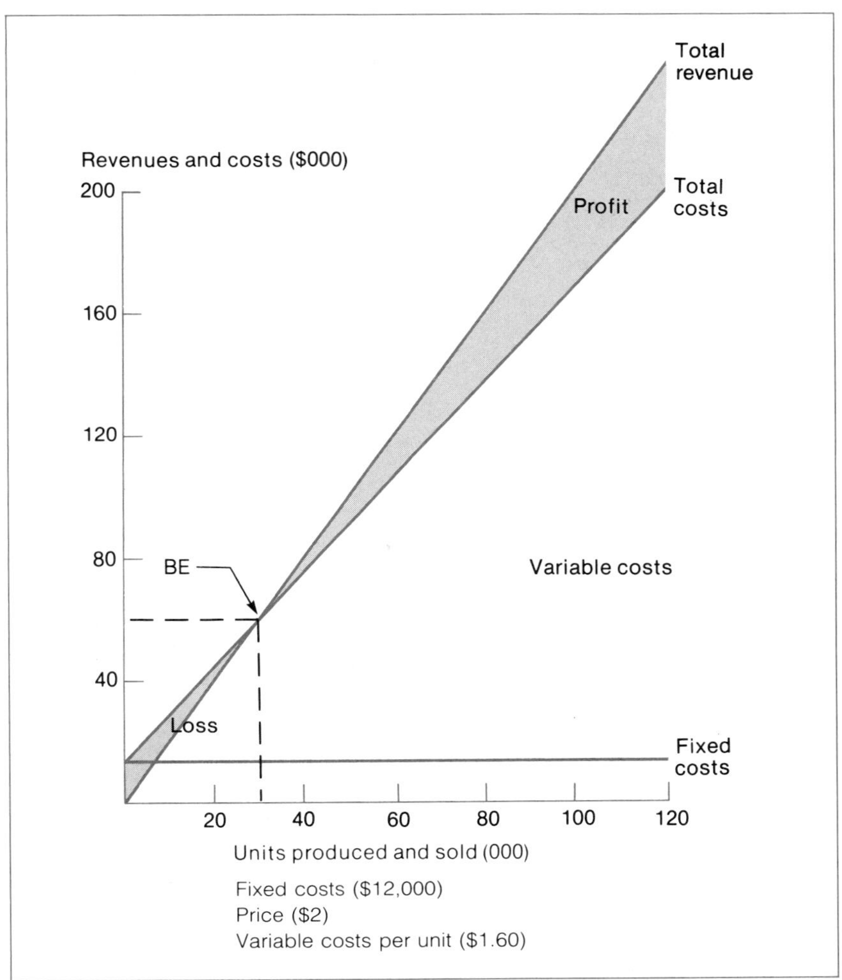


## The Risk Factor

Whether management follows the path of the leveraged firm or of the more conservative firm depends on its perceptions about the future. If the vice president of finance is apprehensive about economic conditions, the conservative plan may be undertaken. For a growing business, in times of relative prosperity, management might maintain a more aggressive, leveraged position. The firm's competitive position

**Table 5–3**
**Volume-cost-profit analysis: Conservative firm**

| Units Sold | Total Variable Costs | Fixed Costs | Total Costs | Total Revenue | Operating Income (loss) |
|---|---|---|---|---|---|
| 0 | 0 | $12,000 | $ 12,000 | 0 | $(12,000) |
| 20,000 | $ 32,000 | 12,000 | 44,000 | $ 40,000 | (4,000) |
| 30,000 | 48,000 | 12,000 | 60,000 | 60,000 | 0 |
| 40,000 | 64,000 | 12,000 | 76,000 | 80,000 | 4,000 |
| 60,000 | 96,000 | 12,000 | 108,000 | 120,000 | 12,000 |
| 80,000 | 128,000 | 12,000 | 140,000 | 160,000 | 20,000 |
| 100,000 | 160,000 | 12,000 | 172,000 | 200,000 | 28,000 |

within its industry will also be a factor. Does the firm desire to merely maintain stability or to become a market leader? To a certain extent, management should tailor the use of leverage to meet its own risk-taking desires. Those who are risk averse (prefer less risk to more risk) should anticipate a particularly high return before contracting for heavy fixed costs. Others, less averse to risk, may be willing to leverage under more normal conditions. Simply taking risks is not a virtue—our prisons are full of risk takers. The important idea, which is stressed throughout the text, is to match an acceptable return with the desired level of risk.

## Cash Break-Even Analysis

Our discussion to this point has dealt with break-even analysis in terms of accounting flows rather than cash flows. For example, depreciation has been implicitly included in fixed expenses, but it represents an accounting entry rather than an explicit expenditure of funds. To the extent that we were doing break-even analysis on a strictly cash basis, depreciation would be excluded from fixed expenses. In the example of the leveraged firm in Formula 5–1, if we eliminate $20,000 of "assumed" depreciation from fixed costs, the break-even level is reduced to 33,333 units.

$$\frac{FC}{P - VC} = \frac{(\$60{,}000 - \$20{,}000)}{\$2.00 - \$0.80} = \frac{\$40{,}000}{\$1.20} = 33{,}333 \text{ units}$$

Other adjustments could also be made for noncash items. For example, sales may initially take the form of accounts receivable rather than cash, and the same can be said for the purchase of materials and accounts payable. An actual weekly or monthly cash budget would be necessary to isolate these items.

While cash break-even analysis is helpful in analyzing the short-term outlook of the firm, particularly when it may be in trouble, most break-even analysis is conducted on the basis of accounting flows rather than strictly cash flows. Most of the assumptions throughout the chapter are based on concepts broader than pure cash flows.

## Degree of Operating Leverage

Degree of operating leverage (*DOL*) may be defined as the percentage change in operating income that takes place as a result of a percentage change in units sold.

$$DOL = \frac{\text{Percent change in operating income}}{\text{Percent change in unit volume}} \qquad (5\text{–}2)$$

Highly leveraged firms, such as those in the auto or construction industry, are likely to enjoy a rather substantial increase in income as volume expands, while more conservative firms will participate to a lesser extent. Degree of operating leverage (DOL) should only be computed over a profitable range of operations. However, the closer DOL is computed to the company break-even point, the higher the number will be due to a large percentage increase in operating income.[1]

Let us apply the formula to the leveraged and conservative firms previously discussed. Their income or losses at various levels of operation are summarized in Table 5–4.

**Table 5–4**
**Operating income or loss**

| *Units* | *Leveraged Firm (Table 5–2)* | *Conservative Firm (Table 5–3)* |
|---|---|---|
| 0 | $(60,000) | $(12,000) |
| 20,000 | (36,000) | (4,000) |
| 40,000 | (12,000) | 4,000 |
| 60,000 | 12,000 | 12,000 |
| 80,000 | 36,000 | 20,000 |
| 100,000 | 60,000 | 28,000 |

[1]While the value of DOL varies at each level of output, the beginning level of volume determines the DOL regardless of the location of the end point.

We will now consider what happens to operating income as volume moves from 80,000 to 100,000 units.

### Leveraged Firm

$$DOL = \frac{\text{Percent change in operating income}}{\text{Percent change in unit volume}} = \frac{\frac{\$24{,}000}{\$36{,}000} \times 100}{\frac{20{,}000}{80{,}000} \times 100}$$

$$= \frac{67\%}{25\%} = 2.7$$

### Conservative Firm

$$DOL = \frac{\text{Percent change in operating income}}{\text{Percent change in unit volume}} = \frac{\frac{\$8{,}000}{\$20{,}000} \times 100}{\frac{20{,}000}{80{,}000} \times 100}$$

$$= \frac{40\%}{25\%} = 1.6$$

We see the $DOL$ is much greater for the leveraged firm, indicating at 80,000 units, a 1 percent increase in volume will produce a 2.7 percent change in operating income versus a 1.6 percent increase for the conservative firm.

The formula for degree of operating leverage ($DOL$) may be algebraically manipulated to read:

$$DOL = \frac{Q(P - VC)}{Q(P - VC) - FC} \qquad (5\text{–}3)$$

where

$Q$ = Quantity at which $DOL$ is computed
$P$ = Price per unit
$VC$ = Variable costs per unit
$FC$ = Fixed costs

Using the newly stated formula for the first firm at $Q = 80{,}000$, with $P = \$2$, $VC = \$0.80$, and $FC = \$60{,}000$:

$$DOL = \frac{80{,}000\ (\$2.00 - \$0.80)}{80{,}000\ (\$2.00 - \$0.80) - \$60{,}000}$$

$$= \frac{80{,}000\ (\$1.20)}{80{,}000\ (\$1.20) - 60{,}000} = \frac{96{,}000}{96{,}000 - 60{,}000}$$

$$= 2.7$$

We once again derive an answer of 2.7.[2] The same type of calculation could also be performed for the conservative firm.

## Limitations of Analysis

Throughout our analysis of operating leverage, we have assumed that a constant or linear function exists for revenues and costs as volume changes. For example, we have used \$2 as the hypothetical sales price at all levels of operation. In the "real world," however, we may face price weakness as we attempt to capture an increasing market, or we may face cost overruns as we move beyond an optimum-size operation. Relationships are not so fixed as we have assumed.

Nevertheless, the basic patterns we have studied are reasonably valid for most firms over an extended operating range (in our example that might be between 20,000 and 100,000 units). It is only at the extreme levels that linear assumptions break down, as indicated in Figure 5–3.

---

[2]The formula for DOL may also be rewritten as:

$$DOL = \frac{Q(P - VC)}{Q(P - VC) - FC} = \frac{QP - QVC}{QP - QVC - FC}$$

We can rewrite the second terms as:

$QP = S$, or Sales (Quantity $\times$ Price)
$QVC = TVC$, or Total variable costs (Quantity $\times$ Variable costs per unit)
$FC =$ Total fixed costs (remains the same term)

We then have:

$$DOL = \frac{S - TVC}{S - TVC - FC}, \text{ or } \frac{\$160{,}000 - \$64{,}000}{\$160{,}000 - \$64{,}000 - \$60{,}000} = \frac{\$96{,}000}{\$36{,}000} = 2.7$$

Figure 5–3
Nonlinear break-even analysis

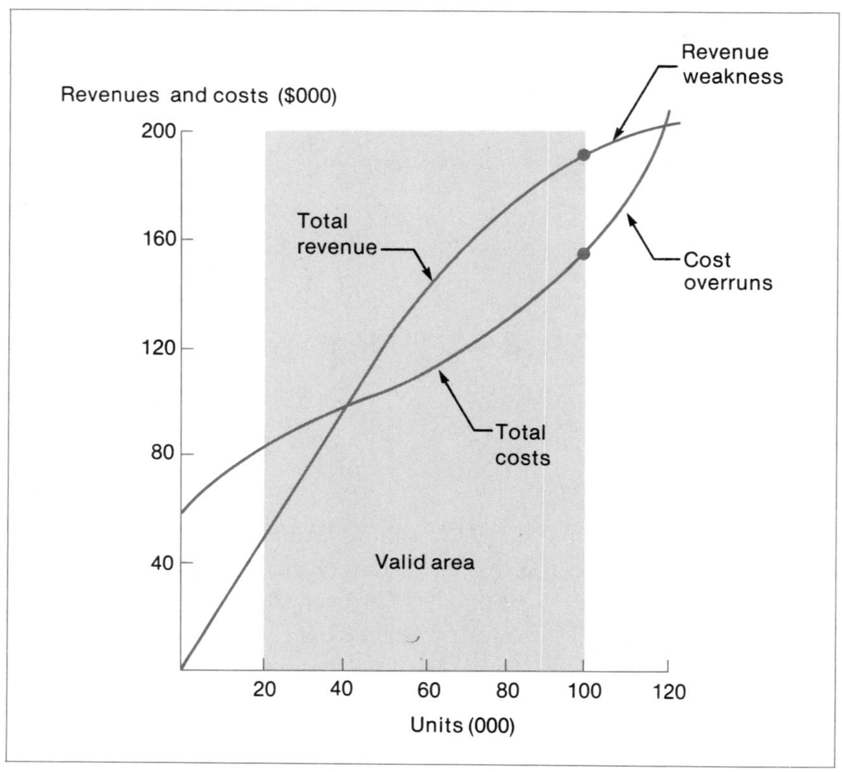


## Financial Leverage

Having discussed the effect of fixed costs on the operations of the firm (operating leverage), we now turn to the second form of leverage. Financial leverage reflects the amount of debt used in the capital structure of the firm. Because debt carries a fixed obligation of interest payments, we have the opportunity to greatly magnify our results at various levels of operation. You may have heard of the real estate developer who borrows 100 percent of the costs of his project and will enjoy an infinite return on his zero investment if all goes well.

It is helpful to think of *operating leverage* as primarily affecting the left-hand side of the balance sheet and *financial* leverage as affecting the right-hand side.

Balance Sheet

| Assets | Liabilities and Net Worth |
|---|---|
| Operating leverage | Financial leverage |

Whereas operating leverage influences the mix of plant and equipment, financial leverage determines how the operation is to be financed. It is entirely possible for two firms to have equal operating capabilities and yet show widely different results because of the use of financial leverage.

## Impact on Earnings

In studying the impact of financial leverage, we shall examine two financial plans for a firm, each employing a significantly different amount of debt in the capital structure. Financing totaling $200,000 is required to carry the assets of the firm.

Total assets—$200,000

| | *Plan A (leveraged)* | *Plan B (conservative)* |
|---|---|---|
| Debt (8% interest) . . . . . | $150,000 ($12,000 interest) | $ 50,000 ($4,000 interest) |
| Common stock . . . . . . . | 50,000 (8,000 shares at $6.25) | 150,000 (24,000 shares at $6.25) |
| Total financing . . . . | $200,000 | $200,000 |

Under *leveraged* Plan A we will borrow $150,000 and sell 8,000 shares of stock at $6.25 to raise an additional $50,000, whereas *conservative* Plan B calls for borrowing only $50,000 and acquiring an additional $150,000 in stock with 24,000 shares.

In Table 5–5, we compute earnings per share for the two plans at various levels of "earnings before interest and taxes" (EBIT). These earnings represent the operating income of the firm—before deductions have been made for financial charges or taxes. We assume EBIT levels of 0, $12,000, $36,000, and $60,000.

The impact of the two financing plans is dramatic. Although both plans assume the same operating income, or EBIT, for comparative purposes at each level (say $36,000 in calculation 4) the reported income per share is vastly different ($1.50 versus $0.67). It is also evident that the conservative plan will produce better results at low income levels—but that the leveraged plan will generate much better earnings per share as operating income, or EBIT, goes up. The firm would be indifferent between the two plans at an EBIT level of $16,000 as indicated in Table 5–5.

In Figure 5–4, we graphically demonstrate the effect of the two financing plans on earnings per share.

With an *EBIT* of $16,000, we are earning *8 percent* on total assets of $200,000—precisely the percentage cost of borrowed funds to the firm. The use or nonuse of debt does not influence the answer. Beyond $16,000, Plan A, employing heavy financial leverage, really goes to work, allowing the firm to greatly expand earnings per share as a result of a change in *EBIT*. For example, at the *EBIT* level of $36,000, an 18 percent return on assets of $200,000 takes place—and financial leverage is clearly working to our benefit as earnings greatly expand.

## Degree of Financial Leverage

As was true of operating leverage, degree of financial leverage measures the effect of a change in one variable on another variable. Degree of financial leverage (*DFL*) may be defined as the percentage change in earnings (*EPS*) that takes place as a result of a percentage change in earnings before interest and taxes (*EBIT*).

$$DFL = \frac{\text{Percent change in } EPS}{\text{Percent change in } EBIT} \qquad (5\text{–}4)$$

For purposes of computation, the formula for *DFL* may be conveniently restated as:

$$DFL = \frac{EBIT}{EBIT - I} \qquad (5\text{–}5)$$

Let's compute the degree of financial leverage for Plan A and Plan B, presented in Table 5–5, at an *EBIT* level of $36,000. Plan A calls for $12,000 of interest at all levels of financing, and Plan B requires $4,000.

**Table 5–5**
**Impact of financing plan on earnings per share**

| | Plan A (leveraged) | Plan B (conservative) |
|---|---|---|
| **1. EBIT (0)** | | |
| Earnings before interest and taxes (EBIT) | 0 | 0 |
| − Interest (I) | $(12,000) | $ (4,000) |
| Earnings before taxes (EBT) | (12,000) | (4,000) |
| − Taxes (T)* | (6,000) | (2,000) |
| Earnings after taxes (EAT) | $ (6,000) | $ (2,000) |
| Shares | 8,000 | 24,000 |
| Earnings per share (EPS) | $(0.75) | $(0.08) |
| **2. EBIT ($12,000)** | | |
| Earnings before interest and taxes (EBIT) | $ 12,000 | $ 12,000 |
| − Interest (I) | 12,000 | 4,000 |
| Earnings before taxes (EBT) | 0 | 8,000 |
| − Taxes (T) | 0 | 4,000 |
| Earnings after taxes (EAT) | $ 0 | $ 4,000 |
| Shares | 8,000 | 24,000 |
| Earnings per share (EPS) | 0 | $0.17 |
| **3. EBIT ($16,000)** | | |
| Earnings before interest and taxes (EBIT) | $ 16,000 | $ 16,000 |
| − Interest (I) | 12,000 | 4,000 |
| Earnings before taxes (EBT) | 4,000 | 12,000 |
| − Taxes (T) | 2,000 | 6,000 |
| Earnings after taxes (EAT) | $ 2,000 | $ 6,000 |
| Shares | 8,000 | 24,000 |
| Earnings per share (EPS) | $0.25 | $0.25 |
| **4. EBIT (36,000)** | | |
| Earnings before interest and taxes (EBIT) | $ 36,000 | $ 36,000 |
| − Interest (I) | 12,000 | 4,000 |
| Earnings before taxes (EBT) | 24,000 | 32,000 |
| − Taxes (T) | 12,000 | $ 16,000 |
| Earnings after taxes (EAT) | $ 12,000 | $ 16,000 |
| Shares | 8,000 | 24,000 |
| Earnings per share (EPS) | $1.50 | $0.67 |
| **5. EBIT ($60,000)** | | |
| Earnings before interest and taxes (EBIT) | $ 60,000 | $ 60,000 |
| − Interest (I) | 12,000 | 4,000 |
| Earnings before taxes (EBT) | 48,000 | 56,000 |
| − Taxes (T) | 24,000 | 28,000 |
| Earnings after taxes (EAT) | $ 24,000 | $ 28,000 |
| Shares | 8,000 | 24,000 |
| Earnings per share (EPS) | $3.00 | $1.17 |

*The assumption is that large losses can be written off against other income, perhaps in other years, thus providing the firm with a tax savings benefit. The tax rate is 50 percent.

**Figure 5–4**
**Financing plans and earnings per share**

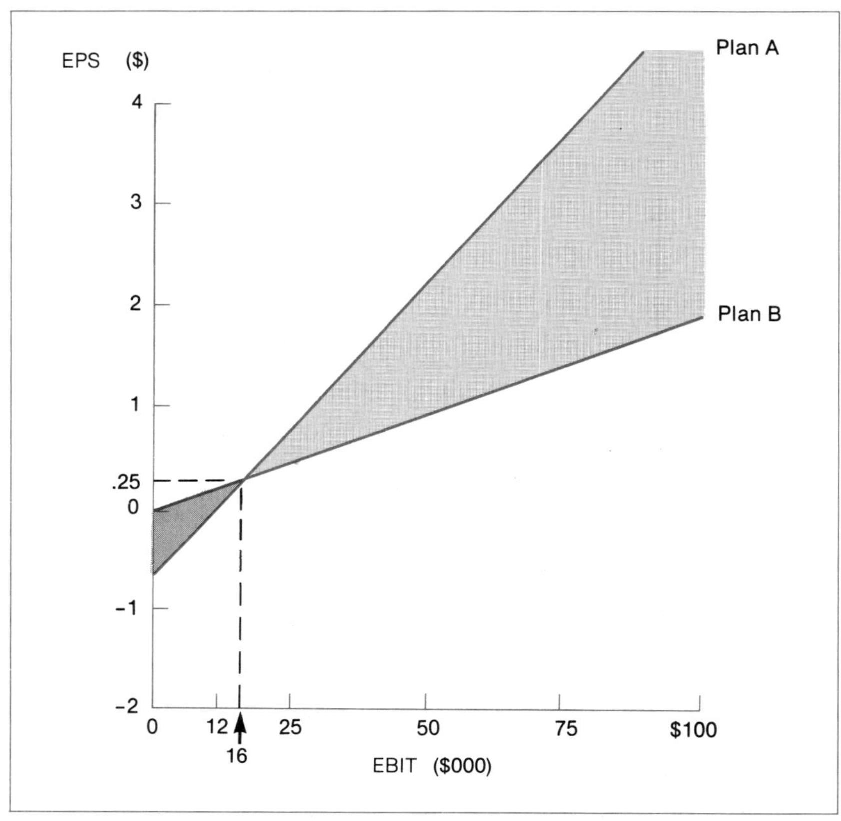


**Plan A (leveraged)**

$$DFL = \frac{EBIT}{EBIT - I} = \frac{\$36{,}000}{\$36{,}000 - \$12{,}000} = \frac{\$36{,}000}{\$24{,}000} = 1.5$$

**Plan B (conservative)**

$$DFL = \frac{EBIT}{EBIT - I} = \frac{\$36{,}000}{\$36{,}000 - \$4{,}000} = \frac{\$36{,}000}{\$32{,}000} = 1.1$$

As expected, Plan A has a much higher degree of financial leverage. At an *EBIT* level of $36,000, a 1 percent increase in earnings will produce a 1.5 percent increase in earnings per share under Plan A but only a 1.1 percent increase under Plan B. *DFL* may be computed for any level of operation, and it will change from point to point, but Plan A will always exceed Plan B.

### Limitations to Use of Financial Leverage

The alert student may quickly observe that if debt is such a good thing, why sell any stock at all? (Perhaps one share to yourself.) With exclusive debt financing at an *EBIT* level of $36,000, we would have a degree of financial leverage factor (*DFL*) of 1.8.

$$DFL = \frac{EBIT}{EBIT - I} = \frac{\$36{,}000}{\$36{,}000 - \$16{,}000} = \frac{\$36{,}000}{\$20{,}000} = 1.8$$

(With no stock, we would borrow the full $200,000.)

$$(8\% \times \$200{,}000 = \$16{,}000 \text{ interest})$$

As stressed throughout the text, debt financing and financial leverage offer unique advantages, but only up to a point—beyond that point, debt financing may be detrimental to the firm. For example, as we expand the use of debt in our capital structure, lenders will perceive a greater financial risk for the firm. For that reason, they may raise the average interest rate to be paid and they may demand that certain restrictions be placed on the corporation. Furthermore, concerned common stockholders may drive down the price of the stock—forcing us away from the *objective of maximizing the firm's overall value* in the market. The impact of financial leverage must be carefully weighed.

This is not to say that financial leverage does not work to the benefit of the firm—it very definitely does if properly used. Further discussion of appropriate debt–equity mixes is covered in Chapter 11, Cost of Capital. For now, we accept the virtues of financial leverage, knowing that all good things must be used in moderation. For firms in industries that offer some degree of stability, are in a positive stage of growth, and are operating in favorable economic conditions, the use of debt is recommended.

## Combining Operating and Financial Leverage

If both operating and financial leverage allow us to magnify our returns, then we will get maximum leverage through their combined use. We have said that operating leverage affects primarily the asset structure of the firm, while financial leverage affects the debt–equity mix. From an income statement viewpoint, operating leverage determines return from operations, while financial leverage determines how the "fruits of our labor" will be allocated to debt holders and, more importantly, to stockholders in the form of earnings per share. In Table 5–6, we show the combined influence of operating and financial leverage on the income statement. The values in Table 5–6 are drawn from earlier material in the chapter (Tables 5–2 and 5–5). We assumed in both cases a high degree of operating and financial leverage. The sales volume is 80,000 units.

The student will observe, first, that operating leverage influences the top half of the income statement—determining operating income. The last item under operating leverage, operating income, then becomes the initial item for determination of financial leverage. "Operating income" and "earnings before interest and taxes" are one and the same, representing the return to the corporation after production, marketing, and so forth—but before interest and taxes are paid. In the second half of the income statement, we then show the extent to which earnings before interest and taxes are translated into earnings per share. A graphical representation of these points is provided in Figure 5–5.

**Table 5–6**
**Income statement**

| | | |
|---|---|---|
| Sales (total revenue) (80,000 units @ $2) | $160,000 | Operating leverage |
| – Fixed costs | 60,000 | |
| – Variable costs ($0.80 per unit) | 64,000 | |
| Operating income | $ 36,000 | |
| Earnings before interest and taxes | $ 36,000 | Financial leverage |
| – Interest | 12,000 | |
| Earnings before taxes | 24,000 | |
| – Taxes | 12,000 | |
| Earnings after taxes | $ 12,000 | |
| Shares | 8,000 | |
| Earnings per share | $1.50 | |

Figure 5–5
Combining operating and financial leverage

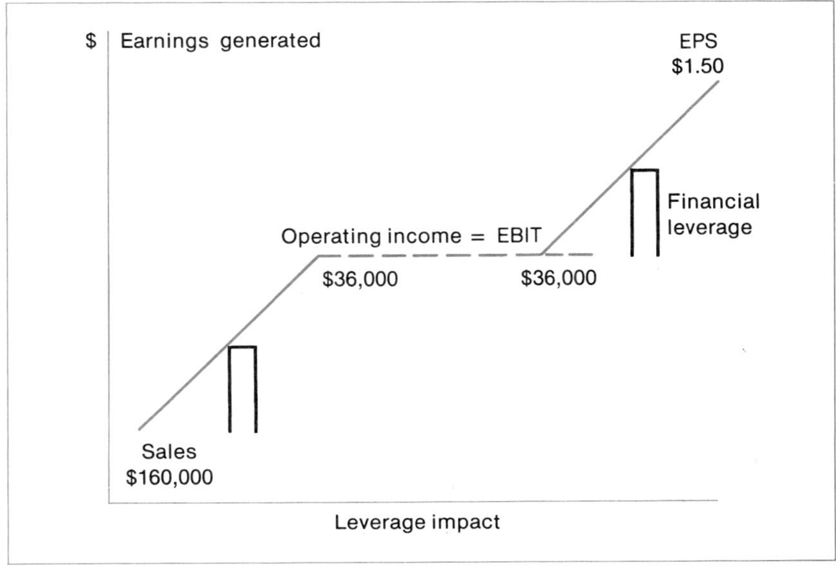


## Degree of Combined Leverage

Degree of combined leverage utilizes the entire income statement and shows the impact of a change in sales or volume on bottom-line earnings per share. Degree of operating leverage and degree of financial leverage are, in effect, being combined. Table 5–7 shows what happens

Table 5–7
Operating and financial leverage

| | *(Taken from Table 5–6)* | | |
|---|---|---|---|
| Sales—$2 per unit (80,000 units) | $160,000 | (100,000 → | $200,000 |
| – Fixed costs | 60,000 | units) | 60,000 |
| – Variable costs ($0.80 per unit) | 64,000 | | 80,000 |
| Operating income = EBIT | 36,000 | | 60,000 |
| – Interest | 12,000 | | 12,000 |
| Earnings before taxes | 24,000 | | 48,000 |
| – Taxes | 12,000 | | 24,000 |
| Earnings after taxes | $ 12,000 | | $ 24,000 |
| Shares | 8,000 | | 8,000 |
| Earnings per share | $1.50 | | $3.00 |

to profitability as the firm's sales go from \$160,000 (80,000 units) to \$200,000 (100,000 units).

The formula for degree of combined leverage is stated as:

$$\text{Degree of combined leverage } (DCL) = \frac{\text{Percent change in } EPS}{\text{Percent change in sales (or volume)}} \tag{5–6}$$

$$\frac{\text{Percent change in } EPS}{\text{Percent change in sales}} = \frac{\dfrac{\$1.50}{\$1.50} \times 100}{\dfrac{\$\ 40{,}000}{\$160{,}000} \times 100} = \frac{100\%}{25\%} = 4$$

Every percentage point change in sales will be reflected in a 4 percent change in earnings per share at this level of operation (quite an impact).

An algebraic statement of the formula is:

$$DCL = \frac{Q(P - VC)}{Q(P - VC) - FC - I} \tag{5–7}$$

From Table 5–7: $Q$ (quantity) = 80,000; $P$ (price per unit) = \$2.00; $VC$ (variable costs per unit) = \$0.80; $FC$ (fixed costs) = \$60,000; $I$ (interest) = \$12,000.

$$DCL = \frac{80{,}000\ (\$2.00 - \$0.80)}{80{,}000\ (\$2.00 - \$0.80) - \$60{,}000 - \$12{,}000}$$

$$= \frac{80{,}000\ (\$1.20)}{80{,}000\ (\$1.20) - \$72{,}000}$$

$$= \frac{\$96{,}000}{\$96{,}000 - \$72{,}000} = \frac{\$96{,}000}{\$24{,}000} = 4$$

The answer is once again shown to be 4.[3]

---

[3]The formula for $DCL$ may be rewritten as:

$$DCL = \frac{Q(P - VC)}{Q(P - VC) - FC - I} = \frac{QP - QVC}{QP - QVC - FC - I}$$

*(continued on the bottom of page 135)*

### A Word of Caution

In a sense, we are piling risk upon risk as the two different forms of leverage are combined. Perhaps a firm carrying heavy operating leverage may wish to moderate its position financially, and vice versa. One thing is certain—the decision will have a major impact on the operations of the firm.

## Summary

Leverage may be defined as the use of fixed cost items to magnify returns at high levels of operation. Operating leverage primarily affects fixed versus variable cost utilization in the operation of the firm. An important concept—degree of operating leverage (*DOL*)—measures the percentage change in operating income as a result of a percentage change in volume. The heavier the utilization of fixed cost assets, the higher *DOL* is likely to be.

Financial leverage reflects the extent to which debt is used in the capital structure of the firm. Substantial use of debt will place a great burden on the firm at low levels of profitability, but it will help to magnify earnings per share as volume or operating income increases. We combine operating and financial leverage to assess the impact of all types of fixed costs on the firm. There is a multiplier effect when we use the two different types of leverage.

Because leverage is a two-edged sword, management must be sure that the level of risk assumed is in accord with its desires for risk and its perceptions of the future. High operating leverage may be balanced off against lower financial leverage if this is deemed desirable, and vice versa.

---

We rewrite the second terms as:

$QP$ = $S$, or Sales (Quantity × Price)
$QVC$ = $TVC$, or Total variable costs (Quantity × Variable cost per unit)
$FC$ = Total fixed costs (remains the same term)
$I$ = Interest (remains the same term)

We then have:

$$DCL = \frac{S - TVC}{S - TVC - FC - I}$$

$$= \frac{\$160{,}000 - \$64{,}000}{\$160{,}000 - \$64{,}000 - \$60{,}000 - \$12{,}000} = \frac{\$96{,}000}{\$24{,}000} = 4$$

## List of Terms

**break-even analysis**
**fixed costs**
**variable costs**
**contribution margin**
**nonlinear break-even analysis**
**leverage (concept in general)**
**operating leverage**
**degree of operating leverage (DOL)**
**financial leverage**
**degreee of financial leverage (DFL)**
**combined leverage**
**degree of combined leverage (DCL)**

## Discussion Questions

1. Discuss the various uses for break-even analysis.
2. What factors would cause a difference in the use of financial leverage for a utility company and an automobile company?
3. Explain how the break-even point and operating leverage are affected by the choice of manufacturing facilities (labor intensive versus capital intensive).
4. What role does depreciation play in break-even analysis based on accounting flows? Based on cash flows? Which perspective is longer term in nature?
5. What does risk taking have to do with the use of operating and financial leverage?
6. Discuss the limitations of financial leverage.
7. How does the interest rate on new debt influence the use of financial leverage?
8. Explain how combined leverage brings together operating income and earnings per share.
9. Explain why operating leverage decreases as a company increases sales and shifts away from the break-even point.

10. Why does the starting level of sales determine the degree of operating leverage rather than the ending level of sales?

11. One could say that financial leverage has its most important impact on earnings per share rather than net income after taxes. How would you support this statement?

12. Does being at the *EPS* indifference point mean that you are always indifferent between two financing plans? Explain.

## Problems

1. The Harmon Corporation manufactures baseball bats with Pete Rose's autograph stamped on. Each bat sells for $12 and has a variable cost of $7.00. There are $20,000 in fixed costs involved in the production process.

   *a.* Compute the break-even point in units.
   *b.* Find the sales (in units) needed to earn a profit of $15,000.

2. Draw two break-even graphs—one for a conservative firm using labor-intensive production and another for a capital-intensive firm. Assuming that these companies compete within the same industry and have identical sales, explain the impact of changes in sales volume on both firms' profits.

3. The Morgan Tire Company income statement for 1987 is as follows:

MORGAN TIRE COMPANY
Income Statement
For the Year Ended December 31, 1987

| | |
|---|---|
| Sales (20,000 tires at $60 each) | $1,200,000 |
| Less: Variable costs (20,000 tires at $30) | 600,000 |
| Fixed costs | 400,000 |
| Earnings before interest and taxes (EBIT) | 200,000 |
| Interest expense | 50,000 |
| Earnings before taxes (EBT) | 150,000 |
| Income tax expense (40%) | 60,000 |
| Earnings after taxes (EAT) | $ 90,000 |

Given this income statement, compute the following:

*a.* Degree of operating leverage.
*b.* Degree of financial leverage.

*c*. Degree of combined leverage.
*d*. Break-even point in units.

**4.** The Prima Donna Company provides studios for musicians to give music lessons. The company's income statement for the year 1987 is as follows:

PRIMA DONNA COMPANY
Income Statement
For the Year Ended December 31, 1987

| | |
|---|---|
| Sales (10,000 lessons @ $20 each) | $200,000 |
| Less: Variable costs (10,000 lessons at $5) | 50,000 |
| Fixed costs | 50,000 |
| Earnings before interest and taxes (EBIT) | 100,000 |
| Interest expense | 20,000 |
| Earnings before taxes (EBT) | 80,000 |
| Income tax expense (40%) | 32,000 |
| Earnings after taxes (EAT) | $ 48,000 |

Given this income statement, compute the following:

*a*. Degree of operating leverage.
*b*. Degree of financial leverage.
*c*. Degree of combined leverage.
*d*. Break-even point in units (number of music lessons).

**5.** University Catering sells 50-pound bags of popcorn to university dormitories for $10 a bag. The fixed costs of this operation are $80,000, while the variable costs of the popcorn are $.10 per pound.

*a*. What is the break-even point in bags?
*b*. Calculate the profit or loss on 12,000 bags and 25,000 bags.
*c*. What is the degree of operating leverage at 20,000 bags and 25,000 bags? Why does the degree of operating leverage change as quantity sold increases?
*d*. If University Catering has an annual interest payment of $10,000, calculate the degree of financial leverage at both 20,000 and 25,000 bags.
*e*. What is the degree of combined leverage at both sales levels?

**6.** Sinclair Manufacturing and Boswell Brothers Inc. are both involved in the production of tile for the homebuilding industry. Their financial information is as follows:

Capital Structure

| | *Sinclair* | *Boswell* |
|---|---|---|
| Debt @ 12% | $ 600,000 | 0 |
| Common stock, $10 per share | 400,000 | $1,000,000 |
| Total | $1,000,000 | $1,000,000 |
| Common shares | 40,000 | 100,000 |

Operating Plan

| | | |
|---|---|---|
| Sales (50,000 units at $20 each) | $1,000,000 | $1,000,000 |
| Less: Variable costs | 800,000 ($16 per unit) | 500,000 ($10 per unit) |
| Fixed costs | 0 | 300,000 |
| Earnings before interest and taxes (EBIT) | $ 200,000 | $ 200,000 |

*a.* If you combine Sinclair's capital structure with Boswell's operating plan, what is the degree of combined leverage? (Round to two places to the right of the decimal point.)

*b.* If you combine Boswell's capital structure with Sinclair's operating plan, what is the degree of combined leverage?

*c.* Explain why you got the result you did in part *b*.

*d.* In part *b*, if sales double, by what percent will EPS increase?

**7.** Cain Auto Supplies and Able Auto Parts are competitors in the aftermarket for auto supplies. The separate capital structures for Cain and Able are presented below.

| *Cain* | | *Able* | |
|---|---|---|---|
| Debt @ 10% | $ 50,000 | Debt @ 10% | $100,000 |
| Common stock, $10 par | 100,000 | Common stock, $10 par | 50,000 |
| Total | $150,000 | Total | $150,000 |
| Common shares | 10,000 | Common shares | 5,000 |

*a.* Compute earnings per share if earnings before interest and taxes are $10,000, $15,000, and $50,000 (assume a 30 percent tax rate).

*b.* Explain the relationship between earnings per share and the level of EBIT.

*c.* If the cost of debt went up to 12 percent and all other factors remained equal, what would be the break-even level for EBIT?

**8.** In Problem 7, compute the stock price for Cain if it sells at 12 times earnings per share and EBIT are $40,000.

9. The Norman Automatic Mailer Machine Company is planning to expand production because of the increased volume of mailouts. The increased mailout capacity will cost $2,000,000. The expansion can be financed either by bonds at an interest rate of 14 percent or by selling 40,000 shares of common stock at $50 per share. The current income statement (before expansion) is as follows:

NORMAN AUTOMATIC MAILER
Income Statement
198X

| | | |
|---|---|---|
| Sales | | $3,500,000 |
| Less: Variable costs | $1,400,000 | |
| Fixed costs | 900,000 | |
| Earnings before interest and taxes | | 1,200,000 |
| Less: interest expense | | 400,000 |
| Earnings before taxes | | 800,000 |
| Less taxes @ 40% | | 320,000 |
| Earnings after taxes | | 480,000 |
| Shares | | 100,000 |
| Earnings per share | | $4.80 |

Assume that after expansion, sales are expected to increase by $1,500,000. Variable costs will be 40 percent of sales, and fixed costs will increase by $600,000. The tax rate is 40 percent.

*a.* Calculate the degree of operating leverage, the degree of financial leverage, and the degree of combined leverage before expansion. (For the degree of operating leverage, use the formula developed in footnote 2; for the degree of combined leverage, use the formula developed in footnote 3. These instructions apply throughout this problem.)
*b.* Construct the income statement for the two financing plans.
*c.* Calculate the degree of operating leverage, the degree of financial leverage, and the degree of combined leverage, after expansion, for the two financing plans.
*d.* Explain which financial plan you favor and the risks involved.

10. Dickinson Company has $12 million in assets. Currently half of these assets are financed with long-term debt at 10 percent and half with common stock having a par value of $8. Ms. Smith, vice president of finance, wishes to analyze two refinancing plans, one with more debt (D) and one with more equity (E). The company

earns a return on assets before interest and taxes of 10 percent. The tax rate is 45 percent.

Under Plan D, a $3 million long-term bond would be sold at an interest rate of 12 percent and 375,000 shares of stock would be purchased in the market at $8 per share and retired.

Under Plan E, 375,000 shares of stock would be sold at $8 per share and the $3,000,000 in proceeds would be used to reduce long-term debt.

*a.* How would each of these plans affect earnings per share? Consider the current plan and the two new plans.
*b.* Which plan would be most favorable if return on assets fell to 5 percent? Increased to 15 percent? Consider the current plan and the two new plans.
*c.* If the market price for common stock rose to $12 before the restructuring, which plan would then be most attractive? Continue to assume that $3 million in debt will be used to retire stock in Plan D and $3 million of new equity will be sold to retire debt in Plan E. Also assume for calculations in part *c* that return on assets is 10 percent.

**11.** Richards Manufacturing Company has $20 million in assets; 80 percent is financed by debt, and 20 percent is financed by common stock. The interest rate on the debt is 14 percent, and the price of the stock is $20 per share. The firm's president is considering two financing plans for an expansion to $30 million in assets.

Under Plan A, the high debt-to-assets ratio will be maintained, but new debt will cost an expensive 18 percent! (The stock will be sold at $20 per share).

Under Plan B, only new common stock at $20 per share will be issued. The tax rate is 40 percent.

*a.* If EBIT is 16 percent on assets, compute earnings per share (EPS) before the expansion and under the two alternatives.
*b.* What is the degree of financial leverage under each of the three plans?
*c.* If stock can be sold at $32 per share due to increased expectations about the firm's sales and earnings, what impact would

this have on earnings per share for the two expansion alternatives? Compute earnings per share for each.

*d*. Explain why corporate financial officers are concerned about their stock values.

**12.** Using Standard & Poor's data or annual reports, compare the financial and operating leverage of IBM, Polaroid, and Delta Airlines for the most current year. Explain the relationship between operating and financial leverage for each company and the resultant combined leverage. What accounts for the differences in leverage of these companies?

**13.** Mr. Gold is in the widget business. He currently sells 1 million widgets a year at $5 each. His variable cost to produce the widgets is $3 per unit, and he has $1,500,000 in fixed costs. His sales-to-assets ratio is five times, and 40 percent of his assets are financed with 8 percent debt, with the balance financed by common stock at $10 per share. The tax rate is 40 percent.

His brother-in-law, Mr. Silverman, says he is doing it all wrong. By reducing his price to $4.50 a widget, he could increase his volume of units sold by 40 percent. Fixed costs would remain constant, and variable costs would remain $3 per unit. His sales-to-assets ratio would be 6.3 times. Furthermore, he could increase his debt-to-assets ratio to 50 percent, with the balance in common stock. It is assumed that the interest rate would go up by 1 percent and that the price of stock would remain constant.

*a*. Compute earnings per share under the Gold plan.
*b*. Compute earnings per share under the Silverman plan.
*c*. Mr. Gold's wife does not think that fixed costs would remain constant under the Silverman plan but that they would go up by 15 percent. If this is the case, should Mr. Gold shift to the Silverman plan, based on earnings per share?

**14.** Reynolds Calculators Inc. (RCI) is in the process of evaluating the company's break-even position and its operating and financial leverage. RCI has been selling 50,000 calculators per year for the last five years at $10 each. The fixed costs associated with this production are $250,000, and variable costs are $2 per calculator. RCI is currently producing at full capacity and has no debt. Management is expecting sales to increase by 10,000 units per year. To plan for this increase over the next five years, RCI is considering a program which would increase capacity to 100,000 units. The company would borrow $1,000,000 at 12 percent to finance the expansion. They currently have no debt. Fixed costs would immediately rise to $400,000, and variable costs would remain at $2 per unit. The price would stay at $10 per unit.

*a.* What is the break-even point before expansion and after expansion?

*b.* What is the degree of operating leverage before expansion? (Use the formula in footnote 2.) What will DOL be one year and five years after expansion?

*c.* Calculate the degree of financial leverage and the degree of combined leverage before expansion, one year after expansion, and five years after expansion. (For degree of combined leverage, use the formula in footnote 3.) Note that in some calculations degree of financial leverage or degree of combined leverage may be negative.

*d.* Explain what causes the changes in break-even and leverage measures in calculations in parts *a*, *b*, and *c*.

**15.** Bertel Bottling Company is considering an expansion of its facilities. Its current income statement is as follows:

| | |
|---|---|
| Sales | $4,000,000 |
| Less: Variable expense (45% of sales) | 1,800,000 |
| Fixed expense | 1,600,000 |
| Earnings before interest and taxes (EBIT) | 600,000 |
| Interest (6% cost) | 120,000 |
| Earnings before taxes (EBT) | 480,000 |
| Tax (50%) | 240,000 |
| Earnings after taxes (EAT) | $ 240,000 |
| Shares of common stock—200,000 | |
| Earnings per share | $1.20 |

Bertel Bottling Company is currently financed with 50 percent debt and 50 percent equity (common stock, par value of $10). In order to expand its facilities, Mr. Bertel estimates a need for $2 million in additional financing. His investment banker has laid out three plans for him to consider:

1. Sell $2 million of debt at 9 percent.
2. Sell $2 million of common stock at $20 per share.
3. Sell $1 million of debt at 8 percent and $1 million of common stock at $25 per share.

Variable costs are expected to stay at 45 percent of sales, while fixed expenses will increase to $2,100,000 per year. Mr. Bertel is not sure how much this expansion will add to sales, but he estimates that sales will rise by $800,000 per year for the next five years. Occasionally when the weather is cool in early spring and late fall, sales fall about 10 percent, but they usually return to their normal growth pattern the following year.

Mr. Bertel is interested in a thorough analysis of his expansion plans and methods of financing. He would like you to analyze the following:

*a.* The break-even point for operating expenses before and after expansion (in sales dollars).
*b.* The degree of operating leverage before and after expansion.
*c.* The degree of financial leverage before expansion and for all three methods of financing after expansion.
*d.* In addition, he would like an indifference graph of the three financing methods and your selection of the financing method which best suits his objective of maximizing shareholders' wealth.

**16.** (*Comprehensive problem for Chapters 2–5.*)

ASPEN SKI COMPANY
Balance Sheet
December 31, 1986

| *Assets* | | *Liabilities and Stockholders' Equity* | |
|---|---|---|---|
| Cash | $ 40,000 | Accounts payable | $1,800,000 |
| Marketable securities | 60,000 | Accrued expenses | 100,000 |
| Accounts receivable | 1,000,000 | Notes payable (current) | 600,000 |
| Inventory | 3,000,000 | Bonds (10%) | 2,000,000 |
| Gross plant and equipment | 5,000,000 | Common stock (1.5 million shares, par value $1) | 1,500,000 |
| Less: Accumulated depreciation | 2,000,000 | Retained earnings | 1,100,000 |
| Total assets | $7,100,000 | Total liabilities and stockholders' equity | $7,100,000 |

Income Statement 1986

| | |
|---|---|
| Sales (credit) | $6,000,000 |
| Fixed costs* | 1,800,000 |
| Variable costs (0.60) | 3,600,000 |
| Earnings before interest and taxes | 600,000 |
| Less: Interest | 200,000 |
| Earnings before taxes | 400,000 |
| Less: Taxes @ 40% | 160,000 |
| Earnings after taxes | 240,000 |
| Dividends | 43,200 |
| Increased retained earnings | $ 196,800 |

*Fixed costs include (*a*) lease expense of $190,000 and (*b*) depreciation of $400,000.

Note: Aspen Ski also has $100,000 per year in sinking fund obligations associated with their bond issue. The sinking fund represents an annual repayment of the principal amount of the bond. It is not tax deductible.

Ratios

| | *Aspen Ski (To be filled in)* | *Industry* |
|---|---|---|
| Profit margin | | 6.1% |
| Return on assets | | 6.5% |
| Return on equity | | 8.9% |
| Receivables turnover | | 4.9× |
| Inventory turnover | | 4.4× |
| Fixed asset turnover | | 2.1× |
| Total asset turnover | | 1.06× |
| Current ratio | | 1.4× |
| Quick ratio | | 1.1× |
| Debt to total assets | | 27% |
| Interest coverage | | 4.2× |
| Fixed charge coverage | | 3.0× |

*a*. Analyze Aspen Ski Company, using ratio analysis. Compute the ratios above for Aspen and compare them to the industry data that is given. Discuss the weak points, strong points, and what you think should be done to improve the company's performance.

*b*. In your analysis, calculate the overall break-even point in sales and the cash break-even point. Also compute the degree of operating leverage, degree of financial leverage, and degree of combined leverage.

*c*. Use the information in parts *a* and *b* to discuss the risk associated with this company. Given the risk, decide whether a bank should loan funds to Aspen Ski.

Aspen Ski Company is trying to plan their funds needed for 1987. The management anticipates an increase in sales of 20 percent, which can be absorbed without increasing fixed assets.

*d*. What would be Aspen's needs for external funds, based on the current balance sheet? Compute RNF (required new funds).

*e*. What would be the required new funds if the company brings its ratios into line with the industry average during 1987? Specifically examine receivables turnover, inventory turnover, and the profit margin. Use the new values to recompute the factors in RNF (assume liabilities stay the same).

*f*. Do not calculate, only comment on these questions. How would required new funds change if the company:
(1) Were at full capacity?
(2) Raised the dividend payout ratio?
(3) Suffered a decreased growth in sales?
(4) Faced an accelerated inflation rate?

## Selected References

Crowningshield, Gerald R., and George L. Battista. "Cost–Volume–Profit Analysis in Planning and Control." *N.A.A. Bulletin* 45 (July 1963), pp. 3–15.

Ghandhi, J. K. S. "On the Measurement of Leverage." *Journal of Finance* 21 (December 1966), pp. 15–26.

Hobbs, J. B. "Volume–Mix–Price Cost Budget Variance Analysis: A Proper Approach." *Accounting Review* 39 (October 1964), pp. 905–13.

Hugon, J. H. "Break-even Analysis in Three Dimensions." *Financial Executive* 33 (December 1965), pp. 22–26.

Hunt, Pearson. "A Proposal for Precise Definitions of 'Trading on the Equity' and 'Leverage.' " *Journal of Finance* 16 (September 1961), pp. 377–86.

Jaedicke, Robert K., and Alexander A. Robichek. "Cost–Volume–Profit Analysis under Conditions of Uncertainty." *Accounting Review* 39 (October 1964), pp. 917–26.

Kelvie, W. E., and J. M. Sinclair. "New Technique for Break-even Charts." *Financial Executive* 36 (June 1968), pp. 31–43.

Krainer, Robert W. "Interest Rates, Leverage, and Investor Rationality." *Journal of Financial and Quantitative Analysis* 12 (March 1977), pp. 1–16.

Lee, Wayne Y., and Henry H. Barker. "Bankruptcy Costs and the Firm's Optimal Debt Capacity: A Positive Theory of Capital Structure." *Southern Economic Journal* 43 (April 1977), pp. 1453–65.

Lev, Baruch. "On the Association between Operating Leverage and Risk." *Journal of Financial and Quantitative Analysis* 9 (September 1974), pp. 627–42.

Percival, John R. "Operating Leverage and Risk." *Journal of Business Research* 2 (April 1974), pp. 223–27.

Raun, D. L. "The Limitations of Profit Graphs, Break-Even Analysis, and Budgets." *Accounting Review* 39 (October 1964), pp. 927–45.

Rendleman, Richard J., Jr. "The Effects of Default Risk on the Firm's Investment and Financing Decisions." *Financial Management* 7 (Spring 1978), pp. 45–53.

Salit, Sol S. "On the Mathematics of Financial Leverage." *Financial Management* 4 (Spring 1975), pp. 57–66.

Sarig, Oded, and James Scott. "The Puzzle of Financial Leverage Clienteles." *Journal of Finance* 40 (December 1985), pp. 1459–67.

Scott, David F., and J. D. Martin. "Industry Influence on Financial Structure." *Financial Management* 4 (Spring 1975), pp. 67–73.

Scott, David F., and Dana J. Johnson. "Financing Policies and Practices in Large Corporations." *Financial Management* 11 (Summer 1982), pp. 51–57.

PART

# THREE

# Working Capital Management

## Introduction

Working capital policy involves the management of the current assets of the firm and the acquisition of the appropriate financing for those assets. While a firm may be able to sustain a decrease in sales or profitability for some period of time, the need for current assets and the associated financing is now.

Typical working capital decisions involve a determination of the appropriate level of cash, accounts receivable, and inventory that the firm should maintain. On the financing side, we must determine whether to carry these assets through credit extension from our supplier, short-term bank loans, or longer-term credit arrangements. The smaller firm usually has a limited number of options.

As we shall see, one of the unfortunate choices of terms in the vernacular of finance and accounting is the phrase "current asset." The normal definition of a current asset is a short-term asset that can be converted to cash within one year or within the normal operating cycle of the firm. Regrettably, as a business begins to grow, some current assets become more "permanent" in nature—perhaps a portion of inventory is not liquidated and a growing volume of receivables, in aggregate, remains on the books. All too often, firms think of current assets as being temporary, when, in fact, a rather sizable portion require longer-term financing. The lesson about the true nature of current assets is well taught every three or four years, as the U.S. economy finds itself in a credit crunch and financing cannot be found for "permanent" current assets.

In the initial chapter on working capital, Chapter 6, we examine some of the basic conceptual items related to working capital and the financing decision, with an eye toward the various risk-return alternatives that are available to the financial manager. We also look at the effects of various production policies on the financing requirements of the firm. In Chapter 7, we look at specific techniques for the management of cash, marketable securities, accounts receivable, and inventory.

Finally, in Chapter 8, we examine the various sources of short-term financing that are available to the firm. The emphasis is on trade credit, bank financing, and the use of secured loans through the pledging of receivables or inventory as collateral. The relative costs, advantages, and disadvantages of these financing outlets are considered. Also, at the end of the chapter, we examine how the financial futures market can be used to hedge the firm's exposure to changing interest rates.

# 6 Working Capital and the Financing Decision

The rapid growth of business firms in the post–World War II period has challenged the ingenuity of financial managers to provide adequate financing. Rapidly expanding sales may cause intense pressure for inventory and receivables buildup—draining the cash resources of the firm. As indicated in Chapter 4, Financial Forecasting, a large sales increase creates an expansion of current assets, especially accounts receivable and inventory. Some of the increased current assets can be financed by the firm's retained earnings, but in most cases internal funds will not provide enough financing and some external sources of funds must be found. In fact, the faster the growth in sales, the more likely it is that an increasing percentage of financing will be external to the firm. These funds could come from the sale of common stock, preferred stock, long-term bonds, short-term securities, and bank loans, or from a combination of short- and long-term sources of funds.

Working capital management involves the financing and management of the current assets of the firm. The financial executive probably devotes more time to working capital management than to any other activity. Current assets, by their very nature, are changing daily, if not hourly, and managerial decisions must be made. "How much inventory is to be carried, and how do we get the funds to pay for it?" Unlike long-term decisions, there can be no deferral of action. While long-term decisions, involving plant and equipment or market strategy, may well determine the eventual success of the firm, short-term decisions on working capital determine whether the firm gets to the long term.

In this chapter, we examine the nature of asset growth, the process of matching sales and production, financial aspects of working capital management, and finally, the factors that go into the development of an optimum policy.

## The Nature of Asset Growth

Any company that produces and sells a product, whether the product is consumer or manufacturer oriented, will have current assets and fixed assets. If a firm grows, those assets are likely to increase over time. The key to current asset planning is the ability of management to forecast sales accurately and then to match the production schedules with the sales forecast. Whenever actual sales are different from forecasted sales, unexpected buildups or reductions in inventory will occur that will eventually affect receivables and cash flow.

In the simplest case, all of the firm's current assets will be self-liquidating (sold off at the end of a specified time period). Assume that at the start of the summer you buy 100 tires to be disposed of by September. It is your intention that all tires will be sold, receivables collected, and bills paid over this time period. In this case, your working capital (current asset) needs are truly short term.

Now let us begin to expand the business. In stage two, you add radios, seat covers, and batteries to your operation. Some of your inventory will again be completely liquidated, while other items will form the basic stock for your operation. In order to stay in business, you must maintain floor displays and multiple items for selection. Furthermore, not all items will sell. As you eventually grow to more than one store, this "permanent" aggregate stock of current assets will continue to increase. Problems of inadequate financing arrangements are often the result of the businessperson's failure to realize that the firm is carrying not only self-liquidating inventory—but also the anomaly of "permanent" current assets.

The movement from stage one to stage two growth for a typical business is depicted in Figure 6–1. In Panel A, the buildup in current

Figure 6–1
The nature of asset growth

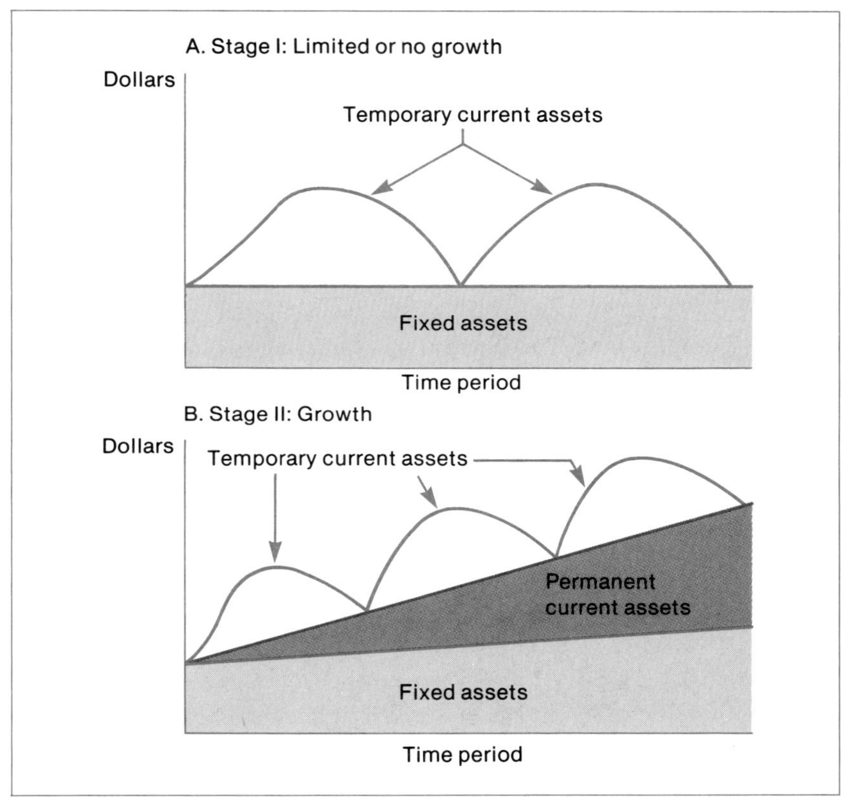


assets is temporary—while in Panel B, part of the growth in current assets is temporary and part is permanent. (Fixed assets are included in the illustrations, but they are not directly related to the present discussion.)

## Controlling Assets—Matching Sales and Production

In most firms, fixed assets grow slowly as productive capacity is increased and old equipment is replaced, but current assets fluctuate in the short run, depending on the level of production versus the level of sales. When the firm produces more than it sells, inventory rises.

When sales rise faster than production, inventory declines and receivables rise.

As discussed in the treatment of the cash budgeting process in Chapter 4, some firms employ level production methods to smooth production schedules and use manpower and equipment efficiently at a lower cost. One consequence of level production is that current assets go up and down when sales and production are not equal. Other firms may try to match sales and production as closely as possible in the short run. This allows current assets to increase or decrease with the level of sales and eliminates the large seasonal bulges or sharp reductions in current assets that occur under level production.

Publishing companies are good examples of companies with seasonal sales and an inventory problem. By the nature of the textbook market, heavy sales are made in the third quarter of the year for Fall semester sales. The bulk of the sales occurs in July and August, and again in December for the second semester. The actual printing and binding of a book has fixed costs that make printing a large number of copies more efficient. Since publishing companies cannot reproduce books on demand, they contract with the printing company to print a fixed number of copies, depending upon expected sales over at least a one-year time period and sometimes based on sales over several years. If the books sell better than expected, the publishing company will order a second or third printing. Orders may have to be placed as much as nine months before the books will actually be needed, and reorders will be placed as much as three or four months ahead of actual sales. If the book declines in popularity, the publisher could get stuck with a large inventory of obsolete books.

Figure 6–2 depicts quarterly sales and earnings per share of two book publishers, Harcourt Brace Jovanovich and Houghton Mifflin. These are good examples of companies with seasonal sales. Both companies have their largest sales and earnings in the third and fourth quarter of each year. If they have not planned their inventory correctly, the lost sales or excess inventory could be a serious problem.

Retail firms such as J. C. Penney and K mart Corp. also have seasonal sales patterns. Figure 6–3 shows the quarterly sales and earnings per share of these two companies, with the quarters ending in January, April, July, and October. These retail companies do not stock a year or more of inventory at one time as do the publishers. They are either

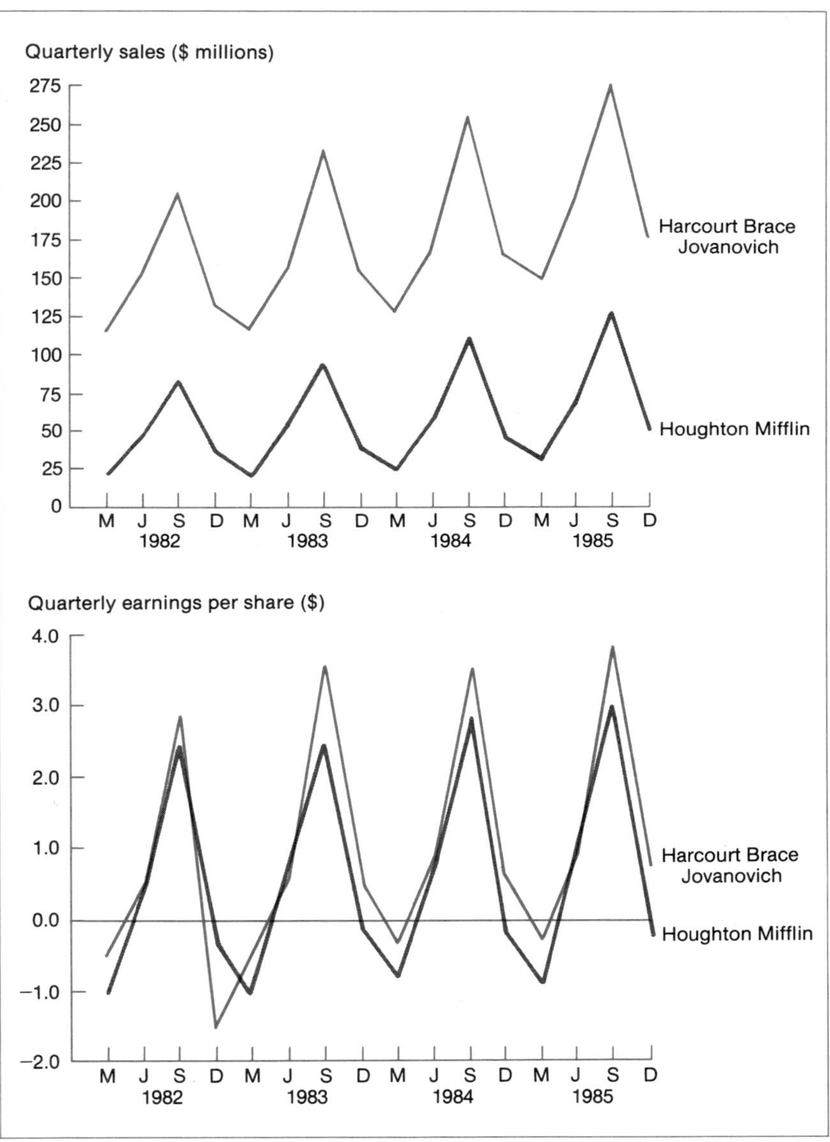


**Figure 6–2**
**Sales and earnings for Harcourt Brace Jovanovich and Houghton Mifflin**

Figure 6–3
Sales and earnings for J. C. Penney and K mart

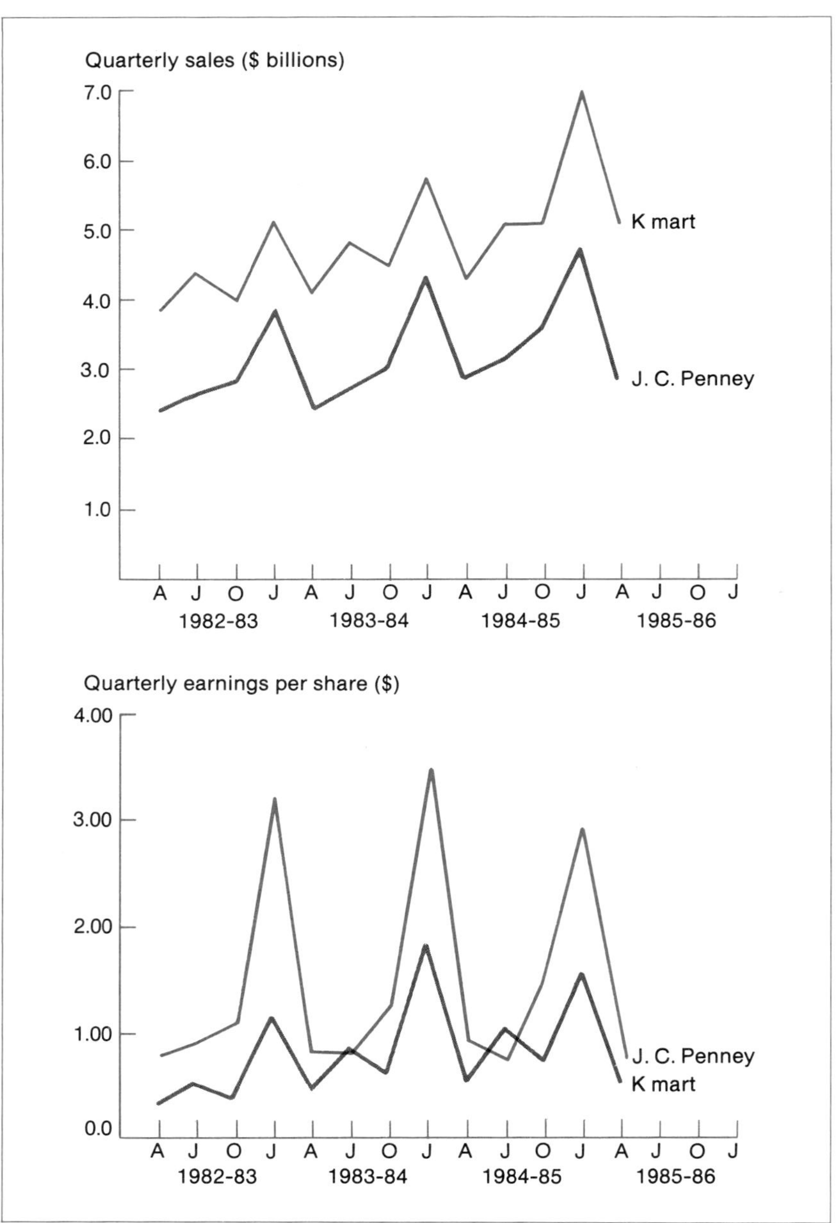

selling products manufactured for them by others or manufactured by their subsidiaries. Most retail stores are not involved in deciding on level versus seasonal production but rather in matching sales and inventory. Their suppliers must make the decision to produce on either a level or a seasonal production basis. Since the selling seasons are very much impacted by the weather and holiday periods, the suppliers and retailers cannot avoid the inventory risk. The fourth quarter beginning in October and ending in December is the biggest quarter for retailers and accounts for as much as one half of their earnings. You can be sure that inventory not sold during the Christmas season will be put on sale during January.

Figure 6–3 demonstrates that over several years, each peak and trough in quarterly sales is higher for both companies. These seasonal peaks and troughs will also be reflected in cash, receivables, and inventory. J. C. Penney has slightly less volatile sales than K mart, but both companies demonstrate the impact of leverage on earnings as discussed in Chapter 5. Notice that when J. C. Penney's sales surge, earnings per share rise by a far greater percentage. We shall see as we go through the chapter that seasonal sales can cause asset management problems. A financial manager must be aware of these to avoid getting caught short of cash or unprepared to borrow when necessary.

Many retail-oriented firms have been more successful in matching sales and orders in recent years because of new, computerized inventory control systems linked to on-line point-of-sales terminals. These point-of-sales terminals either allow digital input or use of optical scanners to record the inventory code numbers and the amount of each item sold. At the end of the day, managers are able to examine sales and inventory levels item by item and, if need be, to adjust orders or production schedules. The predictability of the market will influence the speed with which the manager reacts to this information, while the length and complexity of the production process will dictate just how fast production levels can be changed.

## Temporary Assets under Level Production—An Example

In order to get a better understanding of how current assets fluctuate, let us use the example of the Yawakuzi Motorcycle Company, which manufactures and sells in the snowy U.S. midwest. Not too many people will be buying motorcycles during October through March, but

**Table 6–1**
**Yawakuzi sales forecast (in units)**

| *1st Quarter* | | *2nd Quarter* | | *3rd Quarter* | | *4th Quarter* | |
|---|---|---|---|---|---|---|---|
| October | 300 | January | 0 | April | 1,000 | July | 2,000 |
| November | 150 | February | 0 | May | 2,000 | August | 1,000 |
| December | 50 | March | 600 | June | 2,000 | September | 500 |

Total sales of 9,600 units at $3,000 each = $28,800,000 in sales.

sales will pick up in early spring and summer and will trail off during the fall. Because of the fixed assets and the skilled labor involved in the production process, Yawakuzi decides that level production is the least expensive and the most efficient production method. The marketing department provides a sales forecast for October through September (Table 6–1).

After reviewing the sales forecast, Yawakuzi decides to produce 800 motorcycles per month, or one year's production of 9,600 divided by 12. A look at Table 6–2 shows how level production and seasonal sales combine to create fluctuating inventory. Assume that October's beginning inventory is one month's production of 800 units. The production cost per unit is $2,000.

The inventory level at cost fluctuates from a high of $9 million in March, the last consecutive month in which production is greater than

**Table 6–2**
**Yawakuzi's production schedule and inventory**

| | *Beginning inventory* | + | *Production (level production)* | – | *Sales* | = | *Ending inventory* | *Inventory (at cost of $2,000 per unit)* |
|---|---|---|---|---|---|---|---|---|
| October | 800 | | 800 | | 300 | | 1,300 | $2,600,000 |
| November | 1,300 | | 800 | | 150 | | 1,950 | 3,900,000 |
| December | 1,950 | | 800 | | 50 | | 2,700 | 5,400,000 |
| January | 2,700 | | 800 | | 0 | | 3,500 | 7,000,000 |
| February | 3,500 | | 800 | | 0 | | 4,300 | 8,600,000 |
| March | 4,300 | | 800 | | 600 | | 4,500 | 9,000,000 |
| April | 4,500 | | 800 | | 1,000 | | 4,300 | 8,600,000 |
| May | 4,300 | | 800 | | 2,000 | | 3,100 | 6,200,000 |
| June | 3,100 | | 800 | | 2,000 | | 1,900 | 3,800,000 |
| July | 1,900 | | 800 | | 2,000 | | 700 | 1,400,000 |
| August | 700 | | 800 | | 1,000 | | 500 | 1,000,000 |
| September | 500 | | 800 | | 500 | | 800 | 1,600,000 |

sales, to a low of $1 million in August, the last month in which sales are greater than production. Table 6–3 combines a sales forecast, a cash receipts schedule, a cash payments schedule, and a brief cash budget in order to examine the buildup in accounts receivable and cash.

In Table 6–3 the *sales forecast* is based on assumptions in Table 6–1. The unit volume of sales is multiplied by a sales price of $3,000 to get sales dollars in millions. Next, *cash receipts* represent 50 percent collected in cash during the month of sale and 50 percent from the prior month's sales. For example, in October this would represent $0.45 million from the current month plus $0.75 million from the prior month's sales.

Cash payments in Table 6–3 are based on an assumption of level production of 800 units per month at a cost of $2,000 per unit, or $1.6 million, plus payments for overhead, dividends, interest and taxes.

Finally, the *cash budget* in Table 6–3 represents a comparison of the cash receipts and cash payments schedules to determine cash flow. We further assume that the firm desires a minimum cash balance of $0.25 million. Thus in October, a negative cash flow of $1.1 million brings the cumulative cash balance to a negative $0.85 million and $1.1 million must be borrowed to provide an ending cash balance of $0.25 million. Similar negative cash flows in subsequent months necessitate expanding the bank loan. For example, in November there is a negative cash flow of $1.325 million. This brings the cumulative cash balance to $ – 1.075 million, requiring additional borrowings of $1.325 million to ensure a minimum cash balance of $0.25 million. The cumulative loan through November (October and November borrowings) now adds up to $2.425 million. Our cumulative bank loan is highest in the month of March.

We now wish to ascertain our total current asset buildup as a result of level production and fluctuating sales for October through September. The analysis is presented in Table 6–4. The cash figures come directly from the last line of Table 6–3. The accounts receivable balance is based on the assumption that accounts receivable represent 50 percent of sales in a given month, as the other 50 percent is paid for in cash. Thus, the accounts receivable figure in Table 6–4 represents 50 percent of the sales figure from the second numerical line in Table 6–3. Finally, the inventory figure is taken directly from the last column of Table 6–2, which presented the production schedule and inventory data.

**Table 6–3 Sales forecast, cash receipts and payments, and cash budget**

| | Oct. | Nov. | Dec. | Jan. | Feb. | March | April | May | June | July | Aug. | Sept. |
|---|---|---|---|---|---|---|---|---|---|---|---|---|
| | | | | *Sales Forecast ($ millions)* | | | | | | | | |
| Sales (units) | 300 | 150 | 50 | 0 | 0 | 600 | 1,000 | 2,000 | 2,000 | 2,000 | 1,000 | 500 |
| Sales (unit price, $3,000) | $0.9 | $0.45 | $0.15 | $ 0 | $ 0 | $1.8 | $3.0 | $6.0 | $6.0 | $6.0 | $3.0 | $1.5 |
| | | | | *Cash Receipts Schedule ($ millions)* | | | | | | | | |
| 50% cash | $0.45 | $0.225 | $0.075 | $ 0 | $ 0 | $0.9 | $1.5 | $3.0 | $3.0 | $3.0 | $1.5 | $0.75 |
| 50% from prior month's sales | 0.75* | 0.450 | 0.225 | 0.075 | 0 | 0 | 0.9 | 1.5 | 3.0 | 3.0 | 3.0 | 1.50 |
| Total cash receipts | $1.20 | $0.675 | $0.300 | $0.075 | 0 | $0.9 | $2.4 | $4.5 | $6.0 | $6.0 | $4.5 | $2.25 |

*Assumes September sales of $1.5 million.

| | Oct. | Nov. | Dec. | Jan. | Feb. | March | April | May | June | July | Aug. | Sept. |
|---|---|---|---|---|---|---|---|---|---|---|---|---|
| | | | | *Cash Payments Schedule ($ millions)* | | | | | | | | |
| Constant production of 800 units/month (cost, $2,000 per unit) | $1.6 | $1.6 | $1.6 | $1.6 | $1.6 | $1.6 | $1.6 | $1.6 | $1.6 | $1.6 | $1.6 | $1.6 |
| Overhead | 0.4 | 0.4 | 0.4 | 0.4 | 0.4 | 0.4 | 0.4 | 0.4 | 0.4 | 0.4 | 0.4 | 0.4 |
| Dividends and interest | — | — | — | — | — | — | — | — | — | — | 1.0 | — |
| Taxes | 0.3 | — | — | 0.3 | — | — | 0.3 | — | — | 0.3 | — | — |
| Total cash payments | $2.3 | $2.0 | $2.0 | $2.3 | $2.0 | $2.0 | $2.3 | $2.0 | $2.0 | $2.3 | $3.0 | $2.0 |
| | | | | *Cash Budget ($ millions; required minimum balance is $0.25 million)* | | | | | | | | |
| Cash flow | $(1.1) | $(1.325) | $(1.7) | $(2.225) | $(2.0) | $(1.1) | $0.1 | $2.5 | $4.0 | $3.7 | $1.5 | $0.25 |
| Beginning cash | 0.25† | 0.25 | 0.25 | 0.250 | 0.25 | 0.25 | 0.25 | 0.25 | 0.25 | 0.25 | 1.1 | 2.60 |
| Cumulative cash balance | $(0.85) | $(1.075) | $(1.45) | $(1.975) | $(1.75) | $(0.85) | $0.35 | $2.75 | $4.25 | $3.95 | $2.6 | $2.85 |
| Monthly loan or (repayment) | 1.1 | 1.325 | 1.7 | 2.225 | 2.0 | 1.1 | (0.1) | (2.5) | (4.0) | (2.85) | 0 | 0 |
| Cumulative loan | 1.1 | 2.425 | 4.125 | 6.350 | 8.350 | 9.45 | 9.35 | 6.85 | 2.85 | 0 | 0 | 0 |
| Ending cash balance | 0.25 | 0.25 | 0.25 | 0.25 | 0.25 | 0.25 | 0.25 | 0.25 | 0.25 | 1.1 | 2.6 | 2.85 |

†Assumes cash balance of $0.25 million at the beginning of October and that this is the desired minimum cash balance.

**Table 6–4**
**Total current assets, first year ($ millions)**

| | Cash | Accounts Receivable | Inventory | Total Current Assets |
|---|---|---|---|---|
| October | $0.25 | $0.45 | $2.6 | $ 3.3 |
| November | 0.25 | 0.225 | 3.9 | 4.375 |
| December | 0.25 | 0.075 | 5.4 | 5.725 |
| January | 0.25 | 0.000 | 7.0 | 7.25 |
| February | 0.25 | 0.000 | 8.6 | 8.85 |
| March | 0.25 | 0.90 | 9.0 | 10.15 |
| April | 0.25 | 1.50 | 8.6 | 10.35 |
| May | 0.25 | 3.00 | 6.2 | 9.45 |
| June | 0.25 | 3.00 | 3.8 | 7.05 |
| July | 1.10 | 3.00 | 1.4 | 5.50 |
| August | 2.60 | 1.50 | 1.0 | 5.10 |
| September | 2.85 | 0.75 | 1.6 | 5.20 |

Total current assets start at $3.3 million in October and rise to $10.35 million in the peak month of April. From April through August, sales are larger than production and inventory falls to its low of $1.0 million in August, but accounts receivables peak at $3.0 million in the highest sales months of May, June, and July. The cash budget in Table 6–3 explains the cash flows and external funds borrowed to finance asset accumulation. From October to March, Yawakuzi borrows more and more money to finance the inventory buildup, but from April to July it eliminates all borrowing as inventory is liquidated and cash balances rise to complete the cycle. In October the cycle starts all over again; but now the firm has accumulated cash which it can use to finance next year's asset accumulation, pay a larger dividend, replace old equipment, or—if growth in sales is anticipated—invest in new equipment to increase productive capacity. Table 6–5 presents the cash budget and total current assets for the second year. Under a simplified no-growth assumption, the monthly cash flow is the same as that of the first year, but beginning cash in October is much higher from the first year's ending cash balance and this lowers the borrowing requirement and increases the ending cash balance and total current assets at year-end. Higher current assets are present in spite of the fact accounts receivable and inventory do not change.

Figure 6–4 is a graphic presentation of the current asset cycle. It includes the two years covered in Tables 6–4 and 6–5 assuming level production and no sales growth.

**Table 6–5 Cash budget and assets for second year with no growth in sales ($ millions)**

| | *End of First Year* | *Second Year* | | | | | | | | | | | |
|---|---|---|---|---|---|---|---|---|---|---|---|---|---|
| | *Sept.* | *Oct.* | *Nov.* | *Dec.* | *Jan.* | *Feb.* | *March* | *April* | *May* | *June* | *July* | *Aug.* | *Sept.* |
| Cash flow | $0.25 | $(1.1) | $(1.325) | $(1.7) | $(2.225) | $(2.0) | $(1.1) | $0.1 | $2.5 | $4.0 | $3.7 | $1.5 | $0.25 |
| Beginning cash | 2.60 | 2.85 | 1.750 | 0.425 | 0.25 | 0.25 | 0.25 | 0.25 | 0.25 | 0.25 | 0.25 | 3.7 | 5.2 |
| Cumulative cash balance | | 1.75 | 0.425 | (1.275) | (1.975) | (1.75) | (0.85) | 0.35 | 2.75 | 4.25 | 3.95 | 5.2 | 5.45 |
| Monthly loan or (repayment) | | — | — | 1.525 | 2.225 | 2.0 | 1.1 | (0.1) | (2.5) | (4.0) | (0.25) | — | — |
| Cumulative loan | | — | — | 1.525 | 3.750 | 5.75 | 6.85 | 6.75 | 4.25 | 0.25 | 0 | — | — |
| Ending cash balance | $2.85 | $1.75 | $0.425 | $0.25 | $0.25 | $0.25 | $0.25 | $0.25 | $0.25 | $0.25 | $3.70 | $5.2 | $5.45 |
| | | *Total Current Assets* | | | | | | | | | | | |
| Ending cash balance | $2.85 | $1.75 | $0.425 | $0.25 | $0.25 | $0.25 | $0.25 | $0.25 | $0.25 | $0.25 | $3.70 | $5.2 | $5.45 |
| Accounts receivable | 0.75 | 0.45 | 0.225 | 0.075 | 0 | 0 | 0.90 | 1.50 | 3.0 | 3.0 | 3.0 | 1.5 | 0.75 |
| Inventory | 1.6 | 2.6 | 3.9 | 5.4 | 7.0 | 8.6 | 9.0 | 8.6 | 6.2 | 3.8 | 1.4 | 1.0 | 1.60 |
| Total current assets | $5.2 | $4.8 | $4.55 | $5.725 | $7.25 | $8.85 | $10.15 | $10.35 | $9.45 | $7.05 | $8.1 | $7.7 | $7.80 |

Figure 6–4
The nature of asset growth (Yawakuzi)

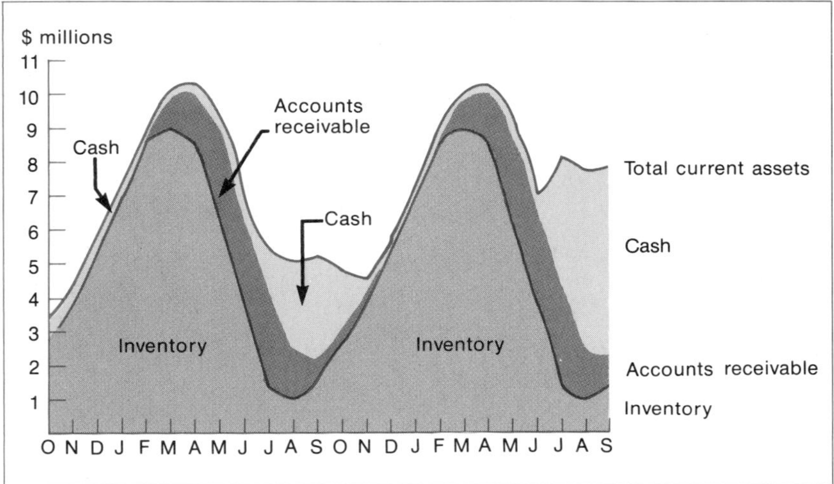


## Patterns of Financing

The financial manager's selection of external sources of funds may be one of the firm's most important decisions. The axiom that all current assets should be financed by current liabilities (accounts payable, bank loans, commercial paper, etc.) is subject to challenge when one sees the permanent buildup that can take place in current assets. In the Yawakuzi example, the buildup in inventory was substantial, at $9.0 million. The example had a logical conclusion in that the motorcycles were sold, cash was generated, and current assets became very liquid. What if a much smaller level of sales had occurred? Yawakuzi would be sitting on a large inventory which needed to be financed and would be generating no cash. Theoretically, the firm could be declared technically insolvent (bankrupt) if short-term sources of funds were used but were unable to be renewed when they came due. How would the interest and principal be paid without cash flow from inventory liquidation? The most appropriate financing pattern would be one in which asset buildup and length of financing terms are perfectly matched, as indicated in Figure 6–5.

In the upper part of Figure 6–5 we see that the temporary buildup in current assets is financed by short-term funds. More important, however, permanent current assets, as well as fixed assets, are financed

Figure 6–5
Matching long-term and short-term needs

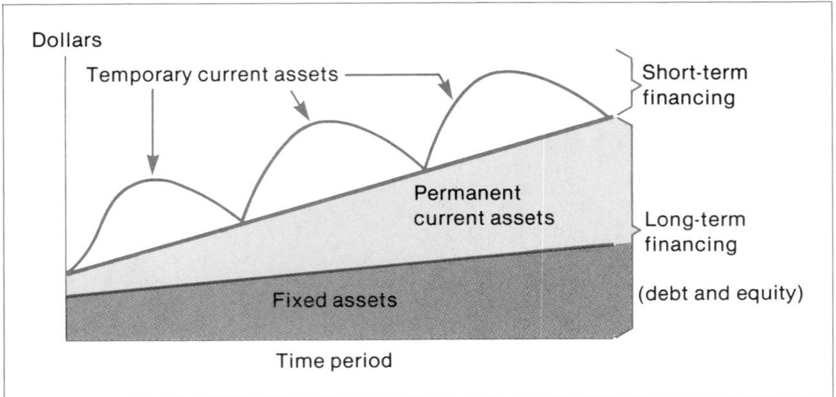


with long-term funds from the sale of stock, the issuance of bonds, or retention of earnings.

### Alternative Plans

Only a financial manager with unusual insight and timing could construct a financial plan for working capital that adhered perfectly to the design in Figure 6–5. The difficulty rests in precisely determining what part of current assets is temporary and what part is permanent. Even if dollar amounts could be ascertained, the exact timing of asset liquidation is a difficult matter. To compound the problem, we are never quite sure how much short-term or long-term financing is available at a given point in time. While the precise synchronization of temporary current assets and short-term financing depicted in Figure 6–5 may be the most desirable and logical plan, other alternatives must be considered.

### Long-Term Financing

To protect against the danger of not being able to provide adequate short-term financing in tight money periods, the financial manager may rely on long-term funds to cover some short-term needs. As indicated in Figure 6–6, long-term capital is now being used to finance fixed

Figure 6–6
Using long-term financing for part of short-term needs

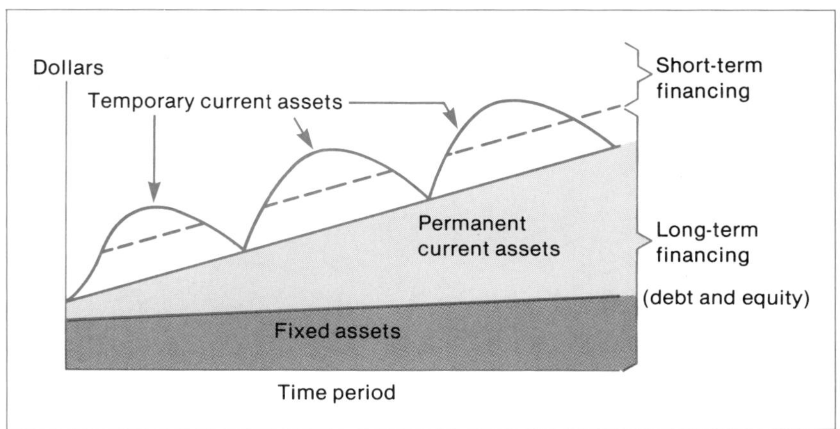


assets, permanent current assets, and part of *temporary current assets*.

By using long-term capital to cover short-term needs, the firm virtually assures itself of having adequate capital at all times. The firm may prefer to borrow a million dollars for 10 years—rather than attempt to borrow a million dollars at the beginning of each year for 10 years and paying it back at the end of each year.

## Short-Term Financing (opposite approach)

This is not to say that all financial managers utilize long-term financing on a large scale. In order to acquire long-term funds, the firm must generally go to the capital markets with a bond or stock offering or must privately place longer-term obligations with insurance companies, wealthy individuals, and so forth. Many small businesses do not have access to such long-term capital and are forced to rely heavily on short-term bank and trade credit. In the capital shortage era of the last decade, even some large businesses were forced to operate with short-term funds.

Furthermore, short-term financing does offer some advantages over more extended financial arrangements. As a general rule, the interest rate on short-term funds is lower than that on long-term funds. We might surmise then that a firm could develop a working capital financing plan in which short-term funds are used to finance not only temporary current assets but also part of the permanent working capital

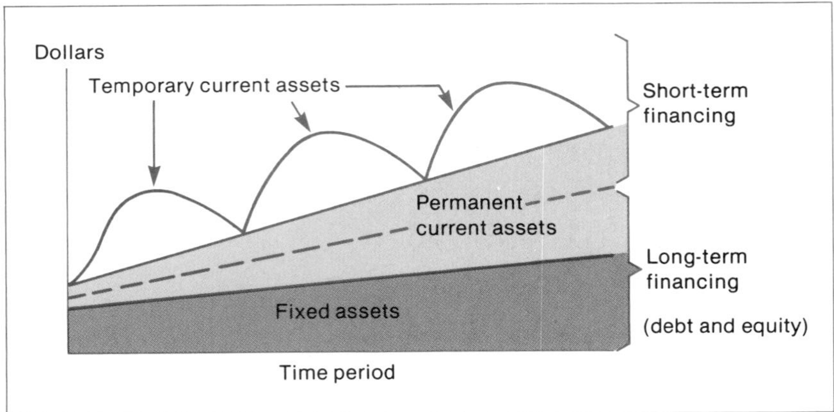


**Figure 6–7**
**Using short-term financing for part of long-term needs**

needs of the firm. As depicted in Figure 6–7, bank and trade credit as well as other sources of short-term financing are now supporting part of the permanent current asset needs of the firm.

## The Financing Decision

Some corporations are more flexible than others because they are not locked into a few available sources of funds. Corporations would like many financing alternatives in order to minimize their cost of funds at any point in time. Unfortunately, not many firms are in this enviable position through the duration of a business cycle. During an economic boom period, a shortage of low-cost alternatives exists and firms often minimize their financing costs by raising funds in advance of forecasted asset needs.

Not only does the financial manager encounter a timing problem, but he also needs to select the right type of financing. Even for companies having many alternative sources of funds, there may be only one or two decisions that will look good in retrospect. At the time the financing decision is made, the financial manager is never sure it is the right one. Should the financing be long-term or short-term, debt or equity, and so on? Figure 6–8 is a decision-tree diagram which shows many of the financing decisions that can be made. At each point a decision is made until a final financing method is reached. In most

Figure 6–8
Decision tree of the financing decision

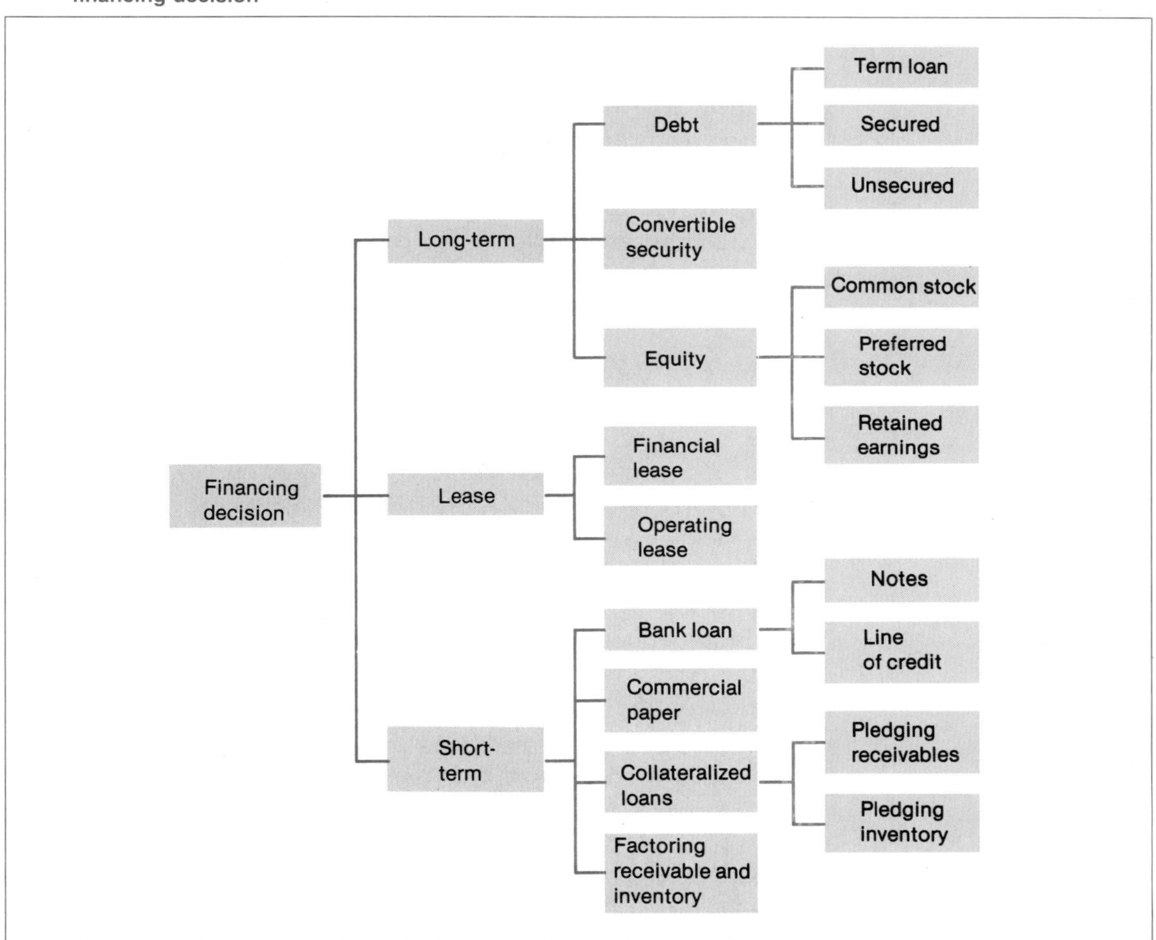


cases a corporation will use a combination of these financing methods. At all times the financial manager will balance short-term versus long-term considerations against the composition of the firm's assets and the firm's willingness to accept risk. The ratio of long-term financing to short-term financing at any point in time will be greatly influenced by the term structure of interest rates.

## Term Structure of Interest Rates

The term structure of interest rates is often referred to as a yield curve. It shows the interest rate at a specific point in time for all securities having equal risk but different maturity dates. Generally U.S. government securities are used to construct yield curves because they have many maturities and each of the securities has an equally low risk of default. Corporate securities will move in the same direction as government securities but will have higher interest rates because of their greater financial risk. Yield curves for both corporations and government securities change daily to reflect current competitive conditions in the money and capital markets, expected inflation, and changes in economic conditions.

Figure 6–9 depicts four panels of term structures (yield curves) covering 11 years. These four panels present very different pictures of interest rate cycles over perhaps some of the most unusual economic times in U.S. history. Panel A shows five yield curves in a period of falling interest rates—from August 1974 to November 1976.

Each yield curve in Panel A has a different shape. The August 1974 curve is called *downward sloping*, or *inverted*, because short-term interest rates are higher than long-term rates. This shape is usually present at peak periods in economic expansions and sometimes well into economic recessions. The September 1975 curve is called a *humped* curve because the intermediate rates are higher than both the short- and long-term rates. The other three yield curves are all *upward sloping*, which is considered to be the normal case.

Panel B represents interest rate changes in a period of rising rates. If you start with the December 1976 yield curve and move to each successive curve, you will trace the most dramatic rise in interest rates in U.S. history, caused by record high inflation rates. In Panel C you can see that short-term rates on U.S. Treasury bills reached historic levels in September of 1981. The Federal Reserve Board maintained high interest rates during this period in an attempt to break the back of inflation even though the economy was quite weak. By 1982 Federal Reserve Board policy had reduced inflation to its lowest level since 1971 but had also created a 16-month recession that ended in November of 1982. However, the recession finally caused interest rates to decline, as evidenced by the May, November, and December 1982 yield curves. One interesting observation is that interest rates can change dramatically in a short period of time. Between November and December of 1982, interest rates on intermediate- and long-term securities dropped as much as 2 percent. This rapid drop in interest rates during 1982 caused long-term bond prices to rise substantially and rewarded long-term bond investors with over a 40 percent annual return.

Interest rates are influenced by many variables, but in recent years inflation has had a large effect in boosting interest rates to record levels. As inflation increases, lenders charge a premium for the lost purchasing power that they will have when their loan is repaid in "cheaper" inflated dollars. Short-term rates are influenced more by current demands for money than by inflation, but long-term rates are greatly affected by expected inflation over the maturity of the bond. The shift in yield curves from August 1974 to November 1976 can be partly attributed to a decline in the rate of inflation, while the increased interest rates in the 1976–81 period were directly linked to the spiraling (double digit) rate of inflation and soaring government deficits.

A business recovery began in December of 1982 and Panel D of Figure 6–9 shows the resulting rise in rates from June of 1983 to April of 1984. As economic growth slowed in late 1984 and 1985, interest rates dropped to their lowest level in many years but still not as low as those depicted in Panel A. During 1983, 1984, and 1985 the inflation rate was stable at a fairly low rate of between 3.0 to 4.0 percent.

In designing working capital policy, the astute financial manager is interested not only in the term structure of interest rates but also in the relative volatility and the historical level of short-term and long-term rates. Figure 6–10 uses long-term AAA-rated corporate bonds and short-term commercial paper to provide insight into interest rate volatility over a long period of time.

The period between 1970 and 1983 demonstrates the large historical differences in relative volatility, with short-term rates being much more volatile than long-term rates. As a general rule short-term rates have been lower than long-term rates, with a few exceptions of course. For example, as indicated in Figure 6–10, in the period before 1930 and after 1971, short-term rates fluctuated around long-term rates quite a bit, even though long-term AAA corporate bond yields soared to dramatic historical highs in the later period. Notice that both long-term and short-term rates have been increasing since about 1953 and that the major increase in rates began in 1965, which is defined by some economists as the beginning of a long inflationary spiral.

**Figure 6–9**
**Yield curves: Yields on U.S. government securities**

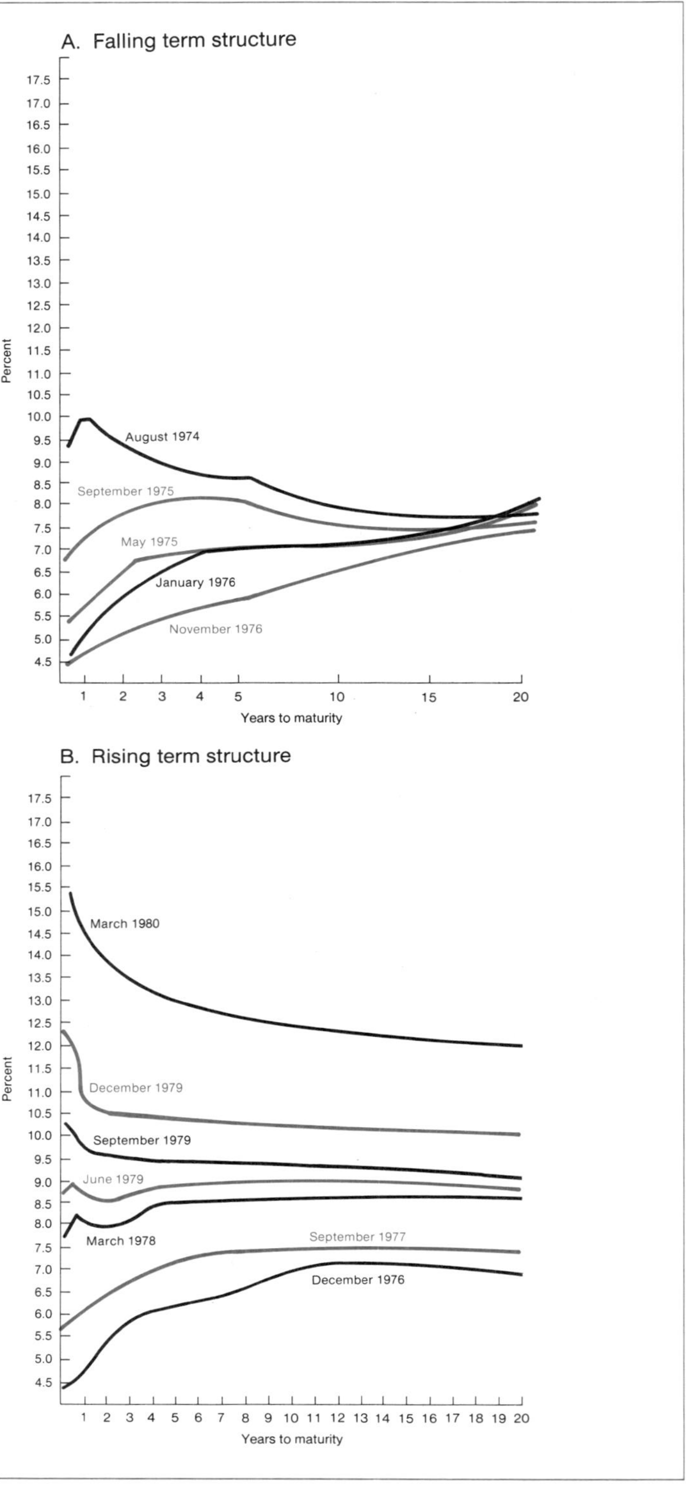

**Figure 6–9**
**(*concluded*)**

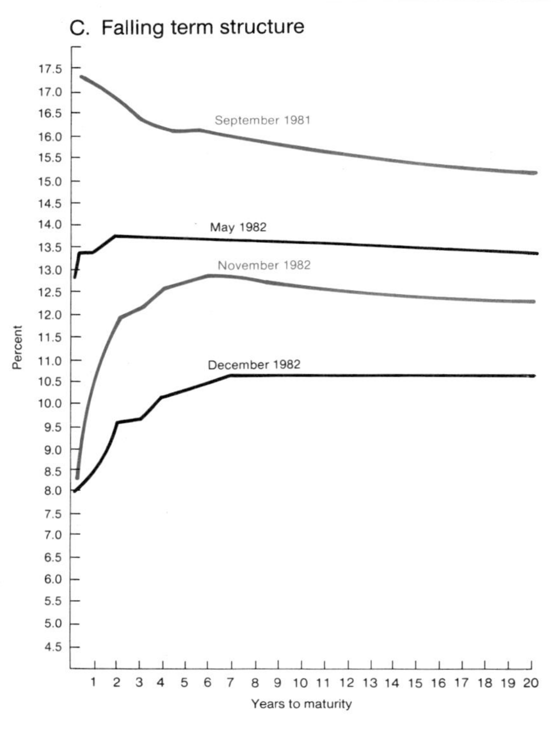


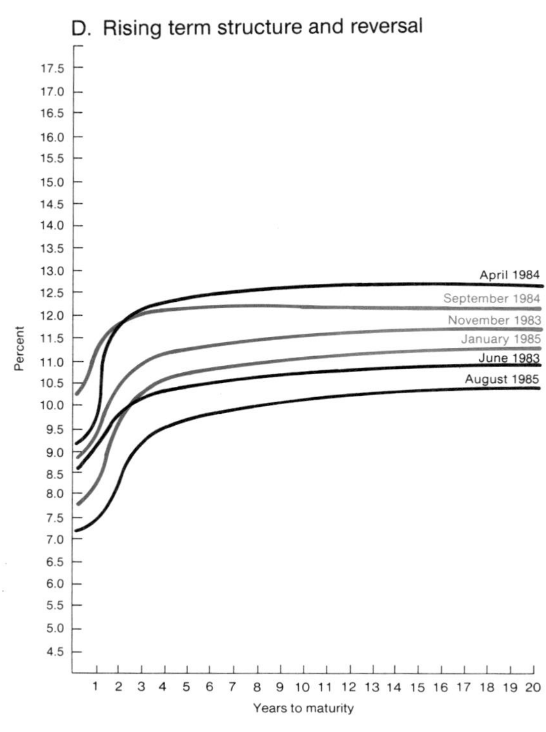

Figure 6–10
Long- and short-term interest rates (annually)

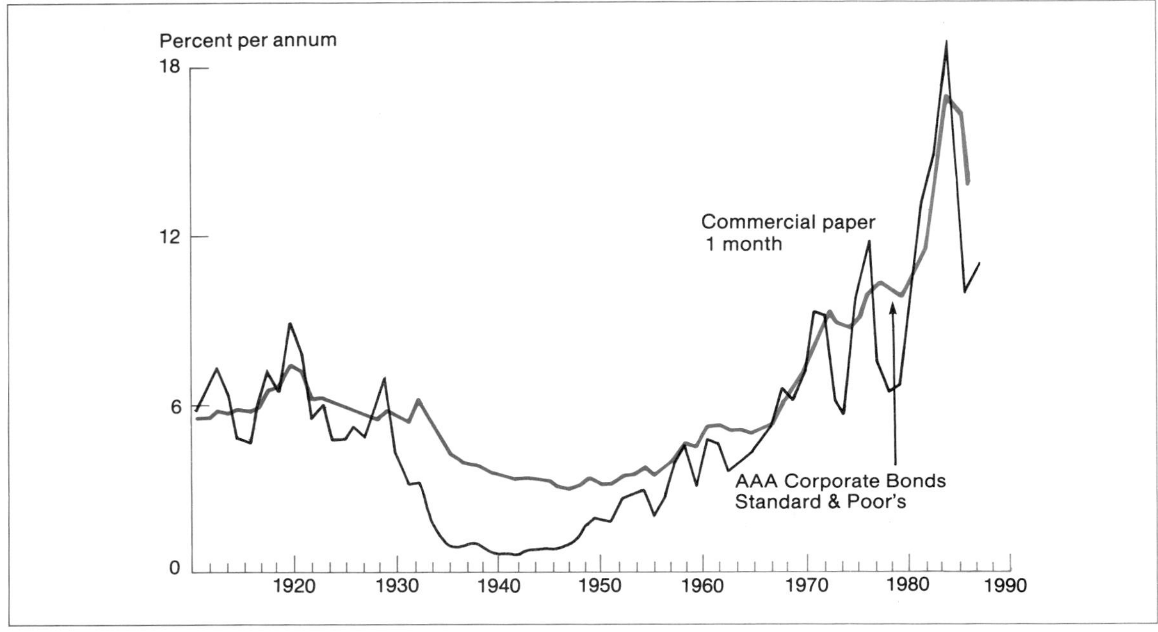


How should the financial manager respond to fluctuating interest rates and changing term structures? When interest rates are high, the financial manager generally tries to borrow short term (if funds are available). As rates decline, the chief financial officer will try to lock in the lower rates with heavy long-term borrowing. Some of these long-term funds will be used to reduce short-term debt and the rest will be available for future expansion of plant and equipment and working capital if necessary.

## A Decision Process

Assume that we are comparing alternative financing plans for working capital. As indicated in Table 6–6, $500,000 of working capital (current assets) must be financed for the Edwards Corporation. Under Plan A, we will finance all our current asset needs with short-term funds, while under Plan B we will finance only a relatively small portion of working capital with short-term money—relying heavily on long-term funds. In

**Table 6–6**
**Alternative financing plans**

EDWARDS CORPORATION

| | Plan A | Plan B |
|---|---|---|
| *Part 1. Current assets* | | |
| Temporary | $250,000 | $250,000 |
| Permanent | 250,000 | 250,000 |
| Total current assets | 500,000 | 500,000 |
| Short-term financing (6%) | 500,000 | 150,000 |
| Long-term financing (10%) | 0 | 350,000 |
| | $500,000 | $500,000 |
| *Part 2. Fixed assets* | $100,000 | $100,000 |
| Long-term financing (10%) | $100,000 | $100,000 |
| *Part 3. Total financing* (summary of parts 1 and 2) | | |
| Short-term (6%) | $500,000 | $150,000 |
| Long-term (10%) | 100,000 | 450,000 |
| | $600,000 | $600,000 |

either case, we will carry $100,000 of fixed assets with long-term financing commitments. As indicated in part 3 of Table 6–6, under Plan A we will finance total needs of $600,000 with $500,000 of short-term financing and $100,000 of long-term financing, whereas with Plan B we will finance $150,000 short term and $450,000 long term.

Plan A carries the lower cost of financing, with interest of 6 percent on $500,000 of the $600,000 required. We show the impact of both plans on bottom-line earnings in Table 6–7.[1] Assuming that the firm generates $200,000 in earnings before interest and taxes, Plan A will provide aftertax earnings of $80,000, while Plan B will generate only $73,000.

## Introducing Varying Conditions

Although Plan A, employing cheaper short-term sources of financing, appears to provide $7,000 more in return, this is not always the

[1]Common stock is eliminated from the example to simplify the analysis. If it were included, all of the basic patterns would still hold.

**Table 6–7**
**Impact of financing plans on earnings**

EDWARDS CORPORATION

| | |
|---|---|
| *Plan A* | |
| Earnings before interest and taxes | $200,000 |
| Interest (short-term), 6% × $500,000 | − 30,000 |
| Interest (long-term), 10% × $100,000 | − 10,000 |
| Earnings before taxes | 160,000 |
| Taxes (50%) | 80,000 |
| Earnings after taxes | $ 80,000 |
| *Plan B* | |
| Earnings before interest and taxes | $200,000 |
| Interest (short-term), 6% × $150,000 | − 9,000 |
| Interest (long-term), 10% × $450,000 | − 45,000 |
| Earnings before taxes | 146,000 |
| Taxes (50%) | 73,000 |
| Earnings after taxes | $ 73,000 |

case. During tight money periods, short-term financing may be difficult to find or may carry exorbitant rates. Furthermore, inadequate financing may mean lost sales or financial embarrassment. For these reasons, the firm may wish to evaluate Plans A and B based on differing assumptions about the economy and the money markets.

## Expected Value

Past history combined with economic forecasting may indicate an 80 percent probability of normal events and a 20 percent chance of extremely tight money. Using Plan A, under normal conditions the Edwards Corporation will enjoy a $7,000 superior return over Plan B (as indicated in Table 6–7). Let us now assume that under disruptive tight money conditions, Plan A would provide a $15,000 lower return than Plan B because of high short-term interest rates. These conditions are summarized in Table 6–8, and an expected value of return is computed. The expected value represents the sum of the expected outcomes under the two conditions.

We see that even when downside risk is considered, Plan A carries a higher expected return of $2,600. For another firm in the same industry that might suffer $50,000 lower returns during tight money

Table 6–8
**Expected returns under different economic conditions**

EDWARDS CORPORATION

| | | | | | | |
|---|---|---|---|---|---|---|
| 1. Normal conditions | Expected higher return under Plan A | | Probability of normal conditions | | Expected outcome |
| | $7,000 | × | .80 | = | + $5,600 |
| 2. Tight money | Expected lower return under Plan A | | Probability of tight money | | |
| | ($15,000) | × | .20 | = | (3,000) |
| Expected value of return for Plan A versus Plan B | | | | = | + $2,600 |

conditions, Plan A becomes too dangerous to undertake, as indicated in Table 6–9. Plan A's expected return is now $4,400 less than that of Plan B.

Table 6–9
**Expected returns for high-risk firm**

| | | | | | |
|---|---|---|---|---|---|
| 1. Normal conditions | Expected higher return under Plan A | | Probability of normal conditions | | Expected outcome |
| | $7,000 | × | .80 | = | + $5,600 |
| 2. Tight money | Expected lower return under Plan A | | Probability of tight money | | |
| | ($50,000) | × | .20 | = | (10,000) |
| Negative expected value of return for Plan A versus Plan B | | | | = | ($4,400) |

## Shifts in Asset Structure

Thus far, our attention has been directed to the risk associated with various financing plans. Risk-return analysis must also be carried to the asset side. A firm with heavy risk exposure due to short-term borrowing may compensate in part by carrying highly liquid assets. Conversely, a firm with established long-term debt commitments may choose to carry a heavier component of less liquid, highly profitable assets.

Either through desire or compelling circumstances, business firms have decreased the liquidity of their current asset holdings since the early 1960s. The rise in interest rates and the cost of financing current assets may be a major reason for this decline. For example, in Table 6–10 we see that for U.S. nonfinancial corporations, cash and equivalents have decreased from 18.98 percent of current assets in 1963 to 11.16 percent in 1985, while inventory increased from 30.44 percent

**Table 6–10** **Current asset positions ($ billions): U.S. nonfinancial corporations**

| | Cash and Equivalents | | | Inventory | | |
|---|---|---|---|---|---|---|
| Year | Amount | Percent of Current Assets | Percent of Current Liabilities | Amount | Percent of Current Assets | Percent of Current Liabilities |
| 1963 . . . | $ 66.7 | 18.98% | 35.44% | $107.0 | 30.44% | 56.85% |
| 1974 . . . | 84.3 | 11.48 | 18.66 | 318.9 | 43.41 | 70.58 |
| 1979 . . . | 134.7 | 11.09 | 16.69 | 505.1 | 41.58 | 62.57 |
| 1981 . . . | 153.1 | 10.79 | 15.78 | 583.7 | 41.15 | 60.18 |
| 1983 . . . | 196.4 | 12.61 | 18.83 | 599.3 | 38.48 | 57.46 |
| 1985 . . . | 189.1 | 11.16 | 16.31 | 664.6 | 39.23 | 57.73 |

Source: *Federal Reserve Bulletin*, selected issues.

of current assets in 1963 to 39.23 percent in 1985. The ratio of cash and cash equivalents to current liabilities has fallen from 35 percent at the end of 1963 to approximately 16 percent by 1985, or nearly a 50 percent decline. Clearly, U.S. nonfinancial corporations are less liquid today than 20 years ago.

The reasons for diminishing liquidity can be traced in part to more sophisticated, profit-oriented financial management as well as better utilization of cash balances via the computer. Less liquidity can also be traced to the long-term effect inflation has had on corporate balance sheets—forcing greater borrowing to carry more expensive assets and to decreasing profitability during recessions. The average current ratio for nonfinancial corporations is presented in Figure 6–11. After the recession in 1974–75, corporate liquidity increased to the highest level of the 1970s in the third quarter of 1976. Since reaching that peak, corporate liquidity has been squeezed. Generally speaking, corporations are relying more and more on short-term borrowings to carry less liquid assets—a potentially dangerous situation.

## Toward an Optimal Policy

As previously indicated, the firm should attempt to relate asset liquidity to financing patterns, and vice versa. In Table 6–11, a number of different working capital alternatives are presented. Along the top of the table we show asset liquidity; along the side, the type of financing

Figure 6–11 Nonfinancial corporations' current ratio

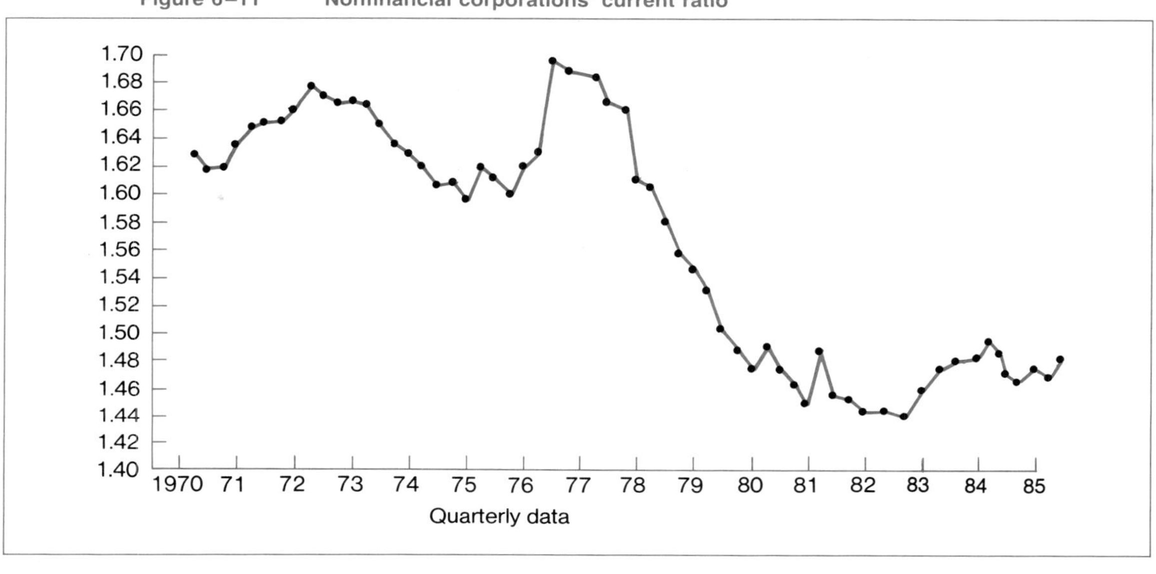


arrangement. The combined impact of the two variables is shown in each of the four panels of the table.

Each firm must decide how it wishes to combine asset liquidity and financing needs. The aggressive, risk-oriented firm in Panel 1 of Table 6–11 will borrow short term and maintain relatively low levels of liquidity, hoping to increase profit. It will benefit from low-cost financing and high-return assets, but it will be vulnerable to a credit crunch. The more conservative firm, following the plan in Panel 4, will utilize established long-term financing and maintain a high degree of liquidity. In Panels 2 and 3, we see more moderate positions in which

Table 6–11
Asset liquidity and financing assets

| *Financing Plan* | *Low Liquidity* | *High Liquidity* |
|---|---|---|
| Short-term | 1<br>High profit<br>High risk | 2<br>Moderate profit<br>Moderate risk |
| Long-term | 3<br>Moderate profit<br>Moderate risk | 4<br>Low profit<br>Low risk |

the firm compensates for short-term financing with highly liquid assets (2) or balances off low liquidity with precommitted, long-term financing (3).

Each financial manager must structure his or her working capital position and the associated risk-return trade-off to meet the company's needs. For firms whose cash flow patterns are predictable, typified by the public utilities sector, a low degree of liquidity can be maintained. Immediate access to capital markets, such as that enjoyed by large, prestigious firms, also allows a greater risk-taking capability. In each case, the ultimate concern must be for maximizing the overall valuation of the firm through a judicious consideration of risk-return options.

In the next two chapters, we will examine the various methods for managing the individual components of working capital. In Chapter 7 we consider the techniques for managing cash, marketable securities, receivables, and inventory. In Chapter 8 we look at trade and bank credit and also at other sources of short-term funds.

## Summary

Working capital management involves the financing and management of the current assets of the firm. A firm's ability to properly manage current assets and the associated liability obligations may determine how well it is able to survive in the short run. To the extent that part of the buildup in current assets is permanent, financial arrangements should carry longer maturities.

The financial manager must also give careful attention to the relationship of the production process to sales. Level production in a seasonal sales environment increases operating efficiency, but it also calls for more careful financial planning. The astute financial manager must also keep an eye on the general cost of borrowing, the term structure of interest rates, and the relative volatility of short- and long-term rates.

The firm has a number of risk-return decisions to consider. Though long-term financing provides a safety margin in availability of funds, its higher cost may reduce the profit potential of the firm. On the asset side, carrying highly liquid current assets assures the bill-paying capability of the firm—but detracts from profit potential. Each firm must tailor the various risk-return trade-offs to meet its own needs. The peculiarities of a firm's industry will have a major impact on the options open to management.

## List of Terms

**working capital management**
**self-liquidating assets**
**"permanent" current assets**
**temporary current assets**
**trade credit**
**level production**
**point-of-sales terminals**
**liquidity**
**term structure of interest rates**
**expected value**
**tight money**
**normal yield curve**
**inverted yield curve**

## Discussion Questions

1. Explain how rapidly expanding sales can drain the cash resources of the firm.
2. Discuss the relative volatility of short- and long-term interest rates.
3. What is the significance to working capital management of matching sales and production?
4. How is a cash budget used to help manage current assets?
5. Discuss the impact of inflation on working capital management.
6. "The most appropriate financing pattern would be one in which asset buildup and length of financing terms are perfectly matched." Discuss the difficulty involved in achieving this financing pattern.
7. By using long-term financing to finance part of temporary current assets, a firm may have less risk but lower returns than a firm with a normal financing plan. Explain the significance of this statement.
8. A firm that uses short-term financing methods for a portion of permanent current assets is assuming more risk but expects higher returns than a firm with a normal financing plan. Explain.
9. Since the early 1960s, corporate liquidity has been declining. What reasons can you give for this trend?

## Problems

1. Randolph Equipment Company expects sales next year to be $600,000. Inventory and accounts receivable will have to be increased by $110,000 to accommodate this sales level. The company has a steady profit margin of 10 percent and a 30 percent dividend payout.

   How much external funding will Randolph Equipment Company have to seek? Assume there is no increase in liabilities other than that which will occur with the external funding.

2. Austin Electronics expects sales next year to be $900,000 if the economy is strong, $650,000 if the economy is steady, and $375,000 if the economy is weak. The firm believes there is a 15 percent probability that the economy will be strong, a 60 percent probability of a steady economy, and a 25 percent probability of a weak economy.

   What is the expected level of sales next year?

3. Doris Daycare Centers, Inc., has decided to buy a new computer system with an expected useful life of three years. The cost is $200,000. The company can borrow $200,000 for three years at 12 percent annual interest or for one year at 10 percent annual interest.

   How much would Doris Daycare Centers save in interest over the three-year life of the computer system if the one-year loan is utilized, and the loan is rolled over (reborrowed) each year at the same 10 percent rate? Compare this to the 12 percent three-year loan. What if interest rates go up to 15 percent in year two and 18 percent in year three? What is the total interest cost now compared to the 12 percent, three-year loan?

4. Assume that Hogan Surgical Instruments Co. has $2,000,000 in assets. If it goes with a low liquidity plan for the assets, it can earn a return of 18 percent, but with a high liquidity plan, the return will be 14 percent. If the firm goes with a short-term financing plan, the financing costs on the $2,000,000 will be 10 percent, and with a long-term financing plan, the financing costs on the $2,000,000 will be 12 percent.

*a*. Compute the anticipated return after financing costs on the most aggressive asset-financing mix (review Figure 6–11).
*b*. Compute the anticipated return after financing costs on the most conservative asset-financing mix.
*c*. Compute the anticipated return after financing costs on the two moderate approaches to the asset-financing mix.
*d*. Would you necessarily accept the plan with the highest return after financing costs? Briefly explain.

**5.** Sherlock Homes, a manufacturer of low-cost mobile housing, has $4,500,000 in assets.

| | |
|---|---|
| Temporary current assets . . . . | $1,000,000 |
| Permanent current assets . . . . | 1,500,000 |
| Fixed assets . . . . . . . . . . . | 2,000,000 |
| Total assets . . . . . . . . . . . | $4,500,000 |

Short-term rates are 8 percent. Long-term rates are 13 percent. Earnings before interest and taxes are $960,000. The tax rate is 40 percent.

If long-term financing is perfectly matched (synchronized) with long-term asset needs, and the same is true of short-term financing, what will earnings after taxes be? For an example of perfectly matched plans, see Figure 6–5.

**6.** In Problem 5, assume the term structure of interest rates becomes inverted, with short-term rates going to 12 percent and long-term rates 4 percentage points lower than short-term rates.

If all other factors in the problem do not change, what will earnings after taxes be?

**7.** Plaza Square Inc. has $600,000 in current assets, $250,000 of which are considered permanent current assets. In addition, the firm has $500,000 invested in fixed assets.

*a*. Plaza wishes to finance all long-term assets and one half of its permanent current assets with long-term financing costing 10 percent. Short-term financing currently costs 5 percent. Plaza's earnings before interest and taxes are $200,000. Determine Plaza's earnings after taxes under this financing plan. The tax rate is 50 percent.

*b*. As an alternative, Plaza might wish to finance all long-term assets and permanent current assets plus one half of its temporary current assets with long-term financing. The same interest rates apply as in part *a*. Earnings before interest and taxes will be $200,000. What will be Plaza's earnings after taxes? The tax rate is 50 percent.

*c*. What are some of the risks associated with each of these alternative financing strategies?

**8.** Guardian Inc. is trying to develop an asset financing plan. The firm has $400,000 in temporary current assets and $300,000 in permanent current assets. Guardian also has $500,000 in fixed assets. The tax rate is 40 percent.

*a*. Construct two alternative financing plans for Guardian. One of the plans should be conservative, with 75 percent of assets financed by long-term sources, and the other should be aggressive, with only 56.25 percent of assets financed by long-term sources. The current interest rate is 15 percent on long-term funds and 10 percent on short-term financing.

*b*. Given that Guardian's earnings before interest and taxes are $200,000, calculate earnings after taxes for each of your alternatives.

*c*. What would happen if the short- and long-term rates were reversed?

**9.** Liz's Health Food Stores has estimated monthly financing requirements for the next six months as follows:

| | | | |
|---|---|---|---|
| January | $8,000 | April | $8,000 |
| February | 2,000 | May | 9,000 |
| March | 3,000 | June | 4,000 |

Short-term financing will be utilized for the first four months and long-term financing for the last two months. Projected annual interest rates are:

| *Short-term* | | *Long-term* | |
|---|---|---|---|
| January | 8.07% | May | 12% |
| February | 9.0% | June | 12% |
| March | 12.0% | | |
| April | 15.0% | | |

*a*. Compute total dollar interest payments for the six months. To convert an annual rate to a monthly rate, divide by 12.

*b.* If long-term financing at 12 percent had been utilized throughout the six months, would the total-dollar interest payments be larger or smaller?

**10.** Garza Electronics expects to sell 500 units in January, 250 units in February, and 1,000 units in March. December's ending inventory is 700 units. Expected sales for the year are 7,200 units. Garza has decided on a level production schedule of 600 units (7,200 units for the year/12 months = 600 units per month). What is the expected end-of-month inventory for January, February, and March? Show the beginning inventory, production, and sales for each of the three months that is used to derive the ending inventory.

**11.** Bombs Away Video Games Corporation has forecasted the following monthly sales:

| | | | |
|---|---|---|---|
| January . . . . . | $95,000 | July . . . . . . . . | $ 40,000 |
| February . . . . | 88,000 | August . . . . . . | 40,000 |
| March . . . . . | 20,000 | September . . . . | 50,000 |
| April . . . . . . | 20,000 | October . . . . . | 80,000 |
| May . . . . . . | 15,000 | November . . . . | 100,000 |
| June . . . . . . | 30,000 | December . . . . | 118,000 |

Total sales = $696,000

Bombs Away Video Games sells the popular Strafe and Capture video game cartridge. It sells for $5 per unit and costs $2 per unit to produce. A level production policy is followed. Each month's production is equal to annual sales (in units) divided by twelve.

Of each month's sales, 30 percent are for cash and 70 percent are on account. All accounts receivable are collected in the month after the sale is made.

*a.* Construct a monthly production and inventory schedule in units. Beginning inventory in January is 20,000 units. (Note: To do part *a*, you should work in terms of units of production and units of sales.)

*b.* Prepare a monthly schedule of cash receipts. Sales in the December before the planning year are $100,000. Work part *b* using dollars.

*c.* Determine a cash payments schedule for January through December. The production costs of $2 per unit are paid for in the month in which they occur. Other cash payments, besides those for production costs, are $40,000 per month.

*d.* Prepare a monthly cash budget for January through December. The beginning cash balance is $5,000 and that is also the minimum desired.

**12.** Esquire Products, Inc., expects the following monthly sales:

| Month | Sales | Month | Sales | Month | Sales |
|---|---|---|---|---|---|
| January . . . . | $24,000 | May . . . . . | $ 4,000 | September . . . . | $25,000 |
| February . . . . | 15,000 | June . . . . . | 2,000 | October . . . . . | 30,000 |
| March . . . . . | 8,000 | July . . . . . | 18,000 | November . . . . | 38,000 |
| April . . . . . . | 10,000 | August . . . . | 22,000 | December . . . . | 20,000 |

Total sales = $216,000

Cash sales are 40 percent in a given month, with the remainder going into accounts receivable. All receivables are collected in the month following the sale. Esquire sells all of its goods for $2 each and produces them for $1 each. Esquire uses level production and average monthly production is equal to annual production divided by 12.

*a.* Generate a monthly production and inventory schedule in units. Beginning inventory in January is 8,000 units. (Note: To do part *a*, you should work in terms of units of production and units of sales.)

*b.* Determine a cash receipts schedule for January through December. Assume that dollar sales in the prior December were $20,000. Work *b* using dollars.

*c.* Determine a cash payments schedule for January through December. The production costs ($1 per unit produced) are paid for in the month in which they occur. Other cash payments (besides those for production costs) are $7,000 per month.

*d.* Construct a cash budget for January through December. The beginning cash balance is $3,000, and that is also the required minimum.

*e.* Determine total current assets for each month. (Note: accounts receivable equals sales minus 40 percent of sales for a given month.)

**13.** Pick a day within the past week and construct a yield curve for that day. Pick a day approximately a year ago and construct a yield curve for that day. How are interest rates different? *The Wall Street Journal* and the *Federal Reserve Bulletin* should be of help in solving this problem.

## Selected References


Archer, Stephen H. "A Model for the Determination of Firm Cash Balances." *Journal of Financial and Quantitative Analysis* 1 (March 1966), pp. 1–11.

Bean, Virginia L., and Reynolds Griffith. "Risk and Return in Working Capital Management." *Mississippi Valley Journal of Business and Economics* 1 (Fall 1966), pp. 28–48.

Bogen, Jules T., ed. *Financial Handbook*. 4th ed. New York: Ronald, 1968, sec. 16.

Brick, John R., and Howard E. Thompson. "Time Series Analysis of Interest Rates: Some Additional Evidence." *Journal of Finance* 33 (March 1978), pp. 93–103.

Budin, Morris, and Van Handel, Robert J. "A Rule-of-Thumb Theory of Cash Holdings by Firm." *Journal of Financial and Quantitative Analysis* 10 (March 1975), pp. 85–108.

Cossaboom, Roger A. "Let's Reassess the Profitability-Liquidity Tradeoff." *Financial Executive* 39 (May 1971), pp. 46–51.

Glautier, M. W. E. "Towards a Reformation of the Theory of Working Capital." *Journal of Business Finance* 3 (Spring 1971), pp. 37–42.

Jennings, Joseph A. "A Look at Corporate Liquidity." *Financial Executive* 39 (February 1971), pp. 26–32.

Knight, W. D. "Working Capital Management—Satisfying versus Optimization." *Financial Management* 1 (Spring 1972), pp. 33–40.

Mehta, Dileep R. *Working Capital Management*. Englewood Cliffs, N.J.: Prentice-Hall, 1974.

Smith, Keith V. *Management of Working Capital*. St. Paul: West, 1974.

Stancill, James McN. *The Management of Working Capital*. Scranton, Pa.: Intext, 1971, chaps. 1, 6, and 7.

Van Horne, James C. "A Risk-Return Analysis of a Firm's Working Capital Position." *Engineering Economist* 14 (Winter 1969), pp. 71–89.

Walker, Ernest W. "Towards a Theory of Working Capital." *Engineering Economist* 9 (January–February 1964), pp. 21–35.

Walter, James E. "Determination of Technical Solvency." *Journal of Business* 30 (January 1959), pp. 39–43.

Welter, Paul. "How to Calculate Savings Possible through Reduction of Working Capital." *Financial Executive*, October 1970, pp. 50–58.

# 7 Current Asset Management

The financial manager must carefully allocate resources among the current assets of the firm—cash, marketable securities, accounts receivable, and inventory. In managing cash and marketable securities, the primary concern should be for safety and liquidity—with secondary attention placed on maximizing profitability. As we move to accounts receivable and inventory, a stiffer profitability test must be met. The investment level should not be a matter of happenstance or historical determination, but must meet the same return-on-investment criteria applied to any decision. We may need to choose between a 20 percent increase in inventory and a new plant location or a major research program. We shall examine the decision techniques that are applied to the various forms of current assets.

## Cash Management

In the parlance of corporate financial management, the less cash you have, the better off you are. In spite of whatever lifelong teachings you might have learned about the virtues of cash, the corporate manager actively seeks to keep this nonearning asset to a minimum.

The first consideration is to ensure that inflows and outflows of cash are properly synchronized for transaction purposes. Interest-paying marketable securities, held for precautionary purposes, should only be transferred into cash when there is a scheduled need for disbursement. In determining the appropriate cash balance, the firm must carefully assess the payment pattern of customers, the speed at which suppliers and creditors process checks, and the efficiency of the banking system.

## Float

Some people are shocked to realize that even the most trusted asset on a corporation's books, "cash," may not portray actual dollars at a given point in time. There are, in fact, two cash balances of importance: the corporation's recorded amount and the amount credited to the corporation by the bank. The difference between the two is labeled *float,* and it exists as a result of the lag between the time when a check is written and the eventual clearing of the check against a corporate bank account.

Let us examine the use of float. A firm has deposited $1,000,000 in checks received from customers during the week and has written $900,000 in checks to suppliers. If the initial balance were $100,000, the corporate books would show $200,000. But what will the bank records show in the way of usable funds? Perhaps $800,000 of the checks from customers will have cleared their accounts at other banks and been credited to us, while only $400,000 of our checks may have completed a similar cycle. As indicated in Table 7–1, we have used "float" to provide us with $300,000 extra in available short-term funds.

Some companies actually operate with a negative cash balance on the corporate books, knowing that float will carry them through at the bank. In the above example, the firm may write $1.2 million in checks

**Table 7–1**
**The use of float to provide funds**

| | *Corporate Books* | *Bank Books (usable funds) (amounts actually cleared)* |
|---|---|---|
| Initial amount . . . | $ 100,000 | $100,000 |
| Deposits . . . . . | + 1,000,000 | + 800,000 |
| Checks . . . . . . | − 900,000 | − 400,000 |
| Balance . . . . . | +$ 200,000 | +$500,000 |
| | +$300,000 float | |

**Table 7–2**
**Playing the float**

| | Corporate Books | Bank Books (usable funds) (amounts actually cleared) |
|---|---|---|
| Initial amount | $ 100,000 | $100,000 |
| Deposits | + 1,000,000* | + 800,000* |
| Checks | − 1,200,000 | − 800,000 |
| Balance | −$ 100,000 | +$100,000 |
| | +$200,000 float | |

*Assumed to remain the same as in Table 7–1.

on the assumption that only $800,000 will clear by the end of the week, thus leaving it with surplus funds in its bank account. The results, shown in Table 7–2, represent the phenomenon known as "playing the float." A float of $200,000 turns a negative balance on the corporation's books into a positive temporary balance on the bank's books. Obviously, float can also work against you if checks going out are being processed more quickly than checks coming in.

## Improving Collections

We may expedite the collection and check-clearing process through a number of strategies.[1] A popular method is to utilize a variety of collection centers throughout our marketing area. A dress manufacturer with headquarters in Chicago may have 75 collection offices disbursed throughout the country, each performing a billing and collection-deposit function. One of the collection offices in San Francisco, using a local bank, may be able to clear a check on a San Jose bank in one day—whereas a Chicago bank would require a substantially longer time to remit and clear the check at the California bank.[2] Excess cash balances at the local banks throughout the collection system are remitted to the home office bank through a daily wire transfer.

[1] Larger banks have cash management advisory groups that can offer valuable consultation on these matters.

[2] Checks deposited with a bank are cleared through the Federal Reserve System, through a correspondent bank, or through a locally established clearinghouse system. A check is collected when it is remitted to the payer's bank and actually paid by that bank to the payee's bank.

For those who wish to enjoy the benefits of expeditious check clearance at lower costs, a *lockbox system* may replace the network of regional collection offices. Under this plan, customers are requested to forward their checks to a post-office box in their geographic region and a local bank picks up the checks and processes them to other banks in the locality for rapid collection. Funds are then wired to the corporate home office for immediate use. The company retains many of the benefits of regional collection centers, but with reduced corporate overhead.

### Extending Disbursements

Perhaps you have heard of the multimillion-dollar corporation with its headquarters located in the most exclusive office space in downtown Manhattan, but with its primary check disbursement center in Fargo, North Dakota. Though the firm may engage in aggressive speedup techniques in the processing of incoming checks, a slowdown pattern more aptly describes the payment procedures.

While the preceding example represents an extreme case, the slowing of disbursements is not an uncommon practice in cash management. It has even been given the title "extended disbursement float."[3] Many full-service banks offer customers consulting services pointing out structural defects in the Federal Reserve and other collection systems that allow the firm to extend the payment period. While it is not the intent of this text to encourage or discourage such practices, their fairly widespread use is worthy of note.

### Cost-Benefit Analysis

An efficiently maintained cash management program can be an expensive operation. The utilization of remote collection and disbursement centers involves additional costs, and banks involved in the process will require that the firm maintain adequate deposit balances or pay sufficient fees to justify their services. Though the use of a lockbox

---

[3] "Making Millions by Stretching the Float," *Business Week*, November 23, 1974, p. 88.

system may reduce total corporate overhead, the costs may still be substantial.

These expenses must be compared to the benefits that may accrue. If a firm has an average daily remittance of $2 million and 1.5 days can be saved in the collection process by establishing a sophisticated collection network, the firm has freed up $3 million for investment elsewhere. Also, through stretching the disbursement schedule by one day, perhaps another $2 million will become available for alternate uses. An example of this process is shown in Figure 7–1. If the firm is able to earn 10 percent on the $5 million that is freed up, as much as $500,000 may be expended on the administrative costs of cash management before the new costs are equal to the generated revenue.

**Figure 7–1**
**Cash management network**

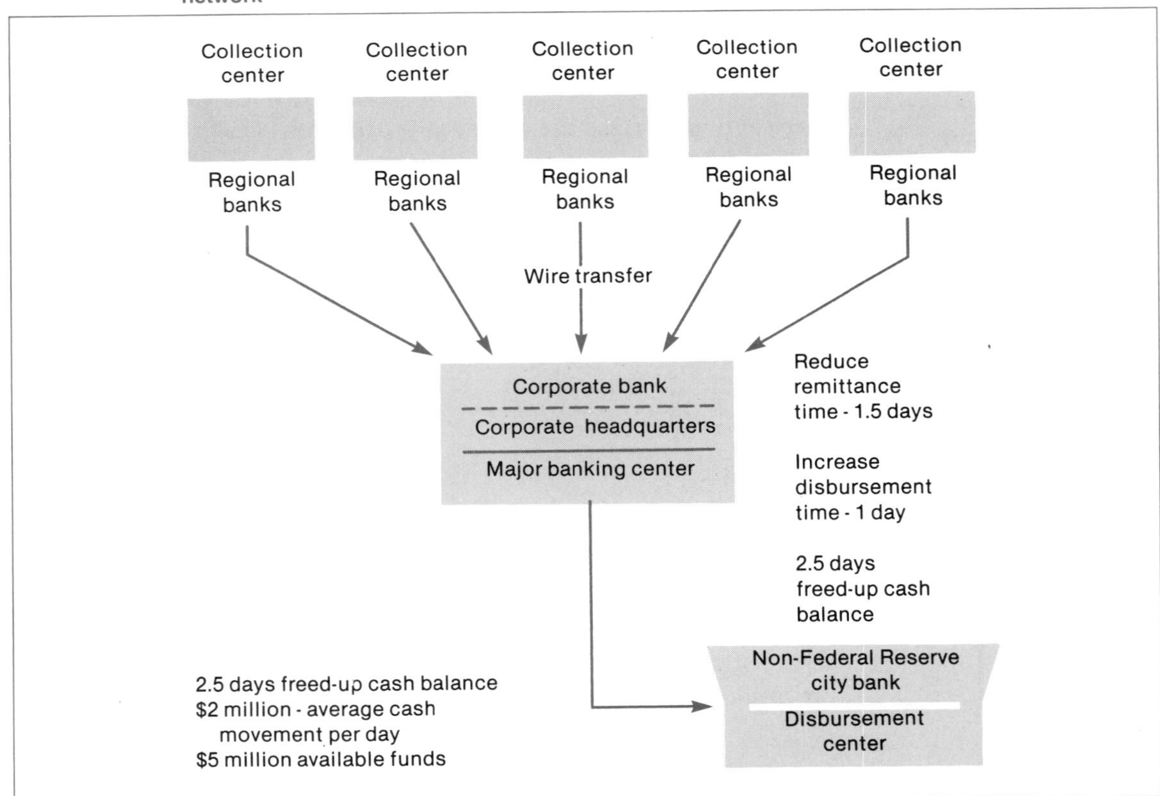

## Electronic Funds Transfer

As we move into the mid-1980s, some of the techniques of delaying payment will be reduced through the techniques of *electronic funds transfer,* a system in which funds are moved between computer terminals without the use of a "check." Through the use of terminal communication between the store and the bank, your payment to the supermarket will be automatically charged against your account at the bank before you walk out the door.

Many large corporations have computerized cash management systems. For example, a firm may have 55 branch offices and 56 banks, one bank for each branch office and a lead bank in which the major corporate account is kept. At the end of each day the financial manager can check all the company's bank accounts through an on-line computer terminal. He or she can then transfer through the computer all excess cash balances from each branch or regional bank to the corporate lead bank for overnight investment in money market securities.

It has been reported that close to 77 percent of large companies use computers to initiate money transfers and that about 70 percent now use computers to receive reports from their banks on lockbox receipts and bank balances to judge the amount of float available.

Automated clearinghouses (ACHs) are becoming an important element in electronic funds transfer. An ACH transfers information between one financial institution and another and from account to account via computer tape. There are approximately 30 regional automated clearinghouses throughout the United States, claiming total membership of over 10,000 financial institutions. The biggest use of ACHs so far has been in payroll processing, as more banks are offering direct deposit options. In the future more companies will use these automated clearinghouses for transfer of payments between the company and customers, suppliers, and utilities.

## International Cash Management

Multinational corporations can shift funds around from country to country much as a firm may transfer funds from regional banks to the lead bank. Just as financial institutions in the United States have become more involved in electronic funds transfer there has also developed an international payments system. This international funds transfer system is called SWIFT.

A company may prefer to hold cash balances in one currency rather than another or to take advantage of the high interest rates that are available in a particular country for short-term investments in marketable securities. In periods in which one country's currency is rising in value relative to other currencies, an astute financial manager will try to keep as much cash as possible in the country with the strong currency. In periods in which the dollar is rising relative to other currencies, many balances are held in U.S. bank accounts or in dollar-denominated bank accounts in foreign banks, more commonly known as Eurodollar deposits. The international money markets have been growing in scope and size, so that these markets have become a much more important aspect of efficient cash management. Cash management at the international level employs the same techniques as domestic cash management, using such forecasting devices as the cash budget and daily cash reports, so that excess funds may be collected and invested until needed in Eurodollar money market securities or other appropriate investments in securities denominated by strong currencies. An in-depth coverage of international cash and asset management is presented in Chapter 21.

## Marketable Securities

The firm may hold excess funds in anticipation of some major cash outlay, such as a dividend payment or partial retirement of debt or as a precaution against an unexpected event. When funds are being held for other than immediate transaction purposes they should be converted from cash into interest-earning marketable securities.[4]

The financial manager has a virtual supermarket of securities from which to choose. Among the factors influencing that choice are yield, maturity, minimum investment required, safety, and marketability. Under normal conditions, the longer the maturity period of the security, the higher the yield, as indicated in Figure 7–2.

[4]The one possible exception to this principle is found in the practice of holding compensating balances at commercial banks—a topic for discussion in Chapter 8.

Figure 7–2
An examination of yield and maturity characteristics

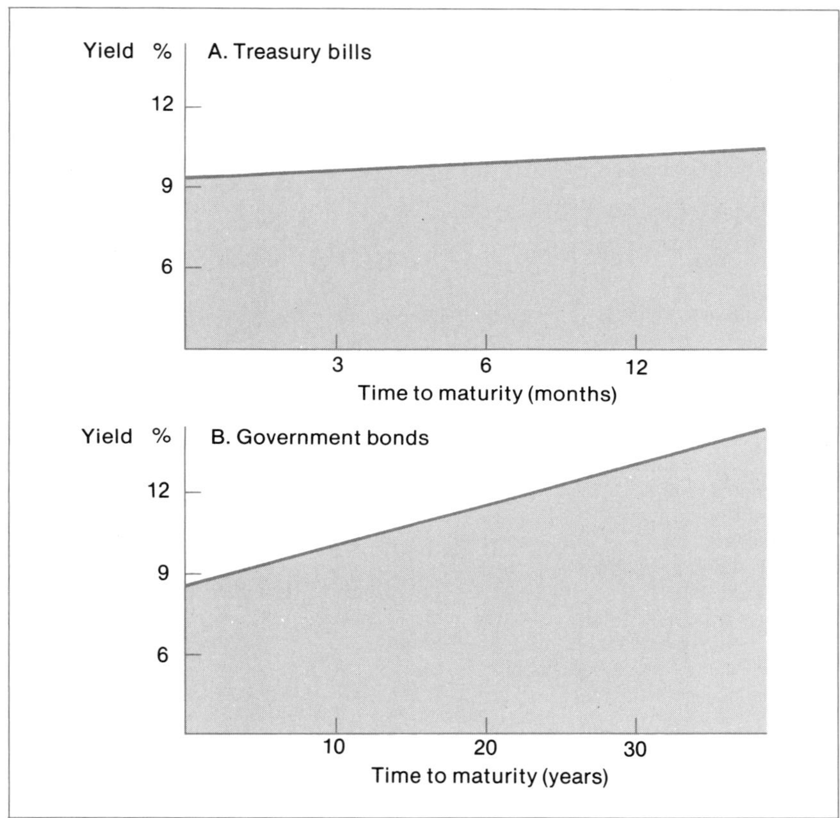


The problem in "stretching out" the maturity of your investment is not that you are legally locked in (you can generally sell your security when you need funds) but that you may have to take a loss. A $5,000 Treasury note issued initially at 9.5 percent, with three years to run, may only bring $4,500 if the going interest rate climbs to 11 percent. This risk is considerably greater as the maturity date is extended. A complete discussion of the "interest rate risk" is presented in Chapter 16, Long-Term Debt and Lease Financing.

The various forms of marketable securities and investments, emphasizing the short term, are presented in Table 7–3. The key characteristics of each investment are delineated along with examples of

**Table 7–3**
**Types of short-term investments**

| Investment | Maturity* | Minimum Amount | Safety | Marketability | Yield March 22, 1980 | Yield January 6, 1986 |
|---|---|---|---|---|---|---|
| Federal government securities | | | | | | |
| Treasury bills . . . . . . . . . . . . | 3 months | $ 10,000 | Excellent | Excellent | 14.76 | 7.25 |
| Treasury bills . . . . . . . . . . . . | 1 year | 10,000 | Excellent | Excellent | 13.89 | 7.74 |
| Treasury notes . . . . . . . . . . . | 3–5 years | 5,000 | Excellent | Excellent | 13.86 | 8.56 |
| Federal agency securities | | | | | | |
| Federal Home Loan Bank . . . . . | 1–5 years | 5,000 | Excellent | Excellent | 14.40 | 7.73 |
| Fannie Mae (Federal National Mortgage Association) . . . . . | 1–5 years | 5,000 | Excellent | Excellent | 14.32 | 7.64 |
| Nongovernment securities | | | | | | |
| Certificates of deposit (large) . . . | 1 month | 100,000 | Good | Good | 16.97 | 7.70 |
| Certificates of deposit (small) . . . | 90 days | 500 | Good | Poor | 15.90 | 7.50 |
| Commercial paper . . . . . . . . . | 3 months | 25,000 | Good | Fair | 17.04 | 7.75 |
| Banker's acceptances . . . . . . . . | 90 days | None | Good | Good | 17.22 | 7.62 |
| Eurodollar deposits . . . . . . . . . | 3 months | 25,000 | Good | Excellent | 18.98 | 8.00 |
| LIBOR (London Interbank Offered Rates) . . . . . . . . . . | 3 months | 100,000 | Good | Excellent | — | 8.06 |
| Savings accounts . . . . . . . . . . | Open | None | Excellent | None† | 5–5½ | 5.25 |
| Money market funds . . . . . . . . | Open | 500 | Good | None† | 14.50 | 7.20 |
| Money market deposit accounts (financial institutions) . . . . . . . | Open | 1,000 | Excellent | None† | — | 6.82 |

*Several of the above securities can be purchased with maturities longer than those indicated. The above maturities are the most commonly quoted.
†Though not marketable, these investments are still highly liquid in that funds may be withdrawn without penalty.

yields on March 22, 1980, when interest rates were extremely high, and January 6, 1986, a period of disinflation and declining interest rates. Rates at the beginning of 1986 were less than half the level of rates in 1980.

Let us examine the characteristics of each security. *Treasury bills* are short-term obligations of the federal government and are a popular place to "park funds" because of a large and active market. Although these securities are originally issued with maturities of 91 days, 182 days, and one year, the investor may buy an outstanding T-bill with as little as one day remaining (perhaps two prior investors have held it for 45 days each). With the government issuing new Treasury bills weekly, a wide range of choices is always available. Treasury bills are unique in that they trade on a discount basis—meaning that the yield you receive takes place as a result of the difference between the price you pay and the maturity value.

*Treasury notes* are government obligations with a maturity of three to five years, and they may be purchased with short- to intermediate-term funds. *Federal agency* securities represent the offerings of such governmental organizations as the Federal Land Bank, the Federal Home Loan Bank, and the Federal National Mortgage Association (Fannie Mae). Though lacking the direct backing of the U.S. Treasury, they are guaranteed by the issuing agency and provide all the safety that one would normally require. There is an excellent secondary market, meaning that an investor may sell an outstanding issue in an active and liquid market prior to the maturity date. Government agency issues pay slightly higher yields than direct Treasury issues.

Another outlet for investment is the *certificates of deposit* (CD's), offered by commercial banks, savings and loans, and other financial institutions. The investor places his or her funds on deposit at a specified rate over a given time period as evidenced by the certificate received. This is a two-tier market, with small CDs ($500 to $10,000) carrying lower interest rates, while larger CDs ($100,000 and more) have higher interest provisions and a degree of marketability for those who wish to turn over their CDs prior to maturity. The CD market became fully deregulated by the federal government in 1986.

Comparable in yield and quality to large certificates of deposit, *commercial paper* represents unsecured promissory notes issued to the public by large business corporations. When Ford Motor Credit Corporation is in need of short-term funds, it may choose to borrow at the bank or expand its credit resources by issuing its commercial paper to the general public in minimum units of $25,000. Commercial paper is usually held to maturity by the investor, with no active secondary market in existence.

*Banker's acceptances* are short-term securities that generally arise from foreign trade. The acceptance is a draft which is drawn on a bank for payment when presented to the bank. The difference between a draft and a check is that a company does not have to deposit funds at the bank to cover the draft until the bank has accepted the draft for payment and presented it to the company. In the case of banker's acceptances arising from foreign trade, the draft may be accepted by the bank for *future* payment of the required amount. This means that the exporter who now holds the banker's acceptance may have to wait 30, 60, or 90 days to collect the money. Because there is an active market for banker's acceptances, the exporter can sell the acceptance on a discount basis to any buyer and in this way receive the money before the importer receives the goods. This provides a good investment opportunity in banker's acceptances. Banker's acceptances rank close behind Treasury bills and certificates of deposits as a vehicle for viable short-term investments.

Another popular international short-term investment arising from foreign trade is the *Eurodollar certificate of deposit*. The rate on this investment is usually higher than the rates on U.S. Treasury bills and bank certificates of deposit at large U.S. money market banks. Eurodollars are U.S. dollars held on deposit by foreign banks and in turn loaned out by those banks to anyone seeking dollars. Since the U.S. dollar is the only international currency that is also used as a domestic currency abroad, any country can use it to help pay for goods. Therefore, there is a large market for Eurodollar deposits and loans, mostly centered in the London international banking market.

In this edition we have added *LIBOR* (London Interbank Offered Rate) to the investment table. The LIBOR rate is the rate offered for dollar deposits in the London market. While this is essentially a Eurodollar deposit, the difference is that the deposit is centered in London rather than Paris or Frankfurt or some other part of Europe. LIBOR is often used as a base lending rate for U.S. companies who may borrow at a floating interest rate of LIBOR plus a small premium. LIBOR is even being used as a base rate for some U.S. domestic loans to corporations. The use of LIBOR is discussed further in Chapter 21, International Financial Management.

The lowest yielding investment may well be a passbook *savings account* at a bank or a savings and loan. Although rates on savings accounts are no longer prescribed by federal regulation, they are still a relatively unattractive form of investment in terms of yield.

Of particular interest to the smaller investor is the *money market fund*—a product of the tight money periods of the 1970s and early 1980s. For as little as $500 or $1,000, an investor may purchase shares in a money market fund, which in turn reinvests the proceeds in high-yielding $100,000 bank CDs, $25,000–$100,000 commercial paper, and other large-denomination, high-yielding securities. The investor then receives his pro rata portion of the interest proceeds daily as a credit to his shares.

The money market funds allow the small businessperson or investor to participate directly in higher yielding securities. All too often in the past, the small investor was forced to place funds in savings accounts yielding 5–5½ percent, while "smart" money was parked at higher yields in large-unit investments. Examples of money market funds are Dreyfus Liquid Assets, Inc., and Fidelity Daily Income Trust.

Beginning in December 1982, money market funds got new competition when commercial banks, savings and loans, and credit unions were permitted by the regulatory agencies and Congress to offer new *money market accounts* modeled after money market funds. Due to deregulation, financial institutions are now able to pay competitive market rates on money market deposit accounts. While there is no longer a federally prescribed minimum balance, the normal minimum is $1,000. Terms do vary from institution to institution. Generally these accounts may have only three deposits and three withdrawals per month, and are not meant to be transaction accounts, but a place to keep minimum and excess cash balances. They may be used by individuals or corporations, but are more attractive to smaller firms than to larger firms (which have many more alternatives available). These accounts are insured up to $100,000 by federal agencies, which make them slightly less risky than money market funds. Obviously these funds have been well received, because by September of 1985 money market deposit accounts at commercial banks and thrifts had a combined balance of almost $500 billion, more than twice that of money market funds.

## Management of Accounts Receivable

An increasing portion of the investment in corporate assets has been in accounts receivable as expanding sales, fostered to some extent by inflationary pressures, have placed additional burdens on firms to carry larger balances for their customers. Frequently, recessions have also stretched out the terms of payment as small customers have had to rely on suppliers for credit. Accounts receivable as a percentage of total assets has almost doubled between 1950 and the mid 1980s, representing over 20 percent of total assets for the average U.S. corporation.[5]

[5]Federal Trade Commission and Securities and Exchange Commission, *Quarterly Report for Manufacturing Corporations*, 4th quarter, 1951, and 4th quarter, 1985.

## Accounts Receivable as an Investment

As is true of other current assets, accounts receivable should be thought of as an investment. The level of accounts receivable should not be adjudged too high or too low based on historical standards of industry norms, but rather the test should be whether the level of return we are able to earn from this asset equals or exceeds the potential gain from other commitments. For example, if we allow our customers five extra days to clear their accounts, our accounts receivable balance will increase—draining funds from marketable securities and perhaps drawing down the inventory level. We must ask whether we are optimizing our return, in light of appropriate risk and liquidity considerations.

An example of a buildup in accounts receivable is presented in Figure 7–3, with supportive financing provided through reducing lower yielding assets and increasing lower cost liabilities.

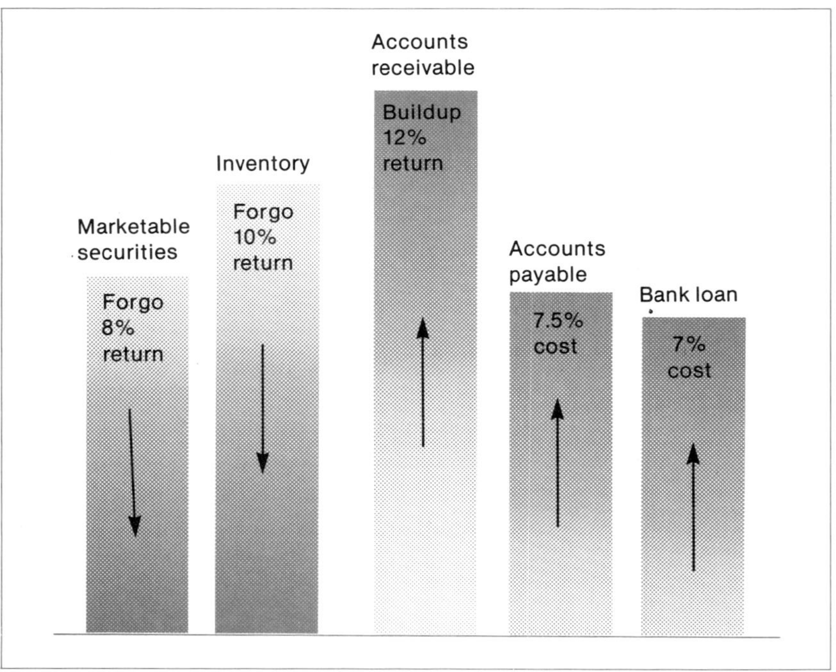


**Figure 7–3**
**Financing growth in accounts receivable**

## Credit Policy Administration

In considering the extension of credit, there are three primary policy variables to consider in conjunction with our profit objective.

1. Credit standards.
2. Terms of credit.
3. Collection policy.

**Credit standards** The firm must determine the nature of the credit risk on the basis of prior record of payment, financial stability, current net worth, and other factors. An extensive network of credit information has been developed by credit agencies throughout the country (Big Brother is watching). The most prominent source is Dun & Bradstreet, which publishes a *Reference Book* listing over 3 million business establishments. Information is given on the firm's line of business, net worth, and creditworthiness. An example of the rating system used by Dun & Bradstreet is presented in Table 7–4.

A firm with a BB2 rating has estimated financial strength, based on net worth, of $200,000–$300,000, with an overall composite credit rating of "Good." Besides the *Reference Book,* Dun & Bradstreet can

**Table 7–4**
**Dun & Bradstreet credit rating system**

| Key to Ratings | | | | | | |
|---|---|---|---|---|---|---|
| Estimated Financial Strength | | | Composite Credit Appraisal | | | |
| | | | *High* | *Good* | *Fair* | *Limited* |
| 5A . . . | Over | $50,000,000 | 1 | 2 | 3 | 4 |
| 4A . . . | $10,000,000 to | 50,000,000 | 1 | 2 | 3 | 4 |
| 3A . . . | 1,000,000 to | 10,000,000 | 1 | 2 | 3 | 4 |
| 2A . . . | 750,000 to | 1,000,000 | 1 | 2 | 3 | 4 |
| 1A . . . | 500,000 to | 750,000 | 1 | 2 | 3 | 4 |
| BA . . | 300,000 to | 500,000 | 1 | 2 | 3 | 4 |
| (BB) . . | 200,000 to | 300,000 | 1 | (2) | 3 | 4 |
| CB . . | 125,000 to | 200,000 | 1 | 2 | 3 | 4 |
| CC . . | 75,000 to | 125,000 | 1 | 2 | 3 | 4 |
| DC . . | 50,000 to | 75,000 | 1 | 2 | 3 | 4 |
| DD . . | 35,000 to | 50,000 | 1 | 2 | 3 | 4 |
| EE . . . | 20,000 to | 35,000 | 1 | 2 | 3 | 4 |
| FF . . . | 10,000 to | 20,000 | 1 | 2 | 3 | 4 |
| GG . . | 5,000 to | 10,000 | 1 | 2 | 3 | 4 |
| HH . . | Up to | 5,000 | 1 | 2 | 3 | 4 |

also provide extensive individualized credit reports on potential customers.

Certain industries have also developed their own special credit reporting agencies, such as the Lyon Furniture Mercantile Agency and the National Credit Office (textiles). Even more important are the local credit bureaus that keep close tabs on day-to-day transactions in a given community.

**Terms of trade** The stated terms of credit extension will have a strong impact on the eventual size of the accounts receivable balance. If a firm averages $5,000 in daily credit sales and allows 30-day terms, the average accounts receivable balance will be $150,000. If customers are carried for 60 days, we must maintain $300,000 in receivables and much additional financing will be required.

In establishing credit terms the firm should also consider the use of a cash discount. Offering the terms 2/10, net 30, enables the customer to deduct 2 percent from the face amount of the bill when paying within the first 10 days, but if the discount is not taken, the customer must remit the full amount within 30 days. As later demonstrated in Chapter 8, Sources of Short-Term Financing, the annualized cost of not taking a cash discount may be substantial.

**Collection policy** A third area for consideration under credit policy administration is the collection function. A number of quantitative measures may be applied to the credit department of the firm.

*a.* Average collection period $= \dfrac{\text{Accounts receivable}}{\text{Average daily credit sales}}$

(See ratio 5 in Chapter 3.) An increase in the average collection period may be the result of a predetermined plan to extend credit terms or the consequence of poor credit administration.

*b.* Ratio of bad debts to credit sales.

An increasing ratio may indicate too many weak accounts or an aggressive market expansion policy.

*c.* Aging of accounts receivables.

We may wish to determine the amount of time that the various accounts have been on our books. If there is a buildup in receivables beyond our normal credit terms, we may wish to take remedial action. Such a buildup is shown in the table presented here.

*Age of receivables, May 31, 1987*

| *Month of Sales* | *Age of Account (days)* | *Amounts* |
|---|---|---|
| May | 0–30 | $ 60,000 |
| April | 31–60 | 25,000 |
| March | 61–90 | 5,000 |
| February | 91–120 | 10,000 |
| Total receivables | | $100,000 |

If our normal credit terms are 30 days, we may be doing a poor job of collecting our accounts, with particular attention required on the over-90-day accounts.

## An Actual Credit Decision

We now examine a credit decision that brings together the various elements of accounts receivable management. Assume that a firm is considering selling to a group of customers that will bring $10,000 in new annual sales, of which 10 percent will be uncollectible. While this is a very high rate of nonpayment, the critical question is, What is the potential contribution to profitability?

Assume the collection cost on these accounts is 5 percent and the cost of producing and selling the product is 77 percent of the sales dollar. We are in a 40 percent tax bracket. The profit on new sales is as follows:

| | |
|---|---|
| Additional sales | $10,000 |
| Accounts uncollectible (10% of new sales) | 1,000 |
| Annual incremental revenue | 9,000 |
| Collection costs (5% of new sales) | 500 |
| Production and selling costs (77% of new sales) | 7,700 |
| Annual income before taxes | 800 |
| Taxes (40%) | 320 |
| Annual incremental income after taxes | $ 480 |

Though the return on sales is only 4.8 percent ($480/$10,000), the return on invested dollars may be considerably higher. Let us assume that the only new investment in this case is a buildup in accounts receivable. (Present working capital and fixed assets are sufficient to support the higher sales level.) Assume analysis of our accounts indicates a turnover ratio of 6 to 1 between sales and accounts receivable. Our new accounts receivable balance will average $1,667.

$$\frac{\text{Sales}}{\text{Turnover}} = \frac{\$10{,}000}{6}^{6} = \$1{,}667$$

Thus, we are committing an average investment of only $1,667 to provide an aftertax return of $480, so that the yield is a very attractive 28.8 percent. If the firm had a minimum required aftertax return of 10 percent, this would clearly be an acceptable investment. We might ask next if we should consider taking on 12 percent or even 15 percent in uncollectible accounts—remaining loyal to our concept of maximizing profit and forsaking any notion about risky accounts being inherently good or bad.

## Inventory Management

Inventory can create financing and profit problems for a company. The automobile industry in 1985 and 1986 is a case in point. In the Fall of 1985, with bulging inventories of 1985 models, the automobile industry instituted a discount financing plan of 7.9 percent interest. While this stimulated sales and cleared 1985 cars out of the dealer showrooms, profits suffered—at General Motors especially. The discount financing was discontinued, but late in 1985 and early in 1986, General Motors found that it had over 80 days of inventory when 60 days is the normal target. Again GM led the industry with 7.9 percent financing.

Inventory is the least liquid of current assets, and it should provide the highest yield to justify investment. While the financial manager may have direct control over the cash management, marketable securities, and accounts receivable, control over inventory policy is generally shared with production management and marketing. Let us examine some key factors influencing inventory management.

---

[6] We could actually argue that our out-of-pocket commitment to sales is 82 percent times $10,000, or $8,200. This would indicate an even smaller commitment to receivables.

## Level versus Seasonal Production

A manufacturing firm must determine whether a plan of level or seasonal production should be followed. Level production was discussed in Chapter 6. While level (even) production throughout the year allows for maximum efficiency in the use of manpower and machinery, it may result in unnecessarily high inventory buildups prior to shipment, particularly in a seasonal business. We may have 10,000 bathing suits in stock in November.

If we produce on a seasonal basis, the inventory problem is eliminated, but we will then have unused capacity during slack periods. Furthermore, as we shift to maximum operations to meet seasonal needs, we may be forced to pay overtime wages to labor and to sustain other inefficiencies as equipment is overused.

We have a classic problem in financial analysis. Are the cost savings from level production sufficient to justify the extra expenditure in carrying inventory? Let us look at a typical case.

| | *Production* | |
|---|---|---|
| | *Level* | *Seasonal* |
| Average inventory . . . . . . . . . | $100,000 | $70,000 |
| Operating costs—after tax . . . . | 50,000 | 60,000 |

Though we will have to invest $30,000 more in average inventory under level production, we will save $10,000 in operating costs. This represents a 33 percent return on investment. If our required rate of return is 10 percent, this would clearly be an acceptable alternative.[7]

## Inventory Policy in Inflation (and Deflation)

The price of copper went from $0.50 to $1.40 a pound and back again in 1973–75 and also showed sharp price volatility in the 1979–

[7]The problem may be further evaluated by using the capital budgeting techniques presented in Chapter 12.

82 period. Similar price instability has taken place in wheat, sugar, lumber, and a number of other commodities. Only the most astute inventory manager can hope to prosper in this type of environment. The problem can be partially controlled by taking moderate inventory positions (do not fully commit at one price).

Another way of protecting your inventory position would be by hedging with a futures contract to sell at a stipulated price some months from now.

Rapid price movements in inventory may also have a major impact on the reported income of the firm, a process described in Chapter 3, Financial Analysis. A firm using FIFO (first-in, first-out) accounting may experience large inventory profits when old, less expensive inventory is written off against new high prices in the marketplace. The benefits may be transitory, as the process reverses itself when prices decline.

## The Inventory Decision Model

Substantial research has been devoted to the problem of determining optimum inventory size, order quantity, usage rate, and similar considerations. An entire branch in the field of operations research is dedicated to the subject.

In developing an inventory model, we must evaluate the two basic costs associated with inventory: the carrying costs and the ordering costs. Through a careful analysis of both of these variables, we can determine the optimum order size to place to minimize costs. Carrying costs include interest on funds tied up in inventory, the cost of warehouse space, insurance premiums, and material handling expenses. There is also an implicit cost associated with the dangers of obsolescence and rapid price change. The larger the order we place, the greater the average inventory we will have on hand, and the higher the carrying cost.

As a second factor, we must consider the cost of ordering and processing inventory into stock. If we maintain a relatively low average inventory in stock, we must order many times and total ordering cost will be high. The opposite patterns associated with the two costs are portrayed in Figure 7–4.

As the order size increases, carrying costs go up because we have more inventory on hand. With larger orders, of course, we will order less frequently and overall ordering costs will go down. The approximate trade-off between the two can best be judged by examining the

Figure 7–4
Determining the optimum inventory level

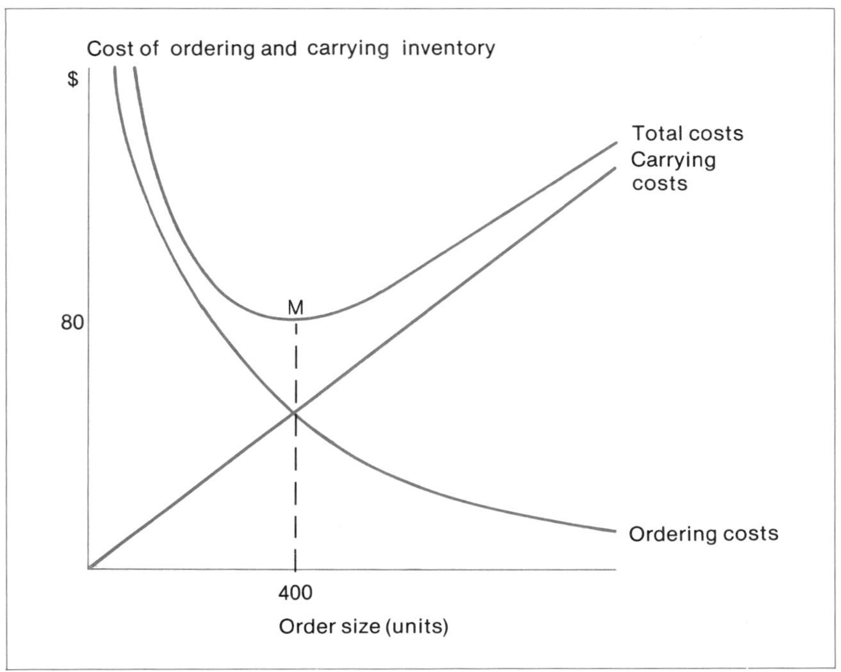


total cost curve. At point $M$, we have appropriately played the advantages and disadvantages of the respective costs against each other. With larger orders, carrying costs will be excessive, while at a reduced order size, constant ordering will put us at an undesirably higher point on the ordering cost curve.

The question becomes, How do we mathematically determine the minimum point ($M$) on the total cost curve? Under certain fairly reasonable assumptions,[8] we may use the following formula as the first step.

$$EOQ = \sqrt{\frac{2SO}{C}} \qquad (7\text{–}1)$$

[8]The assumptions are that inventory usage is at a constant rate, that the amount of time to deliver each order is consistent, and that the delivery date coincides with the point at which we reach a zero level of inventory. It does not consider the problem of stock-outs. A stock-out occurs when a firm is out of a specific inventory item and is unable to sell or deliver the product. Relaxation of these assumptions does not greatly change the calculations.

*EOQ* is the "economic ordering quantity," the amount which it is most advantageous for the firm to order each time. We will determine this value, translate it into average inventory size, and determine the minimum total cost amount (*M*). The terms in the *EOQ* formula are defined as follows:

$S$ = Total sales in units
$O$ = Ordering cost for each order
$C$ = Carrying cost per unit in dollars

Let us assume that we anticipate selling 2,000 units, that it will cost us $8 to place each order, and that the price per unit is $1, with a 20 percent carrying cost to maintain the average inventory (the carrying charge per unit is $0.20). Plugging these values into our formula, we show:

$$EOQ = \sqrt{\frac{2SO}{C}} = \sqrt{\frac{2 \times 2{,}000 \times \$8}{\$0.20}} = \sqrt{\frac{\$32{,}000}{\$0.20}} = \sqrt{160{,}000}$$
$$= 400 \text{ units}$$

The optimum order size is 400 units. On the assumption that we will use up inventory at a constant rate throughout the year, our average inventory on hand will be 200 units, as indicated in Figure 7–5. Average inventory equals *EOQ*/2.

Our total costs with an order size of 400 and an average inventory size of 200 units are computed in Table 7–5.

Figure 7–5
Inventory usage pattern

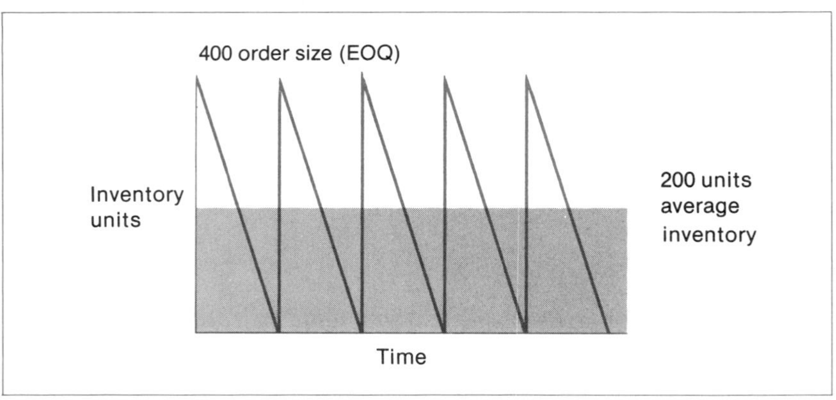

**Table 7–5**
**Total costs for inventory**

1. Ordering costs $= \dfrac{2{,}000 \text{ units}}{400 \text{ order size}} = 5$ orders

   5 orders at \$8 per order = \$40

2. Carrying costs = Average inventory in units × Carrying cost per unit

   200 × \$0.20 = \$40

3. | | |
   |---|---|
   | Order cost . . . . . . | \$40 |
   | Carrying cost . . . . . | +40 |
   | Total cost . . . . . . | \$80 |

Point *M* on Figure 7–4 can be equated to a total cost of \$80 at an order size of 400 units. At no other order point can we hope to achieve lower costs. The same basic principles of total cost minimization that we have applied to inventory can be applied to other assets as well. For example, we may assume that cash has a carrying cost (opportunity cost of lost interest on marketable securities as a result of being in cash) and an ordering cost (transaction costs of shifting in and out of marketable securities) and then work toward determining the optimum level of cash. In each case we are trying to minimize the overall costs and increase the profit and valuation of the firm.

## Summary

In cash management our primary goal should be to keep our balances as low as possible consistent with the notion of maintaining adequate funds for transaction purposes. We try to speed the inflow of funds and defer their outflow. Excess short-term funds may be placed in marketable securities—with a wide selection of issues, maturities, and yields from which to choose.

The management of accounts receivable calls for the determination of credit standards and the forms of credit to be offered as well as the development of an effective collection policy. There is no such thing as bad credit—only unprofitable credit extension. Inventory is the least liquid of the current assets, so it should provide the highest yield. We determine the economic ordering quantity and the optimum average inventory size to minimize the total costs of ordering and carrying inventory.

Other assets may also be subjected to decision models similar to that provided for inventory. In each instance we look at the cost of holding the asset versus the cost of transacting in the asset and we strive for a minimum value.

## List of Terms

**float**
**lockbox system**
**electronic funds transfer**
**cost–benefit analysis**
**Treasury bills**
**Treasury notes**
**certificates of deposit**
**commercial paper**
**Dun & Bradstreet**
**hedging**
**futures contract**
**LIBOR (London Interbank Offered Rate)**
**automated clearinghouse (ACH)**
**economic ordering quantity (*EOQ*)**
**carrying costs**
**trade credit**
**credit terms**
**average collection period**
**aging of accounts receivable**
**Eurodollars**
**banker's acceptances**
**money market accounts**
**money market funds**

## Discussion Questions

1. In the management of cash and marketable securities, why should the primary concern be for safety and liquidity rather than maximization of profit?
2. Briefly explain how a corporation may use float to its advantage.
3. Why does float exist at all, and what effect would electronic funds transfer systems have on float?
4. How can a firm operate with a negative cash balance on its corporate books?
5. Explain the similarities and differences of lockbox systems and regional collection offices.

6. Why would a financial manager want to slow down disbursements?
7. Use *The Wall Street Journal* or some other financial publication to find the going interest rates for the list of marketable securities in Table 7–3. Which security would you choose for a short-term investment? Why?
8. Why are Treasury bills a favorite place for financial managers to invest excess cash?
9. Explain why the bad debt percentage or any other similar credit-control percentage is not the ultimate measure of success in the management of accounts receivable. What is the key consideration?
10. Precisely what does the *EOQ* formula tell us? What assumption is made about the usage rate for inventory?

## Problems

1. Shelia's Society Clothing Manufacturer has collection centers across the country to speed up collections. The company also makes distributions from remote disbursement centers so the firm's checks take longer to clear the bank. Collection time has been reduced by two and one half days and disbursement time increased by one and one half days because of these policies. Excess funds are being invested in short-term instruments yielding 11 percent per annum.

   *a*. If the firm has $4 million per day in collections and $3 million per day in disbursements, how many dollars has the cash management system freed up?
   *b*. How much can the firm earn in dollars per year on short-term investments made possible by the freed-up cash?
2. Barney's Antique Shop has annual credit sales of $1,080,000 and an average collection period of 40 days in 1986. Assume a 360-day year.

   What is the company's average accounts receivable balance?
3. In Problem two, if accounts receivable change in 1987 to $140,000, while credit sales are $1,440,000, should we assume the firm has a more or a less lenient credit policy?

**4.** Midwest Tires has expected sales of 12,000 tires this year, an ordering cost of $6 per order, and carrying cost of $1.60 per tire.

*a.* What is the economic ordering quantity?
*b.* How many orders will be placed during the year?
*c.* What will the average inventory be?

**5.** Fisk Corporation is trying to improve its inventory control system and has installed an on-line computer at its retail stores. Fisk anticipates sales of 75,000 units per year, an ordering cost of $8 per order, and carrying costs of $1.20 per unit.

*a.* What is the economic ordering quantity?
*b.* How many orders will be placed during the year?
*c.* What will the average inventory be?
*d.* What is the total cost of ordering and carrying inventory?

**6.** (See Problem 5 for basic data.) In the second year, Fisk Corporation finds it can reduce ordering costs to $2 per order but that carrying costs stay the same at $1.20. Also, volume remains at 75,000 units.

*a.* Recompute *a,b,c,* and *d* in Problem 5 for the second year.
*b.* Now compare years one and two and explain what happened.

**7.** Johnson Electronics is considering extending trade credit to some customers previously considered poor risks. Sales would increase by $100,000 if credit is extended to these new customers. Of the new accounts receivable generated, 10 percent will prove to be uncollectible. Additional collection costs will be 3 percent of sales, and production and selling costs will be 79 percent of sales. The firm is in the 40 percent tax bracket.

*a.* Compute the incremental income after taxes.
*b.* What will Johnson's incremental return on sales be if these new credit customers are accepted?
*c.* If the receivable turnover ratio is 6 to 1, and no other asset buildup is needed to serve the new customers, what will Johnson's incremental return on new average investment be?

**8.** Oscar's checkbook shows a balance of $600. A recent statement from the bank (received last week) shows that all checks written as of the date of the statement have been paid except numbers 423 and 424, which were for $62 and $40, respectively. Since the statement date, checks 425, 426, 427, have been written for $32, $70, and $44, respectively.

There is a 75 percent probability that checks 423 and 424 have been paid by this time. There is a 40 percent probability that checks 425, 426, and 427 have been paid.

*a.* What is the total value of the five checks outstanding?
*b.* What is the expected value of payments for the five checks outstanding?
*c.* What is the difference between parts *a* and *b*? This represents a type of float.

**9.** North Pole Snowmobile is considering a switch to level production. Cost efficiencies would occur under level production, and aftertax costs would decline by $30,000, but inventory would increase by $250,000. North Pole Snowmobile would have to finance the extra inventory at a cost of 13.5 percent. Should the company go ahead and switch to level production? How low would interest rates need to fall before level production would be feasible?

**10.** Anderson Corporation is considering a more liberal credit policy to increase sales, but expects that 8 percent of the new accounts will be uncollectible. Collection costs are 5 percent of new sales, production and selling costs are 77 percent, and accounts receivable turnover is five times. Assume income taxes of 40 percent and an increase in sales of $60,000. No other asset buildup will be required to service the new accounts.

*a.* What is the level of accounts receivable to support this sales expansion?
*b.* What would be Anderson's incremental aftertax return on investment?
*c.* Should Anderson liberalize credit if a 15 percent aftertax return on investment is required?

Assume that Anderson also needs to increase its level of inventory to support new sales and that inventory turnover is four times.

*d.* What would be the total incremental investment in accounts receivable and inventory to support a $60,000 increase in sales?

*e*. Given the income determined in part *b* and the investment determined in part *d*, should Anderson extend more liberal credit terms?

**11.** Fashion Furniture is evaluating the extension of credit to a new group of customers. Although these customers will provide $180,000 in additional credit sales, 12 percent are likely to be uncollectible. The company will also incur $14,000 in additional collection expense. Production and marketing costs represent 70 percent of sales. The firm is in a 40 percent tax bracket and has a receivables turnover of 5 times. No other asset buildup will be required to service the new customers.

*a*. Should Fashion Furniture extend credit to these customers, assuming that it has a 10 percent desired return?
*b*. Should credit be extended if 15 percent of the new sales prove uncollectible?
*c*. Should credit be extended if the receivables turnover drops to 1.5, and 12 percent of the accounts are uncollectible?

**12.** Reconsider Problem 11. Assume the average collection period is 120 days. All other factors are the same (including 12 percent uncollectibles). Should credit be extended?

(*Problems 13–16 are a series and should be taken in order.*)

**13.** Dome Metals has credit sales of $144,000 yearly with credit terms of net 30 days, which is also the average collection period. Dome does not offer a discount for early payment, so its customers take the full 30 days to pay.

What is the average receivables balance? Receivables turnover?

**14.** If Dome offered a 2 percent discount for payment in 10 days and every customer took advantage of the new terms, what would the new average receivables balance be? Use the full sales of $144,000 for your calculation of receivables.

**15.** If Dome reduces its bank loans, which cost 10 percent, by the cash generated from reduced receivables, what will be the net gain or loss to the firm (don't forget the 2 percent discount)? Should it offer the discount?

**16.** Assume that the new trade terms of 2/10, net 30 will increase sales by 15 percent because the discount makes Dome price competitive. If Dome earns 20 percent on sales before discounts, should it offer the discount? (Consider the same variables as you did for Problems 13 through 15.)

**17.** (*Comprehensive problem on receivables and inventory policy*)

Logan Distributing Company of Atlanta sells fans and heaters to retail outlets throughout the Southeast. Joe Logan, the president of the company, is thinking about changing the firm's credit policy to attract customers away from competitors. The present policy calls for a 1/10, net 30 cash discount. The new policy would call for a 3/10, net 50 cash discount. Currently, 30 percent of Logan customers are taking the discount, and it is anticipated that this number would go up to 50 percent with the new discount policy. It is further anticipated that annual sales would increase from a level of $400,000 to $600,000 as a result of the change in the cash discount policy.

The increased sales would also affect the inventory level carried by Logan. The average inventory carried by Logan is based on a determination of an EOQ. Assume sales of fans and heaters increase from 15,000 to 22,500 units. The ordering cost for each order is $200, and the carrying cost per unit is $1.50 (these values will not change with the discount). The average inventory is based on EOQ/2. Each unit in inventory has an average cost of $12.

Cost of goods sold is equal to 65 percent of net sales, general and administrative expenses are 15 percent of net sales, and interest payments of 14 percent will only be necessary for the increase in the accounts receivable and inventory balances. Taxes will be 40 percent of before-tax income.

*a.* Compute the accounts receivable balance before and after the change in the cash discount policy. Use the net sales (total sales minus cash discounts) to determine the average daily sales.

*b.* Determine EOQ before and after the change in the cash discount policy. Translate this into average inventory (in units and dollars) before and after the change in the cash discount policy.

*c.* Complete the income statement.

| | Before Policy Change | After Policy Change |
|---|---|---|
| Net sales (sales − cash discount) . . . . . . . | | |
| Cost of goods sold . . . . . . . . . . . . . . | | |
| Gross profit . . . . . . . . . . . . . . . . . | | |
| General and administrative expenses . . . . . | | |
| Operating profit . . . . . . . . . . . . . . . | | |
| Interest on increase in accounts receivable and inventory (14 percent) . . . . | | |
| Income before taxes . . . . . . . . . . . . . | | |
| Taxes . . . . . . . . . . . . . . . . . . . . | | |
| Income after taxes . . . . . . . . . . . . . . | | |

*d*. Should the new cash discount policy be utilized? Briefly comment.

## Selected References

Batlin, C. A., and Susan Hinko. "Lockbox Management and Value Maximization." *Financial Management* 10 (Winter 1981), pp. 39–44.

Baumol, William J. "The Transactions Demand for Cash: An Inventory Theoretic Approach." *Quarterly Journal of Economics* 65 (November 1952), pp. 545–56.

Beman, Lewis. "A Big Payoff from Inventory Controls." *Fortune* 104 (July 27, 1981), pp. 76–80.

Block, Stanley B. "Accounts Receivable as an Investment." *Credit and Financial Management* 76 (May 1974), pp. 32–35, 40.

Budin, Morris, and Robert J. Van Handel. "Rule-of-Thumb Theory of Cash Holdings by Firm." *Journal of Financial and Quantitative Analysis* 10 (March 1975), pp. 85–108.

Emery, Gary W. "Some Empirical Evidence on the Properties of Daily Cash Flow." *Financial Management* 10 (Spring 1981), pp. 21–28.

Hofer, C. F. "Analysis of Fixed Costs in Inventory." *Management Accounting* (September 1970), pp. 15–17.

Kim, Yong H.; Joseph C. Atkins; and Walter Dolde. "Evaluating Investments in Accounts Receivable: A Maximizing Framework." *Journal of Finance* 33 (May 1978), pp. 403–12.

Magee, John F. "Guides to Inventory Policy, 1–3." *Harvard Business Review* 34 (January–February 1956), pp. 49–60; 34 (March–April 1956), pp. 103–16; and 34 (May–June 1956), pp. 57–70.

Miller, Merton H., and Daniel Orr. "The Demand for Money by Firms: Extension of Analytic Results." *Journal of Finance* 23 (December 1968), pp. 735–59.

———. "A Model of the Demand for Money by Firms." *Quarterly Journal of Economics* 80 (August 1966), pp. 413–35.

Miller, Tom W., and Bernell K. Stone. "Daily Cash Modeling and Seasonal Resolution: Alternative Models and Techniques for Using the Distribution Approach." *Journal of Financial and Quantitative Analysis* 20 (September 1985), pp. 335–51.

Patterson, Harlan R. "New Life in the Management of Corporate Receivables." *Credit and Financial Management* 72 (February 1970), pp. 15–18.

Rodriguez, Rita M., and Eugene E. Carter. *International Financial Management*. 2d. Englewood Cliffs, N.J.: Prentice Hall, 1979.

Schiff, Michael. "Credit and Inventory Management." *Financial Executive* 40 (November 1972), pp. 28–33.

Smith, Keith V. *Management of Working Capital*. St. Paul: West 1974, sec. 4.

# 8 Sources of Short-Term Financing

In Chapter 8 we examine the cost and availability of the various outlets for short-term funds, with primary attention to trade credit from suppliers, bank loans, corporate promissory notes, foreign borrowing, and loans against receivables and inventory. It is sometimes said the only way to be sure a bank loan will be approved is to convince the banker that you don't really need the money. The learning objective of this chapter will be quite the opposite—namely, to demonstrate how badly needed funds can be made available on a short-term basis from the various suppliers of credit.

## Trade Credit

The largest provider of short-term credit is usually at the firm's doorstep—the manufacturer or seller of goods and services. Approximately 40 percent of short-term financing is in the form of accounts payable or trade credit. Accounts payable is a spontaneous source of funds, growing as the business expands on a seasonal or long-term basis and contracting in a like fashion.

### Payment Period

Trade credit is usually extended for 30 to 60 days. Many firms attempt to "stretch the payment period" in order to provide additional short-term financing. This is an acceptable form of financing as long as it is not carried to an abusive extent. Going from a 30- to a 35-day average payment period may be tolerated within the trade, while stretching payments to 65 days might alienate suppliers and cause a diminishing credit rating with Dun & Bradstreet and local credit bureaus. A major variable in determining the payment period is the possible existence of a cash discount.

### Cash Discount Policy

A cash discount allows for a reduction in price if payment is made within a specified time period. A 2/10, net 30 cash discount means that we can deduct 2 percent if we remit our funds 10 days after billing, but failing this, we must pay the full amount by the 30th day.

On a \$100 billing, we could pay \$98 up to the 10th day or \$100 at the end of 30 days. If we fail to take the cash discount, we will get to use \$98 for 20 more days at a \$2 fee. The cost is a whopping 36.72 percent. Note that we first consider the interest cost and then convert this to an annual basis. The standard formula is:

$$\text{Cost of failing to take a cash discount} = \frac{\text{Discount percent}}{\text{100 percent} - \text{Discount percent}} \times \frac{360}{\text{Final due date} - \text{Discount period}} \quad (8\text{–}1)$$

$$= \frac{2\%}{100\% - 2\%} \times \frac{360}{(30 - 10)}$$

$$= 2.04\% \times 18 = 36.72\%$$

Cash discount terms may vary. For example, on a 2/10, net 90 basis, it would cost us only 9.18 percent not to take the discount and to pay the full amount after 90 days.

$$\frac{2\%}{100\% - 2\%} \times \frac{360}{(90 - 10)} = 2.04\% \times 4.5 = 9.18\%$$

In each case, we must ask ourselves whether bypassing the discount and using the money for a longer period of time is the cheapest means of financing. In the first example, with a cost of 36.72 percent, it probably is not. We would be better off borrowing $98 for 20 days at some lesser rate. For example, at 10 percent interest we would pay 54 cents[1] in interest as opposed to $2 under the cash discount policy. With the 2/10, net 90 arrangement, the cost of missing the discount is only 9.18 percent and we may choose to let our suppliers carry us for an extra 80 days.

### Net Credit Position

In Chapter 2, Review of Accounting, we defined accounts receivable as a use of funds and accounts payable as a source. The firm should closely watch the relationship between the two to determine its net credit position. If a firm has average daily sales of $5,000 and collects in 30 days, the accounts receivable balance will be $150,000. If this is associated with average daily purchases of $4,000 and a 25-day average payment period, the average accounts payable balance is $100,000—indicating $50,000 more in credit extended than received. Changing this situation to an average payment period of 40 days increases the accounts payable to $160,000 ($4,000 × 40). Accounts payable now exceeds accounts receivable by $10,000, thus leaving funds for other needs. Larger firms tend to be net providers of trade credit (relatively high receivables), with smaller firms in the user position (relatively high payables).

## Bank Credit

Banks may provide funds to finance seasonal needs, product line expansion, and long-term growth. The typical banker prefers a self-liquidating loan in which the use of funds will ensure a built-in or automatic repayment scheme. Actually, two thirds of bank loans are short term in nature. Nevertheless, through the process of renewing old loans, many of these 90- or 180-day agreements take on the characteristics of longer-term financing.

---

[1] $\frac{20}{360} \times 10\% \times \$98 = 54¢$

Major changes are taking place in banking today that are centered on the concept of "full-service banking." The modern banker's function is much broader than merely accepting deposits, making loans, and processing checks. At present, a banking institution may be providing trust and investment services, a credit card operation, real estate lending, data processing services, and helpful advice in cash management or international trade. This wide array of services has been made possible through the development of the bank holding company—a legal entity in which one key bank owns a number of affiliate banks as well as other nonbanking subsidiaries engaged in closely related activities.

As we enter the mid-to-late 1980s, more and more banks may also engage in interstate banking activities as legislative barriers come down. Even Illinois, which has been a bastion of unit banks (no statewide branching), has entered into a regional agreement with several neighboring Midwest states to allow interregional banking. Bank deregulation has also created greater competition among financial institutions, such as commercial banks, savings and loans, credit unions, and brokerage houses.

We will look at a number of terms generally associated with banking (and other types of lending activity) and consider the significance of each. Attention is directed to the prime interest rate, compensating balances, the term loan arrangement, and methods of computing interest.

### Prime Rate

This is the rate that the bank charges its most creditworthy customers, and it is scaled up proportionally to reflect the various credit classes. At certain slack loan periods in the economy, banks may actually charge top customers less than the published prime rate; however, such activities are difficult to track. The average customer can expect to pay 1 or 2 percent above prime, while in tight money periods a builder in a speculative construction project may pay 5 or more percentage points over prime.

Figure 8–1 presents the annual average prime rate from 1961 through 1985. While the period before 1961 does not show up, it should be pointed out that interest rates in the 1950s and early 1960s were relatively stable, moving between 3 percent and 5 percent. Beginning in 1965 and continuing into the present, the prime rate became highly

Figure 8–1
Pattern of prime interest rate movements

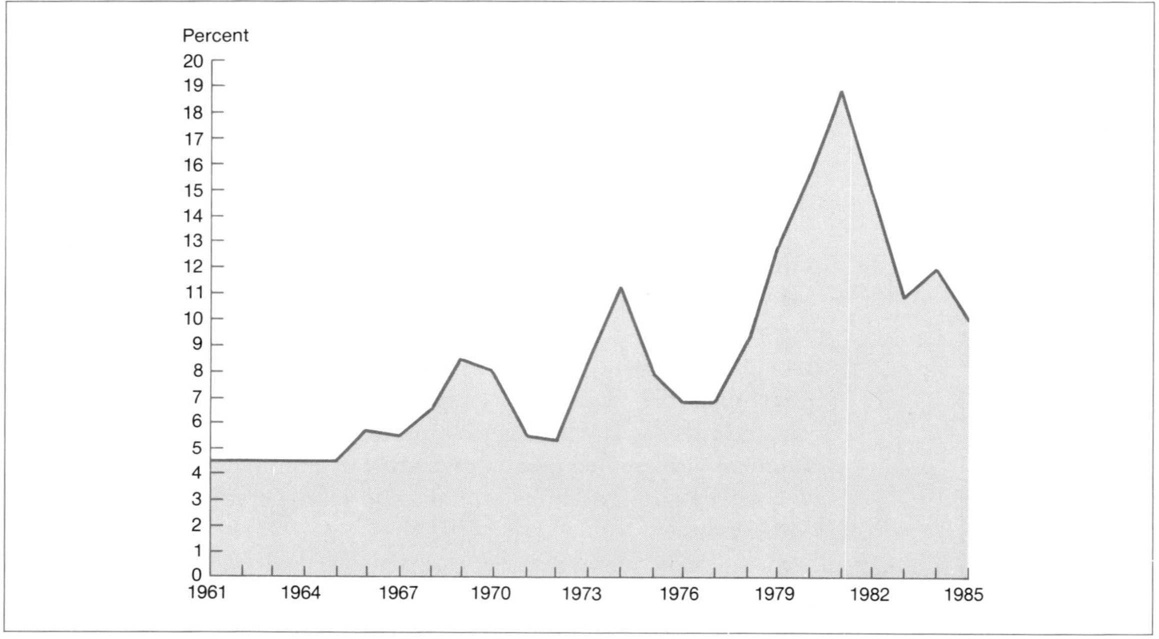


volatile, moving as much as 8 percentage points in a 12-month period. In the early 1980s, the prime rate went above 20 percent for several months (the annual average in 1981 reached 18.87 percent) before sharply declining. With lower inflation from 1982 to 1985, interest rates followed the same pattern, and the prime began 1986 at 9½ percent and reached 8½ percent in April of 1986.

## Compensating Balances

In providing loans and other services, the bank may require that *business* customers maintain a minimum average account balance, herein referred to as a compensating balance. The required amount is usually computed as a percentage of customer loans outstanding or as a percentage of bank commitments toward future loans to a given account. A common ratio is 20 percent against outstanding loans or 10 percent against total future commitments, though market conditions tend to influence the percentages.

Some view the compensating balance requirement as an unusual arrangement. Where else would you walk into a business establishment, buy a shipment of goods, and then be told that you could not take 20 percent of the purchase home with you? If you borrow $100,000, paying 8 percent interest on the full amount with a 20 percent compensating balance requirement, you will be paying $8,000 for the use of $80,000 in funds, or an effective rate of 10 percent.

The amount that must be borrowed to end up with the desired sum of money is simply figured by taking the needed funds and dividing by $(1 - c)$, where $c$ is the compensating balance expressed as a decimal. For example, if you need $100,000 in funds, you must borrow $125,000 to ensure that the intended amount will be available. This would be calculated as follows:

$$\text{Amount to be borrowed} = \frac{\text{Amount needed}}{(1 - c)} = \frac{\$100{,}000}{(1 - 0.2)} = \$125{,}000$$

A check on this calculation could be done to see if we actually end up with the use of $100,000

| | |
|---|---|
| $125,000 | Loan |
| −25,000 | 20% compensating balance requirement |
| $100,000 | Available funds |

The intent here is not to suggest that the compensating balance requirement represents an unfair or hidden cost. If it were not for compensating balances, quoted interest rates would be higher or gratuitous services now offered by banks would carry a price tag. Some authorities in the banking community think that this would be a move in a positive direction, forcing both banker and customer to unbundle and evaluate the full cost of services provided.[2]

[2] A number of enlightened bankers have begun moving in this direction. Paul Nadler, "Compensating Balances and the Prime at Twilight," *Harvard Business Review* 50 (January–February 1972), pp. 112–20.

## Maturity Provisions

As previously indicated, bank loans have been traditionally short term in nature (though perhaps renewable). In the last decade there has been a movement to the use of the term loan, in which credit is extended for a period of one to seven years. The loan is usually repaid in monthly or quarterly installments over its life rather than in one single payment. Only superior credit applicants, as measured by working capital strength, potential profitability, and competitive position, can qualify for term loan financing. Here the banker and the business firm are said to be "climbing into bed together" because of the length of the loan.

Bankers are hesitant to fix a single interest rate to a term loan. The more common practice is to allow the interest rate to change with market conditions. Thus the interest rate on a term loan may be tied to the prime rate and will change (float) with it. Perhaps it is set at prime plus 1 percent.

## Cost of Commercial Bank Financing

The effective interest rate on a loan is based on the loan amount, the dollar interest paid, the length of the loan, and the method of repayment. It is easy enough to observe that $60 interest on a $1,000 loan for one year would carry a 6 percent interest rate, but what if the same loan were for 120 days? We use the formula:

$$\text{Effective rate} = \frac{\text{Interest}}{\text{Principal}} \times \frac{\text{Days in the year (360)}}{\text{Days loan is outstanding}} \qquad (8\text{–}2)$$

$$= \frac{\$60}{\$1000} \times \frac{360}{120} = 6\% \times 3 = 18\%$$

Since we have use of the funds for only 120 days, the effective rate is 18 percent. To highlight the effect of time, if you borrowed $20 for only ten days and paid back $21, the effective interest rate would be 180 percent—a violation of almost every usury law.

$$\frac{\$1}{\$20} \times \frac{360}{10} = 5\% \times 36 = 180\%$$

Not only is the time dimension of a loan important, but also the way in which interest is charged. We have assumed that interest would be paid when the loan comes due. If the bank deducts the interest in advance (discounts the loan), the effective rate of interest increases. For example, a $1,000 one-year loan with $60 of interest deducted in advance represents the payment of interest on only $940, or an effective rate of 6.38 percent.

$$\text{Effective rate on discounted loan} = \frac{\text{Interest}}{\text{Principal} - \text{Interest}} \times \frac{\text{Days in the year (360)}}{\text{Days loan is outstanding}} \tag{8–3}$$

$$= \frac{\$60}{\$1{,}000 - \$60} \times \frac{360}{360} = \frac{\$60}{\$940} = 6.38\%$$

## Interest Costs with Compensating Balances

When a loan is made with compensating balances, the effective interest rate is the stated interest rate divided by (1 − c), where c is the compensating balance expressed as a decimal. Assume that 6 percent is the stated annual rate and that a 20 percent compensating balance is required.

$$\text{Effective rate with compensating balances} = \frac{\text{Interest rate}}{(1 - c)} \tag{8–4}$$

$$= \frac{6\%}{(1 - 0.2)}$$

$$= 7.5\%$$

If dollar amounts are used and the stated rate is unknown, Formula 8–5 can be used. The assumption is that we are paying $60 interest on a $1,000 loan, but are only able to use $800 of the funds. The loan is for a year.

$$\text{Effective rate with compensating balances} = \frac{\text{Interest}}{\text{Principal} - \text{Compensating balance in dollars}} \times \frac{\text{Days in the years (360)}}{\text{Days loan is outstanding}} \tag{8–5}$$

$$= \frac{\$60}{\$1{,}000 - \$200} \times \frac{360}{360} = \frac{\$60}{\$800} = 7.5\%$$

Only when a firm had idle cash balances that could be used to cover compensating balance requirements would the firm not use the higher effective-cost formulas (8–4 and 8–5).

## Rate on Installment Loans

The most confusing borrowing arrangement to the average bank customer or a consumer is the installment loan. An installment loan calls for a series of equal payments over the life of the loan. Though federal legislation prohibits a misrepresentation of interest rates on loans to customers, a loan officer or an overanxious salesperson may quote a rate on an installment loan that is approximately half the true rate.

Assume that you borrow \$1,000 on a 12-month installment basis, with regular monthly payments to apply to interest and principal, and that the interest requirement is \$60. Though it might be suggested that the rate on the loan is 6 percent, this is clearly not the case. Though you are paying a total of \$60 in interest, you do not have the use of \$1,000 for one year—rather, you are paying back the \$1,000 on a monthly basis, with an average outstanding loan balance for the year of approximately \$500. The effective rate of interest is 11.08 percent.

$$\text{Rate on installment loan} = \frac{2 \times \text{Annual no. of payments} \times \text{Interest}}{(\text{Total no. of payments} + 1) \times \text{Principal}} \qquad (8\text{–}6)$$

$$= \frac{2 \times 12 \times \$60}{13 \times \$1{,}000} = \frac{\$1{,}440}{\$13{,}000} = 11.08\%$$

## The Credit Crunch Phenomenon

In 1969–70, 1973–74, and 1979–81, the economy went through a period of extreme credit shortage in the banking sector and other financial markets. We seem to find ourselves in the midst of a tight money situation every three to five years. The anatomy of a credit crunch is as follows. The Federal Reserve tightens the growth in the money supply in its battle against inflation, causing a decrease in lendable funds and an increase in interest rates. To compound the difficulty, business requirements for funds may be increasing to carry inflation-laden inventory and receivables. A third problem is the massive withdrawal of savings deposits at our banking and thrift institutions, all in search of higher returns. There simply are not enough lendable funds to "go around."

Recent history has taught us that the way *not* to deal with credit shortages is to impose artificial limits on interest rates in the form of restrictive usury laws or extreme governmental pressure. In 1969–70 the prime rate went to 8.5 percent in a tight money period—a level not high enough to bring the forces of demand and supply together, and little credit was available. In 1974 the prime rose to 12 percent, a rate truly reflecting market conditions, and funds were available. The same was true in 1980 and 1981 as the prime went to 20 percent and higher, but lendable funds were available.

Since late 1979 the Federal Reserve has put increasing emphasis on "attempting" to control the rate of growth in the money supply at a steady pace and allowing interest rates to move freely. This helps to explain part of the volatility in interest rates in the last few years. No one can be sure what future Fed policy will be in regard to growth of the money supply and interest rates.

## Financing through Commercial Paper

For large, prestigious firms, commercial paper may provide an outlet for raising funds. Commercial paper represents a short-term, unsecured promissory note issued to the public in minimum units of $25,000. As Figure 8–2 indicates, the amount of commercial paper outstanding has increased dramatically, rising from $83 billion in 1978 to over $273 billion in 1985. This large increase in the commercial paper market reflects the willingness of qualified companies to borrow at the lowest rate available. The larger market that has emerged in the last five years has improved the ability of corporations to raise short-term funds.

Commercial paper falls into two categories. First, there are finance companies, such as General Motors Acceptance Corporation (GMAC), General Electric Credit, and CIT Financial Corporation, that issue paper primarily to institutional investors such as pension funds, in-

Figure 8–2
Total commercial paper outstanding

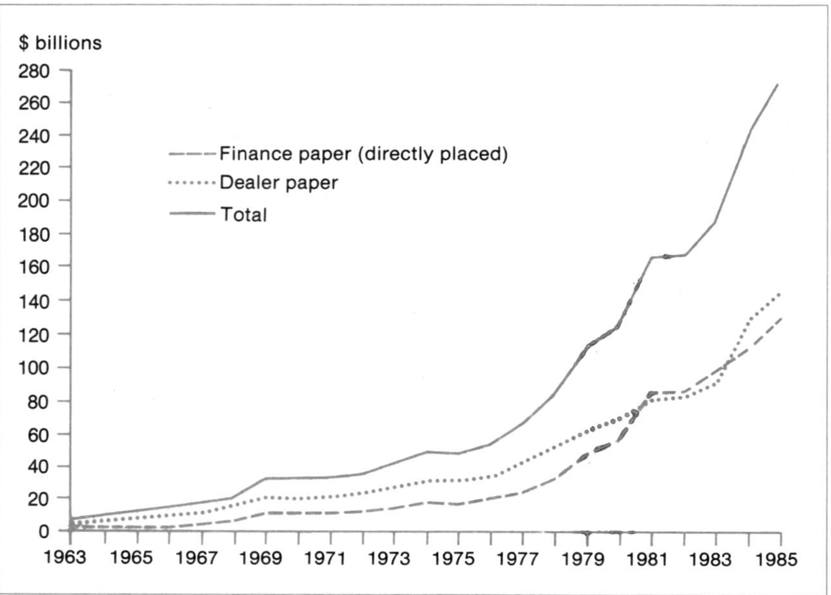


surance companies, and money market mutual funds. It is probably the growth of money market mutual funds that has had such a great impact on the ability of companies to sell such an increased amount of commercial paper in the market. Paper sold by financial firms such as GMAC is referred to as *finance paper,* and since it is usually sold directly to the lender by the finance company, it is also referred to as *direct paper*. The second type of commercial paper is sold by industrial or utility firms that use an intermediate dealer network to distribute their paper. This is referred to as *dealer paper*.

## Advantages of Commercial Paper

The growing popularity of commercial paper can be attributed to other factors besides the rapid growth of money market mutual funds and their need to find short-term securities for investment. For example, commercial paper may be issued at below the prime interest.

**Table 8–1**
**Comparison of commercial paper rate to bank prime rate (annual rate)***

| Year | Finance Co. Paper (directly placed) 4–6 months | Other Paper (dealer-placed) 4–6 months | Average Bank Prime Rate | Prime Rate Minus Dealer Paper |
|---|---|---|---|---|
| 1961 | 2.97 | 2.68 | 4.50 | 1.82 |
| 1962 | 3.26 | 3.07 | 4.50 | 1.43 |
| 1963 | 3.55 | 3.40 | 4.50 | 1.10 |
| 1964 | 3.97 | 3.83 | 4.50 | 0.67 |
| 1965 | 4.38 | 4.27 | 4.50 | 0.23 |
| 1966 | 5.55 | 5.42 | 5.75 | 0.33 |
| 1967 | 5.10 | 4.89 | 5.50 | 0.61 |
| 1968 | 5.90 | 5.69 | 6.50 | 0.81 |
| 1969 | 7.83 | 7.16 | 8.50 | 1.34 |
| 1970 | 7.72 | 7.20 | 8.00 | 0.80 |
| 1971 | 5.11 | 4.89 | 5.50 | 0.61 |
| 1972 | 4.69 | 4.55 | 5.25 | 0.70 |
| 1973 | 8.15 | 7.38 | 8.30 | 0.92 |
| 1974 | 9.84 | 8.61 | 11.12 | 2.51 |
| 1975 | 6.32 | 6.16 | 7.86 | 1.70 |
| 1976 | 5.35 | 5.22 | 6.84 | 1.62 |
| 1977 | 5.60 | 5.50 | 6.82 | 1.32 |
| 1978 | 7.99 | 7.78 | 9.06 | 1.28 |
| 1979 | 10.91 | 10.25 | 12.67 | 2.42 |
| 1980 | 12.29 | 11.28 | 15.27 | 3.99 |
| 1981 | 14.76 | 13.73 | 18.87 | 5.14 |
| 1982 | 11.89 | 11.20 | 14.86 | 3.66 |
| 1983 | 8.89 | 8.69 | 10.79 | 2.10 |
| 1984 | 10.16 | 9.65 | 12.04 | 2.39 |
| 1985 | 8.11 | 7.81 | 9.93 | 2.12 |

*Averages for the year.
Source: *Federal Reserve Bulletins, Business Statistics.*

As indicated in the last column of Table 8–1, this rate differential reached over 5 percent in the tight money markets of 1981.

A second advantage of commercial paper is that no compensating balance requirements are associated with its issuance, though the firm is generally required to maintain commercial bank lines of approved credit equal to the amount of the paper outstanding (a procedure somewhat less costly than compensating balances). Finally, a number of firms enjoy the prestige associated with being able to float their commercial paper in what is considered a "snobbish market" for funds.

### Limitations on the Issuance of Commercial Paper

The commercial paper market is not without its problems. When the Penn Central Railroad went bankrupt in 1970 with its $85 million in "bad" commercial paper floating around, many lenders in the market panicked and refused to roll over (renew) existing paper as it came due. The market shrank by 15 percent from May to December, and the unnerving situation almost caused Chrysler Financial Corporation to be towed away.

The lesson to be learned is that although the funds provided through the issuance of commercial paper are cheaper than bank loans, they are also less predictable. Although a firm may pay a higher rate for a bank loan, it is also buying a degree of loyalty and commitment that is unavailable in the commercial paper market.

## Foreign Borrowing

An increasing source of funds for U.S. firms has been the large Eurodollar market. Loans from foreign banks denominated in dollars are called Eurodollar loans. Such loans are usually short term to intermediate term in maturity. Many multinational corporations are finding cheaper ways of borrowing in foreign markets. A new approach in the 1980s has been for financial managers to borrow *foreign currencies* either directly or through foreign subsidiaries at very favorable interest rates. The companies *convert* the borrowed francs or marks to dollars, which are then sent to the United States to be used by the parent company. There is, however, foreign exchange exposure risk associated with these loans. This topic is given greater coverage in Chapter 21.

As an example of an international loan, IBM arranged a seven-year loan in Swiss francs at an interest rate of 6 percent at a time when the prime rate in the United States was 19 percent. Because of the different financial practices in foreign countries, the differential is not as great as it seems, but this did save IBM several percent in borrowing costs. A foreign subsidiary of a large U.S. drug and medical supply company borrowed from its foreign banks at rates below prevailing U.S. interest rates and then loaned the money back to its parent firm. These examples simply show that the world financial markets have become more sophisticated, and so must financial managers.

## Use of Collateral in Short-Term Financing

Almost any firm would prefer to borrow on an unsecured (no-collateral) basis; but if the borrower's credit rating is too low or its need for funds too great, the lending institution will require that certain assets be pledged. A secured credit arrangement might help the borrower to obtain funds that would otherwise be unavailable.

In any loan the lender's primary concern, however, is whether the borrower's capacity to generate cash flow is sufficient to liquidate the loan as it comes due. Few lenders would make a loan strictly on the basis of collateral. Collateral is merely a stopgap device to protect the lender when all else fails. The bank or finance company is in business to collect interest, not to repossess and resell assets.

Though a number of different types of assets may be pledged, our attention will be directed to accounts receivable and inventory. All states have now adopted the Uniform Commercial Code, which standardizes and simplifies the procedures for establishing the security on a loan.

## Accounts Receivable Financing

Accounts receivable financing may include *pledging* accounts receivable as collateral for a loan or an outright *sale* (factoring) of receivables. Receivables financing is popular because it permits borrowing to be tied directly to the level of asset expansion at any point in time. As the level of accounts receivable goes up, we are able to borrow more.

A drawback is that this is a relatively expensive method of acquiring funds, so that it must be carefully compared to other forms of credit. Accounts receivable represent one of the firm's most valuable short-term assets, and they should be committed only where the appropriate circumstances exist. An ill-advised accounts receivable financing plan may exclude the firm from a less expensive bank term loan. Let us investigate more closely the characteristics and the costs associated with the pledging and selling of receivables.

**Table 8–2**
**Receivable loan balance**

| | Month 1 | Month 2 | Month 3 | Month 4 |
|---|---|---|---|---|
| Total accounts receivable | $11,000 | $15,100 | $19,400 | $16,300 |
| Acceptable accounts receivable (to finance company) | 10,000 | 14,000 | 18,000 | 15,000 |
| Loan balance (80%) | 8,000 | 11,200 | 14,400 | 12,000 |
| Interest 12% annual—1% per month | 80 | 112 | 144 | 120 |

## Pledging Accounts Receivable

The lending institution will generally stipulate which of the accounts receivable are of sufficient quality to serve as collateral for a loan. On this basis, we may borrow 60–80 percent of the value of the acceptable collateral. The loan percentage will depend on the financial strength of the borrowing firm and on the creditworthiness of its accounts. The lender will have full recourse against the borrower in the event that any of the accounts go bad. The interest rate in a receivables borrowing arrangement is generally well in excess of the prime rate.

The interest is computed against the loan balance outstanding, a figure that may change quite frequently, as indicated in Table 8–2. In the illustration, interest is assumed to be 12 percent annually, or 1 percent per month. In month 1, we are able to borrow $8,000 against $10,000 in acceptable receivables and we must pay $80 in interest. Similar values are developed for succeeding months.

## Factoring Receivables

When we factor our receivables, they are sold outright to the finance company. Our customers may be instructed to remit the proceeds directly to the purchaser of the account. The factoring firm generally does not have recourse against the seller of the receivables. As a matter of practice, the finance company may do part or all of the credit analysis directly to ensure the quality of the accounts. As a potential sale is being made, the factoring firm may give immediate feedback to the seller on whether the account will be purchased.

When the factoring firm accepts an account, it may forward funds immediately to the seller, in anticipation of receiving payment 30 days later as part of the normal billing process. The factoring firm is not only absorbing risk, but is actually advancing funds to the seller a month earlier than the seller would normally receive them.

For taking the risk, the factoring firm is generally paid on a fee or commission basis equal to 1 to 3 percent of the invoices accepted. In addition, it is paid a lending rate for advancing the funds early. If $100,000 a *month* is processed at a 1 percent commission and a 12 percent annual borrowing rate, the total effective cost will be 24 percent on an *annual* basis.

| | |
|---|---|
| 1% | Commission |
| 1% | Interest for one month (12% annual/12) |
| 2% | Total fee monthly |
| 2% | Monthly × 12 = 24% annual rate |

If one considers that the firm selling the accounts is transferring risk as well as receiving funds early, which may allow it to take cash discounts, the rate may not be considered exorbitant. Also, the firm is able to pass on much of the credit-checking cost to the factor.

### Asset-Backed Public Offerings

A new wrinkle in accounts receivable financing is the sale of receivables by large firms in public offerings. While factoring has long been one way of selling receivables, public offerings of securities backed by receivables as collateral gained respectability when General Motors Acceptance Corporation made a public offering of $500 million of asset-backed securities in December of 1985.

These asset-backed securities are nothing more than the sale of receivables. In former years companies that sold receivables were viewed as short of cash, financially shaky, or in some sort of financial trouble. While this negative perception has yet to be overcome, new issues of receivables-backed securities by companies such as Sperry Corporation, Marine Midland Bank, and General Motors may succeed in changing this perception. Sperry's securities are backed by computer leases, and so far the others are backed by automobile loans. If these new offerings are successful, more firms such as Ford, Chrysler, and other large companies may follow suit.

There are several problems facing the public sale of receivables besides the image problem. Computer systems need to be upgraded to service securities and handle the paperwork. In order for GMAC to offer such a large public issue, they had to change their whole data-processing system to keep track of the loans for the investors in the securities. Additionally, regulatory roadblocks stand in the way of banks (which have the potential to be the largest segment of this new market). Not all loans are repaid, and risk to the purchaser of receivables-backed securities exists. Even though current loss rates on loans were about one half of one percent in late 1985, bad debts can be as much as 5 to 10 percent in tight money markets. What may develop is either self-insured guaranteed payment by the selling company or outside insurance firms guaranteeing the repayment of the offering in total. While this short-term market is still relatively small by money market standards, it could provide an important avenue for corporate liquidity and short-term financing.[3]

## Inventory Financing

We may also borrow against inventory to acquire funds. The extent to which inventory financing may be employed is based on the marketability of the pledged goods, their associated price stability, and the perishability of the product. Another significant factor is the degree of physical control that can be exercised over the product by the lender. We can relate some of these factors to the stages of inventory production and the nature of lender control.

### Stages of Production

Raw materials and finished goods are likely to provide the best collateral, while goods in process may only qualify for a small percentage loan. To the extent that a firm is holding such widely traded raw materials as lumber, metals, grain, cotton, and wool, a loan of 70–80

[3]Ann Monroe, "Sales of Receivables by Big Firms Gain Respect in Public Offerings," *The Wall Street Journal*, December 2, 1985, p. 41.

percent or higher is possible. The lender may only have to place a few quick phone calls to dispose of the goods at market value if the borrower fails to repay the loan. For standardized finished goods, such as tires, canned goods, and building products, the same principle would apply. Goods in process, representing altered but unfinished raw materials, may qualify for a loan of only one fourth their value or less.

### Nature of Lender Control

The methods for controlling pledged inventory go from the simple to the complex, providing ever greater assurances to the lender but progressively higher administrative costs.

**Blanket inventory liens** The simplest method is for the lender to have a general claim against the inventory of the borrower. Specific items are not identified or tagged, and there is no physical control.

**Trust receipts** A trust receipt is an instrument acknowledging that the borrower holds the inventory and proceeds from sales in trust for the lender. Each item is carefully marked and specified by serial number. When sold, the proceeds are transferred to the lender and the trust receipt is cancelled. Also known as *floor planning,* this financing device is very popular among auto and industrial equipment dealers and in the television and home appliance industries. Although it provides tighter control than does the blanket inventory lien, it still does not give the lender direct control over inventory—only a better and more legally enforceable system of tracing the goods.

**Warehousing** Under this arrangement, goods are physically identified, segregated, and stored under the direction of an independent warehousing company. The firm issues a warehouse receipt to the lender, and goods can be moved only with the lender's approval.

The goods may be stored on the premises of the warehousing firm, an arrangement known as *public warehousing,* or on the *borrower's premises*—under a *field warehousing* agreement. When field warehousing is utilized, it is still an independent warehousing company that exercises control over inventory.

### Appraisal of Inventory Control Devices

While the more structured methods of inventory financing appear somewhat restrictive, they are well accepted in certain industries. For example, field warehousing is popular in grain storage and food canning. Well-maintained control measures do involve substantial administrative expenses, and they raise the overall costs of borrowing. The costs of inventory financing may run 15 percent or higher. As is true of accounts receivable financing, the extension of funds is well synchronized with the need.

## Hedging to Reduce Borrowing Risk

Those who are in continual need of borrowed funds for the operations of their firm are exposed to the risk of interest rate changes. One way to partially reduce that risk is through interest rate hedging activities in the financial futures market. Hedging means to engage in a transaction that partially or fully reduces a prior risk exposure.

The financial futures market is set up to allow for the trading of a financial instrument at a future point in time. For example, in January of 1987, one might sell a Treasury bond contract that is to be closed out in June of 1987. The sales price of the June 1987 contract is established by the initial January transaction. However, a subsequent purchase of a June 1987 contract at a currently unknown price will be necessary to close out the transaction. In the futures market, you do not physically deliver the goods; you merely execute a later transaction that reverses your initial position. Thus if you initially sell a futures contract, you later buy a contract that covers your initial sale. If you initially buy a futures contract, the opposite is true and you later sell a contract that covers your initial purchase position.

In the case of selling a Treasury bond futures contract, the subsequent pattern of interest rates will determine whether it is profitable or not. If interest rates go up, Treasury bond prices will go down and you will be able to buy a subsequent contract at a lower price than the sales value you initially established. This will result in a profitable transaction. Note the following example.

| | |
|---|---|
| Sales price, June 1987 Treasury bond contract[4] (sale takes place in January 1987) | $95,000 |
| Purchase price, June 1987 Treasury bond contract (the purchase takes place in June 1987) | 90,000 |
| Profit on futures contract | $ 5,000 |

The reason Treasury bond prices went down is that, as previously mentioned, interest rates and bond prices move in opposite directions, and interest rates went up. The lesson to be learned from this example is that rising interest rates can mean profits in the financial futures market if you initially sell a contract and later buy it back.

The financial manager who continually needs to borrow money and fears changes in interest rates can partially hedge his or her position by engaging in the type of futures contract described above. If interest rates do rise, the extra cost of borrowing money to actually finance the business can be offset by the profit on a futures contract. If interest rates go down, there will be a loss on the futures contract as bond prices go up, but this will be offset by the more desirable lower borrowing costs of financing the firm.

The financial futures market can be used to partially or fully hedge against almost any financial event. In addition to Treasury bonds, trades may be initiated in Treasury bills, certificates of deposits, GNMA certificates[5] and many other instruments.[6] The trades may be executed on such exchanges as the Chicago Board of Trade, the Chicago Mercantile Exchange, or the New York Futures Exchange.

## Summary

A firm in search of short-term financing must be aware of all the institutional arrangements that are available. The easiest access is to trade credit provided by suppliers as a natural outgrowth of the buying

[4]Only a small percentage of the actual dollars involved must be invested to initiate the contract. This is known as margin.

[5]GNMA stands for Government National Mortgage Association, also known as Ginnie Mae.

[6]For a more complete discussion of corporate hedging in the futures market, see "Commodities and Financial Futures" in Chapter 15 of Geoffrey Hirt and Stanley Block, *Fundamentals of Investment Management*, 2nd ed. (Homewood, Ill.: Richard D. Irwin, 1986).

and reselling of goods. Larger firms tend to be net providers of trade credit, while smaller firms are net users.

Bank financing is usually in the form of short-term, self-liquidating loans. A financially strong customer will be offered the prime, or lowest rate, with the rates to other accounts scaled up appropriately. The use of compensating balances tends to increase the effective yield to the bank and serves as a device to compensate the bank for the many services it provides to a commercial account.

An alternative to bank credit for the large, prestigious firm is the use of commercial paper. Though generally issued at a rate below prime, it is an impersonal means of financing that may "dry up" during difficult financing periods.

Firms are also turning to foreign sources of funds, either through the Eurodollar market (foreign dollar loans) or through borrowing foreign currency directly.

By using a secured form of financing, the firm ties its borrowing requirements directly to its asset buildup. We may pledge our accounts receivable as collateral or sell them outright, as well as borrow against inventory. Though secured-asset financing devices may be expensive, they may well fit the credit needs of the firm, particularly those of a small firm that cannot qualify for premium bank financing or the commercial paper market.

Finally, the financial manager may wish to consider the use of hedging through the financial futures market. The consequences of rapid interest rate changes can be reduced through participation in the financial futures market.

## List of Terms

**spontaneous sources of funds**
**net trade credit**
**self-liquidating loan**
**prime rate**
**compensating balances**
**term loan**
**commercial paper**
**installment loan**
**Eurodollar loan**
**discounted loan**
**factoring receivables**
**asset-backed public offerings**
**pledging receivables**
**blanket inventory liens**
**trust receipt**
**public warehousing**
**field warehousing**
**financial futures market**
**hedging**

## Discussion Questions

1. Under what circumstances would it be advisable to borrow money to take a cash discount?
2. Discuss the relative use of credit between large and small firms. Which group is generally in the net creditor position, and why?
3. What is the prime interest rate? How does the average bank customer fare in regard to the prime interest rate? Are companies ever allowed by banks to borrow at less than prime?
4. What advantages do compensating balances have for banks? Are the advantages to banks necessarily disadvantages to corporations?
5. A borrower is often confronted with a stated interest rate and an effective interest rate. What is the difference, and which one should the financial manager recognize as the true cost of borrowing?
6. Commercial paper may show up on corporate balance sheets as either a current asset or a current liability. Explain this statement.
7. What are the advantages of commercial paper in comparison with bank borrowing at the prime rate? What are the disadvantages?
8. Discuss the major types of collateralized short-term loans.
9. What is an asset-backed public offering?
10. What is meant by hedging in the financial futures market to offset interest rate risks?

## Problems

1. Compute the cost of not taking the following cash discounts:

   *a.* 2/10, net 50.
   *b.* 2/15, net 40.
   *c.* 3/10, net 45.
   *d.* 3/10, net 180.

2. Your bank will lend you $2,000 for 45 days at a cost of $25 interest. What is your effective rate of interest?

3. Dr. Sixkiller is going to borrow $3,000 for one year at 12 percent interest. What is the effective rate of interest if the loan is discounted?

4. Beasley Furniture Company is borrowing $300,000 for one year at 11 percent from Gateway National Bank. The bank requires a 20 percent compensating balance. What is the effective rate of interest? What would the effective rate be if the company were required to make 12 monthly payments to retire the loan? The principal, as used in Formula 8–6, refers to funds the firm can effectively utilize (amount borrowed − compensating balance).

5. Randall Corporation plans to borrow $200,000 for one year at 12 percent from the Waco State Bank. There is a 20 percent compensating balance requirement. Randall Corporation keeps minimum transaction balances of $10,000 in the normal course of business. This idle cash counts toward meeting the compensating balance requirement.

   What is the effective rate of interest?

6. The treasurer for the Ogden Gold Sox baseball team is seeking a $20,000 loan for 180 days from the 3d National Bank of Ogden. The stated interest rate is 14 percent, and there is a 10 percent compensating balance requirement. The treasurer always keeps a minimum of $1,500 in the baseball team's checking account. These funds count toward meeting any compensating balance requirements.

   What is the effective rate of interest on this loan?

7. Spicer Corporation plans to borrow $100,000. Northwest Bank will lend the money at ½ percent over the prime rate of 11½ percent (12 percent total) and requires a compensating balance of 20 percent. Principal in this case refers to funds that the firm can effectively use in the business.

   What is the effective rate of interest?

   What would the effective rate be if Spicer were required to make four quarterly payments to retire the loan?

8. Your company plans to borrow $5 million for 12 months, and your banker gives you a stated rate of 14 percent interest. You would like to know the effective rate of interest for the following types of loans. (Each of the following parts stands alone.)

*a.* Simple 14 percent interest with a 10 percent compensating balance.
*b.* Discounted interest.
*c.* An installment loan (12 payments).
*d.* Discounted interest with a 5 percent compensating balance.

**9.** If you borrow $4,000 at $500 interest for one year, what is your effective interest cost for the following payment plans?

*a.* Annual payment.
*b.* Semiannual payments.
*c.* Quarterly payments.
*d.* Monthly payments.

**10.** Lewis and Clark Camping-Supplies Inc. is borrowing $45,000 from Western State Bank. The total interest is $12,000. The loan will be paid by making equal monthly payments for the next three years.

What is the effective rate of interest on this installment loan?

**11.** Mr. Hugh Warner is a very cautious business man. His supplier offers trade credit terms of 3/10, net 80. Mr. Warner never takes the discount offered, but he pays his suppliers in 70 days rather than the 80 days allowed so he is sure the payments are never late.

What is Mr. Warner's cost of not taking the cash discount?

**12.** The Reynolds Corporation buys from its suppliers on terms of 2/10, net 40. Reynolds has not been utilizing the discount offered and has been taking 55 days to pay its bills. The suppliers seem to accept this payment pattern, and Reynold's credit rating has not been adversely affected.

Mr. Duke, Reynolds Corporation vice president, has suggested that the company begin to take the discount offered. Duke proposes that the company borrow from its bank at a stated rate of 14 percent. The bank requires a 20 percent compensating balance on these loans. Current account balances would not be available to meet any of this compensating balance requirement.

Do you agree with Mr. Duke's proposal?

**13.** In Problem 12, if the compensating balance requirement were 10 percent instead of 20 percent, would you change your answer? Do the appropriate calculation.

**14.** Burt's Department Store needs $300,000 to take a cash discount of 3/10, net 70. A banker will loan the money for 60 days at an interest rate of $8,100.

*a.* What is the effective rate on the bank loan?
*b.* How much would it cost (in percentage terms) if Burt did not take the trade discount, but paid the bill in 70 days instead of 10 days?
*c.* Should Burt borrow the money to take the discount?
*d.* If the banker requires a 20 percent compensating balance, how much must Burt borrow to end up with the $300,000?
*e.* What would be the effective interest rate in part *d* if the interest charge for 60 days were $10,125? Should Burt borrow with the 20 percent compensating balance? (he has no funds to count against the compensating balance requirement).

**15.** Ajax Box Company is negotiating with two banks for a $100,000 loan.

Midland Bank requires a 20 percent compensating balance, discounts the loan, and wants to be paid back in four quarterly payments. Central Bank requires a 10 percent compensating balance, does not discount the loan, but wants to be paid back in 12 monthly installments. The stated rate for both banks is 8 percent. Compensating balances will be subtracted from the $100,000 in determining the available funds in part *a*.

*a.* Which loan should Ajax accept?
*b.* Recompute the effective cost of interest, assuming that Ajax ordinarily maintains at each bank $20,000 in deposits which will serve as compensating balances.
*c.* How much did the compensating balances inflate your interest costs? Does your choice of banks change if the assumption in part *b* is correct?

**16.** Ewing Oil Supplies sells to the 12 accounts listed below.

| Account | Receivable Balance Outstanding | Average Age of the Account over the Last Year |
|---|---|---|
| A | $ 50,000 | 35 |
| B | 80,000 | 25 |
| C | 120,000 | 47 |
| D | 10,000 | 15 |

| | | |
|---|---|---|
| E . . . . . . | 250,000 | 35 |
| F . . . . . . | 60,000 | 51 |
| G . . . . . . | 40,000 | 18 |
| H . . . . . . | 180,000 | 60 |
| I . . . . . . | 15,000 | 43 |
| J . . . . . . | 25,000 | 33 |
| K . . . . . . | 200,000 | 41 |
| L . . . . . . | 60,000 | 28 |

J&R Financial Corporation will lend 90 percent against account balances that have averaged 30 days or less; 80 percent for account balances between 30 and 40 days; and 70 percent for account balances between 40 and 45 days. Customers that take over 45 days to pay their bills are not considered as adequate accounts for a loan.

The current prime rate is 12 percent, and J&R Financial Corporation charges 3 percent over prime to Ewing Oil Supplies as its annual loan rate.

*a.* Determine the maximum loan for which Ewing Oil Supplies could qualify.

*b.* Determine how much one month's interest expense would be on the loan balance determined in part *a*.

**17.** The treasurer for Fletcher Iron Works wishes to use financial futures to hedge her interest rate exposure. She will sell five Treasury futures contracts at $72,000 per contract. It is July and the contracts must be closed out in December of this year. Long-term interest rates are currently 12.5 percent. If they increase to 14 percent, assume the value of the contracts will go down by 10 percent. Also, if interest rates do increase by 1.5 percent, assume the firm will have additional interest expense on its business loans and other commitments of $40,500. This expense, of course, is separate from the futures contracts.

*a.* What will be the profit or loss on the futures contract if interest rates go to 14 percent?

*b.* Explain why a profit or loss took place on the futures contracts.

*c.* After considering the hedging in part *a*, what is the net cost to the firm of the increased interest expense of $40,500. What percent of this increased cost did the treasurer effectively hedge away?

*d.* Indicate whether there would be a profit or loss on the futures contracts if interest rates went down.

## Selected References

Abraham, Alfred B. "Factoring—The New Frontier for Commercial Banks." *Journal of Commercial Bank Lending* 53 (April 1971), pp. 32–43.

Baxter, Nevins D., and Harold T. Shapiro. "Compensating Balance Requirements: The Results of a Survey." *Journal of Finance* 19 (September 1964), pp. 483–96.

Block, Stanley B. "Financial and Management Strategy for Bank Holding Companies." *Bank Administration* 48 (August 1972), pp. 14–16.

Crane, Dwight B., and William L. White. "Who Benefits from a Floating Prime Rate?" *Harvard Business Review* 50 (January–February 1972), pp. 121–29.

Denonn, Lester E. "The Security Agreement." *Journal of Commercial Bank Lending* 50 (February 1968), pp. 32–40.

Hawkins, Gregory D. "An Analysis of Revolving Credit Agreements." *Journal of Financial Economics* 59 (March 1982), pp. 59–81.

Hirt, Geoffrey A., and Stanley B. Block. *Fundamentals of Investment Management*, 2nd ed. Homewood, Ill.: Richard D. Irwin, 1986.

James, Christopher. "An Analysis of Bank Loan Rate Indexation." *Journal of Finance* 37 (June 1982), pp. 809–25.

Kolb, Robert W., and Chiang, Raymond. "Improving Performance Using Interest-Rate Futures." *Financial Management* 10 (Autumn 1981), pp. 72–79.

Lev, Baruch. *Financial Statement Analysis: A New Approach*. Englewood Cliffs, N.J.: Prentice-Hall, 1974, chap. 11.

Monroe, Ann. "Sales of Receivables by Big Firms Gain Respect in Public Offerings." *The Wall Street Journal* (December 2, 1985), p. 41.

Nadler, Paul S. "Compensating Balances and the Prime at Twilight." *Harvard Business Review* 50 (January–February 1972), pp. 112–20.

Quarles, J. Carson. "The Floating Lien." *Journal of Commercial Bank Lending* 53 (November 1970), pp. 51–58.

Robichek, Alexander A., and Stewart C. Myers. *Optimal Financing Decisions*. Englewood Cliffs, N.J.: Prentice-Hall, 1965, chap. 5.

Schwartz, Robert A. "An Economic Model of Trade Credit." *Journal of Financial and Quantitative Analysis* 9 (September 1974), pp. 643–58.

Seiden, Martin H. "The Quality of Trade Credit." Occasional Paper No. 87. New York: National Bureau of Economic Research, 1964.

Selden, Richard T. *Trends and Cycles in the Commercial Paper Market.* New York: National Bureau of Economic Research, 1963.

Selected issues of *Federal Reserve Bulletin.*

Smith, Keith V. *Management of Working Capital.* St. Paul: West, 1974.

PART

# FOUR

# The Capital Budgeting Process

## Introduction

A capital budgeting decision is one that involves the allocation of funds to projects that will have a life of at least one year and usually much longer. Examples might include the development of a major new product, a plant site location, or an equipment replacement decision. Because we may be locked into our decision for 10–20 years and large sums of money are usually involved, the capital budgeting decision must be approached with great care. Basic capital budgeting decisions determine whether there is under- or overcapacity in a given firm or within an industry. The problem has been complicated by the introduction of nonprofitable, but at times necessary, government regulations for pollution control and safety provisions.

The capital budgeting decision is of interest not only to students of finance, but also to those who desire careers in accounting, marketing, production management, and a number of other areas. Whether the marketing manager gets a new product approved for production and distribution may be a function of how well he or she provides data into the capital budgeting process and understands the analysis.

Because the capital budgeting process is long term in nature, we must develop a methodology for translating future inflows and outflows to the present. Thus, our first step will be to consider the time value of money in Chapter 9. Our understanding of compound sum, present value, annuities, and yields allows us to move back and forth between the future and the present. The student may be particularly interested in the extensive summary and review material at the end of the chapter.

We then move to the topic of valuation of sources of financing in Chapter 10. By understanding what measures investors use to determine required rates of return and current values for bonds, preferred stock, and common stock, we are also considering what the corporation must pay for these funds. The chapter on valuation thus naturally extends into the next chapter on cost of capital (financing) to the firm. As described in Chapter 11, the cost of capital represents the weighted cost of the various sources of financing to the firm and is generally a minimum standard for accepting an investment. The capital asset pricing model, an analytical approach to relating individual asset returns to market returns, is considered briefly in Chapter 11 and is also covered on an optional basis in Appendix 11A.

In Chapter 12 we bring together the concepts of time value of money and cost of capital to develop actual investment decisions. Though a number of methods of evaluating capital investments are discussed, such as the payback method and the internal rate of return method, the primary emphasis is on the net present value method. Here we discount future flows from an investment at the cost of capital to see whether they equal or exceed the required investment. If the answer is positive, we know that we have earned the cost of financing the project. Because these investment decisions depend upon the aftertax cash flow-generating capability of a project, the tax impact is carefully considered.

In Chapter 13 we study risk in the capital budgeting decision process. Most managers and investors are risk averse—that is, all things being equal, they would prefer a certain predictable outcome of 10 percent, rather than a 50–50 chance of going broke or doubling their money (this is an extreme case). To reflect these preferences we incorporate a penalty for large risk in our decision-making process. A more risky investment may have to provide a higher return than a less risky investment. Since the objective of financial management is to maximize the market value of the firm and the wealth of its shareholders, we must determine the appropriate mix of profitability and risk to achieve this objective. As part of the analytical procedures introduced in the chapter, simulation techniques to approximate future outcomes are considered.

# 9 The Time Value of Money

In 1624 the Indians sold Manhattan Island at the ridiculously low figure of $24. But wait, was it really ridiculous? If the Indians had merely taken the $24 and reinvested it at 6 percent annual interest up to 1987, they would have had $37.0 billion, an amount sufficient to repurchase most of New York City. If the Indians had been slightly more astute and had invested the $24 at 7.5 percent compounded annually, they would now have close to $6,000,000,000,000 ($6 trillion)—and tribal chiefs would now rival oil sheikhs as the richest people in the world. Another popular example is that $1 received 1,987 years ago, invested at 6 percent, could now be used to purchase all the wealth in the world.

While not all examples are this dramatic, the time value of money figures in many day-to-day decisions. Understanding the effective rate on a business loan, the mortgage payment in a real estate transaction, or the true return on an investment is dependent on understanding the time value of money. As long as an investor is able to garner a positive return on idle dollars, distinctions must be made between money received today and money received in the future. The investor/

lender essentially demands that a financial "rent" be paid on his or her funds as current dollars are set aside today in anticipation of higher returns in the future.

## Relationship to the Capital Outlay Decision

The decision to purchase new plant and equipment or to introduce a new product in the market requires using capital allocating or capital budgeting techniques. Essentially, we must determine whether future benefits are sufficiently large to justify current outlays. It is important that we develop the mathematical tools of the time value of money as the first step toward making capital allocating decisions. Let us now examine the basic terminology of "time value of money."

## Compound Sum—Single Amount

In determining the compound sum, we measure the future value of an amount that is allowed to grow at a given interest rate over a period of time. Assume that an investor has $1,000 and wishes to know its worth after four years if it grows at 10 percent per year. At the end of the first year, he will have $1,000 × 1.10, or $1,100. By the end of year two, the $1,100 will have grown to $1,210 ($1,100 × 1.10). The four-year pattern is indicated below.

1st year $1,000 × 1.10 = $1,100
2nd year $1,100 × 1.10 = $1,210
3rd year $1,210 × 1.10 = $1,331
4th year $1,331 × 1.10 = $1,464

After the fourth year, the investor has accumulated $1,464. Because compounding problems often cover a long period of time, a more generalized formula is necessary to describe the compounding procedure. We shall let:

$S$ = Compound sum
$P$ = Principal or present value

$i$ = Interest rate
$n$ = Number of periods

The simple formula is:

$$S = P(1 + i)^n$$

In the present case, $P = \$1000$, $i = 10$ percent, $n = 4$, so we have:

$$S = \$1000(1.10)^4, \text{ or } \$1,000 \times 1.464 = \$1,464$$

The term $(1.10)^4$ is found to equal 1.464 by multiplying 1.10 four times itself (the fourth power) or by using logarithms. An even quicker process is using an interest rate table, such as Table 9–1 for the compound sum of a dollar. With $n = 4$ and $i = 10$ percent, the value is also found to be 1.464.

The table tells us the amount that $1 would grow to if it were invested for any number of periods at a given interest rate. We multiply this factor times any other amount to determine the compound sum. An expanded version of Table 9–1 is presented at the back of the text in Appendix A.

In determining the compound sum, we will shorten our formula from $S = P(1 + i)^n$ to:

$$S = P \times IF_s \qquad (9\text{–}1)$$

where $IF_s$ equals the interest factor found in the table.

If $10,000 were invested for 10 years at 8 percent, the compound sum, based on Table 9–1, would be:

$$S = P \times IF_s \ (n = 10, i = 8\%)$$
$$S = \$10,000 \times 2.159 = \$21,590$$

**Table 9–1**
**Compound sum of $1 ($IF_s$)**

| *Periods* | *1%* | *2%* | *3%* | *4%* | *6%* | *8%* | *10%* |
|---|---|---|---|---|---|---|---|
| 1 . . . | 1.010 | 1.020 | 1.030 | 1.040 | 1.060 | 1.080 | 1.100 |
| 2 . . . | 1.020 | 1.040 | 1.061 | 1.082 | 1.124 | 1.166 | 1.210 |
| 3 . . . | 1.030 | 1.061 | 1.093 | 1.125 | 1.191 | 1.260 | 1.331 |
| 4 . . . | 1.041 | 1.082 | 1.126 | 1.170 | 1.262 | 1.360 | 1.464 |
| 5 . . . | 1.051 | 1.104 | 1.159 | 1.217 | 1.338 | 1.469 | 1.611 |
| 10 . . . | 1.105 | 1.219 | 1.344 | 1.480 | 1.791 | 2.159 | 2.594 |
| 20 . . . | 1.220 | 1.486 | 1.806 | 2.191 | 3.207 | 4.661 | 6.727 |

## Present Value—Single Amount

In recent years, the sports pages have been filled with stories of athletes who receive multimillion dollar contracts for signing with sports organizations. Perhaps you have wondered how the Lakers or Yankees can afford to pay such fantastic sums. The answer may lie in the concept of present value—a sum payable in the future is worth less today than the stated amount.

The present value is the exact opposite of the compound sum. For example, earlier we determined that the compound sum of $1,000 for four periods at 10 percent was $1,464. We could reverse the process to state that $1,464 received four years into the future, with a 10 percent interest or discount rate, is worth only $1,000 today—its present value. The relationship is depicted in Figure 9–1.

The formula for present value is derived from the original formula for the compound sum.

$$S = P(1 + i)^n \text{ Compound sum}$$

$$P = S\left[\frac{1}{(1 + i)^n}\right] \text{Present value}$$

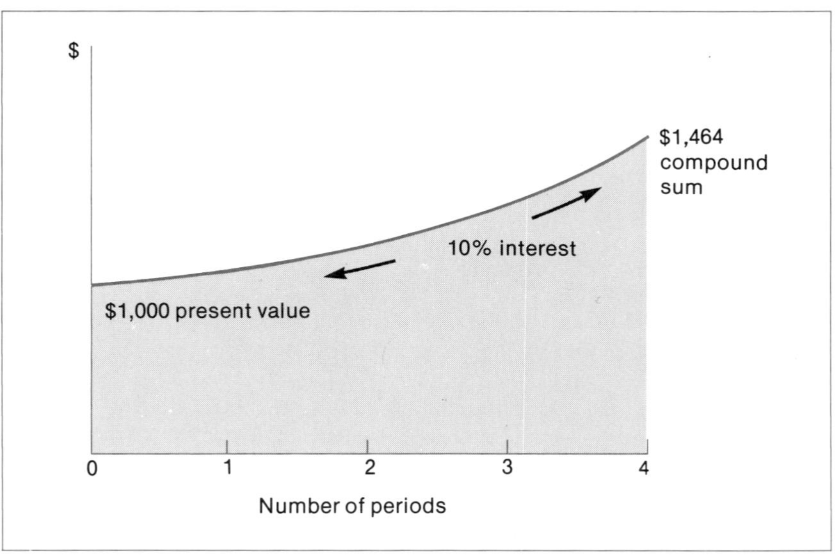


Figure 9–1
Relationship of present value and compound sum

Table 9–2
Present value of $1 ($IF_{pv}$)

| Periods | 1% | 2% | 3% | 4% | 6% | 8% | 10% |
|---|---|---|---|---|---|---|---|
| 1 . . . | 0.990 | 0.980 | 0.971 | 0.962 | 0.943 | 0.926 | 0.909 |
| 2 . . . | 0.980 | 0.961 | 0.943 | 0.925 | 0.890 | 0.857 | 0.826 |
| 3 . . . | 0.971 | 0.942 | 0.915 | 0.889 | 0.840 | 0.794 | 0.751 |
| 4 . . . | 0.961 | 0.924 | 0.888 | 0.855 | 0.792 | 0.735 | 0.683 |
| 5 . . . | 0.951 | 0.906 | 0.863 | 0.822 | 0.747 | 0.681 | 0.621 |
| 10 . . . | 0.905 | 0.820 | 0.744 | 0.676 | 0.558 | 0.463 | 0.386 |
| 20 . . . | 0.820 | 0.673 | 0.554 | 0.456 | 0.312 | 0.215 | 0.149 |

An expanded table is presented in Appendix B.

The present value can be determined by solving for a mathematical solution to the above formula, or by using Table 9–2, the present value of a dollar. In the latter instance, we restate the formula for present value as:

$$P = S \times IF_{pv} \tag{9–2}$$

Once again, $IF_{pv}$ represents the interest factor found in appropriate Table 9–2.

Let's demonstrate that the present value of $1,464, based on our assumptions, is $1,000 today.

$$P = S \times IF_{pv}\,(n = 4,\ i = 10\%)\ [\text{Table 9–2}]$$
$$P = \$1{,}464 \times 0.683 = \$1{,}000$$

## Compound Sum—Annuity

Our calculations up to now have dealt with single amounts rather than annuity values, which may be defined as a series of consecutive payments or receipts of equal amount. The annuity values are generally assumed to occur at the end of each period. If we invest $1,000 at the end of each year for four years and our funds grow at 10 percent, what is the compound sum of this annuity? We may find the compound sum for each payment and then total to find the compound sum of an annuity (Figure 9–2).

The compound sum for the annuity in Figure 9–2 is $4,641. Although this is a four-period annuity, the first $1,000 comes at the *end* of the first period and has but three periods to run, the second $1,000

Figure 9–2
Compounding process for annuity

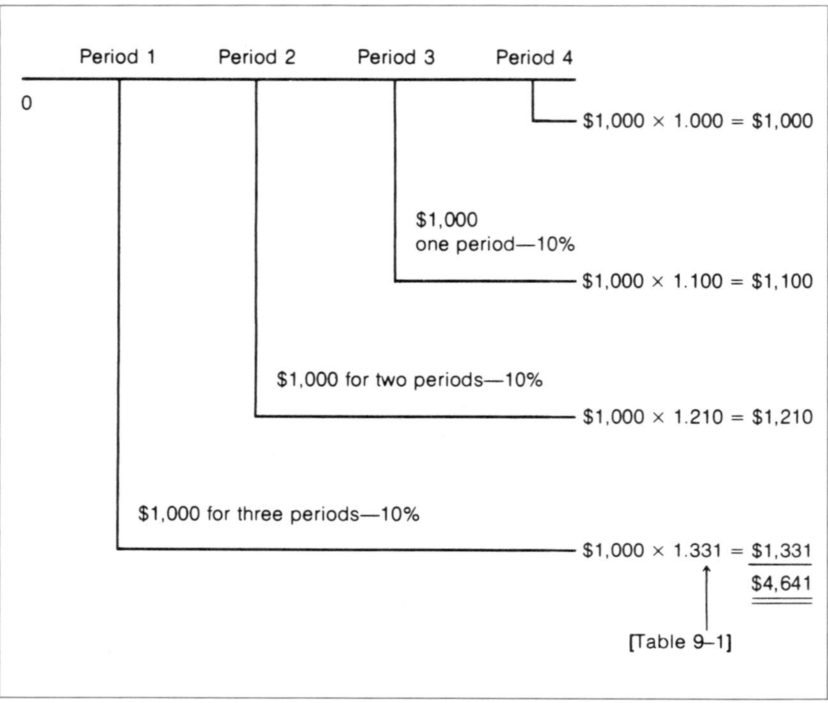


at the end of the second period, with two periods remaining—and so on down to the last $1,000 at the end of the fourth period. The final payment (period 4) is not compounded at all.

Because the process of compounding the individual values is quite tedious, special tables are also available for annuity computations. We shall refer to Table 9–3, the compound sum of an annuity of $1. Let us define $R$ as the annuity value and use Formula 9–3 for the compound sum of an annuity.[1] Note that in the $IF$ term the first subscript, $_s$, indicates compound sum and the second subscript, $_a$, indicates that we are dealing with an annuity.

---

[1] $S = R(1 + i)^{n-1} + R(1 + i)^{n-2} + \ldots R(1 + i)^1 + R(1 + i)^0$

$$= R\left[\frac{(1 + i)^n - 1}{i}\right] = R \times IF_{sa}$$

**Table 9–3**
**Compound sum of an annuity of $1 ($IF_{sa}$)**

| Periods | 1% | 2% | 3% | 4% | 6% | 8% | 10% |
|---|---|---|---|---|---|---|---|
| 1 . . . | 1.000 | 1.000 | 1.000 | 1.000 | 1.000 | 1.000 | 1.000 |
| 2 . . . | 2.010 | 2.020 | 2.030 | 2.040 | 2.060 | 2.080 | 2.100 |
| 3 . . . | 3.030 | 3.060 | 3.091 | 3.122 | 3.184 | 3.246 | 3.310 |
| 4 . . . | 4.060 | 4.122 | 4.184 | 4.246 | 4.375 | 4.506 | 4.641 |
| 5 . . . | 5.101 | 5.204 | 5.309 | 5.416 | 5.637 | 5.867 | 6.105 |
| 10 . . . | 10.462 | 10.950 | 11.464 | 12.006 | 13.181 | 14.487 | 15.937 |
| 20 . . . | 22.019 | 24.297 | 26.870 | 29.778 | 36.786 | 45.762 | 57.275 |
| 30 . . . | 34.785 | 40.588 | 47.575 | 56.085 | 79.058 | 113.280 | 164.490 |

An expanded table is presented in Appendix C.

$$S = R \times IF_{sa}\ (n = 4,\ i = 10\%) \qquad (9\text{–}3)$$
$$S = \$1{,}000 \times 4.641 = \$4{,}641$$

If a wealthy relative offered to set aside $2,500 a year for you for the next 20 years, how much would you have to your credit after 20 years if the funds grew at 8 percent?

$$S = R \times IF_{sa}\ (n = 20,\ i = 8\%)$$
$$S = \$2{,}500 \times 45.762 = \$114{,}405$$

A rather tidy sum considering that only a total of $50,000 has been invested over the 20 years.

## Present Value—Annuity

To find the present value of an annuity, the process is reversed. In theory, each individual payment is discounted back to the present and then all of the discounted payments are added up, yielding the present value of the annuity. Table 9–4 allows us to eliminate extensive calculations and to find our answer directly. In Formula 9–4 the term $A$ refers to the present value of the annuity.[2] Once again, assume that $R = \$1{,}000$, $n = 4$, and $i = 10$ percent—only now we want to know

---

[2] $$A = R\left[\frac{1}{(1+i)}\right]^1 + R\left[\frac{1}{(1+i)}\right]^2 + \ldots R\left[\frac{1}{(1+i)}\right]^n = R\left[\frac{1 - \frac{1}{(1+i)^n}}{i}\right]$$
$$= R \times IF_{pva}$$

**Table 9–4**
**Present value of an annuity of \$1 ($IF_{pva}$)**

| Periods | 1% | 2% | 3% | 4% | 6% | 8% | 10% |
|---|---|---|---|---|---|---|---|
| 1 . . . | 0.990 | 0.980 | 0.971 | 0.962 | 0.943 | 0.926 | 0.909 |
| 2 . . . | 1.970 | 1.942 | 1.913 | 1.886 | 1.833 | 1.783 | 1.736 |
| 3 . . . | 2.941 | 2.884 | 2.829 | 2.775 | 2.673 | 2.577 | 2.487 |
| 4 . . . | 3.902 | 3.808 | 3.717 | 3.630 | 3.465 | 3.312 | 3.170 |
| 5 . . . | 4.853 | 4.713 | 4.580 | 4.452 | 4.212 | 3.993 | 3.791 |
| 8 . . . | 7.652 | 7.325 | 7.020 | 6.733 | 6.210 | 5.747 | 5.335 |
| 10 . . . | 9.471 | 8.983 | 8.530 | 8.111 | 7.360 | 6.710 | 6.145 |
| 20 . . . | 18.046 | 16.351 | 14.877 | 13.590 | 11.470 | 9.818 | 8.514 |
| 30 . . . | 25.808 | 22.396 | 19.600 | 17.292 | 13.765 | 11.258 | 9.427 |

An expanded table is presented in Appendix D.

the present value of the annuity. Note that in the *IF* term the first subscript, $_{pv}$, represents present value and that the second subscript, $_a$, indicates an annuity.

$$A = R \times IF_{pva}(n = 4, i = 10\%) \qquad (9\text{–}4)$$
$$A = \$1{,}000 \times 3.170 = \$3{,}170$$

## Determining the Annuity Value

In our prior discussion of annuities, we assumed that the unknown value was the compound sum or the present value—with specific information available on the annuity value ($R$), the interest rate, and the number of periods or years. In certain cases our emphasis may shift to solving for one of these other values (on the assumption that compound sum or present value is given). For now, we will concentrate on determining an unknown annuity value.

### Annuity Equaling a Compound Sum

Assuming that we wish to accumulate \$4,641 after four years at a 10 percent interest rate, how much must be set aside at the end of each of the four periods? We take the previously developed statement for the compound sum of an annuity and solve for $R$.

$$S = R \times IF_{sa}$$
$$R = \frac{S}{IF_{sa}} \tag{9–5}$$

$S$ is given as $4,641, and $IF_{sa}$ (interest factor) may be determined from Table 9–3 (compound sum of an annuity). Whenever you are working with an annuity problem relating to compound sum, you employ Table 9–3, regardless of the variable that is unknown. For $n = 4$ and $i = 10$ percent, $IF_{sa}$ is 4.641. Thus $R$ equals $1,000.

$$R = \frac{S}{IF_{sa}} = \frac{\$4{,}641}{4.641} = \$1{,}000$$

The solution is the exact reverse of that previously presented under the discussion of the compound sum of an annuity. As a second example, assume that the director of the Women's Tennis Association must set aside an equal amount for each of the next 10 years in order to accumulate $100,000 in retirement funds and that the return on deposited funds is 6 percent. Solve for the annual contribution, $R$.

$$R = \frac{S}{IF_{sa}} \quad (n = 10,\ i = 6\%)$$

$$R = \frac{\$100{,}000}{13.181} = \$7{,}587$$

## Annuity Equaling a Present Value

In this instance, we assume that you know the present value and that you wish to determine what size annuity can be equated to that amount. Suppose that your wealthy uncle presents you with $10,000 now to help you get through the next four years of college. If you are able to earn 6 percent on deposited funds, how much can you withdraw at the end of each year for four years? We need to know the value of an annuity equal to a given present value. We take the previously developed statement for the present value of an annuity and reverse it to solve for $R$.

$$A = R \times IF_{pva} \quad (9\text{–}6)$$

$$R = \frac{A}{IF_{pva}}$$

The appropriate table is Table 9–4 (present value of an annuity). We determine an answer of $2,886.

$$R = \frac{A}{IF_{pva}} \ (n = 4, i = 6\%)$$

$$R = \frac{\$10{,}000}{3.465} = \$2{,}886$$

The flow of funds would follow the pattern in Table 9–5. Annual interest is based on the beginning balance for each year.

**Table 9–5**
**Relationship of present value to annuity**

| Year | Beginning Balance | Annual Interest (6 percent) | Annual Withdrawal | Ending Balance |
|---|---|---|---|---|
| 1 . . . . . | $10,000.00 | $600.00 | $2,886.00 | $7,714.00 |
| 2 . . . . . | 7,714.00 | 462.84 | 2,886.00 | 5,290.84 |
| 3 . . . . . | 5,290.84 | 317.45 | 2,886.00 | 2,722.29 |
| 4 . . . . . | 2,722.29 | 163.71 | 2,886.00 | 0 |

The same process can be used to indicate necessary repayments on a loan. Suppose that a homeowner signs a $40,000 mortgage to be repaid over 20 years at 8 percent interest. How much must he or she pay annually to eventually liquidate the loan? In other words, what annuity paid over 20 years is the equivalent of a $40,000 present value with an 8 percent interest rate?

$$R = \frac{A}{IF_{pva}} \ (n = 20, i = 8\%)$$

$$R = \frac{\$40{,}000}{9.818} = \$4{,}074$$ [3]

[3]The actual mortgage could be further refined into monthly payments of approximately $340.

Part of the payments to the mortgage company will go toward the payment of interest, with the remainder applied to debt reduction, as indicated in Table 9–6.

**Table 9–6**
**Payoff table for loan (amortization table)**

| Period | Beginning Balance | Annual Payment | Annual Interest (8 percent) | Repayment on Principal | Ending Balance |
|---|---|---|---|---|---|
| 1 . . . . | $40,000 | $4,074 | $3,200 | $ 874 | $39,126 |
| 2 . . . . | 39,126 | 4,074 | 3,130 | 944 | 38,182 |
| 3 . . . . | 38,182 | 4,074 | 3,055 | 1,019 | 37,163 |

If this same process is followed over 20 years, the balance will be reduced to zero. The student might note that the homeowner will pay over $41,000 of *interest* during the term of the loan, as indicated below.

| | |
|---|---|
| Total payments ($4,074 for 20 years) . . . . | $81,480 |
| Repayment of principal . . . . . . . . . . . | −40,000 |
| Payments applied to interest . . . . . . . . | $41,480 |

## Determining the Yield on an Investment

In our discussion thus far, we have considered the following time value of money problems.

| | Formula | Table | Appendix |
|---|---|---|---|
| Compound sum—single amount . . . . . . . | (9–1) $S = P \times IF_s$ | 9–1 | A |
| Present value—single amount . . . . . . . | (9–2) $P = S \times IF_{pv}$ | 9–2 | B |
| Compound sum—annuity . . . . . . . . . . | (9–3) $S = R \times IF_{sa}$ | 9–3 | C |
| Present value—annuity . . . . . . . . . . | (9–4) $A = R \times IF_{pva}$ | 9–4 | D |
| Annuity equaling a compound sum . . . . . | (9–5) $R = \frac{S}{IF_{sa}}$ | 9–3 | C |
| Annuity equaling a present value . . . . . . | (9–6) $R = \frac{A}{IF_{pva}}$ | 9–4 | D |

In each case, we knew three out of the four variables and solved for the fourth. We will follow the same procedure once again, but now the unknown variable will be $i$, the interest rate, or yield on the investment.

### Yield—Present Value of a Single Amount

An investment producing \$1,464 after four years has a present value of \$1,000. What is the interest rate, or yield on the investment?

We take the basic formula for the present value of a single amount and rearrange the terms.

$$P = S \times IF_{pv}$$

$$IF_{pv} = \frac{P}{S} = \frac{\$1{,}000}{\$1{,}464} = 0.683 \qquad (9\text{–}7)$$

The determination of $IF_{pv}$ does not give us the final answer—but in effect, it scales down the problem so that we may ascertain the answer from Table 9–2, the present value of \$1. A portion of Table 9–2 is presented below.

| Periods | 1% | 2% | 3% | 4% | 5% | 6% | 8% | 10% |
|---|---|---|---|---|---|---|---|---|
| 2 . . . . . | 0.980 | 0.961 | 0.943 | 0.925 | 0.907 | 0.890 | 0.857 | 0.826 |
| 3 . . . . . | 0.971 | 0.942 | 0.815 | 0.889 | 0.864 | 0.840 | 0.794 | 0.751 |
| 4 . . . . . | 0.961 | 0.924 | 0.888 | 0.855 | 0.823 | 0.792 | 0.735 | 0.683 |

Read down the left-hand column of the table until you have located the number of periods in question (in this case $n = 4$), and read across the table for $n = 4$ until you have located the computed value of $IF_{pv}$. We see that for $n = 4$ and $IF_{pv}$ equal to 0.683, the interest rate, or yield, is 10 percent. This is the rate that will equate \$1,464 received in four years to \$1,000 today.

If an $IF_{pv}$ value does not fall under a given interest rate, an approximation is possible. For example, with $n = 3$ and $IF_{pv} = 0.861$, 5 percent may be suggested as an approximate answer.

*Interpolation* may also be used to find a more precise answer. In the above example, we write out the two $IF_{pv}$ values that the designated $IF_{pv}$ (0.861) falls between and take the difference between the two.

| | |
|---|---|
| $IF_{pv}$ at 5% . . . . | 0.864 |
| $IF_{pv}$ at 6% . . . . | 0.840 |
| | 0.024 |

We then find the difference between the $IF_{pv}$ value at the lowest interest rate and the designated $IF_{pv}$ value.

| | |
|---|---|
| $IF_{pv}$ at 5% . . . . . . . | 0.864 |
| $IF_{pv}$ designated . . . . | 0.861 |
| | 0.003 |

We next express this value (0.003) as a fraction of the preceding value (0.024) and multiply by the difference between the two interest rates (6 percent minus 5 percent). The value is added to the lower interest rate (5 percent) to get a more exact answer of 5.125 percent rather than the estimated 5 percent.

$$5\% + \frac{0.003}{0.024}(1\%) =$$

$$5\% + 0.125\ (1\%) =$$

$$5\% + 0.125\% = 5.125\%$$

### Yield—Present Value of an Annuity

We may also find the yield related to any other problem. Let's look at the present value of an annuity. Take the basic formula for the present value of an annuity, and rearrange the terms.

$$A = R \times IF_{pva} \qquad \text{(9–8)}$$

$$IF_{pva} = \frac{A}{R}$$

The appropriate table is Table 9–4 (the present value of an annuity of \$1). Assuming that a \$10,000 investment will produce \$1,490 a year for the next 10 years, what is the yield on the investment?

$$IF_{pva} = \frac{A}{R} = \frac{\$10,000}{\$1,490} = 6.710$$

If the student will flip back to Table 9–4 and read across the columns for $n = 10$ periods, he will see that the yield is 8 percent.

The same type of approximated or interpolated yield that applied to a single amount can also be applied to an annuity when necessary.

## Special Considerations in Time Value Analysis

We have assumed that interest was compounded or discounted on an annual basis. This assumption will now be relaxed. Contractual arrangements, such as an installment purchase agreement or a corporate bond contract, may call for semiannual, quarterly, or monthly compounding periods. The adjustment to the normal formula is quite simple. To determine $n$, multiply the number of years by the number of compounding periods during the year. The factor for $i$ is then determined by dividing the quoted annual interest rate by the number of compounding periods.

*Case 1*—Find the compound sum of a \$1,000 investment after five years at 8 percent annual interest, compounded semiannually.

$$n = 5 \times 2 = 10 \qquad i = 8 \text{ percent} \div 2 = 4 \text{ percent}$$

Since the problem calls for the compound sum of a single amount, the formula is $S = P \times IF_s$. Using Table 9–1 for $n = 10$ and $i = 4$ percent, the answer is \$1,480.

$$S = P \times IF_s$$
$$S = \$1{,}000 \times 1.480 = \$1{,}480$$

*Case 2*—Find the present value of 20 quarterly payments of \$2,000 each to be received over the next five years. The stated interest rate is 8 percent per annum. The problem calls for the present value of an annuity.

$$A = R \times IF_{pva}\ (n = 20,\ i = 2\%)\ \text{[Table 9–4]}$$
$$A = \$2{,}000 \times 16.351 = \$32{,}702$$

### Patterns of Payment

Time value of money problems may evolve around a number of different payment or receipt patterns. Not every situation will involve a single amount or an annuity. For example, a contract may call for the payment of a different amount each year over a three-year period. To determine present value, each payment is discounted (Table 9–2) to the present and then summed.

(Assume 8% discount rate)

| | | |
|---|---|---|
| 1. | 1,000 × 0.926 = | $ 926 |
| 2. | 2,000 × 0.857 = | 1,714 |
| 3. | 3,000 × 0.794 = | 2,382 |
| | | $5,022 |

A more involved problem might include a combination of single amounts and an annuity. If the annuity will be paid at some time in the future, it is referred to as a deferred annuity and it requires special treatment. Assume the same problem as above, but with an annuity of $1,000 that will be paid at the end of each year from the fourth through the eighth year. With a discount rate of 8 percent, what is the present value of the cash flows?

| | | |
|---|---|---|
| 1. | $1,000 | Present value = $5,022 |
| 2. | 2,000 | |
| 3. | 3,000 | |
| 4. | 1,000 | Five-year annuity |
| 5. | 1,000 | |
| 6. | 1,000 | |
| 7. | 1,000 | |
| 8. | 1,000 | |

We know that the present value of the first three payments is $5,022, but what about the annuity? Let's diagram the five annuity payments.

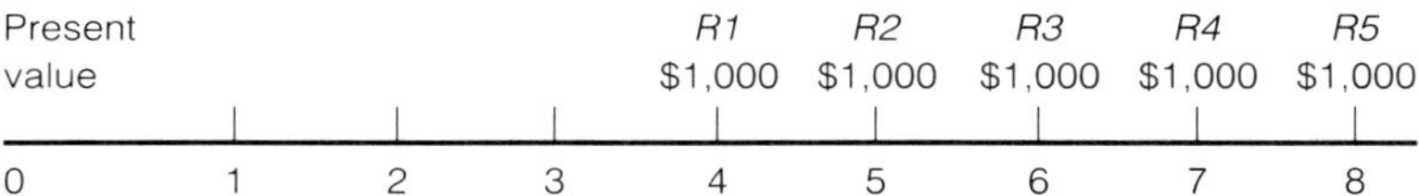


The information source is Table 9–4, the present value of an annuity of $1. For $n = 5$, $i = 8$ percent, the discount factor is 3.993—leaving a "present value" of the annuity of $3,993. However, tabular values only discount to the beginning of the first stated period of an annuity—in this case the beginning of the fourth year, as diagramed below.

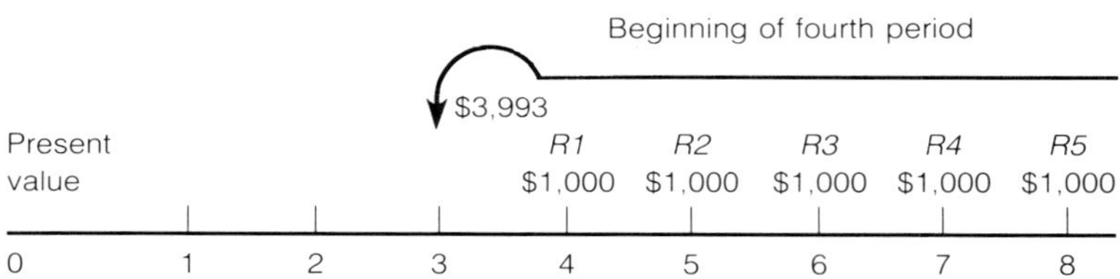


The $3,993 must finally be discounted back to the present. Since this single amount falls at the beginning of the fourth period—in effect, the equivalent of the end of the third period—we discount back for three periods at the stated 8 percent interest rate. Using Table 9–2, we have:

$$P = S \times IF_{pv}(n = 3, i = 8\%)$$
$$P = \$3{,}993 \times 0.794 = \$3{,}170 \text{ (actual present value)}$$

The last step in the discounting process is shown below.

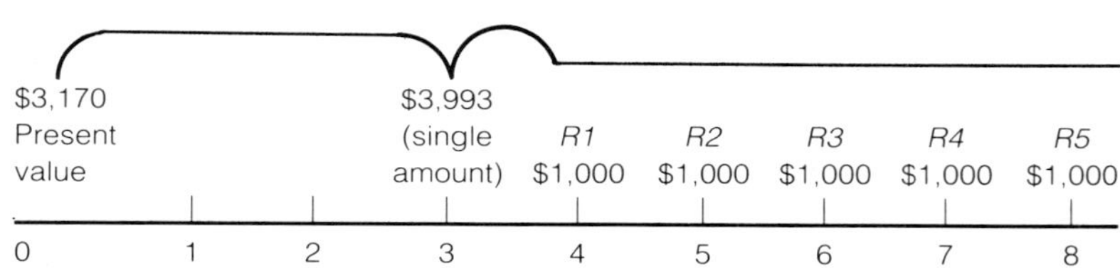


A *second method* for finding the present value of a deferred annuity is to:

1. Find the present value factor of an annuity for the total time period. In this case, where $n = 8$, $i = 8\%$, the $IF_{pva}$ is 5.747.

2. Find the present value factor of an annuity for the total time period (8) minus the deferred annuity period (5).

$$8 - 5 = 3$$
$$n = 3, i = 8\%$$

The $IF_{pva}$ value is 2.577.

3. Subtract the value in step 2 from the value in step 1, and multiply by $R$.

$$\begin{array}{r} 5.747 \\ -\underline{2.577} \\ 3.170 \end{array}$$

$3.170 \times \$1{,}000 = \$3{,}170$ (present value of the annuity)

$3,170 is precisely the same answer for the present value of the annuity as that reached by the first method. The present value of the five-year annuity may now be added to the present value of the inflows over the first three years to arrive at the total value.

| | |
|---|---|
| $5,022 | First three period flows |
| +3,170 | Five-year annuity |
| $8,192 | Total present value |

## Special Review of the Chapter

In working a time value of money problem, the student should determine, first, whether the problem deals with compound sum or present value and, second, whether a single sum or an annuity is involved. The major calculations in Chapter 9 are summarized below.

1. *Compound sum of a single amount.*
   Formula: $S = P \times IF_s$
   Table: 9–1 or Appendix A.
   When to use: In determining the future value of a single amount.
   Sample problem: A invests $1,000 for four years at 10 percent interest. What is the value at the end of the fourth year?

2. *Present value of a single amount.*
   Formula: $P = S \times IF_{pv}$
   Table: 9–2 or Appendix B.
   When to use: In determining the present value of an amount to be received in the future.

Sample problem: A will receive $1,000 after four years at a discount rate of 10 percent. How much is this worth today?

3. *Compound sum of an annuity.*
   Formula: $S = R \times IF_{sa}$
   Table: 9–3 or Appendix C.
   When to use: In determining the future value of a series of consecutive, equal payments (an annuity).
   Sample problem: A will receive $1,000 at the end of each period for four periods. What is the accumulated value (future worth) at the end of the fourth period if money grows at 10 percent?

4. *Present value of an annuity.*
   Formula: $A = R \times IF_{pva}$
   Table: 9–4 or Appendix D.
   When to use: In determining the present worth of an annuity.
   Sample problem: A will receive $1,000 at the end of each period for four years. At a discount rate of 10 percent, what is the current worth?

5. *Annuity equaling a compound sum.*

$$\text{Formula: } R = \frac{S}{IF_{sa}}$$

   Table: 9–3 or Appendix C.
   When to use: In determining the size of an annuity that will equal a future value.
   Sample problem: A needs $1,000 after four periods. With an interest rate of 10 percent, how much must be set aside at the end of each period to accumulate this amount?

6. *Annuity equaling a present value.*

$$\text{Formula: } R = \frac{A}{IF_{pva}}$$

   Table: 9–4 or Appendix D.
   When to use: In determining the size of an annuity equal to a given present value.
   Sample problems:
   *a.* What four-year annuity is the equivalent of $1,000 today with an interest rate of 10 percent?

*b.* A deposits \$1,000 today and wishes to withdraw funds equally over four years. How much can he withdraw at the end of each year if funds earn 10 percent?

*c.* A borrows \$1,000 for four years at 10 percent interest. How much must be repaid at the end of each year?

7. *Determining the yield on an investment.*

| *Formulas* | *Tables* | |
|---|---|---|
| a. $IF_{pv} = \frac{P}{S}$ | 9–2, Appendix B | Yield—present value of a single amount |
| b. $IF_{pva} = \frac{A}{R}$ | 9–4, Appendix D | Yield—present value of an annuity |

When to use: In determining the interest rate ($i$) that will equate an investment with future benefits.

Sample problem: A invests \$1,000 now, and the funds are expected to increase to \$1,360 after four periods.

What is the yield on the investment:

$$\text{Use } IF_{pv} = \frac{P}{S}.$$

8. *Less than annual compounding periods.*

| | | | |
|---|---|---|---|
| Semiannual | Multiply $n \times 2$ | Divide $i$ by 2 | (then use normal formula) |
| Quarterly | Multiply $n \times 4$ | Divide $i$ by 4 | |
| Monthly | Multiply $n \times 12$ | Divide $i$ by 12 | |

When to use: If the compounding period is more (or perhaps less) frequent than once a year.

Sample problem: A invests \$1,000 compounded semiannually at 8 percent per annum over four years. Determine the future sum.

9. *Patterns of payment—deferred annuity.*

| *Formulas* | *Tables* | |
|---|---|---|
| $A = R \times IF_{pva}$ | 9–4, Appendix D | Method 1 |
| $P = S \times IF_{pv}$ | 9–2, Appendix B | |

When to use: If an annuity begins in the future.

Sample problem: A will receive \$1,000 per period, starting at the end of the fourth period and running through the end of the eighth period. With a discount rate of 8 percent, determine the present value.

The student is encouraged to work the many problems found at the end of the chapter.

## List of Terms

| | |
|---|---|
| **compound sum** | **compound sum of annuity** |
| **present value** | **semiannual compounding** |
| **interest factor (*IF*)** | **annuity** |
| **discount rate** | **yield** |

## Discussion Questions

1. How is the compound sum (Appendix A) related to the present value of a single sum (Appendix B)?
2. How is the present value of a single sum (Appendix B) related to the present value of an annuity (Appendix D)?
3. Why does money have a time value?
4. Does inflation have anything to do with making a dollar today worth more than a dollar tomorrow?
5. Adjust the annual formula for a compound sum of a single amount at 12 percent for 10 years to a semiannual compounding formula. What are the interest factors ($IF_s$) for the two assumptions? Why are they different?
6. If, as an investor, you had a choice of daily, monthly, or quarterly compounding, which would you choose? Why?
7. What is a deferred annuity?
8. List five different financial applications of the time value of money.

## Problems

1. What is the present value of:

   *a.* $8,000 in 10 years at 6 percent?
   *b.* $16,000 in 5 years at 12 percent?

*c.* $25,000 in 15 years at 8 percent?
*d.* $1,000 in 40 periods at 20 percent?

**2.** If you invest $12,000 today, how much will you have:

*a.* In 6 years at 7 percent?
*b.* In 15 years at 12 percent?
*c.* In 25 years at 10 percent?
*d.* In 25 years at 10 percent (compounded semiannually)?

**3.** How much would you have to invest today to receive:

*a.* $12,000 in 6 years at 12 percent?
*b.* $8,000 in 5 years at 20 percent?
*c.* $20,000 in 10 years at 6 percent?
*d.* $15,000 in 15 years at 8 percent?
*e.* $10,000 in 20 years at 25 percent?
*f.* $5,000 each year for 10 years at 8 percent?
*g.* $30,000 each year for 20 years at 6 percent?
*h.* $40,000 each year for 40 years at 5 percent?

**4.** Mr. Elite invests $80,000 in an old, classic Rolls-Royce. He expects it to increase 12 percent per year for the next five years. How much will his car be worth after five years?

**5.** Mr. Sampson will receive $6,500 a year for the next 14 years from his trust. If an 8 percent interest rate is applied, what is the current value of their future payments?

**6.** Ms. Graham has been depositing $1,500 in her savings account every December starting in 1977. Her account earns 5 percent, compounded annually. How much will she have on December of 1986? (Assume that a deposit is made in 1986.)

**7.** At a growth rate (interest) rate of 8 percent annually, how long will it take for a sum to double? to triple? Select the year that is closest to the correct answer.

**8.** If you owe $4,000 payable at the end of five years, what amount should your creditor accept in payment immediately if he or she could earn 7 percent on his or her money?

**9.** Mr. Flint retired as president of the Color Tile Company but is currently on a consulting contract for $45,000 per year for the next 10 years.

*a*. If Mr. Flint's opportunity cost (potential return) is 10 percent, what is the present value of his consulting contract?
*b*. Assuming that Mr. Flint will not retire for two more years and will not start to receive his 10 payments until the end of the third year, what would be the value of his deferred annuity?

**10.** Your grandfather has offered you a choice of one of the three following alternatives: $5,000 now; $1,000 a year for eight years; or $12,000 at the end of eight years. Assuming you could earn 11 percent annually, which alternative should you choose? If you could earn 12 percent annually, would you still choose the same alternative?

**11.** You need $30,750 at the end of eight years, and your only investment outlet is a 12 percent long-term certificate of deposit (compounded annually). With the certificate of deposit, you make an initial investment at the beginning of the first year.

*a*. What single payment could be made at the beginning of the first year to achieve this objective?
*b*. What amount could you pay at the end of each year annually for eight years to achieve this same objective?

**12.** On January 1, 1985, Mr. Strong bought 100 shares of stock for $13 per share. On December 31, 1987, he sold the stock for $20.50 per share.

What is his annual rate of return? Interpolate to find the exact answer.

**13.** Dr. Emily Smart bought 1,000 shares of Quality Steel Products stock for $5 per share on January 1, 1982. Using interpolation, find her exact annual rate of return if she sells the stock:

*a*. On December 31, 1983, for $6 per share.
*b*. On December 31, 1986, for $7.85 per share.
*c*. On December 31, 1989, for $11 per share.

**14.** Dr. John Foresight has just invested $2,790 for his son (age one). This money will be used for his son's education 17 years from now. He calculates that he will need $30,000 for his son's education by the time the boy goes to school.

What rate of return will Mr. Foresight need in order to achieve this goal?

**15.** Donald Johnson has just given an insurance company $20,000. In return, he will receive an annuity of $1,800 for 20 years.

At what rate of return must the insurance company invest this $20,000 in order to make the annual payments? Interpolate.

**16.** Brian Hirt started a paper route on January 1, 1980. Every three months, he deposits $250 in his bank account, which earns 8 percent annually but is compounded quarterly. On December 31, 1984, he used the entire balance in his bank account to invest in a certificate of deposit at 12 percent annually.

How much will he have on December 31, 1987?

**17.** Mary Mills has retired after 35 years with the Electric Company. Her total pension funds have an accumulated value of $300,000, and her life expectancy is 18 more years. Her pension fund manager assumes that she can earn an 8 percent return on her assets.

What will her yearly annuity be for the next 18 years?

**18.** Dr. T. Account, an accounting professor, invests $50,000 in a dude ranch that is expected to increase in value by 9 percent per year for the next five years. He will take the proceeds and provide himself with a 10-year annuity.

Assuming a 9 percent interest rate, how much will this annuity be?

**19.** You wish to retire in 20 years, at which time you want to have accumulated enough money to receive an annuity of $12,000 for 25 years after retirement. During the period before retirement you can earn 8 percent annually, while after retirement you can earn 10 percent on your money.

What are your annual contributions to the retirement fund to allow you to receive the $12,000 annuity?

**20.** If you borrow $9,725 and are required to repay the loan in five equal annual installments of $2,500, what is the interest rate associated with the loan?

**21.** If your uncle borrows $50,000 from the bank at 10 percent interest over the eight-year life of the loan, what equal annual payments must be made to discharge the loan, plus pay the bank its required rate of interest (round to the nearest dollar)? How much of his first payment will be applied to interest? To principal? How much of his second payment will be applied to each?

**22.** Darla Lewis has purchased an annuity to begin payment at the end of 1989 (that is the date of the first payment). Assume it is now the end of 1986. The annuity is for $12,000 per year and is designed to last eight years.

If the discount rate for this problem is 11 percent, what is the most she should have paid for this annuity?

**23.** Jim Thomas borrows $70,000 at 12 percent interest toward the purchase of a home. His mortgage is for 30 years.

*a.* How much will his annual payments be? (Although home payments are usually on a monthly basis, we shall do our analysis on an annual basis for ease of computation. We get a reasonably accurate answer.

*b.* How much interest will he pay over the life of the loan?

*c.* How much should he be willing to pay to get out of a 12 percent mortgage and into a 10 percent mortgage with 30 years remaining on the mortgage? Assume that current interest rates are 10 percent. Disregard taxes.

**24.** Your younger sister, Susie, will start college in five years. She has just informed your parents that she wants to go to Collegiate U., which will cost $8,000 per year for four years (assumed to come at the end of each year). Anticipating Susie's ambitions, your parents started investing $1,000 per year five years ago and will continue to do so for five more years.

How much *more* will your parents have to invest each year for the next five years to have the necessary funds for Susie's education? Use 10 percent as the appropriate interest rate throughout this problem (for discounting or compounding).

**25.** Susie (from Problem 24) is now 18 years old (five years have passed), and she wants to get married instead of going to school. Your parents have accumulated the necessary funds for her education.

Instead of her schooling, your parents are paying $2,433 for her current wedding and plan to take a year-end vacation costing $4,000 per year each year for the next three years.

How much will your parents have at the end of three years to help you with graduate school, which you will start then? You plan to work on a master's and perhaps a Ph.D. If graduate school costs \$5,450 per year, approximately how long will you be able to stay in school based on these funds? Use 10 percent as the appropriate interest rate throughout this problem.

**26.** You are chairperson of the investment retirement fund for the local Actors Guild. You are asked to set up a fund of semiannual payments to be compounded semiannually to accumulate a sum of \$50,000 after 10 years at an 8 percent annual rate (20 payments). The first payment into the fund is to take place six months from today, and the last payment is to take place at the end of the tenth year.

*a.* Determine how much the semiannual payment should be. (Round all values to whole numbers.)

On the day after the sixth payment is made (the beginning of the fourth year), the interest rate goes up to a 10 percent annual rate, and you can earn a 10 percent annual rate on the funds that have accumulated as well as on all future payments into the fund. Interest is to be compounded semiannually on all funds.

*b.* Determine how much the revised semiannual payments should be after this rate change (there are 14 remaining payments and compounding dates). The next payment will be in the middle of the fourth year. (Round all values to whole numbers.)

## Selected References

Bierman, Harold, Jr.; Charles P. Bonini; and Warren H. Hausman. *Quantitative Analysis for Business Decisions*. 7th ed. Homewood, Ill.: Richard D. Irwin, 1986.

———; and Seymour Smidt. *The Capital Budgeting Decision*. 5th ed. New York: Macmillan, 1980.

Boness, A. James. *Capital Budgeting*. New York: Praeger, 1972.

Cissell, Robert, and Helen Cissell. *Mathematics of Finance*. 4th ed. Boston: Houghton Mifflin, 1972.

Draper, Jean E., and Jane S. Klingman. *Mathematical Analysis*. New York: Harper & Row, 1967.

Howell, James E., and Daniel Teichroew. *Mathematical Analysis for Business Decisions*. Rev. ed. Homewood, Ill.: Richard D. Irwin, 1971.

Jean, William H. *Capital Budgeting: The Economic Evaluation of Investment Projects*. Scranton, Pa.: International Textbook, 1969.

Johnson, R. W. *Capital Budgeting*. Belmont, Calif.: Wadsworth, 1970.

Osteryoung, Jerome. *Capital Budgeting: Long-Term Asset Selection*. Columbus, Ohio: Grid, 1974, chap. 3.

Peterson, David E. *A Quantitative Framework for Financial Management*. Homewood, Ill.: Richard D. Irwin, 1969.

Solomon, Ezra. "The Arithmetic of Capital-Budgeting Decisions." *Journal of Business* 29 (April 1956), pp. 124–29.

# 10 Valuation and Rates of Return

In Chapter 9 we considered the basic principles of the time value of money. In this chapter, we will use many of those concepts to determine how financial assets (bonds, preferred stock, and common stock) are valued and how investors establish the rates of return they demand. In the next chapter we will use material from this chapter to determine the overall cost of financing to the firm. We merely turn the coin over. Once we know how much bondholders and stockholders demand in the way of rates of return, we then observe what the corporation is required to pay them in order to attract their funds. The cost of corporate financing (capital) is subsequently used in analyzing whether a project is acceptable for investment or not. These relationships are depicted in Figure 10–1.

## Valuation Concepts

The valuation of a financial asset is based on determining the present value of future cash flows. Thus, we need to know the value of future cash flows and the discount rate to be applied to the future cash flows to determine the current value.

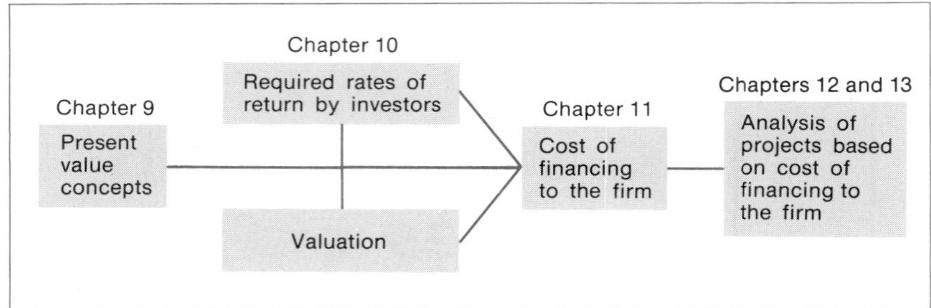


**Figure 10–1**
**The relationship between time value of money, required return, cost of financing, and investment decisions**

The market-determined required rate of return, which is the discount rate, depends on the market's perceived level of risk associated with the individual security. Also important is the idea that required rates of return are competitively determined among the many companies seeking financial capital. For example, IBM, due to its low financial risk, relatively high return, and strong market position in computers, is likely to raise debt capital at a significantly lower cost than can Armco Steel or LTV, two financially troubled firms. This implies that investors are willing to accept low return for low risk, and vice versa. In the way described above, the market allocates capital to companies based on risk, efficiency, and expected returns—which are based to a large degree on past performance. The reward to the financial manager for efficient use of capital in the past is a lower required return for investors than that of competing companies that did not manage their financial resources as well.

Throughout the balance of this chapter, we apply concepts of valuation to corporate bonds, preferred stock, and common stock. Although we describe the basic characteristics of each form of security as part of the valuation process, extended discussion of each security is deferred until later chapters.

## Valuation of Bonds

As previously stated, the value of a financial asset is based on the concept of the present value of future cash flows. Let's apply this approach to bond valuation. A bond provides an annuity stream of interest payments and a $1,000 principal payment at maturity.[1] These cash flows are discounted at $Y$, the yield to maturity. The value of $Y$ is determined in the bond markets and represents the required rate of return for bonds of a given risk and maturity. More will be said about the concept of yield to maturity in the next section.

The price of a bond is thus equal to the present value of regular interest payments discounted by the yield to maturity added to the present value of the principal (also discounted by the yield to maturity).

This relationship can be expressed mathematically as follows.

$$P_b = \sum_{t=1}^{n} \frac{I_t}{(1 + Y)^t} + \frac{P_n}{(1 + Y)^n} \qquad (10\text{–}1)$$

where

$P_b$ = Price of the bond
$I_t$ = Interest payments
$P_n$ = Principal payment at maturity
$t$ = Number corresponding to a period; running from 1 to $n$
$n$ = Total number of periods
$Y$ = Yield to maturity (or required rate of return)

The first term in the equation says to take the sum of the present values of the interest payments ($I_t$); the second term directs you to take the present value of the principal payment at maturity ($P_n$). The discount rate used throughout the analysis is the yield to maturity ($Y$). The answer derived is referred to as $P_b$ (the price of the bond). The analysis is carried out for $n$ periods.

Let's assume that $I_t$ (interest payments) equals $100; $P_n$ (principal payment at maturity) equals $1,000; $Y$ (yield to maturity) is 10 percent; and $n$ (total number of periods) equals 20. We could say that $P_b$ (the price of the bond) equals:

$$P_b = \sum_{t=1}^{20} \frac{\$100}{(1 + .10)^t} + \frac{\$1{,}000}{(1 + .10)^{20}}$$

Although the price of the bond could be determined with logarithms, it is much simpler to use present value tables. We take the present

---

[1]The assumption is that the bond has a $1,000 par value. If the par value is higher or lower, then this value would be discounted to the present from the maturity date.

value of the interest payments and then add this value to the present value of the principal payment at maturity.

**Present value of interest payments** In this case, we determine the present value of a $100 annuity for 20 years.[2] The discount rate is 10 percent. Using Appendix D, the present value of an annuity, we find the following:

$$A = R \times IF_{pva}\ (n = 20, i = 10\%)$$
$$A = \$100 \times 8.514 = \$851.40$$

**Present value of principal payment (par value) at maturity** This single value of $1,000 will be received after 20 years. Note the term *principal payment at maturity* is used interchangeably with *par value* or *face value* of the bond. We discount $1,000 back to the present at 10 percent. Using Appendix B, the present value of a single amount, we find the following:

$$P = S \times IF_{pv}\ (n = 20, i = 10\%)$$
$$P = \$1{,}000 \times .149 = \$149$$

The current price of the bond, based on the present value of interest payments and the present value of the principal payment at maturity, is $1,000.40.

| | |
|---|---|
| Present value of interest payments . . . . . . . . . . | $ 851.40 |
| Present value of principal payment at maturity . . . . | 149.00 |
| Total present value, or price, of the bond . . . . . . | $1,000.40 |

The price of the bond in this case is essentially the same as its par, or stated, value to be received at maturity of $1,000.[3] This is because the annual interest rate is 10 percent (the annual interest payment of $100 divided by $1,000) and the yield to maturity, or discount rate, is also 10 percent. When the interest rate on the bond and the yield to maturity are equal, the bond will trade at par value. Later, we shall

---

[2] For now we are using *annual* interest payments for simplicity. Later in the discussion, we will shift to semiannual payments, and more appropriately determine the value of a bond.

[3] The slight difference is due to the rounding procedures in the tables.

examine the mathematical effects of varying the yield to maturity above or below the interest rate on the bond. But first, let's more fully examine the concept of yield to maturity.

## Concept of Yield to Maturity

In the previous example the yield to maturity that was used as the discount rate was 10 percent. The yield to maturity, or discount rate, is the required rate of return by bondholders. The bondholder, or any investor for that matter, will allow *three* factors to influence his or her required rate of return.

*1. The required Real Rate of Return*—This is the rate of return that the investor demands for giving up current use of the funds on a noninflation-adjusted basis. It is the financial "rent" that the investor charges for using his or her funds for one year, five years, or any given time period. Historically, the real rate of return demanded by investors has been about 2 to 3 percent. Throughout the 1980s the real rate of return has been much higher; that is, 5 to 7 percent.

*2. Inflation Premium*—In addition to the real rate of return discussed above, the investor requires a premium to compensate for the eroding effect of inflation on the value of the dollar. It would hardly satisfy an investor to have a 3 percent total rate of return in a 5 percent inflationary economy. Under such circumstances, the lender (investor) would be paying the borrower 2 percent (in purchasing power) for use of the funds. This would represent an irrational course of action. No one wishes to *pay* another party to use his or her funds. The inflation premium added to the real rate of return ensures that this will not happen. The size of the inflation premium will be based on the investor's expectations about future inflation. In the 1980s the inflation premium has been of the magnitude of 3 to 4 percent. In the late 1970s it was in excess of 10 percent.

If one combines the real rate of return (part *a*) and the inflation premium (part *b*), the *risk-free rate of return* is determined. This is the rate that compensates the investor for the current use of his or her funds and for the loss in purchasing power due to inflation, but not for taking risks. As an example, if the real rate of return were 3 percent and the inflation premium were 4 percent, we would say the risk-free rate of return is 7 percent.[4]

*3. Risk Premium*—We must now add the risk premium to the risk-free rate of return. This is a premium associated with the special risks of a given investment. Of primary interest to us are two types of risks: *business risk* and *financial risk*. Business risk relates to the inability of the firm to hold its competitive position and maintain stability and growth in its earnings. Financial risk relates to the inability of the firm to meet its debt obligations as they come due. In addition to the two forms of risk mentioned above, the risk premium will be greater or less for different types of investments. For example, because bonds possess a contractual obligation for the firm to pay interest to bondholders, they are considered less risky than common stock where no such obligation exists.[5]

The risk premium of an investment may range from as low as zero on a very short-term U.S. government-backed security to 10 to 15 percent on a gold mining expedition. The typical risk premium is 2 to 6 percent. We shall assume that in the investment we are examining that the risk premium is 3 percent. If we add this risk premium to the two components of the risk-free rate of return developed in parts *a* and *b*, we arrive at an overall required rate of return of 10 percent.

| | |
|---|---|
| + Real rate of return . . . . . . | 3% |
| + Inflation premium . . . . . . | 4 |
| = Risk-free rate . . . . . . . . | 7% |
| + Risk premium . . . . . . . . | 3 |
| = Required rate of return . . . . | 10% |

In this instance, we assume we are evaluating the required return on a bond issued by a firm. If the security had been the common stock of the same firm, the risk premium might be 5 to 6 percent and the required rate of return 12 to 13 percent.

[4]Actually, a slightly more accurate representation would be: Risk-free rate = (1 + real rate of return) (1 + inflation premium) − 1. We would show: (1.03) (1.04) − 1 = 1.0712 − 1 = .0712 = 7.12 percent.

[5]On the other hand, common stock carries the potential for unlimited return when the corporation is very profitable.

Finally, in concluding this section, you should recall that the required rate of return on a bond is effectively the same concept as required yield to maturity.

### Changing the Yield to Maturity and the Impact on Bond Valuation

In the earlier bond value calculation, we assumed the interest rate was 10 percent ($100 annual interest on a $1,000 par value bond) and the yield to maturity was also 10 percent. Under those circumstances, the price of the bond was basically equal to par value. Now let's assume that conditions in the market cause the yield to maturity to change.

**Increase in inflation premium** For example, assume the inflation premium goes up from 4 to 6 percent. All else remains constant. The required rate of return would now be 12 percent.

| | |
|---|---|
| + Real rate of return . . . . . . | 3% |
| + Inflation premium . . . . . . | ⑥ |
| = Risk-free rate . . . . . . . . | 9% |
| + Risk premium . . . . . . . . | 3 |
| = Required rate of return . . . . | 12% |

With the required rate of return, or yield to maturity, now at 12 percent, the price of the bond will change.[6] A bond that only pays 10 percent interest when the required rate of return (yield to maturity) is 12 percent will fall below its current value of approximately $1,000. The new price of the bond, as computed below, is $850.90.

*Present value of interest payments*—We take the present value of a $100 annuity for 20 years. The discount rate is 12 percent. Using Appendix D:

$$A = R \times IF_{pva} \, (n = 20, i = 12\%)$$
$$A = \$100 \times 7.469 = \$746.90$$

[6]Of course, the required rate of return on all other financial assets will also go up proportionally.

*Present value of principal payment at maturity*—We take the present value of \$1,000 after 20 years. The discount rate is 12 percent. Using Appendix B:

$$P = S \times IF_{pv} (n = 20, i = 12\%)$$
$$P = \$1{,}000 \times .104 = \$104$$

*Total present value*—

| | |
|---|---|
| Present value of interest payments . . . . . . . . . . | \$746.90 |
| Present value of principal payment at maturity . . . . | 104.00 |
| Total present value, or price, of the bond . . . . . . | \$850.90 |

In this example, we assumed that increasing inflation caused the required rate of return (yield to maturity) to go up and the bond price to fall by approximately \$150. The same effect would take place if the business risk increased or the demanded level for the *real* rate of return became higher.

**Decrease in inflation premium** Of course, the opposite effect would happen if the required rate of return went down because of lower inflation, less risk, or other factors. Let's assume the inflation premium declines and the required rate of return (yield to maturity) goes down to 8 percent.

The 20-year bond with the 10 percent interest rate would now sell for \$1,196.80.

*Present value of interest payments*—

$$A = R \times IF_{pva} (n = 20, i = 8\%) \quad \text{[Appendix D]}$$
$$A = \$100 \times 9.818 = \$981.80$$

*Present value of principal payment at maturity*—

$$P = S \times IF_{pv} (n = 20, i = 8\%) \quad \text{[Appendix B]}$$
$$P = \$1{,}000 \times .215 = \$215$$

*Total present value*—

| | |
|---|---|
| Present value of interest payments . . . . . . . . . . | \$ 981.80 |
| Present value of principal payment at maturity . . . . | 215.00 |
| Total present value, or price, of the bond . . . . . . | \$1,196.80 |

The price of the bond is now trading at $196.80 over par value. This is certainly the expected result because the bond is paying 10 percent interest when the yield in the market is only 8 percent. The 2 percent differential on a $1,000 par value bond represents $20 per year. The investor will receive this differential for the next 20 years. The present value of $20 for the next 20 years at the current market rate of interest of 8 percent is approximately $196.80. This explains why the bond is trading at $196.80 over its stated, or par, value.

The further the yield to maturity on a bond falls away from the stated interest rate on the bond, the greater the price change effect will be. This is illustrated in Table 10–1 on page 284 for the 10 percent interest rate, 20-year bonds discussed in this chapter.

We clearly see the impact that different yields to maturity have on the price of a bond.[7]

## Time to Maturity

The impact of a change in yield to maturity on valuation is also affected by the remaining time to maturity. The effect of a bond paying 2 percent more or less than the going rate of interest is quite different for a 20-year bond than it is for a 1-year bond. In the latter case, the investor will only be gaining or giving up $20 for one year. That is certainly not the same as having this differential for an extended period of time. Let's once again return to the 10 percent interest rate bond and show the impact of a 2 percent decrease or increase in yield to maturity for varying *times* to maturity. The values are shown in Table 10–2 and graphed in Figure 10–2. The upper part of Figure 10–2 shows how the amount (premium) above par value is reduced as the number of years to maturity becomes smaller and smaller. Figure 10–2 should be read from left to right. The lower part of the figure shows

---

[7]The reader may observe that the impact of a decrease or increase in interest rates is not equal. For example, a 2 percent decrease in interest rates will produce a $196.80 gain in the bond price and an increase of 2 percent causes a $149.10 loss. While price movements are not symmetrical around the price of the bond when the time dimension is the maturity date of the bond, they are symmetrical around the duration of the bond. The duration represents the weighted average time period to recapture the interest and principal on the bond. While these concepts go beyond that appropriate for an introductory finance text, the interested reader may wish to consult Geoffrey A. Hirt and Stanley B. Block, *Fundamentals of Investment Management*, 2nd ed. (Homewood, Ill.: Richard D. Irwin, 1986) or Frank K. Reilly, *Investments*, 2nd ed. (Hinsdale, Ill.: Dryden Press, 1985).

**Table 10–1**
**Bond price table**

(10 Percent Interest Payment, 20 Years to Maturity)

| Yield to Maturity | Bond Price |
|---|---|
| 2% | $2,308.10 |
| 4 | 1,825.00 |
| 6 | 1,459.00 |
| 7 | 1,317.40 |
| 8 | 1,196.80 |
| 9 | 1,090.90 |
| 10 | 1,000.00* |
| 11 | 920.30 |
| 12 | 850.90 |
| 13 | 789.50 |
| 14 | 735.30 |
| 16 | 643.90 |
| 20 | 513.00 |
| 25 | 407.40 |

*This value was computed earlier as $1,000.40 due to rounding. The correct value is $1,000.00.

how the amount (discount) below par value is reduced with progressively fewer years to maturity. Clearly, the longer the maturity, the greater the impact of changes in yield.

**Table 10–2**
**Impact of time to maturity on bond prices**

| Time Period in Years (of 10 percent bond) | Bond Price with 8 Percent Yield to Maturity | Bond Price with 12 Percent Yield to Maturity |
|---|---|---|
| 0 | $1,000.00 | $1,000.00 |
| 1 | 1,018.60 | 982.30 |
| 5 | 1,080.30 | 927.50 |
| 10 | 1,134.00 | 887.00 |
| 15 | 1,170.90 | 864.11 |
| 20 | 1,196.80 | 850.90 |
| 25 | 1,213.50 | 843.30 |
| 30 | 1,224.80 | 838.50 |

## Determining Yield to Maturity from the Bond Price

Up until now, we have used yield to maturity as well as other factors, such as the interest rate on the bond and number of years to maturity, to determine the price of the bond. We shall now assume that we know

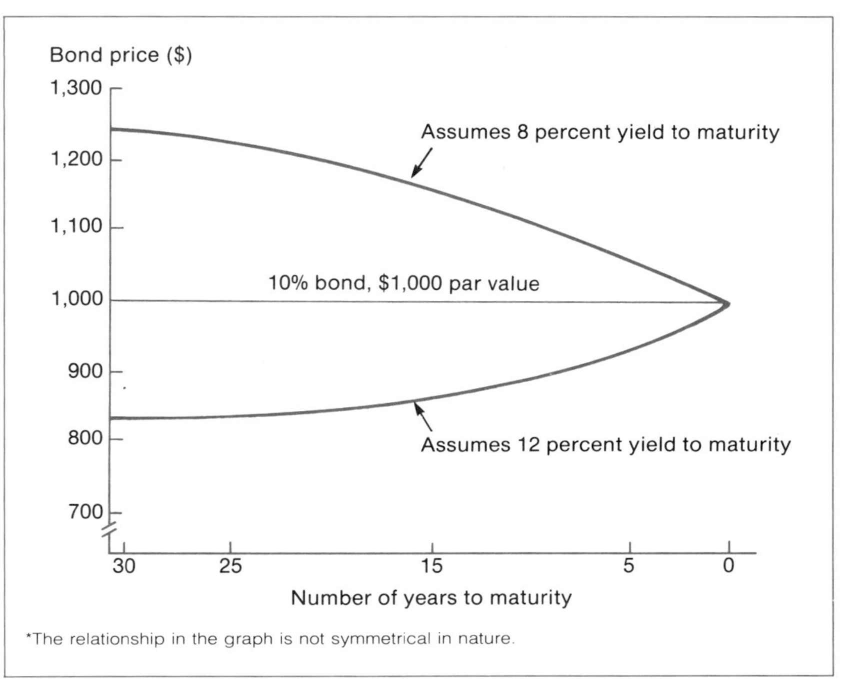


**Figure 10–2**
**Relationship between time to maturity and bond price***

the price of the bond, the interest rate on the bond, and the years to maturity, and we wish to determine the yield to maturity. Once we have computed this value, we have determined the rate of return that investors are demanding in the marketplace to provide for inflation, risk, and other factors.

Let's once again present Formula 10–1.

$$P_b = \sum_{t=1}^{n} \frac{I_t}{(1 + Y)^t} + \frac{P_n}{(1 + Y)^n}$$

We now try to determine the value $Y$, the yield to maturity, that will equate the interest payments ($I_t$) and the principal payment ($P_n$) to the price of the bond ($P_b$). This is similar to the calculations to determine yield in the prior chapter.

Assume a 15-year bond pays $110 per year (11 percent) in interest and $1,000 after 15 years in principal repayment. The current price of the bond is $932.21. We wish to determine the yield to maturity, or discount rate, that equates future flows with the current price.

In this trial and error process, the first step is to choose an initial percentage in the tables to try as the discount rate. Since the bond is trading below the par value of $1,000, we can assume the yield to maturity (discount rate) must be above the quoted interest rate of 11 percent. Let's begin the trial and error process.

**A 13 percent discount rate** As a first approximation, we might try 13 percent and compute the present value of the bond as follows:

*Present value of interest payments—*

$$A = R \times IF_{pva}\ (n = 15, i = 13\%) \qquad \text{[Appendix D]}$$
$$A = \$110 \times 6.462 = \$710.82$$

*Present value of principal payment at maturity—*

$$P = S \times IF_{pv}\ (n = 15, i = 13\%) \qquad \text{[Appendix B]}$$
$$P = \$1{,}000 \times .160 = \$160$$

*Total present value—*

| | |
|---|---|
| Present value of interest payments . . . . . . . . . . | $710.82 |
| Present value of principal payment at maturity . . . . | 160.00 |
| Total present value, or price, of the bond . . . . . . . | $870.82 |

The answer of $870.82 is below the current bond price of $932.21. This indicates we have used too high a discount rate in creating too low a value.

**A 12 percent discount rate** As a next step in the trial and error process, we will try 12 percent.

*Present value of interest payments—*

$$A = R \times IF_{pva}\ (n = 15, i = 12\%) \qquad \text{[Appendix D]}$$
$$A = \$110 \times 6.811 = \$749.21$$

*Present value of principal payment at maturity—*

$$P = S \times IF_{pv}\ (n = 15, i = 12\%) \qquad \text{[Appendix B]}$$
$$P = \$1{,}000 \times .183 = \$183$$

*Total present value—*

| | |
|---|---|
| Present value of interest payments . . . . . . . . . . | $749.21 |
| Present value of principal payment at maturity . . . . | 183.00 |
| Total present value, or price, of the bond . . . . . . . | $932.21 |

The answer precisely matches the bond price of $932.21 that we are evaluating. That indicates that the correct yield to maturity for the bond is 12 percent. Of course, if the computed value were slightly different from the price of the bond, we could use interpolation to arrive at the correct answer. An example of interpolating to derive yield to maturity is presented in Appendix 10A.

**Formula for bond yield** Because it is a tedious process to determine the bond yield to maturity through trial and error, an approximate answer can also be found by using Formula 10–2.

$$\text{Approximate yield to maturity } (Y') = \frac{\text{Annual interest payment} + \dfrac{\text{Principal payment} - \text{price of the bond}}{\text{Number of years to maturity}}}{\dfrac{\text{Price of the bond} + \text{Principal payment}}{2}} \quad (10\text{–}2)$$

Plugging in the values from the just completed analysis of yield to maturity, we show:

$$= \frac{\$110 + \dfrac{\$1{,}000 - \$932.21}{15}}{\dfrac{\$932.21 + \$1{,}000}{2}}$$

$$= \frac{\$110 + \dfrac{\$67.79}{15}}{\dfrac{\$932.21 + \$1{,}000}{2}}$$

$$= \frac{\$110 + \$4.52}{\$966.11}$$

$$= \frac{\$114.52}{\$966.11} = 11.84\%$$

The answer of 11.84 percent is a reasonably good approximation of the exact yield to maturity of 12 percent.[8] We use the prime (′) symbol after $Y$ to indicate the answer based on Formula 10–2 is only an approximation.

Note the numerator of Formula 10–2 represents the average annual income over the life of the bond and the denominator represents the average investment. That is, in the numerator, we take the annual interest payment of $110 and add that to the average annual change in the bond value over 15 years which is computed as $4.52. This provides average annual income of $114.52. In the denominator, we average the original price of $932.21 with the final value of $1,000 that we will receive at maturity to get the average investment over the 15-year holding period.

It should be pointed out that in computing yield to maturity on a bond, financially oriented hand-held calculators and software programs for microcomputers can be extremely helpful. There are also useful bond tables in libraries. Nevertheless, it is important that students also understand the mechanics that go into the calculations.

As we have discussed throughout, the yield to maturity is the required rate of return that bondholders demand. More importantly for our purposes here, it also indicates the current cost to the corporation to issue bonds. In the prior example, the corporation had issued bonds at 11 percent, but market conditions changed and the current price of the bond fell to $932.21. At this current price, the ongoing yield to maturity increased to 12 percent (11.84 percent, using the approximation method). If the corporate treasurer were to issue new bonds today, he would have to respond to the current market-demanded rate of 12 percent rather than the initial yield of 11 percent. Only by understanding how investors value bonds in the marketplace can the corporate financial officer properly assess the cost of that source of financing to the corporation.

## Semiannual Interest and Bond Prices

We have been assuming that interest was paid annually in our bond analysis. In actuality, most bonds pay interest semiannually. Thus, a

---

[8]The greater the premium or discount and the longer the period to maturity, the less accurate the approximation.

10 percent interest rate bond may actually pay $50 twice a year instead of $100 annually. To make the conversion from an annual to semiannual analysis, we follow three steps.

1. Divide the annual interest rate by two.
2. Multiply the number of years by two.
3. Divide the annual yield to maturity by two.

Assume a 10 percent, $1,000 par value bond has a maturity of 20 years. The annual yield to maturity is 12 percent. In following the three steps above, we would show:

1. 10%/2 = 5% semiannual interest rate; therefore, 5% × $1,000 = $50 semiannual interest.
2. 20 × 2 = 40 periods to maturity.
3. 12%/2 = 6% yield to maturity, expressed on a semiannual basis.

In computing the price of the bond issued, on a semiannual analysis, we show:

*Present value of interest payments*—We take the present value of a $50 annuity for 40 periods. The semiannual discount rate is 6 percent. Using Appendix D:

$$A = R \times IF_{pva}\ (n = 40,\ i = 6\%)$$
$$A = \$50 \times 15.046 = \$752.30$$

*Present value of principal payment at maturity*—We take the present value of $1,000 after 40 periods, using a 6 percent discount rate. Note that once we go to a semiannual analysis with the interest payments, we consistently follow the same approach in discounting back the principal payment; otherwise, we would be using semiannual and annual calculations on the same bond. Using Appendix B:

$$P = S \times IF_{pv}\ (n = 40,\ i = 6\%)$$
$$P = \$1{,}000 \times .097 = \$97$$

*Total present value*—

| | |
|---|---|
| Present value of interest payments . . . . . . . . . . | $752.30 |
| Present value of principal payment at maturity . . . . | 97.00 |
| Total present value, or price, of the bond . . . . . . | $849.30 |

The answer of \$849.30 is slightly below that which we found previously for the same bond, assuming an annual interest rate (\$850.90). In terms of accuracy, the semiannual analysis is a more acceptable method. It is the method used in most bond tables, for example. As is true in many finance texts, the annual interest rate approach is given first for ease of presentation, and then the semiannual basis is given. In the problems at the back of the chapter, you will be asked to do problems on both an annual and semiannual interest payment basis.

## Valuation and Preferred Stock

Preferred stock usually represents a perpetuity or, in other words, has no maturity date. It is valued in the market without any principal payment since it has no ending life. If preferred stock had a maturity date, the analysis would be similar to that of the preceding bond example. Preferred stock has a fixed dividend payment carrying a higher order of precedence than common stock dividends, but not the binding contractual obligation of interest on debt. Preferred stock, being a hybrid security, has neither the ownership privilege of common stock nor the legally enforceable provisions of debt. To value a perpetuity such as preferred stock, we first consider the formula:

$$P_p = \frac{D_p}{(1 + k_p)^1} + \frac{D_p}{(1 + k_p)^2} + \frac{D_p}{(1 + k_p)^3} + \ldots + \frac{D_p}{(1 + k_p)^\infty} \qquad (10\text{–}3)$$

Where:

$P_p$ = the price of preferred stock
$D_p$ = the annual dividend for preferred stock. It is a constant value
$K_p$ = the required rate of return, or discount rate, applied to preferred stock dividends

Note the formula calls for taking the present value of an infinite stream of constant dividend payments at a discount rate equal to $K_p$. Because we are dealing with an infinite stream of payments, Formula 10–3 can be reduced to a much more usable form as indicated in Formula 10–4.

$$P_p = \frac{D_p}{K_p} \qquad (10\text{–}4)$$

According to Formula 10–4, all we have to do to find the price of preferred stock ($P_p$) is to divide the constant annual dividend payment

($D_p$) by the required rate of return that preferred stockholders are demanding ($K_p$). For example, if the annual dividend were $10 and the stockholder required a 10 percent rate of return, the price of preferred stock would be $100.

$$P_p = \frac{D_p}{K_p} = \frac{\$10}{.10} = \$100$$

As was true in our bond valuation analysis, if the rate of return required by security holders changes, the value of the financial asset (in this case, preferred stock) will change. You may also recall that the longer the life of an investment, the greater the impact of a change in required rate of return. It is one thing to be locked into a low-paying security for one year when the rate goes up; it is quite another to be locked in for 10 or 20 years. With preferred stock, you have a *perpetual* security, so the impact is at a maximum. Assume in the prior example that because of higher inflation or increased business risk that $K_p$ (the required rate of return) increases to 12 percent. The new value for the preferred stock shares is:

$$P_p = \frac{D_p}{K_p} = \frac{\$10}{.12} = \$83.33$$

Of course, if the required rate of return were reduced to 8 percent, the opposite effect would take place. The preferred stock price would be computed as:

$$P_p = \frac{D_p}{K_p} = \frac{\$10}{.08} = \$125$$

It is not surprising that preferred stock is now trading well above its original price of $100. It is still offering a $10 dividend (10 percent of original offering price of $100), and the market is only demanding an 8 percent yield. In order to match the $10 dividend with the 8 percent rate of return, the market price will advance to $125.

### Determining the Required Rate of Return (Yield) from the Market Price

In our analysis of preferred stock, we have used the value of the annual dividend ($D_p$) and the required rate of return ($K_p$) to solve for the price of preferred stock ($P_p$). We could change our analysis to solve for the required rate of return ($K_p$) as the unknown, given that we knew the annual dividend ($D_p$) and the preferred stock price ($P_p$). We take Formula 10–4 and rewrite it as Formula 10–5, where the unknown is the required rate of return ($K_p$).

$$P_p = \frac{D_p}{K_p} \quad \text{(reverse the position of } K_p \text{ and } P_p\text{)} \tag{10–4}$$

$$K_p = \frac{D_p}{P_p} \tag{10–5}$$

Using Formula 10–5, if the annual preferred dividend ($D_p$) is \$10 and the price of preferred stock ($P_p$) is \$100, the required rate of return (yield) would be 10 percent.

$$K_p = \frac{D_p}{P_p} = \frac{\$10}{\$100} = 10\%$$

If the price goes up to \$130, the yield will only be 7.69 percent.

$$K_p = \frac{\$10}{\$130} = 7.69\%$$

We see the higher market price provides quite a decline in the yield.

## Valuation of Common Stock

The value of a share of common stock may be interpreted by the shareholder as the *present value* of an expected stream of *future dividends*. Although in the short run stockholders may be influenced by a change in earnings or other variables, the ultimate value of any holding rests with the distribution of earnings in the form of dividend payments. Though the stockholder may benefit from the retention and reinvestment of earnings by the corporation, at some point the earnings must be translated into cash flow for the stockholder. A stock valuation model based on future expected dividends can be stated as:

$$P_0 = \frac{D_1}{(1 + K_e)^1} + \frac{D_2}{(1 + K_e)^2} + \frac{D_3}{(1 + K_e)^3} + \ldots + \frac{D_\infty}{(1 + K_e)^\infty} \tag{10–6}$$

where

$P_0$ = Price of the stock today

$D$ = Dividend for each year

$K_e$ = the required rate of return for common stock (discount rate)

This formula, with modification, is generally applied to three different circumstances.

1. No growth in dividends.
2. Constant growth in dividends.
3. Variable growth in dividends.

## No Growth in Dividends

Under the no-growth circumstance, common stock is very similar to preferred stock. The common stock pays a constant dividend each year. For that reason, we merely translate the terms in Formula 10–5, which applies to preferred stock, to apply to common stock. This is shown as new Formula 10–7.

$$P_0 = \frac{D_0}{K_e} \qquad (10\text{–}7)$$

$P_0$ = Price of common stock today
$D_0$ = Current annual common stock dividend (a constant value)
$K_e$ = Required rate of return for common stock

Assume $D_0$ = \$1.86 and $K_e$ = 12 percent; the price of the stock would be \$15.50

$$P_0 = \frac{\$1.86}{.12} = \$15.50$$

A no-growth policy for common stock dividends does not hold much appeal for investors and so is seen infrequently in the real world.

## Constant Growth in Dividends

A firm that increases dividends at a constant rate is a more likely circumstance. Perhaps a firm decides to increase its dividends by 5 or 7 percent per year. The general valuation approach is shown in Formula 10–8.

$$P_0 = \frac{D_0(1+g)^1}{(1+K_e)^1} + \frac{D_0(1+g)^2}{(1+K_e)^2} + \frac{D_0(1+g)^3}{(1+K_e)^3} + \ldots + \frac{D_0(1+g)^\infty}{(1+K_e)^\infty} \quad (10\text{–}8)$$

where

$P_0$ = Price of common stock today
$D_0(1 + g)^1$ = Dividend in year 1, $D_1$
$D_0(1 + g)^2$ = Dividend in year 2, $D_2$, and so on
$g$ = Constant growth rate in dividends
$K_e$ = Required rate of return for common stock (discount rate)

In other words, the current price of the stock is the present value of the future stream of dividends growing at a constant rate. If we can anticipate the growth pattern of future dividends and determine the discount rate, we can ascertain the price of the stock.

For example, assume the following information:

$D_0$ = Latest 12-month dividend (assume \$1.87)
$D_1$ = First year, \$2.00 (growth rate, 7%)
$D_2$ = Second year, \$2.14 (growth rate, 7%)
$D_3$ = Third year, \$2.29 (growth rate, 7%)
etc., etc.
$K_e$ = Required rate of return (discount rate), 12%

then:

$$P_0 = \frac{\$2.00}{(1.12)^1} + \frac{\$2.14}{(1.12)^2} + \frac{\$2.29}{(1.12)^3} + \ldots + \frac{\text{Infinite dividend}}{(1.12)^\infty}$$

To find the price of the stock, we take the present value of each year's dividend. This is no small task when the formula calls for us to take the present value of an *infinite* stream of growing dividends. Fortunately, Formula 10–8 can be compressed into a much more usable form if two circumstances are satisfied.

1. The firm must have a constant growth rate ($g$).
2. The discount rate ($K_e$) must exceed the growth rate ($g$).

For most introductory courses in finance, these assumptions are usually made to reduce the complications in the analytical process. This then allows us to reduce or rewrite Formula 10–8 as Formula

10–9. Formula 10–9 is the basic equation for finding the value of common stock and is referred to as the dividend valuation model.

$$P_0 = \frac{D_1}{K_e - g} \qquad (10\text{–}9)$$

This is an extremely easy formula to use in which:

$P_0$ = Price of the stock today
$D_1$ = Dividend at the end of the first year (or period)
$K_e$ = Required rate of return (discount rate)
$g$ = Constant growth rate in dividends

Based on the current example:

$D_1$ = \$2.00
$K_e$ = .12
$g$ = .07

and $P_0$ is computed as:

$$P_0 = \frac{D_1}{K_e - g} = \frac{\$2.00}{.12 - .07} = \frac{\$2.00}{.05} = \$40$$

Thus, given that the stock has a \$2 dividend at the end of the first period, a discount rate of 12 percent, and a constant growth rate of 7 percent, the current price of the stock is \$40.

Let's take a closer look at Formula 10–9 and the factors that influence valuation. For example, what is the anticipated effect on valuation if $K_e$ (the required rate of return, or discount rate) increases as a result of inflation or increased risk? Intuitively, we would expect the stock price to decline if investors demand a higher return and the dividend and growth rate remain the same. This is precisely what happens.

If $D_1$ remains at \$2.00 and the growth rate ($g$) is 7 percent, but $K_e$ increases from 12 percent to 14 percent, using Formula 10–9, the price of the common stock will now be \$28.57. This is considerably lower than its earlier value of \$40.

$$P_0 = \frac{D_1}{K_e - g} = \frac{\$2.00}{.14 - .07} = \frac{\$2.00}{.07} = \$28.57$$

Similarly, if the growth rate ($g$) increases while $D_1$ and $K_e$ remain constant, the stock price can be expected to increase. Assume

$D_1 = \$2.00$, $K_e$ is set at its earlier level of 12 percent, and $g$ increases from 7 percent to 9 percent. Using Formula 10–9 once again, the new price of the stock would be \$66.67.

$$P_0 = \frac{D_1}{K_e - g} = \frac{\$2.00}{.12 - .09} = \frac{\$2.00}{.03} = \$66.67$$

We should not be surprised to see that an increasing growth rate has enhanced the value of the stock.

**Stock valuation based on future stock value** The discussion of stock valuation to this point has related to the concept of the present value of future dividends. This is a valid concept, but suppose we wish to approach the issue from a slightly different viewpoint. Assume we are going to buy a stock and hold it for three years and then sell it. We wish to know the present value of our investment. This is somewhat like the bond valuation analysis. We will receive a dividend for three years ($D_1$, $D_2$, $D_3$) and then a price (payment) for the stock at the end of three years ($P_3$). What is the present value of the benefits? What we do is add the present value of three years of dividends and the present value of the stock price after three years. Assuming a constant-growth dividend analysis, the stock price after three years is simply the present value of all future dividends after the third year (from the fourth year on). Thus, the current price of the stock in this case is nothing other than the present value of the first three dividends, plus the present value of all future dividends (which is equivalent to the stock price after the third year). Saying the price of the stock is the present value of all future dividends is also the equivalent of saying it is the present value of a dividend stream for a number of years, plus the present value of the price of the stock after that time period. The appropriate formula is still $P_0 = D_1/(K_e - g)$, which we have been using throughout this part of the chapter. This point is demonstrated in Problem 22 at the back of the chapter.

## Determining the Required Rate of Return from the Market Price

In our analysis of common stock, we have used the first year's dividend ($D_1$), the required rate of return ($K_e$), and the growth rate ($g$) to solve for the stock price ($P_0$) based on Formula 10–9.

$$P_0 = \frac{D_1}{K_e - g} \qquad \text{(Previously presented Formula 10–9)}$$

We could change the analysis to solve for the required rate of return ($K_e$) as the unknown, given that we know the first year's dividend ($D_1$), the stock price ($P_0$), and the growth rate ($g$). We take the formula above and algebraically change it to provide Formula 10–10.

$$P_0 = \frac{D_1}{K_e - g} \tag{10–9}$$

$$K_e = \frac{D_1}{P_0} + g \tag{10–10}$$

This formula allows us to compute the required return ($K_e$) from the investment. Returning to the basic data, from the common stock example:

$K_e$ = Required rate of return (to be solved)
$D_1$ = Dividend at the end of the first year \$2.00
$P_0$ = Price of the stock today, \$40
$g$ = Constant growth rate .07

$$K_e = \frac{\$2.00}{\$40} + 7\% = 5\% + 7\% = 12\%$$

In this instance, we would say the stockholder demands a 12 percent return on his common stock investment. Of particular interest are the individual parts of the formula for $K_e$ that we have been discussing. Let's write out Formula 10–10 again.

$$K_e = \frac{\text{First year's dividend}}{\text{Common stock price}}\left(\frac{D_1}{P_0}\right) + \text{Growth } (g)$$

The first term represents the dividend yield that the stockholder will receive, and the second term represents the anticipated growth in dividends, earnings, and stock price. While we have been describing the growth rate primarily in terms of dividends, it is assumed that the earnings and stock price will also grow at that same rate over the long term if all else holds constant. You should also observe that the formula above represents a total return concept. The stockholder is receiving a current dividend plus anticipated growth in the future. If the dividend yield is low, the growth rate must be high to provide the necessary return. Conversely, if the growth rate is low, a high dividend yield will be expected.

## The Price–Earnings Ratio Concept and Valuation

In Chapter 2 we introduced the concept of the price–earnings ratio. The price–earnings ratio represents a multiplier applied to current earnings to determine the value of a share of stock in the market. It is considered a pragmatic, everyday approach to valuation. If a stock has earnings per share of $3 and a price–earnings (P/E) ratio of 12 times, it will carry a market value of $36. Another company with the same earnings but a P/E ratio of 15 times will enjoy a market price of $45.

The price–earnings ratio is influenced by the earnings and sales growth of the firm, the risk (or volatility in performance), the debt–equity structure of the firm, the dividend policy, the quality of management, and a number of other factors. Firms that have bright expectations for the future tend to trade at high P/E ratios while the opposite is true of low P/E firms.

For example, the average P/E for all New York Stock Exchange firms was 14 in early 1986, but Capital Cities Communication Corporation traded at a P/E of 21 because of unusually bright prospects for the broadcasting/publishing industry. At the same time, Mobil Corporation traded at a relatively low P/E of eight because of less than favorable factors influencing the petroleum market.

Actually, P/E ratios can be looked up in *The Wall Street Journal* or the business section of most newspapers. Quotations from *The Wall Street Journal* are presented in Table 10–3. The first column (Div.) after the company name shows the annual dividend, and the second column (Yld) shows the dividend yield. This represents the annual dividend divided by the closing stock price. The third column after the company name (PE) is of primary interest in that it shows the current price–earnings ratio. For Aetna Life, it is 16, indicating that the current stock price of 47-1/4 represents 16 times annual earnings.[9] The remaining columns show the high, low, and closing prices for the day, plus any changes from the previous day.

The P/E ratio represents an easily understood, pragmatic approach to valuation that is widely used by stockbrokers and individual inves-

[9]The price–earnings ratio is not shown for some companies because they do not have positive earnings on which to base the calculation, or because it is the preferred stock of the company which is shown, in which case, the P/E ratio is not relevant because preferred stock does not have earnings per share as such.

Table 10–3
Quotations from *The Wall Street Journal*

| 52-week High | 52-week Low | Stock | Div. | Yld. | PE | Sales 100s | High | Low | Last | Chg. |
|---|---|---|---|---|---|---|---|---|---|---|
| | | – A–A–A – | | | | | | | | |
| 24⅜ | 16 | AAR | .56 | 2.5 | 15 | 38 | 23 | 22⅜ | 22½ | − ½ |
| 17⅜ | 9¾ | AGS | | .. | 12 | 226 | 15½ | 15 | 15⅜ | + ⅛ |
| 50¾ | 29¾ | AMR | | .. | 7 | 3092 | 40⅞ | 39⅞ | 40 | − ½ |
| 23⅝ | 18⅝ | AMR | pf2.18 | 9.4 | .. | 5 | 23¼ | 23¼ | 23¼ | ..... |
| 25⅞ | 23 | ANR | pf 2.67 | 11. | .. | 3 | 23⅝ | 23⅝ | 23⅝ | − ⅛ |
| 61⅛ | 34¾ | ASA | 2 | 5.5 | .. | 143 | 37⅛ | 36½ | 36⅝ | − ¼ |
| 27 | 10½ | AVX | .32 | 2.9 | 16 | 215 | 11¼ | 10⅞ | 10⅞ | − ⅝ |
| 28⅛ | 19¼ | AZP | 2.72 | 11. | 7 | 546 | 25⅝ | 25¼ | 25¼ | − ¼ |
| 60 | 38⅝ | AbtLab | 1.40 | 2.5 | 15 | 838 | 57¾ | 56¾ | 56¾ | − ⅝ |
| 25⅞ | 19⅝ | AccoWd | .50 | 2.2 | 17 | 83 | 23⅜ | 23⅛ | 23⅛ | ..... |
| 24¾ | 12 | AcmeC | .40 | 3.4 | .. | 45 | 12⅛ | d11½ | 11¾ | − ¼ |
| 10½ | 7⅜ | AcmeE | .32b | 4.3 | 11 | 8 | 7½ | 7½ | 7½ | ..... |
| 19 | 15½ | AdaEx | 1.92e | 11. | .. | 35 | 17⅝ | 17⅜ | 17⅜ | ..... |
| 20 | 13½ | AdmMI | .32 | 1.7 | 8 | 20 | 18½ | 18¼ | 18½ | − ⅛ |
| 16⅛ | 8⅝ | AdvSys | .53t | 3.7 | 21 | 95 | 14⅜ | 14⅛ | 14⅜ | + ½ |
| 36⅞ | 22⅛ | AMD | | .. | 37 | 7685 | 25⅞ | 24⅞ | 25 | + ⅝ |
| 12⅛ | 6⅞ | Advest | .12 | 1.4 | 19 | 89 | 8¾ | 8½ | 8½ | − ¼ |
| 15⅞ | 10 | Aerflex | | .. | 13 | 147 | 15½ | 15¼ | 15⅜ | + ⅛ |
| → 49⅝ | 34⅜ | AetnLf | 2.64 | 5.6 | 16 | 3805 | 48½ | 47 | 47¼ | − 1 |
| 57½ | 53¼ | AetL | pf5.41e | 9.7 | .. | 28 | 56 | 55⅞ | 56 | ..... |
| 37⅜ | 22⅛ | Ahmns | 1.20 | 3.3 | 6 | 2158 | 36 | 35½ | 36 | + ¾ |
| 3⅝ | 2½ | Alleen | | .. | .. | 29 | 2¾ | 2⅝ | 2⅝ | ..... |
| 57 | 43⅜ | AirPrd | 1.48 | 2.7 | 12 | 731 | 54⅞ | 54⅜ | 54¾ | + ⅜ |
| 24⅜ | 17½ | AirbFrt | .60 | 2.7 | 13 | 56 | 22 | 21¾ | 21⅞ | ..... |
| 2⅛ | 1¼ | AlMoa | s.10e | 6.2 | .. | 163 | 1¾ | 1⅝ | 1⅝ | ..... |
| 33⅜ | 29¼ | AlaP | pfA3.92 | 13. | .. | 9 | 31⅜ | 31⅛ | 31¼ | − ⅛ |
| 8⅛ | 6⅝ | AlaP | dpf .87 | 10. | .. | 79 | u 8⅜ | 7⅞ | 8⅜ | + ⅜ |
| 82 | 65¼ | AlaP | pf 9 | 11. | .. | z400 | 80⅛ | 80⅛ | 80⅛ | − ¼ |
| 26⅜ | 12½ | AlskAir | .16 | .8 | 8 | 1979 | 20 | 19 | 19⅝ | + ¾ |
| 25 | 12½ | Albrto | s .38 | 1.6 | 17 | 31 | 23¾ | 23¼ | 23¼ | − ¾ |
| 33¼ | 26⅜ | Albtsns | .76 | 2.5 | 12 | 166 | 30⅛ | 29⅝ | 30 | + ⅛ |
| 31¼ | 23¼ | Alcan | 1.20 | 5.0 | 46 | 1014 | 24¼ | 24 | 24⅛ | + ⅛ |
| 38⅞ | 27⅛ | AlcoStd | 1.20 | 3.5 | 12 | 200 | 34 | 33⅞ | 34 | ..... |
| 32 | 21 | AlexAlx | 1 | 3.4 | .. | 619 | 29⅝ | 29⅛ | 29¼ | − ¼ |
| 30 | 20⅜ | Alexdr | | .. | 25 | 12 | 27⅞ | 27¾ | 27⅞ | ..... |
| 89½ | 72¼ | AllgCp | 1.54t | 1.9 | .. | 34 | 80 | 79½ | 80 | + ¼ |
| 26¾ | 24½ | AlgCp | pf2.86 | 11. | .. | 3 | 26½ | 26½ | 26½ | ..... |
| 28¾ | 20¼ | AlgInt | 1.40 | 5.3 | .. | 296 | 26¾ | 25¾ | 26¼ | − ⅜ |
| 20¾ | 16⅞ | AlgIn | pf2.19 | 12. | .. | 6 | 18⅝ | 18⅝ | 18⅝ | − ⅛ |
| 34⅜ | 28⅛ | AllgPw | 2.70 | 8.9 | 9 | 1085 | 30⅜ | 30¼ | 30¼ | + ⅛ |
| 24 | 16¼ | AllenG | .60b | 2.5 | 16 | 94 | 24 | 23¾ | 23¾ | ..... |
| 23¼ | 15⅞ | AlldPd | | .. | 11 | 14 | 17¾ | 17½ | 17½ | − ⅛ |
| 45 | 42 | AldSgn | n | .. | 9 | 3139 | 43¼ | 42¾ | 43⅛ | − ⅛ |
| 66½ | 62 | AldS | pfA4.12 | 6.6 | .. | 7 | 62¾ | 62¾ | 62¾ | ..... |
| 63 | 58¾ | AldS | pfC6.74 | 11. | .. | 59 | 60 | 59⅝ | 59¾ | + ¼ |
| 111 | 105½ | AldS | pfD 12 | 11. | .. | 60 | 107¼ | 106⅜ | 107¼ | + ¾ |
| 61 | 47¾ | AlldStr | 2.20 | 3.7 | 8 | 1713 | 60¾ | 59⅝ | 60¼ | − ½ |
| 9½ | 3¼ | AllisCh | | .. | .. | 88 | 4¼ | 4⅛ | 4⅛ | − ⅛ |
| 34⅞ | 24 | AllisC | pf | .. | .. | 3 | 29¾ | 29¾ | 29¾ | − ¼ |
| 29¾ | 22¾ | ALLTL | 1.96 | 6.8 | 9 | 90 | 29⅛ | 28¾ | 28⅞ | − ⅛ |
| 38½ | 30 | ALLT | pf2.06 | 5.5 | .. | 5 | 37½ | 37½ | 37½ | + ½ |
| 39⅞ | 29¾ | Alcoa | 1.20 | 3.7 | 30 | 1154 | 32⅝ | 32¼ | 32½ | + ⅜ |
| 19⅝ | 11⅝ | Amax | .10i | .. | .. | 2579 | 11⅞ | d11¼ | 11½ | − ⅜ |
| 38½ | 29¼ | Amax | pf 3 | 9.8 | .. | 6 | 30½ | 29½ | 30½ | + 1 |
| 34 | 22¾ | AmHes | 1.10 | 3.7 | 24 | 10111 | 29½ | 29 | 29⅝ | + ⅝ |

Source: Reprinted by permission of *The Wall Street Journal*,  (October 25, 1985), p. 44. 

tors. The dividend valuation approach (based on the present value of dividends) that we have been using throughout the chapter is more theoretically sound and likely to be used by sophisticated financial analysts. Actually, to some extent, the two concepts can be brought together. A stock that has a high required rate of return ($K_e$) because of its risky nature will generally have a low P/E ratio. Similarly, a stock with a low required rate of return ($K_e$) because of the likelihood of positive future performance will normally have a high P/E ratio. In the first example, both methods provide a low valuation, while in the latter case, both methods provide a high valuation.

## Variable Growth in Dividends

In the discussion of common stock valuation, we have considered procedures for firms that had no growth in dividends and for firms that had a constant growth. Most of the discussion and literature in finance assumes a constant growth dividend model. However, there is also a third case, and that is one of variable growth in dividends. The most common variable growth model is one in which the firm experiences supernormal (very rapid) growth for a number of years and then levels off to more normal, constant growth. The supernormal growth pattern is often experienced by firms in emerging industries, such as in the early days of electronics or microcomputers.

In evaluating a firm with an initial pattern of supernormal growth, we first take the present value of dividends during the exceptional growth period. We then determine the price of the stock at the end of the supernormal growth period by taking the present value of the normal, constant dividends that follow the supernormal growth period. We discount this price to the present and add it to the present value of the supernormal dividends. This gives us the current price of the stock.

A numerical example of a supernormal growth rate evaluation model is presented in Appendix 10B at the end of this chapter. (The appendix is optional and not essential to the continued development of the material in the text.)

Finally, in the discussion of common stock valuation models, readers may ask about the valuation of companies that currently pay no dividends. Since virtually all our discussion has been based on values associated with dividends, how can this "no dividend" circumstance be handled? One approach is to assume that even for the firm that pays no current dividends, at some point in the future, stockholders will be rewarded with cash dividends. We then take the present value of their deferred dividends.

A second approach to valuing a firm that pays no cash dividend is to take the present value of earnings per share for a number of periods and add that to the present value of a future anticipated stock price. The discount rate applied to future earnings is generally higher than the discount rate applied to future dividends.

## Summary and Review of Formulas

The primary emphasis in this chapter is on valuation of financial assets: bonds, preferred stock, and common stock. Regardless of the security being analyzed, valuation is normally based on the concept of determining the present value of future cash flows. Thus, we draw on many of the time-value-of-money techniques developed in Chapter 9. Inherent in the valuation process is a determination of rate of return that investors demand. When we have computed this value, we have also identified what it will cost the corporation to raise new capital. Let's specifically review the valuation techniques associated with bonds, preferred stock, and common stock.

### Bonds

The price, or current value, of a bond is equal to the present value of interest payments ($I_t$) over the life of the bond plus the present value of the principal payment ($P_n$) at maturity. The discount rate used in the analytical process is the yield to maturity ($Y$). The yield to maturity (required rate of return) is determined in the marketplace by such factors as the *real* rate of return, an inflation premium, and a risk premium.

The equation for bond valuation was presented as Formula 10–1.

$$P_b = \sum_{t=1}^{n} \frac{I_t}{(1 + Y)^t} + \frac{P_n}{(1 + Y)^n} \qquad [10\text{–}1]$$

The actual terms in the equation are solved by the use of present value tables. We say the present value of interest payments is:

$$A = R \times IF_{pva}\,(n = \_\_,\ i = \_\_) \qquad \text{[Appendix D]}$$

the present value of the principal payment at maturity is:

$$P = S \times IF_{pv}\,(n = \_\_,\ i = \_\_) \qquad \text{[Appendix B]}$$

We add these two values together to determine the price of the bond. We may use annual or semiannual analysis.

The value of the bond will be strongly influenced by the relationship of the yield to maturity in the market to the interest rate on the bond and also the length of time to maturity.

If you know the price of the bond, the size of the interest payments, and the maturity of the bond, you can solve for the yield to maturity through a trial and error approach (discussed in the chapter and expanded in Appendix 10A), by an approximation approach as presented in Formula 10–2, or by using financially oriented calculators or appropriate computer software.

## Preferred Stock

In determining the value of preferred stock, we are taking the present value of an infinite stream of level dividend payments. This would be a tedious process if it were not for the fact that the mathematical calculations can be compressed into a simple formula. The appropriate equation is Formula 10–4.

$$P_p = \frac{D_p}{K_p} \qquad [10\text{–}4]$$

According to Formula 10–4, to find the preferred stock price ($P_p$) we take the constant annual dividend payment ($D_p$) and divide this value by the rate of return that preferred stockholders are demanding ($K_p$).

If, on the other hand, we know the price of the preferred stock and the constant annual dividend payment, we can solve for the required rate of return on preferred stock as:

$$K_p = \frac{D_p}{P_p} \qquad [10\text{–}5]$$

## Common Stock

The value of common stock is also based on the concept of the present value of an expected stream of future dividends. Unlike preferred stock, the dividends are not necessarily level. The firm and shareholders may experience:

1. No growth in dividends.
2. Constant growth in dividends.
3. Variable or supernormal growth in dividends.

It is the second circumstance that receives most of the attention in the financial literature. If a firm has constant growth ($g$) in dividends ($D$) and the required rate of return ($K_e$) exceeds the growth rate, Formula 10–9 can be utilized.

$$P_0 = \frac{D_1}{K_e - g} \qquad [10\text{–}9]$$

In using Formula 10–9, all we need to know is the value of the dividend at the end of the first year, the required rate of return, and the discount rate. Most of our valuation calculations with common stock utilize Formula 10–9.

If we need to know the required rate of return ($K_e$) for common stock, Formula 10–10 can be employed.

$$K_e = \frac{D_1}{P_0} + g \qquad [10\text{–}10]$$

The first term represents the dividend yield on the stock and the second term the growth rate. Together they provide the total return demanded by the investor.

## List of Terms

**yield to maturity**
**real rate of return**
**inflation premium**
**risk premium**
**perpetuity**
**dividend valuation model**
**dividend yield**
**price–earnings ratio (P/E)**
**supernormal growth**
**discount rate**
**required rate of return**

## Discussion Questions

1. How is valuation of financial assets by investors related to the cost of financing (cost of capital) for the firm?
2. How is valuation of any financial asset related to future cash flows?
3. Why might investors demand a lower rate of return for an investment in IBM as compared to Armco Steel or LTV?
4. What are the three factors that influence the demanded rate of return by investors?
5. If inflationary expectations increase, what is likely to happen to yield to maturity on bonds in the marketplace? What is also likely to happen to the price of bonds?
6. Why is the remaining time to maturity an important factor in evaluating the impact of a change in yield to maturity on bond prices?
7. What are the three adjustments that have to be made in going from annual to semiannual bond analysis?
8. Why is a change in required yield for preferred stock likely to have a greater impact on price than a change in required yield for bonds?
9. What type of dividend pattern for common stock is similar to the dividend payment for preferred stock?
10. What two conditions must be met to go from Formula 10–8 to Formula 10–9 in using the dividend valuation model?

$$P_0 = \frac{D_1}{K_e - g} \qquad \text{[Formula 10–9]}$$

11. What are the two components that make up the required rate of return on common stock?
12. What are some factors that might influence a firm's price–earnings ratio?
13. How is the supernormal growth pattern likely to vary from the more normal, constant growth pattern?

14. What approaches can be taken in valuing a firm's stock when there is no cash dividend payment?

## Problems

*(For the first nine bond problems, assume interest payments are on an annual basis)*

1. The Lone Star Company has $1,000 par value bonds outstanding at 9 percent interest. The bonds will mature in 20 years. Compute the current price of the bonds if the present yield to maturity is:

   *a.* 6 percent.
   *b.* 8 percent.
   *c.* 12 percent.

2. The Hartford Telephone Company has a $1,000 par value bond outstanding that pays 11 percent annual interest. The current yield to maturity on such bonds in the market is 14 percent. Compute the price of the bond based on these maturity dates:

   *a.* 30 years.
   *b.* 15 years.
   *c.* 1 year.

3. For Problem 2 graph the relationship in a manner similar to the bottom half of Figure 10–2 in the chapter. Also explain why the pattern of price change takes place.

4. The Perry Refrigerator Company issued bonds in 1981 at $1,000 per bond. The bonds had a 25-year life when issued and the annual interest payment was then 12 percent. This return was in line with required returns by bondholders at that point in time as described below:

| | |
|---|---|
| Real rate of return . . . . | 3% |
| Inflation premium . . . . | 6 |
| Risk premium . . . . . . | 3 |
| Total return . . . . . . | 12% |

   Assume that in 1986 the inflation premium is only 4 percent and is appropriately reflected in the required return (or yield to maturity) of the bonds. The bonds have 20 years remaining until maturity.

Compute the new price of the bond.

5. Ron Rhodes calls his broker to inquire about purchasing a bond of Golden Years Recreation Corporation. His broker quotes him a price of $1,170. Ron is concerned that the bond might be overpriced based on the factors involved. The $1,000 par value bond pays 13 percent annual interest, and it has 18 years remaining until maturity. The current yield to maturity on similar bonds is 11 percent.

   Do you think the bond is overpriced? Do the necessary calculations.

6. Lawrence Alexander III specializes in buying deep discount bonds. These represent bonds that are trading at well below par value. He has his eye on a bond issued by the Fulton Steamship Company. The $1,000 par value bond pays 5 percent annual interest and has 15 years remaining to maturity. The current yield to maturity on similar bonds is 12 percent.

   *a.* What is the current price of the bonds?
   *b.* By what percent will the price of the bonds increase between now and maturity?
   *c.* What is the annual compound rate of growth in the value of the bonds? (An approximate answer is acceptable.)

7. Bonds issued by the Lawton Corporation have a par value of $1,000, which, of course, is also the amount of principal to be paid at maturity. The bonds are currently selling for $870. They have 10 years remaining to maturity. The annual interest payment is 10 percent ($100).

   Compute the approximate yield to maturity, using Formula 10–2.

8. Bonds issued by the Norton Corporation have a par value of $1,000, are selling for $1,075, and have 15 years remaining to maturity. The annual interest payment is 12.5 percent ($125).

   Compute the approximate yield to maturity, using Formula 10–2.

9. *Optional*—for Problem 8, use the techniques in Appendix 10A to combine a trial and error approach with interpolation to find a more exact answer.

*(For the next two problems, assume interest payments are on a semiannual basis)*

**10.** Ami Brian is considering a bond investment in Wilmette Music Company. The $1,000 par value bonds have a quoted annual interest rate of 12 percent and interest is paid semiannually. The yield to maturity on the bonds is 10 percent annual interest. There are 15 years to maturity.

Compute the price of the bonds based on semiannual analysis.

**11.** You are called in as a financial analyst to appraise the bonds of Granny's Karate and Judo Schools, a national chain of self-defense programs. The $1,000 par value bonds have a quoted annual interest rate of 9 percent, which is paid semiannually. The yield to maturity on the bonds is 12 percent annual interest. There are 20 years to maturity.

*a.* Compute the price of the bonds based on semiannual analysis.

*b.* With 20 years remaining to maturity, if yield to maturity goes down to 8 percent, what will be the new price of the bonds?

**12.** The preferred stock of the Hilton Chocolate Company pays an annual dividend of $6. It has a required return of 8 percent.

Compute the price of the preferred stock.

**13.** The Shipley Software Corporation has preferred stock outstanding that pays an annual dividend of $12. It has a price of $108.

What is the required rate of return (yield) on the preferred stock?

**14.** X-Tech Company issued preferred stock many years ago. It carries a fixed dividend of $5.00 per share. With the passage of time, yields have soared from the original 5 percent to 12 percent (yield is the same as required rate of return).

*a.* What was the original issue price?

*b.* What is the current value of this preferred stock?

*c.* If the yield on the Standard & Poor's Preferred Stock Index declines, how will the price of the preferred stock be affected?

*(All of the following problems pertain to the common stock section of the chapter)*

**15.** Stagnant Iron and Steel currently pays a $4.20 annual cash dividend ($D_0$). They plan to maintain the dividend at this level for the foreseeable future as no future growth is anticipated.

If the required rate of return by common stockholders ($K_e$) is 12 percent, what is the price of the common stock?

**16.** Allied Coal will pay a common stock dividend of $3.40 at the end of the year ($D_1$). The required return on common stock ($K_e$) is 14 percent. The firm has a constant growth rate ($g$) of 8 percent.

Compute the current price of the stock ($P_0$).

**17.** Matson Chemical Company will pay a dividend of $2.50 per share in the next 12 months ($D_1$). The required rate of return ($K_e$) is 12 percent and the constant growth rate is 5 percent.

*a.* Compute $P_0$.

(In the remaining questions in this problem all variables remain the same except the one specifically changed. Each question is independent of the others.)

*b.* Assume $K_e$, the required rate of return, goes up to 14 percent, what will be the new value of $P_0$?

*c.* Assume the growth rate ($g$) goes up to 8 percent, what will be the new value of $P_0$?

*d.* Assume $D_1$ is $3.00, what will be the new value of $P_0$?

**18.** The Fleming Corporation paid a dividend of $4.00 last year. Over the next 12 months, the dividend is expected to grow at 8 percent, which is the constant growth rate for the firm ($g$). The new dividend after 12 months will represent $D_1$. The required rate of return ($K_e$) is 13 percent.

Compute the price of the stock ($P_0$).

**19.** Rick's Department Stores has had the following pattern of earnings per share over the last five years.

| *Year* | *Earnings per Share* |
|---|---|
| 1982 | $4.00 |
| 1983 | 4.20 |
| 1984 | 4.41 |
| 1985 | 4.63 |
| 1986 | 4.86 |

The earnings per share have grown at a constant rate (on a rounded basis) and will continue to do so in the future. Dividends represent 40 percent of earnings.

Project earnings and dividends for the next year (1987).

If the required rate of return ($K_e$) is 13 percent, what is the anticipated stock price at the beginning of 1987?

**20.** A firm pays a \$4.00 dividend at the end of year one ($D_1$), has a stock price of \$50 ($P_0$), and a constant growth rate ($g$) of 5 percent.

Compute the required rate of return ($K_e$).

**21.** A firm pays a \$2.20 dividend at the end of year one ($D_1$), has a stock price of \$80 ($P_0$), and a constant growth rate ($g$) of 13 percent.

*a.* Compute the required rate of return ($K_e$).

Indicate whether each of the following changes would make the required rate of return ($K_e$) go up or down. (Each question is separate from the others. No actual numbers are necessary.)

*b.* The stock price increases.
*c.* The dividend payment increases.
*d.* The expected growth rate increases.

**22.** Hunter Petroleum Corporation paid a \$2 dividend last year. The dividend is expected to grow at a constant rate of 5 percent over the next three years. The required rate of return is 12 percent (this will also serve as the discount rate in this problem). Round all values to three places to the right of the decimal point where appropriate.

*a.* Compute the anticipated value of the dividends for the next three years. That is, compute $D_1$, $D_2$, and $D_3$; for example, $D_1$ is \$2.10 (\$2.00 $\times$ 1.05).

*b.* Discount each of these dividends back to the present at a discount rate of 12 percent and then sum them.

*c.* Compute the price of the stock at the end of the third year ($P_3$).

$$P_3 = \frac{D_4}{K_e - g}$$

($D_4$ is equal to $D_3$ times 1.05)

*d.* After you have computed $P_3$, discount it back to the present at a discount rate of 12 percent for three years.

*e.* Add together the answers in part *b* and part *d* to get $P_0$, the current value of the stock. This answer represents the present value of the first three periods of dividends plus the present value of the price of the stock after three periods (which, in turn, represents the value of all future dividends).

*f.* Use Formula 10–9 to show that it will provide approximately the same answer as part *e*.

$$P_0 = \frac{D_1}{K_e - g} \qquad [(10\text{–}9)]$$

For Formula 10–9, use $D_1$ = \$2.10, $K_e$ = 12 percent, and $g$ = 5 percent. (The slight difference between the answers to part *e* and part *f* is due to rounding.)

## Selected References

Barnes, Amir, and Dennis E. Logue. "The Evaluation Forecasts of a Security Analyst." *Financial Management* 2 (Summer 1975), pp. 38–45.

Friend, Irwin, and Marshall Blume. "The Demand for Risky Assets." *American Economic Review* 75 (December 1975), pp. 900–22.

Gooding, Arthur E. "Quantification of Investors' Perceptions of Common Stocks: Risk and Return Dimensions." *Journal of Finance* 30 (December 1975), pp. 1301–16.

Hirt, Geoffrey A., and Stanley B. Block. *Fundamentals of Investment Management*. 2d ed. Homewood, Ill.: Richard D. Irwin, 1986.

McEnally, Richard W. "A Note on the Return of High Risk Common Stock." *Journal of Finance* 29 (March 1974), pp. 199–202.

Nelson, Charles R. "Inflation and Rates of Return on Common Stocks." *Journal of Finance* 31 (May 1976), pp. 471–83.

Norgaard, Richard L. "An Examination of the Yields of Corporate Bonds and Stocks." *Journal of Finance* 29 (September 1974), pp. 1275–86.

Olsen, I. J. "Valuation of a Closely Held Corporation." *Journal of Accounting* 128 (August 1969), pp. 35–47.

Reilly, Frank K. *Investments*. 2d ed. Hinsdale, Ill.: Dryden Press, 1985.
Vandell, Robert F., and Jerry L. Stevens. "Personal Taxes and Equity Security Pricing." *Financing Management* 11 (Spring 1984), pp. 31–40.

## Appendix 10A: The Bond Yield to Maturity Using Interpolation

We will use a numerical example to demonstrate this process. Assume a 20-year bond pays $118 per year (11.8 percent) in interest and $1,000 after 20 years in principal repayment. The current price of the bond is $1,085. We wish to determine the yield to maturity or discount rate that equates the future flows with the current price.

Since the bond is trading above par value at $1,085, we can assume the yield to maturity must be below the quoted interest rate of 12 percent (the yield to maturity would be the full 12 percent at a bond price of $1,000). As a first approximation, we will try 10 percent. Annual analysis is used.

*Present value of interest payments*

$$A = R \times IF_{pva}\,(n = 20,\ i = 10\%) \qquad \text{[Appendix D]}$$
$$A = \$118 \times 8.514 = \$1{,}004.65$$

*Present value of principal payment at maturity*

$$P = S \times IF_{pv}\,(n = 20,\ i = 10\%) \qquad \text{[Appendix B]}$$
$$P = \$1{,}000 \times .149 = \$149$$

*Total present value*

| | |
|---|---|
| Present value of interest payments . . . . . . . . . . | $1,004.65 |
| Present value of principal payment at maturity . . . . | 149.00 |
| Total present value or price of the bond . . . . . . . . | $1,153.65 |

The discount rate of 10 percent gives us too high a present value in comparison to the current bond price of $1,085. Let's try a higher discount rate to get a lower value. We will use 11 percent.

*Present value of interest payments*

$$A = R \times IF_{pva}\ (n = 20,\ i = 11\%) \qquad \text{[Appendix D]}$$
$$A = \$118 \times 7.963 = \$939.63$$

*Present value of principal payment at maturity*

$$P = S \times IF_{pv}\ (n = 20,\ i = 11\%) \qquad \text{[Appendix B]}$$
$$P = \$1{,}000 \times .124 = \$124.00$$

*Total present value*

| | |
|---|---|
| Present value of interest payments . . . . . . . . . . | $ 939.63 |
| Present value of principal payment at maturity . . . . | 124.00 |
| Total present value or price of the bond . . . . . . . . | $1,063.63 |

The discount rate of 11 percent gives us a value slightly lower than the bond price of $1,085. The rate for the bond must fall between 10 and 11 percent. Using linear interpolation, the answer is 10.76 percent.

| | |
|---|---|
| $1,153.65 *PV* @ 10% | $1,153.65 *PV* @ 10% |
| 1,063.63 *PV* @ 11% | 1,085.00 bond price |
| $ 90.02 | $ 68.65 |

$$10\% + \frac{\$68.65}{\$90.02}(1\%) = 10\% + .76(1\%) = 10.76\%$$

## Problem

**10A–1.** Bonds issued by the Peabody Corporation have a par value of $1,000, are selling for $890, and have 18 years to maturity. The annual interest payment is 8 percent.

Find yield to maturity by combining the trial and error approach with interpolation, as shown in this appendix. (Use an assumption of annual interest payments.)

## Appendix 10B: Valuation of a Supernormal Growth Firm

The equation for the valuation of a supernormal growth firm is:

$$P_0 = \sum_{t=1}^{n} \frac{D_t}{(1 + K_e)^t} + P_n \left(\frac{1}{1 + K_e}\right)^n \qquad \text{(10B–1)}$$

(Supernormal growth period) (After supernormal growth period)

Actually, the formula is not difficult to use. The first term calls for determining the present value of the dividends during the supernormal growth period. The second term calls for computing the present value of the future stock price as determined at the end of the supernormal growth period. If we add the two together, we arrive at the current stock price. We are adding together the two benefits the stockholder will receive: a future stream of dividends during the supernormal growth period and the future stock price.

Let's assume the firm paid a dividend over the last 12 months of \$1.67; this represents the current dividend rate. Dividends are expected to grow by 20 percent per year over the supernormal growth period ($n$) of three years. They will then grow at a normal constant growth rate ($g$) of 5 percent. The required rate of return (discount rate) as represented by $K_e$ is 9 percent. We first find the present value of the dividends during the supernormal growth period.

*(1) Present value of supernormal dividends*

$D_0$ = \$1.67. We allow the value to grow at 20 percent per year over the three years of supernormal growth.

$D_1 = D_0\,(1 + .20) = \$1.67\,(1.20) = \$2.00$
$D_2 = D_1\,(1 + .20) = \$2.00\,(1.20) = \$2.40$
$D_3 = D_2\,(1 + .20) = \$2.40\,(1.20) = \$2.88$

We then discount these values back at 9 percent to find the present value of dividends during the supernormal growth period.

| | Supernormal Dividends | Discount Rate $K_e$ = 9% | Present Value of Dividends during the Supernormal Period |
|---|---|---|---|
| $D_1$ . . . . . . | \$2.00 | .917 | \$1.83 |
| $D_2$ . . . . . . | 2.40 | .842 | 2.02 |
| $D_3$ . . . . . . | 2.88 | .772 | 2.22 |
| | | | \$6.07 |

The present value of the supernormal dividends is \$6.07. We now turn to the future stock price.

*(2) Present value of future stock price*

We first find the future stock price at the end of the supernormal growth period. This is found by taking the present value of the dividends that will be growing at a normal, constant rate after the supernormal period. This will begin *after* the third (and last) period of supernormal growth.

Since after the supernormal growth period the firm is growing at a normal, constant rate ($g$ = 5 percent) and $K_e$ (the discount rate) of 9 percent exceeds the new, constant growth rate of 5 percent, we have fulfilled the two conditions for using the constant dividend growth model after three years. That is, we can apply Formula 10–9 (without subscripts for now).

$$P = \frac{D}{K_e - g}$$

In this case, however, $D$ is really the dividend at the end of the fourth period because this phase of the analysis starts at the beginning of the fourth period and $D$ is supposed to fall at the *end* of the first period of analysis in the formula. Also, the price we are solving for now is the price at the beginning of the fourth period which, of course, is the same concept as the price at the end of the third period ($P_3$).

We thus say:

$$P_3 = \frac{D_4}{K_e - g} \qquad (10\text{–B2})$$

$D_4$ is equal to the previously determined value for $D_3$ of \$2.88 moved forward one period at the constant growth rate of 5 percent.

$$D_4 = \$2.88\ (1.05) = \$3.02$$

Also:

$$K_e = .09 \text{ discount rate (required rate of return)}$$
$$g = .05 \text{ constant growth rate}$$

$$P_3 = \frac{D_4}{K_e - g} = \frac{\$3.02}{.09 - .05} = \frac{\$3.02}{.04} = \$75.50$$

This is the value of the stock at the end of the third period. We discount this value back to the present.

| *Stock Price after Three Years* | *Discount Rate* $K_e$ = 9%* | *Present Value of Future Price* |
|---|---|---|
| $75.50 | .772 | $58.29 |

*Note: *n* is equal to 3.

The present value of the future stock price ($P_3$) of $75.50 is $58.29.

By adding together the answers in part (1) and part (2) of this appendix, we arrive at the total present value, or price, of the supernormal growth stock.

| | |
|---|---|
| (1) Present value of dividends during the normal growth period . . . . . . | $ 6.07 |
| (2) Present value of the future stock price . . . . . . . . . . . . . . . . | 58.29 |
| Total present value, or price . . . . . . . . . . . . . . . . . . . . | $64.36 |

The process we have just completed is presented in Figure 10B–1. The student who wishes to develop skills in growth analysis should work Problem 10B–1.

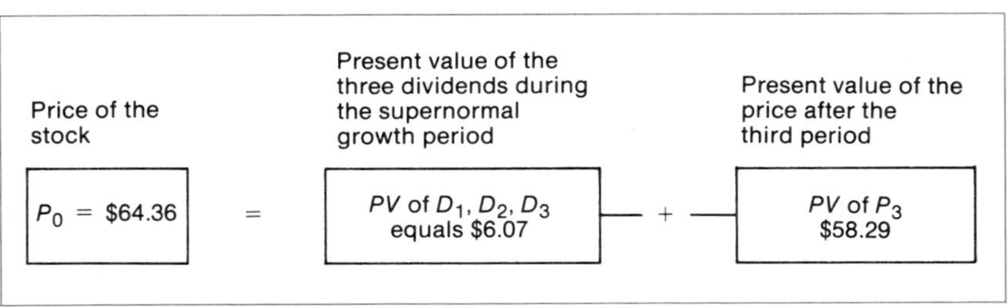


**Figure 10B–1**
**Stock valuation under supernormal growth analysis**

## Problem

**10B–1.** The McMillan Corporation paid a dividend of \$2.40 over the last 12 months. The dividend is expected to grow at a rate of 25 percent over the next three years (supernormal growth). It will then grow at a normal, constant rate of 6 percent for the foreseeable future. The required rate of return is 14 percent (this will also serve as the discount rate).

*a.* Compute the anticipated value of the dividends for the next three years ($D_1$, $D_2$, and $D_3$).

*b.* Discount each of these dividends back to the present at a discount rate of 14 percent and then sum them.

*c.* Compute the price of the stock at the end of the third year ($P_3$).

$$P_3 = \frac{D_4}{K_e - g}$$ [Review Appendix 10B–1 for the definition of $D_4$]

*d.* After you have computed $P_3$, discount it back to the present at a discount rate of 14 percent for three years.

*e.* Add together the answers in part *b* and part *d* to get the current value of the stock. (This answer represents the present value of the first three periods of dividends plus the present value of the price of the stock after three periods.)

# 11 Cost of Capital

Throughout the previous two chapters, a number of references were made to discounting future cash flows in solving for the present value. How do you determine the appropriate interest rate or discount rate in a problem situation? Suppose that a young doctor is rendered incapable of practicing medicine due to an auto accident in the last year of his residency. The court determines that he could have made $100,000 a year for the next 30 years. What is the present value of these inflows? We must know the appropriate discount rate. If 10 percent is used, the value is $942,700; with 5 percent, the answer is $1,537,300—over half a million dollars is at stake.

In the corporate finance setting, the more likely circumstance is that an investment will be made today—promising a set of inflows in the future and we need to know the appropriate discount rate. The purpose of this chapter is to set down the methods and procedures for making such a determination.

First of all, the student should observe that if we invest money today to receive benefits in the future, we must be absolutely certain we are earning at least as much as it costs us to acquire the funds for investment—that, in essence, is the minimum acceptable return. If funds cost the firm 10 percent, then all projects must be tested to make sure they earn at least 10 percent. By using this as the discount rate, we can ascertain whether we have earned the financial cost of doing business.

## The Overall Concept

How does the firm determine the cost of its funds or, more properly stated, the *cost of capital?* Suppose the plant superintendent wishes to borrow money at 6 percent to purchase a conveyor system, while a division manager suggests stock be sold at an effective cost of 12 percent to develop a new product. Not only would it be foolish indeed for each investment to be judged against the specific means of financing used to implement it, but this would also make investment selection decisions inconsistent. For example, picture financing a conveyor system having an 8 percent return with 6 percent debt and also evaluating a new product having an 11 percent return but financed with 12 percent common stock. If projects and financing are matched in this way, the project with the lower return would be accepted and the project with the higher return would be rejected. In reality, if stock and debt are sold in equal proportions, the average cost of financing would be 9 percent (one half debt at 6 percent and one half stock at 12 percent). With a 9 percent average cost of financing, we would now reject the 8 percent conveyor system and accept the 11 percent new product. This would be a rational and consistent decision. Though an investment financed by low-cost debt might appear acceptable at first glance, the use of debt might increase the overall risk of the firm and eventually make all forms of financing more expensive. Each project must be measured against the overall cost of funds to the firm. We now consider cost of capital in a broader context.

The determination of cost of capital can best be understood by examining the capital structure of a hypothetical firm, the Baker Corporation, in Table 11–1. Note that the aftertax costs of the individual sources of financing are shown, then weights are assigned to each, and finally a weighted average cost is determined. (The costs under consideration are those related to new funds which can be used for future financing, rather than historical costs.) In the remainder of the chapter, each of these procedural steps is examined.

**Table 11–1**
**Cost of capital—Baker Corporation**

| | | (1) Cost (aftertax) | (2) Weights | (3) Weighted Cost |
|---|---|---|---|---|
| Debt | $K_d$ | 6.34% | 30% | 1.90% |
| Preferred stock | $K_p$ | 10.94 | 10 | 1.09 |
| Common equity (retained earnings) | $K_e$ | 12.00 | 60 | 7.20 |
| Weighted average cost of capital | $K_a$ | | | 10.19% |

Each element in the capital structure has an explicit or opportunity cost associated with it, herein referred to by the symbol $K$. These costs are directly related to the valuation concepts developed in the previous chapter. If a reader understands how a security is valued, then there is little problem in determining its cost. The mathematics involved in the cost of capital are not difficult. We begin our analysis with a consideration of the cost of debt.

## Cost of Debt

The cost of debt is measured by the interest rate, or yield, paid to bondholders. The simplest case would be a $1,000 bond paying $100 annual interest, thus providing a 10 percent yield. The computation may be more difficult if the bond is priced at a discount or premium from par value. Techniques for computing such bond yields were presented in Chapter 10, Valuation and Rates of Return.

For example, assume the firm is preparing to issue new debt. To determine the likely cost of the new debt in the marketplace, the firm will compute the yield on its currently outstanding debt. This is not the rate at which the old debt was issued, but the rate that investors are demanding today. Assume the debt issue pays $112 per year in interest, has a 20-year life, and is currently selling for $950. In order to find the current yield to maturity on the debt, we could use the trial-and-error process described in the previous chapter. That is, we would experiment with discount rates until we found the rate that would equate interest payments of $112 for 20 years and a maturity payment of \$1,000 with \$950 today. A simpler process would be to use Formula 10–2 from the prior chapter which gives us the approximate yield to maturity. We reproduce the formula below and relabel it Formula 11–1 to fit the numbering system in this chapter.

$$\text{Approximate yield to maturity } (Y') = \frac{\text{Annual interest payment} + \dfrac{\text{Principal payment} - \text{Price of the bond}}{\text{Number of years to maturity}}}{\dfrac{\text{Price of the bond} + \text{Principal payment}}{2}} \quad (11\text{–}1)$$

For the bond under discussion, the approximate yield to maturity $(Y')$ would be:

$$= \frac{\$112 + \dfrac{\$1{,}000 - \$950}{20}}{\dfrac{\$950 + \$1{,}000}{2}}$$

$$= \frac{\$112 + \dfrac{\$50}{20}}{\dfrac{\$1{,}950}{2}}$$

$$= \frac{\$112 + \$2.50}{\$975}$$

$$= \frac{\$114.50}{\$975} = 11.74\%$$

In many cases, you will not have to compute the yield to maturity. It will simply be given to you. The practicing corporate financial manager also can normally consult a source such as *Moody's Bond Record* to determine the yield to maturity on his firm's outstanding debt. An excerpt from this bond guide is presented in Table 11–2. If the firm involved is Ohio Power Co., for example, the financial manager could observe that debt maturing in 2007 would have a yield to maturity of 12.51 percent. This is true in spite of the fact that the debt was originally issued at 9 percent.

Once the bond yield is determined through the formula or the tables (or is given to you), you must adjust the yield for tax considerations. In other words, yield to maturity indicates how much the corporation

**Table 11–2**
**Excerpt from *Moody's Bond Guide***

62 Ohio-Otte **MOODY'S BOND RECORD**

| Issue | Interest Dates | Current Call Price | Moody's Rating | Current Price | Yield to Mat. | Price Range 1985 High | 1985 Low | 1946-84 High | 1946-84 Low | Amt. Outst. Mil. $ | Sink. Fund Prov. | Legal Status | Fed. Tax | Issued | Price | Yld* |
|---|---|---|---|---|---|---|---|---|---|---|---|---|---|---|---|---|
| Ohio Power Co. 1st 9.00 1994 | J&D 1 | 104.04* | A3 r | 85¼ bid | 11.66 | 85¼ | 67 | 109 | 58 | 80.0 | Alt | 1 | N | 12-9-69 | 101.75 | 8.825 |
| do 1st 5.00 1996 | J&J 1 | 102.33* | A3 r | 59¼ bid | 12.02 | 59¼ | 45 | 101¾ | 35½ | 48.1 | Alt | 1 | N | 1-5-66 | 101.75 | 4.89 |
| do 1st 6.50 1997 | F&A 1 | 103.32* | A3 r | 66 bid | 11.93 | 66 | 49½ | 103¼ | 42 | 49.9 | Alt | 1 | N | 8-16-67 | 102.309 | 6.45 |
| do 1st 6.75 1998 | M&S 1 | 103.60* | A3 r | 66¾ bid | 11.95 | 66¾ | 50¼ | 108 | 43 | 59.8 | Alt | 1 | N | 2-27-68 | 101.948 | 6.60 |
| do 1st 7.75 1999 | M&S 1 | 104.54* | A3 r | 72¼ bid | 11.95 | 72¼ | 55 | 104½ | 47¾ | 70.0 | Alt | 1 | N | 3-5-69 | 102.362 | 7.55 |
| do 1st 7.625 2002 | A&O 1 | 104.18* | A3 r | 69 bid | 11.97 | 69 | 51½ | 101½ | 45 | 25.0 | Alt | 1 | N | 3-28-72 | 101.483 | 7.35 |
| do 1st 7.75 2002 | A&O 1 | 104.09* | A3 r | 69½ bid | 11.99 | 69½ | 52 | 102 | 46 | 25.0 | Alt | 1 | N | 10-16-72 | 101.169 | 7.65 |
| do 1st 8.375 2003 | F&A 1 | 104.60* | A3 r | 73¾ bid | 11.96 | 73¾ | 55¼ | 101¾ | 49 | 40.0 | Alt | 1 | N | 7-23-73 | 100.824 | 8.30 |
| do 1st 9.25 2006 | M&N 1 | 107.19* | A3 r | 78 bid | 12.16 | 78 | 59 | 105½ | 53 | 80.0 | Alt | 1 | N | 11-17-76 | 101.53 | 9.10 |
| do 1st10.00 2006 | M&N 1 | 106.25* | A3 r | 84¼ bid | 12.09 | 84¼ | 63¼ | 105½ | 57 | 80.0 | Alt | 1 | N | 5-12-76 | 100.00 | 10.00 |
| → do 1st 9.00 2007 | A&O 1 | 107.05* | A3 r | 74 bid | 12.51 | 75¾ | 57¼ | 101⅝ | 51½ | 40.0 | Alt | 1 | N | 4-13-77 | 101.57 | 8.85 |
| do 1st 9.25 2008 | M&S 1 | 106.91* | A3 r | 77½ bid | 12.20 | 77½ | 58½ | 100½ | 53 | 38.0 | Alt | 1 | N | 3-14-78 | 100.50 | 9.20 |
| do 1st12.875 2013 | J&D 1 | §111.81* | A3 r | 104 bid | 12.36 | 104 | 80 | 96⅞ | 80 | 70.0 | Alt | 1 | N | Ref. fr. 6-1-88@ 110.20 | | |
| do 1st12.75 2013 | J&J 1 | §111.69* | A3 r | 101 bid | 12.62 | 101¼ | 79¼ | 96 | 79¼ | 60.0 | Alt | 1 | N | Ref. fr. 7-1-88@ 110.10 | | |
| do s.f.deb. 5.125 1996 | J&J 1 | 102.44* | Baa1 r | 58¾ bid | 12.31 | 58⅞ | 44¼ | 101⅞ | 36 | 22.6 | Yes | 1 | N | 1-13-66 | 101.931 | 5.00 |
| do s.f.deb. 6.625 1997 | F&A 1 | 103.39* | Baa1 r | 64¼ bid | 12.49 | 64¼ | 50 | 103⅝ | 42 | 14.4 | 101.53 | 1 | N | 8-17-67 | 102.309 | 6.45 |
| do s.f.deb. 7.875 1999 | M&S 1 | 104.45* | Baa1 r | 71½ bid | 12.25 | 71½ | 55½ | 105½ | 48 | 10.3 | Yes | 1 | N | 3-5-69 | 102.037 | 7.70 |
| • Oklahoma Gas & Elec. 1st 4.50 1987 | J&J 1 | 100.20* | Aa2 | 95¼ bid | 8.58 | 89½ | 87⅞ | 105 | 58 | 20.0 | Yes | 123 | N | 1-18-57 | 101.155 | 4.43 |
| • do 1st 3.875 1988 | J&D 1 | 100.34* | Aa2 | 86¾ bid | 9.62 | — | — | 101 | 52 | 15.0 | 100.40 | 123 | N | 6-17-58 | 101.00 | 3.83 |
| • do 1st 4.25 1993 | M&S 1 | 101.09* | Aa2 | 68½ bid | 10.46 | 62⅝ | 62⅝ | 100¼ | 44 | 15.0 | 100.17 | 123 | N | 3-13-63 | 100.25 | 4.23 |
| • do 1st 4.50 1995 | M&S 1 | 101.40 | Aa2 | 62⅛ bid | 11.08 | 58 | 58 | 100⅝ | 42 | 25.0 | 100.00 | 123 | N | 3-10-65 | 100.00 | 4.50 |
| do 1st 5.125 1997 | J&J 1 | 102.39* | Aa2 r | 60 bid | 11.57 | 60 | 45¾ | 101⅛ | 37 | 15.0 | 100.71 | 123 | N | 1-24-67 | 101.152 | 5.05 |
| do 1st 6.375 1998 | J&J 1 | 102.64* | Aa2 r | 66¾ bid | 11.50 | 66¾ | 51½ | 100½ | 43 | 25.0 | 100.00 | 123 | N | 1-24-68 | 100.00 | 6.375 |
| do 1st 7.125 1999 | J&J 1 | 103.34* | Aa2 r | 70¾ bid | 11.47 | 70¾ | 55 | 101 | 47 | 12.5 | 100.69 | 123 | N | 1-28-69 | 100.93 | 7.05 |
| do 1st 8.625 2000 | J&J 1 | 104.17* | Aa2 r | 80½ bid | 11.42 | 80½ | 63¼ | 109½ | 53¾ | 30.0 | Yes | 123 | N | 1-13-70 | 100.00 | 8.63 |
| do 1st 7.125 2002 | J&J 1 | 104.17* | Aa2 r | 68 bid | 11.52 | 68 | 52 | 101 | 43½ | 40.0 | 100.78 | 123 | N | 1-11-72 | 100.93 | 7.05 |
| do 1st 8.375 2004 | J&J 1 | 106.06* | Aa2 r | 76½ bid | 11.47 | 76½ | 58¾ | 105 | 50½ | 75.0 | 101.24 | 123 | N | 1-8-74 | 101.38 | 8.25 |
| do 1st 9.125 2005 | J&J 1 | 106.47* | Aa2 r | 81 bid | 11.61 | 81 | 62¾ | 108 | 55½ | 60.0 | 101.18 | 123 | N | 1-14-75 | 101.29 | 8.99 |
| do 1st 8.625 2006 | J&J 1 | 106.54* | Aa2 r | 76½ bid | 11.67 | 76½ | 59 | 102⅝ | 51½ | 55.0 | 101.24 | 123 | N | 1-13-76 | 101.35 | 8.50 |
| do 1st 8.625 2007 | M&N 1 | 107.58* | Aa2 r | 74 bid | 12.00 | 74¼ | 60 | 101½ | 49¾ | 35.0 | 101.35 | 123 | N | 11-1-77 | 101.35 | 8.50 |
| do 1st 8.375 2007 | J&J 1 | 107.23* | Aa2 r | 75¾ bid | 11.43 | 75¾ | 57½ | 101⅝ | 49½ | 75.0 | 101.49 | 123 | N | 1-10-77 | 101.61 | 8.23 |
| Old Republic Int'l s.f.deb.11.50 2015 | J&D1 | §111.06* | Aa2 r | | — | — | — | — | — | 30.0 | Yes | — | N | Ref. fr. 6-1-95@ 105.53 | | |
| Oneok, Inc. nts.15.375 1991 | J&D1 | '100.00 | A2 r | 103 bid | 14.62 | 105 | 101 | 108 | 97 | 50.0 | No | 13 | N | 12-10-81 | 100.00 | 15.38 |
| Ontario (Prov. of) deb. 4.75 1990 | M&S15 | 102.75* | Aaa | 80¼ bid | 9.88 | 82½ | 62⅛ | 98¾ | 49⅞ | 44.0 | No | 13 | F | 1965 | | |
| do nts.12.50 1994 | ²A&O4 | N.C. | Aaa r | 111 bid | 10.51 | 117⅞ | 91½ | 103¾ | 91½ | 250 | No | 3 | F | 3-13-84 | 99.33 | 12.62 |
| do deb. 5.50 1996 | A&O 1 | 102.00* | Aaa | 69⅛ bid | 10.40 | 70 | 51⅛ | 103½ | 43⅝ | 30.0 | No | 13 | F | 3-16-66 | 100.00 | 5.50 |
| do deb. 6.875 1997 | J&D 1 | 102.20* | Aaa | 76 bid | 10.39 | 77¾ | 56½ | 114½ | 50¼ | 62.6 | No | 13 | F | 11-15-67 | 99.00 | 6.95 |
| do deb. 5.625 1997 | A&O15 | 102.21* | Aaa | 67⅞ bid | 10.49 | 83¾ | 50 | 100 | 43½ | 55.8 | No | 13 | F | 3-21-67 | 100.00 | 5.625 |
| do deb. 7.125 1998 | F&A 1 | 100.00 | Aaa | 76¼ bid | 10.54 | 90⅛ | 57⅛ | 104 | 51 | 61.5 | No | 13 | F | 7-11-68 | 99.25 | 7.19 |
| do deb. 8.375 1999 | M&S 1 | 102.60* | Aaa | 83 bid | 10.75 | 96 | 63⅝ | 107 | 57¾ | 74.2 | No | 13 | F | 8-19-69 | 98.25 | 8.54 |
| do deb. 7.375 1999 | F&A15 | 102.44* | Aaa | 76⅜ bid | 10.74 | 90⅛ | 58⅛ | 100 | 52 | 63.0 | No | 13 | F | 2-4-69 | 99.10 | 7.45 |
| do deb. 9.25 2000 | F&A 1 | 103.70* | Aaa | 88 bid | 10.90 | 88¼ | 68¾ | 111½ | 62½ | 64.4 | No | 13 | F | 7-14-70 | 100.00 | 9.25 |
| do deb. 9.25 2000 | F&A15 | 103.15* | Aaa | 88⅛ bid | 10.90 | 88⅛ | 68½ | 114½ | 62½ | 81.8 | No | 13 | F | 1-27-70 | 99.00 | 9.35 |
| do deb. 7.85 2001 | M&N15 | '103.14* | Aaa | 76⅛ bid | 11.10 | 79¾ | 59¼ | 104½ | 53¾ | 75.1 | No | 13 | F | 4-22-70 | 100.00 | 7.85 |
| do deb. 7.30 2002 | J&D15 | '102.92* | Aaa | 71⅛ bid | 11.09 | 74⅝ | 54⅝ | 100 | 49¾ | 78.2 | No | 13 | F | 12-6-72 | 100.00 | 7.30 |
| do deb. 7.70 2002 | M&N15 | '102.98* | Aaa | 74½ bid | 11.09 | 78⅛ | 57½ | 103½ | 52½ | 84.6 | No | 13 | F | 5-5-72 | 99.75 | 7.72 |
| do deb. 7.90 2003 | A&O15 | '103.16* | Aaa | 75½ bid | 11.06 | 79 | 58⅛ | 100 | 53¼ | 91.0 | No | 13 | F | 1-3-73 | 100.00 | 7.90 |
| do deb.10.25 2004 | A&O 1 | '104.10* | Aaa | 92⅝ bid | 11.19 | 94¾ | 74⅝ | 114¼ | 67½ | 172 | No | 13 | F | 10-2-74 | 100.00 | 10.25 |
| do deb. 8.60 2004 | M&S15 | 103.44* | Aaa | 80¼ bid | 11.14 | 82⅛ | 62½ | 100 | 57¼ | 110 | No | 13 | F | 3-12-74 | 100.00 | 8.60 |
| do deb. 9.25 2005 | M&N15 | '103.50* | Aaa | 84⅞ bid | 11.15 | 86⅝ | 66 | 107½ | 61 | 192 | No | 13 | F | 1975 | | |

Source: *Moody's Bond Record*, October 1985, p. 62.

has to pay on a *before tax* basis. But keep in mind the interest payment on debt is a tax-deductible expense. Since interest is tax deductible, its true cost is less than its stated cost, because the government is picking up part of the tab by allowing the firm to pay less taxes. The aftertax cost of debt is actually the yield to maturity times one minus the tax rate.[1] This is presented as Formula 11–2.

$$K_d \text{ (Cost of debt)} = Y \text{ (Yield) } (1 - T) \qquad (11\text{–}2)$$

[1]The yield may also be thought of as representing the interest cost to the firm after consideration of all selling and distribution costs, though no explicit representation is given to these costs in relationship to debt. These costs are usually quite small, and they are often bypassed entirely in some types of loans. For those who wish to explicitly include this factor in Formula 11–1, we would have:

$$K_d = [\text{Yield} / (1 - \text{Distribution costs})]\,(1 - \text{T})$$

The term *yield* in the formula is interchangeable with yield to maturity or approximate yield to maturity. In using the approximate-yield-to-maturity formula earlier in this section, we determined that the *current* required yield on existing debt was 11.74 percent. We shall assume that new debt can be issued at the same going market rate,[2] and that the firm is in a 46 percent tax bracket. Applying the tax adjustment factor, the aftertax cost of debt would be 6.34 percent.

$$\begin{aligned} K_d \text{ (Cost of debt)} &= Y \text{ (Yield) } (1 - T) \\ &= 11.74\% \ (1 - .46) \\ &= 11.74\% \ (.54) \\ &= 6.34\% \end{aligned}$$

Please refer back to Table 11–1 and observe in column (*1*) that the aftertax cost of debt is the 6.34 percent that we have just computed.

## Cost of Preferred Stock

The cost of preferred stock is similar to the cost of debt in that a constant annual payment is made, but dissimilar in that there is no maturity date in which a principal payment must be made. In truth, the determination of the yield on preferred stock is simpler than determining the yield on debt. All you have to do is divide the annual dividend by the current price (this process was discussed in Chapter 10). This represents the rate of return to preferred stockholders as well as the annual cost to the corporation for the preferred stock issue.

Actually, we need to make one slight alteration to this process by dividing the dividend payment by the *net* price or proceeds received by the firm. Since a new share of preferred stock has a selling cost (flotation cost), the proceeds to the firm are equal to the selling price in the market minus the flotation cost. The cost of preferred stock is presented as Formula 11–3.[3]

---

[2] Actually, the rate might be slightly higher to reflect that bonds trading at a discount from par ($950 in this case) generally pay a lower yield to maturity than par value bonds because of potential tax advantages and higher leverage potential. This is not really a major issue in this case.

[3] Note that in Chapter 10, $K_p$ was presented without any adjustment for flotation costs. The instructor may wish to indicate that we have altered the definition slightly. Some may wish to formally add an additional subscript to $K_p$ to indicate we are now talking about the cost of *new* preferred stock. The adjusted symbol would be $K_{pn}$.

$$K_p \text{ (cost of preferred stock)} = \frac{D_p}{P_p - F} \quad (11\text{–}3)$$

Where:

$K_p$ = Cost of preferred stock
$D_p$ = The annual dividend on preferred stock
$P_p$ = The price of preferred stock
$F$ = Flotation, or selling, cost

In the case of the Baker Corporation, we shall assume the annual dividend is $10.50, the preferred stock price is $100, and the flotation, or selling, cost is $4. The effective cost is:

$$K_p = \frac{D_p}{P_p - F} = \frac{\$10.50}{\$100 - 4} = \frac{\$10.50}{\$96} = 10.94\%$$

Because a preferred stock dividend is not a tax deductible expense, there is no downward tax adjustment.

Please refer back to Table 11–1 and observe in column (*1*) that 10.94 percent is the value we used for the cost of preferred stock.

## Cost of Common Equity

Determining the cost of common stock in the capital structure is a more involved task. The out-of-pocket cost is the cash dividend, but is it prudent to assume that the percentage cost of common stock is simply the current year's dividend divided by the market price?

$$\frac{\text{Current dividend}}{\text{Market price}}$$

If such an approach were followed, the common stock costs for selected U.S. corporations in January 1986 would be Disney (1.1 percent), Motorola (1.6 percent), Texas Instruments (1.9 percent), and Delta Airlines (2.5 percent). Ridiculous, you say! If new common stock were assumed to cost such low amounts, the firms would have no need to issue other securities and could profitably finance projects that earned only 2 or 3 percent. How, then, do we find the correct theoretical cost of common stock to the firm?

## Valuation Approach

In determining the cost of common stock, the firm must be sensitive to the pricing and performance demands of current and future stockholders. An appropriate approach is to develop a model for valuing common stock and to extract from this model a formula for the required return on common stock.

In Chapter 10 we discussed the constant dividend growth model and said that the current price of common stock could be stated to equal:

$$P_0 = \frac{D_1}{K_e - g}$$

in which:

$P_0$ = Price of the stock today
$D_1$ = Dividend at the end of the first year (or period)
$K_e$ = Required rate of return
$g$ = Constant growth rate in dividends

We then stated that we could rearrange the terms in the formula to solve for $K_e$ instead of $P_0$. This was presented in Formula 10–10 in the prior chapter. We present the formula once again and relabel it Formula 11–4.

$$K_e = \frac{D_1}{P_0} + g \qquad (11\text{–}4)$$

The required rate of return ($K_e$) is equal to the dividend at the end of the first year ($D_1$), divided by the price of the stock today ($P_0$), plus a constant growth rate ($g$). Although the growth rate basically applies to dividends, it is also assumed to apply to earnings and stock price over the long term.

If $D_1$ = \$2, $P_0$ = \$40, and $g$ = 7%, we would say $K_e$ equals 12 percent.

$$K_e = \frac{D_1}{P_0} + g = \frac{\$2}{\$40} + 7\% = 5\% + 7\% = 12\%$$

This means that stockholders expect to receive a 5 percent dividend yield on the stock price plus a 7 percent growth in their investment, making a total return of 12 percent.

## Alternate Calculation of the Required Return on Common Stock

The required return on common stock can also be calculated by an alternate approach called the capital asset pricing model (CAPM). This topic is covered in Appendix 11A, so only brief mention will be made at this point. Some accept the capital asset pricing model as an important approach to common stock valuation, while others suggest it is not a valid description of how the real world operates.

Under the capital asset pricing model, the required return for common stock (or other investments) can be described by the following formula.

$$K_j = R_f + \beta (K_m - R_f) \qquad (11\text{–}5)$$

where

$K_j$ = Required return on common stock
$R_f$ = Risk-free rate of return; usually the current rate on Treasury bill securities
$\beta$ = Beta coefficient. The beta measures the historical volatility of an individual stock's return relative to a stock market index. A beta greater than 1 indicates greater volatility (price movements) than the market, while the reverse would be true for a beta less than 1.
$K_m$ = Return in the market as measured by an appropriate index

For the Baker Corporation example, we might assume the following values:

$$R_f = 9\%$$
$$K_m = 11\%$$
$$\beta = 1.5$$

$K_j$, based on Formula 11–5, would then equal:

$$K_j = 9\% + 1.5(11\% - 9\%) = 9\% + 1.5(2\%)$$
$$= 9\% + 3\% = 12\%$$

In this case, we have assumed that $K_j$ (the required return under the capital asset pricing model) would equal $K_e$ (the required return under the dividend valuation model). They are both computed to equal

12 percent. Under this equilibrium circumstance, the dividend valuation model and the capital asset pricing model would produce the same answer.

For now, we shall use the dividend valuation model exclusively; that is, we shall use $K_e = D_1/P_0 + g$ in preference to $K_j = R_f + \beta(K_m - R_f)$.

Those who wish to study the capital asset pricing model further are referred to Appendix 11A. This appendix is optional and not required for further reading in the text.

## Cost of Retained Earnings

Up to this point, we have discussed the cost (required return) on common stock in a general sense. We have not really specified who is supplying the funds. One obvious supplier of common stock equity capital is the purchaser of new shares of common stock. But this is not the only source. For many corporations, the most important source of ownership or equity capital is in the form of retained earnings, an internal source of funds.

Accumulated retained earnings represent the past and present earnings of the firm minus previously distributed dividends. Retained earnings, by law, belong to the current stockholders. They can either be paid out to the current stockholders in the form of dividends or reinvested in the firm. As current funds are retained in the firm for reinvestment, they represent a source of equity capital to the firm that is being supplied by the current stockholders. They, however, should not be considered as free in nature. There is an opportunity cost involved. Why? As previously indicated, the funds could be paid out to the current stockholders in the form of dividends, and then redeployed by the stockholders in other stocks, bonds, real estate, etc. What is the expected rate of return on these alternative investments? That is, what is the opportunity cost? We assume that stockholders could at least earn an equivalent return to that provided by their present investment in the firm (on an equal risk basis). This represents $D_1/P_0 + g$. In the security markets, there are literally thousands of investments from which to choose, so that it is not implausible to assume that the stockholder can take dividend payments and reinvest them for a comparable yield.

Thus, when we compute the cost of retained earnings, this takes us back to the point at which we began our discussion of the cost of common stock. The cost of retained earnings is equivalent to the rate of return on the firm's common stock. This is the opportunity cost. Thus, we say the cost of common equity in the form of retained earnings is equal to the required rate of return on the firm's stock.[4]

$$K_e \text{ (Cost of common equity in the form of retained earnings)} = \frac{D_1}{P_0} + g \qquad (11\text{–}6)$$

Thus, $K_e$ not only represents the required return on common stock as previously defined, but it also represents the cost of equity in the form of retained earnings. It is a symbol that has double significance.

For ease of reference, the terms in Formula 11–6 are reproduced in the box. They are based on prior values presented in this section on the cost of common stock.

$K_e$ = Cost of common equity in the form of retained earnings
$D_1$ = Dividend at the end of the first year, \$2
$P_0$ = Price of the stock today, \$40
$g$ = Constant growth rate in dividends, 7%

We arrive at the value of 12%.

$$K_e = \frac{D_1}{P_0} + g = \frac{\$2}{\$40} + 7\% = 5\% + 7\% = 12\%$$

[4]One could logically suggest that this is not a perfectly equivalent relationship. For example, if stockholders receive a distribution of retained earnings in the form of dividends, they will have to pay taxes on the dividends before they can reinvest them in equivalent yield investments. Also, the stockholder may incur brokerage costs in the process. For these reasons, one might suggest that the opportunity cost of retained earnings is less than the rate of return on the firm's common stock. The authors have generally supported this position in the past. However, the current predominant view is probably that the appropriate cost for retained earnings is equal to the rate of return on the firm's common stock. The strongest argument for this equality position is that, in a publicly traded company, a firm always has the option of buying back its stock in the market. Given that this is the case, it is assured a return of $K_e$. Thus, the firm should not make a physical asset investment that has an expected equity return of less than $K_e$. Having presented both sides of the argument, the authors have adopted the equality position in the fourth edition and have used it throughout this chapter. Nevertheless, some instructors may wish to discuss both sides of the issue. In the event a tax adjustment is made, the cost of retained earnings can be shown as $K_r = K_e (1 - {}_{tr})$; where $K_r$ equals the cost of retained earnings, $K_e$ equals the required rate of return on common stock, and *tr* equals the average stockholder marginal tax rate.

The cost of common equity in the form of retained earnings is to be equal to 12 percent. Please refer back to Table 11–1 and observe in column (*1*) that 12 percent is the value we have used for common equity.

### Cost of New Common Stock

Let's now consider the other source of equity capital, new common stock. If we are issuing *new* common stock, we must earn a slightly higher return than $K_e$, which represents the required rate of return of *present* stockholders. The higher return is needed to cover the distribution costs of the new securities. Assume that the required return for present stockholders is 12 percent and that shares are quoted to the public at $40. A new distribution of securities must earn slightly more than 12 percent to compensate the corporation for not receiving the full $40 because of sales commissions and other expenses. The formula for $K_e$ is restated as $K_n$ (the cost of new common stock) to reflect this requirement.

Common stock $\qquad K_e = \frac{D_1}{P_0} + g$

↘

New common stock $\qquad K_n = \frac{D_1}{P_0 - F} + g \qquad$ (11–7)

The only new term is $F$ (flotation, or selling, costs).

Assume:

$$D_1 = \$2$$
$$P_0 = \$40$$
$$F = \$4$$
$$g = 7\%$$

then

$$K_n = \frac{\$2}{\$40 - \$4} + 7\%$$
$$= \frac{\$2}{\$36} + 7\%$$
$$= 5.6\% + 7\% = 12.6\%$$

The cost of new common stock to the Baker Corporation is 12.6 percent. This value will be used more extensively later in the chapter. New common stock is not assumed to be in the original capital structure for the Baker Corporation presented in Table 11–1.

### Overview of Common Stock Costs

For those of you who are suffering from an overexposure to *K*s in the computation of cost of common stock, let us boil down the information to the only two common stock formulas that you will be using in the rest of the chapter and in the problems at the back of the chapter.

$$K_e \text{ (Cost of common equity in the form of retained earnings)} = \frac{D_1}{P_0} + g$$

$$K_n \text{ (Cost of new common stock)} = \frac{D_1}{P_0 - F} + g$$

The primary emphasis will be on $K_e$ for now, but later in the chapter we will also use $K_n$ when we discuss the marginal cost of capital.

## Optimal Capital Structure—Weighting Costs

Having established the techniques for computing the cost of the various elements in the capital structure, we must now discuss methods of assigning weights to these costs. We will attempt to weight capital components in accordance with our desire to achieve a minimum overall cost of capital. For purpose of this discussion, Table 11–1 (Cost of Capital for the Baker Corporation) is *reproduced* in this section.

| | | *Cost (aftertax)* | *Weights* | *Weighted Cost* |
|---|---|---|---|---|
| Debt . . . . . . . . . . . . | $K_d$ | 6.34% | 30% | 1.90% |
| Preferred stock . . . . . . . | $K_p$ | 10.94 | 10 | 1.09 |
| Common equity (retained earnings) . . . . | $K_e$ | 12.00 | 60 | 7.20 |
| Weighted average cost of capital . . . . . . | $K_a$ | | | 10.19% |

How does the firm decide on the appropriate weights for debt, preferred stock, and common stock financing? Though debt is the cheapest form of financing, it should be used only within reasonable limits. In the Baker Corporation example, debt carried an aftertax cost of 6.34 percent, while other sources of financing cost at least 10.94 percent. Why not more debt? The answer is that the use of debt beyond a reasonable point may greatly increase the firm's financial risk and thereby drive up the costs of all sources of financing.

Assume you are going to start your own company and are considering three different capital structures. For ease of presentation, only debt and equity (common stock) are being considered. The costs of the components in the capital structure change each time we vary the debt–equity mix (weights).

| | Cost (aftertax) | Weights | Weighted Cost |
|---|---|---|---|
| *Financial Plan A* | | | |
| Debt . . . . . . . . . . | 6.5% | 20% | 1.3% |
| Equity . . . . . . . . . . | 12.0 | 80 | 9.6 |
| | | | 10.9% |
| *Financial Plan B* | | | |
| Debt . . . . . . . . . . | 7.0% | 40% | 2.8% |
| Equity . . . . . . . . . . | 12.5 | 60 | 7.5 |
| | | | 10.3% |
| *Financial Plan C* | | | |
| Debt . . . . . . . . . . | 9.0% | 60% | 5.4% |
| Equity . . . . . . . . . . | 15.0 | 40 | 6.0 |
| | | | 11.4% |

The firm is able to initially reduce the cost of capital with debt financing, but beyond Plan B the continued use of debt becomes unattractive and greatly increases the costs of the sources of financing. Traditional financial theory maintains that there is a U-shaped cost-of-capital curve relative to debt–equity mixes for the firm, as illustrated in Figure 11–1.[5] In this example, the optimum capital structure occurs at a 40 percent debt-to-equity ratio.

---

[5] A dissenting viewpoint was expressed by Professors Modigliani and Miller in which they maintained that the cost of capital is constant over all debt–equity mixes. Their assumption of perfect markets and their neglect of tax considerations were strongly challenged. They later modified their positions to include tax and bankruptcy considerations and the possibility of an optimal debt–equity mix.

Figure 11–1
Cost of capital curve

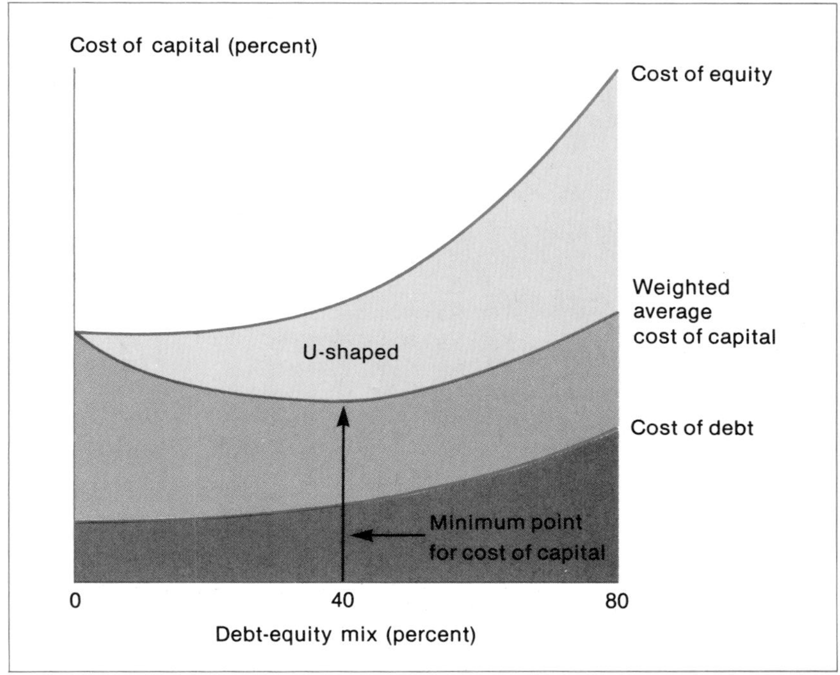


Most firms are able to use 30–50 percent debt in their capital structure without exceeding norms acceptable to creditors and investors. Distinctions should be made, however, between firms that carry high or low business risks. As discussed in Chapter 5, Operating and Financial Leverage, a growth firm in a reasonably stable industry can afford to absorb more debt than its counterpart in cyclical industries. Examples of debt use by companies in various industries are presented in Table 11–3.

In determining the appropriate capital mix, the firm generally begins with its present capital structure and ascertains whether its current position is optimal.[6] If not, subsequent financing should carry the firm toward a mix that is deemed more desirable. Only the costs of new or incremental financing should be considered.

---

[6] Market value rather than book value should be used—though in practice book value is commonly used.

**Table 11–3**
**Debt as a percentage of total assets**

| Selected Companies, with Industry Designation | Percent |
|---|---|
| American Home Products (drugs and food) | 23% |
| Lilly (Eli) & Co. (ethical drugs) | 29 |
| Polaroid (photographic equipment and film) | 30 |
| Quaker State (petroleum refining) | 33 |
| Weyerhaeuser (lumber and wood products) | 34 |
| Phelps Dodge (copper) | 37 |
| Standard Oil of Ohio (domestic crude oil) | 39 |
| General Motors (motor vehicles) | 40 |
| Gannett (newspaper and publishing) | 42 |
| American brands (tobacco and food) | 45 |
| Gulf and Western Industries (conglomerate) | 47 |
| Bethlehem Steel (blast furnaces and steelworks) | 48 |
| Dow Chemical (chemicals) | 50 |
| American Standard, Inc. (heating and plumbing equip.) | 53 |
| Levitz Furniture (retail furniture sales) | 57 |
| DiGiorgio (wholesale groceries) | 68 |
| Pan American Corp. (airline service) | 77 |

Source: Annual reports, Standard & Poor's *Compustat* tapes and *Moody's Industrial Manual.*

## Capital Acquisition and Investment Decision Making

So far, the various costs of financial capital and the optimum capital structure have been discussed. Financial capital, as you may have figured out, consists of bonds, preferred stock, and common equity. These forms of financial capital appear on the corporate balance sheet under liabilities and equity. The money raised by selling these securities and retaining earnings is invested in the real capital of the firm, the long-term productive assets of plant and equipment.

Long-term funds are usually invested in long-term assets, with several asset–financing mixes possible over the business cycle. Obviously, a firm wants to provide all of the necessary financing at the lowest possible cost. This means selling common stock when prices are relatively high to minimize the cost of equity. The financial manager also wants to sell debt at low interest rates. Since there is short-term and long-term debt, he needs to know how interest rates move over the business cycle and when to use short-term versus long-term debt.

A firm has to find a balance between debt and equity to achieve its

Figure 11–2
Cost of capital over time

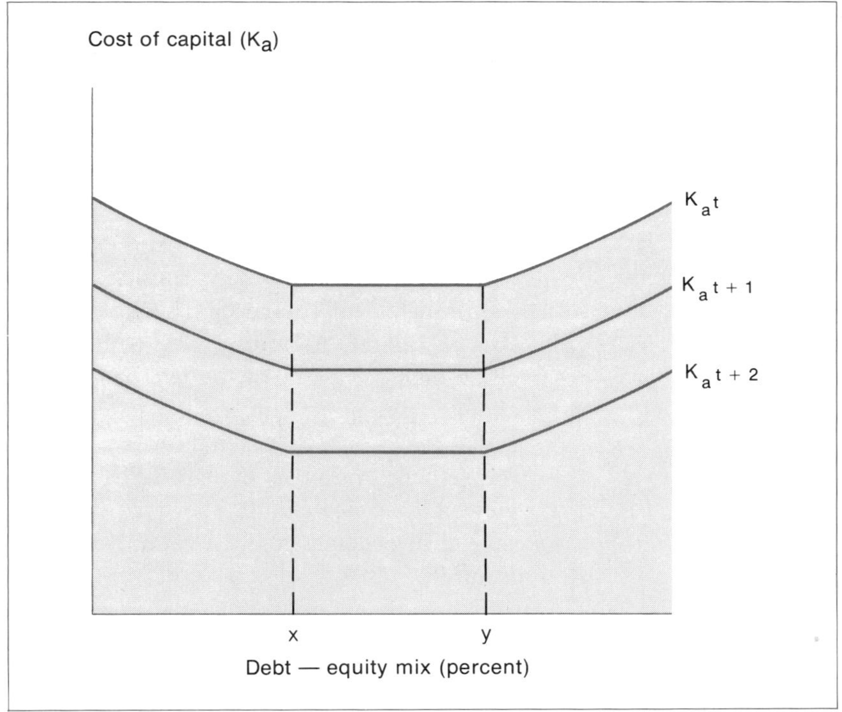


minimum cost of capital. Although we discussed minimizing the overall cost of capital ($K_a$) at a single debt-to-equity ratio, in reality a firm operates within a relevant range of debt to equity before it becomes penalized with a higher overall cost because of increased risk.

Figure 11–2 shows a theoretical cost-of-capital curve at three different points in time. As we move from time period $t$ to time period $t + 2$, falling interest rates and rising stock prices cause a downward shift in $K_a$. This graph illuminates two basic points: (1) the firm wants to keep its debt-to-equity ratio between $x$ and $y$ at all times; and (2) the firm would rather finance its long-term needs at $K_a t + 2$ than at $K_a t$. Corporations are allowed some leeway in the money and capital markets, and it is not uncommon for the debt-to-equity ratio to fluctuate between $x$ and $y$ over a business cycle. The firm that is at point $y$ has lost the flexibility of increasing its debt-to-equity ratio without incurring the penalty of higher capital costs.

## Cost of Capital in the Capital Budgeting Decision

It is always the current cost of capital for each source of funds that is important when making a capital budgeting decision. Historical costs for past fundings may have very little to do with current costs against which present returns must be measured. When raising new financial capital, a company will tap the various sources of financing over a reasonable period of time. Regardless of the particular source of funds that the company is using for the purchase of an asset, the required rate of return or discount rate will be the weighted average cost of capital. As long as the company earns its cost of capital, the common stock value of the firm will be maintained, since stockholder expectations are being met. For example, assume the Baker Corporation was considering making an investment in eight projects with the returns and costs shown in Table 11–4. These projects could be viewed graphically and merged with the weighted average cost of capital in order to make a capital budgeting decision, as indicated in Figure 11–3.

Notice that the Baker Corporation is facing a total of $95 million in projects, but given the weighted average cost of capital of 10.19 percent it will choose only projects A through E, or $50 million in new assets. Selecting assets F, G, and H would probably reduce the market value of the common stock because these projects do not provide a return equal to the overall costs of raising funds. We cannot forget that the use of the weighted average cost of capital assumes that the Baker Corporation is in its optimum capital structure range.

**Table 11–4**
**Investment projects available to the Baker Corporation**

| *Projects* | *Expected Returns* | *Cost ($ millions)* |
|---|---|---|
| A | 16.00% | $10 |
| B | 14.00 | 5 |
| C | 13.50 | 4 |
| D | 11.80 | 20 |
| E | 10.40 | 11 |
| F | 9.50 | 20 |
| G | 8.60 | 15 |
| H | 7.00 | 10 |
| | | $95 million |

Figure 11–3
Cost of capital and investment projects for the Baker Corporation

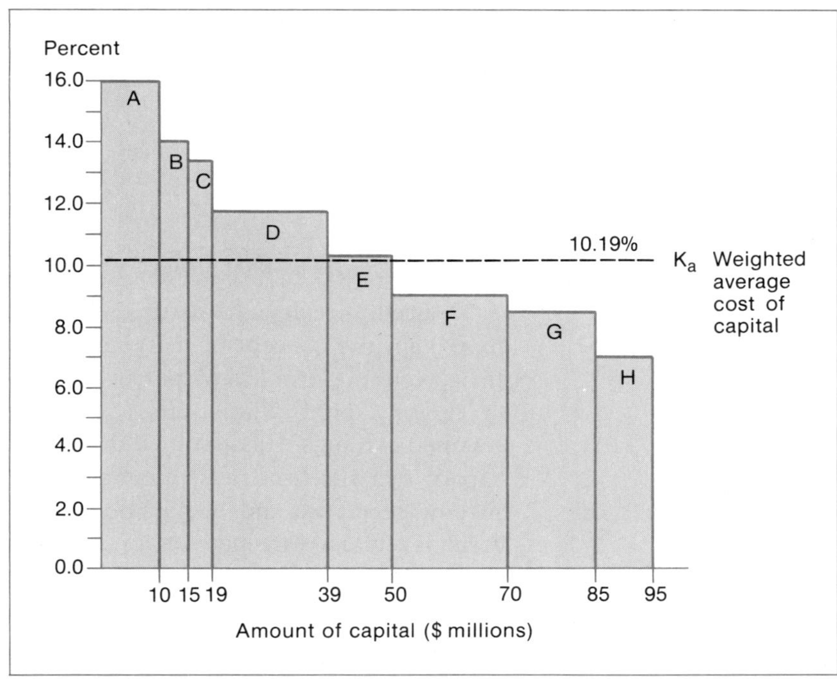


## The Marginal Cost of Capital

Nothing guarantees the Baker Corporation that its component cost of capital will stay constant for as much money as it wants to raise even if a given capital structure is maintained. If a large amount of financing is desired, the market may demand a higher cost of capital for each amount of funds desired. The point is analogous to the fact that you may be able to go to your relatives and best friends and raise funds for an investment at 10 percent. After you have exhausted the lending or investing power of those closest to you, you will have to look to other sources and the marginal cost of your capital will go up.

As a background for this discussion, the cost of capital table for the Baker Corporation is reproduced again.

| | | *Cost (aftertax)* | *Weights* | *Weighted Cost* |
|---|---|---|---|---|
| Debt . . . . . . . . . . . . . | $K_d$ | 6.34% | 30% | 1.90% |
| Preferred stock . . . . . . . . | $K_p$ | 10.94 | 10 | 1.09 |
| Common equity (retained earnings) . . . . | $K_e$ | 12.00 | 60 | 7.20 |
| Weighted average Cost of capital . . . . . . | $K_a$ | | | 10.19% |

We need to review the nature of the firm's capital structure in order to explain the concept of marginal cost of capital as it applies to the firm. Note the firm has 60 percent of the capital structure in the form of equity capital. The equity (ownership) capital is represented by retained earnings. It is assumed that 60 percent is the amount of equity capital that the firm must maintain to keep a balance between fixed income securities and ownership interest. But equity capital in the form of retained earnings can not grow indefinitely as the firm's capital needs expand. Retained earnings is limited to the amount of past and present earnings that can be redeployed into the investment projects of the firm. Let's assume the Baker Corporation has $23.40 million of retained earnings available for investment. Since retained earnings is to represent 60 percent of the capital structure, there is adequate retained earnings to support a capital structure of $39 million. More formally, we say that:

$$X = \frac{\text{Retained earnings}}{\text{Percent of retained earnings in the capital structure}} \qquad (11\text{–}8)$$

(Where $X$ represents the size of the capital structure that retained earnings will support.)

$$X = \frac{\$23.40 \text{ million}}{.60}$$
$$= \$39 \text{ million}$$

After the first $39 million of capital is raised, retained earnings will no longer be available to provide the 60 percent equity position in the capital structure. Nevertheless, lenders and investors will still require that 60 percent of the capital structure be in the form of common equity (ownership) capital. Because of this, *new* common stock will replace

**Table 11–5 Cost of capital for different amounts of financing**

| First $39 Million | | | | | Next $11 Million | | | | |
|---|---|---|---|---|---|---|---|---|---|
| | | A/T Cost | Wts. | Weighted Cost | | | A/T Cost | Wts. | Weighted Cost |
| Debt . . . . . . . | $K_d$ | 6.34% | .30 | 1.90% | Debt . . . . . . . | $K_d$ | 6.34% | .30 | 1.90% |
| Preferred . . . . | $K_p$ | 10.94 | .10 | 1.09 | Preferred . . . . | $K_p$ | 10.94 | .10 | 1.09 |
| Common equity* . . . . | $K_e$ | 12.00 | .60 | 7.20 | Common equity† . . . . | $K_n$ | 12.60 | .60 | 7.56 |
| | | | $K_a$ = | 10.19% | | | | $K_{mc}$ = | 10.55% |

*Retained earnings.

†New common stock.

retained earnings to provide the 60 percent common equity component for the firm. That is, after $39 million, common equity capital will be in the form of new common stock rather than retained earnings.

In the left-hand portion of Table 11–5, we see the original cost of capital that we have been discussing throughout the chapter. This applies up to $39 million. After $39 million, the concept of marginal cost of capital becomes important. The cost of capital goes up as shown on the right-hand portion of the table.

$K_{mc}$, in the right-hand portion of the table, represents the *marginal* cost of capital, and it is 10.55 percent after $39 million. What has happened is that the cost of capital has increased after $39 million because common equity is now in the form of new common stock rather than retained earnings. The aftertax (A/T) cost of the latter is slightly more expensive than the former because of flotation costs ($F$). The equation for the cost of new common stock was shown earlier in the chapter as Formula 11–7. For the example we are doing:

$$K_n = \frac{D_1}{P_0 - F} + g = \frac{\$2}{\$40 - \$4} + 7\%$$

$$= \frac{\$2}{\$36} + 7\% = 5.6\% + 7\% = 12.6\%$$

The flotation cost ($F$) is $4 and the cost of new common stock is 12.60 percent.

This is higher than the 12 percent cost of retained earnings that we have been using and causes the increase in the marginal cost of capital.

To carry the example a bit further, we will assume that the cost of debt of 6.34 percent applies to the first $15 million of debt that the firm raises. After that, the aftertax cost of debt will rise to 7.90 percent. Since debt represents 30 percent of the capital structure for the Baker Corporation, the cheaper form of debt can be used to support the capital structure up to $50 million. We derive the $50 million by using Formula 11–9.

$$Z = \frac{\text{Amount of lower cost debt}}{\text{Percent of debt in the capital structure}} \quad (11\text{–}9)$$

(Where $Z$ represents the size of the capital structure in which lower cost debt can be utilized.)

$$Z = \frac{\$15 \text{ million}}{.30}$$
$$= \$50 \text{ million}$$

After the first $50 million of capital is raised, lower-cost debt will no longer be available to provide 30 percent of the capital structure. After $50 million in total financing, the aftertax cost of debt will go up to the previously specified 7.90 percent. The marginal cost of capital for over $50 million in financing is shown in Table 11–6.

The change in the cost of debt gives way to a new marginal cost of capital ($K_{mc}$) of 11.02 percent after $50 million of financing. You should observe that the capital structure with over $50 million of financing reflects not only the change in the cost of debt, but also the continued exclusive use of new common stock to represent common equity capital. Of course, this change took place at $39 million, but must be carried on indefinitely as the capital structure expands.

**Table 11–6**
**Cost of capital for increasing amounts of financing**

| *Over $50 million* | | | | |
|---|---|---|---|---|
| | | *Cost (aftertax)* | *Weights* | *Weighted Cost* |
| Debt (higher cost) . . . . . | $K_d$ | 7.90% | .30 | 2.37% |
| Preferred stock . . . . . . . . | $K_p$ | 10.94 | .10 | 1.09 |
| Common equity (new common stock) . . . | $K_n$ | 12.60 | .60 | 7.56 |
| | | | $K_{mc}$ = | 11.02% |

We could carry on this process by next indicating a change in the cost of preferred stock, or continually increasing the cost of debt or new common stock as more and more capital is used. For now, it is sufficient that you merely observe the basic process. To summarize, we have said that the Baker Corporation has a basic weighted average cost of capital of 10.19 percent. This value was developed throughout the chapter and was originally presented in Table 11–1. However, as the firm began to substantially expand its capital structure, the weighted average cost of capital increased. This gave way to the concept of marginal cost of capital. The first increase or break point was at $39 million in which the marginal cost of capital went up to 10.55 percent as a result of replacing retained earnings with new common stock. The second increase or break point was at $50 million in which the marginal cost of capital increased to 11.02 percent as a result of the utilization of more expensive debt. The changes are summarized below.

| *Amount of Financing* | *Marginal Cost of Capital* |
|---|---|
| 0–$39 million | 10.19% |
| $39–50 million | 10.55 |
| Over $50 million | 11.02 |

In the previously presented Figure 11–3, we showed returns from investments A through H. In Figure 11–4, we reproduce the returns originally shown in Figure 11–3, but now include the concept of marginal cost of capital. Observe the increasing cost of capital (dotted lines) in relationship to the decreasing returns (straight lines).

In the earlier presentation in Figure 11–3, the Baker Corporation was justified in choosing projects A through E for a capital expenditure of $50 million. This is no longer the case in Figure 11–4. Because of the increasing marginal cost of capital, the returns exceed the cost of capital only up to $39 million and now only projects A through D are acceptable.

Although the concept of marginal cost of capital is very important, for most of our capital budgeting decisions in the next chapter, we will assume we are operating on the initial flat part of the marginal cost of capital curve in Figure 11–4, and that most of our decisions can be made based on the initial weighted average cost of capital.

**Figure 11–4**
**Marginal cost of capital and Baker Corporation projects**

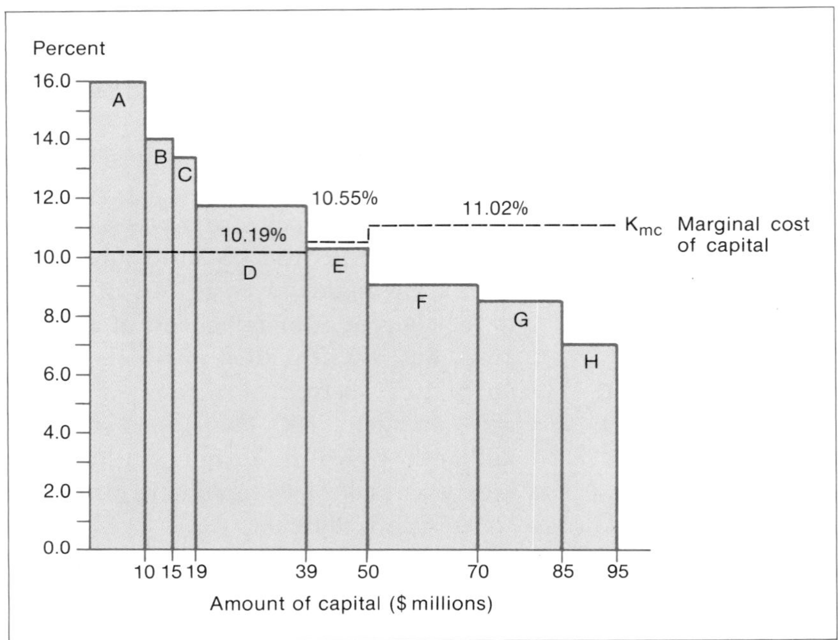


## Summary

The cost of capital for the firm is determined by computing the costs of various sources of financing and weighting them in proportion to their representation in the capital structure. The cost of each component in the capital structure is closely associated with the valuation of that source. For debt and preferred stock, the cost is directly related to the current yield, with debt adjusted downward to reflect the tax deductible nature of interest.

For common stock, the cost of retained earnings ($K_e$) is the current dividend yield on the security plus an anticipated rate of growth for the future. Minor adjustments are made to the formula to determine the cost of new common stock. A summary of the Baker Corporation's capital costs is presented in Table 11–7.

We weigh the elements in the capital structure in accordance with our desire to achieve a minimum overall cost. While debt is usually the "cheapest" form of financing, excessive debt use may increase the financial risk of the firm and drive up the costs of all sources of financing. The wise financial manager attempts to ascertain what debt

**Table 11–7**
**Cost of components in the capital structure**

| | | |
|---|---|---|
| 1. Cost of debt . . . . . . . . . . . . | $K_d = \text{Yield}\ (1 - T) = 6.34\%$ | Yield = 11.74%<br>$T$ = Corporate tax rate, 46% |
| 2. Cost of preferred stock . . . . . . | $K_p = \dfrac{D_p}{P_p - F} = 10.94\%$ | $D_p$ = Preferred dividend, \$10.50<br>$P_p$ = Price of preferred stock, \$100<br>$F$ = Flotation costs, \$4 |
| 3. Cost of common equity (retained earnings) . . . . . . . . . | $K_e = \dfrac{D_1}{P_0} + g = 12\%$ | $D_1$ = First year common dividend, \$2<br>$P_0$ = Price of common stock, \$40<br>$g$ = Growth rate, 7% |
| 4. Cost of new common stock . . . . | $K_n = \dfrac{D_1}{P_0 - F} + g = 12.60\%$ | Same as above, with $F$ = flotation costs, \$4 |

component will result in the lowest overall cost of capital. Once this has been determined, the weighted average cost of capital is the discount rate we use in present-valuing future flows to ensure we are earning at least the cost of financing.

The marginal cost of capital is also introduced to explain what happens to a company's cost of capital as it tries to finance a large amount of funds. First, the company will use up retained earnings, and the cost of financing will rise as higher-cost new common stock is substituted for retained earnings in order to maintain the optimum capital structure with the appropriate debt-to-equity ratio. Larger amounts of financial capital can also cause the individual means of financing to rise by raising interest rates or by depressing the price of the stock because more is sold than the market wants to absorb.

## List of Terms

**financial capital**
**optimum capital structure**
**common equity**
**cost of capital**
**weighted average cost of capital**
**marginal cost of capital**
**dividend valuation model**
**flotation costs**
**capital asset pricing model (CAPM)**

## Discussion Questions

1. Why do we use the overall cost of capital for investment decisions even when only one source of capital will be used (e.g., debt)?
2. How does the cost of a source of capital relate to the valuation concepts presented in Chapter 10?
3. In computing the cost of capital, do we use the historical costs of existing debt and equity or the current costs as determined in the market? Why?
4. Why is the cost of debt less than the cost of preferred stock if both securities are priced to yield 10 percent in the market?
5. What are the two sources of equity (ownership) capital for the firm?
6. Explain why retained earnings has an opportunity cost associated with it?
7. Why is the cost of retained earnings the equivalent of the firm's own required rate of return on common stock ($K_e$)?
8. Why is the cost of new common stock ($K_n$) higher than the cost of retained earnings? ($K_e$)?
9. How are the weights determined to arrive at the optimal weighted average cost of capital?
10. Modigliani and Miller previously maintained that the cost of capital is constant for all debt–equity mixes. The traditional approach maintains that it is U-shaped. Explain the logic of the traditional approach.
11. Identify other variables (ratios) besides the debt-to-equity ratio that you think will influence a company's cost of capital. You may wish to refer to Chapter 3 for possibilities.
12. It has often been said that if the company can't earn a rate of return greater than the cost of capital it should not make investments. Explain.

**13.** What effect would inflation have on a company's cost of capital? (Hint: Think about how inflation influences interest rates, stock prices, corporate profits, and growth.)

**14.** What is the concept of marginal cost of capital?

## Problems

**1.** Orbit Enterprises can issue debt yielding 12 percent. The company is in a 40 percent tax bracket.

What is the aftertax cost of debt?

**2.** Calculate the aftertax cost of debt under each of the following conditions.

| | *Yield* | *Corporate Tax Rate* |
|---|---|---|
| *a.* | 8.0% | 16% |
| *b.* | 14.0 | 46 |
| *c.* | 11.5 | 24 |

**3.** Calculate the aftertax cost of debt on a bond issue yielding 12 percent. The issuing company pays tax at a rate of 42 percent, and will incur distribution costs of 1 percent on this bond issue. (See text footnote 1.)

**4.** Oxford Clothiers has a $1,000 par value bond outstanding with 20 years to maturity. The bond carries an annual interest payment of $95 and is currently selling for $920 per bond. Oxford Clothiers is in a 35 percent tax bracket. The firm wishes to know what the aftertax cost of a new bond issue is likely to be. The yield to maturity on the new issue will be the same as the yield to maturity on the old issue because the risk and maturity date will be similar.

*a.* Compute the approximate yield to maturity on the old issue and use this as the yield for the new issue.

*b.* Make the appropriate tax adjustment to determine the aftertax cost of debt.

**5.** Oklahoma Gas and Electric is planning to issue debt that will mature in the year 2000. In many respects the issue is similar to currently outstanding debt of the corporation. Using Table 11–2 in the chapter, identify:

*a.* The yield to maturity on similarly outstanding debt for the firm, in terms of maturity.
*b.* Assume that because the new debt will be issued at par, the required yield to maturity will be 0.15 percent higher than the value determined in part *a*. Add this factor to the answer in *a*. (New issues at par sometimes require a slightly higher yield than old issues that are trading below par. There is less leverage and tax advantages.)
*c.* If the firm is in a 46 percent tax bracket, what is the aftertax cost of debt?

**6.** Schuss, Inc., can sell preferred stock for $60 with an estimated flotation cost of $3. The preferred stock is anticipated to pay $7 per share in dividends.

*a.* Compute the cost of preferred stock for Schuss, Inc.
*b.* Do we need to make a tax adjustment for the issuing firm?

**7.** The Holtz Corporation issued $100 par value stock 10 years ago. The stock provided a 9 percent preferred stock yield at the time of issue. The preferred stock is now selling for $85.

*a.* What is the current yield or cost of preferred stock? (Disregard flotation costs.)
*b.* If a 5 percent flotation (selling) cost is presently involved in issuing new preferred stock, what is the current cost to issue preferred stock? [Hint: divide the answer in part *a* by (1 − flotation percentage).]

**8.** Ellington Electronics wants you to calculate its cost of common stock. During the next 12 months, the company expects to pay dividends ($D_1$) of $1.50 per share, and the current price of its common stock is $30 per share. The expected growth rate is 8 percent.

*a.* Compute the cost of retained earnings ($K_e$). Use Formula 11–6.
*b.* If a $2 flotation cost is involved, compute the cost of new common stock ($K_n$). Use Formula 11–7.

**9.** Compute $K_e$ and $K_n$ under the following circumstances:

*a.* $D_1 = \$4.60$, $P_0 = \$60$, $g = 6\%$, $F = \$4.00$
*b.* $D_1 = \$0.25$, $P_0 = \$20$, $g = 10\%$, $F = \$1.50$.
*c.* $E_1$ (earnings at the end of period one) $= \$6$, payout ratio equals 30 percent, $P_0 = \$25$, $g = 4.5\%$, $F = \$2$.
*d.* $D_0$ (dividend at the *beginning* of the first period) $= \$3$, growth rate for dividends and earnings ($g$) $= 7\%$, $P_0 = \$42$, $F = \$3$.

**10.** Sam's Fine Garments sells jackets and sport coats in suburban shopping malls throughout the country. Business has been good as indicated by the six-year growth in earnings per share. The earnings have grown from \$1.00 to \$1.87.

*a.* Use Appendix A at the back of the text to determine the compound annual rate of growth in earnings ($n = 6$).
*b.* Based on the growth rate determined in part *a*, project earnings for next year ($E_1$). Round to two places to the right of the decimal point.
*c.* Assume the dividend payout ratio is 40 percent. Compute ($D_1$). Round to two places to the right of the decimal point.
*d.* The current price of the stock is \$15. Using the growth rate ($g$) from part *a* and $D_1$ from part *c*, compute $K_e$.
*e.* If the flotation cost is \$1.75, compute the cost of new common stock ($K_n$).

**11.** The Tyler Oil Company's capital structure is as follows:

| | |
|---|---|
| Debt . . . . . . . . . | 35% |
| Preferred stock . . . . | 15 |
| Common equity . . . . | 50 |

The aftertax cost of debt is 7 percent; the cost of preferred stock is 10 percent; and the cost of common equity (in the form of retained earnings) is 13 percent.

Calculate Tyler Oil Company's weighted average cost of capital in a manner similar to Table 11–1.

**12.** As an alternative to the capital structure shown in Problem 11 for the Tyler Oil Company, an outside consultant has suggested the following modifications.

| | |
|---|---|
| Debt | 60% |
| Preferred stock | 5 |
| Common equity | 35 |

Under this new, more debt-oriented arrangement, the aftertax cost of debt is 8.8 percent, the cost of preferred stock is 10.5 percent, and the cost of common equity (in the form of retained earnings) is 15.5 percent.

Recalculate Tyler Oil Company's weighted average cost of capital.

Which plan is optimal in terms of minimizing the weighted average cost of capital?

**13.** Given the following information, calculate the weighted average cost of capital for Genex Corporation. Line up the calculations in the order shown in Table 11–1.

Percent of capital structure:

| | |
|---|---|
| Debt | 35% |
| Preferred stock | 10 |
| Common equity | 55 |

Additional information:

| | |
|---|---|
| Bond coupon rate | 13% |
| Bond yield | 11% |
| Dividend, expected common | \$3.00 |
| Dividend, preferred | \$10.00 |
| Price, common | \$50.00 |
| Price, preferred | \$98.00 |
| Flotation cost, preferred | \$5.50 |
| Growth rate | 8% |
| Corporate tax rate | 30% |

**14.** Georgia Atlantic Corporation is trying to calculate its cost of capital for use in a capital budgeting decision. Mr. Krone, the vice president of finance, has given you the following information and has asked you to compute the weighted average cost of capital. The company currently has outstanding a bond with a 9 percent coupon rate and a convertible bond with a 6½ percent coupon rate. Georgia Atlantic's investment banker has informed Mr. Krone that bonds of equal risk and credit rating are currently selling to yield 13 percent. The common stock has a price of \$30 per share and an expected dividend ($D_1$) of \$1 per share. Georgia Atlantic's historical growth rate of dividends and earnings per share has been 15 percent, but security analysts on Wall Street expect this growth to slow to 12 percent in future years. The preferred stock is selling at $50 per share and carries a dividend of $5 per share. The corporate tax rate is 40 percent. The flotation costs are 4 percent of the selling price for preferred stock. The optimum capital structure for Georgia Atlantic seems to be 30 percent debt, 10 percent preferred stock, and 60 percent common equity in the form of retained earnings.

Compute the cost of capital for the individual components in the capital structure and then calculate the weighted average cost of capital (similar to Table 11–1).

**15.** Southeast Electric Utility Company faces increasing needs for capital. Fortunately, it has an Aa2 credit rating. The corporate tax rate is 46 percent. Southeast's treasurer is trying to determine the corporation's current weighted average cost of capital in order to assess the profitability of capital budgeting projects. Historically, the corporation's earnings and dividends per share have increased at about a 5 percent annual rate. Southeast common stock is selling at $50 per share, and the company will pay a $4 per share dividend ($D_1$). The company's $100 preferred stock has been yielding 9 percent in the current market. Flotation costs for the company have been estimated by its investment banker to be $2 for preferred stock. The company's optimum capital structure is 40 percent debt, 15 percent preferred stock, and 45 percent common equity in the form of retained earnings. Refer to the table below on bond issues for comparative yields on bonds of equal risk to Southeast.

*Data on Bond Issues*

| *Issue* | *Moody's Rating* | *Price* | *Yield to Maturity* |
|---|---|---|---|
| Utilities: | | | |
| Balt. G&E 8–3/8's 2006 | Aa1 | $753.75 | 11.38% |
| New Jersey Bell 6–5/8's 2008 | Aa2 | 601.00 | 11.70 |
| Miss. Pow. 9.62's 2008 | A1 | 821.00 | 11.97 |
| Industrials: | | | |
| IBM 9–3/8's 2004 | Aaa | 912.00 | 10.61 |
| N'west Corp. 10–1/2's 2000 | Aa3 | 909.00 | 11.81 |
| General Mills 9–3/8's 2009 | A2 | 800.50 | 12.06 |

Compute the following from the preceding information.

*a.* Cost of debt, $K_d$ (use the table on page 347—relate to utility bond credit rating for yield.)
*b.* Cost of preferred stock, $K_p$.
*c.* Cost of common equity in the form of retained earnings, $K_e$.
*d.* Weighted average cost of capital.

**16.** The Nolan Corporation finds that it is necessary to determine its marginal cost of capital. Nolan's current capital structure calls for 45 percent debt, 15 percent preferred stock, and 40 percent common equity. Initially, common equity will be in the form of retained earnings ($K_e$) and then new common stock ($K_n$). The costs of the various sources of financing are as follows: debt, 5.6 percent; preferred stock, 9 percent; retained earnings, 12 percent; and new common stock, 13.2 percent.

*a.* What is the initial weighted average cost of capital? (Include debt, preferred stock, and common equity in the form of retained earnings, $K_e$.)
*b.* If the firm has $12 million in retained earnings, at what size capital structure will the firm run out of retained earnings?
*c.* What will the marginal cost of capital be immediately after that point? (Equity will remain at 40 percent of the capital structure, but will all be in the form of new common stock, $K_n$.)
*d.* The 5.6 percent cost of debt referred to above applies only to the first $18 million of debt. After that the cost of debt will be 7.2 percent. At what size capital structure will there be a change in the cost of debt?
*e.* What will the marginal cost of capital be immediately after that point? (Consider the facts in both parts *c* and *d*.)

**17.** Hailey Mills, an apparel manufacturer, is in the process of expanding its productive capacity to introduce a new line of products. Current plans call for a possible expenditure of $100 million on four projects of equal size ($25 million), but different returns. Project A will increase the firm's processed yarn capacity and has an expected return of 15 percent after taxes. Project B will increase the capacity for woven fabrics and carries a return of 13.5 percent. Project C, a venture into synthetic fibers, is expected to earn 11.2

percent, and Project D, an investment into dye and textile chemicals, is expected to show a 10.5 percent return.

The firm's capital structure consists of 40 percent debt and 60 percent common equity, and this will continue in the future. There is no preferred stock.

Hailey Mills has $15 million in retained earnings. After a capital structure with $15 million in retained earnings is reached (in which retained earnings represent 60 percent of the financing), all additional equity financing must come in the form of new common stock.

Common stock is selling for $30 per share and underwriting costs are estimated at $3 if new shares are issued. Dividends for the next year will be $1.50 per share ($D_1$), and earnings and dividends have grown consistently at 9 percent per year.

The yield on comparative bonds has been hovering at 11 percent. The investment banker feels that the first $20 million of bonds could be sold to yield 11 percent while additional debt might require a 2 percent premium and be marketed to yield 13 percent. The corporate tax rate is 45 percent.

*a.* Based on the two sources of financing, what is the initial weighted average cost of capital? (Use $K_d$ and $K_e$.)

*b.* At what size capital structure will the firm run out of retained earnings?

*c.* What will the marginal cost of capital be immediately after that point?

*d.* At what size capital structure will there be a change in the cost of debt?

*e.* What will the marginal cost of capital be immediately after that point?

*f.* Based on the information about potential returns on investments in the first paragraph and information on marginal cost of capital (in parts *a*, *c*, and *e*), how large a capital investment budget should the firm use?

*g.* Graph the answer determined in part *f*.

**18.** (*Comprehensive problem*)

Logan Manufacturing is a very large company with common stock listed on the New York Stock Exchange and bonds traded over-the-counter. As of the current balance sheet, it has three bond issues outstanding:

$100 million of 8–3/4 percent series 1999
$ 50 million of 6 percent series 1989
$150 million of 4 percent series 1988

The vice president of finance is planning to sell $150 million of bonds next year to replace the debt due to expire in 1988. At present, market yields on similar Aaa bonds are 10.8 percent.

Logan also has $100 million of 4.5 percent noncallable preferred stock outstanding, and it has no intentions of selling any preferred stock at any time in the future. The preferred stock is currently priced at $47 per share, and its dividend per share is $4.50.

The company has had very volatile earnings, but its dividends per share have had a very stable growth rate of 5 percent and this will continue. The expected dividend ($D_1$) is $2.80 per share, and the common stock is selling for $45 per share. The company's investment banker has quoted Logan the following flotation costs: $2 per share for preferred stock and $1.90 per share for common stock.

On the advice of its investment banker, Logan has kept its debt at 50 percent of assets and its equity at 50 percent. Logan sees no need to sell either common or preferred stock in the foreseeable future as it generates enough internal funds for its investment needs when these funds are combined with debt financing. Logan's corporate tax rate is 46 percent.

Compute the cost of capital for the following:

*a.* Bond (debt) ($K_d$).
*b.* Preferred stock ($K_p$).
*c.* Common equity in the form of retained earnings ($K_e$).
*d.* New common stock ($K_n$).
*e.* Weighted average cost of capital.

## Selected References

Alberts, W. W., and S. H. Archer. "Some Evidence on the Effect of Company Size on the Cost of Equity Capital." *Journal of Financial and Quantitative Analysis* 8 (March 1973), pp. 229–42.

Archer, Stephen H., and Leroy G. Faerber. "Firm Size and the Cost of Equity Capital." *Journal of Finance* 21 (March 1966), pp. 69–84.

Arditti, F. D. "The Weighted Average Cost of Capital: Some Questions on Its Definition, Interpretation, and Use." *Journal of Finance* 28 (September 1973), pp. 1001–8.

Beranek, William. "The Cost of Capital, Capital Budgeting, and the Maximization of Shareholder Wealth." *Journal of Financial and Quantitative Analysis* 10 (March 1975), pp. 1–21.

Bierman, Harold, Jr., and Jerome E. Hass. "Capital Budgeting under Uncertainty: A Reformulation." *Journal of Finance* 28 (March 1973), pp. 119–20.

Brennan, Michael J. "A New Look at the Weighted Average Cost of Capital." *Journal of Business Finance* 5, no. 1 (1973), pp. 24–30.

Brigham, Eugene F., and Keith V. Smith. "The Cost of Capital to the Small Firm." *Engineering Economist* 13 (Fall 1967), pp. 1–26.

Conine, Thomas E., Jr., and Maury Tamarkin. "Divisional Cost of Capital Estimation: Adjusting for Leverage." *Financial Management* 14 (Spring 1985), pp. 54–58.

Elton, Edwin J., and Martin J. Gruber. "The Cost of Retained Earnings—Implications of Share Repurchase." *Industrial Management Review* 9 (Spring 1968), pp. 87–104.

Fuller, Russell J. and Halbert S. Kerr. "Estimating the Divisional Cost of Capital: An Analysis of the Pure-Play Technique." *Journal of Finance* 36 (December 1981), pp. 997–1009.

Gordon, Myron J., and Paul J. Halpern. "Cost of Capital for a Division of a Firm." *Journal of Finance* 29 (September 1974), pp. 1153–63.

Lewellen, Wilbur G. *The Cost of Capital*. Belmont, Calif.: Wadsworth, 1969.

Lintner, John. "The Cost of Capital and Optimal Financing of Corporate Growth." *Journal of Finance* 18 (May 1963), pp. 292–310.

Long, Susan W. "Risk-Premium Curve vs. Capital Market Line: Differences Explained." *Financial Management* 7 (Spring 1978), pp. 60–64.

Modigliani, F., and M. Miller. "The Cost of Capital, Corporation Finance, and the Theory of Investment." *American Economic Review* 48 (June 1958), pp. 261–96.

Nantell, Timothy J., and C. Robert Carlson. "The Cost of Capital as a Weighted Average." *Journal of Finance* 30 (December 1975), pp. 1343–55.

Ofer, Aharon R. "Investors' Expectations of Earnings Growth, Their Accuracy, and Effects on the Structure of Realized Rates of Return." *Journal of Finance* 30 (May 1975), pp. 509–23.

Roll, Richard. "A Critique of the Asset Pricing Theory's Test. Part 1; On the Past and Potential Testability of the Theory." *Journal of Financial Economics* 4 (March 1977), pp. 129–76.

———. "Ambiguity When Performance is Measured by the Securities Market Line." *Journal of Finance* 33 (September 1978), pp. 1051–70.

Sharpe, William F. "Capital Asset Prices: A Theory of Market Equilibrium under Conditions of Risk." *Journal of Finance* 19 (September 1964), pp. 425–42.

Solomon, Ezra. "Measuring a Company's Cost of Capital." *Journal of Business* 28 (October 1955), pp. 240–52.

## Appendix 11A: Cost of Capital and the Capital Asset Pricing Model (Optional)

### The Capital Asset Pricing Model

The capital asset pricing model (CAPM) relates the risk-return tradeoffs of individual assets to market returns. Common stock returns over time have generally been used to test this model since stock prices are widely available and efficiently priced, as are market indexes of stock performance. In theory the CAPM encompasses all assets, but in practice it is difficult to measure returns on all types of assets or to find an all-encompassing market index. For our purposes, we will use common stock returns to explain the model and occasionally we will generalize to other assets.

The basic form of the CAPM is a linear relationship between returns on individual stocks and the market over time. By using least squares regression analysis, the return on an individual stock, $K_j$, is expressed in Formula 11A–1.

$$K_j = \alpha + \beta K_m + e \qquad (11A\text{–}1)$$

where

$K_j$ = Return on individual common stock of a company
$\alpha$ = Alpha, the intercept on the y-axis
$\beta$ = Beta, the coefficient
$K_m$ = Return on the market (usually an index of stock returns is used)
$e$ = Error term of the regression equation

As indicated in Table 11A–1 and Figure 11A–1, this equation uses historical data to generate the beta coefficient ($\beta$), a measurement of the return performance of a given stock versus the return performance of the market. Assume that we want to calculate a beta for Parts Associates, Inc. (PAI), and that we have the performance data for that company and the market shown in Table 11A–1. The relationship between PAI and the market appears graphically in Figure 11A–1.

The alpha term in Figure 11A–1 of 2.8 percent is the *y*-intercept of the linear regression. It is the expected return on PAI stock if returns on the market are zero. However, if the returns on the market are expected to approximate the historical rate of 12.4 percent, the expected return on PAI would be $K_j = 2.8 + 0.9(12.4) = 14.0$ percent. This maintains the historical relationship. If the returns on the market are expected to rise to 18 percent next year, expected return on PAI would be $K_j = 2.8 + 0.9\ (18.0) = 19$ percent.

Notice that we are talking in terms of expectations. The CAPM is an exceptional (ex ante) model, and there is no guarantee that historical data will reoccur. One area of empirical testing involves the stability

**Table 11A–1**
**Performance of PAI and the market**

| | Rate of Return on Stock | |
|---|---|---|
| *Year* | *PAI* | *Market* |
| 1 | 12.0% | 10.0% |
| 2 | 16.0 | 18.0 |
| 3 | 20.0 | 16.0 |
| 4 | 16.0 | 10.0 |
| 5 | 6.0 | 8.0 |
| Mean return | 14.0% | 12.4% |
| Standard deviation | 4.73% | 3.87% |

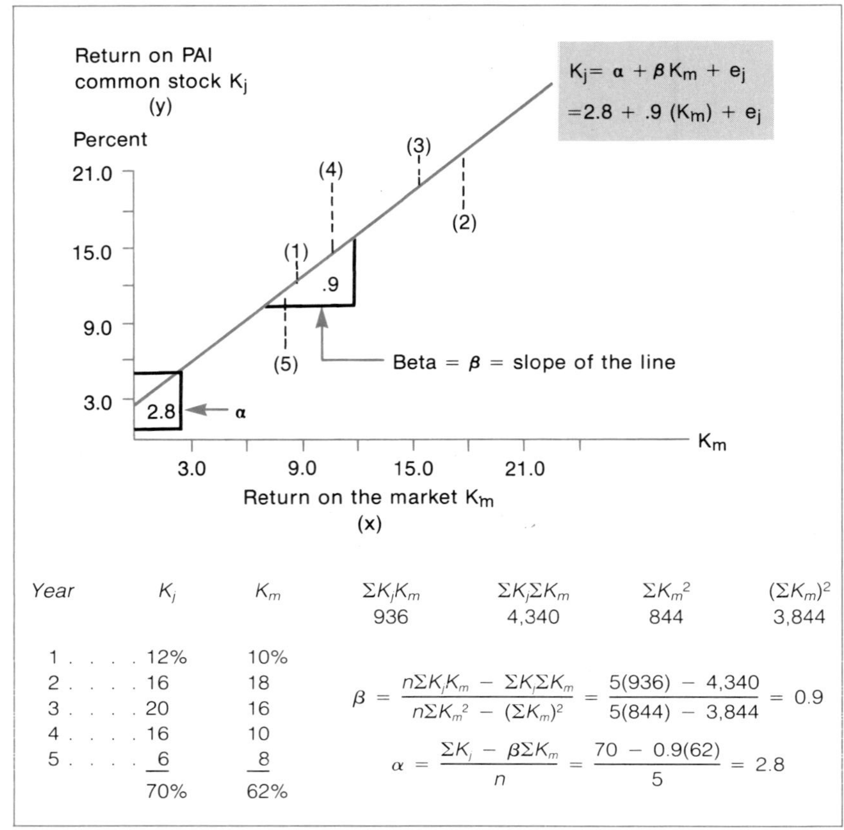


| Year | $K_j$ | $K_m$ |
|---|---|---|
| 1 . . . . | 12% | 10% |
| 2 . . . . | 16 | 18 |
| 3 . . . . | 20 | 16 |
| 4 . . . . | 16 | 10 |
| 5 . . . . | 6 | 8 |
| | 70% | 62% |

| $\Sigma K_j K_m$ | $\Sigma K_j \Sigma K_m$ | $\Sigma K_m^2$ | $(\Sigma K_m)^2$ |
|---|---|---|---|
| 936 | 4,340 | 844 | 3,844 |

$$\beta = \frac{n\Sigma K_j K_m - \Sigma K_j \Sigma K_m}{n\Sigma K_m^2 - (\Sigma K_m)^2} = \frac{5(936) - 4{,}340}{5(844) - 3{,}844} = 0.9$$

$$\alpha = \frac{\Sigma K_j - \beta \Sigma K_m}{n} = \frac{70 - 0.9(62)}{5} = 2.8$$

**Figure 11A–1**
**Linear regression of returns between PAI and the market**

and predictability of the beta coefficient based on historical data. Research has indicated that betas are more useful in a portfolio context (for groupings of stocks) because the betas of individual stocks are less stable from period to period than portfolio betas. In addition, there seems to be a tendency for individual betas to approach 1.0 over time.

## The Security Market Line

The capital asset pricing model evolved from Formula 11A–1 into a risk premium model where the basic assumption is that in order for investors to take more risk they must be compensated by larger expected returns. Investors should also not accept returns that are less than they can get from a riskless asset. For CAPM purposes it is assumed that short-term U.S. Treasury bills may be considered a riskless asset.[1] When viewed in this context, an investor must achieve an extra return above that obtainable from a Treasury bill in order to induce the assumption of more risk. This brings us to the more common and theoretically useful model:

$$K_j = R_f + \beta(K_m - R_f) \qquad (11A\text{–}2)$$

where

$R_f$ = Risk-free rate of return
$\beta$ = Beta coefficient from Formula 11A–1
$K_m$ = Return on the market index
$K_m - R_f$ = Premium or excess return of the market versus the risk-free rate (since the market is riskier than $R_f$, the assumption is that the expected $K_m$ will be greater than $R_f$)
$\beta(K_m - R_f)$ = Expected return above the risk-free rate for the stock of Company $j$, given the level of risk.

The model centers on "beta," the coefficient of the premium demanded by an investor to invest in an individual stock. For each individual security, beta measures the sensitivity (volatility) of the security's return to the market. By definition, the market has a beta of 1.0, so that if an individual company's beta is 1.0, it can expect to have returns as volatile as the market and total returns equal to the market. A company with a beta of 2.0 would be twice as volatile as the market and would be expected to generate more returns, whereas a company with a beta of 0.5 would be half as volatile as the market. For example, assuming that the risk-free rate is 9.0 percent and that the expected return in the market is 11 percent, the following returns would occur with betas of 2.0, 1.0, and 0.5.

$$K_2 = 9.0\% + 2.0\,(11.0\% - 9.0\%) = 13\%$$
$$K_1 = 9.0\% + 1.0\,(11.0\% - 9.0\%) = 11\%$$
$$K_{.5} = 9.0\% + 0.5\,(11.0\% - 9.0\%) = 10\%$$

[1] A number of studies have also indicated that longer-term government securities may appropriately represent $R_f$, or the risk-free rate.

Basically beta measures the riskiness of an investment relative to the market. In order to outperform the market, one would have to assume more risk by selecting assets with betas greater than 1.0. Another way of looking at the risk-return trade-off would be that if less risk than the market is desired, an investor would choose assets with a beta of less than 1.0. Beta is a good measure of a stock's risk when the stock is combined into a portfolio, and therefore it has some bearing on the assets that a company acquires for its portfolio of real capital.

In Figure 11A–1, individual stock returns were compared to market returns and the beta from Formula 11A–1 was shown. From Formula 11A–2, the risk premium model, a generalized risk-return graph called the security market line (SML) can be constructed that identifies the risk-return trade-off of any common stock (asset) relative to the company's beta. This is shown in Figure 11A–2.

The required return for all securities can be expressed as the risk-free rate plus a premium for risk. Thus, we see that a stock with a beta of 1.0 would have a risk premium of 2 percent added to the risk-free rate of 9 percent to provide a required return of 11 percent. Since a beta of 1.0 implies risk equal to the market, the return is also at the overall market rate. If the beta is 2.0, twice the market risk premium of 2 percent must be earned and we add 4 percent to the risk-free rate of 9 percent to determine the required return of 13 percent. For a beta of 0.5, the required return is 10 percent.

**Figure 11A–2**
**The security market line (SML)**

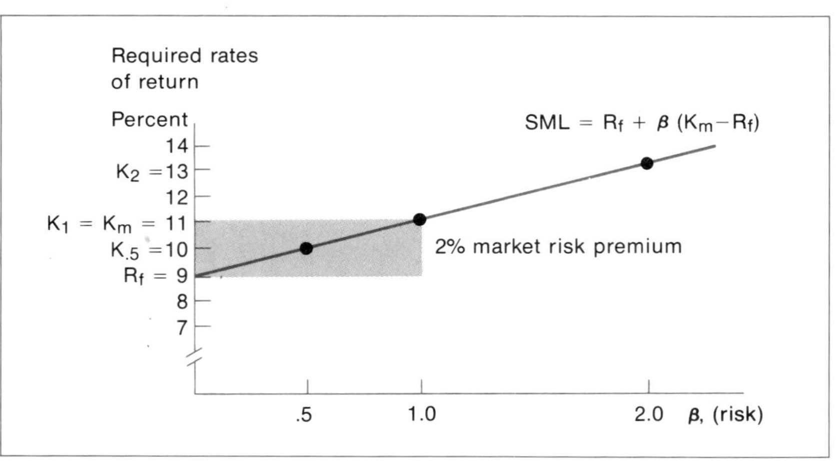

## Cost of Capital Considerations

When calculating the cost of capital for common stock, remember that $K_e$ is equal to the expected total return from the dividend yield and capital gains.

$$K_e = \frac{D_1}{P_0} + g$$

$K_e$ is the return required by investors based on expectations of future dividends and growth. The SML provides the same information, but in a market-related risk-return model. As required returns rise, prices must fall to adjust to the new equilibrium return level, and as required returns fall, prices rise. Stock markets are generally efficient and when stock prices are in equilibrium, the $K_e$ derived from the dividend model will be equal to $K_j$ derived from the SML.

The SML helps us to identify several circumstances that can cause the cost of capital to change. Figure 11–2 in Chapter 11 examined required rates of returns over time with changing interest rates and stock prices. Figure 11A–3 does basically the same thing, only through the SML format.

When interest rates increase from the initial period ($R_{f1}$ versus $R_{f0}$), the security market line in the next period is parallel to $SML_0$, but higher. What this means is that required rates of return have risen for

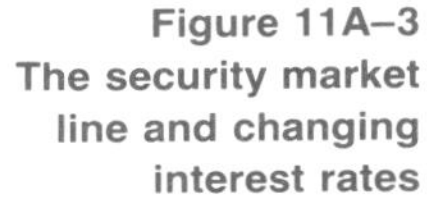
**Figure 11A–3**
**The security market line and changing interest rates**

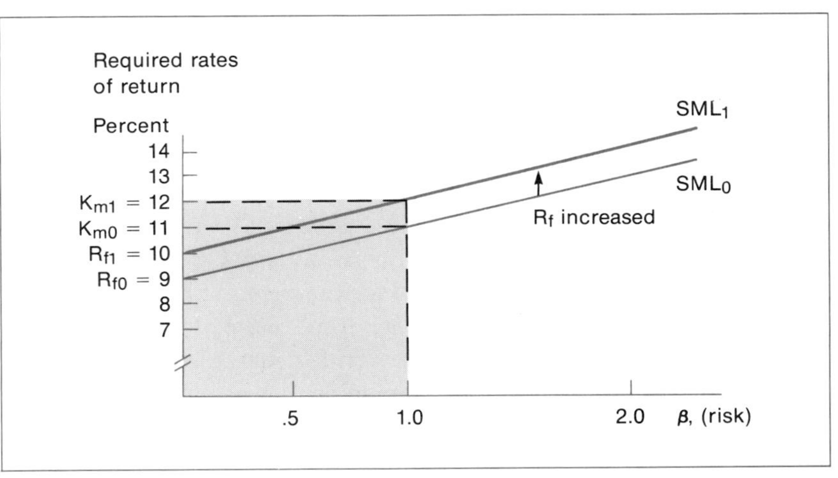

every level of risk, as investors desire to maintain their risk premium over the risk-free rate. The market rate will not always change by a percentage equal to that of the change in the risk-free rate. A steeper slope for the SML could cause a greater change in the required market returns.

One very important variable influencing interest rates is the rate of inflation. As inflation increases, lenders try to maintain their real dollar purchasing power, so they increase the required interest rates to offset inflation. The risk-free rate can be thought of as:

$$R_f = RR + IP$$

where

$RR$ is the real rate of return on a riskless government security when inflation is zero.

$IP$ is an inflation premium that compensates lenders (investors) for loss of purchasing power.

An upward shift in the SML indicates that the prices of all assets will shift downward as interest rates move up. In Chapter 10, Valuation and Rates of Return, this was demonstrated in the discussion which showed that when market interest rates went up, bond prices adjusted downward to make up for the lower coupon rate (interest payment) on the old bonds.

Another factor affecting the cost of capital is a change in risk preferences by investors. As investors become more pessimistic about the economy, they require larger premiums for assuming risks. This desire for more returns per unit of risk causes the SML to increase its slope, as indicated in Figure 11A–4. This change in risk premiums causes $(K_{m0} - R_f)$ to increase from 11 percent minus 9 percent, a 2 percent risk premium, to $(K_{m1} - R_f)$, a 4 percent risk premium (13 percent minus 9 percent). Any asset riskier than the market would have a larger increase in the required return. In many instances, rising interest rates and pessimistic investors go hand in hand, so that the SML may change its slope and intercept at the same time. This combined effect would cause severe drops in the prices of risky assets and much larger required rates of return for such assets.

The capital asset pricing model and the security market line have been presented to further your understanding of market-related events

Figure 11A–4
The security market line and changing investor expectations

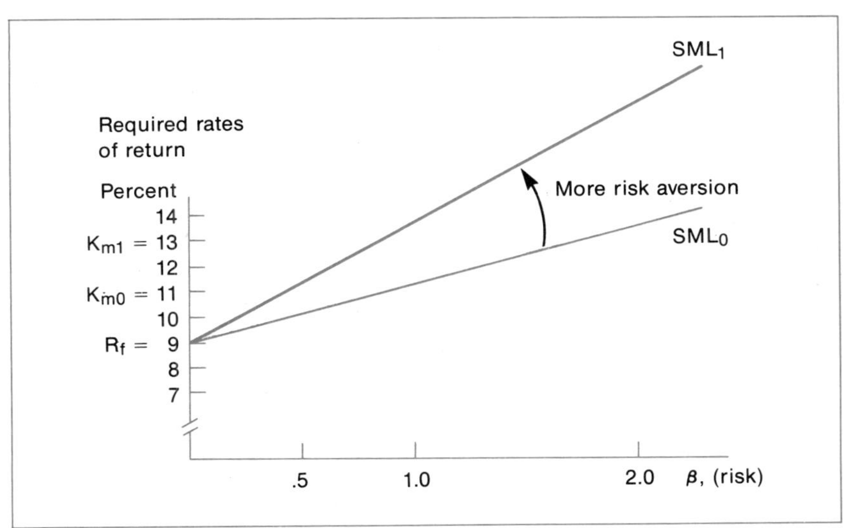


that impact the firm's cost of capital, such as market returns and risk, changing interest rates, and changing risk preferences.

While the capital asset pricing model has received criticism because of the difficulties of dealing with the betas of individual securities and because of the problems involved in consistently constructing the appropriate slope of the SML to represent reality, it provides some interesting insights into risk-return measurement.

## List of Terms

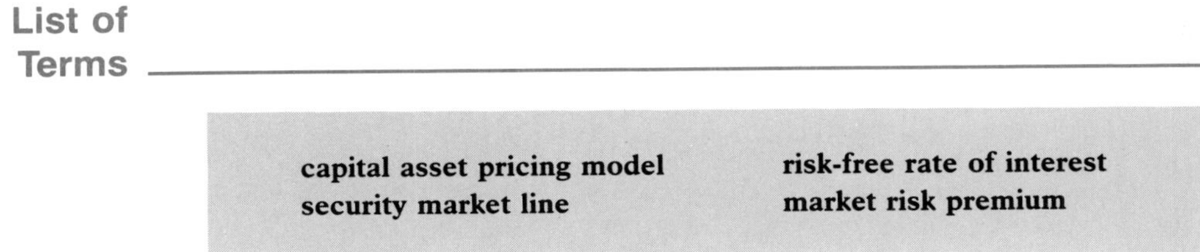


## Discussion Questions

**11A–1.** How does the capital asset pricing model help explain changing costs of capital?

**11A–2.** Why does $K_e$ approximate $K_j$, or why does $D_1/(P_0 - g)$ approximate $R_f + \beta\ (K_m - R_f)$?

**11A–3.** How does the SML react to changes in the rate of interest, changes in the rate of inflation, and changing investor expectations?

## Problems

**11A–1.** Assume that $R_f$ = 6 percent and $K_m$ = 10 percent. Compute $K_j$ for the following betas, using Formula 11A–2.

*a.* 0.7
*b.* 1.4
*c.* 2.0

**11A–2.** In the preceding problem, an increase in interest rates increases $R_f$ to 7.5 percent, and other factors increase $K_m$ to 11 percent. Compute $K_j$ for the three betas of 0.7, 1.4, and 2.0.

# 12 The Capital Budgeting Decision

The decision on capital outlays is among the most significant that a firm will have to make. A decision to build a new plant or expand into a foreign market may influence the performance of the firm over the next decade. The airline industry has shown a tendency to expand in excess of its needs, while other industries have insufficient capacity. The auto industry has often miscalculated its product mix and has had to shift down from one car size to another at an enormous expense.

The capital budgeting decision involves the planning of expenditures for a project with a life of at least one year, and usually a considerably longer period. In the public utilities sector, a time horizon of 25 years is not unusual. The capital expenditure decision requires extensive planning to ensure that engineering and marketing information is available, product design is completed, necessary patents are acquired, and the capital markets are tapped for the necessary funds. Throughout this chapter, we will use techniques developed under the discussion of the time value of money to equate future flows to the present, while using the cost of capital as the basic discount rate.

A problem a manager faces is that as the time horizon moves farther into the future, uncertainty becomes a greater hazard. The manager is uncertain about annual costs and inflows, product life, interest rates, economic conditions, and technological change. A good example of the vagueness of the marketplace can be observed in the hand calculator industry in the mid-1970s. A number of firms tooled up in the early 1970s in the hope of being first to break through the $100 price range for pocket calculators, assuming that penetration of the $100 barrier would bring a larger market share and high profitability. However, technological advancement, price cutting, and the appearance of Texas Instruments in the consumer market drove prices down by 60–90 percent and made the $100 pocket calculator a museum piece. Rapid Data Systems, the first entry into the under-$100 market, went into bankruptcy. Of course, not all new developments are quite so perilous, and a number of techniques, which will be treated in the next chapter, have been devised to cope with the impact of uncertainty on decision making.

In this chapter, capital budgeting will be studied under the following major topical headings: administrative considerations, accounting flows versus cash flows, methods of ranking investment proposals, selection strategy, combining cash flow and selection strategy, and the replacement decision. Later in the chapter, emphasis is placed on tax laws and their impact on depreciation and capital budgeting decisions.

## Administrative Considerations

A good capital budgeting program requires that a number of steps be taken in the decision-making process.

1. Search and discovery of investment opportunities.
2. Collection of data.
3. Evaluation and decision making.
4. Reevaluation and adjustment.

The search for new opportunities is the least emphasized, though perhaps the most important, of the four steps. Although it is outside the scope of this book to suggest procedures for developing an organization that is conducive to innovation and creative thinking, the

Figure 12–1
Capital budgeting procedures

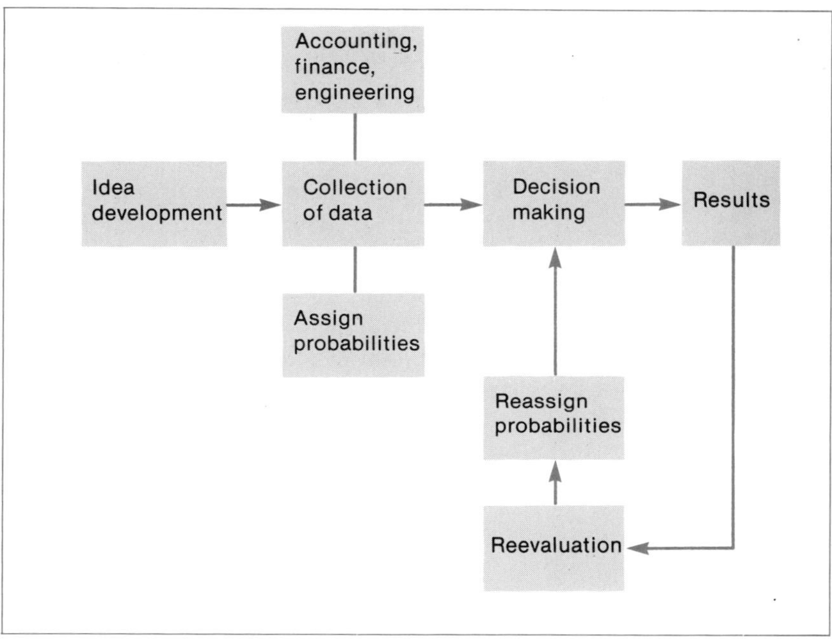


marginal return of such an organization is likely to be high (and a high marginal return is the essence of capital budgeting).

The collection of data should go beyond engineering data and market surveys and should attempt to capture the relative likelihood of the occurrence of various events. The probabilities of increases or slumps in product demand may be evaluated from statistical analysis, while other outcomes may be estimated subjectively.

After all data have been collected and evaluated, the final decision must be made. Generally, determinations involving relatively small amounts will be made at the department or division level, while major expenditures can only be approved by top management. A constant monitoring of the results of a given decision may indicate that a whole new set of probabilities must be developed, based on first-year experience, and the initial decision to choose Product A over Product B must be reevaluated and perhaps reversed. The preceding factors are delineated in Figure 12–1.

## Accounting Flows versus Cash Flows

In most capital budgeting decisions the emphasis is on cash flow rather than reported income. Let us consider the logic of using cash flow in the capital budgeting process. Because depreciation does not represent an actual expenditure of funds in arriving at profit, it is added back to profit to determine the amount of cash flow generated.[1] Assume that the Alston Corporation has $50,000 of new equipment to be depreciated straight-line over 10 years ($5,000 per year). The firm has $20,000 in earnings before depreciation and taxes and is in a 50 percent tax bracket, as indicated in Table 12–1.

The firm shows $7,500 in earnings after taxes, but it adds back the noncash deduction of $5,000 in depreciation to arrive at a cash flow figure of $12,500. The logic of adding back depreciation becomes even greater if we consider the impact of *$20,000* in depreciation for the Alston Corp. (Table 12–2). Net earnings before and after taxes are zero, but the company has $20,000 cash in the bank.

To the capital budgeting specialist, the use of cash flow figures is well accepted. However, top management does not always take a similar viewpoint. Assume you are the president of a firm listed on the New York Stock Exchange and must select between two alternatives. Pro-

**Table 12–1**
**Cash flow for Alston Corporation**

| | |
|---|---|
| Earnings before depreciation and taxes (cash inflow) | $20,000 |
| Depreciation (noncash expense) | 5,000 |
| Earnings before taxes | 15,000 |
| Taxes (cash outflow) | 7,500 |
| Earnings after taxes | 7,500 |
| Depreciation | +5,000 |
| Cash flow | $12,500 |

**Alternative method of cash flow calculation**

| | |
|---|---|
| Cash inflow (EBDT) | $20,000 |
| Cash outflow (taxes) | −7,500 |
| Cash flow | $12,500 |

[1] As explained in Chapter 2, depreciation is not a new source of funds (except in tax savings), but represents a noncash outlay to be added back.

Table 12–2
Revised cash flow for Alston Corporation

| | |
|---|---|
| Earnings before depreciation and taxes | $20,000 |
| Depreciation | 20,000 |
| Earnings before taxes | 0 |
| Taxes | 0 |
| Earnings after taxes | 0 |
| Depreciation | +20,000 |
| Cash flow | $20,000 |

posal A will provide zero in aftertax earnings and $100,000 in cash flow, while Proposal B, calling for no depreciation, will provide $50,000 in aftertax earnings and cash flow. As president of a publicly traded firm, you have security analysts constantly penciling in their projections of your earnings for the next quarter and you fear your stock may drop dramatically if earnings are too low by even a small amount. Although Proposal A is superior, you may be more sensitive to aftertax earnings than to cash flow and you may therefore select Proposal B. Perhaps you are also overly concerned about the short-term impact of a decision rather than the long-term economic benefits that might accrue.

The student must be sensitive to the concessions to short-term pressures that are sometimes made by top executives. Nevertheless, in the material that follows, the emphasis is on the use of proper evaluation techniques to make the best economic choice and assure long-term wealth maximization.

## Methods of Ranking Investment Proposals

Three widely used methods for evaluating capital expenditures will be considered, along with the shortcomings and advantages of each.

1. Payback method.
2. Internal rate of return.
3. Net present value.

The first method, while not conceptually sound, is often used. Approaches 2 and 3 are more acceptable, and one or the other should be applied to most situations.

## Payback Method

Under the payback method, we compute the time required to recoup the initial investment. Assume that we are called upon to select between Investment A and Investment B in Table 12–3.

The payback period for Investment A is 2 years, while Investment B requires 3.8 years. In the latter case, we recover $6,000 in the first three years, leaving us with the need for another $4,000 to recoup the full $10,000 investment. Since the fourth year has a total inflow of $5,000, $4,000 represents .8 of that value. Thus, the payback period for Investment B is 3.8 years.

In using the payback method to select Investment A, two important considerations are ignored. First of all, there is no consideration of inflows after the cutoff period. The $2,000 in year 3 for investment A is ignored, as is the $5,000 in year 5 for Investment B. Even if the $5,000 were $50,000, it would have no impact on the decision.

Second, the method fails to consider the concept of the time value of money. If we had two $10,000 investments with the following inflow patterns, the payback method would rank them equally.

| Year | Early Returns | Late Returns |
|---|---|---|
| 1 . . . . | $9,000 | $1,000 |
| 2 . . . . | 1,000 | 9,000 |
| 3 . . . . | 1,000 | 1,000 |

Although both investments have a payback period of two years, the first alternative is clearly superior because the $9,000 comes in the first year rather than the second.

**Table 12–3**
**Investment alternatives**

| | Cash Inflows (of $10,000 investment) | |
|---|---|---|
| Year | Investment A | Investment B |
| 1 . . . . . | $5,000 | $1,500 |
| 2 . . . . . | 5,000 | 2,000 |
| 3 . . . . . | 2,000 | 2,500 |
| 4 . . . . . | | 5,000 |
| 5 . . . . . | | 5,000 |

The payback method does have some features that help to explain its use by U.S. corporations. It is easy to understand, and it places a heavy emphasis on liquidity. An investment must recoup the initial investment quickly or it will not qualify (most corporations use a maximum time horizon of three to five years). A rapid payback may be particularly important to firms in industries characterized by rapid technological developments.

Nevertheless, the payback method, concentrating as it does on only the initial years of investment, fails to discern the optimum or most economic solution to a capital budgeting problem. The analyst is therefore required to consider the more theoretically correct methods.

## Internal Rate of Return

The internal rate of return (IRR) calls for determining the yield on an investment, that is, calculating the interest rate that equates the cash outflows (cost) of an investment with the subsequent cash inflows. The simplest case would be an investment of $100 which provides $120 after one year, or a 20 percent internal rate of return. For more complicated situations, we use Appendix B (present value of a single amount) and Appendix D (present value of an annuity) and the techniques described in Chapter 9, The Time Value of Money. For example, a $1,000 investment returning an annuity of $244 per year for five years provides an internal rate of return of 7 percent, as indicated by the following calculations.

1. First divide the investment (present value) by the annuity.

$$\frac{\text{(Investment)}}{\text{(Annuity)}} = \frac{\$1,000}{\$244} = 4.1\ (IF_{pva})$$

2. Then proceed to Appendix D (present value of an annuity). The factor of 4.1 for five years indicates a yield of 7 percent.

Whenever an annuity is being evaluated, annuity interest factors ($IF_{pva}$) can be used to find the final IRR solution. If an uneven cash inflow is involved, we are not so lucky. We need to use a trial and error method. The first question is, Where do we start? What interest rate should we pick for our first trial? Assume that we are once again called upon to evaluate the two investment alternatives in Table 12–3, only this time using the internal rate of return to rank the two projects. Because neither proposal represents a precise annuity stream, we must use the trial and error approach to determine an answer. We begin with Investment A.

| | Cash Inflows (of $10,000 investment) | |
|---|---|---|
| *Year* | *Investment A* | *Investment B* |
| 1 . . . . . . | $5,000 | $1,500 |
| 2 . . . . . . | 5,000 | 2,000 |
| 3 . . . . . . | 2,000 | 2,500 |
| 4 . . . . . . | | 5,000 |
| 5 . . . . . . | | 5,000 |

1. In order to find a beginning value to start our first trial, we average the inflows as if we were really getting an annuity.

   $ 5,000
   5,000
   2,000
   $12,000 ÷ 3 = $4,000

2. Then divide the investment by the "assumed" annuity value in step 1.

$$\frac{\text{(Investment)}}{\text{(Annuity)}} = \frac{\$10,000}{\$4,000} = 2.5\ (IF_{pva})$$

3. Proceed to Appendix D to arrive at a *first approximation* of the internal rate of return, using:

$$IF_{pva} \text{ factor} = 2.5$$
$$n \text{ (period)} = 3$$

   The factor falls between 9 and 10 percent. This is only a first approximation—our actual answer will be closer to 10 percent or higher because our method of average cash flows theoretically moved receipts from the first two years into the last year. This averaging understates the actual internal rate of return. The same method would overstate the IRR for Investment B because it would move cash from the last two years into the first three years. Since we know that cash flows in the early years are worth more and increase our return, we can usually gauge whether our first approximation is overstated or understated.

4. We now enter into a trial and error process to arrive at an answer. Because these cash flows are uneven rather than an annuity, we need to use Appendix B. We will begin with 10 percent and then try 12 percent.

| Year | 10 percent | | Year | 12 percent | |
|---|---|---|---|---|---|
| 1 . . . . | $5,000 × 0.909 = | $ 4,545 | 1 . . . . | $5,000 × 0.893 = | $4,465 |
| 2 . . . . | 5,000 × 0.826 = | 4,130 | 2 . . . . | 5,000 × 0.797 = | 3,985 |
| 3 . . . . | 2,000 × 0.751 = | 1,502 | 3 . . . . | 2,000 × 0.712 = | 1,424 |
| | | $10,177 | | | $9,874 |

At 10 percent, the present value of the inflows exceeds $10,000—we therefore use a higher discount rate.

At 12 percent, the present value of the inflows is less than $10,000—thus the discount rate is too high

The answer must fall between 10 percent and 12 percent, indicating an approximate answer of 11 percent.

If we want to be more accurate, the results can be *interpolated.* Because the internal rate of return is determined when the present value of the inflows ($PV_I$) equals the present value of the outflows ($PV_O$), we need to find a discount rate that equates the $PV_I$ to the cost of $10,000 ($PV_O$). The total difference in present values between 10 percent and 12 percent is $303.

| | | | |
|---|---|---|---|
| $10,177 . . . . | $PV_I$ @ 10% | $10,177 . . . . | $PV_I$ @ 10% |
| 9,874 . . . . | $PV_I$ @ 12% | 10,000 . . . . | (cost) |
| $ 303 | | $ 177 | |

The solution at 10 percent is $177 away from $10,000. Actually the solution is ($177/$303) percent of the way between 10 and 12 percent. Since there is a 2 percent difference between the two rates used to evaluate the cash inflows, we need to multiply the fraction by 2 percent and then add our answer to 10 percent for the final answer of:

$$10\% + (\$177/\$303)\,(2\%) = 11.17\%\ \text{IRR}$$

In Investment B, the same process will yield an answer of 14.33 percent (you may wish to confirm this). The use of the internal rate of return calls for the prudent selection of Investment B in preference to Investment A, the exact opposite of the conclusion reached under the payback method.

| | *Investment A* | *Investment B* | *Selection* |
|---|---|---|---|
| Payback method . . . . . . | 2 years | 3.8 years | Quickest payback: Investment A |
| Internal rate of return . . . . | 11.17% | 14.33% | Highest yield: Investment B |

The final selection of any project under the internal rate-of-return method will also depend upon the yield exceeding some minimum cost standard, such as the cost of capital to the firm.

### Net Present Value

The final method of investment selection is to determine the net present value of an investment. This is done by discounting back the inflows over the life of the investment to determine whether they equal or exceed the required investment. The basic discount rate is usually the cost of capital to the firm. Thus, inflows that arrive in later years must provide a return that at least equals the cost of financing those returns. If we once again evaluate Investments A and B—using an assumed cost of capital or a discount rate of 10 percent—we arrive at the following figures for net present value.

*$10,000 investment, 10-percent discount rate*

| *Year* | *Investment A* | | *Year* | *Investment B* | |
|---|---|---|---|---|---|
| 1 . . . . | $5,000 × 0.909 = | $ 4,545 | 1 . . . . | $1,500 × 0.909 = | $ 1,364 |
| 2 . . . . | 5,000 × 0.826 = | 4,130 | 2 . . . . | 2,000 × 0.826 = | 1,652 |
| 3 . . . . | 2,000 × 0.751 = | 1,502 | 3 . . . . | 2,500 × 0.751 = | 1,878 |
| | | $10,177 | 4 . . . . | 5,000 × 0.683 = | 3,415 |
| | | | 5 . . . . | 5,000 × 0.621 = | 3,105 |
| | | | | | $11,414 |
| Present value of inflows . . . | | $10,177 | Present value of inflows . . . | | $11,414 |
| Present value of outflows . . | | 10,000 | Present value of outflows . . | | 10,000 |
| Net present value . . . . . | | $ 177 | Net present value . . . . . | | $ 1,414 |

While both proposals appear to be acceptable, Investment B has a considerably higher net present value than Investment A.[2] Under most circumstances the net present value and internal rate of return methods give theoretically correct answers, and the subsequent discussion will be restricted to these two approaches. A summary of the various conclusions reached under the three methods is presented in Table 12–4.

**Table 12–4**
**Capital budgeting results**

| | Investment A | Investment B | Selection |
|---|---|---|---|
| Payback method . . . . . | 2 years | 3.8 years | Quickest payout: Investment A |
| Internal rate of return . . . | 11.17% | 14.33% | Highest yield: Investment B |
| Net present value . . . . . | $177 | $1,414 | Highest net present value: Investment B |

## Selection Strategy

In both the internal rate of return and net present value methods, the profitability must equal or exceed the cost of capital for the project to be potentially acceptable. However, other distinctions are necessary—namely, whether the projects are *mutually exclusive or not*. If investments are mutually exclusive, the selection of one alternative will preclude the selection of any other alternative. Assume we are going to build a specialized assembly plant in the Midwest and four major cities are under consideration, only one of which will be picked. In this situation, we select the alternative with the highest acceptable yield or the highest net present value and disregard all others. Even if certain

[2] A further possible refinement under the net present value method is to compute a profitability index.

$$\text{Profitability index} = \frac{\text{Present value of the inflows}}{\text{Present value of the outflows}}$$

For Investment A the profitability index is 1.0177 ($10,177/$10,000) and for Investment B it is 1.1414 ($11,414/$10,000). The profitability index can be helpful in comparing returns from different size investments by placing them on a common measuring standard. This, of course, was not necessary in this example.

locations provide a marginal return in excess of the cost of capital, they may be rejected. In the table below, the possible alternatives are presented.

**Mutually exclusive alternatives**

| | *IRR* | *Net present value* |
|---|---|---|
| Dayton | 15% | $300 |
| Columbus | 12 | 200 |
| St. Paul | 11 | 100 |
| *Cost of capital* | *10* | — |
| Gary | 9 | (100) |

Among the mutually exclusive alternatives, only Dayton would be selected. Of course, if the alternatives were not mutually exclusive (much-needed multiple retail outlets), we would accept all of the alternatives that provided a return in excess of our cost of capital, and only Gary would be rejected.

Applying this logic to Investments A and B in the prior discussion and assuming a cost of capital of 10 percent, only Investment B would be accepted if the alternatives were mutually exclusive, while both would clearly qualify if they were not mutually exclusive.

| | *Investment A* | *Investment B* | *Accepted if Mutually Exclusive* | *Accepted if Not Mutually Exclusive* |
|---|---|---|---|---|
| Internal rate of return | 11.17% | 14.33% | B | A, B |
| Net present value | $177 | $1,414 | B | A, B |

The discussion to this point has assumed that the internal rate of return and net present value methods will call for the same decision. Although this is generally true, there are exceptions. Two rules may be stated:

1. Both methods will accept or reject the same investments based on minimum return or cost of capital criteria. If an investment has a positive net present value, it will also have a yield in excess of the cost of capital.
2. In certain limited cases, however, the two methods may give different answers in selecting the best investment from a range of acceptable alternatives.

## Reinvestment Assumption

It is only under this second state of events that a preference for one method over the other must be established. A prime characteristic of the internal rate of return is the assumption that all inflows can be reinvested at the yield from a given investment. For example, in the case of the aforementioned Investment A yielding 11.17 percent, the assumption is made that the dollar amounts coming in each year can, in fact, be reinvested at that rate. For Investment B, with a 14.33 percent internal rate of return, the new funds are assumed to be reinvested at this high rate. The relationships are presented in Table 12–5.

For investments with a very high IRR, it may be unrealistic to assume that reinvestment can take place at an equally high rate. The net present value method, depicted in Table 12–6, makes the more conservative assumption that each inflow can be reinvested at the cost of capital or discount rate.

The reinvestment assumption under the net present value method allows for certain consistency. Inflows from each project are assumed to have the same (though conservative) investment opportunity. Although this may not be an accurate picture for all firms, net present value is generally the preferred method.

**Table 12–5**
**The reinvestment assumption—internal rate of return ($10,000 investment)**

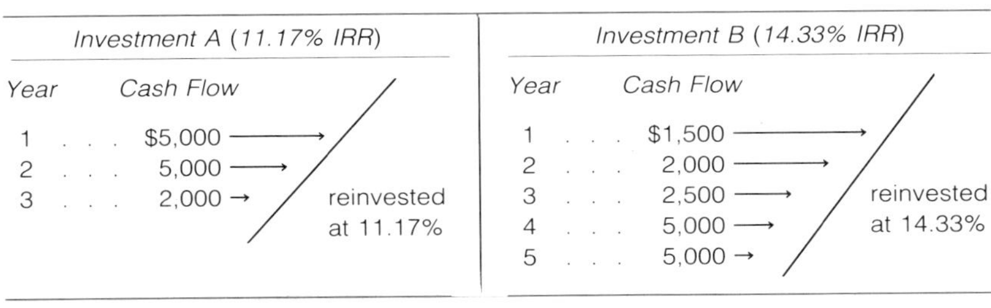

| Investment A (11.17% IRR) | | | Investment B (14.33% IRR) | | |
|---|---|---|---|---|---|
| Year | Cash Flow | | Year | Cash Flow | |
| 1 . . . | $5,000 → | | 1 . . . | $1,500 → | |
| 2 . . . | 5,000 → | | 2 . . . | 2,000 → | |
| 3 . . . | 2,000 → | reinvested at 11.17% | 3 . . . | 2,500 → | reinvested at 14.33% |
| | | | 4 . . . | 5,000 → | |
| | | | 5 . . . | 5,000 → | |

**Table 12–6**
**The reinvestment assumption—net present value ($10,000 investment)**

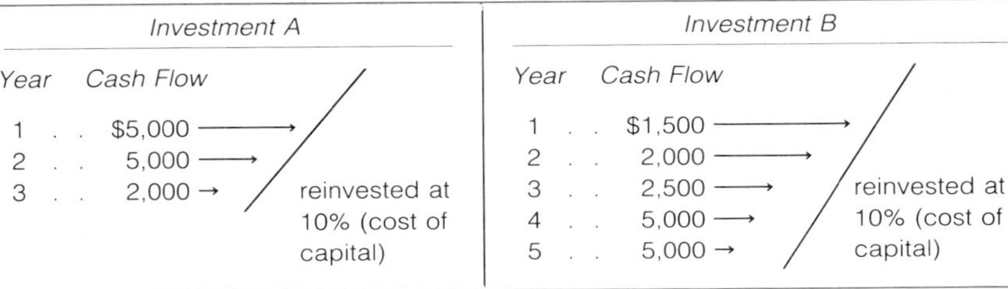

| Investment A | | | Investment B | | |
|---|---|---|---|---|---|
| Year | Cash Flow | | Year | Cash Flow | |
| 1 . . | $5,000 → | | 1 . . | $1,500 → | |
| 2 . . | 5,000 → | | 2 . . | 2,000 → | |
| 3 . . | 2,000 → | reinvested at 10% (cost of capital) | 3 . . | 2,500 → | reinvested at 10% (cost of capital) |
| | | | 4 . . | 5,000 → | |
| | | | 5 . . | 5,000 → | |

## Capital Rationing

At times, management may place an artificial constraint on the amount of funds that can be invested in a given period. The executive planning committee may emerge from a lengthy capital budgeting session to announce that only $5 million may be spent on new capital projects this year. Although $5 million may represent a large sum, it is still an artificially determined constraint and not the product of marginal analysis, in which the return for each proposal is related to the cost of capital for the firm, and projects with positive net present values are accepted.

A firm may adopt a posture of capital rationing because it is fearful of growth or hesitant to use external sources of financing (perhaps debt). In a strictly economic sense, capital rationing hinders a firm from achieving maximum profitability. With capital rationing as indicated in Table 12–7, acceptable projects must be ranked, and only those with the highest positive net present value are accepted.

**Table 12–7**
**Capital rationing**

| | Project | Investment | Total Investment | Net Present Value |
|---|---|---|---|---|
| Capital rationing solution | A | $2,000,000 | | $400,000 |
| | B | 2,000,000 | | 380,000 |
| → | C | 1,000,000 | $5,000,000 | 150,000 |
| | D | 1,000,000 | | 100,000 |
| Best solution → | E | 800,000 | 6,800,000 | 40,000 |
| | F | 800,000 | | (30,000) |

Under capital rationing, only Projects A through C, calling for $5 million in investment, will be accepted. Although Projects D and E have returns exceeding the cost of funds, as evidenced by a positive net present value, they will not be accepted with the capital rationing assumption.

## Net Present Value Profile

An interesting way to summarize the characteristics of an investment is through the use of the net present value profile. The profile allows us to graphically portray the net present value of a project at different discount rates. Let's apply the profile to the investments that we have been discussing. The projects are summarized again below.

| | Cash Inflows (of $10,000 investment) | |
|---|---|---|
| Year | Investment A | Investment B |
| 1 | $5,000 | $1,500 |
| 2 | 5,000 | 2,000 |
| 3 | 2,000 | 2,500 |
| 4 | | 5,000 |
| 5 | | 5,000 |

To apply the net present value profile, you need to know *three* characteristics about an investment:

1. *The net present value at a zero discount rate.* Actually, that is easy to determine. A zero discount rate means no discount rate at all. The values simply retain their original value. For Investment A, the net present value would be $2,000 ($5,000 + $5,000 + $2,000 − $10,000). For Investment B, the answer is $6,000 ($1,500 + $2,000 + $2,500 + $5,000 + $5,000 − $10,000).
2. *The net present value as determined by a normal discount rate* (such as the cost of capital). For these two investments, we used a discount rate of 10 percent. As summarized in Table 12–4, the net present values for the two investments at that discount rate were $177 for Investment A, and $1,414 for Investment B.
3. *The internal rate of return for the investments.* Once again referring to Table 12–4, we see the internal rate of return is 11.17 percent for Investment A, and 14.33 percent for Investment B. The reader should also realize that the internal rate of return is the discount rate that allows the project to have a net present value of zero. This characteristic will become more important when we present our graphic display.

   We summarize the information about discount rates and net present values for each investment here, and graphically in Figure 12–2.

| Investment A | |
|---|---|
| Discount Rate | Net Present Value |
| 0 | $2,000 |
| 10% | 177 |
| 11.17% (IRR) | 0 |

| *Investment B* | |
|---|---|
| *Discount Rate* | *Net Present Value* |
| 0 . . . . . . . . . . . . | $6,000 |
| 10% . . . . . . . . . . . | 1,414 |
| 14.33% (IRR) . . . . . . | 0 |

Note that in Figure 12–2 we have graphed the three points for each investment. For example, for Investment A, we showed a $2,000 net present value at a zero discount rate, a $177 net present value at a 10 percent discount rate, and a zero net present value at an 11.17 percent discount rate. We then connected the points. The same procedure was applied to Investment B. The reader can also visually approximate what the net present value for the investment projects would be at other discount rates (such as 5 percent).

In the above example, the net present value of Investment B was superior to Investment A at every point. This is not always the case in comparing projects. To illustrate, let's introduce a new project, Investment C, and then compare it with Investment B.

**Figure 12–2**
**Net present value profile**

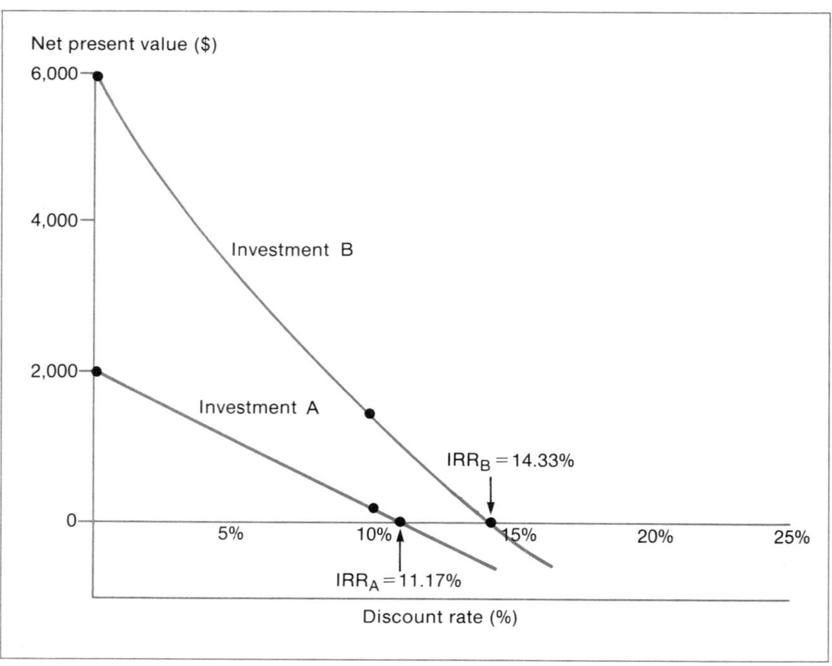

| Investment C ($10,000 Investment) | |
|---|---|
| Year | Cash Inflows |
| 1 . . . . . . . | $9,000 |
| 2 . . . . . . . | 3,000 |
| 3 . . . . . . . | 1,200 |

## Characteristics of Investment C

1. The net present value at a zero discount rate for this project is $3,200 ($9,000 + 3,000 + 1,200 − 10,000).
2. The net present value at a 10 percent discount rate is $1,560.
3. The internal rate of return is 22.51 percent.

You could compute these values for yourself, but that is really not necessary at this point.

Comparing Investment B to Investment C in Figure 12–3, we observe that at low discount rates, Investment B has a higher net present

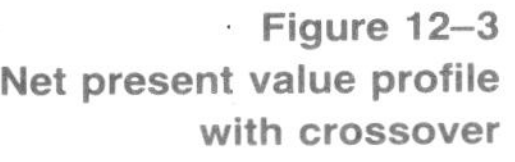
Figure 12–3
Net present value profile with crossover

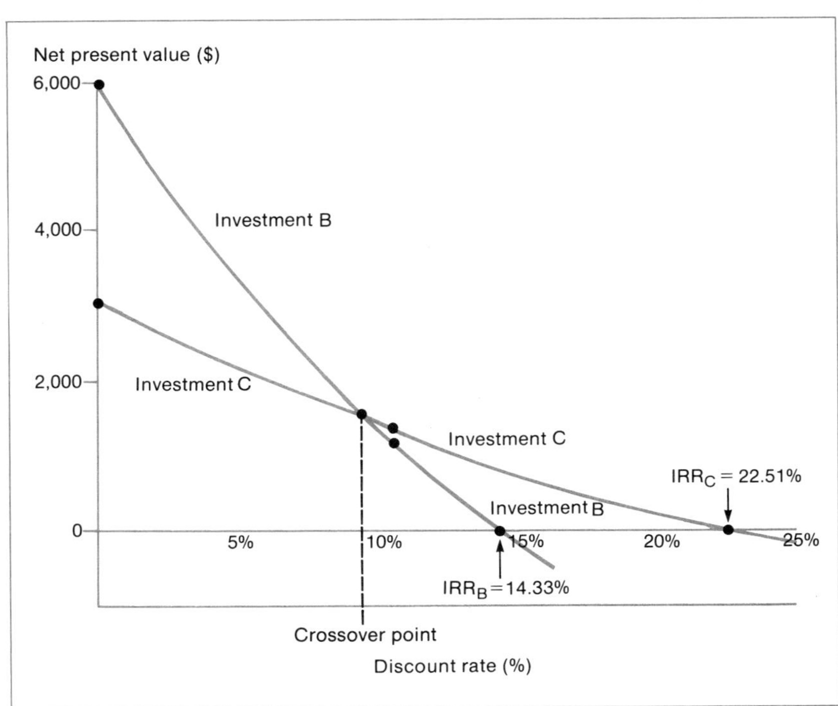

value than Investment C. However, at high discount rates, Investment C has a higher net present value than Investment B. The actual crossover point can be viewed at approximately 8.7 percent. That is to say, if you had to choose between Investment B and Investment C, your answers would be dependent on the discount rate. At low rates (below 8.7 percent), you would opt for Investment B. At higher rates (above 8.7 percent), you would select Investment C. Since the cost of capital is presumed to be 10 percent, you would probably prefer Investment C, but keep in mind the cost of capital can change.

Why does Investment B do well compared to Investment C at low discount rates and relatively poorly compared to Investment C at high discount rates? This difference is related to the timing of inflows. Let's examine the inflows.

| | *Cash Inflows (of $10,000 investment)* | |
|---|---|---|
| *Year* | *Investment B* | *Investment C* |
| 1 . . . . . . . | $1,500 | $9,000 |
| 2 . . . . . . . | 2,000 | 3,000 |
| 3 . . . . . . . | 2,500 | 1,200 |
| 4 . . . . . . . | 5,000 | |
| 5 . . . . . . . | 5,000 | |

Investment B has heavy late inflows ($5,000 in both the fourth and fifth years) and these are more strongly penalized by high discount rates. Investment C has extremely high early inflows and these hold up well with high discount rates.

As previously mentioned in the chapter, if the investments are non-mutually exclusive or there is not capital rationing, we would probably accept both Investment B and Investment C at discount rates below 14.33 percent, because they both would have positive net present values. On the other hand, if we can only select one, the decision may well turn on the discount rate. Observe in Figure 12–3, at a discount rate of 5 percent, we would select Investment B, at 10 percent we would select Investment C, and so on. The net present value profile helps us to make such decisions. Now back to basic capital budgeting issues.

## Combining Cash Flow Analysis and Selection Strategy

Many of the points that we have covered thus far will be reviewed in the context of a capital budgeting decision, in which we determine the annual cash flows from an investment and compare them to the initial outlay. In order to be able to analyze a wide variety of cash flow patterns, we shall first consider the types of depreciation that are allowable under the 1981 Economic Recovery Tax Act.

Allowable depreciation is defined under the Accelerated Cost Recovery System (ACRS) standards that are part of the 1981 tax legislation. Essentially, the 1981 legislation decreased the life span over which an asset may be depreciated. Since depreciation provides tax shield benefits, the sooner the benefits can be taken, the higher the present value of the project.

According to the 1981 act, assets are to be depreciated in one of four categories, as indicated in Table 12–8.

The 1981 legislation also specifies the amount of depreciation that can be taken each year.[3] This information is presented in Table 12–9.

The depreciation schedules in Table 12–9 supersede the old methods of sum-of-the-years' digits, double declining balance, and various other

**Table 12–8**
**Recovery periods for different types of assets**

| Asset type | Recovery period |
|---|---|
| Automobiles, light-duty trucks, research and development equipment, and certain other short-lived assets | 3 years |
| Most machinery and equipment, petroleum storage facilities, and some agricultural structures | 5 years |
| Most public utility property, railroad tank cars, coal-fired burners, and residential mobile homes | 10 years |
| Longer-life public utility property that does not fall into the 10-year category | 15 years |

[3] For firms that wish to extend the write-off period because they are currently experiencing losses and not in need of rapid depreciation, the 1981 legislation also specifies optimal extended recovery periods over which straight-line depreciation may be taken. For example, in the case of an asset such as an automobile, which normally falls into the three-year write-off period, straight-line depreciation may be used for three, five, or even more years.

**Table 12–9**
**Percentage depreciation that is allowable with the Accelerated Cost Recovery System (ACRS) under the 1981 Economic Recovery Tax Act**

| Recovery Period | 3-Year | 5-Year | 10-Year | 15-Year |
|---|---|---|---|---|
| 1 | 25% | 15% | 8% | 5% |
| 2 | 38 | 22 | 14 | 10 |
| 3 | 37 | 21 | 12 | 9 |
| 4 | | 21 | 10 | 8 |
| 5 | | 21 | 10 | 7 |
| 6 | | | 10 | 7 |
| 7 | | | 9 | 6 |
| 8 | | | 9 | 6 |
| 9 | | | 9 | 6 |
| 10 | | | 9 | 6 |
| 11 | | | | 6 |
| 12 | | | | 6 |
| 13 | | | | 6 |
| 14 | | | | 6 |
| 15 | | | | 6 |

techniques for tax purposes.[4] In presenting this material the authors realize that tax laws are subject to rapid change. We are presenting the laws as they existed in mid-1986.

## Actual Decision

Assume a firm is evaluating a decision on whether to purchase five new trucks. The total cost is $35,000. In referring to Table 12–8, we see the trucks can be included in the three-year depreciation recovery period. We then go to Table 12–9 to determine the appropriate annual depreciation for the three-year period. The actual depreciation for the five trucks is presented in Table 12–10.

This is only one part of the analysis. We must also consider any additional possibility or cost saving benefits that will result from the purchase. In the present case, we shall assume the firm is paying transportation fees to others and can save a substantial amount by owning

[4]Although the annual write-off is not as fast as under prior accelerated depreciation methods, the shorter life under a modified version of 150 percent declining balance (with a half year's depreciation in the first year) more than makes up the difference. Other methods of depreciation may still be used for financial accounting purposes.

Table 12–10
Annual dollar depreciation

| Year | Depreciation Base | Percentage Depreciation (Table 12–9) | Depreciation |
|---|---|---|---|
| 1 | $35,000 | 25% | $ 8,750 |
| 2 | 35,000 | 38 | 13,300 |
| 3 | 35,000 | 37 | 12,950 |
| | | | $35,000 |

its own trucks. After all cash outflows (such as labor, maintenance, etc.) are considered, it is determined that the firm can save $15,500 per year for the next three years, and $8,000 per year for two more years. There is no problem with the fact that the productive life of the asset exceeds the depreciation recovery period under the Accelerated Cost Recovery System (ACRS). This is quite often the case. These cash savings are the equivalent of earnings before depreciation and taxes. They can be combined with depreciation write-off to determine cash flow. Using an analysis similar to that in the upper part of Table 12–1, we now compute annual cash flow for the trucks in Table 12–11.

Table 12–11
Cash flow related to truck purchase

| | Year 1 | Year 2 | Year 3 | Year 4 | Year 5 |
|---|---|---|---|---|---|
| Earnings before depreciation and taxes | $15,500 | $15,500 | $15,500 | $8,000 | $8,000 |
| Depreciation | 8,750 | 13,300 | 12,950 | — | — |
| Earnings before taxes | 6,750 | 2,200 | 2,550 | 8,000 | 8,000 |
| Taxes (46%) | 3,105 | 1,012 | 1,173 | 3,680 | 3,680 |
| Earnings after taxes | 3,645 | 1,188 | 1,377 | 4,320 | 4,320 |
| + Depreciation | 8,750 | 13,300 | 12,950 | — | — |
| Cash flow | $12,395 | $14,488 | $14,327 | $4,320 | $4,320 |

We must now discount the annual cash flows back to the present and compare them with the $35,000 initial investment. We will be using the net present value method with an assumed cost of capital of 12 percent. The analysis is presented in Table 12–12.

The investment shows a positive net present value and appears to be acceptable.

**Table 12–12**
**Net present value analysis**

| Year | Cash Flow (inflows) | Present Value Factor (12%) | Present Value |
|---|---|---|---|
| 1 | $12,395 | 0.893 | $11,069 |
| 2 | 14,488 | 0.797 | 11,547 |
| 3 | 14,327 | 0.712 | 10,201 |
| 4 | 4,320 | 0.636 | 2,748 |
| 5 | 4,320 | 0.567 | 2,449 |
| | | | $38,014 |

| | |
|---|---|
| Present value of inflows | $38,014 |
| Present value of outflows (cost) | 35,000 |
| Net present value | $ 3,014 |

## Investment Tax Credit

A potentially important variable in the capital budgeting decision is the investment tax credit (ITC). The credit represents a percentage of the purchase price that may be deducted directly from tax obligations.[5] Under the Economic Recovery Tax Act of 1981, a three-year recovery life asset (autos, trucks etc.) is entitled to a 6 percent ITC. An asset with a life of five years or more is entitled to an ITC of 10 percent.

| *Normal recovery period* | *Investment tax credit* |
|---|---|
| 3 years | 6% |
| 5 years | 10 |
| 10 years | 10 |
| 15 years | 10 |

In 1982 an amendment to the 1981 legislation was passed that requires half of the ITC to be subtracted from the initial depreciation base before allowing for depreciation.[6] Let's see how the investment tax credit actually works.

In the prior example of the five trucks purchased for $35,000, which fell into the three-year recovery period, a 6 percent ITC would be available. Six percent of the $35,000 purchase price represents $2,100.

[5]The investment tax credit actually has a multiplier effect on the amount of equivalent before-tax income necessary to generate aftertax cash flow. See reference for Matukonis.

[6]The legislation was part of the Tax Equity and Fiscal Responsibility Act of 1982.

This $2,100 savings in taxes effectively lowers the purchase price to $32,900.

| | |
|---|---|
| $35,000 | Purchase price |
| −2,100 | ITC |
| $32,900 | Net price |

But now we must subtract half of the ITC from the purchase price to set up the depreciation base.

| | |
|---|---|
| $35,000 | Purchase price |
| 1,050 | Deduction of half the ITC (½ times $2,100) |
| $33,950 | Depreciation base |

With the new depreciation base, the annual depreciation is now amended to the values shown below.

| *Year* | *Depreciation Base* | *Percentage Depreciation (Table 12–9)* | *Depreciation* |
|---|---|---|---|
| 1 | $33,950 | 25% | $ 8,488 |
| 2 | 33,950 | 38 | 12,901 |
| 3 | 33,950 | 37 | 12,561 |
| | | | $33,950 |

The prior analysis in Table 12–11 is then changed to include the effect of the ITC on the depreciation values as shown in Table 12–13.

**Table 12–13**
**Cash flow related to truck purchases, including ITC**

| | *Year 1* | *Year 2* | *Year 3* | *Year 4* | *Year 5* |
|---|---|---|---|---|---|
| Earnings before depreciation and taxes | $15,500 | $15,500 | $15,500 | $8,000 | $8,000 |
| Depreciation | 8,488 | 12,901 | 12,561 | — | — |
| Earnings before taxes | 7,012 | 2,599 | 2,939 | 8,000 | 8,000 |
| Taxes (46%) | 3,226 | 1,196 | 1,352 | 3,680 | 3,680 |
| Earnings after taxes | 3,786 | 1,403 | 1,587 | 4,320 | 4,320 |
| + Depreciation | 8,488 | 12,901 | 12,561 | — | — |
| Cash flow | $12,274 | $14,304 | $14,148 | $4,320 | $4,320 |

We then take the present value of the amended numbers and compute the net present value in Table 12–14. The net present value shown there is $1,717 higher than the net present value that was shown in Table 12–12 ($4,731 versus $3,014). In comparing the values at the bottom of both tables, we can observe that the ITC lowers the present values of the inflows slightly because of the decreased depreciation base, but more substantially decreases the outflow figure because of the tax credit. The net effect is a higher net present value.

**Table 12–14**
**Net present value analysis including the ITC**

| Year | Cash Flow (inflows) | Present Value Factor (12%) | Present Value |
|---|---|---|---|
| 1 | $12,274 | 0.893 | $10,961 |
| 2 | 14,304 | 0.797 | 11,400 |
| 3 | 14,148 | 0.712 | 10,073 |
| 4 | 4,320 | 0.636 | 2,748 |
| 5 | 4,320 | 0.567 | 2,449 |
| | | | $37,631 |

| | |
|---|---|
| Present value of inflows | $37,631 |
| Present value of outflows (net price) | 32,900 |
| Net present value | $ 4,731 |

## The Replacement Decision

So far, our discussion of capital budgeting has centered on projects that are being considered as a net addition to the present plant and equipment. However, many capital budgeting decisions occur because of new technology, and these are considered replacement decisions. The financial manager often needs to determine whether a new machine with advanced technology can do the job better than the machine being used at present.

These replacement decisions include several additions to the basic capital budgeting problems presented thus far in this chapter. For example, we need to include the sale of the old machine in our analysis. This sale will produce a cash inflow that offsets the purchase price of the new machine. In addition, the sale of the old machine will usually have tax consequences. Some of the cash inflow from the sale can be a recovery of depreciation if the old machine is sold for more than book value. If it is sold for less than book value, this will be considered a capital loss and will provide a tax benefit.

The replacement decision can be analyzed by using a total analysis of both the old and new machine or by using an incremental analysis which emphasizes the changes in cash flows between the old and the new machine. We will emphasize the incremental approach.

Assume the Dalton Corporation purchased a computer two years ago for $100,000. The asset is being depreciated over five years under the Accelerated Cost Recovery System (ACRS). It could currently be sold in the market for $40,000. A new computer would cost $150,000 and would also be written off over five years. A 10 percent investment tax credit will be taken on the new computer.[7]

The new computer would provide cost savings and operating benefits of $38,000 per year for the next five years over the old computer. This is the equivalent of increased earnings before depreciation and taxes. The firm is in a 46 percent tax bracket and has a 10 percent cost of capital.

First of all, we need to determine the net cost of the new computer. The initial item for consideration is the price of the new computer less the investment tax credit, which gives us the net price of the new computer (Table 12–15). From this, we shall subtract the cash inflow

**Table 12–15**
**Net price of the new computer**

| | |
|---|---|
| Price of the new computer | $150,000 |
| − Investment tax credit (10%) | 15,000 |
| Net price of new computer | $135,000 |
| − Cash inflow from sale of old computer | – – – |
| Net cost of new computer | – – – |

[7] For purposes of our present analysis, we will assume there is not an investment tax credit associated with the old computer. An ITC would not only change the dollar depreciation on the old computer, but would result in a recapture of part of the tax credit. An investment tax credit is assumed to be earned at the rate of 2 percent per year. If the old five-year depreciated computer is sold after two years, 6 percent of the 10 percent credit is being recaptured and must be returned to the IRS.

**Table 12–16**
**Book value of old computer**

| Year | Depreciation Base | Percentage Depreciation (Table 12–9) | Depreciation |
|---|---|---|---|
| 1 | $100,000 | 15% | $15,000 |
| 2 | 100,000 | 22 | 22,000 |
| Total depreciation to date | | | $37,000 |

| | |
|---|---|
| Purchase price | $100,000 |
| Total depreciation to date | −37,000 |
| Book value | $ 63,000 |

associated with the sale of the old computer to determine the net *cost* of the new computer.

## Sale of Old Assets

The cash inflow from the sale of the old computer is based on the sale price as well as the related tax factors. In order to determine these tax factors, we first determine the book value of the old computer and compare this figure to its sales price to determine if there is a tax gain or loss. The book value of the old computer is shown in Table 12–16. You will recall, it initially cost $100,000, had a five-year depreciation life, and is now two years old.

Since the book value of the old computer is $63,000, and the market value (previously given) is $40,000, there will be a $23,000 tax loss.

| | |
|---|---|
| Book value | $63,000 |
| Market value | −40,000 |
| Tax loss on sale | $23,000 |

A tax loss on the sale of a depreciable asset used in business or trade may be written off against ordinary income (this is true even if it is a long-term capital loss). The Dalton Corporation is in a 46 percent tax bracket so the tax write-off is worth $10,580.

| | |
|---|---|
| Tax loss on sale | $23,000 |
| Tax rate | 46% |
| Tax benefit | $10,580 |

We now add the tax benefit from the sale of the old computer to its sales value to arrive at the cash inflow from the sale of the old computer.[8]

| | |
|---|---|
| Sales price for old computer | $40,000 |
| Tax benefit from sale | + 10,580 |
| Cash inflow from sale of old computer | $50,580 |

The computation of the cash inflow figure now allows us to complete our analysis of the net cost of the new computer in Table 12–17. The value is $84,420.

**Table 12–17**
**Net cost of the new computer**

| | |
|---|---|
| Price of the new computer | $150,000 |
| − Investment tax credit (10%) | 15,000 |
| Net price of new computer | 135,000 |
| − Cash inflow from sale of old computer | 50,580 |
| Net cost of new computer | $ 84,420 |

The question then becomes, are the incremental gains from the new computer compared to the old computer, large enough to justify the net cost of $84,420? We assume both will be operative over the next five years although the old computer will run out of depreciation in three more years.

We will base our cash inflow analysis on (a) the incremental gain in depreciation and the related tax shield benefits and (b) cost savings.

## Incremental Depreciation

The depreciation factors for the new and old computer are as follows:

| | *New Computer* | *Old Computer* |
|---|---|---|
| Purchase price | $150,000 | |
| Deduction of half of ITC | 7,500 | |
| Depreciation base | 142,500<br>(over 5 years) | $100,000<br>(3 years remaining out of original 5) |

[8]There could also be a tax liability from the sale of old equipment if it is sold for more than book value. This matter is covered in Appendix 12–A.

The annual depreciation on the new computer will be:

| Year | Depreciation Base | Percentage Depreciation (Table 12–9) | Depreciation |
|---|---|---|---|
| 1 | $142,500 | 15% | $ 21,375 |
| 2 | 142,500 | 22 | 31,350 |
| 3 | 142,500 | 21 | 29,925 |
| 4 | 142,500 | 21 | 29,925 |
| 5 | 142,500 | 21 | 29,925 |
| | | | $142,500 |

The annual depreciation on the old computer for the remaining three years would be:

| Year* | Depreciation Base | Percentage Depreciation (Table 12–9) | Depreciation |
|---|---|---|---|
| 1 | $100,000 | 21% | $21,000 |
| 2 | 100,000 | 21 | 21,000 |
| 3 | 100,000 | 21 | 21,000 |

*The next three years represent the last three years for the old computer, which is already two years old.

In Table 12–18, we bring together the depreciation on the old and new computer to determine incremental depreciation and the related tax shield benefits. Since depreciation shields off other income from being taxed, it is worth the amount being depreciated times the tax rate. For example, in year one, $375 of incremental depreciation will stop an additional $375 from being taxed, and with the firm in a 46 percent tax bracket, this represents a tax savings of $173. The same type of analysis applies to each subsequent year.

**Table 12–18**
**Analysis of incremental depreciation benefits**

| (1) Year | (2) Depreciation on New Computer | (3) Depreciation on Old Computer | (4) Incremental Depreciation | (5) Tax Rate | (6) Tax Shield Benefits |
|---|---|---|---|---|---|
| 1 | $21,375 | $21,000 | $ 375 | 0.46 | $ 173 |
| 2 | 31,350 | 21,000 | 10,350 | 0.46 | 4,761 |
| 3 | 29,925 | 21,000 | 8,925 | 0.46 | 4,105 |
| 4 | 29,925 | — | 29,925 | 0.46 | 13,766 |
| 5 | 29,925 | — | 29,925 | 0.46 | 13,766 |

## Cost Savings

The second type of benefit relates to cost savings from the new computer. As previously stated, these savings are assumed to be $38,000 per year for the next five years. The aftertax benefits are shown in Table 12–19.

As indicated in Table 12–19, we take the cost savings in column (2) and multiply by one minus the tax rate. This indicates the value of the savings on an aftertax basis.

**Table 12–19**
**Analysis of incremental cost savings benefits**

| (1)<br>Year | (2)<br>Cost Savings | (3)<br>(1 − Tax Rate) | (4)<br>Aftertax Savings |
|---|---|---|---|
| 1 . . . . . . | $38,000 | 0.54 | $20,520 |
| 2 . . . . . . | 38,000 | 0.54 | 20,520 |
| 3 . . . . . . | 38,000 | 0.54 | 20,520 |
| 4 . . . . . . | 38,000 | 0.54 | 20,520 |
| 5 . . . . . . | 38,000 | 0.54 | 20,520 |

We now combine the incremental tax shield benefits from depreciation (Table 12–18) and the aftertax cost savings (Table 12–19) to arrive at total annual benefits in column (3) of Table 12–20. These benefits are discounted to the present at a 10 percent cost of capital. The present value of the inflows is $102,894 as indicated in column (5) of Table 12–20.

**Table 12–20**
**Present value of total incremental benefits**

| Year | (1)<br>Tax Shield Benefits from Depreciation (from Table 12–18) | (2)<br>Aftertax Cost Savings (from Table 12–19) | (3)<br>Total Annual Benefits | (4)<br>Present Value Factor (10%) | (5)<br>Present Value |
|---|---|---|---|---|---|
| 1 . . . . | $ 173 | $20,520 | $20,693 | 0.909 | $ 18,810 |
| 2 . . . . | 4,761 | 20,520 | 25,281 | 0.826 | 20,882 |
| 3 . . . . | 4,105 | 20,520 | 24,625 | 0.751 | 18,493 |
| 4 . . . . | 13,766 | 20,520 | 34,286 | 0.683 | 23,417 |
| 5 . . . . | 13,766 | 20,520 | 34,286 | 0.621 | 21,292 |
| Present value of incremental benefits . . . . . . . . . . . . . . . . | | | | | $102,894 |

We are now in a position to compare the present value of incremental benefits of $102,894 from Table 12–20 to the net cost of the new computer of $84,420 from Table 12–17.

| | |
|---|---|
| Present value of incremental benefits . . . . | $102,894 |
| Net cost of new computer . . . . . . . . . . | 84,420 |
| Net present value . . . . . . . . . . . . . | $ 18,474 |

Clearly, there is a positive net present value, and the purchase of the new computer may be recommended on the basis of the financial analysis (there may be other subjective factors to consider as well). The student will be given the opportunity to examine other replacement decisions in selected end-of-chapter problems.

## Summary

The capital budgeting decision involves the planning of expenditures for a project with a life of at least one year and usually a considerably longer time. Although top management is often anxious about the impact of decisions on short-term reported income, the planning of capital expenditures dictates a longer time horizon. Three primary methods are used to analyze capital investment proposals: the payback method, the internal rate of return, and the net present value. The first method is unsound, while the last two are acceptable, with net present value deserving our greatest attention.

Investment alternatives may be classified as either mutually exclusive or nonmutually exclusive. If they are mutually exclusive, the selection of one alternative will preclude the selection of all other alternatives, and projects with a positive net present value may be eliminated in favor of projects with an even higher net present value. The same is also true under capital rationing, a less than desirable method in which management arbitrarily determines the maximum amount that can be invested in any time period. The student must carefully define each situation and apply the appropriate capital budgeting technique. Tax considerations are also a major factor in capital budgeting decisions. In this chapter, the impact of the 1981 and 1982 tax legislation on depreciation and tax credits is considered in the analysis. In Chapter 13 we will examine how risk fits into the capital budgeting decision-making process.

## List of Terms

**planning horizon**
**payback**
**internal rate of return**
**net present value**
**mutually exclusive**
**reinvestment assumption**
**capital rationing**
**cash flow**
**Accelerated Cost Recovery System**
**normal recovery period**
**investment tax credit**
**net present value profile**

## Discussion Questions

1. What are the important administrative considerations in the capital budgeting process?
2. Why does capital budgeting rely for analysis on cash flows rather than net income?
3. What are the weaknesses of the payback method?
4. What is normally used as the discount rate in the net present value method?
5. What does the term *mutually exclusive investments* mean?
6. If a corporation has projects that will earn more than the cost of capital, should it ration capital? Shouldn't it be able to find external funds and thus increase its wealth?
7. What is the net present value profile? What three points (characteristics) should be determined to compute the profile?
8. Generally speaking, what impact did the 1981 legislation (Economic Recovery Tax Act) have on the life span of depreciation? What are the consequences?
9. What is an investment tax credit? How does the 1982 legislation (Tax Equity and Fiscal Responsibility Act) specify the investment tax credit should be handled in determining the appropriate depreciation base?

## Problems

1. Assume that a corporation has earnings before depreciation and taxes of $60,000, depreciation of $30,000, and that it is in the 46 percent tax bracket. Compute its cash flow.

2. Assume a $50,000 investment and the following cash flows for two alternatives.

| Year | Investment A | Investment B |
|---|---|---|
| 1 . . . . . . . | $10,000 | $20,000 |
| 2 . . . . . . . | 11,000 | 25,000 |
| 3 . . . . . . . | 13,000 | 15,000 |
| 4 . . . . . . . | 16,000 | |
| 5 . . . . . . . | 24,000 | |

   Which alternative would you select under the payback method?

3. Now assume that in Problem 2 you used the net present value method, with a 10 percent discount rate. Would your answer change? Run the numbers and explain the logic behind your answer.

4. You buy a new piece of equipment for $19,254, and you receive a cash inflow of $3,000 per year for 10 years. What is the internal rate of return?

5. Bevan's Department Store is contemplating the purchase of a new machine at a cost of $13,566. The machine will provide $3,000 per year in cash flow for six years. Bevan has a cost of capital of 11 percent.

   Using the internal-rate-of-return method, evaluate this project and indicate whether it should be undertaken. Interpolate to find the exact answer (for this interpolation, refer to techniques in Chapter 9 if necessary).

6. DeBarry Corporation makes an investment of $50,000 which yields the following cash flows:

| Year | Cash Flow |
|---|---|
| 1 . . . . . | $10,000 |
| 2 . . . . . | 10,000 |
| 3 . . . . . | 16,000 |
| 4 . . . . . | 18,000 |
| 5 . . . . . | 20,000 |

*a.* What is the net present value at a 9 percent discount rate?
*b.* What is the internal rate of return? Use the interpolation procedure in this chapter.
*c.* In this problem would you make the same decision under both parts *a* and *b*?

**7.** The Green Goddess Salad Oil Company is considering the purchase of a new machine that would increase the speed of bottling and save money. The net cost of this machine is $45,000. The annual cash flows have the following projections.

| *Year* | *Cash Flow* |
|---|---|
| 1 . . . . . | $15,000 |
| 2 . . . . . | 20,000 |
| 3 . . . . . | 25,000 |
| 4 . . . . . | 10,000 |
| 5 . . . . . | 5,000 |

*a.* If the cost of capital is 10 percent, what is the net present value of selecting the new machine?
*b.* What is the internal rate of return?
*c.* Should the project be accepted? Why?

**8.** You are asked to evaluate the following two projects for the Boring Corporation. Using the net present value method, combined with the profitability index approach described in footnote 2 of this chapter, which project would you select? Use a discount rate of 10 percent.

| *Project X (Videotapes of the Weather Report) ($10,000 Investment)* | | *Project Y (Slow-Motion Replays of Commercials) ($30,000 Investment)* | |
|---|---|---|---|
| *Year* | *Cash Flow* | *Year* | *Cash Flow* |
| 1 . . . . . | $5,000 | 1 . . . . . | $15,000 |
| 2 . . . . . | 3,000 | 2 . . . . . | 8,000 |
| 3 . . . . . | 4,000 | 3 . . . . . | 9,000 |
| 4 . . . . . | 3,600 | 4 . . . . . | 11,000 |

**9.** The Suboptimal Glass Company uses a process of capital rationing in its decision making. The firm's cost of capital is 13 percent. It will only invest $60,000 this year. It has determined the internal rate of return for each of the following projects.

| Project | Project Size | Internal Rate of Return |
|---|---|---|
| A | $10,000 | 15% |
| B | 30,000 | 14 |
| C | 25,000 | 16.5 |
| D | 10,000 | 17 |
| E | 10,000 | 23 |
| F | 20,000 | 11 |
| G | 15,000 | 16 |

*a.* Pick out the projects that the firm should accept.

*b.* If Projects D and E were mutually exclusive, how would that affect your overall answer? That is, which projects would you accept in expending the $60,000?

**10.** Keller Construction Company is considering two new investments. Project E calls for the purchase of earth-moving equipment. Project H represents the investment in a hydraulic lift. Keller wishes to use a net present value profile in comparing the projects. The investment and cash flow patterns are as follows:

| Project E ($20,000 Investment) | | Project H ($20,000 Investment) | |
|---|---|---|---|
| Year | Cash Flow | Year | Cash Flow |
| 1 | $ 5,000 | 1 | $16,000 |
| 2 | 6,000 | 2 | 5,000 |
| 3 | 7,000 | 3 | 4,000 |
| 4 | 10,000 | | |

*a.* Determine the net present value of the projects based on a zero discount rate.

*b.* Determine the net present value of the projects based on a 9 percent discount rate.

*c.* The internal rate of return on Project E is 13.25 percent, and the internal rate of return on Project H is 16.30 percent. Graph a net present value profile for the two investments similar to Figure 12–3. (Use a scale up to $8,000 on the vertical axis, with $2,000 increments. Use a scale up to 20 percent on the horizontal axis, with 5 percent increments.)

*d.* If the two projects are not mutually exclusive, what would your acceptance or rejection decision be if the cost of capital (discount rate) is 10 percent? (Use the net present value profile for your decision; no actual numbers are necessary.)

*e.* If the two projects are mutually exclusive (the selection of one precludes the selection of the other), what would be your decision if the cost of capital is (1) 6 percent, (2) 13 percent, (3) 18 percent? Once again, use the net present value profile for your answer.

**11.** Luft Watch Company is considering an investment of $15,000, which produces the following inflows.

| Year | Cash Flow |
|---|---|
| 1 . . . . . . | $8,000 |
| 2 . . . . . . | 7,000 |
| 3 . . . . . . | 4,000 |

You are going to use the net present value profile to approximate the value for the internal rate of return. Please follow these steps.

*a.* Determine the net present value of the project based on a zero discount rate.

*b.* Determine the net present value of the project based on a 10 percent discount rate.

*c.* Determine the net present value of the project based on a 20 percent discount rate (it will be negative).

*d.* Draw a net present value profile for the investment and observe the discount rate at which the net present value is zero. This is an approximation of the internal rate of return on the project.

*e.* Actually compute the internal rate of return based on the interpolation procedure presented in this chapter. Compare your answers in parts *d* and *e*.

**12.** The Stevens Company will invest $50,000 in a project. The firm's discount rate (cost of capital) is 9 percent. The investment will provide the following inflows.

| | |
|---|---|
| 1 . . . . | $10,000 |
| 2 . . . . | 10,000 |
| 3 . . . . | 16,000 |
| 4 . . . . | 18,000 |
| 5 . . . . | 20,000 |

The internal rate of return is 12.8 percent.

*a.* If the reinvestment assumption of the net present value method is used, what will be the total value of the inflows after five years? (Assume the inflows come at the end of each year).

*b*. If the reinvestment assumption of the internal rate of return method is used, what will be the total value of the inflows after five years?

*c*. Generally, is one reinvestment assumption likely to be better than another?

**13.** A $95,000 investment is to be depreciated using the Accelerated Cost Recovery System (ACRS) shown in Tables 12–8 and 12–9.

*a*. If the investment represents a fleet of automobiles, what will the recovery time period be?

*b*. How much will the annual dollar depreciation be? Do not include an investment tax credit (ITC).

*c*. If the investment represents machinery and equipment, what will the recovery time period be?

*d*. How much will the annual dollar depreciation be under the assumption in part *c*? Do not include an investment tax credit.

*e*. Is salvage value utilized under ACRS depreciation?

**14.** The Pacific Corporation will purchase a $40,000 asset with a five-year life. Increased sales will be $65,000 per year, and increased cost and maintenance will be $35,000 per year. The equipment will be depreciated on a straight-line basis. The firm is in the 46 percent tax bracket. Complete the following table to determine annual cash flow.

| | |
|---|---|
| Increased sales | ________ |
| Increased cost and maintenance | ________ |
| Earnings before depreciation and taxes | ________ |
| Depreciation | ________ |
| Earnings before taxes | ________ |
| Taxes | ________ |
| Earnings after taxes | ________ |
| Depreciation | ________ |
| Cash Flow | ________ |

**15.** Assume the same facts as in Problem 14, but using the Accelerated Cost Recovery System (ACRS), determine the cash flow for each of the five years. Do not include an investment tax credit.

The remaining problems are based on the Accelerated Cost Recovery System (ACRS) for depreciation. You should round to the nearest dollar. For problems that require an investment decision, use the net present value method.

**16.** Assume an asset with a five-year depreciation life is to be purchased for $80,000. The 10 percent investment tax credit will be taken.

*a.* Compute the investment tax credit (ITC).
*b.* What is the depreciation base?
*c.* Compute the annual depreciation.

**17.** (*Basic investment decision*)
The Bryant Corporation is considering the purchase of 25 automobiles for $160,000. The automobiles will fall under the ACRS three-year category for depreciation and the ITC.

Because of fuel efficiency, the automobiles will save the firm $60,000 per year for five years.* (This is the equivalent of earnings before depreciation and taxes.) The firm is in a 40 percent tax bracket and has a 12 percent cost of capital.

Should they purchase the automobiles?

*As explained in the chapter, it is not unusual for the productive life of the asset to exceed the depreciable life under ACRS depreciation (as is true here). In fact, the circumstance is quite common.

**18.** (*Basic investment decision*)
Airway Kite Company is considering the purchase of a new machine that cuts plastic sheets and binds the edges with string. The cost is $60,000. The machine will fall under the five-year category for depreciation and the ITC.

If the machine is purchased, Airway can begin producing an entirely different line of kites. The new product is anticipated to provide a revenue of $58,000 per year for the next seven years, and associated expenses of $44,000 per year for the first five years and $50,500 for the last two years. The firm is in a 46 percent tax bracket and has a cost of capital of 10 percent.

Should Airway Kite Company purchase the new machine?

**19.** (*Basic investment decision*)
The 4-Ward Looking Corporation is considering starting a new subsidiary to make firecrackers and other explosives. The initial

investment in building space and equipment will be $60,000. Of this amount, $45,000 is subject to five-year ACRS depreciation and a 10 percent investment tax credit. The balance is in nondepreciable property. The corporation realizes that state ordinance Number 132 will preclude continued operation of the business at the end of five years and the nondepreciable assets will be sold for $15,000. The depreciated assets will have zero value.

The subsidiary will also require an investment of $20,000 in working capital at the beginning of the first year and of this amount, $16,000 will be returned to the 4-Ward Looking Corporation after five years.

The investment will produce $24,000 in income before depreciation and taxes for each of the five years. The corporation is in a 40 percent tax bracket and has a 13 percent cost of capital.

Should the investment be undertaken?

**20.** (*Basic investment calculation—real property*)
J. B. Lipscomb of North Tex Properties is considering construction of a 6,000 square foot building. In checking the tax code, he determines that most real estate is written off over 18 years. Actually the tax code has changed the depreciation period on real estate almost annually. Eighteen years is merely considered to be representative. The annual depreciation schedule is shown below.

The building will cost $35 a square foot to construct. The land price is $60,000. The property taxes on the building will be $3,900. Insurance and maintenance expenses will total $2,800. The financing costs (interest payments) in year one will be $25,500.

The building can be rented for $7.50 per square foot. The firm is in a 46 percent tax bracket.

*Accelerated Depreciation on Real Estate*

| *Years of Depreciation* | *Percentage Depreciation* |
|---|---|
| 1–2 | 9% |
| 3 | 8 |
| 4–5 | 7 |
| 6 | 6 |
| 7–12 | 5 |
| 13–18 | 4 |

*a.* Determine the cost of the building (excluding land).
*b.* Determine the depreciation schedule for the first five years (only the building and not the land is depreciated). No tax credit is allowable.
*c.* Determine earnings before depreciation and taxes for the first year. (Total rentals minus all expenses except depreciation).
*d.* Determine cash flow for the first year. Use the following format:
(1) Earnings before depreciation and taxes.
(2) Less depreciation.
(3) Earnings (loss) before taxes.
(4) Tax shield benefits from loss (answer to item (3) times the tax rate).
(5) Plus depreciation.
(6) Cash flow* [(3) + (4) + (5)].

*Item (3) (a loss) and items (4) and (5) are added together to arrive at cash flow.

As a matter of procedure, cash flow could be computed for each year and the net present value or internal rate of return computed (if sufficient information were given).

**21.** (*Replacement decision*)
Nelson technology purchased a telecommunication system three years ago for $258,000. It has a five-year life for ACRS depreciation. No investment tax credit was taken. The system can be sold for $78,000.

A new system will cost $320,000 and will be written off over five years. A 10 percent ITC is available on the new equipment.

Assume the new system would provide the following stream of cost savings over the next five years.

| Year | Cash Savings |
|---|---|
| 1 . . . . . . | $87,000 |
| 2 . . . . . . | 86,000 |
| 3 . . . . . . | 72,000 |
| 4 . . . . . . | 60,000 |
| 5 . . . . . . | 58,000 |

The tax rate is 46 percent and the cost of capital is 11 percent.

*a.* What is the cash inflow generated by the sale of the old system? Include tax considerations.

*b*. Compute the net cost of the new system (include consideration of the cash inflow from the sale of the old system).

*c*. Determine the depreciation base and depreciation schedule for the new system.

*d*. Compute the remaining depreciation on the old system.

*e*. Determine the incremental depreciation between the old and new system and the related tax shield benefits.

*f*. Compute the aftertax benefits of the cost savings.

*g*. Add the depreciation tax shield benefits and the aftertax cost savings and determine the present value.

*h*. Compare the present value of incremental benefits (*g*) to the net cost of the new system (*b*).

Should the replacement be undertaken?

**22.** (*Replacement decision—recapture of ITC with instructions*) Tasty Foods is evaluating a decision to replace its computerized model for packaging. The old model was purchased two years ago for $400,000. At the time of purchase the model was set up for a five-year life for purposes of ACRS depreciation. Also a 10 percent investment tax credit was taken.

The old model could be sold in the current market for $180,000. Since the asset has not been held for the full five years, part of the investment tax credit must be returned to the IRS. As indicated in footnote 7 of this chapter, an investment tax credit is assumed to be earned at the rate of 2 percent per year. If a five-year-old asset is sold after two years, 6 percent of the 10 percent credit is being recaptured and must be returned to the IRS (in this case at the end of the second year).

A new computerized model for packaging will cost $500,000 and will be written off over five years under ACRS depreciation. A 10 percent investment tax credit will be taken. The new equipment will provide the following cost savings over the next eight years.

| Year | Savings | Year | Savings |
|---|---|---|---|
| 1 . . . | $92,000 | 5 . . . | $77,000 |
| 2 . . . | 84,000 | 6 . . . | 68,000 |
| 3 . . . | 83,000 | 7 . . . | 63,000 |
| 4 . . . | 81,000 | 8 . . . | 57,000 |

The firm is in a 46 percent tax bracket and the cost of capital is 10 percent.

*a.* What is the book value of the old model after two years? Recall that half of the investment tax credit must be subtracted out in setting up the initial depreciation base.
*b.* What is the tax benefit from the sale of the old model?
*c.* Subtract the recapture of the investment tax credit (6 percent of purchase price) from the answer to part *b* to arrive at the net tax benefit.
*d.* Add the answer to part *c* to the sales price for the old model to arrive at cash inflow from the sale of the old model.
*e.* Compute the net cost of the new model.
*f.* Determine the depreciation base and depreciation schedule for the new model.
*g.* Compute the remaining depreciation on the old model. Use the depreciation base from part *a*.
*h.* Determine the incremental depreciation between the old and new model and the related tax shield benefits.
*i.* Compute the aftertax benefits of the cost savings.
*j.* Determine the present value of the tax shield benefits from depreciation and the aftertax cost savings.
*k.* Compare the present value of the incremental benefits in part *j* to the net cost of the new model in part *e*.
Should the replacement be undertaken?

## Selected References


Abdelsamad, Moustafa. *A Guide to Capital Expenditure Analysis*. New York: American Management Association, 1973.

Bacon, Peter W. "The Evaluation of Mutually Exclusive Investments." *Financial Management* 6 (Summer 1977), pp. 55–58.

Bernhard, Richard H. "Mathematical Programming Models for Capital Budgeting—A Survey, Generalization, and Critique." *Journal of Financial and Quantitative Analysis* 4 (June 1969), pp. 111–58.

Bierman, Harold, Jr., and Seymour Smidt. *The Capital Budgeting Decision*, 4th ed. New York: Macmillan, 1975.

Brick, Ivan, and Daniel G. Weaver. "A Comparison of Capital Budgeting Techniques in Identifying Profitable Investments." *Financial Management* 13 (Winter 1984), pp. 29–39.

Donaldson, Gordon. "Strategic Hurdle Rates for Capital Investment." *Harvard Business Review* 50 (March–April 1972), pp. 50–58.

Dorfman, Robert. "The Meaning of Internal Rates of Return." *Journal of Finance* 36 (December 1981), pp. 1010–21.

Durand, David. "Comprehensiveness in Capital Budgeting." *Financial Management* 10 (Winter 1981), pp. 7–13.

Johnson, Robert W. *Capital Budgeting*. Belmont, Calif.: Wadsworth, 1970.

Klommer, Thomas. "Empirical Evidence of the Adoption of Sophisticated Capital Budgeting Techniques." *Journal of Business* 45 (July 1972), pp. 387–97.

Libscomb, Joseph. "Real Estate Capital Budgeting." *The Real Estate Appraiser and Analyst* 48 (Summer 1982), pp. 23–31.

Mao, James C. T. "The Internal Rate of Return as a Ranking Criterion." *Engineering Economist* 11 (Winter 1966), pp. 1–13.

Matukonis, Michael. "Appropriate Application of the Investment Tax Credit in Capital Budgeting Decisions." State University of New York College at Oneonta, Manuscript, 1985.

Murdick, Robert G., and Donald D. Deming. *The Management of Corporate Expenditures*. New York: McGraw-Hill, 1968.

Oakford, Robert V. *Capital Budgeting*. New York: Ronald, 1970.

Petty, J. William; David F. Scott, Jr.; and Monroe M. Bird. "The Capital Expenditure Decision-Making Process of Large Corporations." *Engineering Economist* 20 (Spring 1975), pp. 159–72.

Rappaport, Alfred, and Robert A. Taggart, Jr. "The Evaluation of Capital Expenditure Proposals Under Inflation." *Financial Management* 11 (Spring 1982), pp. 5–13.

Sarnat, M., and H. Levy. "The Relationship of Rules of Thumb to the Internal Rate of Return: A Restatement and Generalization." *Journal of Finance* 24 (June 1969), pp. 479–89.

Van Horne, James C. "A note of Biases in Capital Budgeting Introduced by Inflation." *Journal of Financial and Quantitative Analysis* 6 (January 1971), pp. 653–58.

Weaver, James B. "Organizing and Maintaining a Capital Expenditure Program." *Engineering Economist* 20 (Fall 1974), pp. 1–36.

## Appendix 12A: Tax Implications for the Disposal of an Asset

There are four different tax implications for the sale of an asset. We will assume that an $80,000 asset, with a five-year life under ACRS depreciation, is disposed of after two years.[1] The book value at that point in time is $50,400, as developed here.

| Year | Depreciation Base | Percentage Depreciation (Table 12–9) | Depreciation |
|---|---|---|---|
| 1 | $80,000 | 15% | $12,000 |
| 2 | 80,000 | 22 | 17,600 |
| Total depreciation to date | | | $29,600 |

| | |
|---|---|
| Purchase price | $80,000 |
| Total depreciation to date | 29,600 |
| Book value | $50,400 |

We now look at the four different tax implications of the sale. Each depends on the sales price of the asset.

**A. The sales price is higher than the purchase price ($95,000 compared to $80,000).**

In this case there is a long-term capital gains tax[2] as well as a tax on the recapture of depreciation.

**Long-term capital gains tax** The long-term capital gain is represented by the difference between the sales price ($95,000) and the purchase price ($80,000). The long-term capital gains tax rate for a corporation is 28 percent or the ordinary tax rate, whichever is lower. In most cases the 28 percent will be lower (since the ordinary tax rate goes up to 46 percent for corporations).

Applying a 28 percent tax rate to the long-term capital gains of $15,000 results in a tax of $4,200.

[1]For the purpose of this analysis, an ITC on the old asset is not considered.

[2]The gain is long-term because the asset has been held for over six months.

| | |
|---|---|
| Sales price . . . . . . . . . . | $95,000 |
| Purchase price | 80,000 |
| Long-term capital gains . . . . | 15,000 |
| Capital gains tax rate . . . . . | 28% |
| Capital gains tax . . . . . . . | $ 4,200 |

**Tax on recaptured depreciation** The recapture of depreciation in this case is represented by the difference between the purchase price ($80,000) and the book value ($50,400). The firm is assumed to be recapturing depreciation it has taken in the past and must pay its ordinary income tax rate on it (presumed to be 46 percent in this instance). The basis of recaptured depreciation is that a firm cannot justify a prior depreciation deduction in writing down an asset when the asset's confirmed exchange value upon sale exceeds that amount. The tax on recaptured depreciation is $13,616.

| | |
|---|---|
| Purchase price . . . . . . . . . . | $80,000 |
| Book value . . . . . . . . . . . | 50,400 |
| Recaptured depreciation . . . . | 29,600 |
| Ordinary tax rate . . . . . . . . | 46% |
| Ordinary income tax . . . . . . | $13,616 |

The total tax is:

| | |
|---|---|
| Capital gains tax . . . . . . | $ 4,200 |
| Ordinary income tax . . . . | 13,616 |
| Total tax . . . . . . . . . | $17,816 |

The actual cash inflow from the sale of the old asset is $77,184.

| | |
|---|---|
| Sales price . . . . | $95,000 |
| Tax . . . . . . . . | − 17,816 |
| Cash inflow . . . . | $77,184 |

We now look at a second tax implication.

**B. Sales price is above book value, but below the purchase price. In this second example, we will assume a sales price of $70,000.**

There are no long-term capital gains because the sales price ($70,000) is below the purchase price ($80,000). However, there is recaptured depreciation in this case because the sales price exceeds the book value. The calculation of recaptured depreciation in this second instance is slightly different from the first example in that we take the difference between the sales price and book value in order to calculate the tax. This is always the procedure when the sales price is above book value, but below the purchase price. The tax on recaptured depreciation is $9,016.

| | |
|---|---|
| Sales price | $70,000 |
| Book value | 50,400 |
| Recaptured depreciation | 19,600 |
| Ordinary tax rate | 46% |
| Ordinary income tax | $ 9,016 |

The actual cash inflow from the sale of the old asset is $60,984.

| | |
|---|---|
| Sales price | $70,000 |
| Tax | −9,016 |
| Cash inflow | $60,984 |

**C. Sales price is at book value. In this third example, we assume a sales price of $50,400.**

Under this circumstance, there are no tax consequences and the cash inflow from the sale of the old asset is the sales price of $50,400.

**D. Sales price is below book value. In this fourth example, we assume a sales price of $40,000.**

There will be a loss in this case. Since this is a depreciable asset used in business or trade, the long-term capital loss may be used to offset ordinary income to the corporation. It provides a tax shield benefit equal to the loss times 46 percent.

| | |
|---|---|
| Book value | $50,400 |
| Sales price | 40,000 |
| Long-term capital loss | 10,400 |
| Ordinary tax rate | 46% |
| Tax benefits (shield) | $ 4,784 |

The cash inflow from the sale of the old asset is $44,784.

| | |
|---|---|
| Sales price . . . . . . . . . . | $40,000 |
| + Tax benefit from sale . . . . | 4,784 |
| Cash inflow . . . . . . . . . . | $44,784 |

## Problems

**12A–1.** The Blackstone Corporation purchased an operating asset three years ago for $130,000. At the time of purchase, the asset had a five-year life for ACRS purposes. No investment tax credit is assumed. The firm is now going to dispose of the asset. The applicable tax rates are 46 percent for ordinary income and 28 percent for capital gains. Determine the (*a*) taxes owed or tax shield benefit and (*b*) the cash inflow from the sale of the asset under the following circumstances.

*a.* The sales price is $145,000.
*b.* The sales price is $92,000.
*c.* The sales price is $54,600.
*d.* The sales price is $33,000.

**12A–2.** (*Comprehensive replacement decision—capital gains, recaptured depreciation*)
Supersoft Products, Inc., is evaluating the possibility of replacing its X-model equipment for producing microcomputer disks. The purchase price of the old model two years ago was $65,000. The company has a firm offer from CPT, Inc., to buy the equipment for $74,000. The equipment is being depreciated over a five-year life under ACRS depreciation provisions. There is no investment tax credit on the old model.

A new piece of equipment would cost $125,000 and would be written off over a five-year time period. A 10 percent investment tax credit would be taken on the purchase. It is anticipated that with the new equipment, 60¢ per disk can be saved on the production of disks over the next seven years. This would represent added before-tax profit per disk. The current production is 10,000 disks, and that is expected to increase 1,000 per year over the next seven years. Thus, for the first year of analysis, use a production level of 10,000 and then show annual increments as specified. The firm has a tax rate of 46 percent for ordinary income and 28 percent for capital gains. The cost of capital is 10 percent.

Should the new equipment be purchased?

# 13 Risk and Capital Budgeting

No one area is more essential to financial decision making than the evaluation and management of risk. The price of a firm's stock is, to a large degree, influenced by the amount of risk that investors perceive to be inherent in the firm. We are constantly trying to achieve the appropriate mix between profitability and risk to satisfy those with a stake in the affairs of the firm and to achieve the goal of wealth maximization for shareholders.

The difficulty is not in finding viable investment alternatives but in determining where we want to be on the risk-return scale. Would we prefer a 25 percent potential return on a new product in oil-sensitive Western Europe or a safe 8 percent return on an extension of our current product line in our home territory? The question can only be answered in terms of profitability, the risk position of the firm, and management and stockholder disposition toward risk. In this chapter, we examine additional definitions of risk, its measurement and its incorporation into the *capital budgeting* process, and the basic tenets of portfolio theory.

## Definition of Risk in Capital Budgeting

Risk may be defined in terms of the variability of possible outcomes from a given investment. If funds are invested in a 30-day U.S. government obligation, the outcome is certain and there is no variability—hence no risk. On the other hand, if we invest the same funds in a gold-mining expedition to the deepest wilds of Africa, the variability of possible outcomes is great and we say the project is replete with risk.

The student should observe that risk is measured not only in terms of losses but also in terms of uncertainty.[1] We say that gold mining carries a high degree of risk not just because you may lose your money but because there is a wide range of possible outcomes. Observe in Figure 13–1 examples of three investments with different risk characteristics. Note that in each case the distributions are centered on the same expected value ($20,000) but that the variability (risk) increases as we move from Investment A to Investment C. Because you may *gain* or *lose* the most in Investment C, it is clearly the riskiest of the three.

## The Concept of Risk Averse

A basic assumption in financial theory is that most investors and managers are risk averse—that is, for a given situation they would prefer relative certainty to uncertainty. In Figure 13–1, they would prefer Investment A over Investments B and C, although all three investments have the same expected value of $20,000. You are probably risk averse too. Assume you have saved $1,000 for your last year in college and are challenged to flip a coin, double or nothing. Heads, you end up with $2,000—tails, you are broke. Given that you are not enrolled at the University of Nevada at Las Vegas or that you are not an inveterate gambler, you will probably stay with your certain $1,000.

This is not to say that investors or businessmen are unwilling to take risks—but rather that they will require a higher expected value or

[1] We use the term *uncertainty* in its normal sense, rather than in the more formalized sense in which it is sometimes used in decision theory to indicate that insufficient evidence is available to estimate a probability distribution.

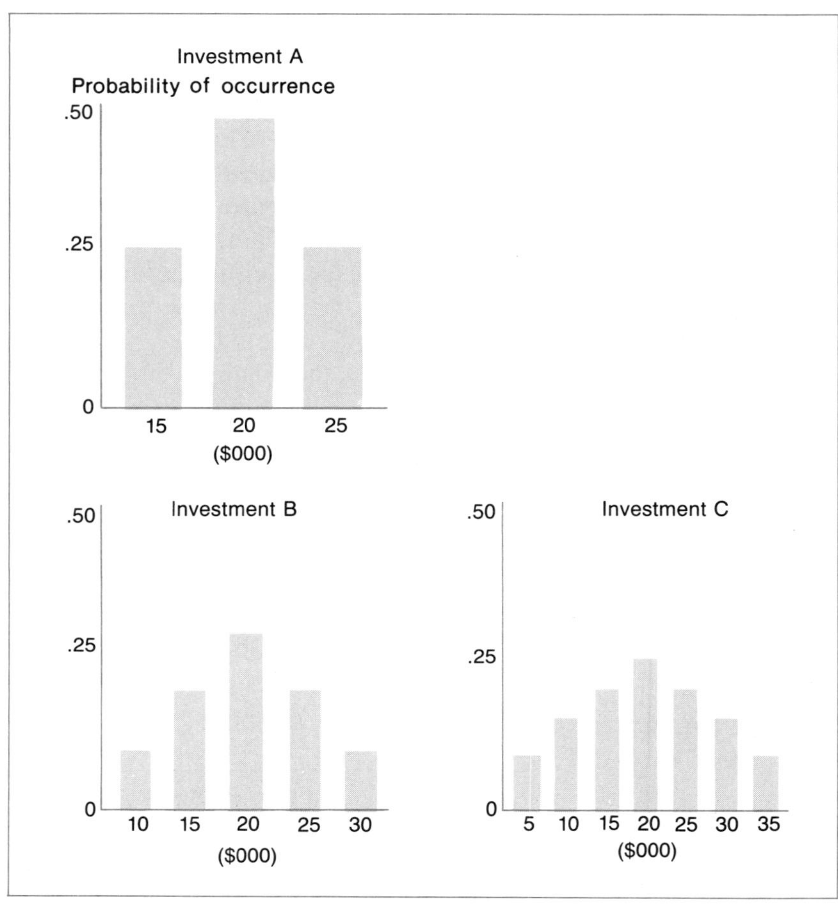


Figure 13–1
Variability and risk

return for risky investments. In Figure 13–2, we compare a low-risk proposal with an expected value of $20,000 to a high-risk proposal with an expected value of $30,000. The higher expected return may well compensate investors for absorbing greater risk.

Throughout the chapter, we will develop methods for incorporating a higher demanded return for risky investments. For Evel Knievel, back in the 1970s, it was $7 million to jump over the Snake River Canyon—for a corporation, it may be a bonus return of 5 percent over the cost of capital.

Figure 13–2
Risk-return trade-off

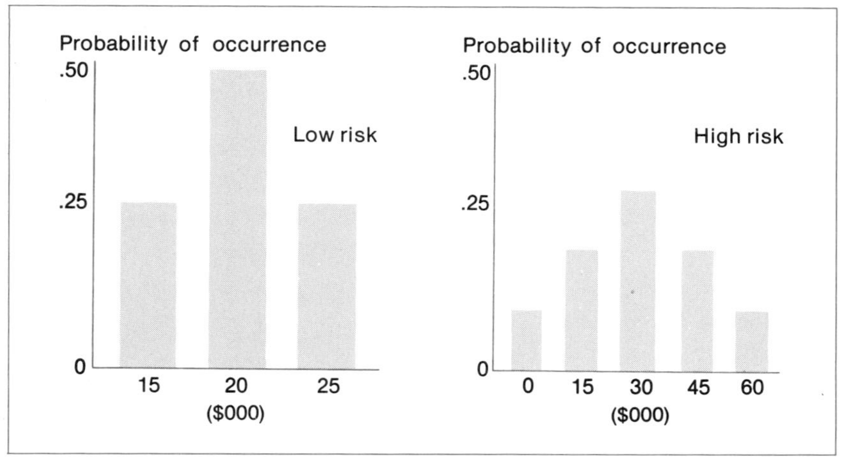


## Actual Measurement of Risk

A number of basic statistical devices may be employed to measure the extent of risk inherent in any given situation. Assume that we are examining an investment with the possible outcomes and probability of outcomes shown in Table 13–1.

The probabilities in Table 13–1 may be based on past experience, industry ratios and trends, interviews with company executives, and sophisticated simulation techniques. The probability values may be quite easy to determine for the introduction of a mechanical stamping process in which the manufacturer has 10 years of past data, but difficult to assess for a new product in a foreign market. In any event, we force ourselves into a valuable analytical process.

With the data before us, we compute two important statistical measures—the expected value and the standard deviation. The ex-

Table 13–1
Probability distribution of outcomes

| *Outcome* | *Probability of Outcome* | *Assumptions* |
|---|---|---|
| $300 | .2 | Pessimistic |
| 600 | .6 | Moderately successful |
| 900 | .2 | Optimistic |

pected value is a weighted average of the outcomes times their probabilities.

$$\bar{D} \text{ (expected value)} = \Sigma DP \qquad (13\text{–}1)$$

| $D$ | | $P$ | | $DP$ |
|---|---|---|---|---|
| 300 | × | .2 | = | \$ 60 |
| 600 | × | .6 | = | 360 |
| 900 | × | .2 | = | 180 |
| | | | | \$600 = $\Sigma DP$ |

The expected value is \$600. We then compute the standard deviation—the measure of dispersion or variability around the expected value. The formula for the standard deviation is quite simple:

$$\sigma \text{ (standard deviation)} = \sqrt{\Sigma(D - \bar{D})^2 P} \qquad (13\text{–}2)$$

The following steps should be followed:

| Step 1: subtract the expected value ($\bar{D}$) from each outcome ($D$) | | | | | Step 2: square ($D - \bar{D}$) | Step 3: multiply by $P$ and sum | | Step 4: determine the square root |
|---|---|---|---|---|---|---|---|---|
| $D$ | | $\bar{D}$ | | $(D - \bar{D})$ | $(D - \bar{D})^2$ | $P$ | $(D - \bar{D})^2 P$ | |
| 300 | − | 600 | = | −300 | 90,000 | × .20 = | 18,000 | |
| 600 | − | 600 | = | 0 | 0 | × .60 = | 0 | |
| 900 | − | 600 | = | +300 | 90,000 | × .20 = | 18,000 | |
| | | | | | | | 36,000 | $\sqrt{36,000}$ = \$190 |

The standard deviation of \$190 gives us a rough average measure of how far each of the three outcomes falls away from the expected value. Generally, the larger the standard deviation (or spread of outcomes), the greater is the risk, as indicated in Figure 13–3.

The student will note that in Figure 13–3 we compare the standard deviation of three investments with the same expected value of \$600. If the expected values of the investments were quite different (such as \$600 versus \$6,000), a direct comparison of the standard deviations for each distribution would not be very helpful in measuring risk. In Figure 13–4 we show such an occurrence.

Note that the investment in Panel A of Figure 13–4 appears to have a high standard deviation—but not when related to the expected value

Figure 13–3
Probability distribution with differing degrees of risk

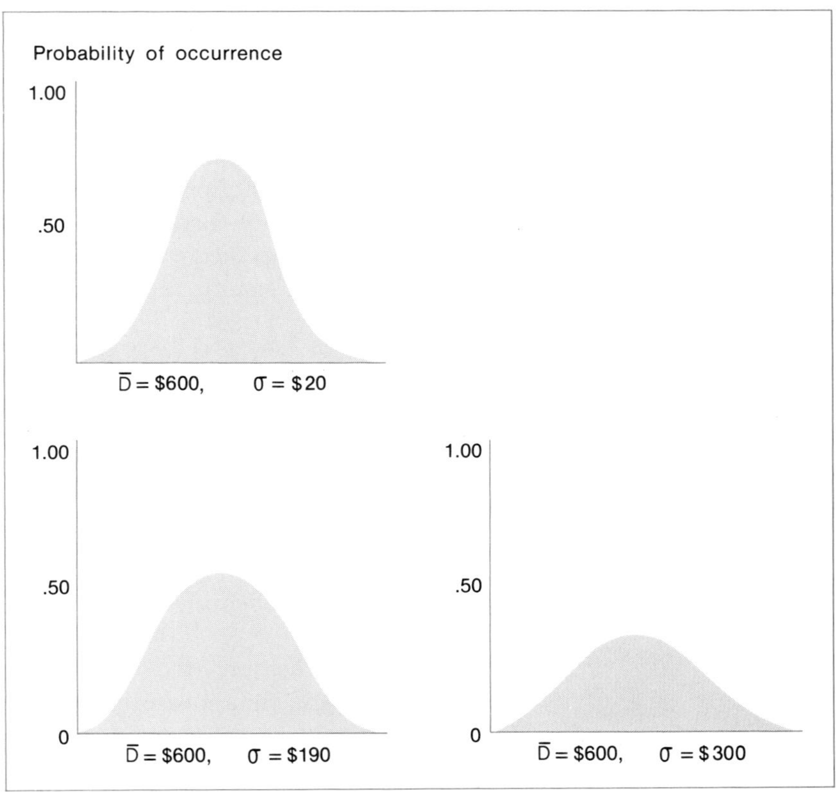


Figure 13–4

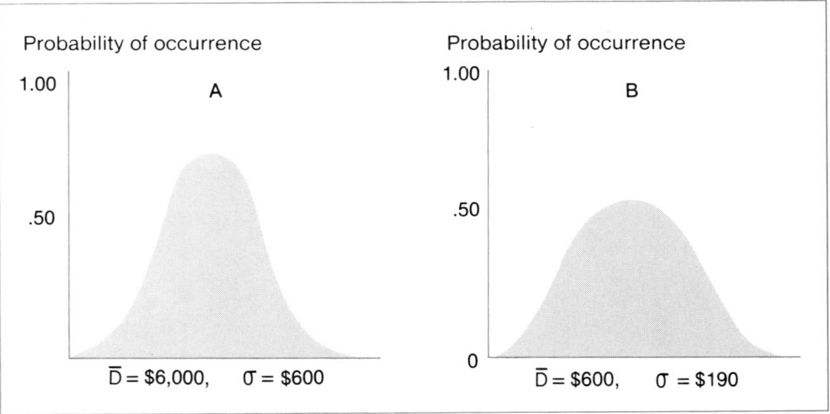

of the distribution. A standard deviation of \$600 on an investment with an expected value of \$6,000 may indicate less risk than a standard deviation of \$190 on an investment with an expected value of only \$600.

We can eliminate the size difficulty by developing a third measure, the coefficient of variation ($V$). This rather imposing term calls for nothing more difficult than dividing the standard deviation of an investment by the expected value. Generally, the larger the coefficient of variation, the greater is the risk.

$$\text{Coefficient of variation } (V) = \frac{\sigma}{\bar{D}} \tag{13–3}$$

For the investments in Panels A and B of Figure 13–4, we show:

$$A \qquad \frac{600}{6{,}000} = .10 \qquad\qquad B \qquad \frac{190}{600} = .317$$

We have correctly identified the second investment as carrying the greater risk.

Another risk measure, the beta ($\beta$), is widely used with portfolios of common stock. Beta measures the volatility of returns on an individual stock relative to a stock market index of returns such as the Standard & Poor's 500-stock index.[2] A common stock with a beta of 1.0 is said to be of equal risk with the market. Stocks with betas greater

**Table 13–2**
**Betas for a five-year period (1980–1985)**

| *Company Name* | *Beta* |
|---|---|
| Anchor Hocking | 0.65 |
| Arizona Public Service | 0.70 |
| Gordon Jewelry | 0.75 |
| United Inns | 0.80 |
| Warner-Lambert | 0.95 |
| Standard & Poor's 500 Stock Index | 1.00 |
| Gulf & Western | 1.10 |
| Citicorp | 1.20 |
| General Dynamics | 1.35 |
| Control Data | 1.50 |
| E. F. Hutton Group | 2.00 |

[2]Other market measures may also be utilized.

than 1.0 are riskier than the market, while stocks with betas of less than 1.0 are less risky than the market. Table 13–2 presents a sample of betas for several well-known companies from 1980–85.

## Risk and the Capital Budgeting Process

How can risk analysis be used effectively in the capital budgeting process? In Chapter 12, The Capital Budgeting Decision, we made no explicit distinction between risky and nonrisky events.[3] We showed the amount of the investment and the annual returns—making no comment about the riskiness or likelihood of achieving these returns. We know that enlightened investors and managers need further information. A $1,400 investment that produces "certain" returns of $600 a year for three years is not the same as a $1,400 investment that produces returns with an expected value of $600 for three years—but a high coefficient of variation. Investors, being risk averse by nature, will apply a stiffer test to the second investment. How can this new criterion be applied to the capital budgeting process?

### Risk-Adjusted Discount Rate

A favored approach to adjusting for risk is to use different discount rates for proposals with different risk levels. A project that carries a normal amount of risk and does not change the overall risk composure of the firm should be discounted at the cost of capital. Investments carrying greater than normal risk will be discounted at a higher rate; and so on. In Figure 13–5, we show a possible risk-discount rate trade-off scheme. Risk is assumed to be measured by the coefficient of variation ($V$).

The normal risk for the firm is represented by a coefficient of variation of 0.30. An investment with this risk would be discounted at the firm's normal cost of capital of 10 percent. As the firm selects riskier projects with, for example, a $V$ of 0.90, a risk premium of 5 percent is added for an increase in $V$ of 0.60. If the company selects a project with a coefficient of variation of 1.20, it will now add another 5 percent

[3]Our assumption was that the risk factor could be considered as constant for various investments.

Figure 13–5
Relationship of risk to discount rate

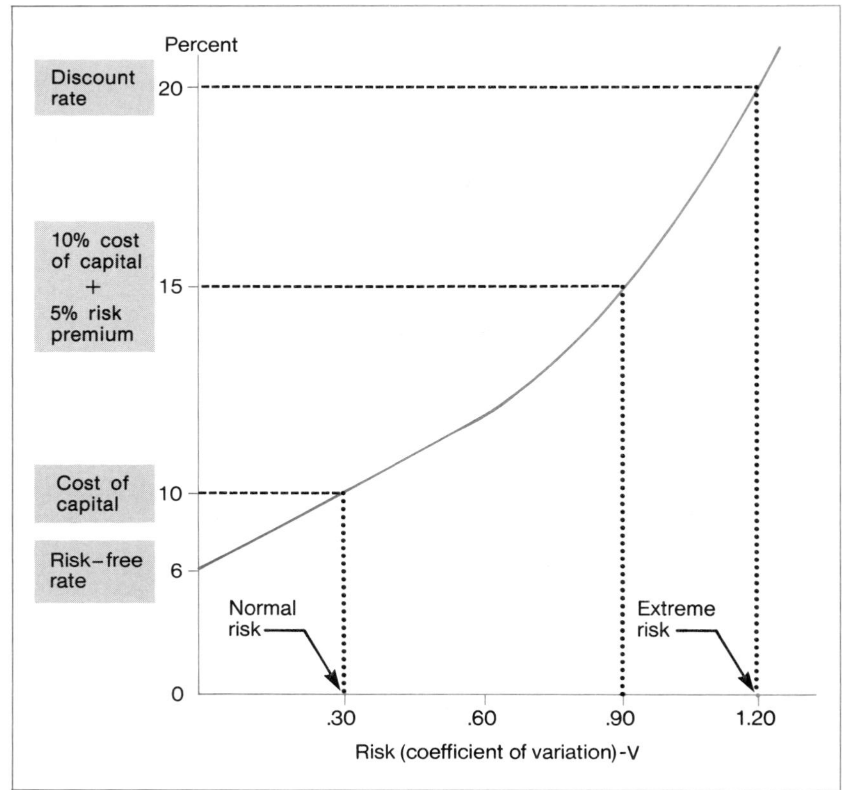


risk premium for this additional $V$ of 0.30. Notice that the same risk premium of 5 percent was added for a smaller increase in risk. This is an example of being increasingly risk averse at higher levels of risk and potential return.

## Increasing Risk over Time

It seems that our ability to forecast accurately diminishes as we forecast farther out in time. As the time horizon becomes longer, more uncertainty enters the forecast. The decline in oil prices sharply curtailed the search for petroleum and left many drillers in serious financial condition in the 1980s after years of expanding drilling activity. The cancellation or delay of aircraft orders during 1982 is another example

Figure 13–6
Risk over time

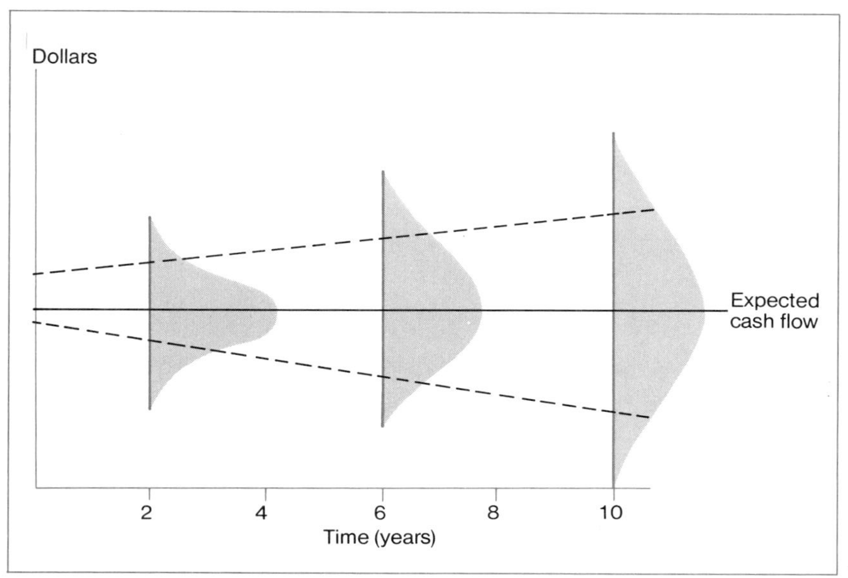


of negative outcomes in an industry that looked so rosy in 1980 that Boeing expected to sell several hundred of its newly designed jetliners. These unexpected events create a higher standard deviation in cash flows and increase the risk associated with long-lived projects. Figure 13–6 depicts the relationship between risk and time.

Even though a forecast of cash flows shows a constant expected value, Figure 13–6 shows that the range of outcomes and probabilities increase as we move from year 2 to 10. The standard deviations increase for each forecast of cash flow. If cash flows were forecast as easily for each period, all distributions would look like the first one for year 2. Using progressively higher discount rates to compensate for risk tends to penalize late flows more than early flows, and this is consistent with the notion that risk is greater for longer-term cash flows than for near-term cash flows.

## Qualitative Measures

Rather than relate the discount rate—or required return—to the coefficient of variation or possibly the beta, management may wish to

**Table 13–3**
**Risk categories and associated discount rates**

| | Discount Rate |
|---|---|
| Low or no risk (repair to old machinery) | 6% |
| Moderate risk (new equipment) | 8 |
| Normal risk (addition to normal product line) | 10 |
| Risky (new product in related market) | 12 |
| High risk (completely new market) | 16 |
| Highest risk (new product in foreign market) | 20 |

set up risk classes based on qualitative considerations. Examples are presented in Table 13–3. Once again, we are equating the discount rate to the perceived risk.

**Example—risk-adjusted discount rate** In Chapter 12 we compared two $10,000 investment alternatives and indicated that each had a positive net present value (at a 10 percent cost of capital). The analysis is reproduced in Table 13–4.

Though both proposals are acceptable, if they were mutually exclusive, only Investment B would be undertaken. But what if we add a risk dimension to the problem? Assume that Investment A calls for an addition to the normal product line and is assigned a discount rate of 10 percent. Further assume that Investment B represents a new product in a foreign market and must carry a 20 percent discount to adjust for

**Table 13–4**
**Capital budgeting analysis**

| Year | *Investment A (10% discount rate)* | | Year | *Investment B (10% discount rate)* | |
|---|---|---|---|---|---|
| 1 | $5,000 × 0.909 = | $ 4,545 | 1 | $1,500 × 0.909 = | $ 1,364 |
| 2 | 5,000 × 0.826 = | 4,130 | 2 | 2,000 × 0.826 = | 1,652 |
| 3 | 2,000 × 0.751 = | 1,502 | 3 | 2,500 × 0.751 = | 1,878 |
| | | $10,177 | 4 | 5,000 × 0.683 = | 3,415 |
| | | | 5 | 5,000 × 0.621 = | 3,105 |
| | | | | | $11,414 |
| Present value of inflows | | $10,177 | Present value of inflows | | $11,414 |
| Investment | | 10,000 | Investment | | 10,000 |
| Net present value | | $ 177 | Net present value | | $ 1,414 |

**Table 13–5**
**Capital budgeting decision adjusted for risk**

| Year | Investment A (10% discount rate) | | Year | Investment B (20% discount rate) | |
|---|---|---|---|---|---|
| 1 . . . . | $5,000 × 0.909 = | $ 4,545 | 1 . . . . | $1,500 × 0.833 = | $ 1,250 |
| 2 . . . . | 5,000 × 0.826 = | 4,130 | 2 . . . . | 2,000 × 0.694 = | 1,388 |
| 3 . . . . | 2,000 × 0.751 = | 1,502 | 3 . . . . | 2,500 × 0.579 = | 1,448 |
| | | $10,177 | 4 . . . . | 5,000 × 0.482 = | 2,410 |
| | | | 5 . . . . | 5,000 × 0.402 = | 2,010 |
| | | | | | $ 8,506 |
| Present value of inflows . . . | | $10,177 | Present value of inflows . . . | | $ 8,506 |
| Investment . . . . . . . . . | | 10,000 | Investment . . . . . . . . . | | 10,000 |
| Net present value . . . . . . | | $ 177 | Net present value . . . . . . | | $ (1,494) |

the large risk component. As indicated in Table 13–5 our answers are reversed and Investment A is now the only acceptable alternative.

Other methods besides the risk-adjusted discount rate approach are also used to evaluate risk in the capital budgeting process. The spectrum runs from a seat-of-the-pants "executive preference" approach to sophisticated computer-based statistical analysis. All methods, however, include a common approach—that is, they must give recognition to the riskiness of a given investment proposal and an appropriate adjustment for risk.[4]

## Simulation Models

Computers make it possible to simulate various economic and financial outcomes, using a large number of variables. Thus simulation is one way of dealing with the uncertainty involved in forecasting the outcomes of capital budgeting projects or other types of decisions. A Monte Carlo simulation model uses random variables for inputs. By

[4]As an example, each value might be penalized for lack of certainty (adjusted for risk) and then a risk-free discount rate might be applied to the resultant values. This is termed the *certainty equivalent approach*. In practice, the expected value for a given year is multiplied by a percentage figure indicating the degree of certainty and then translated back to the present at a risk-free discount rate (less than the cost of capital). Items with a high degree of certainty are multiplied by 100 percent, less certain items by 75 percent, and so on down the scale.

programming the computer to randomly select inputs from probability distributions, the outcomes generated by a simulation are distributed about a mean, and instead of generating one return or net present value, a range of outcomes with standard deviations is provided. A simulation model relies on repetition of the same random process as many as several hundred times. Since the inputs are representative of what one might encounter in the real world, many possible combinations of returns are generated.

One of the benefits of simulation is its ability to test various possible combinations of events. This sensitivity testing allows the planner to ask "what if" questions, such as: What will happen to the returns on this project if oil prices go up? go down? What effect will a 5 percent increase in interest rates have on the net present value of this project? The analyst can use the simulation process to test out possible changes in economic policy, sales levels, inflation or any other variable that is included in the modeling process. Some simulation models are driven by sales forecasts with assumptions to derive income statements and balance sheets. Others generate probability acceptance curves for capital budgeting decisions by informing the analyst about the probabilities of having a positive net present value.

For example, each distribution in Figure 13–7 will have a value picked randomly and used for one simulation. The simulation will be run many times, each time selecting a new random variable to generate the final probability distribution for the net present value (at the bottom). For that probability distribution, the expected values are on the horizontal axis and the probability of occurrence is on the vertical axis. The outcomes also indicate something about the riskiness of the project, which is indicated by the overall dispersion.

## Decision Trees

Decision trees help lay out the sequence of decisions that can be made and present a tabular or graphical comparison resembling the branches of a tree, which highlight the differences between investment choices. In Figure 13–8 we examine a semiconductor firm considering two choices: (A) expanding the production of semiconductors for sale to end users of these tiny chips or (B) entering the highly competitive home computer market by using the firm's technology. The cost of

Figure 13–7
Simulation flow chart

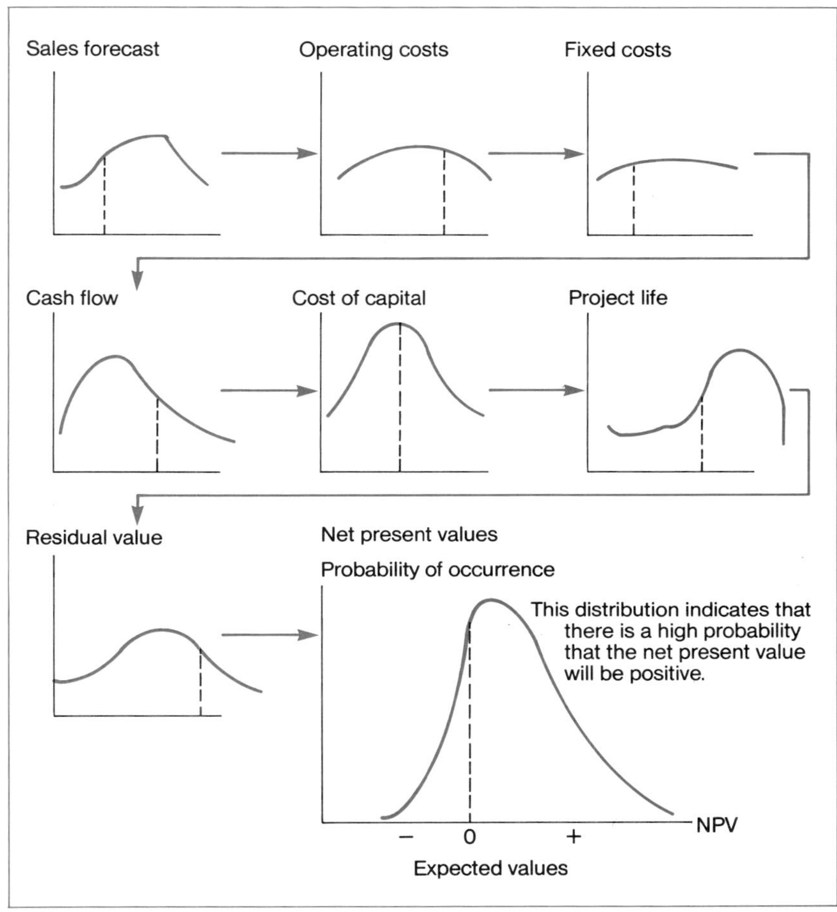


both projects is the same $60 million, but the net present value (NPV) and risk are different.

If the firm expands its semiconductor capacity (Project A), it is assured of some demand so that a high likelihood of a positive rate of return exists. The market demand for these products is volatile over time, but long-run growth seems to be a reasonable expectation as the United States increases the emphasis on technology. If the firm expands into the home computer market (Project B), it faces stiff competition from many existing firms. It stands to lose more money if expected

**Figure 13–8**
**Decision trees**

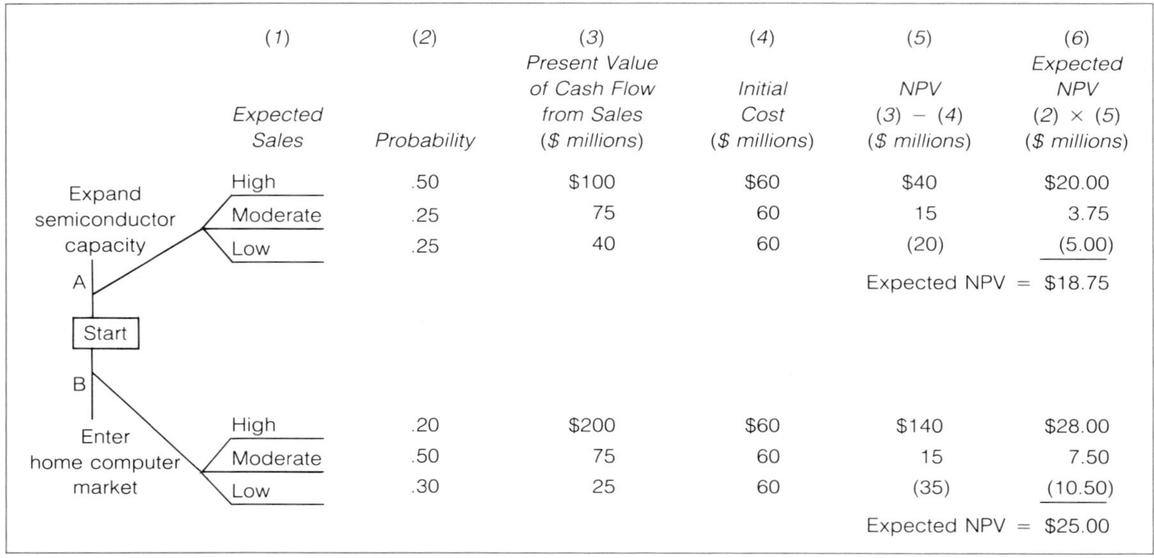

| | (1) Expected Sales | (2) Probability | (3) Present Value of Cash Flow from Sales ($ millions) | (4) Initial Cost ($ millions) | (5) NPV (3) − (4) ($ millions) | (6) Expected NPV (2) × (5) ($ millions) |
|---|---|---|---|---|---|---|
| A: Expand semiconductor capacity | High | .50 | $100 | $60 | $40 | $20.00 |
| | Moderate | .25 | 75 | 60 | 15 | 3.75 |
| | Low | .25 | 40 | 60 | (20) | (5.00) |
| | | | | | Expected NPV = | $18.75 |
| B: Enter home computer market | High | .20 | $200 | $60 | $140 | $28.00 |
| | Moderate | .50 | 75 | 60 | 15 | 7.50 |
| | Low | .30 | 25 | 60 | (35) | (10.50) |
| | | | | | Expected NPV = | $25.00 |



sales are low than it would under option A; but it will make more if sales are high. Even though project B has a higher expected NPV than project A, its extra risk does not make for an easy choice. Clearly, more analysis would have to be done before management made the final decision between these two projects. Nevertheless, the decision tree provides for an important analytical process.

## The Portfolio Effect

Up to this point, we have been primarily concerned with the risk inherent in an *individual* investment proposal. While this approach is quite useful, we also need to consider the impact of a given investment on the overall risk of the firm—the "portfolio effect."[5] For example, we might undertake an investment in the building products industry that appears to carry a high degree of risk—but if our primary business is the manufacture of electronic components for industrial use, we may

[5] Here the portfolio of investments refers to plant, equipment, new products, and so forth, rather than stocks and bonds.

**Figure 13–9**
**Portfolio considerations in evaluating risk**

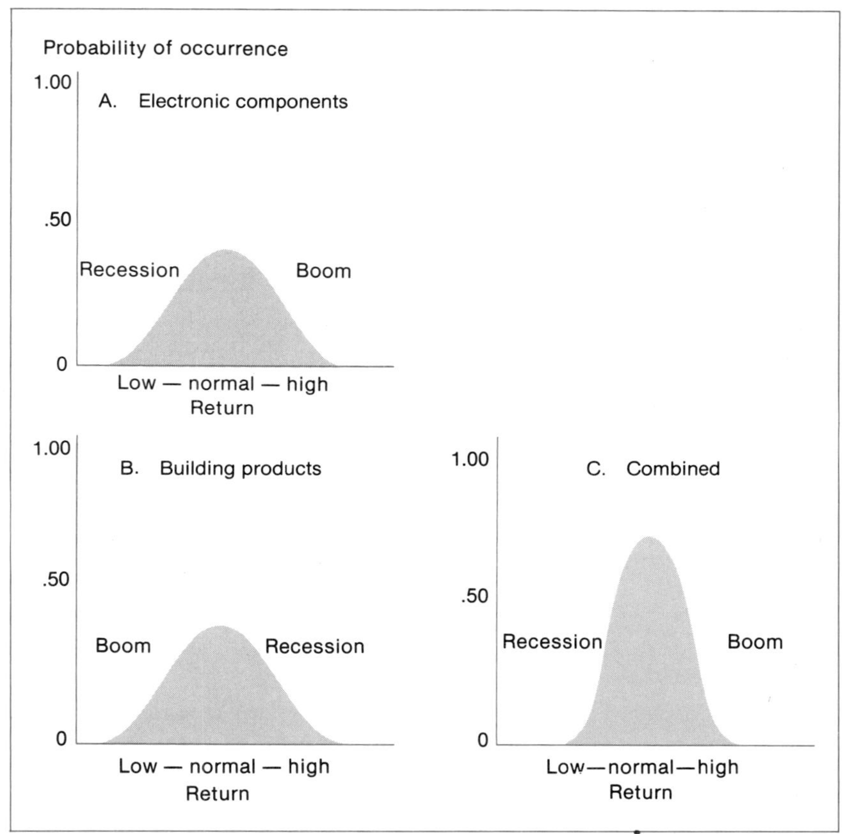


actually diminish the overall risk exposure of the firm. Why? Because electronic component sales expand when the economy does well and falter in a recession. The building products industry reacts in the opposite fashion—performing poorly in boom periods and generally reacting well in recessionary periods. By investing in the building products industry, an electronic components manufacturer could actually smooth out the cyclical fluctuations inherent in its business and reduce overall risk exposure, as indicated in Figure 13–9.

The risk reduction phenomenon is demonstrated by a less dispersed probability distribution. We say the standard deviation for the entire company (the portfolio of investments) has been reduced.

## Portfolio Risk

Whether or not a given investment will change the overall risk of the firm depends on its relationships to other investments. If one airline purchases another, there is very little risk reduction. Highly correlated investments, that is, projects which move in the same direction in good times as well as bad, do little or nothing to diversify away risk. Projects moving in opposite directions (building products and electronic components) are referred to as being negatively correlated and provide a high degree of risk reduction.

Finally, projects which are totally uncorrelated provide some overall reduction in portfolio risk—though not as much as negatively correlated investments. For example, if a beer manufacturer purchases a textile firm, the projects are neither positively nor negatively correlated, but the purchase will reduce the overall risk of the firm simply through the "law of large numbers." If you have enough unrelated projects going on at one time, good and bad events will probably even out.

The extent of correlation among projects is represented by a new term called the *coefficient of correlation*—a measure that may take on values anywhere from −1 to +1.[6] Examples are presented in Table 13–6.

In the real world, very few investment combinations take on values as extreme as −1 or +1, or for that matter exactly 0. The more likely case is a point somewhere in between, such as −.2 negative correlation

**Table 13–6**
**Measures of correlation**

| *Coefficient of Correlation* | *Condition* | *Example* | *Impact on Risk* |
|---|---|---|---|
| −1 . . . . | Negative correlation | Electronic components, building products | Large risk reduction |
| 0 . . . . | No correlation | Beer, textile | Some risk reduction |
| +1 . . . . | Positive correlation | Two airlines | No risk reduction |

[6]Coefficient of correlation is not to be confused with coefficient of variation—a term used earlier in the chapter.

Figure 13–10
Levels of risk reduction as measured by the coefficient of correlation

| | Significant Risk Reduction | | Some Risk Reduction | | Minor Risk Reduction | | |
|---|---|---|---|---|---|---|---|
| Extreme risk reduction | −1 | −.5 | −.2 | 0 | +.3 | +.5 | +1 | No reduction |

or +.3 positive correlation, as indicated along the continuum in Figure 13–10.

The fact that risk can be reduced by combining risky assets with low or negatively correlated assets can be seen by the example of Conglomerate, Inc. Conglomerate has fairly average returns and standard deviations of returns. The company is considering the purchase of two separate but large companies with sales and assets equal to its own. Management is struggling with the decision since both companies have a 14 percent rate of return, which is 2 percent higher than that of Conglomerate, and they have the same standard deviation of returns as that of Conglomerate, at 2.82 percent. This information is presented in the first three columns of Table 13–7.

Table 13–7 Rates of return for Conglomerate, Inc., and two merger candidates

| Year | (1) Conglomerate, Inc. | (2) Positive Correlation, Inc. + 1.0 | (3) Negative Correlation, Inc. −.9 | (1) + (2) Conglomerate, Inc. + Positive Correlation, Inc. | (1) + (3) Conglomerate, Inc. + Negative Correlation, Inc. |
|---|---|---|---|---|---|
| 1 | 14% | 16% | 10% | 15% | 12% |
| 2 | 10 | 12 | 16 | 11 | 13 |
| 3 | 8 | 10 | 18 | 9 | 13 |
| 4 | 12 | 14 | 14 | 13 | 13 |
| 5 | 16 | 18 | 12 | 17 | 14 |
| Mean return | 12% | 14% | 14% | 13% | 13% |
| Standard deviation of returns ($\sigma$) | 2.82% | 2.82% | 2.82% | 2.82% | .63% |
| Correlation coefficients with Conglomerate, Inc. | | | | +1.0 | −.9 |

Since management desires to reduce risk ($\sigma$) and to increase returns at the same time, it decides to analyze the results of each combination.[7] These are shown in the last two columns in Table 13–7. A combination with Positive Correlation, Inc., increases the mean return to 13 percent but maintains the exact same standard deviation of returns (no risk reduction). Why? Because the coefficient of correlation is +1.0 and no diversification benefits are achieved. A combination with Negative Correlation, Inc., also increases the mean return to 13 percent, but it reduces the standard deviation of returns to 0.63 percent, a significant reduction in risk. This occurs because of the offsetting relationship of returns between the two companies, as evidenced by the coefficient of correlation of −.9. When one company has high returns, the other has low returns, and vice versa.

## Evaluation of Combinations

The firm should evaluate all possible combinations of projects, determining which will provide the best trade-off between risk and return. In Figure 13–11, we see a number of alternatives that might be available to a given firm. Each point represents a combination of different possible investments. For example, point *F* might represent a semiconductor manufacturer combining three different types of semiconductors, plus two calculators, and two products in totally unrelated fields. In choosing between the various points or combinations, management should have two primary objectives:

1. Achieve the highest possible return at a given risk level.
2. Allow the lowest possible risk at a given return level.

All the best opportunities will fall along the leftmost sector of the diagram (line *C–F–G*). Each point on the line satisfies the two objectives of the firm. Any point to the right is less desirable.

After we have developed our best risk–return line, known in the financial literature as the "efficient frontier," we must determine where

[7] In Chapter 20, you will evaluate a merger situation in which there is no increase in earnings, only a reduction in the standard deviation. Because the lower risk may mean a higher price–earnings ratio, this could, of course, be beneficial.

Figure 13–11
Risk–return trade-offs

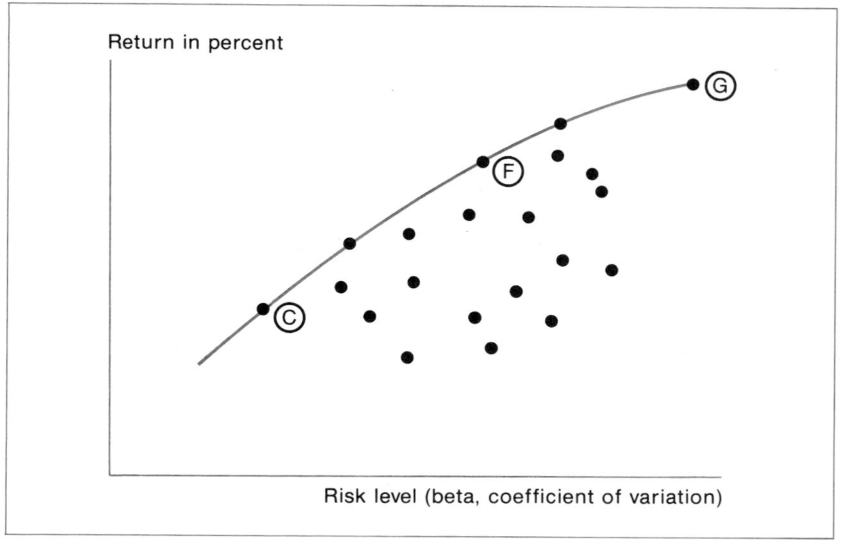


on the line our firm should be. There is no universally correct answer. To the extent we are willing to take large risks for superior returns, we will opt for some point on the upper portion of the line—such as *G*. A more conservative selection might be *C or F*.

## The Share Price Effect

The firm must be sensitive to the wishes and demands of shareholders. To the extent that unnecessary or undesirable risks are taken, a higher discount rate and lower valuation may be assigned to our stock in the market. Higher profits, resulting from risky ventures, could have a result opposite from that intended. In raising the coefficient of variation, or beta, we could be lowering the overall valuation of the firm.

The aversion of investors to nonpredictability (and the associated risk) is confirmed by observing the relative valuation given to cyclical stocks versus highly predictable growth stocks in the market. Metals, autos, and housing stocks generally trade at an earnings multiplier well below that for industries with level, predictable performance such as drugs, soft drinks, and even alcohol or cigarettes. Each company must carefully analyze its own situation to determine the appropriate trade-off between risk and return. The changing desires and objectives of investors tend to make the task somewhat more difficult.

## Summary

Risk may be defined as the potential variability of the outcomes from an investment. The less predictable the outcomes, the greater is the risk. Both management and investors tend to be risk averse—that is, all things being equal, they would prefer to take less risk rather than greater risk.

The most commonly employed method to adjust for risk in the capital budgeting process is to alter the discount rate based on the perceived risk level. High-risk projects will carry a risk premium, producing a discount rate well in excess of the cost of capital.

In assessing the risk components in a given project, management may rely on simulation techniques to generate probabilities of possible outcomes, and decision trees to help isolate the key variables to be evaluated.

Management must consider not only the risk inherent in a given project, but also the impact of a new project on the overall risk of the firm (the portfolio effect). Negatively correlated projects have the most favorable effect on smoothing out business cycle fluctuations. The firm may wish to consider all combinations and variations of possible projects and to select only those that provide a total risk–return trade-off consistent with its goals.

## List of Terms

**risk**
**risk averse**
**expected value**
**standard deviation**
**coefficient of variation**
**risk-adjusted discount rate**
**portfolio effect**
**coefficient of correlation**
**efficient frontier**
**beta**
**simulation**
**decision tree**

## Discussion Questions

1. If corporate managers are risk averse, does this mean that they will not take risks? Explain.
2. Discuss the concept of risk and how it might be measured.
3. When is the coefficient of variation a better measure of risk than the standard deviation?
4. Explain how the concept of risk can be incorporated into the capital budgeting process.
5. If risk is to be analyzed in a qualitative way, place the following investment decisions in order from the lowest risk to the highest risk.

   *a.* New equipment.
   *b.* Completely new market.
   *c.* Repair old machinery.
   *d.* New product in a foreign market.
   *e.* New product in a related market.
   *f.* Addition to a new product line.

6. Assume that a company, correlated with the economy, is evaluating six projects, of which two are positively correlated with the economy, two are negatively correlated, and two are not correlated with it at all. Which two projects would you select to minimize the company's overall risk?
7. Assume that a firm has several hundred possible investments and that it wants to analyze the risk–return trade-off for portfolios of 20 projects. How should it proceed with the evaluation?
8. Explain the effect of the risk–return trade-off on the market value of common stock.
9. What is the purpose of using simulation analysis?
10. Why might an analyst set up a decision tree in attempting to make a decision?

## Problems

1. Pabst Dental Supplies is evaluating the introduction of a new product. The possible levels of unit sales and the probabilities of their occurrence are given.

| Possible Market Reaction | Sales in Units | Probabilities |
|---|---|---|
| Low response | 20 | .10 |
| Moderate response | 40 | .20 |
| High response | 65 | .40 |
| Very high response | 80 | .30 |

   *a.* What is the expected value of unit sales for the new product?
   *b.* What is the standard deviation of unit sales?

2. Possible outcomes for three investment alternatives and their probabilities of occurrence are given below.

| | Alternative 1 | | Alternative 2 | | Alternative 3 | |
|---|---|---|---|---|---|---|
| | Outcomes | Probability | Outcomes | Probability | Outcomes | Probability |
| Failure | 50 | .2 | 90 | .3 | 80 | .4 |
| Acceptable | 80 | .4 | 160 | .5 | 200 | .5 |
| Successful | 120 | .4 | 200 | .2 | 400 | .1 |

   Rank the three alternatives in terms of risk (compute the coefficient of variation).

3. Five investment alternatives have the following returns and standard deviations of returns.

| Alternative | Returns: Expected Value | Standard Deviation |
|---|---|---|
| A | $ 1,000 | $200 |
| B | 3,000 | 300 |
| C | 3,000 | 400 |
| D | 5,000 | 700 |
| E | 10,000 | 900 |

   *a.* Using the coefficient of variation, rank the five alternatives from lowest risk to highest risk.
   *b.* If you were to choose between alternatives B and C only, would you need to use the coefficient of variation? Why?

4. Mary Beth Clothes is considering opening one more suburban outlet. An aftertax cash flow of $100 per week is expected from

two stores that are being evaluated. Both stores have positive net present values.

Which store site would you select based on the distribution of these cash flows? Use the coefficient of variation as your measure of risk.

| Site A | | Site B | |
|---|---|---|---|
| *Probability* | *Cash Flows* | *Probability* | *Cash Flows* |
| .2 . . . . | 50 | .1 . . . . | 20 |
| .3 . . . . | 100 | .2 . . . . | 50 |
| .3 . . . . | 110 | .4 . . . . | 100 |
| .2 . . . . | 135 | .2 . . . . | 150 |
| | | .1 . . . . | 180 |

5. Western Dynamite Co. is evaluating two different methods of blowing up old buildings for commercial purposes over the next five years. Method one (implosion) is relatively low in risk for this business and will carry a 10 percent discount rate. Method two (explosion) is more dangerous and will call for a discount rate of 15 percent. Either investment will require an initial capital outlay of $100,000. The inflows from projected business over the next five years are given below. Which method should be selected, using net present value analysis?

| *Years* | *Method 1* | *Method 2* |
|---|---|---|
| 1 . . . . | $25,000 | $28,000 |
| 2 . . . . | 30,000 | 32,000 |
| 3 . . . . | 38,000 | 39,000 |
| 4 . . . . | 31,000 | 33,000 |
| 5 . . . . | 19,000 | 25,000 |

6. American Metal, Mining, and Petroleum is examining two projects for investment. The first project is an oil-well drilling project in the Beaufort Sea at a cost of $500 million, and the second project is the expansion of an aluminum smelter in Appletree, Washington, at a cost of $500 million. The oil wells are expected to produce a deferred cash flow of $100 million per year in years 5 through 10 and $200 million per year in years 11 through 20. The aluminum smelter is expected to generate cash flows of $80 million yearly in years 2 through 25. The cost of capital is 12 percent.

*a.* Which investment should be made? (Note: In looking up present value factors for this problem, you need to work with the concept of a deferred annuity. The returns in years 5 through 10 actually represent *6* years; the returns in years 11 through 20 represent *10* years; and the returns in years 2 through 25 represent *24* years.)

*b.* If the oil-well project justifies an extra 4 percent premium over the normal cost of capital because of its riskiness, how does the investment decision change?

**7.** Larry's Athletic Lounge is planning an expansion program to increase the sophistication of the exercise equipment. Larry is considering some new equipment priced at $20,000 with an estimated life of five years. Larry is not sure how many members the new equipment will attract, but he estimates that his increased yearly cash flows for the next five years will have the following probability distribution. Larry's cost of capital is 14 percent.

| *P* (*probability*) | *Cash Flow* |
|---|---|
| .2 | $2,400 |
| .4 | 4,800 |
| .3 | 6,000 |
| .1 | 7,200 |

*a.* What is the expected cash flow?

*b.* What is the expected net present value and internal rate of return?

*c.* Should Larry buy the new equipment?

**8.** Mr. John Backster, a retired executive, desires to invest a portion of his assets in rental property. He has narrowed his choices down to two apartment complexes, Windy Acres and Hillcrest Apartments. After conferring with the present owners, Mr. Backster has developed the following estimates of the cash flows for these properties.

| *Windy Acres* | | *Hillcrest Apartments* | |
|---|---|---|---|
| *Probability* | *Yearly Aftertax Cash Flow* | *Probability* | *Yearly Aftertax Cash Flow* |
| .1 | $10,000 | .2 | $15,000 |
| .2 | 15,000 | .3 | 25,000 |
| .4 | 30,000 | .4 | 35,000 |
| .2 | 45,000 | .1 | 45,000 |
| .1 | 50,000 | | |

*a.* Find the expected cash flow from each apartment complex.
*b.* What is the coefficient of variation for each apartment complex?
*c.* Which apartment complex has more risk?

**9.** Mr. Backster, in making his decision, feels that he is likely to hold the complex of his choice for about 10 years, and he will use this time period for decision-making purposes. Either apartment complex can be acquired for $100,000. Mr. Backster uses a risk-adjusted discount rate when considering investments with a coefficient of variation ($V$) greater than .35. He estimates his cost of capital to be 12 percent. For projects with a $V$ between .35 and .40, he adds 2 percent to the cost of capital, and for those with a $V$ between .4 and .5 he adds 4 percent. Mr. Backster would not consider an investment with a $V$ of more than .5.

*a.* Compute the risk-adjusted net present values for Windy Acres and Hillcrest Apartments. (Use cash flow figures from the previous problem.)
*b.* Which investment should Mr. Backster accept if the two investments are mutually exclusive? If the investments are not mutually exclusive and no capital rationing takes place, how would your decision be affected?

**10.** Wardrobe Clothing Manufacturers is preparing a strategy for the fall season. One strategy is to go to a highly imaginative new, four-gold-button sport coat with special emblems on the front pocket. The all-wool product will be available for males and females alike. A second option would be to produce a traditional blue blazer line. The market research department has determined that the new, four-gold-button coat and the traditional blue blazer line offer the following probabilities of outcomes and related cash flows.

| | *New Coat* | | *Blazer* | |
|---|---|---|---|---|
| *Expected Sales* | *Probability* | *Present Value of Cash Flows from Sales* | *Probability* | *Present Value of Cash Flows from Sales* |
| Fantastic | .4 | $240,000 | .2 | $120,000 |
| Moderate | .2 | 180,000 | .6 | 75,000 |
| Dismal | .4 | 0 | .2 | 65,000 |

The initial cost to get into the new coat line is $100,000 in designs, equipment, and inventory. The blazer line would carry an initial cost of $60,000.

*a.* Diagram a complete decision tree of possible outcomes similar to Figure 13–8. Take the analysis all the way through the process of computing expected NPV (last column for each investment).
*b.* Given the analysis in part *a*, would you automatically make the investment indicated?

**11.** The Oklahoma Pipeline Company projects the following pattern of inflows from an investment. The inflows are spread over time to reflect delayed benefits. Each year is independent of the others.

| *Year 1* | | *Year 5* | | *Year 10* | |
|---|---|---|---|---|---|
| *Cash Inflow* | *Probability* | *Cash Inflow* | *Probability* | *Cash Inflow* | *Probability* |
| 65 | .20 | 50 | .25 | 40 | .30 |
| 80 | .60 | 80 | .50 | 80 | .40 |
| 95 | .20 | 110 | .25 | 120 | .30 |

The expected value for all three years is $80.

*a.* Compute the standard deviation for each of the three years.
*b.* Diagram the expected values and standard deviations for each of the three years in a manner similar to Figure 13–6.
*c.* Assuming a 6 percent and a 12 percent discount rate, complete the table below for present value factors.

| *Year* | $IF_{pv}$ *6 Percent* | $IF_{pv}$ *12 Percent* | *Difference* |
|---|---|---|---|
| 1 | .943 | .893 | .050 |
| 5 | ___ | ___ | ___ |
| 10 | ___ | ___ | ___ |

*d.* Is the increasing risk over time, as diagrammed in part *b*, consistent with the larger differences in $IF_{pv}$s over time as computed in part *c*?
*e.* Assume the initial investment is $135. What is the net present value of the investment at a 12 percent discount rate? Should the investment be accepted?

**12.** When returns from a project can be assumed to be normally distributed, such as those shown in Figure 13–6 (represented by a symmetrical, bell-shaped curve), the areas under the curve can be determined from statistical tables based on standard deviations. For example, 68.26 percent of the distribution will fall within one standard deviation of the expected value ($\bar{D} \pm 1\sigma$). Similarly, 95.44 percent will fall within two standard deviations ($\bar{D} \pm 2\sigma$), and so on. An abbreviated table of areas under the normal curve is shown here.

| Number of $\sigma$'s from Expected Value | + or − | + and − |
|---|---|---|
| 0.5 | 0.1915 | 0.3830 |
| 1.0 | 0.3413 | 0.6826 |
| 1.5 | 0.4332 | 0.8664 |
| 1.96 | 0.4750 | 0.9500 |
| 2.0 | 0.4772 | 0.9544 |

Assume Project A has an expected value of \$20,000 and a standard deviation ($\sigma$) of \$4,000.

*a.* What is the probability that the outcome will be between \$16,000 and \$24,000?
*b.* What is the probability that the outcome will be between \$14,000 and \$26,000?
*c.* What is the probability that the outcome will be at least \$12,000?
*d.* What is the probability that the outcome will be less than \$27,840?
*e.* What is the probability that the outcome will be less than \$16,000 or greater than \$26,000?

**13.** Chilton Airlines is seeking to diversify its business and lower its risk. Currently, it is examining three companies—an auto parts company, an airline food service company, and an oil company. Each of these companies can be bought at the same multiple of earnings. The following represents information about the companies.

| Company | Correlation with Chilton Airlines | Sales (\$ millions) | Average Earnings (\$ millions) | Standard Deviation in Earnings (\$ millions) |
|---|---|---|---|---|
| Chilton Airlines | + 1.0 | \$80 | \$15 | \$ 5 |
| Auto Parts Company | + .2 | 80 | 15 | \$ 7.5 |
| Airline Food Service Company | + .8 | 80 | 15 | \$ 5 |
| Oil Company | − .6 | 80 | 15 | \$10 |

*a.* Discuss what would happen to Chilton Airlines' portfolio risk–return if it bought the auto parts company? The airline food service company? The oil company?

*b.* If you were going to buy one company, which would you choose? Why?

*c.* If you were going to buy two companies, which would you choose? Why?

**14.** (*Comprehensive problem*)
Tobacco Company of America is a very stable billion dollar company with sales growth of about 5 percent per year in good or bad economic conditions. Because of this stability (correlation coefficient with the economy of +.3 and a standard deviation of sales of about 5 percent from the mean), Mr. Weed, the vice president of finance, thinks the company can absorb some small risky company which could add quite a bit of return without increasing the company's risk very much. He is currently trying to decide which of two companies he will buy. Tobacco Company of America's cost of capital is 10 percent.

| *Computer Whiz Company (cost $75 million)* | | *American Micro-Technology (cost $75 million)* | |
|---|---|---|---|
| *Probability* | *Aftertax Cash Flows for 10 Years (in $ millions)* | *Probability* | *Aftertax Cash Flows for 10 Years (in $ millions)* |
| .3 | $ 6 | .2 | $ (1) |
| .3 | 10 | .2 | 3 |
| .2 | 16 | .2 | 10 |
| .2 | 25 | .3 | 25 |
| | | .1 | 31 |

*a.* What is the expected cash flow from both companies?

*b.* Which company has the lower coefficient of variation?

*c.* Compute the net present value of each company.

*d.* Which company would you pick, based on net present values?

*e.* Would you change your mind if you added the risk dimensions into the problem? Explain.

*f.* What if Computer Whiz had a correlation coefficient with the economy of +.5 and AMT had one of −.1? Which of the companies would give you the best portfolio effects for risk reduction? Which would give you the highest potential returns?

*g.* What might be the effect of the acquisitions on the market value of Tobacco Company's stock?

**15.** Virgil Trucking Company is considering the purchase of 50 new diesel trucks that are 15 percent more fuel efficient than the ones the firm is now using. Mr. George R. Kell, the president, has found that the company uses an average of 10 million gallons of diesel fuel per year at a price of $1.20 per gallon. If he can cut fuel consumption by 15 percent, he will save $1,800,000 per year (1,500,000 gallons times $1.20).

Mr. Kell assumes that the price of diesel fuel is an external market force that he cannot control and that any increased costs of fuel will be passed on to the shipper through higher rates endorsed by the Interstate Commerce Commission. If this is true, then fuel efficiency would save more money as the price of diesel fuel rose (at $1.30 per gallon he would save $1,950,000 in total if he buys the new trucks). Mr. Kell has come up with two possible forecasts as shown below—each of which he feels has about a 50 percent chance of coming true. Under assumption number one, diesel prices will stay relatively low; under assumption number two, diesel prices will rise considerably.

Fifty new trucks will cost Virgil trucking $4.0 million. Three-year ACRS depreciation will be used. No investment tax credit will be assumed. The firm has a tax rate of 40 percent and a cost of capital of 16 percent.

*a.* First compute the yearly expected costs of diesel fuel for both assumption one (relatively low prices) and assumption two (high prices) from the forecasts below:

*Forecast for assumption one:*

| Probability (Same for Each Year) | Price of Diesel Fuel per Gallon | | |
|---|---|---|---|
| | Year 1 | Year 2 | Year 3 |
| .1 | $ .90 | $1.00 | $1.10 |
| .2 | 1.00 | 1.15 | 1.20 |
| .3 | 1.20 | 1.30 | 1.50 |
| .2 | 1.35 | 1.50 | 1.65 |
| .2 | 1.50 | 1.60 | 1.75 |

*Forecast for assumption two:*

| Probability (Same for Each year) | Price of Diesel Fuel per Gallon | | |
|---|---|---|---|
| | Year 1 | Year 2 | Year 3 |
| .1 . . . . . . . | $1.25 | $1.40 | $1.50 |
| .3 . . . . . . . | 1.30 | 1.70 | 2.00 |
| .4 . . . . . . . | 1.60 | 2.00 | 2.20 |
| .2 . . . . . . . | 1.80 | 2.20 | 2.60 |

*b.* What will be the dollar savings in diesel expenses each year for assumption one and for assumption two?

*c.* Find the cash flow after taxes for both forecasts.

*d.* Compute the net present value of the truck purchases for each fuel forecast assumption and the combined net present value (that is, weight the NPVs by .5).

*e.* If you were Mr. Kell, would you go ahead with this capital investment?

*f.* How sensitive to fuel prices is this capital investment?

## Selected References

Arditti, Fred D. "Risk and the Required Return on Equity." *Journal of Finance* 22 (March 1967), pp. 14–36.

Blume, M. E. "On the Assessment of Risk." *Journal of Finance* 26 (March 1971), pp. 95–117.

Breen, William J., and Eugene M. Lerner. "Corporate Financial Strategies and Market Measures of Risk and Return." *Journal of Finance* 28 (May 1973), pp. 339–51.

Chen, Son-Nan, and William T. Moore. "Investment Decisions under Uncertainty: Application of Estimation Risk in the Hiller Approach." *Journal of Financial and Quantitative Analysis* 17 (September 1982), pp. 425–37.

Fabozzi, Frank J. "The Use of Operations Research Techniques for Capital Budgeting Decisions: A Sample Survey." *Journal of Operations Research Society* 29 (1978), pp. 39–42.

Green, Richard C., and Sanjay Stivastava. "Risk Aversion and Arbitrage." *Journal of Finance* 40 (March 1985), pp. 257–68.

Hayes, Robert H. "Incorporating Risk Aversion into Risk Analysis." *Engineering Economist* 20 (Winter 1975), pp. 99–121.

Hertz, David B. "Investment Policies that Pay Off." *Harvard Business Review* 46 (January–February 1968), pp. 96–108.

———. "Risk Analysis in Capital Investment." *Harvard Business Review* 22 (January–February 1964), pp. 95–106.

Hillier, Frederick S. "A Basic Model for Capital Budgeting of Risky Interrelated Projects." *Engineering Economist* 17 (Fall 1971): pp. 1–30.

Lessard, Donald R., and Richard S. Bower. "Risk-Screening in Capital Budgeting." *Journal of Finance* 28 (May 1973), pp. 331–38.

Levy, Haim, and Marshall Sarnat. "The Portfolio Analysis of Multiperiod Capital Investment under Conditions of Risk." *Engineering Economist* 16 (Fall 1970), pp. 1–19.

Lewellen, Wilber G., and Michael E. Long. "Simulation versus Single-Value Estimates in Capital Expenditure Analysis." *Decision Sciences* 3 (1972), pp. 19–33.

Magee, J. F. "How to Use Decision Trees in Capital Investment." *Harvard Business Review* 42 (September–October 1964), pp. 79–96.

Markowitz, Harry. "Portfolio Selection." *Journal of Finance*, 7 (March 1952), pp. 77–91.

Osteryoung, Jerome S.; Elton Scott; and Gordon S. Roberts. "Selecting Capital Projects with the Coefficient of Variation." *Financial Management* 6 (Summer 1977), pp. 65–70.

Richardson, L. K. "Do High Risks Lead to High Returns?" *Financial Analysts Journal* 26 (March–April 1970), pp. 88–99.

Salazar, Rudolfo C., and Subrata K. Sen. "A Simulation Model of Capital Budgeting under Uncertainty." *Management Science* 15 (December 1968), pp. 161–79.

Sharpe, William F. *Portfolio Theory and Capital Markets*. New York: McGraw-Hill, 1970.

Stapleton, R. C. "Portfolio Analysis, Stock Valuation, and Capital Budgeting Decision Rules for Risky Projects." *Journal of Finance* 26 (March 1971), pp. 95–117.

Van Horne, James C. "Capital Budgeting Decisions Using Combinations of Risky Investments." *Management Science* 13 (October 1966), pp. 84–92.

# PART FIVE

# Long-Term Financing

## Introduction

The methods of long-term financing that are available to the firm are diverse and constantly changing. At times, there appears to be a battleground in which the government, large corporations, and small businesses are fighting one another for a shrinking amount of available funds. There has been much talk of a shortage of capital for investment in the United States, particularly as the government runs up large deficits and draws funds out of the private sector. Whether such a shortage really exists is a debatable point. One thing is certain, however: in the 1980s the average business of small-to-medium size (under $20 million in sales) is facing increasing difficulty in attracting investors and long-term lenders.

In Chapter 14 we take a close look at the security markets, with an eye toward the emerging national market system (in which different security exchanges will act cooperatively in rendering their services). In the next chapter we examine the actual process of selling securities to the public through an investment banker. The investment banker is responsible for the analysis, pricing, and distribution of stocks or bonds and serves as the middleman between the corporation and the public. As part of our discussion of investment banking, we also consider the advantages, disadvantages, and size considerations of going public—that is, of selling corporate stock to the general public in the over-the-counter market or through an organized exchange—rather than maintaining ownership in private hands. H. Ross Perot, at one time depicted by *Fortune* magazine as the "Fastest Richest Texan Ever," is studied in the context of going public during the market hysteria of an earlier time period. Rockefeller Center Properties, Inc., is presented as a recent example of going public.

In Chapters 16 and 17 we study the advantages, disadvantages, and limitations of long-term debt, preferred stock, and common stock. Although the analysis is developed primarily from the corporate viewpoint (should the issue take place or not?), the investor's viewpoint is also considered. Under long-term debt financing, we also consider the lease alternative to borrowing funds and purchasing the asset outright. Significant changes in accounting requirements for leasing dramatize the close parallel between borrowing and leasing.

In Chapter 18 we examine a critically important decision for a corporation: whether it should pay out retained earnings in the form of dividends or hold the funds in the corporation for financing future projects. Retained earnings represent an important form of internal long-term financing and must be related to the growth and the life cycle of the firm. In each case, the impact of dividend policy on stockholder expectations and market value maximization must be considered.

Corporate securities that may be converted into common stock or that have special provisions for the purchase of common stock are considered in Chapter 19. The investment features of convertibles and warrants are evaluated along with their potential usage in corporate finance. The related accounting implications of these securities also receive attention.

# 14 Capital Markets

Security markets are generally separated into short-term and long-term markets. The short-term markets comprise securities with maturities of one year or less and are referred to as *money markets*. The securities most commonly traded in these markets, such as Treasury bills, commercial paper, and negotiable certificates of deposit, were previously discussed under working capital and cash management and will not be covered again.

The long-term markets are called *capital markets* and consist of securities having maturities greater than one year. The most common corporate securities in this category are bonds, common stock, preferred stock, and convertible securities. These securities are found on the firm's balance sheet under the designation long-term liabilities and equities. Taken together, these long-term securities comprise the firm's capital structure.

In the following chapters of this section we will be looking at how the capital markets are organized and integrated into the corporate and economic system of the United States. We will also study how corporate securities are sold by investment bankers and examine the rights, contractual obligations, and unique features of each type of security.

## Competition for Funds in the Capital Markets

In order to put corporate securities into perspective, it is necessary to look at other securities that are available in the capital markets. The federal government, government agencies, state governments, and local municipalities all compete with one another for a limited supply of financial capital. The capital markets serve as a way of allocating the available capital to the most efficient user. Therefore, the ultimate investor must choose among many kinds of securities, both corporate and noncorporate. Before investors part with their money they desire to maximize their return for any given level of risk, and thus the expected return from the universe of securities acts as an allocating mechanism in the markets.

The size of the corporate and noncorporate capital markets is large. The total dollar amount of new security issues with maturities of more than one year rose from $76 billion in 1970 to $422 billion by 1984. This does not include the tremendous amount of funds raised in the short-term money markets. Over this time period, new issues of corporate securities averaged closed to 40 percent of the total, while government securities made up the other 60 percent. Figure 14–1 depicts the specific composition of long-term funds raised from 1970 through 1984.

### Government Securities

**U.S. government securities** In accordance with government fiscal policy, the U.S. Treasury manages the federal government's debt in order to balance the inflows and outflows. When deficits are incurred, the Treasury can sell short-term or long-term securities to finance the shortfall. In Figure 14–1 only long-term financing is depicted. Over the total 15-year period shown, long-term U.S. government financing averaged 21 percent of the total of all long-term financing. Since 1976 the use of long-term U.S. government financing has averaged close to 31 percent as the U.S. government ran up large deficits. During 1979 and 1980 moderately successful attempts were made to reduce the deficit. However, the recessions of the early 1980s and a string of $100 to $200 billion deficits from years 1982 through 1986 caused the U.S.

government to be the biggest demander of long-term capital (38.2 percent of the total over this five-year period).[1] It remains to be seen how effective the 1985 Gramm-Rudman "balanced budget bill" will be in reducing deficits and, ultimately, government borrowing. The legislation calls for the government to have its budget in balance by the year 1991.

Besides the deficits, the relationship between long-term and short-term interest rates affects the government's demand for long-term capital. As the general level of interest rates declined since 1981, the Treasury has relied on more long-term financing. Total long-term funds raised by the U.S. Treasury of $137.5 billion in 1983 and $165.9 billion in 1984 were almost enough to cover the annual deficit entirely. Even so, the average maturity on U.S. government debt is still short—close

Figure 14–1 Composition of long-term funds raised (by corporations and government)

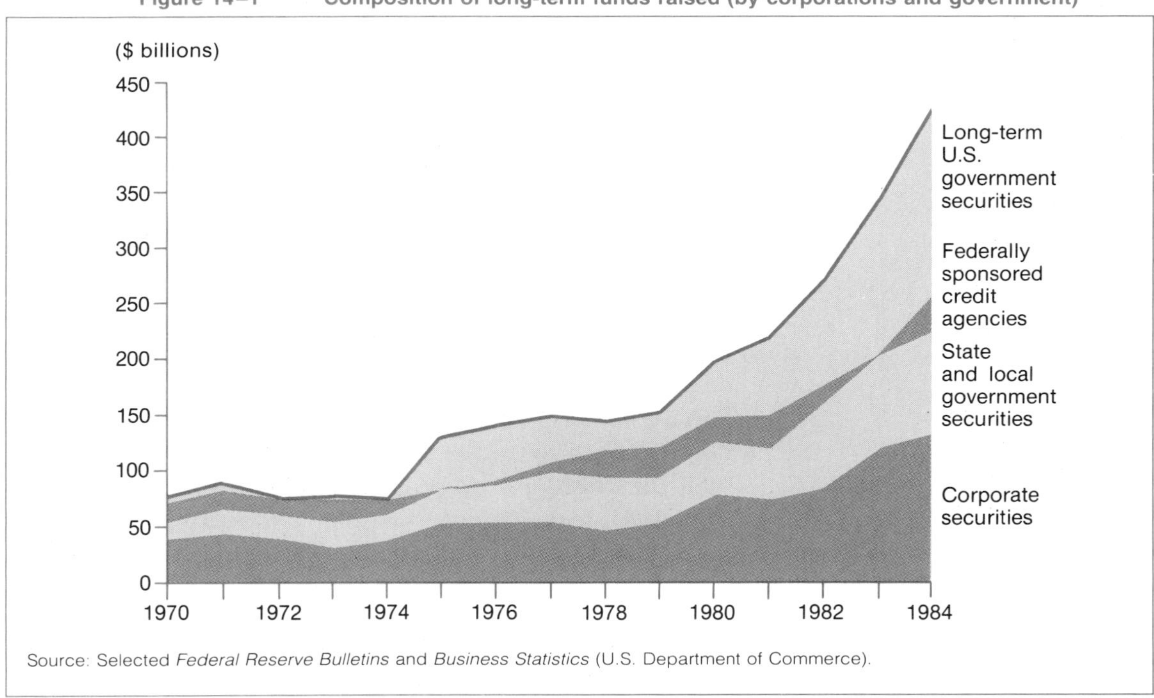


Source: Selected *Federal Reserve Bulletins* and *Business Statistics* (U.S. Department of Commerce).

[1]When short-term U.S. government financing is added to long-term U.S. government financing, the amounts greatly increase.

to three years. With one third of the debt being refunded each year, continual refinancing combined with new financing can cause instability and uncertainty in both the money and capital markets.

**Federally sponsored credit agencies** Most of the federally sponsored credit agencies are involved in making loans to the housing markets or rural farm areas. The largest of these agencies is the Federal National Mortgage Association, which is followed by the Federal Home Loan Banks. Both of these agencies are involved in the housing market. The third largest federally sponsored credit agency is the group of Farm Credit Banks. The depressed farm economy has created many problems for farm lenders as farmers have gone bankrupt and defaulted on their loans. This has had a serious impact on the financial viability of the Farm Credit Banks, and at the end of 1985, the U.S. Congress was considering a bailout or a several-billion-dollar cash infusion into the Farm Credit Banks. Over the period 1970–84, these and other federally sponsored agencies averaged 12.3 percent of the long-term financing shown in Figure 14–1. Long-term financing for government-sponsored agencies has been rather inconsistent, rising from 1.5 percent in 1975 to 16.4 in 1978 but accounting for only 0.5 percent of total long-term financing in 1983.

**State and local issues** These issues are sometimes referred to as municipal securities or tax exempt offerings because the interest on them is exempt from federal income taxes and from state taxes in the state of issue. During the 1970–84 period state and local municipalities were the second largest sellers of long-term securities, averaging 26.6 percent of all long-term issues raised (see Figure 14–1). When huge federal deficits began to mushroom in 1980, long-term municipal financing fell into third place, behind U.S. Treasury and corporate financing. In 1985, federal income tax reform was seriously considered in Congress, which threatened to eliminate the tax exclusion for interest on certain types of municipal bonds (though not on all municipal bonds). This caused a swell of new municipal offerings in order to lock in favored tax treatment in 1985. The total volume of funds raised by state, local, and municipal governments set new records. At the time of writing, the tax reform was not yet complete, and the taxability of interest on municipal securities had not been fully decided. Because of this tax issue, municipal bond financing in 1985 was quite high compared to the pattern over other years.

## Corporate Securities

**Corporate bonds** One misconception held by many investors is that corporate bond markets are dominated in size by the market for common stocks. This is far from the truth. In the new issues market, bonds averaged 73 percent of all long-term corporate securities sold from 1970 through 1985. Bonds as a percentage of total corporate issues have ranged from a high of 83.7 percent in 1974 to a low 57 percent in 1983. It is not surprising that when stock prices reached their lowest level of the seventies decade in 1974, that bonds were the dominant source of external corporate financing. On the other hand, the low point of bond financing was reached in 1983 as stock prices soared and many corporations rushed to take advantage of equity financing. As you remember from Chapter 11, the cost of debt is tax-advantaged because interest is tax deductible. Because of this, the percentage of bond financing is more influenced by common stock prices than by high or low interest rates, which are partially offset by the tax deductibility factor.

**Preferred stock** Preferred stock is the least used of all long-term securities. It has averaged only 6 percent of long-term corporate financing for the period from 1970 to 1985. The major reason for the small amount of financing by preferred stock is that the dividend is not deductible to the corporation before income taxes, as is bond interest. Given a choice between selling bonds and preferred stock, which are both fixed-income securities, most financial managers would choose bonds because they have a lower aftertax cost of capital.

**Common stock** The sale of common stock during the time period 1970–85 averaged approximately 21 percent of total corporate long-term financing. When total long-term funds including government financing are considered, common stock only accounts for about 8 percent of all long-term financing. This small percentage of new common stock financing illustrates that corporations have not been able to rely regularly on common stock for a major portion of their new long-term financing. Figure 14–2 provides comparative data on the various financing alternatives used by U.S. corporations.

**Equity financing in general** When financing by common stock and preferred stock is combined, one industry has been the dominant par-

Figure 14–2
Long-term corporate financing 1970–1985

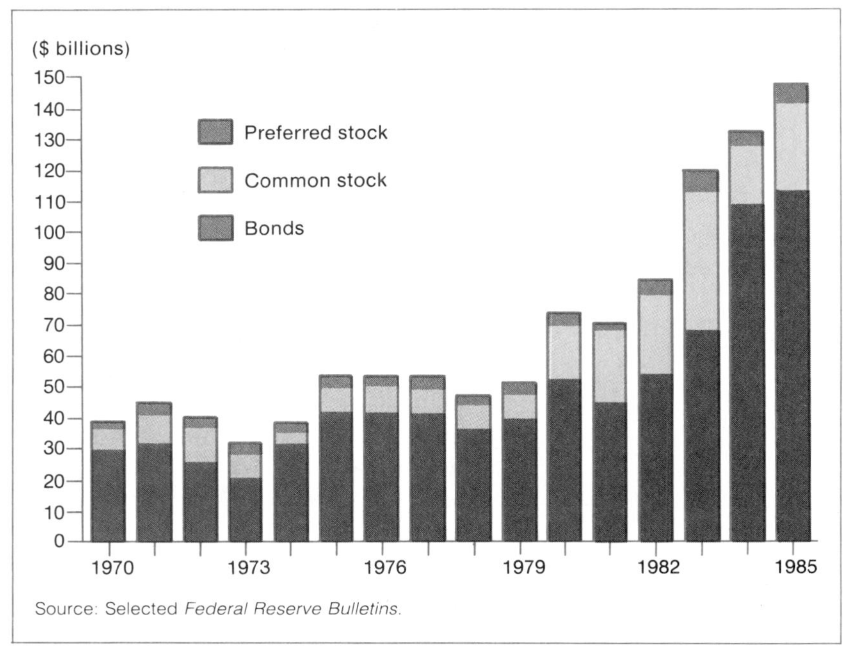


Source: Selected *Federal Reserve Bulletins.*

ticipant, at least until recently. Stock financing of any significance from 1970 through 1982 was done by utility companies. Utilities accounted for an average 41.7 percent of the stock financing during this time period, while manufacturing firms accounted for only 14.1 percent. In 1974 utilities sold 61 percent of all stock offerings and in the following five years averaged over 50 percent of the total stock financing.

It is not hard to understand this trend. Utilities, in general, have very high debt-to-equity ratios relative to manufacturing firms and are, therefore, not very flexible in their financing strategies. They find it necessary to sell stock to keep their debt-to-equity ratios from getting too high and perhaps forcing a reduction in their credit rating. From 1983 to 1985 other firms besides public utilities were also heavy users of equity capital. During this three-year time period, when stock prices reached annual record highs, utilities accounted for only 7 percent of total stock financing, as other industries took advantage of high stock prices to raise equity capital. In particular, manufacturing firms issued $14.1 billion of stock, 27.4 percent of the total.

The overall surge in common stock and preferred stock financing during 1983 can be seen in Figure 14–2. During 1984 and 1985 the relationship of common and preferred stock financing to bond financing was more typical as more firms moved back to the debt market.

## Internal versus External Sources of Funds

So far we have discussed how corporations raise funds externally through long-term financing, using bonds, common stock, and preferred stock. Another extremely important source of funds to the corporation is retained earnings and cash flow added back from depreciation. In our previous discussions of cost of capital (Chapter 11), the cost of retained earnings was considered and our capital budgeting decisions (Chapter 12) also included cash flow from depreciation. These are important sources of funds and it should be pointed out that during the 1950s and early 1960s, corporations relied primarily on internal sources of funds for their capital investment needs.

A look at Figure 14–3 shows that the ratio of external funds to total funds raised rose to extremely high levels in the 1970s and 1980s. This emphasis on external markets makes the need for efficient, liquid markets more important today than ever before. This rise in dependence on external funds is closely related to the inflationary spiral that started in the mid-60s. Corporations were forced to pay more and more for new equipment and capital expansion. At the same time, internally generated funds were not sufficient to replace worn-out equipment and expand capacity with new investments.[2] Relatively low profitability during the recessions of the early 1980s also added to the dependence on externally generated funds.

A New York Stock Exchange report issued in 1975 estimated that the external capital needs of corporations would be approximately $800 billion between 1975 and 1985. In fact the total external funds raised were close to $888 billion. It was also estimated that the average annual equity financing would be $25 billion. In fact it was about $24.5 billion per year. While the estimates were almost on the mark, one concern

[2]Cash flow generated by the tax effects of depreciation has been small relative to the cost of new equipment because depreciation expenses are based on original cost, and replacement of assets is based on inflated costs.

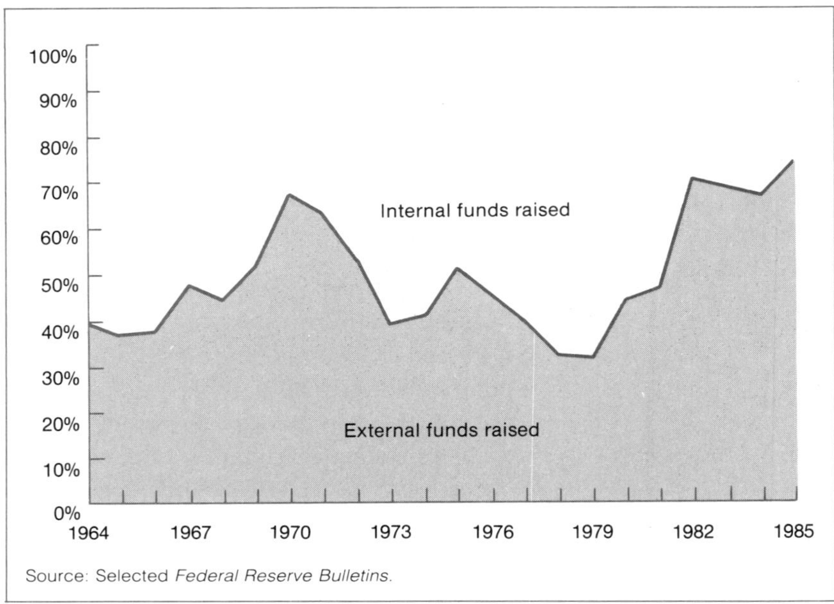


**Figure 14–3**
**External funds raised (as percentage of total funds raised)**

that was expressed in 1975 was that capital shortages of $7 billion per year could occur if savings and investment patterns did not change to accommodate this huge need for funds. Fortunately, no capital shortage occurred. Perhaps this is due to the appearance of new sources of funds such as the Individual Retirement Accounts (IRAs), and to the growing pension funds and other new vehicles for saving and investing. In the next section we look at the flow of funds through the economy and the role of the securities markets in providing capital.

## The Supply of Capital Funds

In a three-sector economy consisting of business, government, and households, the major supplier of funds for investment is the household sector. Corporations and the federal government have traditionally been net demanders of funds. Figure 14–4 diagrams the flow of funds through our basic three-sector economy.

As households receive wages and transfer payments from the government and wages and dividends from corporations, they generally

Figure 14–4
Flow of funds through the economy

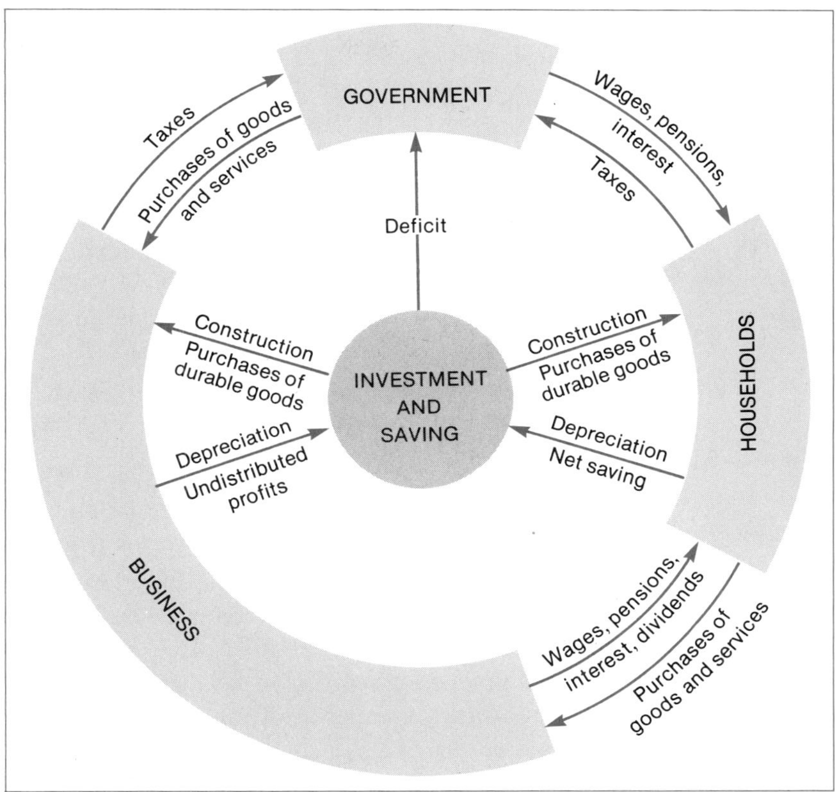


save some portion of their income. These savings are usually funneled to financial intermediaries that in turn make investments in the capital markets with the funds received from the household sector. This is known as indirect investment. The types of financial institutions that channel funds into the capital markets are specialized and diverse. Funds may flow into commercial banks, savings and loans, mutual savings banks, and credit unions. Households may also purchase mutual fund shares, invest in life insurance, or participate in some form of private pension plan or profit sharing. All these financial institutions act as intermediaries; they help make the flow of funds from one sector of the economy to another very efficient and competitive. Without intermediaries, the cost of funds would be higher, and the efficient allocation of funds to the best users at the lowest cost would not take place.

### The Role of the Security Markets

Security markets exist to aid the allocation of capital among households, corporations, and governmental units, with financial institutions acting as intermediaries. Just as financial institutions specialize in their services and investments, so are the capital markets divided into many functional subsets, with each specific market serving a certain type of security. For example, the common stocks of some of the largest corporations are traded on the New York Stock Exchange, whereas government securities are traded by government security dealers in the over-the-counter markets.

Once a security is sold for the first time as an original offering, the security trades in its appropriate market among all kinds of investors. This trading activity is known as *secondary trading* since funds flow among investors rather than to the corporation. The purpose of secondary trading is to provide liquidity to investors and to keep prices competitive among alternative security investments.

Security markets provide liquidity in two ways. First, they enable corporations to raise funds by selling new issues of securities rapidly and at fair, competitive prices. Second, they allow the investor who purchases securities to sell them with relative ease and speed and thereby to turn a paper asset into cash. Ask yourself the question, "Would I buy securities if there were no place to sell them?" You would probably think twice before committing funds to an illiquid investment. Without markets, corporations and governmental units would not be able to raise the large amounts of capital necessary for economic growth.

## The Organization of the Security Markets

The competitive structure and organization of the security markets have changed considerably since the early 1970s. In this section we present the current organization of the markets, provide an update of significant events of the last few years, and make a small conjecture about the nature of the security markets well into the 1980s. The most common division of security markets is between organized exchanges and over-the-counter markets. Each will be examined separately.

## The Organized Exchanges

Organized exchanges are either regional or national in scope. Each exchange has a central location where all buyers and sellers meet in an auction market to transact purchases and sales. Buyers and sellers are not actually present on the floor of the exchange but are represented by brokers who act as their agents. These brokers are registered members of the exchange. On the New York Stock Exchange, the number of members has been fixed at 1,366 since 1953, while the American Stock Exchange has a fixed limit of 650 members.

The New York Stock Exchange (NYSE) and the American Stock Exchange (AMEX) are national exchanges, and each is governed by an elected board of directors, of whom half are public directors and the other half industry representatives. Although the Midwest and Pacific Coast exchanges are the largest of the so-called regional exchanges, they trade primarily issues of large national companies. Some of the smaller exchanges, such as the Detroit, Boston, Cincinnati, and PBW,[3] are more regional in the sense that most of the companies listed on them are headquartered or do their principal business in the region in which the exchange is located. These smaller exchanges account for a very small percentage of trading in listed securities.

Securities can only be listed and traded on an exchange with the approval of the board of governors. Until October 1976, the NYSE and AMEX were mutually exclusive and did not allow shares of stock to be listed on both exchanges. Under prodding from the Securities and Exchange Commission (SEC), both exchanges agreed to allow dual listing so that securities could be traded on both exchanges simultaneously. So far only a few companies have maintained dual listing on the NYSE and AMEX. Dual listing has long been common between the NYSE and the regional exchanges. Approximately 90 percent of the stocks traded on the Pacific and Midwest exchanges are also traded on the NYSE. This means that the shares of many large companies can be purchased on several different exchanges, which helps to make prices more competitive and less volatile.

---

[3]The PBW was formed by a merger of the Philadelphia, Baltimore, and Washington exchanges.

Although dual trading has been a common practice for many years, brokers on the floor of an exchange did not have immediate price information from the other markets. In order to make prices of all competitive trades in the same stock available to all market participants at the same time, the Securities and Exchange Commission applied pressure for creation of a consolidated tape, which became reality on June 16, 1975. The consolidated tape presents the prices and volume of all shares traded on the regional exchanges and the NYSE. This information is visible to all brokers on the floor of each exchange and allows traders on each exchange to follow the activity and prices on all other exchanges as well as any over-the-counter trades in listed securities. Because of the consolidated tape, prices are more competitive and efficient.

## The New York Stock Exchange

**Size and liquidity** The NYSE is the largest and most important of all the exchanges. In 1985 it accounted for over 80 percent of the dollar volume of all listed stocks. Liquidity provided by the NYSE is also evident by the fact that daily average share-trading volume during 1985 ranged from a high of 121.5 million shares per day in January to a low of 94.4 million shares per day for the month of April. By the end of 1985, companies listed on the NYSE had over 51 billion shares of stock listed on the exchange, their worth being close to $2.0 trillion. We can see that the NYSE is certainly an important mechanism in the flow of funds among investors of all types.

**Listing requirements** Each organized exchange has some minimum requirement that a company must meet before the exchange will agree to trade its securities. Most of the largest U.S. companies are traded on the NYSE, although its listing requirements are more stringent than those of the AMEX or the regionals.

Although each case is decided on its own merits, according to the *NYSE Fact Book,* the minimum requirements for a company to be listed on the New York Stock Exchange for the first time are as follows:

1. Demonstrated earning power under competitive conditions of: *either* $2.5 million before federal income taxes for the most recent year

and $2 million pre-tax for each of the preceding two years, *or* an aggregate for the last three fiscal years of $6.5 million *together with* a minimum in the most recent fiscal year of $4.5 million. (All three years must be profitable.)

2. Net tangible assets of $16 million, but greater emphasis is placed on the aggregate market value of the common stock.
3. Market value of publicly held shares, at least equal to $18 million.
4. A total of 1,100,00 common shares publicly held.
5. *Either* 2,000 holders of 100 shares or more, *or* 2,200 total stockholders *together with* average monthly trading volume (for the most recent six months) of 100,000 shares.

Corporations desiring to be listed on exchanges have made the decision that public availability of the stock on an exchange will benefit their shareholders. The benefits will occur either by providing liquidity to owners or by allowing the company a more viable means for raising external capital for growth and expansion. The company must pay annual listing fees to the exchange and some fees based on the number of shares traded each year.

The New York Stock Exchange also has the authority to remove (delist) or suspend a security from trading when the security fails to meet certain criteria. There is much latitude in these decisions but generally a company's security may be considered for delisting if there are fewer than 1,200 round-lot (100 share owners), 600,000 shares or fewer in public hands, and market value of the security is less than $5,000,000. A company that easily exceeded these standards on first being listed may fall below them during hard times.

## The Over-the-Counter Markets

Corporations trading in the over-the-counter market (OTC) are referred to as unlisted. There is no central location for the OTC market but instead a network of dealers all over the country is linked together by computer display terminals, telephones, and teletypes. The difference between *dealers* in the OTC markets and *brokers* on exchanges is that dealers own the securities they trade while brokers act as agents for the buyers and sellers. Dealers are much like any wholesaler or retailer who possesses an inventory of goods. They price the goods to reflect their cost and to manage their inventory by seeking a balance between supply and demand.

Many dealers make markets in the same security and this creates very competitive prices. With the advent of a centralized computer to keep track of all trades and prices, dealers have up-to-the-minute price information on all competing dealers. Many people currently think that the structure of the OTC market is more competitive and cost efficient than organized exchanges.

At least 5,000 stocks are actively traded over-the-counter, but the average price of the securities is low, so the dollar volume of the stocks traded is not as great as that of the organized exchanges. The OTC markets are supervised by the National Association of Securities Dealers (NASD). In recent years the NASD has divided the OTC market into various groupings based on listing requirements. The segment with the biggest companies is the National Market List, followed by the National List and Supplemental List. These categories make it easier to distinguish between various sized companies. The National Market List would include companies such as Apple Computer, MCI Communications, Intel, Coors, Lotus Development, etc., while the National List would include smaller companies centered in one city or state such as Bancorp Mississippi. The Supplemental List would include very small developmental companies with stock priced as low as 25¢ per share or companies that are closely held by the founders with very few shares available for trading. The NASD estimates that at least 600 companies trading on the National Market List would meet the listing requirements of the New York Stock Exchange.

Although the AMEX and NYSE both trade corporate bonds and a small number of government securities, the bulk of all bond trading is done over-the-counter. Trading in government bonds, notes, and Treasury bills through government security dealers makes the OTC the largest market of all for security transactions in total dollars (though the NYSE is clearly the largest for just stocks).

**The third market** Stocks that are listed on organized exchanges but trade in the over-the-counter market as well are said to be trading in the third market.[4] The third market got its start in the early 1970s

[4]There is also a fourth market in which institutions trade among themselves and avoid charges for a middleman.

because institutional investors could buy and sell large blocks of stock (10,000 shares or more) over-the-counter for a fraction of the cost of the prescribed commission on the NYSE. Since the mid-70s the organized exchanges have become more competitive. Under a mandate from the Securities and Exchange Commission, brokers on the exchanges started negotiating commissions with customers when the money involved was over $500,000. In 1972 this limit was reduced to $300,000. Finally, on May 1, 1975 (called May Day in the brokerage industry), commissions on all public transactions became competitive, and for the first time in 183 years fixed minimum commission rates were abolished. These competitive commissions on the organized exchanges have diminished the importance of the third market.

## Security Markets in the Future

Security markets, and especially the stock exchanges as we know them today, may survive, but not in their present form. The U.S. Congress has mandated a national securities market which is currently being studied by the Securities and Exchange Commission advisory panel and the National Market Association, an industry group representing seven major stock markets. The latest proposal of the National Market Association would be a communications system linking the New York, American, Boston, PBW, Midwest, and Pacific Coast stock exchanges and over-the-counter trading in listed stocks. The communications system would be supervised by the National Association of Securities Dealers.

Currently these markets are tied together with the consolidated tape, but the proposed communications system would allow buyers and sellers of securities to make the best competitive trades at all times. The problem is that the end result would not be a national securities market but several different markets competing for business. In September of 1985 the Securities and Exchange Commission brought a national market system a step closer when it allowed the stock exchanges to begin trading in a limited number of over-the-counter stocks on an experimental basis.

This move, which is expected to increase competition, will allow each exchange to request trading privileges in 25 stocks currently trading on the NASD national market system. The experiment will be evaluated at the end of one year to measure any changes in the competitive pricing and market efficiencies as a result of this broadened trading activity. For the time being the decision brings the exchange "auction" markets and the OTC "dealer" markets together and allows a limited number of securities to be priced and traded in either market.

We think it safe to say that over the next decade securities markets will become more competitive as a national market system evolves. Computers will do more of the paperwork and record-keeping, such as the transfer and registration of stock certificates by a central computerized clearinghouse.

## Market Efficiency

We have mentioned competitive and efficient markets all through this chapter, but so far we have not given any criteria to judge whether the U.S. securities markets are indeed competitive and efficient markets.

### Criteria of Efficiency

There are several concepts of market efficiency and there are many degrees of efficiency, depending on which market we are talking about. Markets in general are efficient when: (1) prices adjust rapidly to new information; (2) there is a continuous market in which each successive trade is made at a price close to the previous price (the faster the price responds to new information and the smaller the differences in price changes, the more efficient the market); and (3) the market can absorb large dollar amounts of securities without destabilizing the price.

A key variable affecting efficiency is the certainty of the income stream. The more certain the expected income, the less volatile price movements will be. Fixed income securities, with known maturities, have reasonably efficient markets. The most efficient market is that for U.S. government securities, with the short-term Treasury bill market being exemplary. Corporate bond markets are somewhat efficient, but less so than government bond markets. A question that is still widely debated and researched by academics is whether markets for common stock are truly efficient.

### The Efficient Market Hypothesis

If stock markets are efficient, it is very difficult for investors to select portfolios of common stocks that can outperform the stock market in general. The efficient market hypothesis is stated in three forms—the weak, semistrong, and strong.

The weak form simply states that past price information is unrelated to future prices, and that trends cannot be predicted and taken advantage of by investors. The semistrong form states that prices reflect all *public* information. Most of the research in this area focuses on changes in public information and on the measurement of how rapidly prices converge to a new equilibrium after new information has been released. The strong form states that all information, *both private and public*, is immediately reflected in stock prices. If markets are efficient, insiders and large institutions should not be able to make profits in excess of the market in general. Research on the portfolio performance of mutual funds has shown that this group of investors does no better than the market.

Our objective in bringing up this subject is to make you aware that much current research is focused on the measurement of market efficiency. As communications systems advance, information gets disseminated faster and more accurately. Furthermore, securities laws are forcing fuller disclosure of inside corporate data. It would appear that our security markets are generally efficient, but not perfect, in digesting information and adjusting stock prices.

## Regulation of the Security Markets

Organized securities markets are regulated by the Securities and Exchange Commission (SEC) and by the self-regulation of the exchanges. The OTC market is controlled by the National Association of Securities Dealers. Three major laws govern the sale and subsequent trading of securities. The Securities Act of 1933 pertains to new issues of securities, while the Securities Exchange Act of 1934 deals with trading in the securities markets. The latest legislation is the Securities Acts amendments of 1975, whose main emphasis is on a national securities market. The primary purpose of these laws is to protect unwary investors from fraud and manipulation and to make the markets more competitive and efficient by forcing corporations to make public relevant investment information.

### Securities Act of 1933

The Securities Act of 1933 was enacted after congressional investigations of the abuses present in the securities markets during the 1929 crash. Its primary purpose was to provide full disclosure of all pertinent investment information whenever a corporation sold a new issue of securities. For this reason it is sometimes referred to as the truth-in-securities act. The Securities Act has several important features which follow:

1. All offerings except government bonds and bank stocks that are to be sold in more than one state must be registered with the SEC.[5]
2. The registration statement must be filed 20 days in advance of the date of sale and must include detailed corporate information.[6] If the SEC finds the information misleading, incomplete, or inaccurate, it will delay the offering until the registration statement is corrected. The SEC in no way certifies that the security is fairly priced, but only that the information seems to be accurate.
3. All new issues of securities must be accompanied by a prospectus containing the same information appearing in the registration statement. Usually included in the prospectus are a list of directors and officers; their salaries, stock options, and shareholdings; financial reports certified by a CPA; a list of the underwriters; the purpose and use of the funds to be provided from the sales of securities; and any other reasonable information that investors may need before they can wisely invest their money. A preliminary prospectus may be distributed to potential buyers before the offering date, but it will not contain the offering price or the underwriting fees. It is

---

[5]Actually the SEC was not established until 1934. References to the SEC in this section refer to 1934 to the present. The FTC performed these functions in 1933.

[6]Shelf registration, which was experimentally approved by the SEC in 1982, changes this provision somewhat. Shelf registration is discussed in Chapter 15.

called a "red herring" because stamped on the front in red letters are the words *preliminary prospectus*.

4. For the first time, officers of the company and other experts preparing the prospectus or the registration statement could be sued for penalties and recovery of realized losses if any information presented was fraudulent, factually wrong, or omitted.

### Securities Exchange Act of 1934

This act created the Securities and Exchange Commission to enforce the securities laws. The SEC was empowered to regulate the securities markets and those companies listed on the exchanges. Specifically, the major points of the Securities Exchange Act of 1934 are as follows:

1. Guidelines for inside trading were established. Insiders must hold securities for at least six months before they can sell them. This is to prevent them from taking quick advantage of information which could result in a short-term profit. All short-term profits are payable to the corporation.[7] Insiders were at first generally thought to be officers, directors, employees, or relatives. In the late 1960s, however, the SEC widened its interpretation to include anyone having information that was not public knowledge. This could include security analysts, loan officers, large institutional holders, and many others who had business dealings with the firm.
2. The Federal Reserve's Board of Governors became responsible for setting margin requirements to determine how much credit would be available to purchasers of securities.
3. Manipulation of securities by conspiracies among investors was prohibited.
4. The SEC was given control over the proxy procedures of corporations (a proxy is an absent stockholder's vote).
5. In its regulation of companies traded on the markets, the SEC required that certain reports be filed periodically. Corporations must file quarterly financial statements and annual 10K reports with the SEC and send annual reports to stockholders. The 10K report has

---

[7] In the mid-1980s, Congress and the SEC were considering legislation to make the penalty three times the size of the gain.

more financial data than the annual report and can be very useful to an investor or a loan officer. Most companies will now send 10K reports to stockholders on request.

6. The act required all security exchanges to register with the SEC. In this capacity, the SEC supervises and regulates many pertinent organizational aspects of exchanges, such as the mechanics of listing and trading.

### The Securities Acts Amendments of 1975

The major focus of the Securities Acts amendments of 1975 was to direct the SEC to supervise the development of a national securities market. No exact structure was put forth, but the law did assume that any national market would make extensive use of computers and electronic communication devices. In addition, the law prohibited fixed commissions on public transactions and also prohibited banks, insurance companies, and other financial institutions from buying stock exchange memberships to save commission costs for their own institutional transactions. This act is a worthwhile addition to the securities laws since it fosters greater competition and more efficient prices. As pointed out in the section on the security markets of the future, much progress has already been made on the national market system as mandated by this act.

## Summary

In this chapter we presented the concept of a capital market in which corporations compete for funds not only among themselves but with governmental units of all kinds. Corporations only account for about 40 percent of all funds raised in the capital market, and most of that is obtained through the sale of corporate debt. We also depicted a three-sector economy consisting of households, corporations, and governmental units and showed how funds flow through the capital markets from suppliers of funds to the ultimate users. This process is highly dependent upon the efficiency of the financial institutions that act as intermediaries in channeling the funds to the most productive users.

Security markets are divided into organized exchanges and over-the-counter markets. Brokers act as agents for stock exchange transactions, and dealers make markets over-the-counter at their own risk as owners of the securities they trade. The New York Stock Exchange is the largest of the organized exchanges. We explored some of its major characteristics, such as its relative size, the liquidity it provides corporations and investors, and its requirements for listing securities. Although the OTC market for stock is not as large as that of the organized exchanges, a majority of corporate bond trades and almost all trades in municipal and federal government securities are transacted over-the-counter.

Throughout this chapter we have tried to present the concept of efficient markets doing an important job in allocating financial capital. We find that the existing markets provide liquidity for both the corporation and the investor and that they are efficient in adjusting to new information. Because of the laws governing the markets, much information is available for investors, and this in itself creates more competitive prices. Moreover, there are very few cases of fraud and manipulation. In the future we expect even more efficient markets with a national market system patterned after that of the over-the-counter market.

## List of Terms

**money markets**
**capital markets**
**U.S. Treasury securities**
**municipal securities**
**federally sponsored agency securities**
**internal corporate funds**
**external corporate funds**
**financial intermediaries**
**three-sector economy**
**secondary trading**
**New York Stock Exchange**
**American Stock Exchange**
**dual trading**
**listing requirements**
**regional stock exchanges**
**over-the-counter markets**
**National Market List**
**brokers**
**dealers**
**third market**
**fourth market**
**market efficiency**
**Securities Act of 1933**
**Securities Exchange Act of 1934**
**Securities Acts amendments of 1975**
**Securities and Exchange Commission (SEC)**
**national market system**

## Discussion Questions

1. Name the major competitors for funds in the capital markets.
2. How does the economy influence the amount of funds raised by the federal government in the long-term markets?
3. Discuss the average maturity of the federal government's marketable interest-bearing public debt and the implications for the money and capital markets if the present trend continues.
4. What has been the percentage composition of long-term financing by corporations from 1970 through 1985?
5. Comment on the use of external versus internal sources of funds by corporations in the 1970s and 1980s. What has caused this shifting pattern?
6. Explain the role of financial intermediaries in the flow of funds through the economy.
7. Discuss the importance of security markets for both the corporation and the stockholder or bondholder.
8. What is the difference between organized exchanges and over-the-counter markets?
9. Why does the New York Stock Exchange have listing requirements? What are the major requirements? How do they compare with the listing requirements of the other exchanges?
10. Into what three groupings has the OTC market been divided by the National Association of Security Dealers (NASD)?
11. Explain the third market and the initial reasons for its existence.
12. Congress has mandated a national securities market. What changes do you foresee in the future for stock and bond trading if the national market becomes a reality?
13. How would you define efficient security markets?
14. The efficient market hypothesis is interpreted in a weak form, a semistrong form, and a strong form. How can we differentiate its various forms?

15. Discuss the major implications of the Securities Act of 1933 and the Securities Exchange Act of 1934.

## Problem

1. Go to the latest issue of the *Federal Reserve Bulletin* and see whether you can update Figures 14–1 and 14–2.

## Selected References

Dann, Larry Y.; David Myers; and Robert J. Raab. "Trading Rules, Large Blocks, and the Speed of Price Adjustment." *Journal of Financial Economics* 4 (January 1977); pp. 3–22.

*Demand and Supply of Equity Capital—Projections to 1985*. New York: Research Department of New York Stock Exchange, 1975.

Dougall, Herbert E. *Capital Markets and Institutions*. 2d ed. Englewood Cliffs, N.J.: Prentice-Hall, 1970.

Hempel, George; Bill Marshall; and Jess Yawitz. "The Use of Average Maturity as a Risk Proxy in Investment Portfolios." *Journal of Finance* 30 (May 1975), pp. 325–33.

Henning, Charles N.; William Piggot; and Robert H. Scott. *Financial Markets and the Economy*. Englewood Cliffs, N.J.: Prentice-Hall, 1975.

Homer, Sidney, and Martin L. Leibowitz. *Inside the Yield Book*. Englewood Cliffs, N.J.: Prentice-Hall, 1972.

Jacobs, Donald P.; Loring C. Farwell; and Edwin H. Neave. *Financial Institutions*. 5th ed. Homewood, Ill.: Richard D. Irwin, 1972.

Jensen, Michael C. "Some Anomalous Evidence Regarding Market Efficiency." *Journal of Financial Economics* 5 (June/September 1978).

Lease, Ronald C.; Wilbur G. Lewellen; and Gary G. Schlarbaum. "The Individual Investor: Attributes and Attitudes." In *Issues in Managerial Finance*. Hinsdale, Ill.: Dryden, 1976, pp. 175–98.

Malkiel, Burton. *A Random Walk Down Wall Street*. New York: Norton, 1973.

Marsh, Paul. "The Choice between Equity and Debt: An Empirical Study." *Journal of Finance* 37 (March 1982), pp. 121–44.

Oppenheimer, Henry, and Gary Schlarbaum. "Investing with Ben Graham: An Ex Ante Test of the Efficient Markets Hypothesis." *Journal of Financial and Quantitative Analysis* 16 (September 1981), pp. 341–60.

Polakoff, Murray E., et al. *Financial Institutions and Markets.* Boston: Houghton Mifflin, 1970.

Ritter, Lawrence S. *The Flow of Funds Accounts: A Framework for Financial Analysis.* New York: Institute of Finance, New York University, 1968.

———, and William L. Silber. *Principles of Money, Banking, and Financial Markets.* New York: Basic Books, 1974.

Robinson, Roland I., and Dwayne Wrightsman. *Financial Markets: The Accumulation and Allocation of Wealth.* New York: McGraw-Hill, 1974.

Selected Issues of *Federal Reserve Bulletin.*

Smith, Keith V., and David K. Eiteman. *Essentials of Investing.* Homewood, Ill.: Richard D. Irwin, 1974.

Van Horne, James C. *The Function and Analysis of Capital Market Rates.* Englewood Cliffs, N.J.: Prentice-Hall, 1970.

# 15 Investment Banking: Public and Private Placement

In Chapter 15 we will examine the role of the investment banker, the advantages and disadvantages of selling securities to the public, and the private placement of securities with insurance companies, pension funds, and other lenders. Illustrative material is presented about Electronic Data Systems Corporation and Rockefeller Center Properties, as well as about several companies involved in financing issues.

## The Role of Investment Banking

The investment banker is the great link between the corporation in need of funds and the investor. As a middleman, the investment banker is responsible for designing and packaging a security offering and selling the securities to the public. The investment banking fraternity has long been thought of as an elite group—with appropriate memberships in the country club, the yacht club, and other such venerable institutions. The roller coaster performances of the security markets in the late 1960s and 70s have altered the picture somewhat. Competition has become the new way of doing business in which the fittest survive and prosper, while others drop out of the game.

## Enumeration of Functions

As a middleman in the distribution of securities, the investment banker plays a number of key roles.

**Underwriter** In most cases the investment banker is a risk taker. He will contract to buy securities from the corporation and resell them to other security dealers and the public. By giving a "firm commitment" to purchase the securities from the corporation, he is said to *underwrite* any risks that might be associated with a new issue. While the risk may be fairly low in handling a bond offering for Exxon or General Electric in a stable market, such may not be the case in selling the shares of a less-known firm in a very volatile market environment.

Though most large, well-established investment bankers would not consider managing a public offering without assuming the risk of distribution, smaller investment houses may handle distributions for relatively unknown corporations on a "best-efforts" or commission basis. Some issuing companies even choose to sell their own securities directly. Both the "best efforts" and "direct" methods account for a relatively small portion of total offerings. Table 15–1 shows the distribution of corporate securities by method of sale for registered securities.

**Market maker** During distribution and in later time periods, the investment banker may make a market in a given security—that is,

Table 15–1 **Corporate securities issues by method of distribution**

| | Underwritten | | | Best Efforts Offering | | | Direct by Issuer | | |
|---|---|---|---|---|---|---|---|---|---|
| | Debt | Pref. Stock | Common Stock | Debt | Pref. Stock | Common Stock | Debt | Pref. Stock | Common Stock |
| 1984 . . | 21,770 | 3,258 | 6,128 | 218 | 9 | 8,227 | 520 | 167 | 2,253 |
| 1983 . . | 16,110 | 4,742 | 20,053 | 153 | 16 | 8,448 | 342 | 33 | 2,182 |
| 1982 . . | 21,874 | 4,530 | 10,696 | 1,346 | 13 | 8,644 | 2,591 | 13 | 1,566 |

Source: Securities and Exchange Commission.

engage in the buying and selling of the security to ensure a liquid market. He may also provide research on the firm to encourage active investor interest.

**Adviser** The investment banker may advise clients on a continuing basis about the types of securities to be sold, the number of shares or units for distribution, and the timing of the sale. A company considering a stock issuance to the public may be persuaded, in counsel with an investment banker, to borrow the funds from an insurance company or, if stock is to be sold, to wait for two more quarters of earnings before going to the market. The investment banker also provides important advisory services in the area of mergers and acquisitions, leveraged buy-outs, and corporate restructuring.

**Agency functions** The investment banker may act as an agent for a corporation that wishes to place its securities privately with an insurance company, a pension fund, or a wealthy individual. In this instance, the investment banker will shop around among potential investors and negotiate the best possible deal for the corporation. He may also serve as an agent in merger and acquisition transactions. Because of the many critical roles that the investment banker plays, he may be requested to sit on the board of directors of the client company.

## The Distribution Process

The actual distribution process requires the active participation of a number of parties. The principal or managing investment banker will call upon other investment banking houses to share the burden of risk and to aid in the distribution. To this end, they will form an underwriting syndicate comprising as few as 2 or as many as 200 investment banking houses. In Figure 15–1, we see a typical case in which a hypothetical firm, the Maxwell Corporation, wishes to issue 250,000 additional shares of stock with Merrill Lynch as the managing underwriter and an underwriting syndicate of 15 firms.

The underwriting syndicate will purchase shares from the Maxwell Corporation and distribute them through the channels of distribution. Syndicate members will act as wholesalers in distributing the shares to brokers and dealers who will eventually sell the shares to the public.

Figure 15–1
Distribution process in investment banking

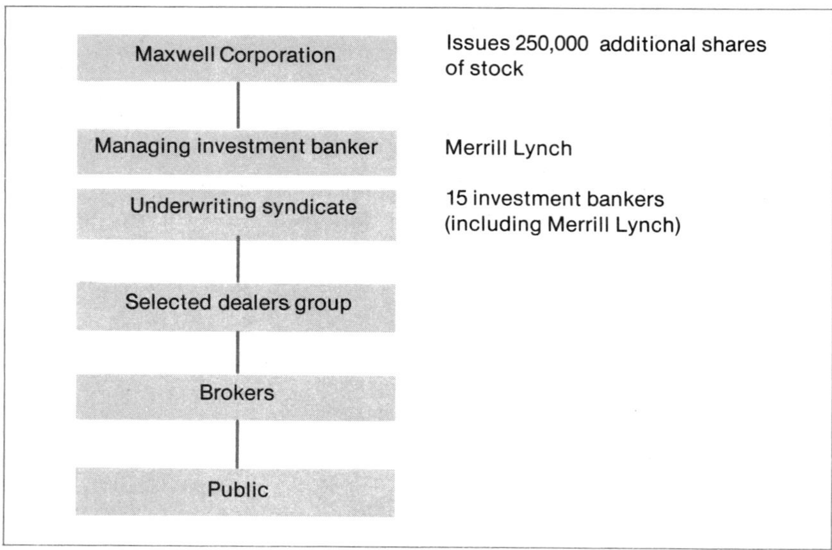


Large investment banking houses may be vertically integrated, acting as underwriter-dealer-broker and capturing all fees and commissions.

**The spread** The spread represents the total compensation for those who participate in the distribution process. If the public or retail price is \$21.50 and the managing investment banker pays a price of \$20.00 to the issuing company, we say there is a total spread of \$1.50. The \$1.50 may be divided up among the participants, as indicated in Figure 15–2.

Note that the lower a party falls in the distribution process, the higher the price for shares. The managing investment banker pays \$20, while dealers pay \$20.75. Also, the farther down the line the securities are resold, the higher is the potential profit. If the managing investment banker resells to dealers, he makes 75 cents per share; if he resells to the public, he makes \$1.50.

The total spread of \$1.50 in the present case represents 7 percent of the offering price (\$1.50/\$21.50). Generally, the larger the dollar value of an issue, the smaller the spread is as a percentage of the offering price. Percentage figures on underwriting spreads for U.S. corporations are presented in Table 15–2. Because there is more uncertainty in the

Figure 15–2
Allocation of underwriting spread

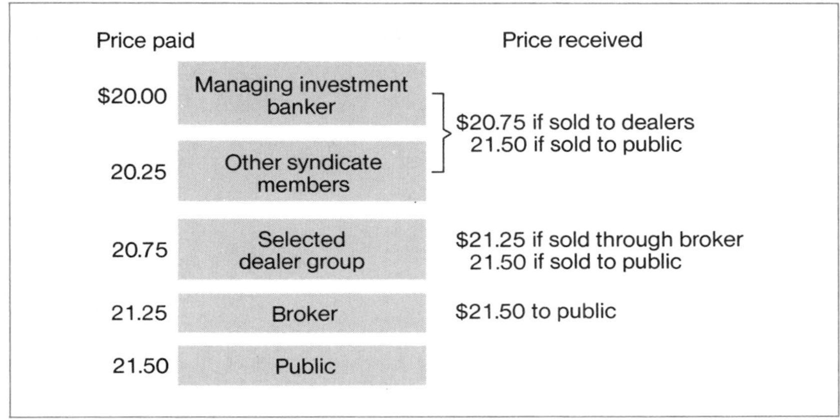


market reaction to common stock, a larger spread often exists for common stock than for other types of offerings.

Since the Maxwell Corporation stock issue is for $5.4 million (250,000 shares × $21.50), the 7 percent spread is in line with SEC figures in Table 15–2. It should be noted that the issuer bears not only the "give-up" expense of the spread in the underwriting process but also out-of-pocket costs related to legal and accounting fees, printing expenses, and so forth. On a small issue, these may represent 6–8 percent of the

Table 15–2
Underwriting compensation as a percentage of proceeds

| Size of Issue ($ millions) | Spread: Common Stock | Spread: Debt |
|---|---|---|
| Under 0.5 | 11.3% | 7.4% |
| 0.5–0.9 | 9.7 | 7.2 |
| 1.0–1.9 | 8.6 | 7.0 |
| 2.0–4.9 | 7.4 | 4.2 |
| 5.0–9.9 | 6.7 | 1.5 |
| 10.0–19.9 | 6.2 | 1.0 |
| 20.0–49.9 | 4.9 | 1.0 |
| 50.0 and over | 2.3 | 0.8 |

Sources: Securities and Exchange Commission, *Cost of Flotation of Registered Equity Issues, 1963–1965* (Washington, D.C.: U.S. Government Printing Office, 1970). Also Irwin Friend et al., *Investment Banking and the New Issues Market* (Cleveland: World, 1967).

**Table 15–3**
**Total costs to issue stock (percentage of total proceeds)**

| Size of Issue ($ millions) | Common Stock Spread | Out-of-Pocket Cost* | Total Expense |
|---|---|---|---|
| Under 0.5 | 11.3% | 7.3% | 18.6% |
| 0.5–0.9 | 9.7 | 4.9 | 14.6 |
| 1.0–1.9 | 8.6 | 3.0 | 11.6 |
| 2.0–4.9 | 7.4 | 1.7 | 9.1 |
| 5.0–9.9 | 6.7 | 1.0 | 7.7 |
| 10.0–19.9 | 6.2 | 0.6 | 6.8 |
| 20.0–49.9 | 4.9 | 0.8 | 5.7 |
| 50.0 and over | 2.3 | 0.3 | 2.6 |

*Out-of-pocket cost of debts is approximately the same.
Source: SEC, *Flotation of Registered Equity Issues, 1963–1965* (Washington, D.C.: U.S. Government Printing Office, 1970). Also Irwin Friend et al., *Investment Banking and the New Issues Market* (Cleveland: World, 1967).

value of the issue. As indicated in Table 15–3, when the spread plus the out-of-pocket costs are considered, the total cost of a new issue is rather high. Of course, substantial benefits may be received in return.

## Pricing the Security

Because the syndicate members purchase the stock for redistribution in the marketing channels, they must be careful about the pricing of the stock. When a stock is sold to the public for the first time (i.e., the firm is going public), the managing investment banker will do an in-depth analysis of the company to determine its value. The study will include an analysis of the firm's industry, financial characteristics, and anticipated earnings and dividend-paying capability. Based on appropriate valuation techniques, a price will be tentatively assigned and will be compared to that enjoyed by similar firms in a given industry. If the industry's average price–earnings ratio is 10, the firm should not stray too far from this norm. Anticipated public demand will also be a major factor in pricing a new issue.

The great majority of the issues handled by investment bankers are, however, additional issues of stocks or bonds for companies already trading publicly. When additional shares are to be issued, the investment bankers will generally set the price at slightly below the current market value. This process, known as underpricing, will help ensure a receptive market for the securities.

At times an investment banker will also handle large blocks of securities for existing stockholders. Because the number of shares may be too large to trade in normal channels, the investment banker will manage the issue and underprice the stock below current prices to the public. Such a process is known as a secondary offering, in contrast to a primary offering in which new corporate securities are sold.

## Dilution

A problem a company faces when issuing additional securities is the actual or perceived dilutive effect on shares currently outstanding. In the case of the Maxwell Corporation, the 250,000 new shares may represent a 10 percent increment to shares currently in existence. Perhaps the firm had earnings of $5 million on 2,500,000 shares prior to the offering, indicating earnings per share of $2. With 250,000 new shares to be issued, earnings per share will temporarily slip to $1.82.

Of course, the proceeds from the sale of new shares may well be expected to provide the increased earnings necessary to bring earnings back to at least $2. While financial theory dictates that a new equity issue should not be undertaken if it diminishes the overall wealth of current stockholders, there may be a perceived time lag in the recovery of earnings per share as a result of the increased shares outstanding. For this reason, there may be a temporary weakness in a stock when an issue of additional shares is proposed. In most cases, this is overcome with the passage of time.

## Market Stabilization

Another problem may set in when the actual public distribution begins—namely, unanticipated weakness in the stock or bond market. Since the sales group normally has made a firm commitment to purchase stock at a given price for redistribution, it is essential that the price of the stock remain relatively strong. Syndicate members, committed to purchasing the stock at $20 or better, could be in trouble if the sales price fell to $19 or $18. The managing investment banker is generally responsible for stabilizing the offering during the distribution period, and may accomplish this by repurchasing securities as the market price moves below the initial public offering price of $21.50.

The period of stabilization usually lasts two or three days after the initial offering, but it may extend up to 30 days for difficult-to-distribute securities. In a very poor market environment, stabilization may be virtually impossible to achieve. For example, when Federal Reserve Board Chairman Paul Volcker announced an extreme credit-tightening policy in October 1979, newly underwritten, high-quality IBM bond prices fell dramatically and Salomon Brothers and other investment bankers got trapped into approximately $10 million in losses. The bonds later recovered in value, but the investment bankers had already taken their losses.

## Aftermarket

The investment banker is also interested in how well the underwritten security behaves after the distribution period—for his ultimate reputation rests on bringing strong securities to the market. This is particularly true of initial public offerings.

Research has indicated that initial public offerings often do well in the immediate aftermarket. For example, one study examined approximately 500 firms and determined that there were 10.9 percent excess returns one week after issue (excess returns refers to movement in the price of the stock above and beyond the market). There were also positive excess returns of 11.6 percent for a full month after issue, but a negative market-adjusted performance of −3.0 percent one full year after issue.[1] Because the managing underwriter may underprice the issue initially to ensure a successful offering, quite often there is a jump in value after the issue first goes public. However, the efficiency of the market eventually takes hold, and sustained long-term performance is

[1]Frank K. Reilly, "New Issues Revisited," *Financial Management* 6 (Winter 1977), pp. 28–42.

very much dependent on the quality of the issue and the market conditions at play.

## Changes in the Investment Banking Industry

The investment banking function has been rapidly expanding. The growth in investment banking revenue has not been predominantly in the underwriting area, but rather in other functions performed. Major increases have taken place in corporate finance and merger/acquisition advisory services. Additionally, investment banking is becoming more internationally oriented, causing many firms (such as First Boston) to become global in nature.

The investment banking industry has remained fiercely competitive on the basis of performance. Furthermore, there has been a tremendous move toward vertical integration. Firms that were at one time primarily investment bankers, specializing in underwriting and corporate client services, have moved into more broadly based brokerage distribution services. Even more significant is the backward vertical integration that has taken place, as retail brokerage firms have acquired investment banking houses. As an example of the latter, in the late 1970s Merrill Lynch acquired White Weld & Company, a firm prominent in the investment banking industry.

In the early 1980s nonbrokerage firms moved into the brokerage area through acquisitions. Since the acquired brokerage houses were also engaged in investment banking activities, acquiring firms obtained investment banking capabilities as well. The merger of Prudential Insurance Company with Bache Halsey Stuart Shields was the first of these types of mergers. In retrospect, as of year-end 1985, Prudential and Sears (who acquired Dean Witter Reynolds) are both having problems generating significant profits from their brokerage and investment banking acquisitions. Only American Express, which acquired the retail broker Shearson Loeb Rhoades and then the investment banker Lehman Brothers, is having some success with the merged firms. However, these acquisitions spurred traditional securities firms such as Merrill Lynch, Salomon Brothers, and others to accelerate their expansion plans and more than triple their staffs over the last 10 years.

Perhaps the biggest change encompassing the investment banking industry is the consolidation of large financial resources among a few very large investment bankers. Underwriting and the mergers and acquisition game is being dominated by Salomon Brothers, First Boston, Goldman Sachs, Drexel Burnham Lambert, and three or four other big houses. Table 15–4 shows the consolidation of capital and clout with a few houses. Salomon Brothers was the lead manager of $21.2 billion in public securities issues in 1984, more than double the dollar amount managed by the second-place investment banker, Drexel Burnham Lambert. When you consider that PaineWebber, the tenth largest investment banker, had a volume less than one twelfth that of Salomon Brothers, you can understand the tremendous resources available to the top five or six investment bankers.

What Table 15–4 does not show is that each firm had its own speciality. Salomon was in first place for mortgage-backed securities, while Drexel dominated the market for low-grade, high-yield "junk bonds." Morgan Stanley, in seventh place, was the leader in common stock

Table 15–4

**Leading Underwriters of Securities in U.S.* 1984**

| MGR RANK† | UNDERWRITER | DOLLAR AMOUNT MANAGED (In billions) | NUMBER OF DEALS MANAGED | NUMBER OF DEALS UNDER-WRITTEN | DOLLAR AMOUNT UNDER-WRITTEN (In billions) | UNDER-WRITER RANK |
|---|---|---|---|---|---|---|
| 1 | Salomon Brothers | $21.2 | 186 | 509 | $12.0 | 1 |
| 2 | Drexel Burnham Lambert | 10.5 | 102 | 545 | 8.4 | 2 |
| 3 | First Boston | 10.0 | 129 | 492 | 7.0 | 4 |
| 4 | Merrill Lynch Capital Mkts. | 8.6 | 125 | 583 | 8.2 | 3 |
| 5 | Goldman Sachs | 7.9 | 97 | 481 | 6.2 | 5 |
| 6 | Shearson Lehman/American Express | 6.9 | 94 | 515 | 4.8 | 6 |
| 7 | Morgan Stanley | 4.9 | 58 | 332 | 3.6 | 7 |
| 8 | Kidder/Peabody | 1.9 | 45 | 509 | 2.6 | 8 |
| 9 | Prudential-Bache | 1.8 | 34 | 548 | 2.6 | 9 |
| 10 | PaineWebber | 1.7 | 33 | 522 | 2.1 | 12 |

*According to IDD Information Services †Credit to lead manager only

Source: Reprinted by permission of *The Wall Street Journal*, © Dow Jones & Company, Inc. (January 2, 1985), p. 16. All rights reserved.

offerings as well as initial offerings. Assessing the international nature of the market, Credit Suisse First Boston, an affiliate of First Boston, was the leading banker in Eurodollar financing, followed by Salomon Brothers.

## Shelf Registration

In February of 1982 the Securities and Exchange Commission began allowing a new filing process, called shelf registration, under SEC Rule 415. Shelf registration permits large companies, such as Exxon or Polaroid, to file one comprehensive registration statement, which outlines the firm's plans for future long-term financing. Then, when market conditions seem appropriate, the firm can issue the securities without further SEC approval. Future issues are thought to be sitting on the shelf, waiting for the appropriate time to appear.

Shelf registration is at variance with the traditional requirement that security issuers file a detailed registration statement for SEC review and approval each and every time they plan a sale. Whether investors are deprived of important "current" information as a result of shelf registration can only be judged with time. While shelf registration was started on an experimental basis by the SEC in 1982, it has now become a permanent part of the underwriting process. Shelf registration has been most frequently used with debt issues, with relatively less utilization in the equity markets (corporations do not wish to announce equity dilution in advance).

Shelf registration has contributed to the concentrated nature of the investment banking business previously discussed. The strong firms are acquiring more and more business, and, in some cases, are less dependent on large syndications to handle debt issues. Only investment banking firms with a big capital base and substantial expertise are in a position to benefit from this new registration process.

## Size Criteria for Going Public

Although there are no prescribed or official size criteria for approaching the public markets, the well-informed corporate financial officer of a private company should have some feel for what his or her options are. Can a company with $10 million in sales even consider a public offering?

A study indicates the following changes in various size considerations between 1969–72 and 1974–78 for 204 new public issues.[2] Note the substantially higher values that apply to the latter period.

| | 1969–1972 ($ millions) | 1974–1978 ($ millions) |
|---|---|---|
| Average sales volume . . . . . | $8.333 | $22.857 |
| Average earnings . . . . . . . | 0.464 | 1.758 |
| Average asset size . . . . . . | 5.833 | 14.643 |

Highly prestigious investment bankers look for larger companies to underwrite than do lesser known or regional investment banking houses.[3] In the preceding data for 1974–78, prestigious underwriters such as First Boston and Goldman Sachs (among others) underwrote companies going public with an average sales volume of $48,486,000 and average earnings of $3,610,000. Smaller underwriters were willing to consider firms with $10–$15 million in sales and at least a million dollars in aftertax earnings.

## Public versus Private Financing

Our discussion to this point has assumed that the firm was distributing stocks or bonds in the public markets (through the organized exchanges or over-the-counter, as explained in Chapter 14). However, many companies, by choice or circumstance, prefer to remain private in nature—restricting their financial activities to direct negotiations with bankers, insurance companies, and so forth. Let us evaluate the advantages and the disadvantages of public versus private financing and then explore the avenues open to a privately financed firm.

[2] Stanley B. Block and Marjorie T. Stanley, "The Price Movement Pattern and Financial Characteristics of Companies Approaching the Unseasoned Securities Market in the Late 1970's." *Financial Management* 9 (Winter 1980), pp. 30–36.

[3] The above figures include both.

### Advantages of Being Public

First of all, the corporation may tap the security markets for a greater amount of funds by selling securities directly to the public. With over 45 million individual stockholders in the country, combined with thousands of institutional investors, the greatest pool of funds is channeled toward publicly traded securities. Furthermore, the attendant prestige of a public security may be helpful in bank negotiations, executive recruitment, and the marketing of products. Some corporations listed on the New York Stock Exchange actually allow stockholders a discount on the purchase of their product lines.

Stockholders of a heretofore private corporation may also sell part of their holdings if the corporation decides to go public. A million-share offering may contain 500,000 authorized but unissued corporate shares (a primary offering) and 500,000 existing stockholder shares (a secondary offering). The stockholder is able to achieve a higher degree of liquidity and to diversify his or her portfolio. A publicly traded stock with an established price may also be helpful for estate planning purposes.

Finally, going public allows the firm to play the merger game, using marketable securities for the purchase of other firms. The high visibility of a public offering may even make the firm a potential recipient of attractive offers for its own securities. (This, of course, may not be viewed as an advantage by some firms who do not wish to be acquired.)

### Disadvantages of Being Public

The company must make all information available to the public through SEC and state filings. Not only is this tedious, time consuming, and expensive, but important corporate information on profit margins and product lines must be divulged. The president must adapt himself to being a public relations representative to all interested members of the securities industry.

Another disadvantage of being public is the tremendous pressure for short-term performance placed on the firm by security analysts and large institutional investors. Quarter-to-quarter earnings reports can become more important to top management than providing a long-run stewardship for the company. A capital budgeting decision calling for the selection of Alternative A—carrying a million dollars higher net present value than Alternative B—may be discarded in favor of the latter because Alternative B adds two cents more to next quarter's earnings per share.

In a number of cases, the blessings of having a publicly quoted security may become quite the opposite. Although a security may have had an enthusiastic reception in a strong "new issues" market such as that of 1961–62, 1967–68, or 1981–83, a dramatic erosion in value may later take place, causing embarrassment and anxiety for stockholders and employers.

A final disadvantage is the high cost of going public. As indicated in Table 15–3, for issues under a million dollars the underwriting spread plus the out-of-pocket cost may run over 15 percent.

## Public Offerings

### A Classic Example of Instant Wealth—EDS Goes Public

Some people are probably more familiar with Apple Computer and Steven Jobs' millionaire status than they are with Electronic Data Systems (EDS) and H. Ross Perot. Perot's success story makes Jobs' pale by comparison. In September 1968 Perot took EDS public, and within one month he found himself worth $300 million. This was no small accomplishment for a man who, six years earlier, had been an IBM salesman with only a few thousand dollars in the bank and a degree from the Naval Academy.

The original EDS offering—managed by P. W. Presprich, a New York investment banker—was at 118 times current earnings (the norm is 10 to 12 times earnings). After one month in the hot new-issues market of 1967–68, the stock was trading at over 200 times earnings. A company with earnings of only $1.5 million had a market value well over $300 million, exceeding many of *Fortune's* 500 largest companies. By 1970, EDS had a quoted market value of $1.5 billion. All of this was accomplished by a firm with a few hundred employees.

It is interesting to note that Perot's main concern in the initial pricing of his stock was not to set too low a value. In the strong new-issues market of the period, too many computer issues, which had been underpriced when they first crossed the tape, quickly doubled or tripled in price. Perot considered this an irrevocable loss to original shareholders who initially sold large blocks of their holdings. He was determined to avoid this by fully pricing his stock and only trading a small percentage of the total capitalization on the initial offering (only 650,000 shares out of 11.5 million). Even at a price–earnings ratio of 118 at initial trading, the stock jumped from $16.50 to $23 in one day.[4]

In the bear markets of the 1970s, EDS suffered more than most companies, and its stock price declined from a high of $161 per share in 1970 to a low of $12½ in 1974. Total market value retreated from a high of $1.5 billion to about $200 million. After recovering to $50 per share in 1983, Perot sold EDS to General Motors Corporation in 1984 for $2.5 billion, and stockholders received Class E common stock of General Motors (discussed more fully in Chapter 17).

## Rockefeller Center Properties, Inc.

The offering of Rockefeller Center Properties, Inc., is one of the biggest initial public offerings of common stock to date and gave the world an inside look at the Rockefeller family's real estate empire which was largely tied up in New York's Rockefeller Center. On September 13, 1985, an offering of 37.5 million shares of Rockefeller Center Properties took place at $20 per share for a grand total of $750 million dollars. The offering set up public ownership (60 percent) along with the Rockefeller family (40 percent) of a public real estate investment trust stock traded on the New York Stock Exchange.

The Rockefeller example is in contrast to the EDS example in several ways. The primary reason for the offering was the Rockefeller family's need for money. There are 79 living descendants of John D. Rockefeller, Jr., and most of their assets (especially the younger generation) had been tied up in the 1934 trusts set up by John D. Rockefeller. Unfortunately the cash flow from these trusts was very small compared to the $1.6 billion size of the underlying assets. EDS, in contrast, raised money for corporate expansion rather than family needs. Second,

---

[4]A. M. Louis, "Fastest Richest Texan Ever," *Fortune*, November 1968, pp. 168–70.

Rockefeller Properties has $1.6 billion of marketable assets as collateral, whereas EDS only had growth prospects with very few assets. Nevertheless, the EDS stock soared to new highs after the stock offering while Rockefeller Properties, in a raging bull market, only hit a high of $20⅜ (recall the offering price was $20) and traded at about 18¾ by year-end 1985. In the Rockefeller case it seems that the underwriters priced the initial offering of stock at a fully valued price of $20 per share.

Table 15–5 is the advertisement of the Rockefeller Center Properties, Inc., stock offering and depicts many of the characteristics of the distribution process discussed earlier in the chapter. The lead underwriters, Goldman, Sachs & Co. and Shearson Lehman Brothers, Inc., are listed on line one. On the following lines the syndicate of investment bankers responsible for the selling and distribution of the common stock are listed by size of their position. For example, Lazard Frères & Co., The First Boston Corporation, Merrill Lynch Capital Markets, and Salomon Brothers Inc. are responsible for millions of shares while those companies listed on the last line such as Stifel, Nicolaus & Co. and Wood Gundy Corp. would be responsible for only thousands of shares. Also there is an international nature to the offering, with firms such as Deutsche Bank Capital, EuroPartners Securities Corp., Swiss Bank Corporation International Securities Inc., and Yamaichi International participating.

## Private Placement

Private placement refers to the selling of securities directly to insurance companies, pension funds, and wealthy individuals rather than through the security markets. The financing device may be employed by a growing firm that wishes to avoid or defer an initial public stock offering or by a publicly traded company that wishes to incorporate private funds into its financing package. Private placement usually takes the form of a debt instrument, though a conversion privilege to common stock is sometimes present. The relative importance of private versus public placement is indicated in Figure 15–3.

The advantages of private placement are worthy of note. First of all, there is no lengthy, expensive registration process with the SEC. Second, the firm has considerably greater flexibility in negotiating with one or a handful of insurance companies, pension funds, or bankers

Table 15–5

## 37,500,000 Shares

# Rockefeller Center Properties, Inc.

**Common Stock**
($.01 par value)

**Price $20 Per Share**

*Upon request, a copy of the Prospectus describing these securities and the business of the Company may be obtained within any State from any Underwriter who may legally distribute it within such State. The securities are offered only by means of the Prospectus, and this announcement is neither an offer to sell nor a solicitation of any offer to buy. Neither the Attorney General of the State of New York nor the Attorney General of the State of New Jersey nor the Bureau of Securities of the State of New Jersey has passed on or endorsed the merits of the Offering. Any representation to the contrary is unlawful.*

Goldman, Sachs & Co. Shearson Lehman Brothers Inc.

Lazard Frères & Co. The First Boston Corporation Merrill Lynch Capital Markets Salomon Brothers Inc

Dillon, Read & Co. Inc. E. F. Hutton & Company Inc. Kidder, Peabody & Co. Incorporated Dean Witter Reynolds Inc.

Bear, Stearns & Co. Alex. Brown & Sons Incorporated Donaldson, Lufkin & Jenrette Securities Corporation Drexel Burnham Lambert Incorporated Hambrecht & Quist Incorporated Montgomery Securities

Nomura Securities International, Inc. Robertson, Colman & Stephens L. F. Rothschild, Unterberg, Towbin Wertheim & Co., Inc.

ABD Securities Corporation Advest, Inc. Allen & Company Incorporated Arnhold and S. Bleichroeder, Inc. Robert W. Baird & Co. Incorporated

Bateman Eichler, Hill Richards Incorporated Sanford C. Bernstein & Co., Inc. William Blair & Company Blunt Ellis & Loewi Incorporated Boettcher & Company, Inc.

J. C. Bradford & Co. Incorporated Butcher & Singer Inc. Cowen & Co. Dain Bosworth Incorporated Daiwa Securities America Inc. Deutsche Bank Capital Corporation

F. Eberstadt & Co., Inc. A. G. Edwards & Sons, Inc. Eppler, Guerin & Turner, Inc. EuroPartners Securities Corporation

First of Michigan Corporation First Southwest Company Robert Fleming Incorporated Gruntal & Co., Incorporated Interstate Securities Corporation

Janney Montgomery Scott Inc. Josephthal & Co. Incorporated Kleinwort, Benson Incorporated Ladenburg, Thalmann & Co. Inc. Legg Mason Wood Walker Incorporated

McDonald & Company Securities, Inc. Moseley, Hallgarten, Estabrook & Weeden Inc. The Nikko Securities Co. International, Inc. The Ohio Company

Oppenheimer & Co., Inc. Piper, Jaffray & Hopwood Incorporated Prescott, Ball & Turben, Inc. Rauscher Pierce Refsnes, Inc.

The Robinson-Humphrey Company, Inc. Rotan Mosle Inc. Sogen Securities Corporation Sutro & Co. Incorporated

Swiss Bank Corporation International Securities Inc. Thomson McKinnon Securities Inc. Tucker, Anthony & R. L. Day, Inc.

UBS Securities Inc. Underwood, Neuhaus & Co. Incorporated Wheat, First Securities, Inc. Yamaichi International (America), Inc.

Baker, Watts & Co. Birr, Wilson & Co., Inc. Brean Murray, Foster Securities Inc. Burgess & Leith Incorporated Cable, Howse & Ragen

Cazenove Inc. The Chicago Corporation Craigie Incorporated D. A. Davidson & Co. Incorporated R. G. Dickinson & Co. Doft & Co., Inc.

Fahnestock & Co. Inc. Ferris & Company Incorporated First Albany Corporation First Manhattan Co. Folger Nolan Fleming Douglas Incorporated

Furman Selz Mager Dietz & Birney Incorporated Gradison & Company Incorporated Herzfeld & Stern Inc. J. J. B. Hilliard, W. L. Lyons, Inc.

Howard, Weil, Labouisse, Friedrichs Incorporated Investment Corporation of Virginia Johnson, Lane, Space, Smith & Co., Inc. Johnston, Lemon & Co. Incorporated

Laidlaw Adams & Peck Inc. Cyrus J. Lawrence Incorporated Lovett Mitchell Webb & Garrison, Inc. Moore & Schley Capital Corporation

Morgan Keegan & Company, Inc. Neuberger & Berman New Japan Securities International Inc. W. H. Newbold's Son & Co., Inc.

Newhard, Cook & Co. Incorporated Nippon Kangyo Kakumaru International, Inc. Parker/Hunter Incorporated Rodman & Renshaw, Inc. R. Rowland & Co. Incorporated

Sanyo Securities America Inc. Scherck, Stein & Franc, Inc. Seidler Amdec Securities Inc. Starr Securities, Inc. Stephens Inc.

Stifel, Nicolaus & Company Incorporated Swergold, Chefitz & Sinsabaugh, Inc. Wedbush, Noble, Cooke, Inc. Wood Gundy Corp.

*September 13, 1985*

Source: An ad that appeared in *The Wall Street Journal,* (September 13, 1985), p. 39.

Figure 15–3
Public versus private placement of bonds

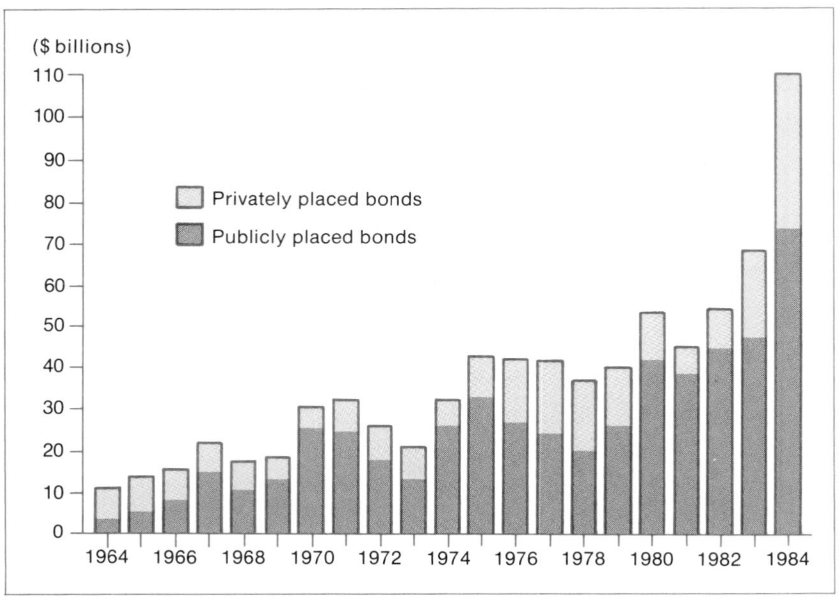


than is possible in a public offering. Because there is no SEC registration or underwriting, the initial costs of a private placement may be considerably lower than those of a public issue. However, the interest rate is usually higher to compensate the investor for holding a less liquid obligation.

## Going Private and Leveraged Buy-Outs

Throughout the years there have always been some firms going from being public to being private. In the 1970s a number of firms gave up their public listings to go private but these were usually small firms. Management figured that they could save several hundred thousand dollars a year in annual report expenses, legal and auditing fees, and security analysts meetings—a significant amount for a small company.

In the 1980s, however, very large corporations have been going private and not just to save several hundred thousand dollars. The answer seems to be in management's desire to manage for the long-term instead of the short-term demands of the stock market. Private firms do not have to please analysts with short-term performance.

There are basically two ways to accomplish going private. First, a publicly owned company can be purchased by a private company or, secondly, the company can repurchase all publicly traded shares from the stockholders. Both methods have been in vogue and are accomplished through the use of a leveraged buy-out. In a leveraged buy-out either the management or some other investor group borrows the needed cash to repurchase all the shares of the company. After the repurchase, the company exists with a lot of debt and heavy interest expense. What worries many analysts is that the borrowing is done at banks rather than through the securities markets. This may cause a misdirection of capital into nonproductive activities (leveraged buy-outs) instead of capital formation for new ventures and products. An additional fallout when a large firm goes private is that common stock outstanding tends to disappear, leaving fewer investment choices for investors.

Usually, management of the private company must sell off assets to reduce the debt load, and a corporate restructuring occurs, wherein divisions and products are sold and assets redeployed into new, higher-return areas. Over the long run these strategies could be rewarding and these companies could again become publicly owned, but that has not been proven yet. Table 15–6 lists nine firms going private in 1985, with prices in excess of one half billion dollars and a total value of over $14 billion.

**Table 15–6**
**Large firms going private in 1985**

| | (*$ millions*) |
|---|---|
| Beatrice Corporation | $ 6,200 |
| Storer Communications Inc. | 2,510 |
| Levi Strauss & Co. | 1,450 |
| Northwest Industries Inc. | 1,000 |
| Uniroyal Inc. | 836 |
| Denny's Inc. | 734 |
| SCOA Industries | 637 |
| Scovill Inc. | 523 |
| Parsons Corp. | 518 |
| Total value | $14,408 |

Source: Reprinted by permission of *The Wall Street Journal*, © Dow Jones & Company, Inc. (August 12, 1985), p. 13. 

## Summary

The role of the investment banker is critical to the distribution of securities in the U.S. economy. The investment banker serves as an underwriter or risk taker by purchasing the securities from the issuing corporation and redistributing them to the public, and he or she may continue to maintain a market in the distributed securities long after they have been sold to the public. The banker can also help a company sell a new issue on a "best efforts" basis. Investment bankers also serve as advisers to corporations and have become more important to corporations in the 1980s in providing advice on mergers, acquisitions, and leveraged buy-outs, and on resisting hostile takeover attempts.

The advantages of selling securities in the public markets must be weighed against the disadvantages. While going public may give the corporation and major stockholders greater access to funds as well as additional prestige, these advantages quickly disappear in a down market. Furthermore, the corporation must open its books to the public and orient itself to the short-term emphasis of investors.

There have been substantial increases in the average size of the corporations going public during the last decade. While during the years 1969–72 the average sales of such corporations were slightly over $8 million, by 1974–78 they had climbed to almost $23 million. The average earnings of these firms had almost quadrupled.

Investment bankers have become larger and consolidated into fewer firms. The industry has become dominated by 5 to 8 large bankers able to take down large blocks of securities and compete in a more international market. Shelf registration has also become an alternative to public syndications, particularly with debt issues, and is advantageous to the larger investment bankers.

Private placement—or the direct distribution of securities to large insurance companies, pension funds, and wealthy individuals—may bypass the rigors of SEC registration and allow more flexibility in terms. A number of corporations actually changed their structure from public to private during the bear market of 1973–74. This trend had become evident again in 1984 and 1985, with many large companies going private through leveraged buy-outs. While much of the debt used in leveraged buy-outs comes from the banking industry, only the public markets can meet the vast capital needs of U.S. corporations.

## List of Terms

**investment banker**
**underwriting**
**market maker**
**underwriting syndicate**
**managing underwriter**
**underwriting spread**
**dilution of earnings**
**market stabilization**
**public placement**
**private placement**
**going private**
**bull market**
**bear market**
**secondary offering**
**shelf registration**
**leveraged buy-out**

## Discussion Questions

1. In what way is an investment banker a risk taker?
2. What is the purpose of market stabilization activities during the distribution process?
3. Discuss how an underwriting syndicate decreases risk for each underwriter and at the same time facilitates the distribution process.
4. Discuss the reason for the differences between underwriting spreads for stocks and bonds.
5. Explain how the price–earnings ratio is related to the pricing of a new security issue and the dilution effect.
6. What is a shelf registration? How does it differ from the traditional requirements for security offerings?
7. Comment on the market performance of companies going public, both immediately after the offering has been made and some time later. Relate this to research that has been done in this area.
8. Discuss key changes that have been going on in the investment banking-brokerage community in terms of vertical integration. Also, who are some of the new participants in the industry?

**9.** Discuss the benefits accruing to a company that is traded in the public securities markets.

**10.** What are some reasons why a corporation may prefer to remain privately held?

**11.** If a company were looking for capital by way of a private placement, where would it look for funds?

**12.** How does a leveraged buy-out work? What does the debt structure of the firm normally look like after a leveraged buy-out? What might be done to reduce the debt?

## Problems

**1.** The Hamilton Corporation currently has four million shares of stock outstanding and will report earnings of $6,000,000 in the current year. The company is considering the issuance of one million additional shares that will net $30 per share to the corporation.

*a.* What is the immediate dilution potential for this new stock issue?

*b.* Assume the Hamilton Corporation can earn 10.5 percent on the proceeds of the stock issue in time to include it in the current year's results. Should the new issue be undertaken based on earnings per share?

**2.** Walton and Company is the managing investment banker for a major new underwriting. The price of the stock to the investment banker is $18 per share. Other syndicate members may buy the stock for $18.25. The price to the selected dealers group is $18.80, with a price to brokers of $19.20. Finally, the price to the public is $19.50.

*a.* If Walton and Company sells its shares to the dealer group, what will the percentage return be?

*b.* If Walton and Company performs the dealer's function also, and sells to brokers, what will the percentage return be?

*c.* If Walton and Company fully integrates its operation and sells directly to the public, what will its percentage return be?

3. Becker Brothers is the managing underwriter for a one million share issue by Jay's Hamburger Heaven. Becker Brothers is "handling" 10 percent of the issue. Their price is $25 and the price to the public is $26.40.

   Becker also provides the market stabilization function. During the issuance, the market for the stock turned soft, and Becker was forced to purchase 40,000 shares in the open market at an average price of $25.75. They later sold the shares at an average value of $23.

   Compute Becker Brothers *overall* gain or loss from managing this issue.

4. Winston Sporting Goods is considering a public offering of common stock. Its investment banker has informed the company that the retail price will be $18 per share for 600,000 shares. The company will receive $16.50 per share and will incur $150,000 in registration, accounting, and printing fees.

   *a.* What is the spread on this issue in percentage terms? What are the total expenses of the issue as a percentage of total value (at retail)?

   *b.* If the firm wanted to net $18 million from this issue, how many shares must be sold?

5. Ashley Homebuilding is about to go public. The investment banking firm of Blake Webber and Company is attempting to price the issue. The homebuilding industry generally trades at a 25 percent discount below the P/E ratio on the Standard & Poor's 500 Stock Index. Assume that Index currently has a P/E ratio of 12. Ashley can be compared to the homebuilding industry as follows:

| | *Ashley* | *Homebuilding Industry* |
|---|---|---|
| Growth rate in earnings per share | 12 percent | 10 percent |
| Consistency of performance . . . . | Increased earnings 4 out of 5 years | Increased earnings 3 out of 5 years |
| Debt to total assets . . . . . . . . . | 55 percent | 40 percent |
| Turnover of product . . . . . . . | Slightly below average | Average |
| Quality of management . . . . . . | High | Average |

Assume, in assessing the initial P/E ratio, the investment banker will first determine the appropriate industry P/E based on the Standard & Poor's 500 Index. Then ½ point will be added to the P/E ratio for each case in which Ashley is superior to the industry norm, and ½ point will be deducted for an inferior comparison. On this basis, what should the initial P/E be for Ashley Homebuilding?

6. The Landry Corporation needs to raise $1 million of debt on a 25-year issue. If it places the bonds privately the interest rate will be 11 percent. Thirty thousand dollars in out-of-pocket costs will be incurred. For a public issue the interest rate will be 10 percent, and the underwriting spread will be 4 percent. There will be $100,000 in out-of-pocket costs.

   Assume interest on the debt is paid semiannually, and the debt will be outstanding for the full 25-year period, at which time it will be repaid.

   Which plan offers the higher net present value? (For each plan, compare the net amount of funds initially available—inflow—to the present value of future payments to determine net present value. Assume the discount rate is 12 percent annually. Use 6 percent semiannually throughout the analysis. Disregard taxes.)

7. Midland Corporation has a net income of $15 million and 6 million shares outstanding. Its common stock is currently selling for $40 per share. Midland plans to sell common stock in order to set up a major new production facility costing $21,660,000. The production facility will not produce a profit for one year, and then is expected to earn a 15 percent return on the investment. Stanley Morgan and Co., an investment banking firm, plans to sell the issue to the public for $38 per share with a spread of 5 percent.

   *a.* How many shares of stock must be sold to net $21,660,000? (Note: No out-of-pocket costs must be taken into consideration in this problem.)
   *b.* Why is the investment banker selling the stock at less then its current market price?
   *c.* What are the current earnings per share (EPS) and the price–earnings ratio before the issue (based on a stock price of $40)? What will be the price per share immediately after the sale of stock if the P/E stays constant?

*d.* Compute the EPS and the price (P/E stays constant) after the new production facility begins to produce a profit.
*e.* Are the shareholders better off because of the sale of stock and the resultant investment? What other financing strategy could the company have tried in order to increase earnings per share?

**8.** The Presley Corporation is about to go public. It currently has aftertax earnings of $7,500,000 and 2,500,000 shares are owned by the present stockholders (the Presley family). The new public issue will represent 600,000 new shares. The new shares will be priced to the public at $20 per share, with a 5 percent spread on the offering price. There will also be $200,000 in out-of-pocket costs to the corporation.

*a.* Compute the net proceeds to the Presley Corporation.
*b.* Compute the earnings per share immediately before the stock issue.
*c.* Compute the earnings per share immediately after the stock issue.
*d.* Determine what rate of return must be earned on the net proceeds to the corporation so that there will not be a dilution in earnings per share during the year of going public.
*e.* Determine what rate of return must be earned on the proceeds to the corporation so that there will be a 5 percent increase in earnings per share during the year of going public.

**9.** I. B. Michaels has a chance to participate in a new public offering by Hi-Tech Micro Computers. His broker informs him that there is a very strong demand for the 500,000 shares to be issued. His broker's firm is assigned 15,000 shares in the distribution and will allow Michaels, a relatively good customer, 1.5 percent of their 15,000 share allocation.

The initial offering price is $30 per share. There is a strong aftermarket, and the stock goes to $33 one week after issue. After the first full month after issue, Mr. Michaels is quite pleased to observe his shares are selling for $34.75. He is content to place his shares in a lockbox and eventually use their anticipated increased value to help send his son to college many years in the future. However, one year after the distribution, he looks up the shares in *The Wall Street Journal* and finds they are trading at $28.75.

*a.* Compute the total dollar profit or loss on Mr. Michael's shares one week, one month, and one year after the purchase. In each case, compute the profit or loss against the initial purchase price.

*b.* Also compute this percentage gain or loss from the initial $30 price and compare this to the results that might be expected in an investment of this nature based on prior research. Assume the overall stock market was basically unchanged during the period of observation.

*c.* Why might a new public issue be expected to have a strong aftermarket?

**10.** (*Comprehensive problem—impact of new public offering*)
The Bailey Corporation, a manufacturer of medical supplies and equipment, is planning to sell its shares to the general public for the first time. The firm's investment banker, Robert Merrill and Company, is working with Bailey Corporation in determining a number of items. Information on the Bailey Corporation follows:

BAILEY CORPORATION
Income Statement
For the Year 198X

| | |
|---|---:|
| Sales (all on credit) | $42,680,000 |
| Cost of goods sold | 32,240,000 |
| Gross profit | 10,440,000 |
| Selling and administrative expense | 4,558,000 |
| Operating profit | 5,882,000 |
| Interest expense | 600,000 |
| Net income before taxes | 5,282,000 |
| Taxes | 2,120,000 |
| Net income | $ 3,162,000 |

BAILEY CORPORATION
Balance Sheet
As of December 31, 198X

*Assets*

| | |
|---|---:|
| Current assets | |
| Cash | $ 250,000 |
| Marketable securities | 130,000 |
| Accounts receivable | 6,000,000 |
| Inventory | 8,300,000 |
| Total current assets | 14,680,000 |
| Net plant and equipment | 13,970,000 |
| Total assets | $28,650,000 |

*Liabilities and Stockholders' Equity*

| | |
|---|---|
| Current liabilities: | |
| Accounts payable | $ 3,800,000 |
| Notes payable | 3,550,000 |
| Total current liabilities | 7,350,000 |
| Long-term liabilities | 5,620,000 |
| Total liabilities | $12,970,000 |
| Stockholders' equity: | |
| Common stock (1,800,000 shares at $1 par) | $ 1,800,000 |
| Capital in excess of par | 6,300,000 |
| Retained earnings | 7,580,000 |
| Total stockholders' equity | 15,680,000 |
| Total liabilities and stockholders' equity | $28,650,000 |

*a.* Assume that 800,000 new corporate shares will be issued to the general public. What will earnings per share be immediately after the public offering? (Round to two places to the right of the decimal point.) Based on a price–earnings ratio of 12, what will the initial price of the stock be? Use earnings per share after the distribution in the calculation.

*b.* Assuming an underwriting spread of 5 percent and out-of-pocket costs of $300,000, what will the net proceeds to the corporation be?

*c.* What return must the corporation earn on the net proceeds to equal earnings per share before the offering? How does this compare with the current return on the total assets on the balance sheet?

*d.* Now assume that of the initial 800,000 share distribution, 400,000 belong to current stockholders and 400,000 are new shares, and the latter will be added to the 1,800,000 shares currently outstanding. What will earnings per share be immediately after the public offering? What will the initial market price of the stock be? Assume a price–earnings ratio of 12 and use earnings per share after the distribution in the calculation.

*e.* Assuming an underwriter spread of 5 percent and out-of-pocket costs of $300,000, what will net proceeds to the corporation be?

*f.* What return must the corporation now earn on the net proceeds to equal earnings per share before the offering? How does this compare with current return on the total assets on the balance sheet?

## Selected References

Bloch, Ernest. "Pricing a Corporate Bond Issue: A Look behind the Scenes." In *Essays in Money and Credit,* New York: Federal Reserve Bank of New York, 1964, pp. 72–76.

Block, Stanley B., and Marjorie T. Stanley. "The Price Movement Pattern and Financial Characteristics of Companies Approaching the Unseasoned Securities Market in the Late 1970s." *Financial Management* 9 (Winter, 1980), pp. 30–36.

Cohan, Avery B. *Private Placements and Public Offerings: Market Shares since 1935.* Chapel Hill: School of Business Administration, University of North Carolina, 1961.

Dougall, Herbert E., and Jack E. Gaumnitz. *Capital Markets and Institutions.* Englewood Cliffs, N.J.: Prentice-Hall, 1975.

Friend, Irwin, et al. *Investment Banking and the New Issues Market.* Cleveland: World, 1967.

Haynes, Samuel L., III. "Investment Banking: Power Structure in Flux." *Harvard Business Review* 49 (March-April 1971), pp. 136–52.

———. "The Transformation of Investment Banking." *Harvard Business Review* 57 (January-February 1979), pp. 153–70.

Hess, Alan C., and Peter A. Frost. "Tests for Price Effects of New Issues of Seasoned Securities." *Journal of Finance* 37 (March 1982), pp. 11–25.

Ibbotsen, Roger G. "Price Performance of Common Stock New Issues." *Journal of Financial Economics* 2 (September 1975), pp. 253–72.

Johnson, Keith B.; T. Gregory Morton; and M. Chapman Findlay III. "An Empirical Analysis of the Flotation Cost of Corporate Securities, 1971–1972." *Journal of Finance* 30 (September 1975), pp. 1129–33.

Logue, Dennis E. "On the Pricing of Unseasoned New Issues, 1965–1969." *Journal of Financial and Quantitative Analysis* 8 (January 1973), pp. 91–103.

Louis, A. M. "Fastest Richest Texan Ever." *Fortune,* November 1968, pp. 168–70.

McDonald, J. G., and A. K. Fisher. "New Issue Stock Price Behavior." *Journal of Finance* 27 (March 1972), pp. 97–102.

Nair, Richards S. "Investment Banking: Judge Medina in Retrospect." *Financial Analysts Journal* 16 (July–August 1960), pp. 35–40.

Reilly, Frank K. "New Issues Revisited." *Financial Management* 6 (Winter 1977), pp. 28–42.

Rogowski, Robert J., and Eric H. Sorensen. "Deregulation in Investment Banking: Shelf Registration, Structure, and Performance." *Financial Management* 14 (Spring 1985), pp. 5–15.

"The Scorecard on New Issues." Underwriters Performance Record, Wayne, New Jersey.

Securities and Exchange Commission, *Cost of Flotation of Registered Equity Issues, 1963–1965*. Washington, D.C.: U.S. Government Printing Office, 1970.

# 16 Long-Term Debt and Lease Financing

The Shakespearean quote of "Neither a borrower nor a lender be" hardly applies to corporate financial management. The virtues and drawbacks of debt usage were considered in Chapter 5, Operating and Financial Leverage, and in Chapter 11, The Cost of Capital. One can only surmise that today's financial managers, many of whom were educated in the 1950s and 1960s, remember the advantages a bit better than the disadvantages. Debt usage has been at unprecedented levels in the late 1970s and 1980s.

In Chapter 16 we will consider the importance of debt in the U.S. economy, the nature of long-term debt instruments, the mechanics of bond yields and pricing, and the decision to call back or refund an existing bond issue. Finally, lease financing will be considered as a special case of long-term debt financing. We give particular attention to accounting rules that affect leasing.

## The Expanding Role of Debt

Corporate debt has increased more than tenfold since World War II. This growth is related to rapid business expansion, the inflation-

Figure 16–1
Times interest earned

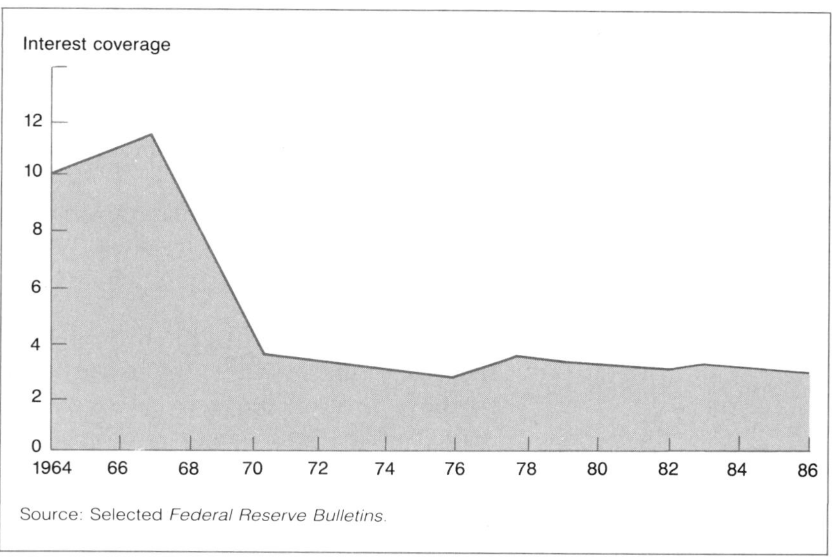


Source: Selected *Federal Reserve Bulletins*.

ary impact on the economy, and, at times, a relatively weak stock market.

The rapid expansion of the U.S. economy has placed pressure on U.S. corporations to raise capital and will continue to do so in the future. In this context, a whole new set of rules has been developed for evaluating corporate bond issues. Much deterioration in borrowing qualifications has taken place. In 1967 the average U.S. manufacturing corporation had its interest payments covered by operating earnings at a rate of 11.7 times (operating earnings were more than 11 times as great as interest). By the mid-1980s the ratio had diminished to approximately three times. Nor has this been a short-term, cyclical phenomenon, but rather a slow, steady decline with only short-term reversals, as indicated in Figure 16–1.

Even with a decline in the interest-paying capability of corporate borrowers, relatively few corporations actually default on their obligations, and an even smaller number are liquidated. Nevertheless, a debt contract dictates the lender's potential influence over a corporation and its relative bargaining position in the event the worst comes to pass.

## The Debt Contract

The corporate bond represents the basic long-term debt instrument for most large U.S. corporations. The bond agreement specifies such basic items as the par value, the coupon rate, and the maturity date.

*Par value (face value)*—The initial value of the bond. Most corporate bonds are traded in $1,000 units.

*Coupon rate*—The actual interest rate on the bond, usually payable in semiannual installments. To the extent that interest rates in the market go above or below the coupon rate after the bond has been issued, the market price of the bond will change from the par value.

*Maturity date*—The final date on which repayment of the bond principal is due.

The bond agreement is supplemented by a much longer document termed a bond indenture. The indenture, often containing over 100 pages of complicated legal wording, covers every minute detail surrounding the bond issue—including collateral pledged, methods of repayment, restrictions on the corporation, and procedures for initiating claims against the corporation. A financially independent trustee is appointed by the corporation to administer the provisions of the bond indenture under the guidelines of the Trust Indenture Act of 1939. Let's examine two items of interest in any bond agreement: the security provisions of the bond and the methods of repayment.

### Security Provisions

A secured claim is one in which specific assets are pledged to bondholders in the event of default. Only infrequently are pledged assets actually sold off and the proceeds distributed to bondholders. Typically, the defaulting corporation is reorganized and existing claims are partially satisfied by issuing new securities to the participating parties. Of course, the stronger and better secured the initial claim, the higher the quality of the new security to be received in exchange. When a defaulting corporation is reorganized for failure to meet obligations, existing management may be terminated and, in extreme cases, held legally responsible for any imprudent actions.

A number of terms are used to denote collateralized or secured debt. Under a *mortgage agreement,* real property (plant and equipment) is pledged as security for the loan. A mortgage may be *senior* or *junior* in nature, with the former requiring satisfaction of claims before payment is given to the latter. Bondholders may also attach an *after-acquired property clause,* requiring that any new property be placed under the original mortgage.

The student should realize that not all secured debt will carry every protective feature, but rather a carefully negotiated position including some safeguards and rejecting others. Generally, the greater the protection offered a given class of bondholders, the lower is the interest rate on the bond. Bondholders are willing to assume some degree of risk to receive a higher yield.

## Unsecured Debt

A number of corporations issue debt that is not secured by a specific claim to assets. In Wall Street jargon, the name *debenture* refers to a long-term, unsecured corporate bond. Among the major participants in debenture offerings are such prestigious firms as American Telephone and Telegraph, Exxon, International Paper, and Dow Chemical. Because of the legal problems associated with "specific" asset claims in a secured bond offering, the trend is decidedly to unsecured debt—allowing the bondholder a general claim against the corporation rather than a specific lien against an asset.

Even unsecured debt may be divided between high-ranking and subordinated debt. A *subordinated debenture* is an unsecured bond in which payment to the holder will take place only after designated senior debenture holders are satisfied. The hierarchy of creditor obligations for secured as well as unsecured debt is presented in Figure 16–2, along with consideration of the position of stockholders. For a further discussion of payment of claims and the hierarchy of obligations, the reader should see Appendix 16A, Financial Alternatives for Distressed Firms, which also covers bankruptcy considerations.

Figure 16–2
Priority of claims

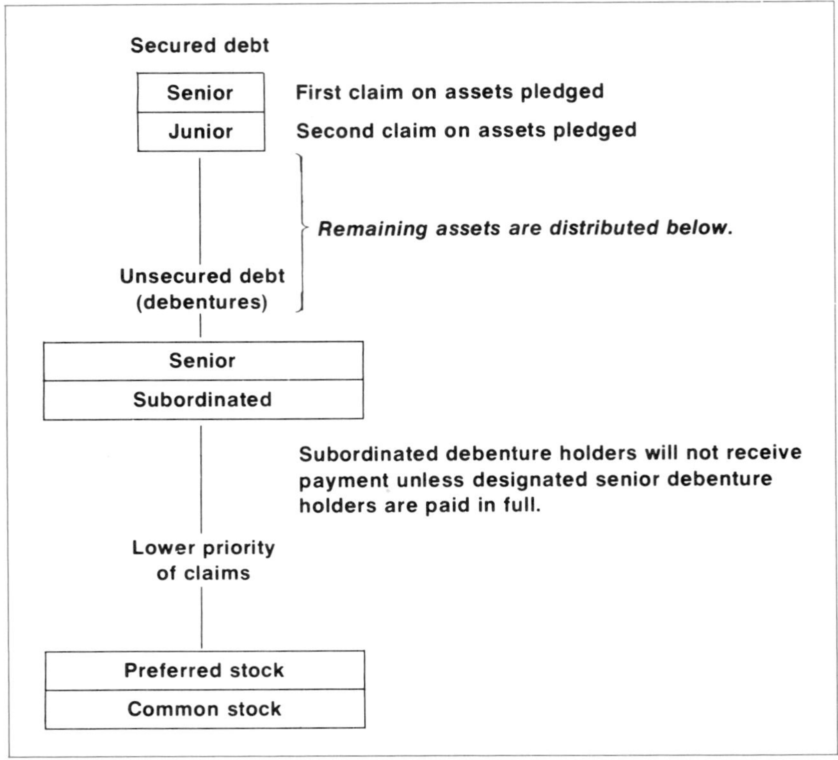


## Methods of Repayment

The method of repayment for bond issues may not always call for one lump-sum disbursement at the maturity date. Some Canadian and British government bonds are perpetual in nature. More interestingly, West Shore Railroad 4 percent bonds are not scheduled to mature until 2361 (almost 400 years in the future). Nevertheless, most bonds have some orderly or preplanned system of repayment. In addition to the simplest arrangement—a single-sum payment at maturity—bonds may be retired by serial payments, through sinking-fund provisions, through conversion, or by a call feature.

**Serial payments** The bonds are paid off in installments over the life of the issue. Each bond has its own predetermined date of maturity and receives interest only to that point. Although the total issue may span over 20 years, 15 or 20 different maturity dates may be assigned specific dollar amounts.

**Sinking-fund provision** A less structured but considerably more popular method of debt retirement is through the use of a sinking fund. Under this arrangement, semiannual or annual contributions are made by the corporation into a fund administered by a trustee for purposes of debt retirement. The trustee takes the proceeds and goes into the market to purchase bonds from willing sellers. If no willing sellers are available, a lottery system may be used among outstanding bondholders.

**Conversion** A more subtle method of reducing debt outstanding is to provide for debt conversion into common stock. Although this feature is exercised at the option of the bondholder, a number of incentives or penalties may be utilized to encourage conversion. The mechanics of convertible bond trading are discussed at length in Chapter 19, Convertibles and Warrants.

**Call feature** A call provision allows the corporation to call in or force in the debt issue prior to maturity. The corporation will pay a premium over par value of 5 to 10 percent—a bargain value to the corporation if bond prices are up. Modern call provisions usually do not take effect until the bond has been outstanding at least 5 to 10 years. Often the call provision declines over time, usually by ½–1 percent per year after the call period begins. A corporation may decide to call in outstanding debt issues when interest rates on new securities are considerably lower than those on previously issued debt (let's get the high cost, old debt off the books).

Now that we have covered the key features of the bond indenture, let us examine an existing bond. Table 16–1 presents a page from *Moody's Bond Record*. We find that Pfizer Incorporated has two bond issues: an 8½ percent sinking fund (S.F.) debenture due in 1999 and a 9¼ percent sinking fund (S.F.) debenture due in the year 2000. More specific features of the bonds are found in Table 16–2 from the *Standard & Poor's Corporate Bond Records*.

Table 16–1

66 Penn-Phil

## MOODY'S BOND RECORD

| Issue | Interest Dates | Current Call Price | Moody's Rating | Current Price | | Yield to Mat. | Price 1985 High | Price 1985 Low | Range 1946-84 High | Range 1946-84 Low | Amt. Outst. Mil. $ | Sink. Fund Prov. | Legal Status | Fed. Tax | Issued | Price | Yld |
|---|---|---|---|---|---|---|---|---|---|---|---|---|---|---|---|---|---|
| Pennzoil O/S Fin NV eurodeb.15.25 1990 | APR 1 | 101.00* | A2 | | | — | — | — | 107 | 107 | 75.0 | No | — | F | 3-15-82 | 99.50 | 15.35 |
| • Penril Corp. sr.sub.nts.10.875 1993 | F&A1 | 100.00 | B3 r | | | — | — | — | — | — | 18.0 | Yes | — | N | 1-28-83 | | |
| People Express Airlines sec.eq.ctf.13.50 A 1990 | J&D 15 | 100.00 | Ba2 r | | | — | — | — | — | — | 25.0 | No | — | N | 6-13-85 | 100.00 | 13.50 |
| do nts.16.50 1991 | J&J 15 | N.C. | Ba3 r | | | — | — | — | 99 | 99 | 40.0 | Yes | — | N | 7-11-84 | 99.05 | 16.73 |
| do sec.eq.ctf.14.00 B 1995 | J&D 15 | 100.00 | Ba2 r | | | — | — | — | — | — | 100 | Yes | — | N | 6-13-85 | 99.75 | 14.05 |
| do sec.eq.ctf.14.75 1999 | A&O15 | 105.54* | Ba2 r | | | — | — | — | 97¼ | 97¼ | 60.0 | Yes | — | N | 4-18-84 | 97.25 | 15.22 |
| Peoples Gas L. & C. 1st&ref. 4.625 J 1986 | M&N 1 | 100.00* | Aa3 | 96½ | bid | 11.00 | 96½ | 91¼ | 104½ | 60⅜ | 18.6 | 100.00 | 13 | N | 5-1-61 | 100.369 | 4.60 |
| do 1st&ref.12.125 T 1990 | F&A15 | 100.00 | Aa3 r | 103½ | bid | 11.17 | 103½ | 98¾ | 102¾ | 73 | 60.0 | Yes | 13 | N | 8-21-80 | 99.00 | 12.30 |
| do 1st&ref. 6.25 L 1992 | F&A15 | 101.82* | Aa3 r | 76¾ | bid | 11.19 | 76¾ | 69 | 103¾ | 52 | 38.2 | 100.55 | 13 | N | 8-24-67 | 101.00 | 6.17 |
| do 1st&ref. 8.875 M 1995 | M&S15 | 103.61* | Aa3 r | 85 | bid | 11.44 | 85 | 76½ | 109⅞ | 60⅜ | 21.0 | 100.53 | 13 | N | 9-16-70 | 100.75 | 8.80 |
| do 1st&ref. 7.625 N 1997 | A&O15 | 103.63* | Aa3 r | 75¾ | bid | 11.46 | 78¼ | 67¼ | 102¾ | 52⅛ | 34.8 | Yes | 13 | N | 4-12-72 | 100.277 | 7.60 |
| do 1st&ref. 8.25 O 1998 | J&J15 | 104.13* | Aa3 r | 78¾ | bid | 11.45 | 78¾ | 69¾ | 101⅝ | 54⅜ | 26.5 | Yes | 13 | N | 7-25-73 | 100.00 | 8.25 |
| • PepsiCo Cap Res Inc. gtd.nts.10.125 1986 | J&D1 | N.C. | Aa2 r | 100¼ | bid | 9.72 | 101½ | 99¾ | 102⅛ | 83⅜ | 150 | No | 13 | N | 6-4-80 | 100.00 | 10.125 |
| do zero cpn.eurodeb. 1988-12 | N.P. | 100.00 | Aa2 | | | — | — | — | — | — | 850 | No | 13 | F | 3-31-82 | — | |
| PepsiCo Cap Corp NV euronts. 1992 | N.P. | 100.00 | Aa2 | k 51⅛ | bid | — | 51¼ | 44½ | 26 | 26 | 00 | No | — | F | 1-82 | 26.00 | |
| do euronts. 1994 | MAR 2 | 100.00 | Aa2 | | | — | — | — | 20¾ | 20¾ | 125 | No | — | F | 2-82 | 20.75 | |
| Pepsico O/S Fin. gtd.eurobonds 7.25 1994 | FEB 26 | 101.25* | Aa2 | | | — | — | — | 100 | 100 | 250 | No | — | F | 2-84 | 100.00 | 7.25 |
| do gtd.euronts. 1994 | N.P. | 100.00 | Aa2 | | | — | — | — | — | — | 125 | No | — | F | 2-82 | 20.75 | |
| Pernambuco (Braz) 2.125 2008 | M&S 1 | 100.00 | — | | | flat | — | — | 88⅞ | 21¼ | 0.24 | Yes | — | F | Mar 1927 | 97.75 | 2.18 |
| • Peru (Rep) ext. 6.00 1960 | †6-1-32 | 100.00 | — | | | flat | — | — | 125 | 14⅜ | 0.66 | Yes | — | F | Dec 1927 | 91.50 | 8.32 |
| Pet Inc. s.f.deb. 8.00 1991 | M&S 1 | 100.50* | — r | 86 | bid | 11.55 | 86 | 78 | 106 | 58 | 16.7 | Yes | — | N | 3-4-71 | 100.00 | 8.00 |
| do s.f.deb. 5.875 1992 | J&D 1 | 100.49* | — | 73 | bid | 11.84 | 73 | 65 | 99 | 50 | 11.6 | 100.00 | — | N | 6-20-67 | 99.00 | 5.95 |
| Petro-Lewis Corp. sr.nts.15.00 1992 | QAPR1 | 115.00* | B3 | | | — | — | — | — | — | | Yes | — | N | MAY 1985 | | |
| • do sr.sub.deb.12.625 2003 | F&A15 | 100.00 | Caa r | 66 | sale | 19.50 | 61 | 61 | 95 | 65 | 45.7 | Yes | — | N | 8-12-81 | 69.83 | 18.25 |
| do sub.deb.13.50 2005 | A&O1 | 100.00 | Caa | | | — | — | — | — | — | | Yes | — | N | MAY 1985 | | |
| • do sub.deb.11.00 1997 | J30&D31 | 103.30 | Caa r | 53⅛ | sale | — | 64 | 45 | 99⅞ | 56⅛ | 20.8 | Yes | — | N | 1-12-78 | | |
| • do sub.deb.12.25 1998 | F&A 1 | 103.68* | Caa r | 60 | sale | — | 68½ | 53 | 4 | 60 | 30.5 | Yes | — | N | 7-25-78 | | |
| • do ver.rt.sub.deb.13.00 2000 | J&J 1 | 106.88* | Caa r | 63 | sale | — | 74¾ | 54⅜ | 96 | 62⅞ | 52.0 | Yes | — | N | 6-25-80 | | |
| • do zero cpn.nts. 1988 | MAR 15 | 100.00 | Caa r | 58⅜ | bid | — | 60 | 55 | 53½ | 46 | 30.9 | No | — | N | 8-2-82 | | |
| • do zero cpn.nts. 1989 | N.P. | 100.00 | Caa r | 43 | sale | — | 45⅜ | 41⅞ | 44 | 27 | 32.1 | No | — | N | 8-12-81 | 25.65 | 17.75 |
| • do sr.sub.nts.11.50 1993 | F&A15 | 100.00 | Caa r | 64½ | sale | — | 71 | 63 | 88¼ | 69 | 85.0 | Yes | — | N | 2-9-83 | 89.47 | 13.44 |
| Petro-Lewis Int'l Fin. euronts. 9.00 1986 | MAY1 | 100.00 | Caa | | | — | — | — | 100 | 100 | 20.0 | Yes | — | F | 4-81 | 100.00 | 9.00 |
| Petro. Heat & Power Co. sub.nts.10.63 1994 | J&J& O 1 | 104.00* | B2 r | | | — | — | — | 99¼ | 99¼ | 20.0 | No | — | N | 6-22-84 | 99.25 | 14.64 |
| PETTIBONE CORP. sub.deb.12.375 2000 | M&S 1 | 100.00 | Caa r | | | — | 76 | 74 | 100 | 65 | 16.8 | Yes | — | N | 8-29-80 | | |
| → • PFIZER INC. s.f.deb. 8.50 1999 | A&O15 | 103.49* | Aa1 r | 81¼ | bid | 11.22 | 83¼ | 75⅜ | 104¾ | 58 | 50.1 | Yes | 123 | N | 4-18-74 | 99.25 | |
| → • do s.f.deb. 9.25 2000 | F&A15 | 104.38* | Aa1 r | 87 | sale | 11.05 | 90 | 78½ | 111 | 61½ | 41.2 | Yes | 123 | N | 8-19-75 | 99.50 | |
| • Phelps Dodge Corp. s.f.deb. 8.10 1996 | J&D15 | 102.43* | Ba1 r | 69⅜ | bid | 13.56 | 65⅛ | 55 | 106½ | 50 | 64.4 | Yes | — | N | 7-16-71 | 100.00 | 8.10 |
| • Phibro-Salomon deb.11.625 2015 | F&A1 | §111.00* | Aa3 r | | | — | 99⅜ | 99⅜ | — | — | 100 | Yes | — | N | Ref. fr 8-1-95@ 105.50 | | |
| do nts.10.70 1992 | F&A1 | 100.00 | Aa3 r | | | — | 100 | 100 | — | — | 100 | No | — | N | 8-1-85 | 100.00 | 10.70 |
| Phila. Balt. & Wash. gen. 5.00 B 1974 | †8-1-70 | N.C. | — | | | flat | — | — | 120 | 23 | 10.0 | No | — | N | 2-1-1924 | | |
| do gen. 4.50 C 1977 | †7-1-70 | N.C. | — | | | flat | — | — | 135 | 16 | 11.3 | No | — | N | Jan 1931 | 102.00 | 4.40 |
| • Phila. Elect. Co. 1st&ref. 4.375 1986 | J&D 1 | 100.20* | Baa3 | 94½ | sale | 9.46 | 94½ | 87⅜ | 104 | 50¼ | 50.0 | No | 1 | N | 12-10-58 | 100.00 | 4.38 |
| • do 1st&ref. 4.625 1987 | M&S 1 | 100.20* | Baa3 | 90⅛ | bid | 10.43 | 87½ | 82 | 109 | 54⅜ | 40.0 | No | 1 | N | 9-13-57 | 100.00 | 4.63 |
| • do 1st&ref. 3.75 1988 | M&N 1 | 100.40* | Baa3 | 84 | bid | 11.04 | 84 | 76⅜ | 100 | 47⅛ | 40.0 | No | 1 | N | 4-30-58 | 99.75 | 3.77 |
| • do 1st&ref. 5.00 1989 | A&O 1 | 100.70* | Baa3 | 82¼ | bid | 10.55 | 77½ | 73¼ | 108⅛ | 51⅜ | 50.0 | No | 1 | N | 10-15-59 | 101.00 | 4.93 |
| • do 1st&ref.13.75 1992 | A&O15 | 103.00* | Baa3 r | 106½ | ask | 12.34 | 103½ | 101⅜ | 107 | 86 | 125 | No | 1 | N | 10-6-80 | 100.00 | 13.75 |
| • do 1st&ref. 6.50 1993 | M&S 1 | 101.90* | Baa3 r | 75 | bid | 11.62 | 74¼ | 65⅜ | 104½ | 49 | 60.0 | No | 1 | N | 3-11-68 | 100.00 | 6.50 |
| • do 1st&ref. 4.50 1994 | M&N 1 | 101.70* | Baa3 r | 63⅛ | bid | 11.33 | 60¼ | 54 | 102½ | 39¼ | 50.0 | No | 1 | N | 5-13-64 | 100.823 | 4.45 |
| • do 1st&ref. 9.00 1995 | F&A1 | 104.30* | Baa3 r | 85 | sale | 11.68 | 86¼ | 75⅛ | 114¾ | 57⅜ | 66.7 | 101.70 | 1 | N | 2-3-70 | 102.25 | 8.78 |
| • do 1st&ref. 8.25 1996 | F&A 1 | 103.70* | Baa3 r | 79¾ | sale | 11.57 | 79¾ | 67⅛ | 108⅜ | 52⅞ | 80.0 | No | 1 | N | 7-26-71 | 100.527 | 8.20 |
| • do 1st&ref. 6.125 1997 | A&O 1 | 102.50* | Baa3 r | 65⅞ | sale | 11.41 | 76½ | 54⅜ | 102 | 41⅜ | 75.0 | No | 1 | N | 10-10-67 | 100.342 | 6.10 |
| • do 1st&ref. 7.50 1998 | J&D15 | 103.90* | Baa3 r | 70 | sale | 12.20 | 70 | 62⅜ | 103¼ | 47⅛ | 100 | No | 1 | N | 6-15-72 | 100.57 | 7.45 |
| • do 1st&ref. 7.50 1999 | J&J15 | 103.90* | Baa3 r | 71 | sale | 11.89 | 71 | 62½ | 101⅜ | 46¼ | 100 | No | 1 | N | 1-22-73 | 100.00 | 7.50 |
| • do 1st&ref.11.00 2000 | F&A 1 | 105.50* | Baa3 r | 95 | sale | 11.71 | 95 | 82½ | 115 | 66 | 72.8 | Yes | 1 | N | 4-23-75 | 101.00 | 11.00 |
| • do 1st&ref. 7.75 2000 | J&D15 | 104.10* | Baa3 r | 70 | sale | 12.11 | 71 | 64⅛ | 107 | 48 | 67.1 | Yes | 1 | N | 12-10-70 | 100.00 | 7.75 |
| • do 1st&ref.11.625 2000 | A&O15 | 107.40* | Baa3 r | 95½ | bid | 12.29 | 98 | 85 | 119⅜ | 66 | 65.0 | No | 12 | N | 4-23-75 | 101.00 | 11.49 |
| • do 1st&ref. 7.375 2001 | J&D15 | 104.60* | Baa3 r | 66⅛ | bid | 12.12 | 69 | 59⅛ | 102½ | 44⅜ | 80.0 | No | 1 | N | 12-13-71 | 100.907 | 7.30 |
| • do 1st&ref. 9.625 2002 | F&A 1 | 106.16* | Baa3 r | 82¼ | bid | 12.12 | 83⅜ | 72⅜ | 109½ | 57⅜ | 100 | No | 1 | N | 7-28-76 | 100.00 | 9.625 |
| • do 1st&ref. 8.625 2003 | J&J15 | 106.05* | Baa3 r | 74⅜ | bid | 12.18 | 75 | 66 | 102¼ | 51½ | 75.0 | No | 1 | N | 7-6-77 | 100.26 | 8.60 |
| • do 1st&ref. 8.50 2004 | J&J15 | 105.90* | Baa3 r | 75⅛ | sale | 11.83 | 75⅛ | 64 | 101⅜ | 50⅛ | 125 | No | 1 | N | 1-16-74 | 100.875 | 8.42 |
| • do 1st&ref.12.50 2005 | A&O15 | 110.00* | Baa3 r | 98⅜ | bid | 12.69 | 103 | 89⅜ | 103 | 72 | 100 | No | 1 | N | 10-10-79 | 100.00 | 12.50 |
| • do 1st&ref. 9.125 2006 | M&S 1 | §105.84* | Baa3 r | 77⅞ | sale | 12.06 | 78 | 68½ | 106¼ | 53½ | 100 | No | 1 | N | Ref. fr 3-1-86@ 105.47 | | |
| • do 1st&ref. 8.625 2007 | M&S15 | 106.30* | Baa3 r | 72¼ | sale | 12.33 | 75⅜ | 64⅛ | 102¼ | 51⅛ | 75.0 | No | 1 | N | 3-8-77 | 100.00 | 8.63 |
| • do 1st&ref. 9.125 2008 | M&S15 | 107.51* | Baa3 r | 77 | sale | 12.12 | 78 | 68 | 100⅜ | 52⅜ | 100 | No | 1 | N | 3-7-78 | 100.77 | 9.05 |
| • do 1st&ref.18.75 2009 | M&S15 | §115.98* | Baa3 r | 121⅜ | sale | 15.36 | 121⅜ | 117⅛ | 127½ | 98⅜ | 125 | No | 1 | N | Ref. fr 9-15-86@ 115.28 | | |
| • do s.f.deb.14.50 2009 | F&A15 | §114.50* | Ba1 r | 107⅜ | bid | 13.46 | 108 | 99 | 101 | 85½ | 150 | Yes | 1 | N | Ref. fr 2-15-89@ 111.21 | | |
| • do 1st&ref.15.375 2010 | A&O1 | §113.70* | Baa3 r | 113⅛ | bid | 13.51 | 113⅜ | 103⅜ | 114¼ | 91⅛ | 100 | No | 1 | N | Ref. fr 10-1-87@ 112.60 | | |
| • do 1st&ref.17.625 2011 | J&J1 | §116.63* | Baa3 r | 115⅜ | bid | 15.19 | 118 | 112⅜ | 122½ | 95⅛ | 125 | No | 1 | N | Ref. fr 7-1-86@ 113.76 | | |
| • do 1st&ref.18.00 2012 | A&O1 | §114.96* | Baa3 r | 120 | sale | 14.94 | 120 | 110 | 124½ | 97½ | 100 | No | 1 | N | Ref. fr 4-1-87@ 113.60 | | |
| • do 1st&ref.13.375 2013 | J&D15 | §111.61* | Baa3 r | 103½ | bid | 12.90 | 104½ | 95 | 99½ | 79⅛ | 125 | No | 1 | N | Ref. fr 6-15-88@ 110.32 | | |
| • do deb.14.125 1990 | A&O15 | 101.60* | Ba1 r | 106½ | sale | 12.21 | 108 | 102½ | 110 | 87⅛ | 50.0 | No | 1 | N | 4-23-80 | 100.13 | 14.10 |
| • do deb.14.75 2005 | A&O15 | §112.10* | Ba1 r | 107½ | sale | 13.64 | 107⅜ | 99½ | 111⅜ | 83½ | 100 | No | 1 | N | Ref. fr 4-15-90@ 108.90 | | |
| Phila. Elect. Pwr. s.f.deb. 4.50 B 1995 | M&S1 | 101.40* | Baa3 r | 58⅛ | bid | 12.03 | 58⅛ | 48⅜ | 99⅜ | 33⅛ | 16.9 | 100.00 | — | N | 4-1-65 | 99.75 | 4.51 |
| Phila. Nat'l. Bank cap.nts. 5.50 1992 | M&S 1 | 100.55* | — r | 73⅜ | bid | 11.41 | 73⅜ | 64⅜ | 69 | 46⅜ | 19.8 | Yes | — | N | 2-23-67 | 100.00 | 5.50 |
| Phila. Sub. Wtr. 1st 4.50 1987 | J&J 1 | 100.20* | A2 | 92 | bid | 11.54 | 92 | 86½ | 102 | 50 | 4.00 | 100.00 | 3 | N | 3-14-57 | 100.00 | 4.50 |
| do 1st 4.125 1988 | M&N 1 | 100.50* | A2 | 85 | bid | 10.95 | 85 | 78 | 101½ | 40 | 4.00 | Yes | 3 | N | 5-8-58 | 101.50 | 4.03 |
| Phila. Sav. Fund. Soc. mtg.bkd.15.50 A 1986 | J&D15 | N.C. | Aaa r | | | — | 109¼ | 95¼ | 111 | 103⅜ | 50.0 | No | 13 | N | 12-17-81 | 100.00 | 15.50 |
| do 11.00 1988 | F&A1 | N.C. | — r | | | — | 102¼ | 97⅜ | 98¼ | 91⅜ | 75.0 | No | — | N | 1-24-83 | | |
| do mtg.bkd.12.00 B 1994 | M&N15 | N.C. | Aaa r | 105½ | bid | 11.02 | 106 | 103 | 99⅜ | 99⅜ | 225 | No | — | N | 11-8-84 | 99.88 | 12.03 |
| • Philip Morris s.f.deb. 6.625 1993 | A&O15 | 100.00 | A1 r | 79 | sale | 10.57 | 79 | 72 | 99 | 53⅜ | 24.6 | 100.00 | 3 | N | 10-15-68 | 98.25 | 6.77 |
| • do s.f.deb. 9.125 2003 | J&J15 | §105.93* | A1 r | 84⅜ | bid | 11.10 | 78 | 78 | 100 | 61 | 150 | Yes | 3 | N | Ref. fr 7-15-88@ 104.56 | | |
| • do s.f.deb. 8.875 2004 | J&D 1 | 104.62* | A1 r | 77⅜ | bid | 11.86 | 82 | 75 | 107 | 57⅜ | 121 | Yes | 3 | N | 5-30-74 | 99.375 | |
| do deb. 6.00 1999 | M&N15 | 100.00 | A1 r | 64 | bid | 11.10 | 64 | 64 | 47⅜ | 47⅜ | 47.4 | No | 3 | N | 11-17-81 | 47.39 | 14.13 |
| do deb. 6.00 2001 | J&J15 | 100.00 | A1 r | 62⅜ | bid | 11.10 | 62⅜ | 62⅜ | 42¾ | 42¾ | 46.3 | No | 3 | N | 7-9-81 | 42.80 | 15.17 |
| • do nts. 9.55 1986 | J&D 1 | 100.00 | A1 r | 100⅜ | sale | 8.95 | 100⅜ | 99 | 100⅜ | 79¼ | 250 | No | 3 | N | 6-5-79 | 100.00 | 9.55 |
| • do nts.14.125 1988 | M&N15 | 100.00 | A1 r | 104⅜ | bid | 12.48 | 107 | 104⅜ | 109⅜ | 93⅜ | 119 | No | 3 | N | 11-17-81 | 99.75 | 14.18 |
| • do nts.14.00 1991 | A&O 1 | 100.00 | A1 r | 108 | sale | 11.97 | 108 | 104⅛ | 110⅜ | 90¼ | 70.9 | No | 3 | N | 4-1-81 | 99.38 | 14.12 |
| • do nts.15.25 1991 | J&J15 | 100.00 | A1 r | 111 | bid | 12.52 | 113 | 108⅜ | 112¼ | 99 | 190 | No | 3 | N | 7-9-81 | 99.63 | 15.32 |
| Philip Morris Cr. Cap. NV zero cpn.eurodeb. 1990 | [illegible] | 100.00 | A1 | | | — | — | — | 22¼ | 22¼ | 200 | No | — | F | 5-18-82 | 22.25 | 13.34 |
| Philip Morris Cr. Corp. eurobonds11.125 1995 | APR15 | 100.75* | A1 | | | — | — | — | 100 | 100 | 70.2 | No | — | F | 3-8-85 | 100.00 | 11.13 |
| Philip Morris Int'l. gtd.s.f.eurodeb. 8.50 1986 | JUN 1 | 100.00 | A1 | k 99½ | bid | 9.20 | 99½ | 98⅜ | 98½ | 98⅜ | 15.0 | Yes | — | F | 5-71 | 98.50 | |
| do eurobonds 9.50 1989 | FEB 1 | 102.00* | A1 | | | — | — | — | 100½ | 100½ | 150 | No | — | F | 2-82 | 100.50 | |

Gtd. by Pennzoil Co. Fr.4-1-87. w.w. Fr. 6-15-92. Fr. 4-15-91. Gtd. by Pepsico, Inc. Due ser. on April 1 fr. 1988-2012. Zero coupon gtd. nts., Gtd. by Pepsico Inc. Due 2-4-92. Gtd. by Pepsico Inc., zero coupon gtd. nts. Gtd. by Pepsico Inc., Bearer Bonds. Fr. 2-26-89. Gtd. by Pepsico Inc., zero coupon. Due 3-2-94. Stamped. See I.C. Ind. Sr. sec. nts. Exchange offer. Fr. 8-15-86. Exchange offer. w.s. Non-Ref.at int.cost less than 11%. w.s. Non-Ref.at int.cost less than 12.25% Int. rt. fr. 7-1-85 thru 6-30-86. Non-Ref.at int.cost less than 13%. Sub. serial. Due 8-15-89. Gtd. Oil Index Note, Gtd. by Petro-Lewis Corp. Sub. exch. var. rt. nts., int. thru 9-30-85. Non-Ref.at int.cost less than 14.94%.

Fr.8-1-90. Fr. 10-15-87. Fr. 2-1-89. Fr. 4-15-87. Cont. by Phila. Elect Co. Now Phila. Sub. Corp. Negotiable Ctfs. of Deposit. S.F. fr. 7-15-89. Fr. 11-15-86. Fr. 4-1-88. Fr 7-15-88. Gtd. by Philip Morris Credit Corp. Thru 4-19-93. Gtd. by Philip Morris Inc. Bearer Bonds, Gtd. by Philip Morris Inc. Fr. 2-1-87.

Note: Moody's ratings are subject to change. Because of the possible time lapse between Moody's assignment or change of a rating and your use of this monthly publication, we suggest you verify the current rating of any security or issuer in which you are interested. For standard abbreviations and symbols, see page 3.

Source: *Moody's Bond Record*, October 1985, p. 66.

**Table 16–2**
**Pfizer Incorporated bonds**

9¼% SINKING FUND DEBS.; Due Aug. 15, 2000
Authorized . . . . . . . . . . . . . . $100,000,000
Outstg. (Dec. 31, 1984) . . . . . . . 41,200,000
Retired or in treas.. . . . . . . . . . . 58,800,000

INDENTURE DATED Aug. 15, 1975. INTEREST PAYABLE Feb. & Aug. 15, to holders registered the preceding Feb. & Aug. 1, respectively. PRINCIPAL & INTEREST PAYABLE at trustee's office. INTEREST GRACE PERIOD—30 days.

TRUSTEE—Chase Manhattan Bank (N.A.), NYC. REGISTRARS—Hartford National Bank & Tr. Co., Conn.; also the trustee.

DENOMINATIONS—Fully registered, $1,000 and multiples thereof.

SINKING FUND requires retirement on 30 days' notice at 100 & int. of $6,500,000 Debs. each Aug. 15, 1986–99, Co. having non-cumulative option to retire up to like amount more each year. Optional redemptions may be used to reduce mandatory requirements. Credit may be taken for Debs. otherwise acquired.

REDEEMABLE OTHERWISE on 30 days' notice at the following prices & int. thru each Aug. 14, with the price declining annually after until Aug. 15, 1995, when the price of 100 is reached:
1985 . . 104.813 1986 . 104.375 1987 . . 103.938

REDEMPTION RESTRICTIONS—No 9¼% Debs. may be redeemed before Aug. 15, 1985, with borrowed funds or net proceeds of any sale and leaseback transaction having an interest cost or factor less than 9.30% per annum.

SECURITY—Same as 8½% Debs. due 1999.

LISTED—NYSE:
1984 . . . . . 81½ 71½ 1983 . . . . . 86¾ 76¾
1982 . . . . . 80 61½ 1981 . . . . . 83 59

8½% SINKING FUND DEBS.; Due Apr. 15, 1999
Authorized . . . . . . . . . . . . . . $125,000,000
Outstg. (Dec. 31, 1984) . . . . . . . 50,100,000
Retired or in treas.. . . . . . . . . . . 74,900,000

INDENTURE DATED Apr. 15, 1974, INTEREST PAYABLE Apr. & Oct. 15 to holders registered the preceding Apr. & Oct. 1, respectively. PRINCIPAL & INTEREST PAYABLE at trustee's office. INTEREST GRACE PERIOD—30 days'.

TRUSTEE & REGISTRAR—Chase Manhattan Bank, N.A., NYC.

DENOMINATIONS—Fully registered, $1,000 & multiples thereof.

SINKING FUND requires retirement on 30 days' notice at 100 & int. of $8,125,000 Debs. each Apr. 15, 1985–98. Co. having non-cumulative option to retire up to a like amount more each year. Optional redemptions may be used to reduce mandatory requirements. Credit may be taken for Debs. otherwise acquired.

REDEEMABLE OTHERWISE on 30 days' notice at the following prices & int. thru each Apr. 14, with price declining each year after to 100:
1986 . . .103.49 1987 . . 103.10 1988 . . 102.71

SECURITY—A direct unsecured obligation. Neither Co. nor any restricted subsidiary may mortgage or pledge any principal property or any shs. or debt of any restricted subsidiary without securing Debs. equally and ratably therewith; excepted are certain permitted liens.

LISTED—NYSE:
1984 . . . . . 77¼ 65⅝ 1983 . . . . . 83⅜ 73¼
1982 . . . . . 80 58 1981 . . . . . 69½ 56

Source: *Standard & Poor's Corporate Records*, June 1985, pp. 3,234–3,235.

As we can see in Table 16–2, the 9¼ percent bond was sold on August 19, 1975, and had an original offering of $100 million. As of December 1984, $41.2 million were still outstanding. A check of the sinking fund requirements indicates that retirement was required beginning in 1986 and ending in 1999. In the case of both bonds, Pfizer decided to use its option to retire a portion of the bonds earlier than specified in the bond indenture. The information in Table 16–2 also provides other pertinent information found in the indenture, such as the interest payment dates, trustees, registrars, denominations of each bond, sinking fund requirements, call features (listed under "redeemable otherwise"), redemption restrictions, security, and a price listing on the NYSE Bond Exchange over the last four years.

## Bond Prices, Yields, and Ratings

The financial manager must be sensitive to interest rate changes and price movements in the bond market. The treasurer's interpretation of market conditions will influence the timing of new issues, the coupon rate offered, the maturity date, and the necessity for a call provision. Lest the student of finance think that bonds maintain stable, long-term price patterns, he or she need merely examine bond pricing during the five-year period 1967–72. When the market interest rate on outstanding 30-year, Aaa corporate bonds went from 5.10 percent to 8.10 percent, the average price of existing bonds dropped 36 percent. A conservative investor would be quite disillusioned to see a $1,000, 5.10 percent bond now quoted at $640.[1] A similar pattern of bond price declines occurred in 1979–82. Though most bonds are virtually certain to be redeemed at their face value at maturity ($1,000 in this case), this is small consolation to the bondholder who has many decades to wait. Of course, at times, bonds also greatly increase in value such as in 1984–85.

As indicated above and in Chapter 10, the price of a bond is intimately tied to current interest rates. A bond paying 5.10 percent ($51 a year) will fare quite poorly when the going market rate is 8.10 percent ($81 a year). In order to maintain a market in the older issue, the price is adjusted downward to reflect current market demands. The longer the life of the issue, the greater the influence of interest rate changes on the price of the bond.[2] The same process will work in reverse if interest

[1] Bond prices are generally quoted as a percentage of original par value. In this case the quote would read 64.

[2] This is known as Malkiel's second theory of bonds. In fact, it is only completely true when the coupon rate of the bond equals or is greater than the original discount rate.

rates go down. A 30-year, $1,000 bond initially issued to yield 8.10 percent would go up to $1,500 if interest rates declined to 5.10 percent (assuming the bond is not callable). A further illustration of interest rate effects on bond prices is presented in Table 16–3 for a bond paying 12 percent interest. Observe that not only interest rates in the market but years to maturity have a strong influence on bond prices.

**Table 16–3**
**Interest rates and bond prices (the bond pays 12 percent interest)**

| *Years to Maturity* | *Rate in the Market (percent)—Yield to Maturity** | | | | |
|---|---|---|---|---|---|
| | *8%* | *10%* | *12%* | *14%* | *16%* |
| 1 . . . . | $1,038.16 | $1,018.54 | $1,000 | $981.48 | $963.98 |
| 15 . . . . | 1,345.52 | 1,153.32 | 1,000 | 875.54 | 774.48 |
| 25 . . . . | 1,429.92 | 1,182.36 | 1,000 | 862.06 | 754.98 |

*This table is based on semiannual interest, but you enter it with annual values.

For the last four decades, the pattern has been for long-term interest rates to move upward (Figure 16–3, p. 506). However, there has been a meaningful decline in long-term interest rates in the mid-1980s.

## Bond Yields

Bond yields are quoted on three different bases; coupon rate, current yield, and yield to maturity. We will apply each to a $1,000 par value bond paying $100 per year interest for 10 years. The bond is currently selling in the market for $900.

*Coupon rate (nominal yield)*—Stated interest payment divided by the par value.

$$\frac{\$100}{\$1,000} = 10\%$$

*Current yield*—Stated interest payment divided by the current price of the bond.

$$\frac{\$100}{\$900} = 11.11\%$$

Figure 16–3
Long-term yields on debt

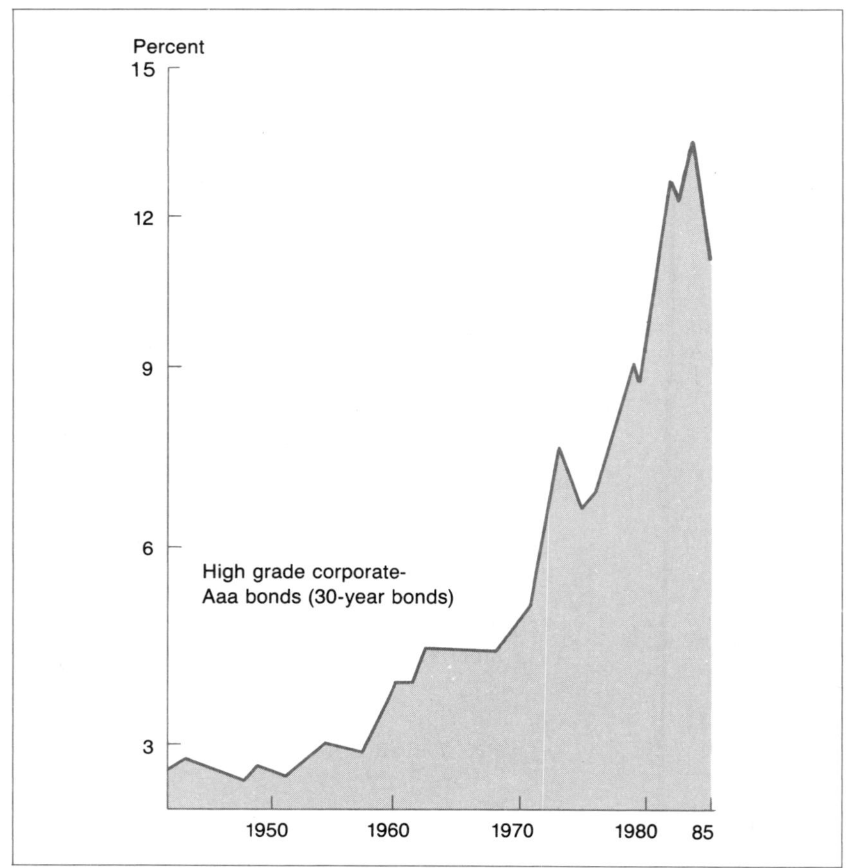


*Yield to maturity*—The interest rate that will equate future interest payments and the payment at maturity to the current market price. This represents the concept of the internal rate of return. In the present case an interest rate of approximately 11.58 percent will equate interest payments of $100 for ten years and a final payment of $1,000 to the current price of $900. A simple formula may be used to approximate yield to maturity.[3] This formula was initially presented in Chapter 10.

[3]The greater the discount or premium and the longer the period to maturity the less accurate is the approximation.

$$\text{Approximate yield to maturity } (Y') = \frac{\text{Annual interest payment} + \dfrac{\text{Principal payment (par)} - \text{Price of the bond}}{\text{Number of years to maturity}}}{\dfrac{\text{Price of the bond} + \text{Principal payment (par)}}{2}} \quad (16\text{–}1)$$

$$= \frac{\$100 + \dfrac{\$1{,}000 - \$900}{10}}{\dfrac{\$900 + \$1{,}000}{2}}$$

$$= \frac{\$100 + \dfrac{\$100}{10}}{\dfrac{\$1{,}900}{2}}$$

$$= \frac{\$100 + \$10}{950} = \frac{\$110}{950} = 11.58\%$$

Extensive bond tables indicating yield to maturity are also available. When financial analysts speak of bond yields, the general assumption is that they are speaking of yield to maturity. This is deemed to be the most significant measure of return.

### Bond Ratings

Both the issuing corporation and the investor are concerned about the rating their bond is assigned by the two major bond rating agencies—Moody's Investor Service and Standard & Poor's Corporation. The higher the rating assigned a given issue, the lower the required interest payments are to satisfy potential investors. This is because highly rated bonds carry lower risk. A major industrial corporation may be able to issue a 30-year bond at 10½ percent yield to maturity because it is rated Aaa, whereas a smaller, regional firm may only qualify for a B rating and be forced to pay 13 or 13½ percent.

As an example of rating systems, Moody's Investor Service provides the following nine categories of ranking:

Aaa Aa A Baa Ba B Caa Ca C

The first two categories represent the highest quality (for example, AT&T and IBM); the next two, medium to high quality; and so on. Beginning in 1982, Moody's began applying numerical modifiers to categories Aa through B. One is the highest in a category, two is the mid-range, and three is the lowest. Thus a Aa2 rating means the bond is in the mid-range of Aa. Standard & Poor's has a similar letter system with + and − modifiers.

Bonds receive ratings based on the corporation's ability to make interest payments, its consistency of performance, its size, its debt–equity ratio, its working capital position, and a number of other factors. The yield spread between higher- and lower-rated bonds changes with the economy. If investors are pessimistic about economic events, they will accept as much as 3 percent less return to go into securities of very high quality, whereas in more normal times the spread may be only 1.5 percent.

## Examining Actual Bond Ratings

Three actual bond offerings are presented in Table 16–4 to illustrate the various terms we have used. The information is taken from *Moody's Bond Record* (October 1985).

The student will recall first of all that the true return on a bond issue is measured by yield to maturity (the last column of Table 16–4). Directing our attention to the Exxon bonds, we note that the oil bonds are unsecured, as indicated by the term *debentures*. Furthermore, they have a sinking-fund provision for retirement of debt. Because of the extremely high quality of the company and the sinking-fund retirement

**Table 16–4**
**Outstanding bond issues**

| | | Rating | Price | Yield to Maturity |
|---|---|---|---|---|
| Exxon 6's . . . . . . . . . . . | Sinking fund debentures due 1997 | Aaa | $700 | 10.60% |
| Duke Power Co. 10⅞'s . . . . | Senior mortgage bonds due 2009 | Aa2 | 955 | 11.39 |
| United Brands 5.5's . . . . . . . | Convertible debentures due 1994 (converts into 18.18 shares) | Ba3 | 650 | 12.20 |

plan, the bonds are accorded a Aaa rating. Nevertheless, the bonds carry a market price of $700 because the interest rate at time of issue (6 percent) is below the demanded rate of interest of 10.6 percent in early 1986 for bonds of similar quality and maturity. Similar observations may be made for the other two bond issues.

## The Refunding Decision

Assume you are the financial vice president for a corporation that has issued bonds at 12.5 percent, only to witness a drop in interest rates to 10 percent. If you do not believe interest rates will go down further, and in fact believe that they will go back up, you may wish to redeem the expensive 12.5 percent bonds and to issue new debt at the prevailing 10 percent rate. This process is labeled a refunding operation. It is made feasible by the call provision which enables a corporation to buy back bonds at close to par, rather than at high market values, when interest rates are declining. Although long-term interest rates tended to move up in the 50s, 60s, 70s, and 80s, there were periods of decline in interest rates that provided an excellent environment for refunding. The mid-1980s was one such period.

### A Capital Budgeting Problem

The refunding decision involves outflows in the form of financing costs related to redeeming and reissuing securities, and inflows represented by savings in annual interest costs and some tax savings. In the present case, we shall assume that the corporation issued $10 million worth of 12.5 percent debt with a 25-year maturity and that the debt has been on the books for five years. The corporation now has the opportunity to buy back the old debt at 10 percent above par (the call premium) and to issue new debt at 10 percent interest with a 20-year life. The underwriting cost for the old issue was $125,000, and the underwriting cost for the new issue is $200,000. We shall also assume that the corporation is in the 40 percent tax bracket and uses a 6 percent discount rate for refunding decisions. Since the savings from a refunding decision are certain—unlike the savings from most other capital budgeting decisions—we use the aftertax cost of new debt as the discount rate rather than the more generalized cost of capital.[4] Actually, in this case the aftertax cost of new debt is 10 percent × (1 − Tax rate), or 6 percent.

Restatement of facts

| | Old Issue | New Issue |
|---|---|---|
| Size | $10,000,000 | $10,000,000 |
| Interest rate | 12.5% | 10% |
| Total life | 25 years | 20 years |
| Remaining life | 20 years | 20 years |
| Call premium | 10% | — |
| Underwriting costs | $125,000 | $200,000 |

| | |
|---|---|
| Tax bracket | 40% |
| Discount rate | 6% |

Let's go through the capital budgeting process of defining our outflows and inflows and determining the net present value.

### Step A—Outflow considerations

1. *Payment of call premium*—The first outflow is the 10 percent call premium on $10 million, or $1 million. This prepayment penalty is necessary to call in the original issue. Being an *out-of-pocket* tax-deductible expense, the $1 million cash expenditure will cost us only $600,000 on an aftertax basis. We multiply the expense by (1 − Tax rate) to get the aftertax cost.

| | |
|---|---|
| Net cost of call premium | $600,000 |

2. *Underwriting cost on new issue*—The second outflow is the $200,000 underwriting cost on the new issue. The actual cost is somewhat less because the payment is tax deductible, though the write-off must be spread over the life of the bond. While the actual $200,000 is being spent now, equal tax deductions of $10,000 a year will take place over the next 20 years (in a manner similar to depreciation).

[4] A minority opinion would be that there is sufficient similarity between the bond refunding decision and other capital budgeting decisions to disallow any specialized treatment. Also, note that although the bondholders must still bear some risk of default, for which they are compensated, the corporation assumes no risk.

The tax savings from a *noncash* write-off equal the amount times the tax rate. For a company in the 40 percent tax bracket, $10,000 of annual tax deductions will provide $4,000 of tax savings each year for the next 20 years. The present value of these savings is the present value of a $4,000 annuity for 20 years at 6 percent interest:

$$\$4,000 \times 11.470\ (n = 20,\ i = 6\%) = \$45,880$$

The net cost of underwriting the new issue is the actual expenditure now, minus the present value of future tax savings:

| | |
|---|---|
| Actual expenditure | $200,000 |
| − PV of future tax savings | 45,880 |
| Net cost of underwriting expense on the new issue | $154,120 |

**Step B—Inflow considerations**

The major inflows in the refunding decision are related to the reduction of annual interest expense and the immediate write-off of the underwriting cost on the old issue.

3. *Cost savings in lower interest rates*—The corporation will enjoy a 2.5 percent drop in interest rates, from 12.5 percent to 10 percent, on $10 million of bonds.

| | |
|---|---|
| 12.5% × $10,000,000 | $1,250,000 |
| 10% × $10,000,000 | 1,000,000 |
| Savings | $ 250,000 |

Since we are in the 40 percent tax bracket, this is equivalent to $150,000 of aftertax benefits per year for 20 years. We have taken the savings and multiplied by one minus the tax rate to get the aftertax benefits. Applying a 6 percent discount rate for a 20-year annuity:

$$\$150,000 \times 11.470\ (n = 20,\ i = 6\%) = \$1,720,500$$

| | |
|---|---|
| Cost savings in lower interest rates | $1,720,500 |

4. *Underwriting cost on old issue*—There is a further cost savings related to immediately writing off the remaining underwriting costs on the old bonds. Note that the initial amount of $125,000 was spent five years

ago and was to be written off for tax purposes over 25 years at $5,000 per year. Since five years have passed, $100,000 of old underwriting costs have not been amortized.

| | |
|---|---|
| Original amount | $125,000 |
| Written off over five years | 25,000 |
| Unamortized old underwriting costs | $100,000 |

There is a tax benefit associated with the immediate write-off of old underwriting costs which we shall consider shortly.

Note, however, that this is not a total gain. We would have gotten the $100,000 additional write-off eventually if we had not called in the old bonds. By calling them in now, we simply take the write-off sooner. If we extended the write-off over the remaining life, we would have taken $5,000 a year for 20 years. Discounting this value, we show:

$$\$5,000 \times 11.470\ (n = 20,\ i = 6\%) = \$57,350$$

Thus we are getting a write-off of $100,000 now rather than a present value of future write-offs of $57,350. The gain in immediate tax write-offs is $42,650. The tax savings from a *noncash* tax write-off equal the amount times the tax rate. Since we are in the 40 percent tax bracket, our savings from this write-off are $17,060.

| | |
|---|---|
| Net gain from the underwriting cost on the old issue | $17,060 |

### Step C—Net present value

We now compare our outflows and our inflows.

| *Outflows* | | *Inflows* | |
|---|---|---|---|
| 1. Net cost of call premium | $600,000 | 3. Cost savings in lower interest rates | $1,720,500 |
| 2. Net cost of underwriting expense on new issue | 154,120 | 4. Net gain from underwriting cost on old issue | 17,060 |
| | $754,120 | | $1,737,560 |

| | |
|---|---|
| Present value of inflows | $1,737,560 |
| Present value of outflows | 754,120 |
| Net present value | $ 983,440 |

The refunding decision has a positive net present value, suggesting that interest rates have dropped to a sufficiently low level to indicate refunding is in order. The only question is, will interest rates go lower—indicating an even better time for refunding? This is a consideration that all firms must face, and there is no easy answer.

A number of other factors could be plugged into the problem. For example, there could be overlapping time periods in the refunding procedure when both issues are outstanding and the firm is paying double interest (hopefully for less than a month). The dollar amount, however, tends to be quite small and is not included in the analysis.

In working problems, the student should have minimum difficulty if he or she follows the four suggested calculations. Note, by way of review, that in each of the four calculations we had the following tax implications:

1. Payment of call premium—the cost equals the amount times (1 − Tax rate) for this *cash tax deductible expense*.
2. Underwriting costs on new issue—we pay an amount now and then amortize it over the life of the bond for tax purposes. This subsequent amortization is similar to depreciation and represents a *noncash write-off* of a tax-deductible expense. The tax savings from the amortization are equal to the amount times the tax rate.
3. Cost savings in lower interest rates—cost savings are like any form of income, and we will retain the cost savings times (1 − Tax rate).
4. Underwriting cost on old issue—once again, the writing off of underwriting costs represents a *noncash write-off* of a tax-deductible expense. The tax savings from the amortization are equal to the amount times the tax rate.

## Innovative Forms of Bond Financing

As interest rates continued to show increasing volatility in the late 70s and early 80s, two innovative forms of bond financing became very popular. We shall examine the zero-coupon rate bond and the floating rate bond.

The zero-coupon rate bond, as the name implies, does not pay interest. It is, however, sold at a deep discount from face value. The return to the investor is the difference between the investor's cost and the face value received at the end of the life of the bond. For example, in early 1982 BankAmerica Corporation offered $1,000 zero-coupon rate bonds with maturities of 5, 8, and 10 years. The 5-year bonds were sold for $500, the 8-year bonds for $333.33, and the 10-year bonds for $250. All three provided an initial yield to maturity (through gain in value) of approximately 14.75 percent. The most dramatic case of a zero-coupon bond was an issue offered by PepsiCo, Inc., in 1982, in which the maturities ranged from 6 to 30 years. The 30-year $1,000 par value issue could be purchased for $26.43, providing a yield of approximately 12.75 percent. The purchase price per bond of $26.43 represents only 2.643 percent of the par value. A million dollars worth of these 30-year bonds could be initially purchased for a mere $26,430.

The advantage to the corporation is that there is immediate cash inflow to the corporation, without any outflow until the bonds mature. Furthermore, the difference between the initial bond price and the maturity value may be amortized for tax purposes by the corporation over the life of the bond. This means that the corporation will be taking annual deductions without current cash outflow.

From the investor's viewpoint, the zero-coupon bonds allow him to lock in a multiplier of the initial investment. For example, an investor may know that he will get four times his or her investment in 10 (or perhaps 12) years. The major drawback is that the annual increase in the value of the bonds is taxable as ordinary income as it accrues even though the bondholder does not have his or her return until maturity. For this reason most investors in zero-coupon rate bonds have tax-exempt or deferred status (pension funds, foundations, charitable organizations, Individual Retirement Accounts, etc.).

The prices of the bonds tend to be highly volatile because of changes in interest rates. Even though the bonds provide no annual interest payment, there is still an initial yield to maturity that may prove to be too high or too low with changes in the marketplace.

In August of 1982, Merrill Lynch and other brokerage houses began offering a variation of the zero-coupon rate bond through selling future interests in government securities. The securities, which are held in custody for the benefit of investors, are sold at a fraction of face value and ultimately redeemed at full value. The investor receives a multiple of the original investment and no interest, or interest which is deferred to the end of the life of the security. These securities tend to be long term (20–30 years).

A second type of innovative bond issue is the floating rate bond (already quite popular in European capital markets). In this case, instead of a change in the price of the bond, the interest rate paid on the bond changes with market conditions (usually weekly). Thus a bond that was initially issued to pay 13 percent may lower the interest payments to 10 percent during some years and raise them to 16 percent in others. The interest rate is usually tied to some overall market rate, such as the yield on Treasury bonds (perhaps 120 percent of the going yield on long-term Treasury bonds).

The advantage to the investor is that he or she has a constant (or almost constant) market value for the security even though interest rates vary. The one exception that can cause a change to this principle is that floating rate bonds often have broad limits that interest payments cannot exceed. For example, the interest rate on a 13 percent initial offering may not be allowed to go over 20 percent or below 6 percent. If long-term interest rates dictated an interest payment of 22 percent, the payment would still remain at 20 percent. This could cause some short-term loss in market value. To date, floating rate bonds have been relatively free of this problem.

To keep matters in perspective, zero-coupon rate bonds and floating rate bonds still represent a relatively small percentage of the total market of new debt offerings. Nevertheless, they are gaining in importance and should be part of a basic understanding of long-term debt instruments.

## Advantages and Disadvantages of Debt

The financial manager must consider whether debt will contribute to or detract from the firm's operations. In certain industries, such as the airlines, very heavy debt utilization is a way of life, whereas in other industries (drugs, photographic equipment) reliance is placed on other forms of capital.

### Benefits of Debt

The advantages of debt may be enumerated as:

1. Interest payments are tax deductible. Because the corporate tax rate approaches 50 percent, the effective aftertax cost of interest is but half the dollar amount expended.

2. The financial obligation is clearly specified and of a fixed nature (with the exception of floating rate bonds). Contrast this with selling an ownership interest in which stockholders have open-end participation in the sharing of profits.
3. In an inflationary economy, debt may be paid back with "cheaper dollars." A $1,000 bond obligation may be repaid in 10 or 20 years with dollars that have shrunk in value by 50 or 60 percent. In terms of "real dollars," or purchasing power equivalents, one might argue that the corporation should be asked to repay something in excess of $2,000. Presumably, high interest rates in inflationary periods compensate the lender for loss in purchasing power, but this is not always the case.
4. The use of debt, up to a prudent point, may lower the cost of capital to the firm. To the extent that debt does not strain the risk position of the firm, its low aftertax cost may aid in reducing the weighted overall cost of financing to the firm.

### Drawbacks of Debt

Finally, we must consider the disadvantages of debt:

1. Interest and principal payment obligations are set by contract and must be met regardless of the economic position of the firm.
2. Bond indenture agreements may place burdensome restrictions on the firm, such as maintenance of working capital at a given level, limits on future debt offerings, and guidelines for dividend policy. Although bondholders generally do not have the right to vote, they may take virtual control of the firm if important indenture provisions are not met.
3. Utilized beyond a given point, debt may serve as a depressant on outstanding common stock values.

### Eurobond Market

A final item of interest in the bond market is the Eurobond. A Eurobond takes us out of the purely domestic framework and into foreign markets. It may be defined as a bond payable in the borrower's currency but sold outside the borrower's country, usually by an international syndicate. An example might be a bond of a U.S. corporation, payable in dollars and sold in London, Paris, or Frankfurt. Disclosure requirements in the Eurobond market are less demanding than those of the Securities and Exchange Commission or other domestic regulatory agencies. Investors in Eurobonds are generally not able to rely on bond-rating agencies, though Moody's and Standard & Poor's have been rating selected Eurobond issues for a fee.

## Leasing as a Form of Debt

When a corporation contracts to lease an oil tanker or a computer and signs a noncancelable, long-term agreement, the transaction has all the characteristics of a debt obligation. Long-term leasing was not recognized as a debt obligation in the early post-World War II period, but since the mid-60s there has been a strong movement by the accounting profession to force companies to fully divulge all information about leasing obligations and to indicate the equivalent debt characteristics.

This position was made official for financial reporting purposes as a result of *Statement No. 13*, issued by the Financial Accounting Standards Board (FASB) in November 1976. In essence, this statement said that certain types of leases must be shown as long-term obligations on the financial statements of the firm. Prior to FASB *Statement No. 13*, lease obligations could merely be divulged in footnotes to financial statements and large lease obligations did not have to be included in the debt structure (except for the upcoming payment). Consider the case of firm ABC, whose balance sheet is shown in Table 16–5.

Prior to the issuance of FASB *Statement No. 13*, a footnote to the financial statements might have indicated a lease obligation of $12

**Table 16–5**
**Balance sheet**
**($ millions)**

| | | | |
|---|---|---|---|
| Current assets | $ 50 | Current liabilities | $ 50 |
| Fixed assets | 150 | Long-term liabilities | 50 |
| | | Total liabilities | $100 |
| | | Stockholders' equity | 100 |
| Total assets | $200 | Total liabilities and stockholders' equity | $200 |

million a year for the next 15 years, with a present value of $100 million dollars. With the issuance of FASB *Statement No. 13,* this information has, of necessity, been moved directly to the balance sheet, as indicated in Table 16–6.

**Table 16–6**
**Revised balance sheet**
**($ millions)**

| | | | |
|---|---|---|---|
| Current assets | $ 50 | Current liabilities | $ 50 |
| Fixed assets | 150 | Long-term liabilities | 50 |
| *Leased property under capital lease | 100 | *Obligation under capital lease | 100 |
| | | Total liabilities | 200 |
| | | Stockholders' equity | 100 |
| Total assets | $300 | Total liabilities and stockholders' equity | $300 |

We see that both a new asset and a new liability have been created, as indicated by the asterisks. The essence of this treatment is that a long-term, noncancelable lease is tantamount to purchasing the asset with borrowed funds, and this should be reflected on the balance sheet. Note that between the original balance sheet (Table 16–5) and the revised balance sheet (Table 16–6) the total-debt-to-total-assets ratio has gone from 50 percent to 66.7 percent.

$$\textit{Original:}\quad \frac{\text{Total debt}}{\text{Total assets}} = \frac{\$100 \text{ million}}{\$200 \text{ million}} = 50\%$$

$$\textit{Revised:}\quad \frac{\text{Total debt}}{\text{Total assets}} = \frac{\$200 \text{ million}}{\$300 \text{ million}} = 66.7\%$$

Though this represents a substantial increase in the ratio, the impact on the firm's credit rating or stock price may be minimal. To the extent that the financial markets are efficient, the information was *already* known by analysts who took the data from footnotes or other sources and made their own adjustments. Nevertheless, corporate financial officers fought long, hard, and unsuccessfully to keep the lease obligation off the balance sheet. They tend to be much less convinced about the efficiency of the marketplace.

## Capital Lease versus Operating Lease

Actually, not all leases must be capitalized (present-valued) and placed on the balance sheet. It is only under circumstances in which substantially all the benefits and risks of ownership are transferred in a lease that this treatment is necessary. Under these circumstances, we have a *capital* (or financing) lease. Identification as a capital lease and the attendant financial treatment are required whenever any *one* of the four following conditions is present:

1. The arrangement transfers ownership of the property to the lessee (the leasing party) by the end of the lease term.
2. The lease contains a bargain purchase price at the end of the lease. The option price will have to be sufficiently low so that exercise of the option appears reasonably certain.
3. The lease term is equal to 75 percent or more of the estimated life of the leased property.
4. The present value of the minimum lease payments equals 90 percent or more of the fair value of the leased property at the inception of the lease.[5]

A lease that does not meet any of these four criteria is not regarded as a *capital* lease, but as an *operating* lease. An operating lease is usually short term and is often cancelable at the option of the lessee. Furthermore, the lessor (the owner of the asset) may provide for the maintenance and upkeep of the asset, since he is likely to get it back. An operating lease does not require the *capitalization*, or presentation, of the full obligation on the balance sheet. Operating leases are used most frequently with such assets as automobiles and office equipment, while capital leases include oil drilling equipment, airplanes and rail equipment, certain forms of real estate, and other long-term assets. The greatest volume of leasing obligations is represented by capital leases.

---

[5]The discount rate used for this test is the leasing firm's new cost of borrowing or the lessor's (the firm that owns the asset) implied rate of return under the lease. The lower of the two must be used when both are known.

## Income Statement Effect

The capital lease calls not only for present-valuing the lease obligation on the balance sheet but also for treating the arrangement for income statement purposes as if it were somewhat similar to a purchase-borrowing arrangement. Thus, under a capital lease the intangible asset account shown in Table 16–6 as "Leased property under capital lease" is amortized or written off over the life of the lease with an annual expense deduction. Also, the liability account shown in Table 16–6 as "Obligation under capital lease" is written off through regular amortization, with an implied interest expense on the remaining balance. Thus, for financial reporting purposes the annual deductions are amortization of the asset, plus implied interest expense on the remaining present value of the liability. Though the actual development of these values and accounting rules is best deferred to an accounting course, the finance student should understand the close similarity between a capital lease and borrowing to purchase an asset, for financial reporting purposes.

An operating lease, on the other hand, usually calls for an annual expense deduction equal to the lease payment, with no specific amortization, as is indicated in Appendix 16B (Lease versus Purchase Decision) at the end of this chapter.

## Advantages of Leasing

Why is leasing so popular? It has emerged as a $100 billion industry, with such firms as Clark Equipment, Citicorp, and U.S. Leasing International providing an enormous amount of financing. Major reasons for the popularity of leasing include the following:

1. The lessee may lack sufficient funds or the credit capability to purchase the asset from a manufacturer, who is willing, however, to accept a lease agreement or to arrange a lease obligation with a third party.
2. The provisions of a lease obligation may be substantially less restrictive than those of a bond indenture.
3. There may be no down payment requirement, as would generally be the case in the purchase of an asset (leasing allows for a larger indirect loan).

4. The lessor may possess particular expertise in a given industry—allowing for expert product selection, maintenance, and eventual resale. Through this process, the negative effects of obsolescence may be lessened.
5. Creditor claims on certain types of leases, such as real estate, are restricted in bankruptcy and reorganization proceedings. Leases on chattels (non-real estate items) have no such limitation.

There are also some tax factors to be considered. Where one party to a lease is in a higher tax bracket than the other party, certain tax advantages, such as an investment tax credit, may be better utilized. For example, a wealthy party may purchase an asset and take an investment tax credit, then lease the asset to another party in a lower tax bracket for actual use. Also, lease payments on the use of land are tax-deductible, whereas landownership does not allow a similar deduction for depreciation.

Finally, a firm may wish to engage in a sale-leaseback arrangement in which assets already owned by the lessee are sold to the lessor and then leased back. This process provides the lessee with an infusion of capital, while allowing the lessee to continue to use the asset. Even though the dollar costs of a leasing arrangement are often higher than the dollar costs of owning an asset, the advantages cited above may outweigh the direct cost factors.

Tax credits and deductions associated with leasing transactions became particularly popular under the 1981 Economic Recovery Tax Act. The Act contained "safe harbor" leasing provisions in which leasing transactions could be arranged for no economic purpose other than tax reduction.[6] These so called "safe harbor" leasing provisions expired in December of 1983 as mandated by the 1982 Tax Equity and Fiscal Responsibility Act.

---

[6]The typical pattern was for an unprofitable company to buy an asset and sell it to a highly profitable company and then lease it back. The profitable company generally paid the unprofitable company a minimum amount of 10 percent in cash and the payments on the balance of the note were assumed to equal to the lease payments owed by the unprofitable company. This was a *wash lease* that required no subsequent lease payments and no economic justification under the "safe harbor" provisions. Sales and leasebacks are still allowable under the law, but because there are no longer "safe harbor" provisions, they must have economic justification.

## Summary

The use of debt financing by corporations has grown very rapidly since the end of World War II, and the quality of corporate debt coverage has deteriorated.

Corporate bonds may be secured by a lien on a specific asset or may carry an unsecured designation, indicating that the bondholder possesses a general claim against the corporation. A special discussion of the hierarchy of claims for firms in financial distress is presented in Appendix 16A.

Bond prices have been in a steady decline for the last four decades due to rising interest rates. Nevertheless, cyclical downturns in interest rates have afforded an excellent opportunity for refunding, that is, replacing high-interest-rate bonds with lower-interest-rate bonds. This was particularly true in the mid-1980s. The financial manager must consider whether the savings in interest will compensate for the additional cost of calling in the old issue and selling a new one.

Finally, the long-term, noncancelable lease should be considered as a special debt form available to the corporation. It is capitalized on the balance sheet to represent both a debt and an asset account and is amortized on a regular basis. Leasing offers a means of financing in which lessor expertise and other financial benefits can be imparted to the lessee (leasing party).

A lease versus purchase decision for an operating lease is presented in Appendix 16B.

## List of Terms

**par value**
**maturity date**
**indenture**
**secured debt**
**mortgage agreement**
**unsecured debt**
**debenture**
**subordinated debenture**
**serial payments**
**sinking fund**
**call feature**
**coupon rate**
**current yield**
**yield to maturity**
**bond ratings**
**refunding**
**capital lease**
**operating lease**
**Eurobond**
**zero-coupon rate bond**
**floating rate bond**

## Discussion Questions

1. Corporate debt has been expanding very dramatically since World War II. What has been the impact on interest coverage, particularly since 1967?
2. What are some of the basic features of bond agreements?
3. What is the difference between a bond agreement and a bond indenture?
4. Discuss the relationship between the coupon rate (original interest rate at time of issue) on a bond and its security provisions.
5. Take the following list of securities and arrange them in order of their priority of claims.

   | | |
   |---|---|
   | Preferred stock | Senior debenture |
   | Subordinated debenture | Senior secured debt |
   | Common stock | Junior secured debt |

6. Which method of "bond repayment" reduces debt and increases the amount of common stock outstanding?
7. What is the purpose of serial repayments and sinking funds?
8. Under what circumstances would a call on a bond be exercised by a corporation? What is the purpose of a deferred call?
9. Discuss the relationship between bond prices and interest rates. What impact do changing interest rates have on the price of long-term bonds versus short-term bonds?
10. What is the difference between the following yields: coupon rate, current yield, yield to maturity?
11. How does the bond rating affect the interest rate paid by a corporation on its bonds?
12. Bonds of different risk classes will have a spread between their interest rates. Is this spread always the same? Why?
13. Explain how the bond refunding problem is similar to a capital budgeting decision?

14. What cost of capital is generally used in evaluating a bond refunding decision? Why?

15. Discuss the advantages and disadvantages of debt.

16. Explain how the zero-coupon rate bond provides return to the investor. What are the advantages to the corporation?

17. Explain how floating rate bonds can save the investor from potential embarrassments in portfolio valuation.

18. What do we mean by capitalizing lease payments?

19. Explain the close parallel between a capital lease and the borrow–purchase decision from the viewpoint of both the balance sheet and the income statement.

## Problems

1. The Milstead Corporation has a bond outstanding with a $90 annual interest payment, a market price of $800, and a maturity date in five years. (Assume that the par value of bonds in all the following problems is $1,000 unless otherwise specified.)
   Find the following:
   *a.* The coupon rate.
   *b.* The current rate.
   *c.* The approximate yield to maturity.

2. The Fletcher Corporation has a bond outstanding with a coupon rate of 14 percent, a maturity of eight years, a par value of $1,000, and a market price of $1,200.
   Compute the yield to maturity, using the approximation method.

3. The Lincoln Investment Fund buys 900 bonds of the Nichols Corporation through its broker. The bonds pay 11 percent annual interest. The yield to maturity (market rate of interest) is 14 percent. The bonds have a 25-year maturity.
   Using an assumption of semiannual interest payments:
   *a.* Compute the price of a bond (refer to "semiannual interest and bond prices" in Chapter 10 for review if necessary).
   *b.* Compute the total value of the 900 bonds.

**4.** The yield to maturity for 20-year bonds is as follows for four different bond rating categories:

| | | | |
|---|---|---|---|
| Aaa | 11.3% | Aa2 | 12.0% |
| Aa1 | 11.6% | Aa3 | 12.3% |

The bonds of Hamilton Corporation were rated as Aa1 and issued at par a few weeks ago. The bonds have just been downgraded to Aa2.

Determine the new price of the bonds, assuming a 20-year maturity and semiannual interest payments.

**5.** A previously issued A2, 20-year industrial bond provides a return one fifth higher than the prime interest rate of 10 percent. Previously issued public utility bonds provide a yield of three eighths of a percentage point higher than previously issued industrial bonds. Finally, new issues of A2 public utility bonds pay one fourth of a percentage point more than previously issued public utility bonds.

What should the interest rate be on a newly issued A2 public utility bond?

**6.** A 20-year, $1,000 par value zero-coupon bond is to be issued to yield 11 percent.

*a.* What should be the initial price of the bond? (Take the present value of $1,000 for 20 years at 11 percent, using Appendix B.)

*b.* If immediately upon issue, interest rates dropped to 9 percent, what would be the value of the zero-coupon rate bond?

*c.* If immediately upon issue, interest rates increased to 13 percent, what would be the value of the zero-coupon rate bond?

**7.** A $1,000 par value bond was issued five years ago, paying 12 percent interest. The bond has 15 years remaining. Interest rates on similar debt obligations are now 10 percent in the market.

*a.* What is the current price of the bond? (Look up the answer in Table 16–3.)

*b.* Assume Mr. Sharp bought the bond three years ago when it had a price of $970. He paid 30 percent of the purchase price in cash and borrowed the rest (known as buying on margin). He used the interest payments from the bond to cover the interest costs on the loan. By what percentage did the bond price increase from the time it was purchased by Mr. Sharp to the present (value computed in part *a*)?

*c.* What is Mr. Sharp's percentage gain on his cash investment?

**8.** Ten years ago the Wilshire Corporation borrowed $5,000,000. Since then, cumulative inflation has been 60 percent (approximately 5 percent per year).

*a.* When the firm repays the original $5,000,000 loan this year, what will be the effective purchasing power of the $5,000,000? (Hint: divide the loan amount by one plus cumulative inflation.)

*b.* In order to maintain the original $5,000,000 purchasing power, how much should the lender be repaid?

*c.* If the lender knows he will only receive $5,000,000 in payment after 10 years, how might he be compensated for the loss in purchasing power?

**9.** The Delta Corporation has a $20 million bond obligation outstanding which it is considering refunding. Though the bonds were initially issued at 13 percent, the interest rates on similar issues have declined to 11.5 percent. The bonds were originally for 20 years and have 16 years remaining. The new issue would be for 16 years. There is a 9 percent call premium on the old issue. The underwriting cost on the new $20,000,000 issue is $560,000 and the underwriting cost on the old issue was $400,000. The company is in a 40 percent tax bracket, and it will use a 7 percent discount rate (rounded aftertax cost of debt) to analyze the refunding decision.

Should the old issue be refunded with new debt?

**10.** The Hopkins Corporation has $60 million of bonds outstanding which were issued at a coupon rate of 14⅛ percent seven years ago. Interest rates have fallen to 13 percent. Mr. Carlson, the vice president of finance, does not expect rates to fall any further. The bonds have 18 years left to maturity, and Mr. Carlson would like to refund the bonds with a new issue of equal amount having 18 years to maturity. The Hopkins Corporation has a tax rate of 40 percent. The underwriting cost on the old issue was 1.25 percent of the total bond value. The underwriting cost on the new issue will be 1.8 percent of the total bond value. The original bond indenture contained a five-year protection against a call, with a 10 percent call premium starting in the sixth year and scheduled to decline by ½ percent each year thereafter. Consider the bond to be seven years old for purposes of computing the premium, with one year of reduction. Assume the discount rate is equal to the aftertax cost of debt rounded to the nearest whole number.

Should the Hopkins Corporation refund the old issue?

**11.** In Problem 10, what would be the aftertax cost of the call premium at the end of the 15th year (in dollar value)?

**12.** The Deluxe Corporation has just signed a 120-month lease on an asset with a 15-year life. The minimum lease payments are $2,000 per month ($24,000 per year) and are to be discounted back to the present at a 7 percent annual discount rate. The estimated fair value of the property is $175,000.

Should the lease be recorded as a capital lease or as an operating lease?

**13.** The Ellis Corporation has heavy lease commitments. Prior to FASB *Statement No. 13,* it merely footnoted lease obligations in the balance sheet, which appeared as follows:

| In $ millions | | In $ millions | |
|---|---|---|---|
| Current assets | $ 50 | Current liabilities | $ 10 |
| Fixed assets | 50 | Long-term liabilities | 30 |
| | | Total liabilities | $ 40 |
| | | Stockholders' equity | 60 |
| Total assets | $100 | Total liabilities and stockholders' equity | $100 |

The footnotes stated that the company had $10 million in annual capital lease obligations for the next 20 years.

*a*. Discount these lease obligations back to the present at a 6 percent discount rate (round to nearest million dollars).

*b*. Construct a revised balance sheet that includes lease obligations, as in Table 16–6.

*c*. Compute total debt to total assets on the original and revised balance sheets.

*d*. Compute total debt to equity on the original and revised balance sheets.

*e*. In an efficient capital market environment, should FASB *Statement No. 13* consequences, as viewed in the answers to parts *c* and *d*, change stock prices and credit ratings?

*f*. Comment on management's perception of market efficiency (the viewpoint of the financial officer).

**14.** The Hegan Corporation plans to lease a $900,000 asset to the Doby Corporation. The lease will be for 10 years.

*a*. If the Hegan Corporation desires a 12 percent return on their investment, how much should the annual lease payments be?

*b*. If the Hegan Corporation is able to take a 10 percent investment tax credit and will pass the benefit along to the Doby Corporation in the form of lower lease payments (related to the Hegan Corporation's lower initial net cost), how much should the revised leased payments be? Continue to assume the Hegan Corporation desires a 12 percent return on the 10-year lease.

## Selected References

Ang, James S. "The Two Faces of Bond Refunding." *Journal of Finance* 30 (June 1975), pp. 869–74.

Bogen, Jules I., ed. *Financial Handbook,* 4th ed. New York: Ronald, 1968, sec. 14.

Boot, John C. G., and George M. Frankfurter. "The Dynamics of Corporate Debt Management, Decision Rules, and Some Empirical Evidence." *Journal of Financial and Quantitative Analysis* 7 (September 1972), pp. 1957–66.

Bowlin, Oswald D. "The Refunding Decision: Another Special Case in Capital Budgeting." *Journal of Finance* 21 (March 1966), pp. 55–68.

Brennan, Michael J., and Eduardo S. Schwartz. "Bond Pricing and Market Efficiency." *Financial Analysts Journal* 38 (September–October 1982), pp. 49–56.

Brick, Ivan, and S. Abraham Ravid. "On the Relevance of Debt Maturity Structure." *Journal of Finance* 40 (December 1985), pp. 1423–37.

Collins, Robert A. "An Empirical Comparison of Bankruptcy Prediction Models." *Financial Management* 9 (Summer 1980), pp. 52–57.

Donaldson, Gordon. "New Framework for Corporate Debt Policy." *Harvard Business Review* 40 (March–April 1962), pp. 117–31.

Everett, Edward. "Subordinated Debt—Nature and Enforcement." *Business Lawyer* 20 (July 1965), pp. 953–87.

Federal Reserve Bank of Cleveland. "Direct Placement of Corporate Debt." *Economic Review* (March 1965), pp. 3–18.

Ferri, Michael G. "An Empirical Examination of the Determinants of Bond Yield Spreads." *Financial Management* 7 (August 1978), pp. 40–46.

Francis, Jack Clark. *Investment Analysis and Management.* New York: McGraw-Hill, 1972, chap. 1.

Hawkins, David M., and Mary M. Wehle. *Accounting for Leases.* New York: Financial Executives Research Foundation, 1973.

Jen, Frank C., and James E. Wert. "The Deferred Call Provision and Corporate Bond Yields." *Journal of Financial and Quantitative Analysis* 3 (June 1968), pp. 157–69.

Kolodny, Richard. "The Refunding Decision in Near Perfect Markets." *Journal of Finance* 29 (December 1974), pp. 1467–78.

Lindvall, John R. "New Issue Corporate Bonds, Seasoned Market Efficiency, and Yield Spreads." *Journal of Finance* 32 (September 1977), pp. 1057–67.

Pinches, George E., and Kent A. Mingo. "The Role of Subordination and Industrial Bond Ratings." *Journal of Finance* 30 (March 1975), pp. 201–6.

Rao, Ramesh K. S. "The Impact of Yield Changes on the Systematic Risk of Bonds." *Journal of Financial and Quantitative Analysis* 17 (March 1982), pp. 115–27.

Schachner, Leopold. "The New Accounting for Leases." *Financial Executive* (February 1978), pp. 40–47.

Sibley, A. M. "Some Evidence on the Cash Flow Effects of Bond Refunding." *Financial Management* 3 (Autumn 1974), pp. 50–53.

Van Horne, James C. *The Function and Analysis of Capital Market Rates.* Englewood Cliffs, N.J.: Prentice-Hall, 1970, chaps. 4–6.

Winn, Willis J., and Arleigh Hess, Jr. "The Value of the Call Privilege." *Journal of Finance* 14 (May 1959), pp. 182–95.

## Appendix 16A: Financial Alternatives for Distressed Firms

A firm may be in financial distress because of *technical insolvency* or *bankruptcy.* The first term refers to a firm's inability to pay its bills as they come due. Thus a firm may be technically insolvent even though it has a positive net worth; there simply may not be sufficient liquid assets to meet current obligations. The second term, bankruptcy, indicates that the market value of a firm's assets are less than its liabilities and the firm has a negative net worth. Under the law, either technical insolvency or bankruptcy may be adjudged as a financial failure of the business firm.

There are also many firms that do not fall into either category, but are still suffering from extreme financial difficulties. Perhaps they are rapidly approaching a situation in which they can not pay their bills or their net worth will soon be negative.

Firms in the types of financial difficulty discussed in the first two paragraphs may participate in out-of-court settlements or in-court settlements through formal bankruptcy proceedings under the National Bankruptcy Act.

Out-of-court settlements, where possible, allow the firm and its creditors to bypass certain lengthy and expensive legal procedures. Of course, if an agreement cannot be reached on a voluntary basis between a firm and its creditors, in-court procedures will be necessary.

## Out-of-Court Settlement

Out-of-court settlements may take many forms. Four alternatives will be examined. The first is an *extension* in which creditors agree to allow the firm more time to meet its financial obligations. A new repayment schedule will be developed, subject to the acceptance of the creditors.

A second alternative is a *composition*, under which creditors agree to accept a fractional settlement of their original claim. They may be willing to do this because they believe the firm is unable to meet its total obligations and they wish to avoid formal bankruptcy procedures. In the case of either a proposed extension or a composition, some creditors may not agree to go along with the arrangements. If their claims are relatively small, major creditors may allow them to be paid off immediately and in full, in order to hold the agreement together. If their claims are large, no out-of-court settlement may be possible, and formal bankruptcy proceedings may be necessary.

A third type of out-of-court settlement may take the form of a *creditor committee* established to run the business. Here the parties involved judge that management can no longer effectively conduct the affairs of the firm. Once the creditors' claims have been partially or fully settled, a new management team may be brought in to replace the creditor committee. Of course, the outgoing management may be willing to accept the imposition of a creditor committee only when formal bankruptcy proceedings appear likely and they wish to avoid that stigma. There are also circumstances in which creditors are unwilling to form such a committee because they fear lawsuits from other dissatisfied creditors or from common or preferred stockholders.

A fourth type of out-of-court settlement is an *assignment,* in which liquidation of assets takes place without going through formal court action. In order to affect an assignment, creditors must agree on liquidation values and the relative priority of claims. This is not an easy task.

In actuality, there may be combinations of two or more of the above-described out-of-court procedures. For example, there may be an extension as well as a composition, or a creditor committeee may help to establish one or more of the alternatives.

## In-Court Settlements—Formal Bankruptcy

When it is apparent that an out-of-court settlement cannot be reached, the next step is formal bankruptcy. Bankruptcy proceedings may be initiated voluntarily by the company or, alternatively, by creditors.

Once the firm falls under formal bankruptcy proceedings, a referee is appointed by the court to oversee the activities. The referee becomes the arbitrator of the proceedings, whose actions and decisions are final, subject only to review by the court. A trustee will also be selected to properly determine the assets and liabilities of the firm and to carry out a plan of reorganization or liquidation for the firm.

### Reorganization

If the firm is to be reorganized (under the Bankruptcy Act's Chapter 11 restructuring), the plan must prove to be fair and feasible. An *internal reorganization* calls for an evaluation of current management and their operating policies. If current management is shown to be incompetent, they will probably be discharged and replaced by new management. An evaluation and possible redesign of the current capital structure is also necessary. If the firm is top-heavy with debt (as is normally the case), alternate securities such as preferred or common stock may replace part of the debt.[1] Of course, it is imperative that any restructuring be fair to all parties involved.

An *external reorganization*, in which a merger partner is found for the firm, may also be considered. The surviving firm must be deemed strong enough to carry out the financial and management obligations of the joint entities. Old creditors and stockholders may be asked to make concessions to ensure that a feasible arrangement is established. Their motivation is that they hope to come out further ahead than if such a reorganization were not undertaken. Ideally, the firm should be merged with a strong firm in its own industry, although this is not always possible. The savings and loan and banking industries have been particularly adept at merging weaker firms with stronger firms within the industry.

## Liquidation

A liquidation or sell-off of assets may be recommended when an internal or external reorganization does not appear possible, and a determination is made that the assets of the firm are worth more in liquidation than through a reorganization. Priority of claims becomes extremely important in a liquidation because it is unlikely that all parties will be fully satisfied in their demands.

The priority of claims in a bankruptcy liquidation is as follows:

1. Cost of administering the bankruptcy procedures (lawyers get in line first).
2. Wages due workers if earned within three months of filing the bankruptcy petition. The maximum amount is $600 per worker.
3. Taxes due at the federal, state, or local level.
4. Secured creditors to the extent that designated assets are sold off to meet their claims. Secured claims that exceed the sales value of

[1] Another possibility is income bonds, in which interest is payable only if earned.

the pledged assets are placed in the same category as other general creditor claims.

5. General or unsecured creditors are next in line. Examples of claims in this category are those held by debenture (unsecured bond) holders, trade creditors, and bankers who have made unsecured loans.

   There may be senior and subordinated positions within category 5, indicating that subordinated debt holders must turn over their claims to senior debt holders until complete restitution is made to the higher ranked category. Subordinated debenture holders may keep the balance if anything is left over after that payment.
6. Preferred stockholders.
7. Common stockholders.

The priority of claims 4 through 7, is similar to that presented in Figure 16–2 of this chapter.

Let us examine a typical situation to determine "who" should receive "what" under a liquidation in bankruptcy. Assume the Mitchell Corporation has a book value and liquidation value as shown in Table 16A–1. Liabilities and stockholders' claims are also presented.

We see that the liquidation value of the assets is far less than the book value ($700,000 versus $1,300,000). Also, the liquidation value of the assets will not cover the total value of liabilities ($700,000 compared to $1,100,000). Since all liability claims will not be met, it is evident that lower-ranked preferred stockholders and common stockholders will receive nothing.

Before a specific allocation is made to the creditors (those with liability claims), the three highest priority levels in bankruptcy must first be covered. That would include the cost of administering the proceedings, allowable past wages due to workers, and overdue taxes. For the Mitchell Corporation, we shall assume these total $100,000. Since the liquidation value of assets was $700,000, that would leave $600,000 to cover creditor demands, as indicated in the left-hand column of Table 16A–2.

Before we attempt to allocate the values in the left-hand column of Table 16A–2 to the right-hand column, we must first identify any creditor claims that are secured by the pledge of a specific asset. In the present case, there is a first lien on the machinery and equipment of $200,000. Referring back to Table 16A–1, we observe that the machinery and equipment has a liquidation value of only $100,000.

**Table 16A–1**
**Financial data for the Mitchell Corporation**

*Assets*

| | *Book Value* | *Liquidation Value* |
|---|---|---|
| Accounts receivable | $ 200,000 | $160,000 |
| Inventory | 410,000 | 240,000 |
| Machinery and equipment | 240,000 | 100,000 |
| Building and plant | 450,000 | 200,000 |
| | $1,300,000 | $700,000 |

*Liabilities and Stockholders' Claims*

| | |
|---|---|
| Liabilities: | |
| Accounts payable | $ 300,000 |
| First lien, secured by machinery and equipment* | 200,000 |
| Senior unsecured debt | 400,000 |
| Subordinated debentures | 200,000 |
| Total liabilities | 1,100,000 |
| Stockholders' claims: | |
| Preferred stock | 50,000 |
| Common stock | 150,000 |
| Total stockholders' claims | 200,000 |
| Total liabilities and stockholders' claims | $1,300,000 |

*A lien represents a potential claim against property. The lien holder has a secured interest in the property.

**Table 16A–2**
**Asset values and claims**

| *Assets* | | *Creditor Claims* | |
|---|---|---|---|
| Asset values in liquidation | $700,000 | Accounts payable | $ 300,000 |
| Administrative costs, wages and taxes | − 100,000 | First lien, secured by machinery and equipment | 200,000 |
| Remaining asset values | $600,000 | Senior unsecured debt | 400,000 |
| | | Subordinated debentures | 200,000 |
| | | Total liabilities | $1,100,000 |

The secured debt holders will receive $100,000, with the balance of their claim placed in the same category as the unsecured debt holders. In Table 16A–3, we show asset values available for unsatisfied secured claims and unsecured debt (top portion) and the extent of the remaining claims (bottom portion).

**Table 16A–3**
**Asset values available for unsatisfied secured claims and unsecured debt holders—and their remaining claims**

| | |
|---|---|
| *Asset values* | |
| Asset values in liquidation | $700,000 |
| Administrative costs, wages and taxes | – 100,000 |
| Remaining asset values | 600,000 |
| Payment to secured creditors | – 100,000 |
| Amount available to unsatisfied secured claims and unsecured debt | $500,000 |
| *Remaining claims of unsatisfied secured debt and unsecured debt* | |
| Secured debt (unsatisfied first lien) | $ 100,000 |
| Accounts payable | 300,000 |
| Senior unsecured debt | 400,000 |
| Subordinated debentures | 200,000 |
| | $1,000,000 |

In comparing the available asset values and claims in Table 16A–3, it appears that the settlement on the remaining claims should be at a 50 percent rate ($500,000/$1,000,000). The allocation will take place in the manner presented in Table 16A–4.

Each category receives 50 percent as an initial allocation. However, the subordinated debenture holders must transfer their $100,000 initial allocation to the senior debt holders in recognition of their preferential position. The secured debt holders and those having accounts payable claims are not part of the senior-subordinated arrangement and thus hold their initial allocation position.

Finally, in Table 16A–5, we show the total amounts of claims, the amount received and the percent of the claim that was satisfied.

The $150,000 in column (3) for secured debt represents the $100,000 from the sale of machinery and equipment, and $50,000 from the

**Table 16A–4**
**Allocation procedures for unsatisfied secured claims and unsecured debt**

| (1)<br>Category | (2)<br>Amount of Claim | (3)<br>Initial Allocation (50%) | (4)<br>Amount Received |
|---|---|---|---|
| Secured debt (unsatisfied 1st lien) | $ 100,000 | $ 50,000 | $ 50,000 |
| Accounts payable | 300,000 | 150,000 | 150,000 |
| Senior unsecured debt | 400,000 | 200,000 | 300,000 |
| Subordinated debentures | 200,000 | 100,000 | 0 |
| | $1,000,000 | $500,000 | $500,000 |

**Table 16A–5**
**Payments and percent of claims**

| (1) Category | (2) Total Amount of Claim | (3) Amount Received | (4) Percent of Claim Satisfied |
|---|---|---|---|
| Secured debt (1st lien) . . . . | $200,000 | $150,000 | 75% |
| Accounts payable . . . . . . . . | 300,000 | 150,000 | 50 |
| Senior unsecured debt . . . . | 400,000 | 300,000 | 75 |
| Subordinated debentures . . . | 200,000 | 0 | 0 |

allocation process in Table 16A–4. The secured debt holders and senior unsecured debt holders come out on top (it is coincidental that they are equal). Furthermore, the subordinated debt holders, and as previously mentioned, the preferred and common stockholders receive nothing. Naturally, allocations in bankruptcy will vary from circumstance to circumstance. Working Problem 16A–1 will help to reinforce many of the liquidation procedure concepts discussed in this section.

## List of Terms

**technical insolvency**
**bankruptcy**
**extension**
**composition**
**assignment**
**internal reorganization**
**external reorganization**
**liquidation**

## Discussion Questions

**16A–1.** What is the difference between technical insolvency and bankruptcy?

**16A–2.** What are four types of out-of-court settlements? Briefly describe each.

**16A–3.** What is the difference between an internal reorganization and an external reorganization under formal bankruptcy procedures?

**16A–4.** What are the first three priority items under liquidation in bankruptcy?

## Problem

**16A–1.** The trustee in the bankruptcy settlement for Nogo Airlines lists the following book values and liquidation values for the assets of the corporation. Liabilities and stockholders' claims are also shown below.

*Assets*

| | *Book Value* | *Liquidation Value* |
|---|---|---|
| Accounts receivable | $1,400,000 | $1,200,000 |
| Inventory | 1,800,000 | 900,000 |
| Machinery and equipment | 1,100,000 | 600,000 |
| Building and plant | 4,200,000 | 2,500,000 |
| Total assets | $8,500,000 | $5,200,000 |

*Liabilities and Stockholders' Claims*

| | |
|---|---|
| Liabilities: | |
| Accounts payable | $2,800,000 |
| First lien, secured by machinery and equipment | 900,000 |
| Senior unsecured debt | 2,200,000 |
| Subordinated debenture | 1,700,000 |
| Total liabilities | 7,600,000 |
| Stockholders' claims: | |
| Preferred stock | 250,000 |
| Common stock | 650,000 |
| Total stockholders' claims | 900,000 |
| Total liabilities and stockholders' claims | $8,500,000 |

*a.* Compute the difference between the liquidation value of the assets and the liabilities.

*b.* Based on the answer to part *a*, will preferred stock or common stock participate in the distribution?

*c.* Assuming that the administrative costs of bankruptcy, workers' allowable wages, and unpaid taxes add up to $400,000, what is the total of remaining asset value available to cover secured and unsecured claims?

*d.* After the machinery and equipment is sold to partially cover the first lien secured claim, how much will be available from the remaining asset liquidation values to cover unsatisfied secured claims and unsecured debt?

*e*. List the remaining asset claims of unsatisfied secured debt holders and unsecured debt holders in a manner similar to that shown at the bottom portion of Table 16A–3.

*f*. Compute a ratio of your answers in part *d* and part *e*. This will indicate the initial allocation ratio.

*g*. List the remaining claims (unsatisfied secured and unsecured) and make an initial allocation and final allocation similar to that shown in Table 16A–4. Subordinated debenture holders may keep the balance after full payment is made to senior debt holders.

*h*. Show the relationship of amount received to total amount of claim in a similar fashion to that of Table 16A–5. (Remember to use the sales liquidation value for machinery and equipment plus the allocation amount in part *g* to arrive at the total received on secured debt).

## Appendix 16B: Lease versus Purchase Decision

The classic lease versus purchase decision does not fit a *capital* leasing decision given the passage of FASB *Statement No. 13* and the similar financial accounting and tax treatment accorded to a capital lease and borrowing to purchase. Nevertheless, the classic lease versus purchase decision is still appropriate for the short-term *operating* lease.

Assume a firm is considering the purchase of a \$5,000 asset with a five-year life or entering into two sequential operating leases, for two years and three years each. Under the operating leases, the annual payments would be \$1,250 on the first lease and \$1,800 on the second lease. If the firm purchased the asset, it would pay \$1,319 annually to amortize a \$5,000 loan over five years at 10 percent interest. This is based on the use of Appendix D for the present value of an annuity.

$$R = \frac{A}{IF_{pva}} = \frac{\$5{,}000}{3.791} = \$1{,}319 \ (n = 5,\ i = 10\%)$$

The firm is in a 40 percent tax bracket. In doing our analysis, we look first of all at the aftertax costs of the operating lease arrangements in Table 16B–1. The tax shield in column (2) indicates the amount

**Table 16B–1**
**Aftertax cost of operating leases**

| Year | (1) Payment | (2) Tax Shield 40% of (1) | (3) Aftertax Cost |
|---|---|---|---|
| 1 . . . . . . | $1,250 | $500 | $ 750 |
| 2 . . . . . . | 1,250 | 500 | 750 |
| 3 . . . . . . | 1,800 | 720 | 1,080 |
| 4 . . . . . . | 1,800 | 720 | 1,080 |
| 5 . . . . . . | 1,800 | 720 | 1,080 |
| | | | $4,740 |

that the lease payments will save us in taxes. In column (3) we see the net aftertax cost of the lease arrangement.

For the borrowing and purchasing decision, we must consider not only the amount of the payment but also separate out those items that are tax deductible. First we consider interest and then depreciation.

In Table 16B–2, we show an amortization table to pay off a $5,000 loan over four years at 10 percent interest with $1,319 annual payments. In column (1), we show the beginning balance for each year. This is followed by the annual payment in column (2). We then show the amount of interest we will pay on the beginning balance at a 10 percent rate in column (3). In column (4) we subtract the interest payment from the annual payment to determine how much is applied directly to the repayment of principal. In column (5) we subtract the repayment of principal from the beginning balance to get the year-end balance.

After determining our interest payment schedule, we look at the depreciation schedule that would apply to the borrow–purchase decision. Assuming five-year depreciation under the Accelerated Cost Re-

**Table 16B–2**
**Amortization table**

| Year | (1) Beginning Balance | (2) Annual Payment | (3) Annual Interest 10% of (1) | (4) Repayment on Principal (2) − (3) | (5) Ending Balance (1) − (4) |
|---|---|---|---|---|---|
| 1 . . . . | $5,000 | $1,319 | $500 | $ 819 | $4,181 |
| 2 . . . . | 4,181 | 1,319 | 418 | 901 | 3,280 |
| 3 . . . . | 3,280 | 1,319 | 328 | 991 | 2,289 |
| 4 . . . . | 2,289 | 1,319 | 229 | 1,090 | 1,199 |
| 5 . . . . | 1,199 | 1,319 | 120 | 1,199 | 0 |

covery System, the asset is depreciated at the rates indicated in Table 16B–3. No investment tax credit (ITC) is used in this analysis.

We now bring our interest and depreciation schedules together in Table 16B–4 to determine the aftertax cost, or cash outflow, associated with the borrow–purchase decision.

The interest and depreciation charges are tax-deductible expenses and provide a tax shield against other income. The total deductions in column (4) are multiplied by the tax rate of 40 percent to show the tax shield benefits in column (5). In column (6) we subtract the tax shield from the payments to get the net aftertax cost, or cash outflow.

Finally, we compare the cash outflows from leasing to the cash outflows from borrowing and purchasing. To consider the time value of money, we discount the annual values at an interest rate of 6 percent. This is the aftertax cost of debt to the firm, and it is computed by multiplying the interest rate of 10 percent by (1 − Tax rate). Because the costs associated with both leasing and borrowing are contractual and certain, we use the aftertax cost of debt as the discount rate rather

**Table 16B–3**
**Depreciation schedule**

| Year | Depreciation Base | Depreciation Percentage | Depreciation |
|---|---|---|---|
| 1 | $5,000 | 15% | $ 750 |
| 2 | 5,000 | 22 | 1,100 |
| 3 | 5,000 | 21 | 1,050 |
| 4 | 5,000 | 21 | 1,050 |
| 5 | 5,000 | 21 | 1,050 |
| | | | $5,000 |

**Table 16B–4**
**Aftertax cost of borrow–purchase**

| Year | (1) Payment | (2) Interest | (3) Depreciation | (4) Total Tax Deductions | (5) Tax Shield 40% × (4) | (6) Net Aftertax Cost (1) − (5) |
|---|---|---|---|---|---|---|
| 1 | $1,319 | $500 | $ 750 | $1,250 | $500 | $819 |
| 2 | 1,319 | 418 | 1,100 | 1,518 | 607 | 712 |
| 3 | 1,319 | 328 | 1,050 | 1,378 | 551 | 768 |
| 4 | 1,319 | 229 | 1,050 | 1,279 | 512 | 807 |
| 5 | 1,319 | 120 | 1,050 | 1,170 | 468 | 851 |

Table 16B–5
Net present value comparison

| Year | Aftertax Cost of Leasing | Present Value Factor at 6% | Present Value | Aftertax Cost of Borrow–Purchase | Present Value Factor at 6% | Present Value |
|---|---|---|---|---|---|---|
| 1 | $ 750 | 0.943 | $ 707 | $819 | 0.943 | $ 772 |
| 2 | 750 | 0.890 | 668 | 712 | 0.890 | 634 |
| 3 | 1,080 | 0.840 | 907 | 768 | 0.840 | 645 |
| 4 | 1,080 | 0.792 | 855 | 807 | 0.792 | 639 |
| 5 | 1,080 | 0.747 | 807 | 851 | 0.747 | 636 |
| | | | $3,944 | | | $3,326 |

than the normal cost of capital. The overall analysis is presented in Table 16B–5.

The borrow–purchase alternative has a lower present value of aftertax costs ($3,326 versus $3,944), which would appear to make it the more desirable alternative. However, many of the previously discussed qualitative factors that support leasing must also be considered in the decision-making process.

## Problem

**16B–1.** The Woodland Corporation is considering whether to borrow funds and purchase an asset or lease the asset under an operating lease arrangement. If it purchases the asset, the cost will be $30,000. It can borrow funds for five years at 12 percent interest. The firm will use the five-year depreciation schedule under the accelerated cost recovery system. Assume a tax rate of 35 percent. No investment tax credit (ITC) is included in the problem.

The other alternative is to sign one lease that calls for payments of $9,500 for the first three years and a second lease that requires payments of $8,400 in years four and five. The leases would be treated as operating leases. (Round all values to the nearest dollar.)

*a.* Compute the aftertax cost of the leases for the five years.
*b.* Compute the annual payment for the loan (round to the nearest dollar).

*c.* Compute the amortization schedule for the loan. (Disregard a small difference from a zero balance at the end of the loan—due to rounding.)

*d.* Determine the depreciation schedule.

*e.* Compute the aftertax cost of the borrow–purchase alternative.

*f.* Compute the present value of the aftertax cost of the two alternatives. The aftertax cost of debt should be rounded to the nearest whole number to determine the discount rate.

*g.* Which alternative should be selected, based on minimizing the present value of aftertax costs?

# 17 Common and Preferred Stock Financing

The ultimate ownership of the firm resides in common stock, whether it is in the form of all outstanding shares of a closely held corporation or one share of IBM. In terms of legal distinctions, it is the common stockholder alone who directly controls the business. While control of the company is legally in the shareholders' hands, it is practically wielded by management on an everyday basis. It is also important to realize that large creditors may exert tremendous pressure on a firm to meet certain standards of performance, even though the creditor has no voting power.

There are over 45 million common stockholders in the United States, and increasingly this ownership is being held by institutional interests rather than the individual investor. As would be expected, management has become increasingly sensitive to these large stockholders who may side with corporate raiders in voting their shares for or against merger offers or takeover attempts (these topics are covered in chapter 20). Mutual funds, pension funds, insurance companies, and bank trust accounts are all examples of institutional investors. For example, in late 1985 institutional investors owned 49

Table 17–1
Institutional ownership of U.S. companies

| Company | Number of Institutions | Percent of Common Stock Stock Held | Dollar Value of Stock Held ($ billions) |
|---|---|---|---|
| IBM | 641 | 49.0% | $37.286 |
| General Electric | 549 | 47.7 | 12.502 |
| Exxon | 533 | 31.3 | 12.211 |
| General Motors | 473 | 37.0 | 7.839 |
| Atlantic Richfield | 463 | 50.4 | 6.235 |
| Amoco | 449 | 35.2 | 6.047 |
| Chevron | 426 | 45.0 | 5.700 |
| Sears Roebuck | 396 | 47.2 | 5.634 |
| American Express | 410 | 60.8 | 5.590 |
| Eastman Kodak | 440 | 53.7 | 5.293 |
| Digital Equipment | 328 | 82.3 | 5.239 |
| Philip Morris | 445 | 58.5 | 5.225 |
| 3M | 433 | 59.2 | 5.243 |
| Du Pont | 406 | 36.2 | 4.994 |
| Coca-Cola | 421 | 54.4 | 4.968 |

Source: *Barron's*, December 2, 1985, p. 22.

percent of IBM, worth $37.286 billion. Table 17–1 presents a list of companies with the 15 largest institutional ownerships by dollar value in late 1985. At the time this list was compiled the stock market was near an all-time high. The values will change with the ups and down of the stock market.

Preferred stock plays a secondary role in financing the corporate enterprise. It represents a hybrid security, combining some of the features of debt and common stock. Though the preferred stockholder does not have an ownership interest in the firm, he or she does have a priority of claims to dividends that is superior to that of the common stockholder.

In order to understand the rights and characteristics of the different means of financing, we shall examine the powers accorded to shareholders under each arrangement. In the case of common stock everything revolves around three key rights; namely, the residual claim to income, the voting right, and the right to purchase new shares. We shall examine each of these in detail and then consider the rights of preferred stockholders.

## Common Stockholder's Claim to Income

All income that is not paid out to creditors or preferred stockholders automatically belongs to common stockholders. Thus, we say they have a residual claim to income. This is true regardless of whether these residual funds are actually paid out in dividends or retained in the corporation. A firm that earns $10 million before capital costs and pays $1 million in interest to bondholders and a like amount in dividends to preferred stockholders will have $8 million available for common stockholders.[1] Perhaps half of that will be paid out as common stock dividends and the balance will be reinvested in the business for the benefit of stockholders, with the hope of providing even greater income, dividends, and price appreciation in the future.

Of course, it should be pointed out that the common stockholder does not have a legal or enforceable claim to dividends. Whereas a bondholder may force the corporation into bankruptcy for failure to make interest payments, the common stockholder must accept circumstances as they are or attempt to change management if a new dividend policy is desired.

Occasionally a company will have several classes of common stock outstanding that carry different rights to dividends and income. For example, Wang Laboratories, a manufacturer of word processors and office computer systems, has Class B and Class C common stock outstanding, where the Class B stock is entitled to 5¢ per share per year more in dividends than the Class C stock. A more recent innovation however has come from General Motors Corporation through two acquisitions. In October of 1984 GM acquired Electronic Data Systems for cash and General Motors Class E common stock (total value $2.5 billion), and in 1985 GM acquired Hughes Aircraft for cash and Class H common stock (total value $5.8 billion).

Both Class E and Class H common stock are distinct from the regular GM common shares in both voting rights and dividend rights. The dividends on the Class E stock are based on the income generated by EDS, and the dividends on the Class H stock are based on the earnings

[1] Tax consequences related to interest payments are ignored for the present.

of Hughes Aircraft. Both of these companies are now subsidiaries of General Motors. However, General Motors has distributed stock dividends of Class E and Class H shares to its regular GM stockholders and has thus created a minority-owned public group of shareholders for these subsidiaries. Both General Motors Class E and H shares are listed on the New York Stock Exchange.

## The Voting Right

Because the common stockholders are the owners of the firm, they are accorded the right to vote in the election of the board of directors and on all other major issues. Common stockholders may cast their ballots as they see fit on a given issue, or assign a proxy, or "power to cast their ballot," to management or some outside contesting group. As mentioned in the previous section, some corporations have different classes of common stock with unequal voting rights. In the case of the Wang Laboratories' Class B and C stock and General Motors' Class E and H stock, not only are dividends unequal but voting rights are also unequal. Regular General Motors common stock is entitled to one vote per share, while each GM Class E share is entitled to .25 vote and each Class H share is entitled to .50 vote per share. At future designated time periods both Class E and H shares will be exchangeable for GM common shares at exchange rates based on future earnings.

In the case of Wang Laboratories, Class B and C shares were used to differentiate the original founders' shares and those shares sold to the public. The founders wanted to preserve their control of the company and assure their continuing management while at the same time raise new capital for expansion. To ensure this result the Class B common stock was sold to the public and carried a higher dividend but had inferior voting rights to the Class C founders' shares. The Class B shares as a group have 1/10 of one vote per share and elect 25 percent of the directors. The Class C shareholders have one vote per share and elect 75 percent of the board of directors. In this way the Wang family is able to maintain control of the company as founders.

Perhaps the Ford Motor Company is the biggest and best example of "founders" stock. The common stock (no class) has one vote and is entitled to elect 60 percent of the board of directors, and the Class B shares have one vote but are entitled as a class of shareholders to elect 40 percent of the board of directors as long as there are at least

10,125,000 Class B shares outstanding. There are currently 129 owners of Class B stock, which is solely reserved for Ford family members or their descendants, trusts, or appointed interests. As of December 31, 1984, there were 171,322,067 shares of Ford common and 13,925,246 shares of Class B. In this way the Ford family has a very important position in Henry Ford's company without owning more than about 7 percent of the current outstanding stock. Both common and Class B stock share in dividends equally, but no stock dividends may be given unless to both common and Class B in proportion to their ownership. Class B is convertible into common on a share-for-share basis.

While common stockholders and the different classes of common stock that they own may, at times, have different voting rights, they do have a vote. Bondholders and preferred stockholders may vote only when a violation of their corporate agreement exists and a subsequent acceleration of their rights takes place. For example, Continental Illinois Corporation, the Chicago banking giant on the edge of bankruptcy in 1984, failed to pay dividends on one series of preferred stock for five quarters from July 1, 1984, to September 30, 1985. The preferred stockholder agreement stated that failure to pay dividends for six consecutive quarters would result in the preferred stockholders being able to elect two directors to the board to represent their interests. Continental Illinois declared a preferred dividend in November of 1985 to pay all current and past dividends on two classes of preferred stock, thus avoiding the voting issue for preferred stockholders.

## Cumulative Voting

The most important voting matter is the election of the board of directors. As indicated in Chapter 1, the board has primary responsibility for the stewardship of the corporation. If illegal or imprudent decisions are made, the board can be held legally accountable. Furthermore, members of the board of directors serve on a number of important subcommittees of the corporation, such as the audit committee, the long-range financial planning committee, and the salary and compensation committee. The board election process may take place through the familiar majority rule system or by cumulative voting. Under majority voting, any group of stockholders owning over 50 percent of the common stock may elect all of the directors. Under cumulative voting, it is possible for those who hold less than a 50 percent interest to elect some of the directors. The provision for some minority interests on the board is important to those who, at times, wish to challenge the prerogatives of management.

How does this cumulative voting process work? A stockholder gets one vote for each share of stock he or she owns times one vote for each director to be elected. The stockholder may then accumulate votes in favor of a specified number of directors.

Assume there are 10,000 shares outstanding, you own 1,001, and nine directors are to be elected. Your total number of votes under a cumulative election system is:

| | |
|---|---|
| Number of shares owned | 1,001 |
| Number of directors to be elected | 9 |
| Number of votes | 9,009 |

Let us assume you cast all your votes for the one director of your choice. With nine directors to be elected, there is no way for the owners of the remaining shares to exclude you from electing a person to one of the top nine positions. If you own 1,001 shares, the majority interest could control a maximum of 8,999 shares. This would entitle them to 80,991 votes.

| | |
|---|---|
| Number of shares owned (majority) | 8,999 |
| Number of directors to be elected | 9 |
| Number of votes (majority) | 80,991 |

These 80,991 votes cannot be spread thinly enough over nine candidates to stop you from electing your one director. If they are spread evenly, each of the majority's nine choices will receive 8,999 votes (80,991/9). Your choice is assured 9,009 votes. Because the nine top vote-getters win, you will claim one position. Note that candidates do not run head-on against each other (such as Place A or Place B on the ballot), but rather that the top nine candidates are accorded directorships.

To determine the number of shares needed to elect a given number of directors under cumulative voting, the following formula is used:

$$\text{Shares required} = \frac{\text{Number of directors desired} \times \text{Total number of shares outstanding}}{\text{Total number of directors to be elected} + 1} + 1 \qquad (17\text{–}1)$$

The formula reaffirms that in the previous instance 1,001 shares would elect one director.

$$\frac{1 \times 10{,}000}{9 + 1} + 1 = \frac{10{,}000}{10} + 1 = 1{,}001$$

If three director positions out of nine are desired, 3,001 shares are necessary.

$$\frac{3 \times 10{,}000}{9 + 1} + 1 = \frac{30{,}000}{10} + 1 = 3{,}001$$

Note that with approximately 30 percent of the shares outstanding, a minority interest can control one third of the board. If instead of cumulative voting a majority rule system were utilized, a minority interest could elect no one. The group that controlled 5,001 or more shares out of 10,000 would elect each and every director.

As a restatement of the problem: If we know the number of minority shares outstanding under cumulative voting and wish to determine how many directors that can be elected, we use the formula:

Number of directors that can be elected

$$= \frac{(\text{Shares owned} - 1) \times (\text{Total number of directors to be elected} + 1)}{(\text{Total number of shares outstanding})} \qquad (17\text{–}2)$$

Plugging 3,001 shares into the formula, we show:

$$\frac{(3{,}001 - 1)(9 + 1)}{10{,}000} = \frac{3{,}000(10)}{10{,}000} = 3$$

If the formula yields an uneven number of directors, such as 3.3 or 3.8, you always round down to the nearest whole number (i.e., 3).

It is not surprising that 22 states require cumulative voting in preference to majority rule, that 18 consider it permissible as part of the corporate charter, and that only 10 make no provision for its use. Such consumer-oriented states as California, Illinois, and Michigan require cumulative voting procedures.

## The Right to Purchase New Shares

In addition to a claim to residual income and the right to vote for directors, the common stockholder may also enjoy a privileged position in the offering of new securities. If the corporate charter contains a *preemptive right* provision, holders of common stock must be given the first option to purchase new shares. While only two states specifically require the use of preemptive rights, most other states allow for its inclusion in the corporation charter.

The preemptive right provision ensures that management cannot subvert the position of present stockholders by selling shares to outside interests without first offering them to current shareholders. If such protection were not afforded, a 20 percent stockholder might find his or her interest reduced to 10 percent through the distribution of new shares to outsiders. Not only would voting rights be diluted, but proportionate claims to earnings per share would be reduced.

### The Use of Rights in Financing

Many corporations also engage in a preemptive rights offering to tap this built-in market for new securities—the current investors. Let us assume that the Walton Corporation has 9 million shares outstanding and that the current market price is $40 a share (the total market value is $360 million). Walton needs to raise $30 million for new plant and equipment and will sell 1 million new shares at $30 per share.[2] As part of the process, it will use a rights offering in which each old shareholder receives a first option to participate in the purchase of new shares.

Each old shareholder will receive one right for each share of stock owned and may combine a specified number of rights plus $30 cash to buy a new share of stock. Let us consider these questions:

---

[2]If this were not a rights offering, the discount from the current market price would be much smaller. The new shares might sell for $38 or $39.

1. How many rights should be necessary to purchase one new share of stock?
2. What is the monetary value of these rights?

**Rights required** Since 9 million shares are currently outstanding and 1 million new shares will be issued, the ratio of old to new shares is 9 to 1. On this basis, the old stockholder may combine nine rights plus $30 cash to purchase one new share of stock.

A stockholder with 90 shares of stock would receive an equivalent number of rights which could be applied toward the purchase of 10 shares of stock at $30 per share. As indicated later in the chapter, stockholders may choose to sell their rights rather than exercise them in the purchase of new shares.

**Monetary value of a right** Anything that contributes toward the privilege of purchasing a considerably higher priced stock for $30 per share must have some market value. Consider the following two-step analysis.

Nine old shares sold at $40 per share, or for $360; now one new share will be introduced for $30. Thus we have a total market value of $390 spread over ten shares. After the rights offering has been completed, the average value of a share is theoretically equal to $39.[3]

| | |
|---|---|
| Nine old shares sold at $40 per share | $360 |
| One new share will sell at $30 per share | 30 |
| Total value of ten shares | $390 |
| Average value of one share | $ 39 |

The rights offering thus entitles the holder to buy a stock that should carry a value of $39 (after the transactions have been completed) for $30. With a differential between the anticipated price and the subscription price of $9 and nine rights required to participate in the purchase of one share, the value of a right in this case is $1.

[3] A number of variables may intervene to change the value. This is a "best" approximation.

| | |
|---|---|
| Average value of one share | $39 |
| Subscription price | 30 |
| Differential | $ 9 |
| Rights required to buy one share | 9 |
| Value of a right ($9 ÷ 9) | $ 1 |

Formulas have been developed to determine the value of a right under any circumstances. Before they are presented, let us examine two new terms that will be part of the calculations—*rights-on* and *ex-rights*. When a rights offering is announced, a stock initially trades rights-on; that is, if you buy the stock, you will also acquire a right toward a future purchase of the stock. After a certain period of time (say four weeks) the stock goes ex-rights—when you buy the stock you no longer get a right toward future purchase of stock. Consider the following:

| Date | Value of Stock | Value of Right |
|---|---|---|
| March 1: Stock trades rights-on | $40 | $1 (part of $40) |
| April 1: Stock trades ex-rights | 39 | $1 |
| April 30: End of subscription period | 39 | — |

Once the ex-right period is reached, the stock will go down by the theoretical value of the right. The remaining value ($39) is the ex-rights value. Though there is a time period remaining between the ex-right date (April 1) and the end of the subscription period (April 30), the market assumes the dilution has already taken place. Thus, the ex-rights value reflects precisely the same value as can be expected when the new, underpriced $30 stock issue is sold. In effect, it projects the future impact of the cheaper shares on the stock price.

The formula for the value of the right when the stock is trading rights-on is:

$$R = \frac{M_o - S}{N + 1} \tag{17–3}$$

where

$M_o$ = Market value—rights-on, $40
$S$ = Subscription price, $30
$N$ = Number of rights required to purchase a new share of stock, in this case 9

$$\frac{\$40 - \$30}{9 + 1} = \frac{\$10}{10} = \$1$$

Using Formula 17–3, we determined that the value of a right in the Walton Corporation offering was $1. An alternative formula giving precisely the same answer is:

$$R = \frac{M_e - S}{N} \tag{17–4}$$

The only new term is $M_e$, the market value of the stock when the shares are trading ex-rights. We show:

$$R = \frac{\$39 - \$30}{9} = \frac{\$9}{9} = \$1$$

These are all theoretical relationships which may be altered somewhat in reality. If there is great enthusiasm for the new issue, the market value of the right may exceed the initial theoretical value (perhaps the right will trade for $1⅜).

## Effect of Rights on Stockholder's Position

At first glance, a rights offering appears to bring great benefits to stockholders. But is this really the case? Does a shareholder really benefit from being able to buy a stock that is initially $40 (and later $39) for $30. Don't answer too quickly!

Think of it this way. Assume 100 people own shares of stock in a corporation and one day decide to sell new shares to themselves at 25 percent below current value. They cannot really enhance their wealth by selling their own product more cheaply to themselves. What is gained by purchasing inexpensive new shares is lost by diluting existing outstanding shares.

Take the case of Stockholder A who owns nine shares before the rights offering and also has $30 in cash. His holdings would appear as follows:

| | |
|---|---|
| Nine old shares at $40 . . . . . | $360 |
| Cash . . . . . . . . . . . . . . | 30 |
| Total value . . . . . . . . | $390 |

If he receives and exercises nine rights to buy one new share at $30, his portfolio will contain:

| | |
|---|---|
| Ten shares at $39 (diluted value) | $390 |
| Cash | 0 |
| Total value | $390 |

Clearly, he is no better off. A second alternative would be for him to sell his rights in the market and stay with his position of owning only nine shares and holding cash.

| | |
|---|---|
| Nine shares at $39 (diluted value) | $351 |
| Proceeds from sale of nine rights | 9 |
| Cash | 30 |
| Total value | $390 |

As indicated above, whether he chooses to exercise his rights or not, the stock will still go down to a lower value (others are still diluting). Once again, his overall value remains constant. The value received for the rights ($9) exactly equals the extent of dilution in the value of the original nine shares.

The only foolish action would be for the stockholder to throw away the rights as worthless securities. He would then suffer the pains of dilution without the offset from the sale of the rights.

| | |
|---|---|
| Nine shares at $39 (diluted value) | $351 |
| Cash | 30 |
| Total value | $381 |

Empirical evidence indicates that this careless activity takes place 1 to 2 percent of the time.

### Desirable Features of Rights Offerings

The student may ask, If the stockholder is no better off in terms of total valuation, why undertake a rights offering? There are a number of possible advantages.

As previously indicated, by giving current stockholders a first option to purchase new shares, we protect their current position in regard to voting rights and claims to earnings. Of equal importance, the use of a rights offering gives the firm a built-in market for new security issues. Because of this built-in base, distribution costs are likely to be considerably lower than under a straight public issue in which investment bankers must underwrite the full risk of distribution.[4]

Also, a rights offering may generate more interest in the market than would a straight public issue. There is a market not only for the stock but also for the rights. Because the subscription price is normally set 15–25 percent below current value, there is the "non-real" appearance of a bargain, creating further interest in the offering.

A last advantage of a rights offering over a straight stock issue is that stock purchased through a rights offering carries lower margin requirements. The margin requirement specifies the amount of cash or equity that must be deposited with a brokerage house or a bank, with the balance of funds eligible for borrowing. Though not all investors wish to purchase on margin, those who do so prefer to put down a minimum amount. While normal stock purchases may require a 50 percent margin (half cash, half borrowed), stock purchased under a rights offering may be bought with as little as 25 percent down, depending on the current requirements of the Federal Reserve Board.

The dollar value of rights traded on the exchanges is small because of the very low prices at which rights trade. Rights also have a short life—of as little as several weeks—and therefore continuous trading in rights is not possible as it is on the common stock of the same company. During 1984 over 6 million rights traded on U.S. securities exchanges and in 1985 this number more than doubled, to over 14 million rights. Clearly the use of rights offerings increased as the stock market made new highs and more common stock was sold to raise capital for corporations.

## Preferred Stock Financing

Having discussed bonds (in Chapter 16) and common stock, we are prepared to look at this intermediate or hybrid form of security known as preferred stock. You may question the validity of the term *preferred*,

[4]Though investment bankers generally participate in a rights offering as well, their fees are less because of the smaller risk factor.

for preferred stock does not possess any of the most desirable characteristics of debt or common stock. In the case of debt, bondholders have a contractual claim against the corporation for the payment of interest and may throw the corporation into bankruptcy if payment is not forthcoming. Common stockholders, of course, are the owners of the firm and have a residual claim to all income not paid out to others. Preferred stockholders, on the other hand, are merely entitled to receive a stipulated dividend, and generally must receive the dividend prior to the payment of dividends to common stockholders. However, their right to annual dividends is not compelling to the corporation, as is true of interest on debt, and the corporation may forgo preferred dividends when this is deemed necessary.

For example, XYZ Corporation might issue 12 percent preferred stock with $100 par value. Under normal circumstances, the corporation would pay the $12 per share dividend. Let us also assume that it has $1,000 bonds carrying 12.2 percent interest and shares of common stock with a market value of $50, normally paying a $1 cash dividend. The 12.2 percent interest *must* be paid on the bonds. The $12 preferred dividend has to be paid before the $1 dividend on common, but both may be waived without threat of bankruptcy. The common stockholder is the last in line to receive payment, but his potential participation is unlimited. Instead of getting a $1 dividend, he may someday receive many times that much.

## Justification for Preferred Stock

Because preferred stock has few unique characteristics, why might the corporation choose to issue it and, equally important, why are investors willing to purchase the security?

Most corporations that issue preferred stock do so to achieve a balance in their capital structure. It is a means of expanding the capital base of the firm without diluting the common stock ownership position or incurring contractual debt obligations. Firms that are heavy users of debt, such as public utilities and capital goods producers, may go to preferred stock to balance their sources of financing.

Even here, there may be a drawback. While interest payments on debt are tax deductible, preferred stock dividends are not. Thus, the interest cost on 12.2 percent debt may be only 6 to 6.5 percent on an aftertax cost basis, while the aftertax cost on 12 percent preferred stock would be the stated amount. A firm issuing the preferred stock may be willing to pay the higher aftertax cost to assure investors that it has a balanced capital structure and because preferred stock may have a positive effect on the costs of the other sources of funds in the capital structure.

**Investor interest** Primary purchasers of preferred stock are corporate investors, insurance companies, and pension funds. To the corporate investor, preferred stock offers a very attractive advantage over bonds. The tax law provides that any corporation which receives either *preferred* or *common* dividends from another corporation must add only 15 percent of such dividends to its taxable income. Thus, 85 percent of such dividends are exempt from taxation. On a preferred stock issue paying a 12 percent dividend, only 1.8 percent would be taxable. By contrast, the interest on bonds is usually taxable to the recipient except for municipal bond interest.

Because of this tax consideration, it is not surprising that corporations are able to issue preferred stock at a slightly lower yield than debt. As indicated in Table 17–2, since the late 1960s preferred stock

**Table 17–2**
**Yields on corporate bonds and high-grade preferred stock**

| *Year** | *Aa Bonds* | *High-Grade Preferred Stock* |
|---|---|---|
| 1947 | 2.70% | 3.79% |
| 1952 | 3.04 | 4.13 |
| 1957 | 4.03 | 4.63 |
| 1962 | 4.47 | 4.50 |
| 1967 | 5.66 | 5.46 |
| 1970 | 8.32 | 7.29 |
| 1972 | 7.49 | 6.85 |
| 1975 | 8.77 | 8.01 |
| 1976 | 8.75 | 7.97 |
| 1977 | 8.24 | 7.60 |
| 1978 | 8.92 | 8.25 |
| 1979 | 10.46 | 9.50 |
| 1980 | 12.50 | 10.57 |
| 1981 | 14.75 | 12.36 |
| 1982 | 14.41 | 12.53 |
| 1983 | 12.42 | 11.02 |
| 1984 | 13.31 | 11.59 |
| 1985† | 12.14 | 10.55 |

*Average value for the year.
†Average for 11 months.
Source: Selected issues of the *Federal Reserve Bulletin*.

has been trading at a 1/4 to 2 1/2 percent lower yield than comparable bonds.

**Summary of tax considerations** Tax considerations work in two opposite directions. First, they make the *aftertax* cost of debt cheaper than preferred stock to the issuing corporation because interest is tax deductible to the payer. (This is true in spite of the fact the quoted rate may be higher.) Second, tax considerations generally make the receipt of preferred dividends more valuable than corporate bond interest to the (corporate) recipient because 85 percent of the dividend is exempt from taxation.

## Provisions Associated with Preferred Stock

A preferred stock issue contains a number of stipulations and provisions that define the stockholder's claim to income and assets.

*1. Cumulative dividends*—Most preferred stock issues have a cumulative claim to dividends. That is, if preferred stock dividends are not paid in any one year, they accumulate and must be paid in total before common stockholders can receive dividends. If preferred stock carries a $12 cash dividend and the company does not pay dividends for three years, preferred stockholders must receive the full $36 before common stockholders can receive anything.

The cumulative dividend feature makes a corporation very cognizant of its obligation to preferred stockholders. When a financially troubled corporation has missed a number of dividend payments under a cumulative arrangement, there may be a financial recapitalization of the corporation in which preferred stockholders receive new securities in place of the dividend arrearage. Assume that the corporation has now missed five years of dividends under a $12 a year obligation and still remains in a poor cash position. Preferred stockholders may be offered $60 or more in new common stock for forgiveness of the missed dividend payments. Preferred stockholders may be willing to cooperate in order to get the corporation "back on its feet."

*2. Conversion feature*—Like certain forms of debt, preferred stock may be convertible into common shares. Thus, $100 in preferred stock may be convertible into *X* number of shares of common stock at the option of the holder. The topic of convertibility is discussed at length in Chapter 19, Convertibles and Warrants. Approximately 40 percent of preferred stock issues have this conversion feature.

3. *Call feature*—Also preferred stock, like debt, may be callable—that is, the corporation may retire the security prior to maturity at some small premium over par. This, of course, accrues to the advantage of the corporation and to the disadvantage of the preferred stockholder. A preferred issue carrying a call provision will be accorded a slightly higher yield than a similar issue without this feature. The same type of refunding decision applied to debt obligations in Chapter 16 could also be applied to preferred stock.

4. *Participation provision*—A *small* percentage of preferred stock issues are participating; that is, they may participate over and above the quoted yield when the corporation is enjoying a particularly good year. Once the common stock dividend equals the preferred stock dividend, the two classes of securities may share equally in additional payouts.

5. *Floating rate*—Beginning in 1982, a few preferred stock issuers made the dividend floating in nature. These issuers include such firms as Alcoa, U.S. Steel, and BankAmerica Corporation. Typically, the dividend is changed on a quarterly basis, based on current market conditions. Because the dividend rate only changes quarterly, there is still some small price change possibility between dividend adjustment dates. Nevertheless, it is less than the price change for regular preferred stock.

6. *Par value*—A final important feature associated with preferred stock is par value. Unlike the par value of common stock, which is often only a small percentage of the actual value, the par value of preferred stock is generally set at the anticipated market value at the time of issue. The par value establishes the amount due to preferred stockholders in the event of liquidation. Also, the par value of preferred stock generally determines the base against which the percentage or dollar return on preferred stock is computed. Thus, 12 percent preferred stock would indicate $12 a year in preferred dividends if the par value were $100, but only $6 annually if the par value were $50.

## Comparing Features of Common and Preferred Stock and Debt

In Table 17–3, we compare the characteristics of common stock, preferred stock, and bonds. The student should carefully consider the comparative advantages and disadvantages of each.

**Table 17–3**
**Features of alternative security issues**

| | *Common Stock* | *Preferred Stock* | *Bonds* |
|---|---|---|---|
| 1. Ownership and control of the firm | Belongs to common stockholders through voting right and residual claim to income | Limited rights when dividends are missed | Limited rights under default in interest payments |
| 2. Obligation to provide return | None | Must receive payment before common stockholder | Contractual obligation |
| 3. Claim to assets in bankruptcy | Lowest claim of any security holder | Bondholders and creditors must be satisfied first | Highest claim |
| 4. Cost of distribution | Highest | Moderate | Lowest |
| 5. Risk–return trade-off | Highest risk, highest return (at least in theory) | Moderate risk, moderate return | Lowest risk, moderate return |
| 6. Tax status of payment by corporation | Not deductible | Not deductible | Tax deductible<br>Cost = Interest payment × (1 − Tax rate) |
| 7. Tax status of payment to recipient | 85 percent of dividend to other corporation is tax exempt. First $100 of dividends to individuals is tax exempt in a given year. | Same as common stock | Municipal bond interest is tax exempt |

In terms of the risk-return features of these three classes of securities and also of the other investments discussed in Chapter 7, we might expect the risk-return patterns depicted in Figure 17–1. The

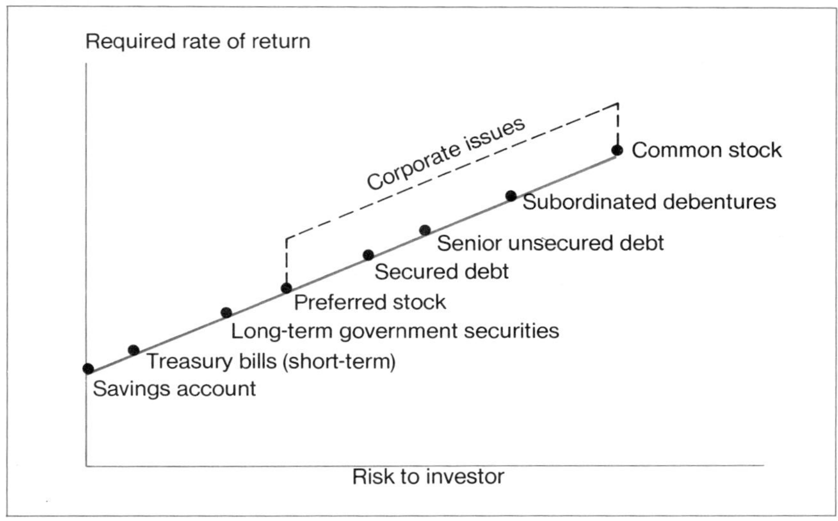


**Figure 17–1**
**Risk and expected return for various security classes**

lowest return is obtained from savings accounts, and the highest return and risk are generally associated with common stock. In between, we note that short-term instruments generally, though not always, provide lower returns than longer-term instruments. We also observe that government securities pay lower returns than issues originated by corporations because of the lower risk involved. Next on the scale after government issues is preferred stock. This hybrid form of security generally pays a lower return than even well-secured corporate debt instruments because of the 85 percent tax-exempt status of preferred stock dividends to corporate purchasers. Thus, the focus on preferred stock is not just on risk-return trade-offs but also on aftertax return.[5]

Next, we observe increasingly high return requirements on debt, based on the presence or absence of security provisions and the priority of claims on unsecured debt. Finally, at the top of the scale is common stock. Because of its lowest priority of claim in the corporation and its volatile price movement, it has the highest demanded return.

[5] In a strict sense, preferred stock does not belong on the straight line because of its relatively high risk and low return.

While extensive research studies have tended to validate these general patterns,[6] short-term or even intermediate-term reversals have taken place, in which investments with lower risk have outperformed investments at the higher end of the risk scale.

## Summary

While common stock is still owned by over 45 million individual investors, institutional ownership through mutual funds, pension funds, insurance companies, and bank trusts is increasing every year.

Common stock ownership carries three primary rights or privileges. First, there is a residual claim to income. All funds not paid out to other classes of securities automatically belong to the common stockholder; the firm may then choose to pay out these residual funds in dividends or to reinvest them for the benefit of common stockholders. Different classes of stock, such as the Wang Class B and Class C stock, may carry different dividends. There are also cases, such as the new GM Class E and H stock, where dividends are tied to the performance of a subsidiary company.

Because common stockholders are the ultimate owners of the firm, they alone have the privilege of voting (except under default or other unusual conditions). There may be more than one class of stock, having differing voting rights. The common example where voting rights are not equal is usually founders' stock, such as in Ford Motor Company's Class B stock and Wang Laboratories' Class C common stock. The General Motors' Class E and H stock also have different rights as a result of acquisitions by General Motors.

To expand the role of minority stockholders, many corporations use a system of cumulative voting, in which each stockholder has voting power equal to the number of shares owned times the number of directors to be elected. By cumulating votes for a small number of

[6]Roger G. Ibbotson and Rex A. Sinquefield, "Stocks, Bonds, Bills and Inflation: Year by Year Historical Returns (1926–1974)," *Journal of Business* 49, no. 1 (January 1976). Also Lawrence Fisher and James H. Lorie, *A Half Century of Returns on Common Stocks and Bonds* (Chicago: University of Chicago Graduate School of Business, 1977). For example, Ibbotson and Sinquefield found, over an almost 50-year period, an average return of 8.5 percent on common stocks, of 3.6 percent on corporate bonds, and of 3.2 percent on U.S. government bonds. A recent study by Robert S. Salomon, Jr., of Salomon Bros. showed a reversal of these patterns for 1969–78.

selected directors, minority stockholders are able to have representation on the board.

Common stockholders may also enjoy a first option to purchase new shares. This privilege is extended through the procedure known as a rights offering. A shareholder receives one right for each share of stock owned, and may combine a certain number of rights, plus cash, to purchase a new share. While the cash or subscription price is usually somewhat below the current market price, the stockholder neither gains nor loses through the process.

A hybrid, or intermediate, security, falling between debt and common stock, is preferred stock. Preferred stockholders are entitled to receive a stipulated dividend and must receive this dividend before any payment is made to common stockholders. Preferred dividends usually accumulate if they are not paid in a given year, though preferred stockholders cannot initiate bankruptcy proceedings or seek legal redress if nonpayment occurs.

Finally, common stock, preferred stock, bonds, and other securities tend to receive returns over the long run in accordance with risk, with corporate issues generally paying a higher return than government securities.

## List of Terms

**common stockholder**
**cumulative voting**
**preemptive right**
**rights offering**
**rights-on**
**ex-rights**
**founders' stock**
**margin requirement**
**floating rate preferred stock**
**preferred stock**
**cumulative preferred stock**
**participating preferred stock**
**majority voting**

## Discussion Questions

1. Why has corporate management become increasingly sensitive to the desires of large institutional investors?

2. What determines the dividend payments on General Motors' Class E and Class H shares?

3. Why might a corporation use a special category such as founders' stock in issuing common stock?

4. What is the purpose of cumulative voting? Are there any disadvantages to management?

5. Why has preferred stock not been popular as a source of funds for corporations?

6. What is the most likely explanation for the use of preferred stock?

7. How does the preemptive right protect stockholders from dilution?

8. If common stockholders are the *owners* of the company, why do they have the last claim on assets and a residual claim on income?

9. Preferred stock is often referred to as a hybrid security. What is meant by this term?

10. During a rights offering the underlying stock is said to sell "rights-on" and "ex-rights." Explain the meaning of these terms and their significance to current stockholders and potential stockholders.

11. If preferred stock is riskier than bonds, why has preferred stock had lower yields than bonds in recent years?

12. A small amount of preferred stock is participating. What would your reaction be if someone said common stock is also participating?

13. What is an advantage of floating rate preferred stock for the risk averse investor?

## Problems

1. Mr. R. C. Cola owns 7,001 shares of Softdrink, Inc. There are 10 seats on the company board of directors, and the company has a total of 77,000 shares outstanding. Softdrinks, Inc., utilizes cumulative voting.

   Can Mr. Cola elect himself to the board when the vote to elect 10 directors is held next week? (Use Formula 17–2 to determine if he can elect one director.)

2. The Lindsey Corporation has been experiencing declining earnings, but has just announced a 50 percent salary increase for top executives. A dissident group of stockholders wants to oust the existing board of directors. There are currently 11 directors and 60,000 shares of stock outstanding. Mr. Perk, the president of the company, has the full support of the existing board. The dissident stockholders control proxies for 20,001 shares. Mr. Perk is worried about losing his job.

   *a.* Under cumulative voting procedures, how many directors can the dissident stockholders elect with the proxies they now hold? How many directors could they elect under majority rule with these proxies?
   *b.* How many shares (or proxies) are needed to elect 6 directors under cumulative voting?

3. Midland Petroleum is holding a stockholders' meeting next month. Ms. Ramsey is president of the company and has the support of the existing board of directors. All 11 members are up for reelection. Mr. T. B. Pickens is a dissident stockholder. He controls proxies for 40,001 shares. Ms. Ramsey and her friends on the board control 60,001 shares. Other stockholders, where loyalties are unknown, will be voting the remaining 19,998 shares. The company uses cumulative voting.

   *a.* How many directors can Mr. Pickens be assured of electing?
   *b.* How many directors can Ms. Ramsey and her friends be assured of electing?
   *c.* How many directors could Mr. Pickens elect if he obtains all the proxies for the uncommitted votes? (Uneven values must be rounded down to the nearest whole number regardless of the amount.) Will he control the board?

4. In Problem 3, if nine directors were to be elected, and Ms. Ramsey and her friends had 60,001 shares and Mr. Pickens had 40,001 shares plus half the uncommitted votes, how many directors could Mr. Pickens elect?

5. Mr. Rogers controls proxies for 38,000 of the 70,000 outstanding shares of Ingot Industrial Company. Mr. Kermit heads a dissident group which controls the remaining 32,000 shares. There are seven board members to be elected and cumulative voting rules apply.

Mr. Rogers does not understand cumulative voting and plans to cast 100,000 of his 266,000 (38,000 × 7) votes for his brother-in-law, Mel. The remaining votes will be spread evenly over three other candidates.

*a.* How many directors can Mr. Kermit elect if Mr. Rogers acts as described above? Use logical analysis rather than a set formula to answer part *a*.
*b.* How many directors can Mr. Kermit elect if Mr. Rogers acts in an optimal manner? (Round down to the nearest whole number.)
*c.* If Mr. Rogers spreads his votes evenly over seven candidates, trying to get all his people on the board, how many directors could Mr. Kermit elect? Use logical analysis rather than a set formula to answer part *c*.

**6.** Madonna Fashions, Inc., has issued rights to its shareholders. The subscription price is $45, and five rights are needed along with the subscription price to buy one of the new shares. The stock is selling for $54 rights-on.

*a.* What would be the value of one right?
*b.* If the stock goes ex-rights, what would the new stock price be?

**7.** Skyway Airlines has announced a rights offering for its shareholders. Mr. Harold Post owns 800 shares of Skyway Airlines' stock. Four rights plus $60 cash are needed to buy one of the new shares. The stock is currently selling for $72 rights-on.

*a.* What is the value of a right?
*b.* How many of the new shares could Mr. Post buy if he exercises all his rights? How much cash would this require?
*c.* Mr. Post does not know if he wants to exercise his rights or sell them. What alternative would have the more positive effect on his wealth?

**8.** Todd Winningham IV has $4,000 to invest. He has been looking at Gallagher Tennis Clubs, Inc., common stock. Gallagher has issued a rights offering to its common stockholders. Six rights plus $38 cash will buy one new share. Gallagher's stock is selling for $50 ex-rights.

*a.* How many rights could Todd buy with his $4,000? Alternatively, how many shares of stock could he buy with the same $4,000 at $50 per share?

*b.* If Todd invests his $4,000 in Gallagher rights and the price of Gallagher stock rises to $59 per share ex-rights, what would his total dollar profit on the rights be? (First compute profits per right.)

*c.* If Todd invests his $4,000 in Gallagher stock and the price of the stock rises to $59 per share ex-rights, what would his total dollar profit be?

*d.* What would the answer be to part *b* if the price of Gallagher's stock falls to $30 per share ex-rights instead of rising to $59?

*e.* What would the answer be to part *c* if the price of Gallagher's stock falls to $30 per share ex-rights?

**9.** Mr. and Mrs. Anderson own five shares of Magic Tricks Corporation common stock. The market value of the stock is $60. They also have $48 in cash. They have just received word of a rights offering. One new share of stock can be purchased at $48 for each five shares currently owned (based on five rights).

*a.* What is the value of a right?

*b.* What is the value of the Andersons' portfolio before the rights offering? (Portfolio in this question represents stock plus cash.)

*c.* If the Andersons participate in the rights offering, what will be the value of their portfolio, based on the diluted value (ex-rights) of the stock?

*d.* If they sell their five rights but keep their stock at its diluted value and hold onto their cash, what will be the value of their portfolio?

**10.** The Hamlin Corporation has some excess cash that it would like to invest in marketable securities for a long-term hold. Its vice president of finance is considering three investments (Hamlin is in a 40 percent tax bracket). Which should he select, based on aftertax return: *(a)* Treasury bonds at 10.5 percent yield, *(b)* Corporate bonds at 12 percent yield, or *(c)* Preferred stock at 10 percent yield.

**11.** National Health Corporation (NHC) has a cumulative preferred stock issue outstanding which has a stated annual dividend of $9 per share. The company has been losing money and has not paid the preferred dividends for the last five years. There are 300,000 shares of preferred stock outstanding and 600,000 shares of common stock.

*a.* How much is the company behind in total preferred dividends?
*b.* If NHC earns $11,000,000 in the coming year after taxes but before dividends, and this is all paid out to the preferred stockholders, how much will the company be in arrears (behind in payments)? Keep in mind the coming year would represent the sixth year.
*c.* How much would be available in common stock dividends in the coming year if $11,000,000 is earned, as indicated in part *b*?

**12.** Franklin Kite Company is four years in arrears on cumulative preferred stock dividends. There are 650,000 preferred shares outstanding and the annual dividend is $7 per share. The vice president of finance sees no real hope of paying the dividends in arrears. He is devising a plan to compensate the preferred stockholders for 90 percent of the dividends in arrears.

*a.* How much should the compensation be?
*b.* Franklin will compensate the preferred stockholders in the form of bonds paying 12 percent interest in a market environment in which the going rate of interest is 14 percent. The bonds will have a 25-year maturity. Using the bond valuation table in Chapter 16 (Table 16–3), indicate the market value of a $1,000 par value bond.
*c.* Based on market value, how many bonds must be issued to provide the compensation determined in part *a*? (Round to the nearest whole number.)

**13.** The treasurer of the Newton Record Company (a corporation) currently has $100,000 invested in preferred stock yielding 9 percent. He appreciates the tax advantages of preferred stock and is considering buying $100,000 more with borrowed funds. The cost of the borrowed funds is 11 percent. He suggests this proposal to his board of directors. They are somewhat concerned by the fact that the treasurer is paying 2 percent more for funds than he is earning. The Newton Record Company is in a 40 percent tax bracket.

*a.* Compute the amount of the aftertax income from the additional preferred stock if it is purchased.
*b.* Compute the aftertax borrowing cost to purchase the additional preferred stock. That is, multiply the interest cost times (1 − T).
*c.* Should the treasurer proceed with his proposal?
*d.* If interest rates and dividend yields in the market go up six months after a decision to purchase is made, what impact will this have on the outcome?

**14.** Walker Machine Tools has 5 million shares of common stock outstanding. The current market price of Walker common stock is $42 per share rights-on. The company's net income this year is $15 million. A rights offering has been announced in which 500,000 new shares will be sold at $36.50 per share. The subscription price plus 10 rights is needed to buy one of the new shares.

*a.* What are the earnings per share and price-earnings ratio before the new shares are sold via the rights offering?
*b.* What would the earnings per share be immediately after the rights offering? What would the price-earnings ratio be immediately after the rights offering? Assume there is no change in the market value of the stock except for the change when the stock begins trading ex-rights. (Round answers to two places after the decimal point.)

**15.** The Crandall Corporation currently has 100,000 shares outstanding which are selling at $50 per share. It needs to raise $900,000. Net income after taxes is $500,000. Its vice president of finance and its outside investment banker have decided on a rights offering, but are not sure how much to discount the subscription price from the current market value. Discounts of 10 percent, 20 percent, and 40 percent have been suggested. Common stock is the sole means of financing for the Crandall Corporation.

*a.* For each discount, determine the subscription price, the number of shares to be issued, and the number of rights required to purchase one share. (Round to one place after the decimal point where necessary.)

*b*. Determine the value of one right under each of the plans. (Round to two places after the decimal point.)
*c*. Compute the earnings per share before and immediately after the rights offering under a 10 percent discount from the subscription price.
*d*. By what percentage has the number of shares outstanding increased?
*e*. Stockholder X has 100 shares before the rights offering and participated by buying 20 new shares. Compute his total claim to earnings both before and after the rights offering (that is, multiply shares by the earnings per share figures computed in part *c*).
*f*. Should Stockholder X be satisfied with this claim over a longer period of time?

**16.** (Comprehensive problem)
Hoffman Bike Parts, Inc., is a small firm which has been very profitable over the past five years and has also exhibited a strong earnings growth trend. Mr. Hoffman owns 35 percent of the two million shares of common stock outstanding, but he is nevertheless worried about being taken over by a larger firm some time in the future. He has read some articles in *The Wall Street Journal* about techniques used to discourage forced mergers and takeovers. Hoffman Bike Parts, Inc., currently uses majority voting for nine directors. Mr. Hoffman wonders which of the following proposals would make it easier for him to reject a takeover bid.

*a*. What would be the effect of cumulative voting?
*b*. What would be accomplished if shareholders could only vote for one third of the directors every year (staggered terms)?
*c*. Should Mr. Hoffman reduce or increase the number of directors? Is the answer to this question dependent on majority rule or cumulative voting?

## Selected References

Bacon, P. W. "The Subscription Price in Rights Offerings." *Financial Management* 1 (September 1972), pp. 59–64.

Baumol, William J. *The Stock Market and Economic Efficiency.* New York: Fordham University Press, 1965.

Bear, Robert M., and Anthony J. Curley. "Unseasoned Financing." *Journal of Financial and Quantitative Analysis* 10 (June 1975), pp. 311–26.

Bloch, Ernest. "Pricing a Corporate Bond Issue: A Look behind the Scenes." *Essays in Money and Credit.* New York: Federal Reserve Bank of New York, 1964, pp. 72–76.

Donaldson, Gordon. "In Defense of Preferred Stock." *Harvard Business Review* 40 (July–August 1962), pp. 123–36.

Dougall, Herbert E., and Jack E. Gaumnitz. *Capital Markets and Institutions.* Englewood Cliffs, N.J.: Prentice-Hall, 1975.

Ederington, Louis H. "Uncertainty, Competition, and Costs in Corporate Bond Underwriting." *Journal of Financial Economics* 2 (March 1975), pp. 71–94.

Edmister, Robert O. "Commission Cost Structure: Shifts and Scale Economies." *Journal of Finance* 33 (May 1978), pp. 477–86.

Eibott, Peter. "Trends in the Value of Individual Stockholdings." *Journal of Business* 47 (July 1974), pp. 339–48.

Evans, G. H., Jr. "The Theoretical Value of Stock Right." *Journal of Finance* 10 (March 1955), pp. 55–61.

Fischer, Donald E., and Glenn A. Wilt, Jr. "Nonconvertible Preferred Stock as a Financing Instrument, 1950–1965." *Journal of Finance* 23 (September 1968), pp. 611–24.

Fisher, Lawrence, and James H. Lorie. *A Half Century of Returns on Common Stocks and Bonds.* Chicago: University of Chicago Graduate School of Business, 1977.

Ibbotson, Roger G., and Rex A. Sinquefield. "Stocks, Bonds, Bills, and Inflation: Year by Year Historical Returns (1926–1974)." *Journal of Business* 49 (January 1976), pp. 11–47.

Keane, S. M. "The Significance of Issue Price in Rights Issues." *Journal of Business Finance* 4 (September 1972), pp. 40–45.

Levy, Haim, and Marshall Sarnat. "Risk, Dividend Policy, and the Optimal Pricing of a Rights Offering." *Journal of Money, Credit, and Banking* 3 (November 1971), pp. 840–49.

Mikkelson, Wayne H., and M. Megan Partch. "Stock Price Effects and Costs of Secondary Distributions." *Journal of Financial Economics* 14 (June 1985), pp. 165–94.

Nelson, J. R. "Price Effects in Rights Offerings." *Journal of Finance* 20 (December 1965), pp. 647–60.

O'Neal, F. H. "Minority Owners Can Avoid Squeeze-Outs." *Harvard Business Review* 41 (March–April 1963), pp. 150–52.

Pinches, George E. "Financing with Convertible Preferred Stock, 1960–1967." *Journal of Finance* 25 (March 1970), pp. 53–63.

Soldofsky, Robert M., and Craig R. Johnson. "Rights Timing." *Financial Analysts Journal* 23 (July–August 1967), pp. 101–4.

# 18 Dividend Policy and Retained Earnings

A successful owner of a small business must continually decide what to do with the profits his firm has generated. One option is to reinvest in the business—purchasing new plant and equipment, expanding inventory, and perhaps hiring new employees. Another alternative, however, is to withdraw the funds from the business and invest them elsewhere. Prospective uses might include buying other stocks and bonds, purchasing a second business, or perhaps spending a "lost weekend" in Las Vegas.

A corporation and its stockholders must face exactly the same type of decision. Should funds associated with profits be retained in the business, or paid out to stockholders in the form of dividends?

## The Marginal Principle of Retained Earnings

In theory, corporate directors should ask, "How can the best use of the funds be made?" The rate of return that the corporation can achieve on retained earnings for the benefit of stockholders must be compared to what stockholders could earn if the funds were paid out to them in dividends. This is known as the marginal principle of retained earnings. Each potential project to be financed by internally generated funds must provide a higher rate of return than the stockholder could achieve for himself. We speak of this as the opportunity cost of using stockholder funds.

## Life Cycle Growth and Dividends

One of the major influences on dividends is the corporate growth rate in sales and the subsequent return on assets. Figure 18–1 shows a corporate life cycle and the corresponding dividend policy that is

**Figure 18–1**
**Life cycle growth and dividend policy**

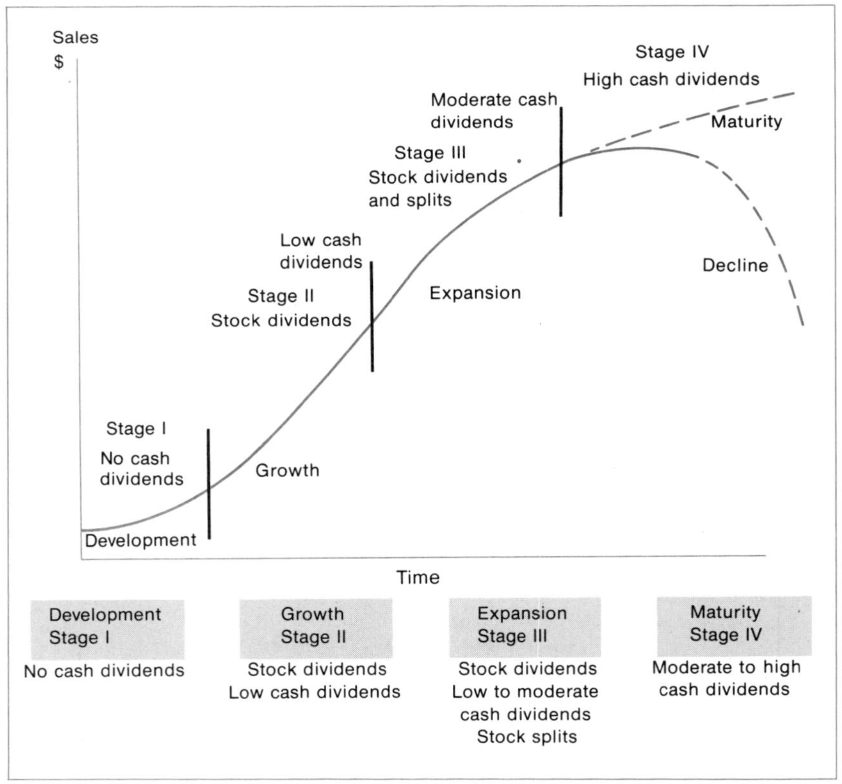

most likely to be found at each stage. A small firm in the initial stages of development (Stage I) pays no dividends because it needs all of its profits (if there are any) for reinvestment in new productive assets. If the firm is successful in the marketplace, the demand for its products will create growth in sales, earnings, and assets, and the firm will move into Stage II. At this stage, sales and returns on assets will be growing at an increasing rate, and earnings will still be reinvested. In the early part of Stage II, stock dividends (distribution of additional shares) may be instituted, and in the latter part of Stage II, *low* cash dividends may be started, to inform investors that the firm is profitable but that cash is needed for internal acquisition.

After the growth period the firm enters Stage III. The expansion of sales continues, but at a decreasing rate, and returns on investment may decline as more competition enters the market and tries to take away the firm's market share. During this period the firm is more and more capable of paying cash dividends, as the asset expansion rate slows and external funds become more readily available. Stock dividends and stock splits are still common in the expansion phase, and the dividend payout ratio usually increases from a low level of 5 to 15 percent of earnings to a moderate level of 25 to 40 percent of earnings. Finally at Stage IV, maturity, the firm maintains a stable growth rate in sales similar to that of the economy as a whole, and when risk premiums are considered, its returns on assets level out to those of the industry and the economy. In unfortunate cases, firms suffer declines in sales if product innovation and diversification have not taken place over the years. In Stage IV, assuming maturity rather than decline, dividends might range from 40 to 60 percent of earnings. These percentages will be different from industry to industry, depending on the individual characteristics of the company, such as operating and financial leverage and the volatility of sales and earnings over the business cycle.

As the chapter continues, more will be said about stock dividends, stock splits, the availability of external funds, and other variables that affect the dividend policy of the firm.

## Dividends as a Passive Variable

In the preceding analysis, dividends were used as a passive decision variable: They are only to be paid out if the corporation cannot make better use of the funds for the benefit of stockholders. The active decision variable is retained earnings: We decide how much to retain, and then the *residual is paid out in dividends.*

## An Incomplete Theory

The only problem with the residual theory is that we have not given recognition to how stockholders feel about receiving dividends. If the stockholders' only concern is with achieving the highest return on their investment, either in the form of *corporate retained earnings remaining in the business* or *as current dividends paid out*, then there is no issue. But if stockholders have a preference for current funds, for example, over retained earnings, then our theory is incomplete. The issue is not only whether reinvestment of retained earnings or dividends provide the highest return, but also how stockholders react to the two alternatives.

While some researchers maintain that stockholders are indifferent to the division of funds between retained earnings and dividends[1] (holding investment opportunities constant), others disagree.[2] Though there is no conclusive proof one way or the other, the judgment of most researchers is that investors do have some preference between dividends and retained earnings.

## Arguments for the Relevance of Dividends

A strong case can be made for the relevance of dividends because they *resolve uncertainty* in the minds of investors. Though retained

---

[1]Merton H. Miller and Franco Modigliani, "Dividend Policy, Growth and Valuation of Shares," *Journal of Business* 34 (October 1961), pp. 411–33. Under conditions of perfect capital markets with an absence of taxes and flotation costs, it is argued that the sum of discounted value per share after dividend payments equals the total valuation before dividend payments.

[2]Myron J. Gordon, "Optimum Investment and Financing Policy," *Journal of Finance* 18 (May 1963), pp. 264–72; and John Lintner, "Dividends, Earnings, Leverage, Stock Prices, and the Supply of Capital to the Corporation," *Review of Economics and Statistics* 44 (August 1962), pp. 243–69.

earnings reinvested in the business theoretically belong to common stockholders, there is still an air of uncertainty about their eventual translation into dividends. Thus, it can be hypothesized that stockholders might apply a higher discount rate ($K_e$) and assign a lower valuation to funds that are retained in the business as opposed to those that are paid out.[3]

It is also argued that dividends may be viewed more favorably than retained earnings because of the *information content* they contain. In essence, the corporation is telling the stockholder, "We are having a good year, and we wish to share the benefits with you." Though the corporation may be able to do just as well with the funds and perhaps provide even greater dividends in the future, some researchers find that "in an uncertain world in which verbal statements can be ignored or misinterpreted, dividend action does provide a clear-cut means of making a statement that speaks louder than a thousand words."[4]

The relevance of dividends in policy determination can also be argued from the viewpoint that the optimum dividend payout rate should be low. Because certain stockholders may be in high tax brackets, retention of funds in excess of investment needs might be recommended.

The primary contention in arguing for the relevance of dividend policy is that stockholders' needs and preferences go beyond the *marginal principle of retained earnings*. The issue is not only who can best utilize the funds (the corporation or the stockholder) but also what are the stockholders' preferences. In practice, it appears that most corporations adhere to the following logic. First, a determination is made of the investment opportunities of the corporation relative to a required return (marginal analysis). This is then tempered by some subjective notion of stockholders' desires. It is not surprising that corporations with unusual growth prospects and high rates of return on internal investments generally pay a relatively low dividend (the small amount may be paid out only for its informational content). For the more mature firm, an analysis of both investment opportunities and stockholder preferences may indicate that a higher rate of payout is necessary. Dividend policies of selected major U.S. corporations are pre-

---

[3] Ibid.

[4] Ezra Solomon, *The Theory of Financial Management* (New York: Columbia University Press, 1963), p. 142.

**Table 18–1**
**Corporate dividend policy**

| | Four-Year Growth Rate in Earnings per Share (1981–85) | Dividend Payout as Percentage of Aftertax Earnings (1985) |
|---|---|---|
| Category 1—rapid growth | | |
| AGS Computers . . . . . . . . . . | 38.1% | 0.0% |
| Christ-Craft (TV stations) . . . . . | 40.0 | 0.0 |
| Heritage Communications . . . . . | 29.5 | 8.0 |
| Marriott . . . . . . . . . . . . . . | 26.1 | 8.6 |
| Category 2—slower growth | | |
| GTE Corporation . . . . . . . . . . | 7.2% | 59.2% |
| Kansas Gas and Electric . . . . . | 3.0 | 64.5 |
| Pacific Lighting . . . . . . . . . . | 4.9 | 64.4 |
| Toledo Edison . . . . . . . . . . . | 2.9 | 72.1 |

sented in Table 18–1. The normal payout has been approximately 50 percent of aftertax earnings in the post-World War II period.

## Dividend Stability

In considering stockholder desires in dividend policy, a primary factor is the maintenance of stability in dividend payments. Thus, corporate management must not only ask, "How many profitable investments do we have this year?" It must also ask, "What has been the pattern of dividend payments in the last few years?" Though earnings may change from year to year, the dollar amount of cash dividends tends to be much more stable, increasing in value only as new permanent levels of income are achieved. Note in Figure 18–2 the considerably greater volatility of earnings compared to dividends for U.S. corporations in the post–World War II period.

By maintaining a record of relatively stable dividends, corporate management hopes to lower the discount rate ($K_e$) applied to future dividends of the firm. The operative rule appears to be that a stockholder would much prefer to receive $1 a year for three years rather than 75 cents for the first year, $1.50 for the second year, and 75 cents for the third year—for the same total of $3. Once again, we temper our policy of marginal analysis of retained earnings to include a notion of stockholder preference, with the emphasis on stability of dividends.

Figure 18–2
Corporate profits
(seasonally adjusted
annual rates, quarterly)

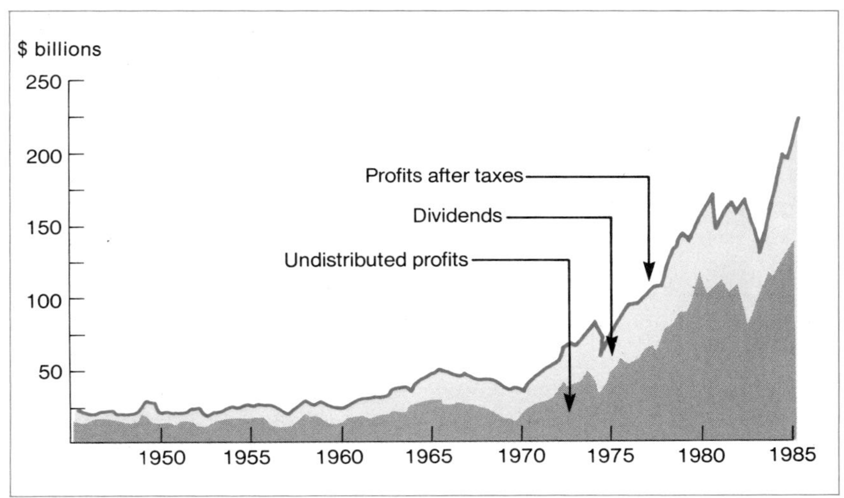


## Other Factors Influencing Dividend Policy

Corporate management must also consider the legal basis of dividends, the cash flow position of the firm, and the corporation's access to capital markets. Other factors that must be considered include management's desire for control, and the tax and financial position of shareholders. Each is briefly discussed.

### Legal Rules

Most states forbid firms to pay dividends that would impair the initial capital contributions to the firm. For this reason, dividends may only be distributed from past and current earnings. To pay dividends in excess of this amount would mean that the corporation is returning to investors their original capital contribution (raiding the capital). If the ABC Company has the following statement of net worth, the maximum dividend payment would be $20 million.

| | |
|---|---|
| Common stock (1 million shares at $10 par value)* . . . . | $10,000,000 |
| Retained earnings . . . . . . . . . . . . . . . . . . . . | 20,000,000 |
| Net worth . . . . . . . . . . . . . . . . . . . . . . . . | $30,000,000 |

*If there is a "paid-in capital in excess of par" account, some states will allow additional dividend payments against capital, while others will not. To simplify the problem for now, paid-in capital in excess of par is not considered.

Why all the concern about impairing permanent capital? Since the firm is going to pay dividends only to those who contributed capital in the first place, what is the problem? Clearly, there is no abuse to the stockholders, but what about the creditors? They have extended credit on the assumption that a given capital base would remain intact throughout the life of the loan. While they may not object to the payment of dividends from past and current earnings, they must have the protection of keeping contributed capital in place.[5]

Even the laws against having dividends exceed the total of past and current earnings (retained earnings) may be inadequate to protect creditors. Because retained earnings is merely an accounting concept and in no way certifies the current liquidity of the firm, a company paying dividends equal to retained earnings may, in certain cases, jeopardize the operation of the firm. Let us examine Table 18–2.

Theoretically, management could pay up to $15,000,000 in dividends by selling off assets even though current earnings are only $1,500,000. In most cases, such frivolous action would not be taken, but the mere possibility encourages creditors to closely watch the balance sheets of corporate debtors and, at times, to impose additional limits on dividend payments as a condition for the granting of credit.

## Cash Position of the Firm

Not only do retained earnings fail to portray the liquidity position of the firm, but there are also limitations to the use of current earnings

**Table 18–2**
**Dividend policy considerations**

| | | | |
|---|---|---|---|
| Cash | $ 1,000,000 | Debt | $10,000,000 |
| Accounts receivable | 4,000,000 | Common stock | 10,000,000 |
| Inventory | 15,000,000 | Retained earnings | 15,000,000 |
| Plant and equipment | 15,000,000 | | $35,000,000 |
| | $35,000,000 | | |

| | |
|---|---|
| Current earnings | $ 1,500,000 |
| Potential dividends | 15,000,000 |

[5] Of course, on liquidation of the corporation, the contributed capital to the firm may be returned to common stockholders after creditor obligations are met. Normally, stockholders who need to recoup all or part of their contributed capital sell their shares to someone else.

to indicate liquidity. As described in Chapter 4, Financial Forecasting, a growth firm producing the greatest gains in earnings may be in the poorest cash position. As sales and earnings expand rapidly, there is an accompanying buildup in receivables and inventory that may far outstrip cash flow generated through earnings. Note that the cash balance in Table 18–2 represents only two thirds of current earnings of $1,500,000. A firm must do a complete funds flow analysis before establishing a dividend policy.

### Access to Capital Markets

The medium-to-large size firm with a good record of performance may have relatively easy access to the financial markets. A company in such a position may be willing to pay dividends now, knowing that it can sell new stocks or bonds in the future if funds are needed. Some corporations may even issue debt or stock *now* and use part of the proceeds to ensure the maintenance of current dividends. Though this policy seems at variance with the concept of a dividend as a reward, management may justify its action on the basis of maintaining stable dividends. It should be clear that in the capital shortage era of the 1970s and 80s only a relatively small percentage of firms have had sufficient ease of entry to the capital markets to modify their dividend policy in this regard. Many firms may actually defer the payment of dividends because they know that they will have difficulty in going to the capital markets for more funds.

### Desire for Control

Management must also consider the effect of the dividend policy on its collective ability to maintain control. The directors and officers of a small, closely held firm may be hesitant to pay any dividends at all for fear of diluting the cash position of the firm and forcing the owners to look to outside investors for financing. The funds may be available only through venture capital sources that wish to have a large say in corporate operations.

A larger firm with a broad base of shareholders may face a different type of threat in regard to dividend policy. Stockholders, spoiled by a past record of dividend payments, may demand the ouster of management if dividends are withheld.

## Tax Position of Shareholders

While the payment of a cash dividend is generally taxable to the recipient, some feel the burden much more heavily than others. To the wealthy doctor or lawyer, dividend income can be taxed up to 50 percent under the tax rate in effect in 1986. Even the average taxpayer will probably pay a 25–30 percent tax. Contrast this with the corporate recipient (such as General Motors owning Xerox stock), in which 85 percent of the dividend payment is tax exempt, and only a maximum tax of 46 percent is paid against the 15 percent balance (the overall rate is 6.9 percent). Furthermore, many large institutional investors, such as pension funds and charitable organizations, are partially or wholly tax exempt.

For the individual, dividends are taxed at an investor's ordinary tax rate. However, $100 of dividends ($200 on a joint return) may be excluded from taxation in a given year. Dividends of $1,000 for an individual investor in a 50 percent tax bracket indicate $900 of dividends would be taxed at a 50 percent rate, for total taxes of $450.

Short-term capital gains (gains on securities held six months or less) are also taxed at the investor's ordinary tax rate, while long-term capital gains are taxed at 40 percent of that rate. For an investor in a 50 percent tax bracket, long-term capital gains would only be taxed at a 20 percent rate (40 percent times 50 percent). For an individual in a 45 percent tax bracket, capital gains would be taxed at 18 percent (40 percent times 45 percent). Thus, an individual in a 45 percent tax bracket would pay $180 in taxes on a $1,000 long-term capital gain.[6]

Because of differences among investors' tax rates, certain investor preferences for dividends versus capital gains have been observed in the market. This investor behavior is called the *clientele effect*. Investors in high marginal tax brackets usually prefer companies that reinvest most of their earnings, thus creating more growth in earnings and stock

[6]The long-term capital gains tax rate for individuals is somewhat different than that for corporations, which is 28 percent of the gain or the ordinary (normal) tax rate, whichever is lower. The attention in this chapter will be primarily directed to individuals.

prices. The returns from such investments will be in the form of long-term capital gains which are taxed at lower rates than dividends. Companies following these dividend policies will most probably be found in the growth and expansion stages (see Figure 18–1). Investors in lower marginal tax brackets will have a greater preference for dividends, since the tax penalty is less at lower marginal tax rates. The clientele effect is also used to explain the advantages of a stable dividend policy that makes investors more certain about the type of return they will receive.

## Dividend Payment Procedures

Now that we have examined the many factors that influence dividend policy, let us track the actual procedures for announcing and paying a dividend. Though dividends are quoted on an annual basis, the payments actually take place over four quarters during the year. For example, in 1985, Procter & Gamble paid $2.60 a year in cash dividends. This meant stockholders could expect to receive 65 cents a quarter in dividends. Because the stock was selling at $70 per share in December of 1985, we say the annual dividend yield is 3.71 percent ($2.60/70).

There are actually three key dates associated with the declaration of a quarterly dividend: the ex-dividend date, the holder-of-record date, and the payment date.

We must begin with the holder-of-record date. On this date, the firm examines its books to determine who is entitled to a cash dividend. In order to have your name included on the corporate books, you must have bought or owned the stock before the ex-dividend date, which is four business days before the holder-of-record date. If you bought the stock on the ex-dividend date or later, your name will eventually be transferred to the corporate books, but you will have bought the stock without the quarterly dividend privilege. Thus we say you bought the stock ex-dividend.[7] As an example, a stock with a holder-of-record date of March 5th will go ex-dividend on March 1st. You must buy the stock by the last day of February to get the dividend. Investors are very conscious of the date on which the stock goes ex-dividend,

[7] In this case, the old stockholder will receive the dividend.

and the value of the stock may go down by the value of the quarterly dividend on the ex-dividend date (all other things being equal). Finally, in our example, we might assume the payment date is April 2 and checks will go out to entitled stockholders on or about this time.

## Stock Dividend

A stock dividend represents a distribution of additional shares to common stockholders. The typical size of such dividends is in the 10 percent range, so that a stockholder with 10 shares might receive 1 new share in the form of a stock dividend. Larger distributions of 20–25 percent or more are usually considered to have the characteristics of a stock split, a topic to be discussed later in the chapter.

### Accounting Considerations for a Stock Dividend

Assume that prior to the declaration of a stock dividend the XYZ Corporation has the net worth position indicated in Table 18–3.

**Table 18–3**
**XYZ Corporation's financial position before stock dividend**

| | | |
|---|---|---|
| Capital accounts | Common stock (1,000,000 shares at $10 par) | $10,000,000 |
| | Capital in excess of par | 5,000,000 |
| | Retained earnings | 15,000,000 |
| | Net worth | $30,000,000 |

If a 10 percent stock dividend is declared, shares outstanding will increase by 100,000 (10 percent times 1,000,000 shares). An accounting transfer will take place between retained earnings and the two capital stock accounts based on the market value of the stock dividend. If the stock is selling at $15 a share, we will assign $1,000,000 to common stock (100,000 shares times $10 par) and $500,000 to capital in excess of par. The net worth position of XYZ after the transfer is shown in Table 18–4.

**Table 18–4**
**XYZ Corporation's financial position after stock dividend**

| | | |
|---|---|---|
| Capital accounts | Common stock (1,100,000 shares at $10) | $11,000,000 |
| | Capital in excess of par | 5,500,000 |
| | Retained earnings | 13,500,000 |
| | Net worth | $30,000,000 |

## Value to the Investor

An appropriate question might be: Is a stock dividend of real value to the investor? Suppose that your finance class collectively purchased \$1,000 worth of assets and issued 10 shares of stock to each class member. Three days later it is announced that each stockholder will receive an extra share. Has anyone benefited from the stock dividend? Of course not! The asset base remains the same (\$1,000), and your proportionate ownership in the business is unchanged (everyone got the same new share). You merely have more paper to tell you what you already knew.

The same logic is essentially true in the corporate setting. In the case of the XYZ Corporation, shown in Tables 18–3 and 18–4, we assumed that 1 million shares were outstanding before the stock dividend and 1.1 million shares afterward. Now let us assume that the corporation had aftertax earnings of \$6.6 million. Without the stock dividend, earnings per share would be \$6.60, and with the dividend \$6.00.

$$\text{Earnings per share} = \frac{\text{Earnings after taxes}}{\text{Shares outstanding}}$$

*Without stock dividend:*

$$= \frac{\$6.6 \text{ million}}{1 \text{ million shares}} = \$6.60$$

*With stock dividend:*

$$= \frac{\$6.6 \text{ million}}{1.1 \text{ million shares}} = \$6.00$$

(10% decline)

Earnings per share have gone down by exactly the same percentage that shares outstanding increased. For further illustration, assuming that Stockholder A had 10 shares before the stock dividend and 11 afterward, what are his total claims to earnings? As expected, they remain the same, at \$66.

$$\text{Claims to earnings} = \text{Shares} \times \text{Earnings per share}$$

*Without stock dividend:*

$$10 \times \$6.60 = \$66$$

*With stock dividend:*

$$11 \times \$6.00 = \$66$$

Taking the analogy one step further, assuming the stock sold at 20 times earnings before and after the stock dividend, what is the total market value of the portfolio in each case?

$$\text{Total market value} = \text{Shares} \times \left(\begin{array}{c}\text{Price/earnings}\\ \text{ratio}\end{array} \times \begin{array}{c}\text{Earnings}\\ \text{per share}\end{array}\right)$$

*Without stock dividend:*

$$10 \times (20 \times \$6.60)$$
$$10 \times \$132 = \$1{,}320$$

*With stock dividend:*

$$11 \times (20 \times \$6.00)$$
$$11 \times \$120 = \$1{,}320$$

The total market value is unchanged. Note that if the stockholder sells off the 11th share to acquire cash, his or her stock portfolio will be worth $120 less than it was worth before the stock dividend.

## Possible Value of Stock Dividends

There are limited circumstances under which a stock dividend may be more than a financial sleight of hand. If at the time a stock dividend is declared, the cash dividend per share remains constant, the stockholder will receive greater total cash dividends. Assume that the annual cash dividend for the XYZ Corporation will remain $1 per share even though earnings per share decline from $6.60 to $6.00. In this instance a stockholder moving from 10 to 11 shares as the result of a stock dividend has a $1 increase in total dividends. The overall value of his portfolio may then increase in response to larger dividends.[8]

---

[8]C. A. Barker, "Evaluation of Stock Dividends," *Harvard Business Review* 36 (July–August 1958), pp. 99–114.

### Use of Stock Dividends

Stock dividends are most frequently used by growth companies as a form of "informational content" in explaining the retention of funds for reinvestment purposes. This was indicated in the discussion of the life cycle of the firm earlier in the chapter. A corporation president may state that "instead of doing more in the way of cash dividends, we are providing a stock dividend. The funds remaining in the corporation will be used for highly profitable investment opportunities." The market reaction to such an approach may be neutral or slightly positive.

A second use of stock dividends may be to camouflage the inability of the corporation to pay cash dividends and to cover up the ineffectiveness of management in generating cash flow. The president may proclaim, "Though we are unable to pay cash dividends, we wish to reward you with a 15 percent stock dividend." Well-informed investors are likely to react very negatively.

## Stock Splits

A stock split is similar to a stock dividend, only more shares are distributed. For example, a two-for-one stock split would double the number of shares outstanding. In general, the rules of the New York Stock Exchange and the Financial Accounting Standards Board encourage distributions in excess of 20–25 percent to be handled as stock splits.

The accounting treatment for a stock split is somewhat different from that for a stock dividend in that there is no transfer of funds from retained earnings to the capital accounts, but merely a reduction in par value and a proportionate increase in the number of shares outstanding. For example, a two-for-one stock split for the XYZ Corporation would necessitate the accounting adjustments shown in Table 18–5.

In this case, all adjustments are in the common stock account. Because the number of shares are doubled and the par value halved, the market price of the stock should drop proportionately. There has been much discussion in the financial literature about the impact of a split on overall stock value. While there might be some positive benefit, that benefit is virtually impossible to capture after the announcement

**Table 18–5**
**XYZ Corporation before and after stock split**

| | |
|---|---|
| *Before* | |
| Common stock (1 million shares at $10 par) . . . . | $10,000,000 |
| Capital in excess of par . . . . . . . . . . . . . . . | 5,000,000 |
| Retained earnings . . . . . . . . . . . . . . . . | 15,000,000 |
| | $30,000,000 |
| *After* | |
| Common stock (2 million shares at $5 par) . . . . . | $10,000,000 |
| Capital in excess of par . . . . . . . . . . . . . . . | 5,000,000 |
| Retained earnings . . . . . . . . . . . . . . . . | 15,000,000 |
| | $30,000,000 |

of a split has taken place.[9] Perhaps a 66 dollar stock will drop only to $36 after a two-for-one split, but one must act very early in the process to benefit.

The primary purpose of a stock split is to lower the price of a security into a more popular trading range. A stock selling for over $50 per share may be excluded from consideration by many small investors. Splits are popular because only the stronger companies that have witnessed substantial growth in market price are in a position to participate in them.

## Repurchase of Stock as an Alternative to Dividends

A firm with excess cash and inadequate investment opportunities may choose to repurchase its own shares in the market rather than pay a cash dividend. For this reason the stock repurchase decision may be thought of as an alternative to the payment of cash dividends.

We will show that the benefits of the stockholder are equal under either alternative, at least in theory. For purposes of study, assume that the Morgan Corporation's financial position may be described by the data in Table 18–6.

The firm has $2 million in excess cash, and it wishes to compare the value to stockholders of a $2 cash dividend (on the million shares

[9]Keith B. Johnson, "Stock Splits and Price Changes," *Journal of Finance* 21 (December 1966), pp. 675–88.

Table 18–6
Financial data of Morgan Corporation

| | |
|---|---|
| Earnings after taxes | $3,000,000 |
| Shares | 1,000,000 |
| Earnings per share | $3 |
| Price–earnings ratio | 10 |
| Market price per share | $30 |
| Excess cash | $2,000,000 |

outstanding) as opposed to spending the funds to repurchase shares in the market. If the cash dividend is paid, the shareholder will have $30 in stock and the $2 cash dividend. On the other hand, the $2 million may be used to repurchase shares at slightly over market value (to induce sale).[10] The overall benefit to stockholders is that earnings per share will go up as the number of shares outstanding is decreased. If the price-earnings ratio of the stock remains constant, then the price of the stock should also go up. If a purchase price of $32 is used to induce sale, then 62,500 shares will be purchased.

$$\frac{\text{Excess funds}}{\text{Purchase price per share}} = \frac{\$2{,}000{,}000}{\$32} = 62{,}500 \text{ shares}$$

Total shares outstanding are reduced to 937,500 (1,000,000 − 62,500). Revised earnings per share for the Morgan Corporation become:

$$\frac{\text{Earnings after taxes}}{\text{Shares}} = \frac{\$3{,}000{,}000}{937{,}500} = \$3.20$$

Since the price–earnings ratio for the stock is 10, the market value of the stock should go to $32. Thus, we see that the consequences of the two alternatives are presumed to be the same.

| (1) Funds Used for Cash Dividend | | (2) Funds Used to Repurchase Stock | |
|---|---|---|---|
| Market value per share | $30 | Market value per share | $32 |
| Cash dividend per share | 2 | | |
| | $32 | | |

[10]In order to derive the desired equality between the two alternatives, the purchase price for the new shares should equal the current market price plus the proposed cash dividend under the first alternative ($30 + $2 = $32).

In either instance, the total value is presumed to be $32. Theoretically, the stockholder would be indifferent with respect to the two alternatives. This changes somewhat, however, when taxes and transaction costs are brought into the decision-making process. Let us look at taxes first. While the cash dividend is immediately taxed as ordinary income in alternative (1), the gain in alternative (2) is likely to be taxed at approximately 40 percent of that rate as a form of capital gains. Furthermore, the tax will be incurred only when the stock is sold. From a tax viewpoint, the repurchase of shares may provide maximum benefits. On the other hand, one can argue that dividends put cash in the stockholder's hands without any transaction costs, while the cash flow from alternative (2) can be realized only by selling stock at the higher price.

### Other Reasons for Repurchase

In addition to using the repurchase decision as an alternative to cash dividends, corporate management may acquire its own shares in the market because it believes they are selling at a low price. A corporation president who sees his firm's stock decline by 50–75 percent over a six-month period may determine that the stock is the best investment available to the corporation.

By repurchasing shares, the corporation is able to maintain a constant demand for its own securities and perhaps to stave off further decline, at least temporarily. Reacquired shares may also be used for employee stock options or as part of a tender offer in a merger or an acquisition. Firms may also reacquire part of their shares as a protective device against being taken over as a merger candidate. In Table 18–7, we see some enormous stock repurchases conducted by major U.S. corporations in 1985.

## Dividend Reinvestment Plans

During the 1970s, many companies started dividend reinvestment plans for their shareholders. These plans take various forms, but basically they provide the investor with an opportunity to buy additional

Table 18–7
Stock repurchases

## The Biggest Stock Buybacks of 1985

| COMPANY | COMMON SHARES* | VALUE* |
|---|---|---|
| **Phillips Petroleum**[1] | 81,480,000 | $4.11 billion[2] |
| **Atlantic Richfield** | 66,945,000 | 4.00 billion |
| **Unocal**[1] | 50,000,000 | 2.37 billion |
| **Exxon**[3] | 46,600,000 | 2.30 billion |
| **Union Carbide** | 23,550,000 | 2.00 billion |
| **Allied-Signal** | 40,000,000 | 1.76 billion |
| **Litton Industries**[1] | 17,500,000 | 1.36 billion |
| **Ford Motor** | 20,000,000 | 980 million |
| **Santa Fe Southern Pacific** | 30,000,000 | 896 million |
| **Westinghouse** | 25,000,000 | 837 million |
| **MidCon**[1] | 10,000,000 | 750 million |
| **Holiday** | 12,640,000 | 749 million |
| **CBS**[1] | 6,365,000 | 738 million |
| **Sun Co.** | 13,423,000 | 700 million |
| **Revlon**[1] | 15,000,000 | 686 million |
| **TRW** | 8,546,000 | 657 million |

[1]Common stock swaps for other securities
[2]Includes $471.6 million repurchase of 8.9 million shares from Mesa Petroleum Co.
[3]Actual 1985 purchases through October 18

*Announcements; plans run various time spans. Values are estimates based on either market prices or securities swaps at announcement time.

Source: Reprinted by permission of *The Wall Street Journal*, © Dow Jones & Company, Inc. (January 2, 1986), p. 63. 

shares of stock with the cash dividend paid by the company. Some plans, such as that of American Telephone and Telegraph, will sell treasury stock or authorized but unissued shares to the stockholders. With this type of plan the company is the beneficiary of increased cash flow, since dividends paid are returned to the company for reinvestment in common stock. These types of plans have been very popular with cash-short utilities, and very often utilities will allow shareholders a 5 percent discount from market value at the time of purchase. This is justified because no investment banking or underwriting fees need be paid.

Under a second popular dividend reinvestment plan, the company's transfer agent, usually a bank, buys shares of stock in the market for the stockholder. This plan provides no cash flow for the company, but it is a service to the shareholder, who benefits from much lower transaction costs, the right to own fractional shares, and more flexibility in choosing between cash and common stock. Usually a shareholder can also add cash payments of up to $1,000 per month to his or her dividend payments and receive the same lower transaction costs. Shareholder accounts are kept at the bank, and quarterly statements are provided. Shares will be sent out to stockholders on request or will be sold on request for a commission that is usually lower than that charged by a broker.

## Summary

The first consideration in the establishment of a dividend policy is the firm's ability to reinvest the funds versus that of the stockholder. To the extent that the firm is able to earn a higher return, reinvestment of retained earnings may be justified. However, we must temper this "highest return theory" with a consideration of stockholder preferences and the firm's need for earnings retention and growth as presented in the life cycle growth curve.

Stockholders may be given a greater payout than the optimum determined by rational analysis in order to resolve their uncertainty about the future and for informational content purposes. Conversely, stockholders may prefer a greater than normal retention in order to defer the income tax obligation associated with cash dividends. Another important consideration in establishing a dividend policy may be the stockholders' desire for steady dividend payments.

Lesser factors influencing dividend policy are legal rules relating to maximum payment, the cash position of the firm, and the firm's access to capital markets. One must also consider the desire for control by corporate management and stockholders.

An alternative (or a supplement) to cash dividends may be the use of stock dividends and stock splits. While neither of these financing devices directly changes the intrinsic value of the stockholder position, they may provide communication to stockholders and bring the stock price into a more acceptable trading range. A stock dividend may take on some actual value when total cash dividends are allowed to increase. Nevertheless, the alert investor will watch for abuses of stock dividends—situations in which the corporation indicates that something of great value is taking place when, in fact, the new shares that are created merely represent the same proportionate interest for each shareholder.

The decision to repurchase shares may be thought of as an alternative to the payment of a cash dividend. Decreasing shares outstanding will cause earnings per share, and perhaps the market price, to go up. The increase in the market price may be equated to the size of the cash dividend forgone.

Many firms are now offering stockholders the option of reinvesting cash dividends in the company's common stock. Cash-short companies have been using dividend reinvestment plans in order to raise external funds. Other companies simply provide a service to stockholders by allowing them to purchase shares in the market for low transaction costs.

## List of Terms

**marginal principle of retained earnings**
**residual dividends**
**declaration date**
**ex-dividend date**
**dividend record date**
**dividend information content**
**dividend payout**
**dividend yield**
**life cycle curve**
**clientele effect**
**dividend payment date**
**stock dividends**
**stock split**
**capital gains taxes**
**dividend reinvestment plans**
**corporate stock repurchase**

## Discussion Questions

1. How does the marginal principle of retained earnings relate to the returns that a stockholder may make in other investments?

2. Discuss the difference between a passive and an active dividend policy.

3. How does the stockholder in general feel about the relevance of dividends?

4. Explain the relationship between a company's growth possibilities and its dividend policy.

5. Discuss the major factors that may influence the firm's willingness and ability to pay dividends.

6. If you buy a stock on the ex-dividend date, will you receive the upcoming quarterly dividend?

7. Describe the importance of stockholder tax rates in setting dividend policy.

8. How is a stock split versus a stock dividend treated on the financial statements of a corporation?

9. Why might a stock dividend or a stock split be of limited value to an investor?

10. Does it make sense for a corporation to repurchase its own stock? Explain.

11. How does the life cycle curve explain the relationship between corporate growth and residual dividend theory?

12. Why might an investor prefer long-term capital gains over dividends?

13. What advantages to the corporation and the stockholder do dividend reinvestment plans offer?

## Problems

1. Sewell Enterprises earned $160 million last year and retained $100 million. What is the payout ratio?

2. In doing a five-year analysis of future dividends, the Dawson Corporation is considering the following two plans. The values represent dividends per share.

| *Year* | *Plan A* | *Plan B* |
|---|---|---|
| 1 . . . . . . | $1.50 | $ .50 |
| 2 . . . . . . | 1.50 | 2.00 |
| 3 . . . . . . | 1.50 | .20 |
| 4 . . . . . . | 1.60 | 4.00 |
| 5 . . . . . . | 1.60 | 1.70 |

*a.* How much in total dividends per share will be paid under each plan over the five years?

*b.* Mr. Bright, the vice president of finance, suggests that stockholders often prefer a stable dividend policy to a highly variable one. He will assume that stockholders apply a lower discount rate to dividends that are stable. The discount rate to be used for Plan A is 10 percent; the discount rate for Plan B is 12 percent. Which plan will provide the higher present value for the future dividends? (Round to two places to the right of the decimal point.)

**3.** The following companies have different financial statistics. What dividend policies would you recommend for them? Explain your reasons.

| | *Turtle Co.* | *Hare Corp.* |
|---|---|---|
| Growth rate in sales and earnings . . . . . | 5% | 20% |
| Cash as a percentage of total assets . . . . | 15% | 2% |

**4.** The Ohio Freight Company's common stock is selling for $40 the day before the stock goes ex-dividend. The annual dividend yield is 6.7 percent, and dividends are distributed quarterly. Based solely on the impact of the cash dividend, by how much should the stock go down on the ex-dividend date? What will the new price of the stock be?

**5.** Below are the earnings per share and the dividends per share of three companies.

| *XYZ Co.* | | *ABC Co.* | | *Widget Co.* | |
|---|---|---|---|---|---|
| *EPS* | *DPS* | *EPS* | *DPS* | *EPS* | *DPS* |
| $2.00 | $1.00 | $2.00 | $1.00 | $2.00 | $1.00 |
| 2.10 | 1.05 | 2.10 | 1.00 | 2.10 | .75 |
| 2.40 | 1.20 | 2.40 | 1.00 | 2.40 | 1.00 |
| 2.80 | 1.40 | 2.80 | 1.00 | 2.80 | 1.50 |
| 3.00 | 1.50 | 3.00 | 1.20 | 3.00 | 1.00 |

*a.* What are the payout ratios for each company on an annual basis?
*b.* Can you explain some of the reasons for such differences in payout patterns?
*c.* Which company would you prefer to own as a stockholder? Why? What other kinds of information would you want before you invested your money?

**6.** The King Petroleum Company has the following capital section on its balance sheet. Its stock is currently selling for $7 per share.

| | |
|---|---|
| Common stock (100,000 shares at $1 par) | $100,000 |
| Capital in excess of par | 150,000 |
| Retained earnings | 250,000 |
| | $500,000 |

The firm intends to declare a 10 percent stock dividend and then pay a 25¢ cash dividend (which also causes a reduction of retained earnings).

Show the capital section of the balance sheet after the first transaction and then after the second transaction.

**7.** Phillips Rock and Mud is trying to determine the maximum amount of cash dividends it can pay this year. Assume its balance sheet is as follows:

| *Assets* | |
|---|---|
| Cash | $ 312,500 |
| Accounts receivable | 800,000 |
| Fixed assets | 987,500 |
| Total assets | $2,100,000 |
| *Liabilities and Stockholders' Equity* | |
| Accounts payable | $ 445,000 |
| Long-term payable | 280,000 |
| Common stock (250,000 shares at $2 par) | 500,000 |
| Retained earnings | 875,000 |
| Total liabilities and stockholders' equity | $2,100,000 |

*a.* From a legal perspective, what is the maximum amount of dividends per share that the firm could pay? Is this realistic?
*b.* In terms of cash availability, what is the maximum amount of dividends per share the firm could pay?

*c.* Assume the firm earned a 16 percent return on stockholders' equity last year. If the board wishes to pay out 60 percent of earnings in the form of dividends, how much will dividends per share be?

**8.** The Adams Corporation has earnings of $750,000, with 300,000 shares outstanding. Its P/E ratio is eight. The firm is holding $400,000 of funds to invest or pay out in dividends. If the funds are retained, the aftertax return on investment will be 15 percent, and this will add to present earnings. The 15 percent is the normal return anticipated for the corporation and the P/E ratio would remain unchanged. If the funds are paid out in the form of dividends, the P/E ratio will increase by 10 percent because the stockholders are in a very low tax bracket and have a preference for dividends over retained earnings. Which plan will maximize the market value of the stock?

**9.** Wilson Pharmaceuticals' stock has done very well in the market during the last three years. It has risen from $45 to $70 per share. The firm's current statement of stockholders' equity is as follows:

| | |
|---|---|
| Common stock (4 million shares issued at par value of $10 per share: 12 million shares authorized) | $ 40,000,000 |
| Paid-in capital in excess of par | 15,000,000 |
| Retained earnings | 45,000,000 |
| Net worth | $100,000,000 |

*a.* What changes would occur in the statement of stockholders' equity after a two-for-one stock split?

*b.* What would the statement of stockholders' equity look like after a three-for-one stock split?

*c.* Assume that Wilson earned $14 million. What would be its earnings per share before and after the two-for-one stock split? The three-for-one stock split?

*d.* What would be the price per share after the two-for-one stock split? The three-for-one stock split? (Assume that the price–earnings ratio stays the same.)

*e.* Should a stock split change the price–earnings ratio for Wilson?

**10.** Slick Products sells marked playing cards to blackjack dealers. It has not paid a dividend in many years, but is currently contemplating some kind of dividend. The capital accounts for the firm are as follows:

| | |
|---|---|
| Common stock (150,000 shares at $1 par) | $150,000 |
| Capital paid in excess of par | 150,000 |
| Retained earnings | 400,000 |
| Net worth | $700,000 |

The company's stock is selling for $6 per share and it earned $0.60 per share this year, indicating a P/E ratio of 10.

*a.* What adjustments would have to be made to the capital accounts for a 10 percent stock dividend?
*b.* What adjustments would be made to EPS and the stock price? (Assume the P/E ratio remains constant.)
*c.* How many shares would an investor end up with if he or she originally had 100 shares?
*d.* What is the investor's total investment worth before and after the stock dividend if the P/E ratio remains constant? (There may be a small difference due to rounding.)
*e.* Has Slick Products pulled a magic trick, or has it given the investor something of value? Explain.

**11.** The purpose of this problem is to compare the aftertax income on a $20,000 investment for the following two investors and two possible investments. Mr. Trucks' marginal tax rate is 30 percent. This is his only investment. Mrs. Carr's marginal tax rate is 50 percent. This is her only investment. Investment A provides $1,500 in dividends and no long-term capital gains. (The first $100 of dividends may be excluded for tax purposes.) Investment B provides no dividends, but $1,500 of long-term capital gains.

*a.* Calculate the aftertax return for Mr. Trucks in Investment A and Investment B.
*b.* Calculate the aftertax return for Mrs. Carr in Investment A and Investment B.
*c.* Indicate the difference in aftertax income between the two investors in Investment A.
*d.* Indicate the difference in aftertax income between the two investors in Investment B.
*e.* In the answers to parts *c* and *d*, why is there a smaller difference between the answers for one investment than for the other?

**12.** The Belton Corporation has $5 in earnings after taxes and 1 million shares outstanding. The stock trades at a P/E of 10. The firm has $4 million in excess cash.

*a.* Compute the current price of the stock.
*b.* If the $4 million is used to pay dividends, how much will dividends per share be?
*c.* If the $4 million is used to repurchase shares in the market at a price of $54 per share, how many shares will be required? (Round to the nearest share.)
*d.* What will the new earnings per share be? (Round to the nearest cent.)
*e.* If the P/E ratio remains constant, what will the price of the securities be? By how much, in terms of dollars, did the repurchase increase the stock price?

Assume Stockholder X has owned 100 shares of Belton stock for a number of years and can easily qualify for long-term capital gains. He owns 12 other stocks and has already used up his $100 dividend exemption, so he will pay full taxes on all cash dividends. He is in a 45 percent tax bracket.

*f.* How much is his aftertax dollar return on his 100 shares with the cash dividend?
*g.* How much is his aftertax return on his 100 shares with the $4 gain from the corporate stock repurchase if he sells his stock? (There, of course, would be no cash dividend.)

**13.** The Hastings Sugar Corporation has the following pattern of net income each year, and associated capital expenditures projects. The firm can earn a higher return on the projects than the stockholders could earn if the funds were paid out as dividends.

| Year | Net Income | Profitable Capital Expenditure |
|---|---|---|
| 1 . . . . . | $10 million | $ 7 million |
| 2 . . . . . | 15 million | 11 million |
| 3 . . . . . | 9 million | 6 million |
| 4 . . . . . | 12 million | 7 million |
| 5 . . . . . | 14 million | 8 million |

The Hastings Corporation has 2 million shares outstanding. (The following questions are separate from each other.)

*a.* If the marginal principle of retained earnings is applied, how much in total cash dividends will be paid over the five years?
*b.* If the firm simply uses a payout ratio of 40 percent of net income, how much in total cash dividends will be paid?
*c.* If the firm pays a 10 percent stock dividend in Years 2 through 5, and also pays a cash dividend of $2.40 per share for each of the five years, how much in total cash dividends will be paid?
*d.* Assume the payout ratio in each year is to be 30 percent of net income, and the firm will pay a 20 percent stock dividend in Years 2 through 5, how much will dividends per share for each year be?

## Selected References

Barker, C. A. "Evaluation of Stock Dividends." *Harvard Business Review* 36 (July–August 1958), pp. 99–114.

Bierman, Harold, Jr., and Richard West. "The Acquisition of Common Stock by the Corporate Issuer." *Journal of Finance* 21 (December 1966), pp. 687–96.

Black, Fischer, and Myron Scholes. "The Effects of Dividend Yield and Dividend Policy on Common Stock Prices and Returns." *Journal of Financial Economics* 1 (May 1974), pp. 1–22.

Brigham, Eugene F., and Myron J. Gordon. "Leverage, Dividend Policy, and the Cost of Capital." *Journal of Finance* 23 (March 1968), pp. 85–104.

Dielmen, T.; R. Wright; and T. Nantell. "Price Effects of Stock Repurchasing: A Random Coefficient Regression Approach." *Journal of Financial and Quantitative Analysis* 15 (March 1980), pp. 175–189.

Elton, Edwin J., and Martin J. Gruber. "The Cost of Retained Earnings—Implications of Share Repurchase." *Industrial Management Review* 9 (Spring 1968), pp. 87–104.

Fama, Eugene F. "The Empirical Relationships between the Dividend and Investment Decisions of Firms." *American Economic Review* 64 (June 1974), pp. 304–18.

Friend, Irwin, and Marshall Puckett. "Dividends and Stock Prices." *American Economic Review* 54 (September 1964), pp. 656–82.

Gordon, Myron J. "Optimum Investment and Financing Policy." *Journal of Finance* 18 (May 1963), pp. 264–72.

Grinblatt, Mark S.; Ronald W. Masulis; and Sheridan Titman. "The Valuation Effects of Stock Splits and Stock Dividends." *Journal of Financial Economics* 13 (December 1984), pp. 461–90.

Johnson, Keith B. "Stock Splits and Price Changes." *Journal of Finance* 21 (December 1966), pp. 675–86.

Kalay, Avner. "Stockholder-Bondholder Conflict and Dividend Constraints." *Journal of Financial Economics* 59 (July 1982), pp. 211–33.

———. "The Ex-dividend Day Behavior of Stock Prices: A Reexamination of the Clientele Effect." *Journal of Finance* 37 (September 1982), pp. 1059–70.

Lintner, John. "Distribution of Income of Corporations among Dividends, Retained Earnings, and Taxes." *American Economic Review* 46 (May 1956), pp. 97–113.

———. "Dividends, Earnings, Leverage, Stock Prices, and the Supply of Capital to Corporations." *Review of Economics and Statistics* 44 (August 1962), pp. 243–69.

Miller, Merton H., and Franco Modigliani. "Dividend Policy, Growth, and the Valuation of Shares." *Journal of Business* 34 (October 1961), pp. 411–33.

Pettit, R. Richardson. "Dividend Announcements, Security Performance, and Capital Market Efficiency." *Journal of Finance* 27 (December 1972), pp. 993–1007.

Solomon, Ezra. *The Theory of Financial Management*. New York: Columbia University Press, 1963.

Terborgh, George. "Inflation and Profits." *Financial Analysts Journal* 30 (May–June 1974), pp. 19–23.

Van Horne, James C., and John G. McDonald. "Dividend Policy and New Equity Financing." *Journal of Finance* 26 (May 1971), pp. 507–19.

Walter, James E. "Dividend Policies and Common Stock Prices." *Journal of Finance* 11 (March 1956), pp. 29–41.

# 19 Convertibles and Warrants

There are as many types of securities as there are innovative corporate treasurers or forward-looking portfolio managers. In the inflation–disinflation, volatile-interest-rate period of the 1970s and 1980s, investors have looked to security features providing special downside protection as well as capital appreciation potential. Many of these securities also are an outgrowth of the wheeler-dealer, fast-buck period of the late 1960s. The particular emphasis in this chapter is on convertible securities and warrants.

## Convertible Securities

A convertible security is a bond or share of preferred stock that can be converted, at the option of the holder, into common stock. Thus, the owner has a fixed income security that can be transferred to a common stock interest if and when the affairs of the firm indicate that such a conversion is desirable. For purposes of discussion, we will refer to convertible bonds (debentures), although the same principles apply to convertible preferred stock.

When a convertible debenture is initially issued, a *conversion ratio* to common stock is specified. The ratio indicates the number of shares of common stock to which the debenture may be converted. Assume that in 1983 the Williams Company issued $10 million of 25-year, 6 percent convertible debentures, with each $1,000 bond convertible into 20 shares of common stock. The conversion ratio of 20 may also be expressed in terms of a *conversion price*. To arrive at the conversion price, we divide the face value of the bond by the conversion ratio of 20. In the case of the Williams Company, the conversion price is $50.

## Value of the Convertible Bond

As a first consideration in evaluating a convertible bond, we must examine the value of the conversion privilege. In the above case, we might assume that the common stock is selling at $45 per share, so that the total conversion value is $900 ($45 × 20). Nevertheless, the bond may sell for par or face value ($1,000) in anticipation of future developments in the common stock and because interest payments are being received on the bonds. With the bond selling for $1,000 and a $900 conversion value, there is a $100 *conversion premium*, representing the dollar difference between market value and conversion value. The conversion premium generally will be influenced by the expectations of future performance of the common stock. If investors are optimistic about the prospects of the common stock, the premium may be large.

If the price of the common stock really takes off and goes to $60 per share, the conversion privilege becomes quite valuable. The bonds, which are convertible into 20 shares, will go up to at least $1,200, and perhaps more. Note that you do not have to convert to common immediately, but may enjoy the movement of the convertible in concert with the common.

What happens if the common stock goes in the opposite direction? Assume that instead of going from $45 to $60 the common stock simply drops from $45 to $25—what will happen to the value of the convertible debentures? We know the value of a convertible bond will go down in response to the drop in the common stock, but will it fall all the way down to $500 (20 × $25 per share)? The answer is clearly no because the debenture still has value as an interest-bearing security. If the going market rate of interest in straight debt issues of similar maturity (25

Figure 19–1
Price movement pattern for a convertible bond

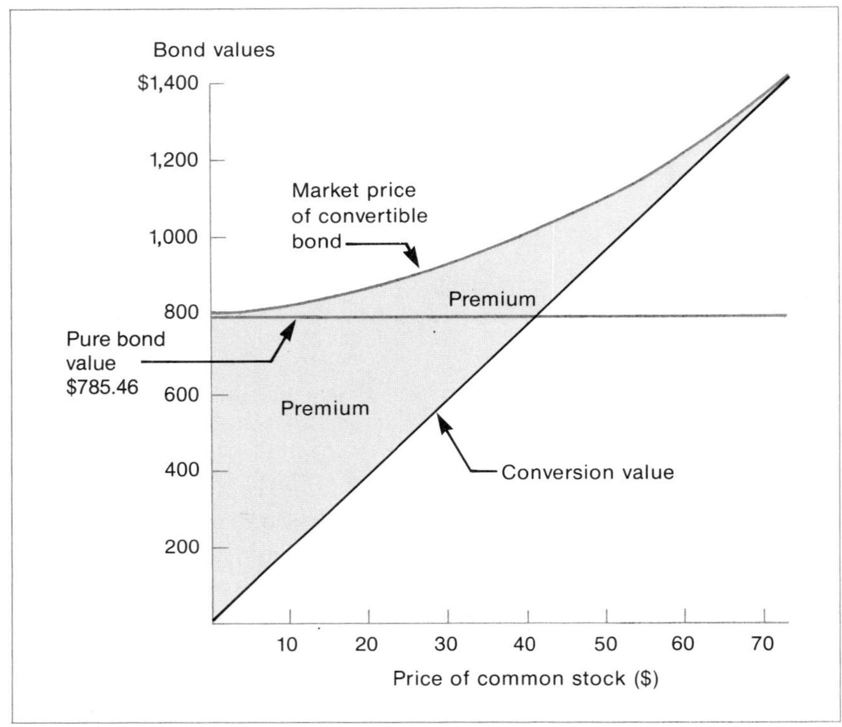


years) and quality is 8 percent, we would say the debenture has a pure bond value of $785.46.[1] Thus, a convertible bond has a floor value,[2] but no upside limitation. The price pattern for the convertible bond is depicted in Figure 19–1.

We see the effect on the convertible bond price as the common stock price, shown along the X-axis, is assumed to change. Note that the floor value for the convertible is well above the conversion value when the common stock price is very low. As the common stock price moves to higher levels, the convertible bond moves in concert with the conversion value. Representative information on outstanding convertible bonds is presented in Table 19–1.

[1] Based on discounting procedures covered in Chapter 10, Valuation and Rates of Return.

[2] The floor value can change if interest rates in the market change. For ease of presentation, we shall assume they are constant for now.

Table 19–1 Pricing pattern for convertible bonds outstanding (October 1985)

| Issue, Coupon, Maturity, and Rating | (1) Conversion Value | (2) Market Value of Bond | (3) Call Price (percent of par) | (4) Yield to Maturity on Bond | (5) Market Rate for Bond of Similar Maturity and Quality |
|---|---|---|---|---|---|
| Anacomp Inc. 13.875, 2002, Ca | $ 171.25 | $ 811.25 | 100.0% | 17.4% | 17.4% |
| Avco Corp. 5½, 1993, Ba2 | 851.25 | 900.00 | 102.2 | 7.1 | 13.3 |
| Pfizer Inc. 8.75, 2006, Aa2 | 1,575.30 | 1,574.75 | 106.91 | 4.5 | 10.9 |
| RCA Corp. 4.5, 1992, A3 | 742.50 | 900.00 | 100.40 | 6.3 | 11.7 |
| Research-Cottrell 10.5, 2006, Ba1 | 1,352.50 | 1,360.00 | 108.93 | 7.2 | 12.4 |

The first bond in Table 19–1 can serve to show what is meant by floor value. Anacomp Inc. had a series of bad years. The common stock declined to $3 per share, and the resulting conversion value fell to $171.25. Because the convertible bond was able to maintain its 13.875 percent coupon payment, the bond price declined to its floor value of $811.25. At this price the bond yields 17.4 percent to maturity, which for a low-rated Ca bond is a high but risky return.

In the cases of Pfizer and Research-Cottrell, the bonds are trading well above the par value of $1,000, indicating that the conversion privilege has become very valuable and that interest payments are probably no factor at all in establishing the bond price. Avco Corporation and RCA Corporation bonds are both selling at a premium over their conversion value, but are at the point where a change in the stock price would affect the market value of the bond. These two bonds would be selling close to the point where the conversion value equals the pure bond value. A decline in stock price would not have too much effect on the bond price, since the yield would support the floor value.

## Is This Fool's Gold?

Have we repealed the old risk–return trade-off principle—that in order to get superior returns we must take larger than normal risks?

With convertible bonds, we appear to limit our risk while maximizing our return potential.

Although there is some truth to this statement, there are many qualifications. For example, once convertible debentures begin going up in value, say to $1,100 or $1,200, the downside protection becomes pretty meaningless. In the case of the Williams Company in our earlier example, the floor is at $785.46. If an investor were to buy the convertible bond at $1,200, he would be exposed to $414.54 in potential losses (hardly adequate protection for a true risk averter). Also, if interest rates in the market rise, the floor price, or pure bond value, could fall, creating more downside risk.

A second drawback with convertible bonds is that the purchaser is invariably asked to accept below-market rates of interest on the debt instrument. The interest rate on convertibles is generally one third below that for instruments in a similar risk class at time of issue. In the sophisticated environment of the bond and stock markets, one seldom gets an additional benefit without having to suffer a corresponding disadvantage.

The student will also recall that the purchaser of a convertible bond pays a premium over the conversion value. For example, if a $1,000 bond were convertible into 20 shares of common at $45 per share, a $100 conversion premium might be involved initially. If the same $1,000 were invested directly in common stock at $45 per share, 22.2 shares could be purchased. If the shares go up in value, we have 2.2 more shares on which to garner a profit.

Lastly, convertibles may suffer from the attachment of a call provision giving the corporation the option of redeeming the bonds at a specified price above par ($1,000) in the future. In a subsequent section, we will see how the corporation can use this device to force the conversion of the bonds.

None of these negatives is meant to detract from the fact that convertibles carry some inherently attractive features if they are purchased with investor objectives in mind. If the investor wants downside protection, he or she should search out convertible bonds trading below par, perhaps within 10–15 percent of the floor value. Though a fairly large move in the stock may be necessary to generate upside profit, the investor has the desired protection and some hope for capital appreciation.

## Advantages and Disadvantages to the Corporation

Having established the fundamental characteristics of the convertible security from the *investor* viewpoint, let us now turn the coin over and examine the factors a corporate financial officer must consider in weighing the advisability of a convertible offer for the firm.

Not only has it been established that the interest rate paid on convertible issues is lower than that paid on a straight debt instrument, but the convertible feature may be the only device for allowing smaller corporations access to the bond market. In this day of debt-ridden corporate balance sheets, investor acceptance of new debt may be contingent upon a special sweetener, such as the ability to convert to common.

Convertible debentures are also attractive to a corporation that believes its stock is currently undervalued. You will recall that in the case of the Williams Company, $1,000 bonds were convertible into 20 shares of common stock at a conversion price of $50. Since the common stock had a current price of $45 and new shares of stock might be sold at only $44,[3] the corporation effectively received $6 over current market price, assuming future conversion. Of course, one can also argue that if the firm had delayed the issuance of common stock or convertibles for a year or two, the stock might have gone up from $45 to $60 and new common stock might have been sold at this lofty price.

To translate this to overall numbers for the firm, if a corporation needs $10 million in funds and offers straight stock now at a net price of $44, it must issue 227,272 shares ($10 million shares/$44). With convertibles, the number of shares potentially issued is only 200,000 shares ($10 million/$50). Finally, if no stock or convertible bonds are issued now and the stock goes up to a level at which new shares can be offered at a net price of $60, only 166,667 will be required ($10 million/$60).

Table 19–2 demonstrates the company's ability to sell stock at premium prices through the use of convertible bonds. The typical convertible bond issued in 1985, according to *Value Line Convertibles*, had a 20 percent conversion premium at issue. The table also provides a

---

[3]There is always a bit of underpricing to ensure the success of a new offering.

**Table 19–2**
**Characteristics of convertible bonds issued in 1985**

| | |
|---|---|
| Yield to maturity | 8.5% |
| Years to maturity | 22.9 |
| Size | $50.4 million |
| Investment value grade | Ba Moody's Rating |
| Initial premium over conversion value | 20.0% |

composite picture of the yield to maturity, years to maturity, size, and investment rating. Notice that the average size of convertibles is quite small with an average offering of only $50.4 million per issue. The typical industrial issue is well in excess of $100 million. This is partially because many small companies with less than a top grade credit rating are primary issuers of convertible bonds.

Another matter of concern to the corporation is the accounting treatment accorded to convertibles. In the funny-money days of the conglomerate merger movement of the 1960s, corporate management often chose convertible securities over common stock because the convertibles had a nondilutive effect on earnings per share. As is indicated in a later section on reporting earnings for convertibles, the rules were changed in 1969, and this is no longer the case.

Inherent in a convertible issue is the presumed ability of the corporation to force the security holder to convert the present instrument to common stock. We will examine this process.

## Forcing Conversion

How does a corporation, desirous of shifting outstanding debt to common stock, force conversion? The principal device is the call provision, as discussed in Chapter 16, Long-Term Debt and Lease Financing. We know that when the value of the common stock goes up, the convertible security will move in a similar fashion. Table 19–3 indicates that convertible debentures may go up substantially in value. Some particularly successful convertibles have actually tripled in price. For this reason, the holder of a convertible bond has no immediate incentive to convert to common unless the company calls the bond.

Notice also that the coupon rates of the convertible bonds in Table 19–3 were relatively low, compared to existing coupon rates of ap-

**Table 19–3**
**Successful convertible bonds not yet called (October 1985)**

| Issue, Coupon, Maturity | Market Price | Call Price |
|---|---|---|
| Allied Stores (4.5%, 1992) . . . . . . . . | $2,420.00 | $1,005.00 |
| Crane Co. (5.00%, 1993) . . . . . . . . . | 3,010.00 | 1,000.00 |
| Pepsico, Inc. (4.75%, 1996) . . . . . . . | 2,827.50 | 1,014.60 |
| Ralston Purina Co. (5.75%, 2000) . . . . | 2,987.50 | 1,028.80 |
| Rockwell Intl. (4.25%, 1991) . . . . . . . | 3,162.50 | 1,001.30 |
| Sherwin-Williams (6.25%, 1995) . . . . . | 3,107.50 | 1,018.80 |

proximately 11.5 to 12.5 percent in October of 1985 for straight bonds of the same risk class.

As an example of forcing a call, we will use the Rockwell International convertible bond from Table 19–3. At the time of issue, the corporation established a future privilege for calling in the bond at 10 percent above par value—thus the $1,000 debenture was redeemable at $1,100. Most bonds have a 5 to 10 percent call premium. This may decline over time. The Rockwell International bond has risen in value to $3,162.50 per $1,000 bond. The conversion value is exactly the same price, and the call price has declined annually to its current level of 100.13 percent of par ($1,001.30). An owner of this bond is entitled to 86.96 common shares per bond. If Rockwell wishes to force conversion, it announces that it is going to call the issue at $1,001.30. Bondholders now have the choice between converting to 86.96 shares of stock worth $3,162.50 or accepting a call price of $1,001.30. Any rational bondholder will take the shares and thus the higher value. This demonstrates the derivation of the term "forced" conversion.

The Pfizer bond in Table 19–1 is a slightly different example. The market must believe that Pfizer will be calling the bond, and therefore the market price is selling at a slight discount from the conversion value. This sometimes also occurs when investors in the market expect the stock price to decline.[4] In case the Pfizer bond did get called, the owner would have a choice of receiving the call price of $1,069.10 or 35.4 shares of common stock selling at 44½ per share and worth $1,575.30. Informed bondholders would take the shares of common stock. By calling the bond, Pfizer would "force" the conversion of

[4]Wayne H. Mikkelson, "Convertible Calls and Stock Price Declines," *Financial Analysts Journal*, January–February 1985, pp. 63–69.

debt to equity. This would change the composition of the balance sheet by decreasing the debt to asset ratio.

Conversion may also be encouraged through a step-up in the conversion price over time. When the bond is issued, the contract may specify the following conversion provisions.

| | *Conversion Price* | *Conversion Ratio* |
|---|---|---|
| First five years . . . . . | $40 | 25.0 shares |
| Next three years . . . . | 45 | 22.2 shares |
| Next two years . . . . . | 50 | 20.2 shares |
| Next five years . . . . . | 55 | 18.2 shares |

At the end of each time period, there is a strong inducement to convert rather than accept an adjustment to a higher conversion price and a lower conversion ratio.

### Euro-Convertible Bonds

Over the past 20 years many companies have been selling convertible bonds to foreign investors, particularly in Europe.[5] The Eurobonds are dollar denominated and sold primarily in western European countries. Foreign investors like convertible Eurobonds because they have the safety of a bond but the chance to grow with U.S. stock prices. U.S. companies like Eurobonds because they skirt U.S. capital transfer restrictions and allow companies to raise dollars outside of the United States for direct investment abroad or for foreign subsidiaries. Table 19–4 presents some selected convertible Eurobonds.

## Accounting Considerations with Convertibles

Prior to 1969, the full impact of the conversion privilege as it applied to convertible securities, warrants (long-term options to buy stock), and other dilutive securities was not adequately reflected in reported

[5]Steve Dawson, "A Somber Fifteenth Euro-Convertible Bond Reunion," *Journal of Portfolio Management*, Winter 1985, pp. 85–87.

**Table 19–4**
**Selected issues of convertible Eurobonds (October 1985)**

| Issue, Coupon, and Maturity | Conversion Value | Market Value of Bond | Call Price (percent) |
|---|---|---|---|
| SCM O/S Cap. Corp. euro, cv.s.f.deb 5.25, 1989 | $1,608.75 | $1,610.00 | 100.00 |
| Southern Cal Ed. Fin euro, c.s.d. 12.50, 1997 | 1,435.00 | 1,490.00 | 103.00 |
| Texaco Cap. N.V. euro, c.s.d. 11.875, 1994 | 730.00 | 1,041.25 | 104.00 |

earnings per share. Since all of these securities may generate additional common stock in the future, the potential effect of dilution should be considered. Let us examine the unadjusted (for conversion) financial statements of the XYZ Corporation in Table 19–5.

An analyst would hardly be satisfied in accepting the unadjusted earnings per share figure of $1 for the XYZ Corporation. In computing earnings per share, we have not accounted for the 400,000 additional shares of common stock that could be created by converting the bonds.

**Table 19–5**

XYZ CORPORATION

1. *Capital section of balance sheet*

| | |
|---|---|
| Common stock (1 million shares at $10 par) | $10,000,000 |
| 4.5% convertible debentures (10,000 debentures of $1,000; convertible into 40 shares per bond, or a total of 400,000 shares) | 10,000,000 |
| Retained earnings | 20,000,000 |
| Net worth | $40,000,000 |

2. *Condensed income statement*

| | |
|---|---|
| Earnings before interest and taxes | $ 2,450,000 |
| Interest (4.5% of $10 million) | 450,000 |
| Earnings before taxes | 2,000,000 |
| Taxes (50%) | 1,000,000 |
| Earnings after taxes | $ 1,000,000 |

3. *Earnings per share*

$$\frac{\text{Earnings after taxes}}{\text{Shares of common outstanding}} = \frac{\$1{,}000{,}000}{1{,}000{,}000} = \$1$$

How then do we make this full disclosure? According to Accounting Principles Board *Opinion No. 15*, issued by the American Institute of Certified Public Accountants in 1969 and amended by the Financial Accounting Standards Board's *Statement No. 55* in 1982, we need to compute earnings per share using two different methods when there is potential dilution of a material nature.

$$\text{1. Primary earnings per share} = \frac{\text{Adjusted earnings after taxes}}{\text{Shares outstanding} + \text{Common stock equivalents}} \tag{19–1}$$

Common stock equivalents include warrants, other options, and any *convertible securities that paid less than two thirds of the average Aa bond yield at time of issue.*

$$\text{2. Fully diluted earnings per share} = \frac{\text{Adjusted earnings after taxes}}{\text{Shares outstanding} + \text{Common stock equivalents} + \textit{All convertibles regardless of the interest rate}} \tag{19–2}$$

The intent in computing both primary and fully diluted earnings per share is to consider the effect of potential dilution. Common stock equivalents represent those securities that are capable of generating new shares of common stock in the future. Note that convertible securities may or may not be required in computing primary earnings per share, depending on rates, but must be included in computing fully diluted earnings per share.

In the case of the XYZ Corporation in Table 19–5, the convertibles pay 4.5 percent interest. We assume that the average Aa bond yield at time of issue was 9 percent, so they are considered as common stock equivalents and are included in both primary and fully diluted earnings per share.

We get new earnings per share for the XYZ Corporation by assuming that 400,000 new shares will be created from potential conversion, while at the same time allowing for the reduction in interest payments that would take place as a result of the conversion of the debt to common stock. Since before-tax interest payments on the convertibles are $450,000 for the XYZ Corporation and a 50 percent tax rate is assumed, the aftertax cost is $225,000. The assumption is that this aftertax interest cost will be saved and can be added back to income.

Making the appropriate adjustments to the numerator and denominator, we show adjusted earnings per share.

$$\text{Primary earnings per share}^{*} = \frac{\text{Adjusted earnings after taxes}}{\text{Shares outstanding} + \text{Common stock equivalents}}$$

$$= \frac{\overset{\textit{Reported earnings}}{\$1{,}000{,}000} + \overset{\textit{Interest savings}}{\$225{,}000}}{1{,}000{,}000 + 400{,}000} = \frac{\$1{,}225{,}000}{1{,}400{,}000} = \$0.88$$

*Same as fully diluted in this instance.

We see a 12 cent reduction from the earnings per share figure of $1 in Table 19–5. The new figure is the value that a sophisticated security analyst would use.

## Financing through Warrants

A warrant is an option to buy a stated number of shares of stock at a specified price over a given time period. For example, the warrants of Wickes Companies enable the holder to buy one share of stock at a price of $4.43 any time between now and January 26, 1992. If the value of Wickes common stock goes up to $15 or $20, the warrants will be quite valuable, while the warrants will eventually be worthless if the stock stays below $4.43 per share.

Warrants are usually issued as a sweetener to a bond offering, and they may enable the firm to issue debt when this would not be feasible otherwise. The warrants are usually detachable from the bond issue, have their own market price, and are generally traded on the New York Stock Exchange or American Stock Exchange. After warrants are exercised, the initial debt to which they are attached remains in existence.

Because a warrant is dependent on the market movement of the underlying common stock and has no "security value" as such, it is highly speculative in nature. If the common stock of the firm is volatile, the value of the warrants may change dramatically.

Tri-Continental Corporation warrants went from 1/32 to 75¾ between 1942 and 1969, while United Airlines warrants moved from 4½ to 126 between 1962 and 1966. Of course, this is not a one-way street, as holders of LTV warrants will attest as they saw their holdings dip from 83 to 2¼ in the 1968–70 bear market.

### Valuation of Warrants

Because the value of a warrant is closely tied to the underlying stock price, we can develop a formula for the minimum value (intrinsic value) of a warrant.

$$\text{Minimum value of a warrant} = \left(\text{Market value of common stock} - \text{Option price of warrant}\right) \times \text{Number of shares each warrant entitles holder to purchase} \quad (19\text{–}3)$$

Using the data from Table 19–6, we see that Navistar International common stock is trading at \$6.88 in October of 1985.[6] Each warrant carries with it the option to purchase one share of Navistar International stock at \$5.00 per share until 1993. Using Formula 19–3, the minimum value (intrinsic value) is \$1.88, or (6.88 − 5.00) × 1. Since the warrant

**Table 19–6** **Relationships determining warrant prices (October 1985)**

| (1) Firm, Place of Warrant Listing, and Stock Listing* | (2) Warrant Price | (3) Stock Price | (4) Option Price | (5) Number of Shares | (6) Intrinsic Value† | (7) Speculative Premium | (8) Due Date |
|---|---|---|---|---|---|---|---|
| Navistar International, NYSE, NYSE | \$ 4.00 | \$ 6.88 | \$ 5.00 | 1.00 | \$ 1.88 | \$ 2.12 | 12/15/93 |
| Public Service N.H., OTC, NYSE | 3.63 | 7.63 | 5.00 | 1.00 | 2.63 | 1.00 | 10/15/91 |
| DNA Plant Technology, OTC, OTC | 1.63 | 7.38 | 7.50‡ | .50 | −.06 | 1.69 | 1/17/90 |
| Pan Am Corp., NYSE, NYSE | 3.13 | 7.88 | 8.00 | 1.00 | −.12 | 3.25 | 5/1/93 |
| Triangle Industries, OTC, NYSE | 36.50 | 26.13 | 9.25 | 2.00 | 33.76 | 2.74 | 9/01/93 |
| Turner Broadcasting, OTC, ASE | 4.75 | 13.25 | 22.50 | 1.00 | −9.25 | 14.00 | 12/15/91 |
| Western Airlines, NYSE, NYSE | 2.75 | 8.13 | 9.50 | 1.00 | −1.37 | 1.38 | 6/15/93 |

*OTC = over-the-counter; NYSE = New York Stock Exchange; ASE = American Stock Exchange.
†Even though the intrinsic value is negative in several cases, a warrant may not have an actual value of less than zero. The negative values are given so that the speculative premium may be calculated easily.
‡DNA Plant Technology's option price per share rises to \$10.50 on 1/17/87.

[6] Navistar International is the new name for the firm formerly known as International Harvester.

has many more years to run and is an effective vehicle for speculative trading, it is trading at $4.00 per warrant. This is $2.12 more than its intrinsic value and is termed the *speculative premium*. Investors are willing to pay a premium because a small percentage gain in the stock price may generate large percentage increases in the warrant price. Formula 19–4 demonstrates the calculation of the speculative premium.

$$\begin{array}{c}\text{Speculative premium}\\ \text{of a warrant}\end{array} = \text{Warrant price} - \text{Intrinsic value} \quad (19\text{–}4)$$

For Navistar International, we use the formula to show the previously stipulated $2.12.

$$\$2.12 = \$4.00 - \$1.88$$

Even if Navistar International stock were trading at less than the option price on the warrant, the warrant might still have some value in the market. Speculators might purchase the warrant in the hope that the common stock would increase sufficiently in the future to make the option provision valuable. As an example of an extreme case of speculative premiums, the warrants of Turner Broadcasting in Table 19–6 are selling at a speculative premium of $14.00 per warrant. Even though the stock price was $9.25 below the option price, the warrant still traded at $4.75. Why? Ted Turner had been attempting a takeover of CBS and other media or broadcasting companies, and evidently, investors were hoping that he would pull off a big merger or takeover before the warrants expire in 1991.

Many warrants continue to trade on this kind of speculation. The typical relationship between the warrant price and the intrinsic value of a warrant is depicted in Figure 19–2. We assume the warrant entitles the holder to purchase one new share of common at $20. Note that although the intrinsic value of the warrant is negative at a common stock price between 0 and 20, the warrant still carries some value in the market. Also, observe that the difference between the market price of the warrant and its intrinsic value is diminished at the upper ranges of value. Two reasons may be offered for the declining premium.

First, the speculator loses the ability to use leverage to generate high returns as the price of the stock goes up. When the price of the stock is relatively low, say $25, and the warrant is in the $5 range, a 10-point movement in the stock could mean a 200 percent gain in the value of the warrant, as indicated in Table 19–7.

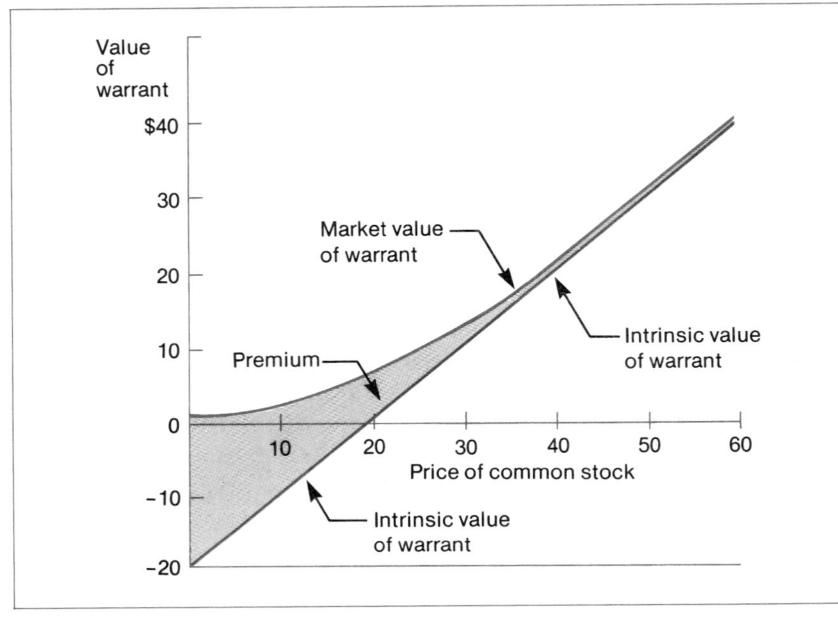


**Figure 19–2 Market price relationships for a warrant**

**Table 19–7 Leverage in valuing warrants**

| *Low Stock Price* | *High Stock Price* |
|---|---|
| Stock price, \$25; warrant price, \$5* | Stock price, \$50; warrant price, \$30 |
| + 10-point movement in stock price | + 10-point movement in stock price |
| New warrant price, \$15 (10-point gain) | New warrant price, \$40 (10-point gain) |
| Percentage gain in warrant $= \frac{\$10}{\$5} \times 100 = 200\%$ | Percentage gain in warrant $= \frac{\$10}{\$30} \times 100 = 33\%$ |

*The warrant price would, of course be greater than \$5 because of the speculative premium. Nevertheless, we use \$5 for ease of computation.

At the upper levels of stock value, much of this leverage is lost. At a stock value of \$50 and a warrant value of approximately \$30, a 10-point movement in the stock would produce only a 33 percent gain in the warrant.

Another reason why speculators pay a very low premium at higher stock prices is that there is less downside protection. A warrant selling at \$30 when the stock price is \$50 is more vulnerable to downside movement than is a \$5–\$10 warrant when the stock is in the 20s.

### Use of Warrants in Corporate Finance

Let us judge the suitability of warrants for corporate financing purposes. As previously indicated, warrants may allow for the issuance of debt under difficult circumstances. While a straight debt issue may not be acceptable or may be accepted only at extremely high rates, the same security may be well received because detachable warrants are included. Warrants may also be included as an add-on in a merger or acquisition agreement. A firm might offer $20 million in cash plus 10,000 warrants in exchange for all the outstanding shares of the acquisition candidate.

The use of warrants has traditionally been associated with such aggressive "high-flying" firms as real estate investment trusts, airlines, and conglomerates. However, in the 1970s staid and venerable American Telephone and Telegraph came out with a $1.57 billion debt offering, sweetened by the use of warrants.

As a financing device for creating new common stock, warrants may not be as desirable as convertible securities. A corporation with convertible debentures outstanding may force the conversion of debt to common stock through a call, while no similar device is available to the firm with warrants. The only possible inducement might be a step-up in option price—whereby the warrant holder may pay a progressively higher option price if he does not exercise by a given date.

The capital structure of the firm after the exercise of a warrant is somewhat different from that created after the conversion of a debenture. In the case of a warrant, the original debt outstanding remains in existence after the detachable warrant is exercised, whereas the conversion of a debenture extinguishes the former debt obligation.[7]

## Accounting Considerations with Warrants

As with convertible securities, the potential dilutive effect of warrants must be considered. All warrants are included in computing both primary and fully diluted earnings per share.[8] The accountant must

[7] It should be pointed out that a number of later financing devices can blur this distinction. See Jerry Miller, "Accounting for Warrants and Convertible Bonds," *Management Accounting*, January 1973, pp. 26–28.

[8] Under most circumstances, if the market price is below the option price, dilution need not be considered. *APB Opinion No. 15*, par. 35.

compute the number of new shares that could be created by the exercise of all warrants, with the provision that the total can be reduced by the assumed use of the cash proceeds to purchase a partially offsetting amount of shares at the market price. Assume that warrants to purchase 10,000 shares at $20 are outstanding and that the current price of the stock is $50. We show the following:

| | |
|---|---|
| 1. New shares created | 10,000 |
| 2. Reduction of shares from cash proceeds (computed below) | 4,000 |
| Cash proceeds—10,000 shares at $20 = $200,000 | |
| Current price of stock—$50 | |
| Assumed reduction in shares outstanding from cash proceeds = $200,000/$50 = 4,000 | |
| 3. Assumed net increase in shares from exercise of warrants (10,000 − 4,000) | 6,000 |

In computing earnings per share, we will add 6,000 shares to the denominator, with no adjustment to the numerator. This, of course will lead to some dilution in earnings per share. Its importance must be interpreted by the financial manager and security analyst.

## Summary

A number of security devices related to the debt and common stock of the firm became popular in the 1960s and in subsequent decades. Each security offers downside protection or upside potential, or a combination of these features.

A convertible security is a bond or share of preferred stock that can be converted into common stock at the option of the holder. Thus the holder has a fixed income security that will not go below a minimum amount because of the interest or dividend payment feature and, at the same time, he or she has a security that is potentially convertible to common stock. If the common stock goes up in value, the convertible security will appreciate as well. From a corporate viewpoint, the firm may force conversion to common stock through a call feature and thus achieve a balanced capital structure. Interest rates on convertibles are usually lower than those on straight debt issues.

A warrant is an option to buy a stated number of shares of stock at a specified price over a given time period. The warrant has a large potential for appreciation if the stock goes up in value. Warrants are used primarily as sweeteners for debt instruments or as add-ons in merger tender offers. When warrants are exercised, the basic debt instrument to which they may be attached is not eliminated, as is the case for a convertible debenture. The potential dilutive effect of warrants and convertible securities must be considered in computing earnings per share.

## List of Terms

**convertible security**
**conversion ratio**
**conversion price**
**conversion value**
**conversion premium**
**pure bond value**
**floor price**
**forced conversion**
**step-up in conversion**
**primary earnings per share**
**fully diluted earnings per share**
**warrant**
**financial sweetener**
**minimum warrant value**
**speculative warrant premium**
**leverage**
**intrinsic value**

## Discussion Questions

1. How can a company force conversion of a convertible bond?
2. What are the basic advantages to the corporation of issuing convertible securities?
3. Explain the difference between primary earnings per share and fully diluted earnings per share.
4. Why are investors willing to pay a premium over the theoretical value (pure bond value or conversion value)?
5. Why is it said that convertible securities have a floor price?
6. Find the prices of the following two convertible bonds in *The Wall Street Journal*: American General cv 11 2008 and Pogo Producing cv 8 2005.
    *a.* Explain what factors cause their prices to be different from their par value of $1,000.

   *b*. What will happen to the pure bond value if long-term interest rates decline?

7. What is meant by a step-up in the conversion price?
8. What adjustments to earnings after taxes are necessary in order to compute primary earnings per share for convertibles?
9. Explain how convertible bonds and warrants are similar and different.
10. Explain why warrants generally are issued (why are they used in corporate finance?)
11. What are the reasons that warrants sell above their intrinsic value?

## Problems

1. National Motors, Inc., has warrants outstanding which allow the holder to purchase 1.5 shares per warrant at $28 per share (option price). Thus, each individual share can be purchased at $28 under the warrant. The common stock is currently selling for $35. The warrant is selling for $14.

   *a*. What is the intrinsic (minimum) value of this warrant?
   *b*. What is the speculative premium on this warrant?
   *c*. What should happen to the speculative premium as the expiration date approaches?

2. H & B Brewing Company has a convertible bond quoted on the NYSE bond market at 85. (Bond quotes represent percentage of par value. Thus 70 represents $700, 80 represents $800 and so on.) It matures in 10 years and carries a coupon rate of 4½ percent. The conversion price is $20, and the common stock is currently selling for $10 per share on the NYSE.

   *a*. Compute the conversion premium.
   *b*. At what price does the common stock need to sell for the conversion value to be equal to the current bond price?

3. The Big Bear Manufacturing Company has a convertible bond outstanding, trading in the marketplace at $850. The par value is

$1,000, the coupon rate is 8 percent, and the bond matures in 20 years. The conversion price is $50, and the company's common stock is selling for $35 per share. Interest is paid semiannually.

*a.* What is the conversion value?
*b.* If similar bonds, which are not convertible, are currently yielding 12 percent, what is the pure bond value of this convertible bond? (Use semiannual analysis as described in Chapter 10.)

**4.** Standard Olive Company of California has a convertible bond outstanding with a coupon rate of 9 percent and a maturity date of 15 years. It is rated Aaa, and competitive, nonconvertible bonds of the same risk class carry a 10 percent return. The conversion ratio is 25. Currently the common stock is selling for $30 per share on the New York Stock Exchange.

*a.* What is the conversion price?
*b.* What is the conversion value?
*c.* Compute the pure bond value. (Use semiannual analysis.)
*d.* Draw a graph that includes the floor price and the conversion value but not the convertible bond price.
*e.* Which will influence the bond price more—the pure bond value or the conversion value?

**5.** Alice Overland Truck Company has convertible bonds outstanding that are callable at $1,080. The bonds are convertible into 22 shares of common stock. The stock is currently selling for $58.75 per share.

*a.* If the firm announces that it is going to call the bonds at $1,080, what action are bondholders likely to take, and why?
*b.* Assume that instead of the call feature, the firm has the right to drop the conversion ratio from 22 down to 20 after 5 years and down to 18 after 10 years. If the bonds have been outstanding for 4 years and 11 months, what will the price of the bonds be if the stock price is $60? Assume the bonds carry no conversion premium.
*c.* Further assume you anticipate in two months that the common stock price will be up to $63. Considering the conversion feature, should you convert now or continue to hold the bond for at least two more months?

6. Assume that you can buy a warrant for $6 which gives you the option to buy one share of common stock at $15 per share. The stock is currently selling at $18 per share.

   *a.* What is the intrinsic value of the warrant?
   *b.* What is the speculative premium on the warrant?
   *c.* If the stock rises to $27 per share and the warrant sells at its theoretical value without a premium, what will be the percentage increase in the stock price and the warrant price if you bought the stock and the warrant at the prices stated above, $6 and $18? Explain this relationship.

7. The Big D Investment Company bought 100 Newsome Corporation warrants one year ago and would like to exercise them today. The warrants were purchased at $30 each, and they expire when trading ends today (assume there is no speculative premium left). Newsome common stock is selling today for $60 per share. The option price is $36, and each warrant entitles the holder to purchase two shares of stock, each at the option price.

   *a.* If the warrants are exercised today, what would Big D's total profit or loss be?
   *b.* What is Big D's percentage rate of return?

8. Assume in Problem 7 that Newsome common stock was selling for $50 per share when Big D Investment Company bought the warrants.

   *a.* What was the intrinsic value of a warrant at that time?
   *b.* What was the speculative premium per warrant when the warrants were purchased? The purchase price, as indicated above, was $30.
   *c.* What would Big D's total dollar profit or loss have been had they invested the $3,000 directly in Newsome Corporation's common stock one year ago at $50 per share? Recall the current value is $60 per share.
   *d.* What would the percentage rate of return be on this common stock investment? Compare this to the rate of return on the warrant computed in Problem 7*b*.

9. Mr. Hymen Flyer has $1,000 to invest in the market. He is considering the purchase of 50 shares of Volatile Corporation at $20 per share. His broker suggests that he may wish to consider pur-

chasing warrants instead. The warrants are selling for $5, and each warrant allows him to purchase one share of Volatile common stock at $18 per share.

*a.* How many warrants can Mr. Flyer purchase for the same $1,000?
*b.* If the price of the stock goes to $30, what would be his total dollar and percentage return on the stock?
*c.* At the time the stock goes to $30, the speculative premium on the warrant goes to 0 (though the intrinsic value of the warrant goes up). What would be Mr. Flyer's total dollar and percentage return on the warrant?
*d.* Assuming that the speculative premium remains $3.50 over the intrinsic value, how far would the price of the stock have to fall before the warrant has no value?

**10.** The Bedrock Tombstone Company has net income of $350,000 in the current fiscal year. There are 100,000 shares of common stock outstanding along with convertible bonds which have a total face value of $800,000. The $800,000 is represented by 800 different $1,000 bonds. Each $1,000 bond pays 5 percent interest and was issued when the average Aa bond yield was 9 percent. The conversion ratio is 20. The tax rate is 46 percent. Calculate Bedrock's primary earnings per share in accordance with *APB Opinion No. 15*. (Note: To get aftertax savings in interest, multiply the before-tax figure by 1 − T.)

**11.** Using the information from Problem 10, assume the average Aa bond yield was 7 percent instead of 9 percent at the time the convertible bonds were issued. All other facts are the same.

*a.* What are the primary earnings per share for Bedrock Tombstone?
*b.* Indicate the value for fully diluted earnings per share.

**12.** Anderson Electronics has 2 million shares of stock outstanding. It also has two convertible bond issues with terms as follows:

10 percent convertible (1999, $15,000,000)
8 percent convertible (2008, $20,000,000).

The issue with the 10 percent coupon rate was first sold when average Aa bonds were yielding 14 percent and is convertible into 400,000 shares. The issue with the 8 percent coupon rate was first sold when Aa bonds were yielding 13 percent and is convertible into 500,000 shares. Earnings after taxes are $6 million and the tax rate is 50 percent.

*a.* Compute both primary and fully diluted earnings per share for Anderson Electronics.

*b.* Now assume Anderson Electronics has warrants outstanding which allow the holder to buy 100,000 shares of stock at $30 per share. The stock is currently selling for $50 per share. Compute primary earnings per share, considering the possible impact of both the warrants and convertibles.

**13.** The Loud Communications Company has $1 million in 10 percent convertible bonds outstanding. Each bond has a $1,000 par value. The conversion ratio is 50, the stock price is $24, and the bond matures in 10 years. The bonds are currently selling at a conversion premium of $100 over their conversion value.

*a.* If the price of Loud Communications common stock rises to $33 this date next year, what would your rate of return be if you bought a convertible bond today and sold it in one year? Assume that on this date next year, the conversion premium has shrunk from $100 to $20.

*b.* Assume that the yield on similar nonconvertible bonds has fallen to 8 percent at the time of sale. What would the pure bond value be at that point in time? (Use semiannual analysis.) Would the pure bond value have a significant effect on valuation then?

**14.** Lomas Exploration Ltd. has 1,000 convertible bonds ($1,000 par value) outstanding, each of which may be converted to 40 shares. The $1 million worth of bonds has 25 years to maturity. The current price of the stock is $32 per share. The firm's net income in the most recent fiscal year was $270,000. The bonds pay 12 percent interest and were issued when the average Aa bond rate was 13.2 percent. The corporation has 160,000 shares of common stock outstanding. Current market rates on long-term bonds of equal quality are 14 percent. A 50 percent tax rate is assumed.

*a.* Compute fully diluted earnings per share.

*b.* Assume the bonds currently sell at a 5 percent conversion premium over straight conversion value (based on a stock price of 32). However, as the price of the stock increases from $32 to $45 due to new events, there will be an increase in the bond price, but the conversion premium will be zero. Under these circumstances, determine the rate of return on a convertible bond investment that is part of this price change, based on the appreciation in value.

*c*. Now assume that the stock price fell to $19 per share because a competitor introduced a new product. Would the straight conversion value be greater than the pure bond value, based on the interest rates stated above? (See Table 16–3 in Chapter 16 to get the bond value without having to go through the actual computation).

*d*. Referring to part *c*, if the convertible traded at a 20 percent premium over the straight conversion value, would the convertible be priced above the pure bond value?

*e*. If long-term interest rates in the market go down to 10 percent while the stock price is $29, with a 6 percent conversion premium, what would the difference be between the market price of the convertible bond and the pure bond value? Assume 25 years to maturity, and once again use Table 16–3 for part of your answer.

*f*. If Lomas were able to retire the convertibles and to replace them with 40,000 shares of common stock selling at $32 per share and paying a 5.5 percent dividend yield (dividend to price ratio), would the aftertax cash outflow related to the convertible be greater or less than the cash outflow related to the stock?

**15.** *(Comprehensive problem)*

AC&C (American Cable and Communications) has $10 million of convertible bonds outstanding with a coupon rate of 9 percent, while interest rates are currently 7 percent for bonds of equal risk. The bonds were originally sold when the average Aa bond rate was 8 percent, and they have 20 years left to maturity. The bond may be called at a 10 percent premium as well as converted into 20 shares of common stock. The tax rate for the company is 50 percent.

AC&C common stock is currently selling for $60 per share, and it pays a dividend of $5 per share. The expected income for the company is $16.15 million on the 2 million shares of common stock currently outstanding.

Make a thorough analysis of this bond, and determine whether AC&C should call the bond at the 10 percent call premium. In your analysis, consider the following:

*a.* The impact of the call on primary and fully diluted earnings per share and the common stock price (assume that the call forces conversion).
*b.* The consequences of your decision on future financing flexibility.
*c.* The net change in cash outflows to the company.
*d.* If the bond is called, will the stockholders take the call price or the 20 shares of common stock?
*e.* Assuming that the bondholders could have converted the bonds into common stock whenever they desired, would you as a bondholder have waited for the company to call your bond and thereby force a decision on your part? Explain.

## Selected References

Accounting Principles Board. *APB Opinion No. 15*. New York: American Institute of Certified Public Accountants.

Alexander, Gordon J., and Roger O. Stover. "Pricing in the New Issue Convertible Debt Market." *Financial Management* 6 (Fall 1977), pp. 35–39.

Bacon, Peter W., and Edward L. Winn, Jr. "The Impact of Forced Conversion on Stock Prices." *Journal of Finance* 24 (December 1969), pp. 871–74.

Baumol, William J.; Burton G. Malkiel; and Richard E. Quandt. "The Valuation of Convertible Securities." *Quarterly Journal of Economics* 80 (February 1966), pp. 48–59.

Black, Fischer, and Myron Scholes. "The Pricing of Options and Corporate Liabilities." *Journal of Political Economy* 81 (May–June 1973), pp. 637–54.

———. "The Valuation of Option Contracts and a Test of Market Efficiency." *Journal of Finance* 27 (May 1972), pp. 399–417.

Brealey, Richard A. *Security Prices in a Competitive Market*. Cambridge, Mass.: MIT Press, 1971, chaps. 16 and 17.

Brennan, M. J., and E. S. Schwartz. "Convertible Bonds: Valuation and Optimal Strategies for Call and Conversion." *Journal of Finance* 32 (December 1977), pp. 1699–1715.

Brigham, Eugene F. "An Analysis of Convertible Debentures: Theory and Some Empirical Evidence." *Journal of Finance* 21 (March 1966), pp. 35–54.

Chen, A. H. Y. "A Model of Warrant Pricing in a Dynamic Market." *Journal of Finance* 25 (December 1970), pp. 1041–59.

Dawson, Steve. "A Somber Fifteenth Euro-Convertible Bond Reunion," *Journal of Portfolio Management,* (Winter 1985), pp. 85–87.

Frank, Werner G., and Jerry J. Weygandt. "Convertible Debt and Earnings per Share: Pragmatism vs. Good Theory." *Accounting Review* 45 (April 1970), pp. 280–89.

Hayes, Samuel L., III, and Henry B. Reiling. "Sophisticated Financing Tool: The Warrant." *Harvard Business Review* 47 (January–February 1969), pp. 137–50.

Lewellen, Wilbur G., and George A. Racette. "Convertible Debt Financing." *Journal of Financial and Quantitative Analysis* 7 (December 1973), pp. 777–92.

Marr, Wayne M., and G. Rodney Thompson. "The Pricing of New Convertible Bond Issues." *Financial Management* 13 (Summer 1984), pp. 38–40.

Mikkelson, Wayne H. "Convertible Calls and Stock Price Declines," *Financial Analysts Journal,* (January–February 1985), pp. 63–69.

Miller, Jerry. "Accounting for Warrants and Convertible Bonds." *Management Accounting* (January 1973), pp. 26–28.

Pinches, George E. "Financing with Convertible Preferred Stocks, 1960–1967." *Journal of Finance* 25 (March 1970), 53–64.

Rush, David F., and Ronald W. Melicher. "An Empirical Examination of Factors which Influence Warrant Prices." *Journal of Finance* 29 (December 1974), pp. 1449–66.

Samuelson, Paul A. "Rational Theory of Warrant Pricing." *Industrial Management Review* 6 (Spring 1965), pp. 13–31.

Schwartz, Eduardo S. "The Valuation of Warrants: Implementing a New Approach." *Journal of Financial Economics* 4 (January 1977), pp. 79–94.

Shelton, John P. "The Relation of the Price of a Warrant to the Price of Its Associated Stock." *Financial Analysts Journal* 23 (May–June and July–August 1967), pp. 143–51 and 88–99.

Sinkey, Joseph F., and James A. Miles. "The Use of Warrants in the Bail Out of First Pennsylvania Bank: An Application of Option Pricing." *Financial Management* 27 (Autumn 1982), pp. 27–32.

Soldofsky, Robert M. "Yield-Risk Performance of Convertible Securities." *Financial Analysts Journal* 39 (March–April 1971), pp. 61–65.

PART

# SIX

# Expanding the Perspective of Corporate Finance

## Introduction

The final two topics, mergers and international finance, are particularly appropriate for the financial environment of the 1980s. Both have achieved increasing importance as financial managers have attempted to grow and diversify away from traditional product lines and across international borders.

Mergers have long been recognized as offering the potential for risk reduction by combining diversified firms under common control. However, the achievement of such risk reduction can be an elusive process, as overly optimistic planners often find obstacles in their way. The successful merger must be based on realistic expectations and a careful consideration of postmerger performance. We shall evaluate both of these factors in Chapter 20.

The latest merger wave is somewhat unique in that it is populated by such high-quality acquiring firms as Du Pont, General Electric, and Colgate Palmolive. The fast-moving conglomerate giants of the late 1960s are no longer strongly in evidence.

In the merger chapter, we examine the significant financial and management variables that influence the merger decision, including the price paid, the accounting implications, the stock market effect, and the motivations of the participating parties. The chapter provides an important overview of topics discussed earlier in the text.

The importance of the multinational business firm is considered in Chapter 21. In an ever-shrinking world, the financial manager must be prepared to make decisions that have worldwide effects. In prior chapters, basic business decisions were considered primarily in terms of the direct "dollar" impact on profitability. As the business firm moves into foreign markets and deals in deutsche marks. Swiss francs, and Japanese yen, the foreign exchange implications of decisions must also be considered. A firm may suddenly have to receive a future payment in a currency that is rapidly declining in value. How is this circumstance to be handled? The international financial manager must understand his or her options.

Although foreign investments may carry unusual political and economic risks, they also allow for expanded market potential. Local customs and requirements in regard to taxation and payment of dividends must be carefully examined. A major example in Chapter 21 considers these factors.

Finally, international financing arrangements, such as the Eurodollar dollar market and Eurobond market, which were touched on in Part Three of the book, are now given expanded coverage. Also, the relationship of the multinational firm to foreign stock markets is considered.

# 20 External Growth through Mergers

Many of the previously discussed points regarding financial planning, risk–return analysis, valuation, capital budgeting, and portfolio management can be examined in the very meaningful context of mergers and acquisitions. To this extent, Chapter 20 may be thought of as an integrative chapter for much of the material discussed throughout the text.

There have been a number of major merger movements in the industrial history of the United States, beginning in the late 1890s with the development of the oil, railroad, tobacco, and steel industries and culminating with the merger mania of the late 1970s and 1980s. This last wave of mergers is of particular interest to us because it has significantly influenced the corporate environment of the 1980s.

The major theme of this latest merger movement is that it is cheaper to acquire other companies than it is to expand through new product development or the purchase of new plant and equipment. This is borne out by the fact that in the late 1970s and 1980s the total market value of the 500 companies listed in the Standard & Poor's index has been consistently below replacement cost.

A second significant feature of the modern merger boom has been that the major participants are no longer the "urge to merge" gunslinger conglomerate giants of the 1960s, but rather old, conservative corporations such as Du Pont, U.S. Steel, R. J. Reynolds, Kennecott Copper, General Electric, Pillsbury, and Colgate Palmolive. In addition, the foreign acquirer has come on the scene in a big way as foreign companies have opted for investment in the relatively stable political climate of the United States.

A final development of the latest merger movement has been the unfriendly buy-out, in which a major acquiring company identifies a target company and attempts to acquire it without management permission. At first this activity was centered in the oil industry with unfriendly takeover attempts by T. Boone Pickens on Gulf Oil, Phillips Petroleum, and Union Oil of California (Unocal). Phillips and Unocal fended off the takeover by restructuring their balance sheet with a heavy debt load and strategies designed to reduce the value of the company if the takeover was successful. These self-emasculating strategies were called "poison pills." Gulf was bought by "white knight" Chevron (formerly Standard Oil of California) for a record $13.3 billion. The next two largest mergers of the mid-1980s were also with oil companies; Texaco bought Getty Oil Co. for $10.125 billion, and Mobil Corporation bought Superior Oil Co. for $5.7 billion.

After oil prices tended to drift lower, corporate raiders began looking for other targets with undervalued assets and found companies like MGM, ABC, and Prentice-Hall in movies, broadcasting, and publishing. Then the move was on to retail stores where hidden real estate values were thought to exist. The wheel next turned to food companies, with the acquisition of General Foods by Philip Morris. Who knows what industry will be the target by the time you read this chapter. Table 20–1 presents a 10-year history of merger activity, and you can see that 1984 was the peak period.

In this chapter, we shall examine the motives for business combinations; the establishment of negotiated terms of exchange, with the associated accounting implications; and the stock market effect of mergers (including unfriendly takeovers). In the final section of the chapter, we examine the holding company device.

**Table 20–1**
**Ten-year merger completion record, 1975–1984**

| Year | Number of Transactions | Percent Change | Value ($ millions) | Percent Change |
|---|---|---|---|---|
| 1975 . . . . . . | 981 | — | * | — |
| 1976 . . . . . | 1,145 | +16.7% | * | — |
| 1977 . . . . . | 1,209 | +5.6 | * | — |
| 1978 . . . . . | 1,452 | +20.1 | * | — |
| 1979 . . . . . | 1,529 | +5.3 | $ 33,964.9 | — |
| 1980 . . . . . | 1,574 | +2.9 | 32,407.4 | −4.6% |
| 1981 . . . . . | 2,326 | +47.8 | 67,545.8 | +108.4 |
| 1982 . . . . . | 2,295 | −1.3 | 64,358.7 | −4.7 |
| 1983 . . . . . | 2,339 | +1.9 | 51,890.9 | −19.4 |
| 1984 . . . . . | 2,946 | +26.0 | 124,027.5 | +139.0 |

*Value not available.
Source: *Mergers & Acquisitions, Almanac & Index*, 1985

## Motives for Business Combinations

A business combination may take the form of either a *merger* or a *consolidation*. A merger is defined as a combination of two or more companies in which the resulting firm maintains the identity of the acquiring company. In a consolidation, two or more companies are combined to form an entirely new entity. A consolidation might be utilized when the firms are of equal size and market power. For purposes of our discussion, the primary emphasis will be on mergers, though virtually all of the principles presented could apply to consolidations as well.

### Financial Motives

The motives for merger and consolidations are both financial and nonfinancial in nature. We examine the financial motives first. As discussed in Chapter 13, a merger allows the acquiring firm to enjoy a potentially desirable *portfolio effect* by achieving risk reduction while perhaps maintaining the firm's rate of return. If two firms that benefit from opposite phases of the business cycle combine, their variability in performance may be reduced. Risk-averse investors may then discount the future performance of the merged firm at a lower rate and thus assign it a higher valuation than was assigned to the separate firms. The same point can be made in regard to multinational mergers. Through merger, a firm that has holdings in diverse economic and political climates can enjoy some reduction in the risks that derive from foreign exchange translation, government politics, military takeovers, and localized recessions.

While the portfolio diversification effect of a merger is intellectually appealing—with each firm becoming a mini-mutual fund unto itself—the practicalities of the situation can become quite complicated. No doubt, one of the major forces of the merger wave of the mid to late 1960s was the desire of the conglomerates for diversification. The lessons we have learned from the LTVs, the Littons, and others is that too much diversification can strain the operating capabilities of the firm. As one form of evidence on the lack of success of some of these earlier mergers, the ratio of divestitures[1] to new acquisitions was only 11 percent in 1967, but it rose to over 50 percent almost a decade later.[2] In 1984 there were 758 divestitures valued at $29.749 billion and equal to 24 percent of the dollar volume of acquisitions.[3] Companies such as Gulf & Western began divesting 20 percent of its assets in 1983 in an attempt to reduce corporate debt. After undertaking large mergers, corporate giants such as Beatrice Companies and Allied Corporation were selling off parts of those companies previously acquired, partly to reduce debt incurred in the acquisition and partly to redeploy assets consistent with corporate strategies.

A second financial motive is the *improved financing posture* that a merger can create as a result of expansion in size. Larger firms may enjoy greater access to financial markets and thus be in a better position to raise debt and equity capital. Such firms may also be able to attract larger and more prestigious investment bankers to handle future financing.

Greater financing capability may also be inherent in the merger itself. This is likely to be the case if the acquired firm has a strong cash position or a low debt–equity ratio that can be used to expand borrowing by the acquiring company.

---

[1] A divestiture is a spin-off or a sell-off of a subsidiary or a division.

[2] James W. Bradley and Donald H. Korn, "Acquisition and Merger Trends Affecting the Portfolio Manager," *Financial Analysts Journal* 33 (November–December 1977), p. 66.

[3] *Mergers & Acquisitions, Almanac and Index,* 1985, p. 25.

One of the popular acquisition devices in the late 1970s and early 1980s was the leveraged buy-out, and by 1984 and 1985 this method of acquisition was still going full steam. As discussed in Chapter 15, the leveraged buy-out results when either existing management or an outsider makes an offer to "go private" by retiring all the shares of the company. The buying group borrows the necessary money, using the assets of the acquired firm as collateral. The buying group then repurchases all the shares and expects to retire the debt over time with the cash flow from operations or the sale of corporate assets. This has been a popular strategy, and in 1984 alone, there were 245 leveraged buy-outs, for a total of $18.6 billion dollars.[4] In November of 1985 Beatrice accepted a record $6.2 billion leveraged buy-out from a New York investor group, Kolberg, Kravis, and Roberts. The Beatrice leveraged buy-out equaled one third of the total leveraged buy-out activity of 1984.

A final financial motive is the *tax loss carry-forward* that might be available in a merger if one of the firms has previously sustained a tax loss. An operating loss may be carried forward up to 15 years, while a capital loss has a five-year potential write-off if necessary. In any event, a tax loss carry-forward must be used up as quickly as possible when there are offsetting profits. As an example of tax loss benefits, assume that Firm A acquires Firm B, which has a $220,000 tax loss carry-forward. We look at Firm A's financial position before and after the merger.

Based on the carry-forward, the company is able to reduce its total taxes from $120,000 to $32,000, and thus it could pay $88,000 for the carry-forward alone (this is on a nondiscounted basis). The tax shield value of a carry-forward is equal to the loss involved times the tax rate ($220,000 × 40 percent = $88,000).

| | *1987* | *1988* | *1989* | *Total Values* |
|---|---|---|---|---|
| *Firm A (without merger)* | | | | |
| Before-tax income | $100,000 | $100,000 | $100,000 | $300,000 |
| Taxes (40%) | 40,000 | 40,000 | 40,000 | 120,000 |
| Income available to stockholders | $ 60,000 | $ 60,000 | $ 60,000 | $180,000 |

[4]Ibid.

| *Firm A (with merger and associated tax benefits)* | | | | |
|---|---|---|---|---|
| Before-tax income | $100,000 | $100,000 | $100,000 | $300,000 |
| Tax loss carry-forward | 100,000 | 100,000 | 20,000 | 220,000 |
| Net taxable income | 0 | 0 | 80,000 | 80,000 |
| Taxes (40%) | 0 | 0 | 32,000 | 32,000 |
| Income available to stockholders | $100,000 | $100,000 | $ 68,000 | $268,000 |

As would be expected, income available to stockholders has gone up by a like amount ($268,000 − $180,000 = $88,000). Of course, Firm B's anticipated operating gains and losses for future years must also be taken into consideration in arriving at a purchase price.

## Nonfinancial Motives

The nonfinancial motives for mergers and consolidations include the desire to expand management and marketing capabilities as well as the acquisition of new products. Particularly popular industries in the latest merger movement—in addition to energy-related companies—have been companies in pharmaceuticals, timber, chemicals, newspapers, and financial services. Companies that are in traditional lines of business may attempt to expand into more dynamic industries in order to upgrade their image.

While mergers may be directed toward either horizontal integration (that is, the acquisition of competitors) or vertical integration (the acquisition of buyers or sellers of goods and services to the company), antitrust policy generally precludes the elimination of competition. For this reason, mergers are often directed toward companies in allied but not directly related fields. The pure conglomerate merger of firms in totally unrelated firms is still undertaken, but less frequently than in the past.

Perhaps the greatest management motive for a merger is the possible synergistic effect. Synergy is said to take place when the whole is greater than the sum of the parts. This "2 + 2 = 5" effect may be the result of eliminating overlapping functions in production and marketing as well as meshing together various engineering capabilities. In terms of planning related to mergers, there is often a tendency to overestimate the possible synergistic benefits that might accrue.[5]

### Motives of Selling Stockholders

Most of our discussion has revolved around the motives of the acquiring firm that initiates a merger. Likewise, the selling stockholders may be motivated by a desire to receive the acquiring company's stock—which may have greater acceptability or activity in the marketplace than the stock they hold. Also, when cash is offered instead of stock, this gives the selling stockholders an opportunity to diversify their holdings into many new investments. As will be discussed later in the chapter, the selling stockholders generally receive an attractive price for their stock that may well exceed its current market or book value. An exchange offer may represent an opportunity to get a value approaching the replacement costs for their assets in an inflationary environment.

In addition, officers of the selling company may receive attractive postmerger management contracts as well as directorships in the acquiring firm. In some circumstances, they may be allowed to operate the company as a highly autonomous subsidiary after the merger (though this is probably the exception).[6]

A final motive of the selling stockholders may simply be the bias against smaller businesses that has developed in this country and around the world. Real clout in the financial markets may dictate being part of a larger organization. These motives should not be taken as evidence that all or even most officers or directors of smaller firms wish to sell out—a matter that we shall examine further when we discuss negotiated offers versus takeover attempts.

## Terms of Exchange

In determining the price that will be paid for a potential acquisition, a number of factors are considered, including earnings, dividends, and growth potential. We shall divide our analysis between cash purchases

[5]T. Hogarty, "The Profitability of Corporate Mergers," *Journal of Business* 43 (July 1970), pp. 317–27.

[6]This is most likely to happen when the acquiring firm is a foreign company.

and stock-for-stock exchanges, in which the acquiring company trades stock rather than paying cash for the acquired firm.

### Cash Purchases

The cash purchase of another company can be viewed within the context of a capital budgeting decision. Instead of purchasing new plant or machinery, the purchaser has opted to acquire a *going concern*. For example, assume that the Invest Corporation is analyzing the acquisition of the Sell Corporation for $1 million. The Sell Corporation has expected cash flow (aftertax earnings plus depreciation) of $100,000 per year for the next 5 years and $150,000 per year for the 6th through the 20th year. Furthermore, the synergistic benefits of the merger (in this case, combining production facilities) will add $10,000 per year to cash flow. Finally, the Sell Corporation has a $50,000 tax loss carry-forward that can be used immediately by the Invest Corporation. Assuming a 40 percent tax rate, the $50,000 loss carry-forward will shield $20,000 of profit from taxes immediately. The Invest Corporation has a 10 percent cost of capital, and this is assumed to remain stable with the merger. Our analysis would be as follows:

| | | | |
|---|---|---|---|
| Cash outflow | | | |
| Purchase price . . . . . . . . . . . . . . . . . . . . . . | | | $1,000,000 |
| Less tax shield benefit from tax loss carry-forward ($50,000 × 40%) . . . . . | | | 20,000 |
| Net cash outflow . . . . . . . . . . . . . . . . . . . . | | | $ 980,000 |
| Cash inflows | | | |
| Years 1–5: | $100,000 | Cash inflow | |
| | 10,000 | Synergistic benefit | |
| | $110,000 | Total cash inflow | |
| Present value of $110,000 × 3.791 . . . . . . . . | | | $ 417,010 |
| Years 6–20: | $150,000 | Cash inflow | |
| | 10,000 | Synergistic benefit | |
| | $160,000 | Total cash inflow | |
| Present value of $160,000 × 4.723 . . . . . . . . | | | 755,680 |
| Total present value of inflows . . . . . . . . . | | | $1,172,690 |

The present value factor for the first five years (3.791) *is* based on $n = 5, i = 10$ percent, and can be found in Appendix D. For the 6th through the 20th year, we take the present value factor in Appendix D for $n = 20, i = 10$ percent, and subtract from this the present value factor for $n = 5, i = 10$ percent. This allows us to isolate the 6th through the 20th year with a factor of 4.723 (8.514 − 3.791).

The net present value of the investment is:

| | |
|---|---|
| Total present value of inflows . . . . . | $1,172,690 |
| Net cash outflow . . . . . . . . . . . | 980,000 |
| Net present value . . . . . . . . . . . | $ 192,690 |

The acquisition appears to represent a desirable alternative for the expenditure of cash with a positive net present value of $192,690. As previously indicated, in the market environment of the late 1970s and 1980s many firms could be purchased at a value below the replacement costs of their assets, and thus represented a potentially desirable capital investment. As an extreme example, Anaconda Copper had an asset replacement value of $1.3 billion when the firm was purchased by Atlantic Richfield for $684 million.

## Stock-for-Stock Exchange

On a stock-for-stock exchange, we use a somewhat different analytical approach, emphasizing the earnings per share impact of exchanging securities (and ultimately the market valuation of those earnings). The analysis is primarily from the viewpoint of the acquiring firm. The shareholders of the acquired firm are concerned mainly about the initial price they are paid for their shares and about the outlook for the acquiring firm.

Assume that Expand Corporation is considering the acquisition of Small Corporation. Significant financial information on the firms before the merger is provided in Table 20–2.

We begin our analysis with the assumption that one share of Expand Corporation ($30) will be traded for one share of Small Corporation ($30). (In actuality, Small Corporation will probably demand more

**Table 20–2**
**Financial data on potential merging firms**

| | *Small Corporation* | *Expand Corporation* |
|---|---|---|
| Total earnings | $200,000 | $500,000 |
| Number of shares of stock outstanding | 50,000 | 200,000 |
| Earnings per share | $4.00 | $2.50 |
| Price–earnings ratio (P/E) | 7.5× | 12× |
| Market price per share | $30.00 | $30.00 |

than $30 per share because the acquired firm usually gets some premium over the current market value. We will later consider the impact of paying such a premium.)

If 50,000 new shares of Expand Corporation are traded in exchange for all the old shares of Small Corporation, Expand Corporation will then have 250,000 shares outstanding. At the same time, its claim to earnings will go to $700,000 when the two firms are combined. Postmerger earnings per share will be $2.80 for the Expand Corporation, as indicated in Table 20–3.

**Table 20–3**
**Postmerger earnings per share**

| | |
|---|---|
| Total earnings: Small ($200,000) + Expand ($500,000) | $700,000 |
| Shares outstanding in surviving corporation: Old (200,000) + New (50,000) | 250,000 |

$$\text{New earnings per share for Expand Corporation} = \frac{\$700,000}{250,000} = \$2.80$$

A number of observations are worthy of note. First, the earnings per share of Expand Corporation have increased as a result of the merger, rising from $2.50 to $2.80. This has occurred because Expand Corporation's P/E ratio was higher than that of Small Corporation at the time of the merger (12 versus 7.5). Whenever a firm acquires another entity whose P/E ratio is lower than its own, there is an immediate increase in earnings per share. The P/E ratio comparison is an important variable that we shall follow closely in our subsequent discussion.

As previously indicated, it is unlikely that Small Corporation will give up its shares at the current market value of $30 per share. We shall now assume that Expand Corporation is willing to pay 33 percent

over market value. This would imply that the shareholders of Small Corporation would receive $40 worth of stock for each share of stock outstanding. Since Expand shares are trading at $30 per share, it must offer 1⅓ shares of Expand Corporation for each share of Small Corporation. This means that Expand Corporation will have to issue 66,667 new shares (50,000 old shares of Small Corporation × 1⅓). Postmerger earnings per share for Expand Corporation are now shown in Table 20–4 to be $2.62.

**Table 20–4**
**Adjusted postmerger earnings per share**

| | |
|---|---|
| Total earnings: Small ($200,000) + Expand ($500,000) | $700,000 |
| Shares outstanding in surviving corporation: | |
| Old (200,000) + New (66,667) | 266,667 |

$$\text{New earnings per share for Expand Corporation} = \frac{\$700{,}000}{266{,}667} = \$2.62$$

Even though Expand Corporation has paid the shareholders of Small Corporation a 33 percent premium over market value, it has still been able to increase its earnings per share from $2.50 premerger (Table 20–2) to $2.62 postmerger (Table 20–4). Why? Well, once again its P/E ratio was higher than that paid to Small Corporation in the exchange transaction. Expand Corporation enjoys a P/E of 12 times earnings, while Small Corporation was purchased at a 33 percent premium over its current P/E of 7.5, or at 10 times earnings. As previously stated, whenever a firm purchases another company at a lower P/E ratio than its own, there is an immediate increase in earnings per share.

One might also wish to determine whether the stockholders of Small Corporation have benefited from the latest suggested merger transaction. In terms of market values they have come out ahead, whereas in terms of earnings per share they have lost out. Both results are indicated in Table 20–5.

Previous research has indicated that stockholders of the *acquired* company are more concerned with the market value exchanged than with the earnings, dividends, or book value exchanged.[7] Thus the $10

[7] Frank K. Reilly, "What Determines the Ratio of Exchange in Corporate Mergers?" *Financial Analysts Journal* 18 (November–December 1962), pp. 47–50. Also Lynn E. Dellenbarger, "A Study of Relative Common Stock Equity Values in Fifty Mergers of Listed Industrial Corporations, 1950–57," *Journal of Finance* 18 (September 1963), p. 565.

**Table 20–5**
**Postmerger analysis of the acquired firm**

A. *Trade in market value*
One share of Small Corporation ($30) traded for 1⅓ shares of Expand Corporation ($40 total value)
Gain: $10

B. *Trade in earnings per share*
One share of Small Corporation previously represented $4.00 in earnings per share (Table 20–2); 1⅓ shares of Expand Corporation represents $3.48 in earnings per share (the $2.62 postmerger value in Table 20–4 times 1.33)
Dilution in earnings per share: $0.52

increase in market value will probably compensate for the decrease in the claims to earnings per share.[8] The stockholders can always sell out after the merger and take a $10 capital gain. At times, however, stockholders may be concerned about trading or maintaining parity in dividends per share. The acquiring company may offer fixed-income securities as well as common stock to maintain parity.

## Long-Term Considerations

In Table 20–4 we showed the earnings per share for Expand Corporation to be $2.62 as a result of the merger—a 12-cent gain over the premerger figure of $2.50. Although Expand Corporation is enjoying an *immediate* appreciation in earnings per share, we must still consider the long-run impact of the merger and its influence on our ultimate objective of market value maximization.

Consider this: The reason Expand Corporation was able to enjoy an immediate appreciation in earnings per share as a result of the merger was that it had a higher P/E ratio than Small Corporation. The reason for Expand's higher P/E ratio may be that it had superior growth prospects, less risk, a better product in the marketplace, more rigorous accounting procedures, or a number of other factors.

We shall assume for now that the differential in the P/E ratios can be explained, in large measure, by differing growth prospects. Perhaps

[8] Earnings-per-share parity would indicate an exchange ratio of 1.6 Expand Corporation shares for each Small Corporation share ($4.00/2.50 = 1.6). The $4.00 represents Small Corporation's premerger EPS, while the $2.50 is Expand Corporation's premerger EPS.

Expand Corporation, without the merger, could be expected to grow at 10 percent per year, while Small Corporation would only grow by 6 percent. Since Expand Corporation is initially contributing $50,000 to earnings and Small Corporation $20,000, the postmerger weighting on earnings is five-sevenths and two-sevenths, respectively. Without considering any postmerger operating benefits (synergy), the new weighted growth rate for Expand Corporation after the merger would be:

$$\tfrac{5}{7}(10\%) + \tfrac{2}{7}(6\%) = 7.14\% + 1.71\% = 8.85\%$$

The net effect is that Expand Corporation will suffer a decline of 1.15 percent in its growth rate at the same time that it enjoys a 12-cent immediate increase in earnings per share ($2.50 to $2.62). We look at the combined effect of these two variables in Table 20–6 as we extend the time horizon to 10 years.

Although earnings per share will be 12 cents higher immediately as a result of the merger, the slower postmerger growth rate of 8.85 percent indicates that after four years there is an indifference point between earnings with and without the merger (at $3.66). After 10 years *nonmerging* would actually provide 42 cents more in earnings per share ($6.49 versus $6.07). The long-term dilutive effect on earnings is the result of the differential growth rates and the absence of synergy.

**Table 20–6**
**Anticipated earnings per share for Expand Corporation with and without the merger, over 10 years**

| | Without Merger | | | With Merger (Small Corporation) | | |
|---|---|---|---|---|---|---|
| Year | Beginning Earnings per Share | Growth Rate | Anticipated Earnings per Share | Beginning Earnings per Share | Growth Rate | Anticipated Earnings per Share |
| 1 | $2.50 | 10% | $2.75 | $2.62 | 8.85% | $2.85 |
| 2 | 2.75 | | 3.03 | 2.85 | | 3.10 |
| 3 | 3.03 | | 3.33 | 3.10 | | 3.37 |
| 4 | 3.33 | | 3.66 | 3.37 | | 3.66 |
| 5 | 3.66 | | 4.03 | 3.66 | | 3.98 |
| 6 | 4.03 | | 4.43 | 3.98 | | 4.33 |
| 7 | 4.43 | | 4.87 | 4.33 | | 4.71 |
| 8 | 4.87 | | 5.36 | 4.71 | | 5.13 |
| 9 | 5.36 | | 5.90 | 5.13 | | 5.58 |
| 10 | 5.90 | | 6.49 | 5.58 | | 6.07 |

If the merger produced synergy by increasing the operating effectiveness of the combined firms by 15 percent, the immediate effect would be to increase earnings per share to $3.01 ($2.62 × 1.15) and tenth-year earnings to $6.98 ($6.07 × 1.15). Nevertheless, as has been pointed out, synergistic benefits may be difficult to achieve.

## Buying a Company at a Higher P/E Ratio

As an alternative strategy, assume that Expand Corporation is considering the acquisition of Growth Corporation. Although Growth Corporation is currently the same in size as Small Corporation, it enjoys a relatively high P/E ratio (14 ×) and a strong anticipated growth in earnings per share (18 percent). Financial information for Growth Corporation is presented in Table 20–7 along with data for Expand Corporation.

**Table 20–7**
**Financial data for potential merging firms**

| | *Growth Corporation* | *Expand Corporation* |
|---|---|---|
| Total earnings | $200,000 | $500,000 |
| Number of shares of stock outstanding | 50,000 | 200,000 |
| Earnings per share | $4.00 | $2.50 |
| Price–earning ratio (P/E) | 14 × | 12 × |
| Market price per share | $56.00 | $30.00 |
| Growth rate in earnings per share | 18% | 10% |

In order to effect a merger, we shall assume that Expand Corporation will pay the shareholders of Growth Corporation a 40 percent premium over market value. With each share of Growth Corporation currently selling at $56 per share, this would indicate a price of $78.40 per share ($56 × 1.4). To purchase 50,000 shares of Growth Corporation, the total value exchanged would be $3,920,000.

| | |
|---|---|
| $78.40 | Price per share |
| × 50,000 | Shares |
| $3,920,000 | Total price |

**Table 20–8**
**Postmerger earnings per share**

| | |
|---|---|
| Total earnings: Growth ($200,000) + Expand ($500,000) . . . . . . . . | $700,000 |
| Shares outstanding in surviving corporation: | |
| Old (200,000) + New (130,667) . . . . . . . . . . . . . . . . . . . | 330,667 |

$$\text{New earnings per share for Expand Corporation} = \frac{\$700{,}000}{330{,}667} = \$2.12$$

Since $30 shares of Expand Corporation are to be traded in the merger, 130,667 shares must be given to the shareholders of Growth Corporation.

$$\frac{\text{Purchase price}}{\text{Value of Expand Corporation shares}} = \frac{\$3{,}920{,}000}{\$30} = 130{,}667 \text{ shares}$$

Postmerger earnings per share are $2.12, as indicated in Table 20–8.

The earnings per share of Expand Corporation have been diluted from $2.50 to $2.12 as a result of the merger. Once again, the reason can be found in the relative P/E ratios. Growth Corporation is being purchased at a 40 percent premium over its current P/E ratio of 14, or at 19.6 times earnings. Since Expand Corporation's P/E ratio is only 12, dilution has set in. Nevertheless, a strong inducement factor for Expand Corporation is the high rate of increase in earnings per share of 18 percent for the Growth Corporation. On a weighted basis, this will increase the postmerger earnings per share growth rate of Expand Corporation to 12.28 percent.

$$\tfrac{5}{7}(10\%) + \tfrac{2}{7}(18\%) = 7.14\% + 5.14\% = 12.28\%$$

Rounding to 12.3 percent, the anticipated stream of future earnings for Expand Corporation with and without the Growth Corporation merger is indicated in Table 20–9.

In spite of the initial dilution in earnings per share, Expand Corporation will eventually benefit from the merger with tenth-year earnings per share at a level 30 cents higher than without merger. If the analysis is extended to 15 years, the difference between the two alternatives becomes approximately $1.70. Although it may take a dilutive, high-growth acquisition longer to show positive benefits, the eventual gains may be substantial. Of course, the presence of synergy would shorten the break-even period and expand the long-term positive benefits.

**Table 20–9**
**Anticipated earnings for Expand Corporation with and without a merger with Growth Corporation, over 10 years**

| | Without Merger | | | With Merger (Growth Corporation) | | |
|---|---|---|---|---|---|---|
| Year | Beginning Earnings per Share | Growth Rate | Anticipated Earnings per Share | Beginning Earnings per Share | Growth Rate | Anticipated Earnings per Share |
| 1 | $2.50 | 10% | $2.75 | $2.12 | 12.3% | $2.38 |
| 2 | 2.75 | | 3.03 | 2.38 | | 2.67 |
| 3 | 3.03 | | 3.33 | 2.67 | | 3.00 |
| 4 | 3.33 | | 3.66 | 3.00 | | 3.37 |
| 5 | 3.66 | | 4.03 | 3.37 | | 3.79 |
| 6 | 4.03 | | 4.43 | 3.79 | | 4.26 |
| 7 | 4.43 | | 4.87 | 4.26 | | 4.79 |
| 8 | 4.87 | | 5.36 | 4.79 | | 5.38 |
| 9 | 5.36 | | 5.90 | 5.38 | | 6.04 |
| 10 | 5.90 | | 6.49 | 6.04 | | 6.79 |

A comparison of the two merger plans with a nonmerger strategy for Expand Corporation is presented in Figure 20–1.

The earnings-per-share impact of a merger is influenced by the exchange ratio (relative price–earnings ratios as reflected in the terms), the relative growth rates of the firms, and the relative sizes of the firms. In regard to the last variable, if Growth Corporation had the same earnings as Expand Corporation, there would be a tremendous dilution in earnings per share down to $1.90, followed by an annual increase in earnings per share of 14 percent. Earnings per share would grow to over $7 after 10 years.

## Market Value Maximization

The basic merger plans diagramed in Figure 20–1 indicate the possibilities in buying a slow-growth firm at a relatively low P/E ratio and a high-growth firm at a relatively high P/E ratio. There is no right or wrong decision as such. The ultimate answer lies in the concept of market value maximization. We must try to assess how shareholders (present and potential) will view the merger. Thus we must consider not only the immediate impact on earnings per share, but also the effect on the surviving firm's postmerger P/E ratio. While the merger

Figure 20–1
Impact of alternative plans on Expand Corporation

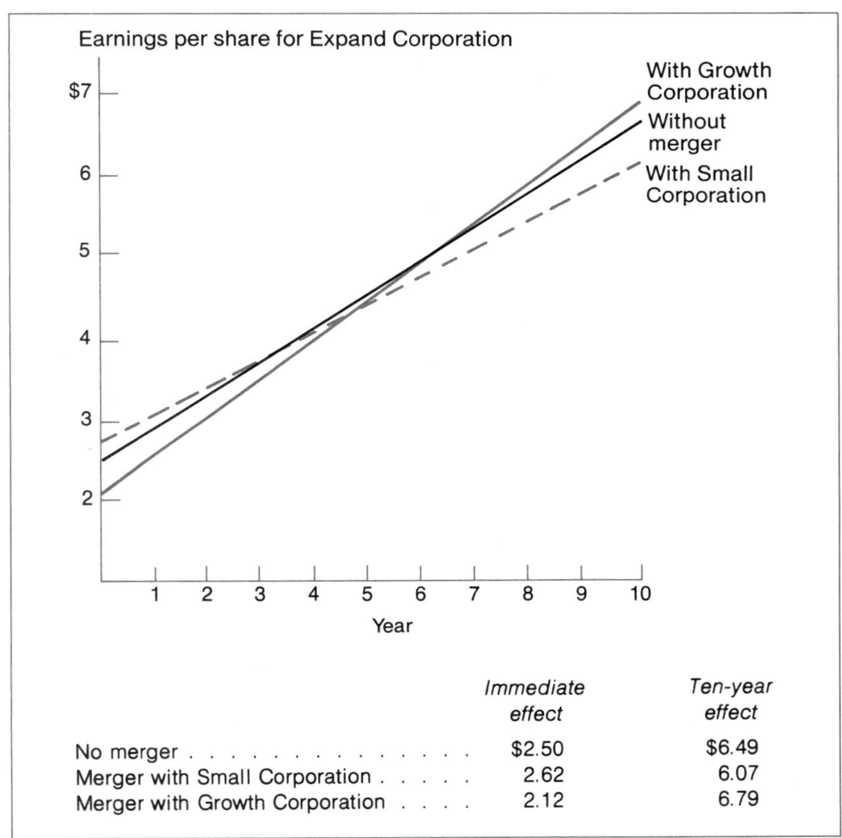


| | Immediate effect | Ten-year effect |
|---|---|---|
| No merger | $2.50 | $6.49 |
| Merger with Small Corporation | 2.62 | 6.07 |
| Merger with Growth Corporation | 2.12 | 6.79 |

with Small Corporation will increase Expand Corporation's earnings per share from $2.50 to $2.62, will there be a decrease in Expand Corporation's postmerger P/E ratio because of the decrease in the corporate growth rate from 10 percent to 8.85 percent? Similarly, will the dilution in earning per share from $2.50 to $2.12 as a result of the Growth Corporation acquisition be more than offset by an imposing increase in the corporate growth rate from 10 percent to 12.3 percent and a possible increase in the P/E ratio? In Table 20–10 we look at possible postmerger P/E ratios and stock prices for Expand Corporation, assuming a merger with *Growth Corporation*.

Undoubtedly, a corporate treasurer would like to study all of these possibilities in the context of a premerger price of $30 per share. Based

**Table 20–10**
**Postmerger valuation based on increased level of P/E ratio (current level of 12)***

| | *Potential Increase in P/E Ratio (percent)* | | | | |
|---|---|---|---|---|---|
| | *1%* | *10%* | *20%* | *30%* | *40%* |
| New P/E ratio | 12.1 × | 13.2 × | 14.4 × | 15.6 × | 16.8 × |
| Postmerger earnings | $2.12 | $2.12 | $2.12 | $2.12 | $2.12 |
| Postmerger market value | $25.65 | $27.98 | $30.53 | $33.07 | $35.62 |

*Additional analysis could also be done based on a declining P/E ratio.

on similar experiences of other companies in the industry or on past corporate history, relative probabilities of outcomes may be assigned and the expected value determined. (See Problem 10 at the end of the chapter.)

## Portfolio Effect

Inherent in all of our discussion is the importance of the merger's portfolio effect on the risk–return posture of the firm. The reduction or increase in risk may influence the P/E ratio as much as the change in the growth rate. To the extent that we are diminishing the overall risk of the firm in a merger, the P/E ratio may increase even if the potential earnings growth is unchanged. Business risk reduction may be achieved through acquiring another firm that is influenced by a set of factors in the business cycle opposite from those that influence our own firm, while financial risk reduction may be achieved by restructuring our postmerger financial arrangements to include less debt.

Perhaps Expand Corporation may be diversifying from a heavy manufacturing industry into the real estate/housing industry. While heavy manufacturing industries move with the business cycle, the real estate/housing industry tends to be countercyclical. Even though the expected value of earnings per share may remain relatively constant as a result of the merger, the standard deviation of possible outcomes may decline as a result of risk reduction through diversification, as is indicated in Figure 20–2.

We see that the expected value of the earnings per share has remained constant in this instance but that the standard deviation has gone down. Because there is less risk in the corporation, the investor may be willing to assign a higher valuation, thus increasing the price–earnings ratio.

Figure 20–2
Risk reduction portfolio benefits

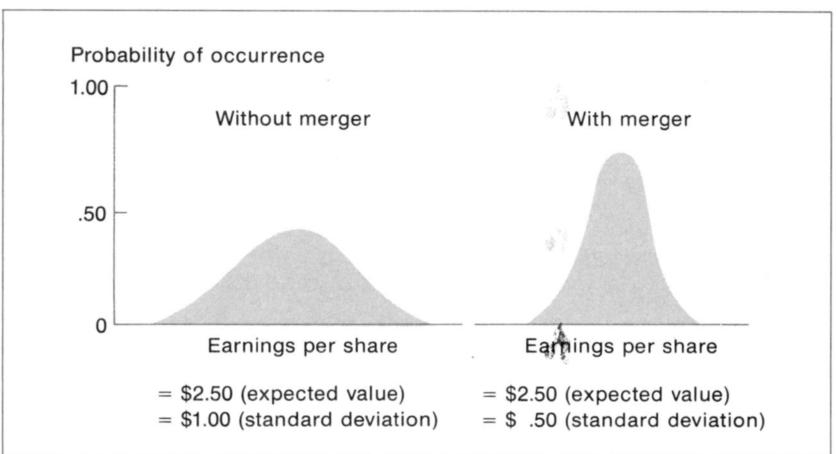


## Accounting Considerations in Mergers and Acquisitions

The role of financial accounting probably has no greater significance than in the area of mergers and acquisitions. When a price substantially above book value is paid for a potential acquisition, goodwill may be created on the books of the acquiring firm and the writing off of this goodwill over time can have a negative impact on earnings per share. Many firms try to avoid the creation of goodwill. Let's see what the issues and the options are.

A merger can be treated on the books of the acquiring firm as either *a pooling of interests* or *a purchase of assets*. Under a pooling of interests, the financial statements of the firms are combined, subject to some minor adjustments, and no goodwill is created. In order to qualify for a pooling of interests, certain criteria must be met, such as:

1. The acquiring corporation issues only common stock, with rights identical to its old outstanding voting stock, in exchange for substantially all of the other company's voting stock.
2. The acquired firm's stockholders maintain an ownership position in the surviving firm.

3. The combined entity does not intend to dispose of a significant portion of the assets of the combined companies within two years.
4. The combination is effected in a single transaction.[9]

Goodwill may be created when the second type of merger recording—a purchase of assets—is used. Because of the criteria described above (particularly items 1 and 2), a purchase of assets treatment rather than a pooling of interests treatment is generally necessary when the tender offer is in cash, bonds, preferred stock, or common stock with restricted rights. Under a purchase of assets accounting treatment, any excess of purchase price over book value must be recorded as goodwill and written off over a maximum period of 40 years.[10] If a company purchases a firm with a $4 million book value (net worth) for $6 million, $2 million of goodwill is created on the books of the acquiring company, and it must be written off over a maximum period of 40 years.[11] This would cause a $50,000-per-year reduction in reported earnings ($2 million/40 years). Because the writing off of goodwill is not a tax-deductible expense, the firm suffers the full amount of the deduction without any tax relief. Under a pooling of interests accounting treatment, you will recall, goodwill is not created.

The main reason we look at the pooling of interests versus the purchase of assets accounting treatment is to recognize the potentially beneficial effect to a corporation of exchanging common stock rather than nonequity compensation (cash, bonds, preferred stock, and so on), and thus perhaps qualifying as a pooling of interests. Common stock compensation also more readily qualifies a merger for a tax-free exchange under Section 368(a) of the Internal Revenue Code. Under a tax-free exchange, the stockholders of the acquired firm may defer any capital gains taxes until the newly acquired shares have actually been sold. Thus, there would be no immediate tax for trading a share

---

[9] Accounting Principles Board, "Business Combinations," *APB Opinion No. 16* (New York: AICPA, 1970). A number of lesser criteria are also involved.

[10] An exception is that certain assets may be revalued upward at the time of merger, thus reducing the magnitude of goodwill creation.

[11] Because of the premiums that are often paid to induce a possible acquisition, payments well in excess of book value are not unusual.

of stock in Growth Corporation that was purchased 10 years ago at $5 for $78.40 in Expand Corporation stock. If and when the Expand Corporation stock is sold, the tax will be recognized. If the tender offer were $78.40 in cash, there would be an immediate tax obligation.

In analyzing accounting and tax considerations, we see that the acquiring corporation has some inducement to offer common stock to qualify as a pooling of interests when the exchange offer exceeds book value; also that the stockholders of the acquired firm have some incentive to receive common stock when the exchange offer exceeds their initial cost basis in order to avoid immediate taxes. During the 1960s and part of the 1970s, common stock, often supplemented by convertible securities and warrants, was a frequently used mode of exchange.[12] In the merger movement of the late 1970s and in the 1980s, cash offers have come into vogue.

Why? First of all, stockholders of the acquired firms have become somewhat disenchanted with the performance of the acquiring companies' stock and, at times, the stock market in general. For this reason they have been willing to take cash, pay a tax and invest in a new, diversified set of investments. Acquiring corporations have gone along with the cash tender offer pattern, in spite of the requirement for purchase of assets accounting treatment, in order to satisfy the demands of selling stockholders.[13]

Also, by using cash instead of stock, a corporation may diminish the perceived dilutive effect of a merger. If Small Corporation or Growth Corporation had been acquired for straight cash by Expand Corporation, no new shares would have been issued and earnings per share would have gone up proportionately by the amount of new aftertax earnings. This latter argument tends to be weakened by recognition of the fact that cash tendered in a merger has a substantial capital cost associated with it and, furthermore, that new shares of stock may later have to be authorized and sold to finance the cash drain.

---

[12]The popularity of the last two items was reduced somewhat by Accounting Principles Board *Opinion No. 15*, "Earnings per Share," issued by the AICPA in May 1969, which required tough standards for the dilutive effects of convertibles and warrants, as described in Chapter 19.

[13]Also where a substantial postmerger asset write-up is possible, the corporation may acquire a beneficial tax base for depreciation rather than non-tax-deductible goodwill.

## Negotiated versus Tendered Offers

Traditionally, mergers have been negotiated in a friendly atmosphere between officers and directors of the participating corporations. Product lines, quality of assets, and future growth prospects are discussed, and eventually an exchange ratio is hammered out and presented to the investment community and the financial press.

As previously mentioned, the merger wave of the late 1970s and the 1980s has helped to create a wholly new atmosphere. The takeover *tender offer,* in which a company attempts to acquire a target firm against its will, has come into vogue. One of the most notorious examples was the announced intent of American Express to take over McGraw-Hill in early 1979. At that time McGraw-Hill was selling at $26 per share. The initial American Express offer was for $34, and eventually the offer went up to $40. McGraw-Hill fought off the offer by maintaining that American Express would obstruct the independent character required of a publisher. McGraw-Hill was able to discourage the unwelcome offer from American Express, but many small McGraw-Hill stockholders sued the publisher, claiming that the calling off of the merger caused them to lose an opportunity to advance the cash value of their holdings.

Not all companies are able to fend off the unwanted advances of suitors. An entire vocabulary has developed on Wall Street around the concept of the target takeover. For example, the *Saturday Night Special* refers to a surprise offer that is made just before the market closes for the weekend and takes the target company's officers by surprise. By the time the officers can react, the impact of the offer has already taken place. Perhaps a stock is trading at $20 and an unfriendly offer comes in at $28. Though the offer may please the company's stockholders, its management faces the dangers of seeing the company going down the wrong path in a merger and perhaps of their being personally ousted.

In order to avoid an unfriendly takeover, management may turn to a *White Knight* for salvation. A White Knight represents a third firm that management calls upon to help it avoid the initial unwanted tender offer. For example, in 1978 Babcock and Wilcox received an unsolicited takeover bid from United Technologies to purchase its stock at $42 per share. Since the stock was currently selling at 34¾, this was not a bad offer. However, the company turned to J. Ray McDermott &

Co. as a friendly suitor. After a bidding war, Babcock and Wilcox was eventually purchased by McDermott for $65 a share. Under similar circumstances in 1982, Conoco turned to DuPont as a suitor after being pursued on an unfriendly basis by Seagrams and others. Also, Marathon Oil merged with U.S. Steel in 1982 to avoid an unfriendly tender offer from Mobil Oil. The biggest "white knight" was Chevron Corporation, who "saved" Gulf Oil from T. Boone Pickens at a cost of $13.3 billion.

Many firms that wish to avoid takeovers have moved their corporate offices to states that have tough prenotification and protection provisions in regard to takeover offers. Other companies have bought in portions of their own shares to restrict the amount of stock available for a takeover or have encouraged employees to buy stock under corporate pension plans. Other protective measures include increasing dividends to keep stockholders happy and staggering the election of members of the board of directors to make outside power plays more difficult to initiate. Possible target companies have also bought up other companies to increase their own size and make themselves more expensive and less vulnerable. One of the key rules for avoiding a targeted takeover is to never get caught with too large a cash position. A firm with large cash balances serves as an ideal target for a *leveraged* takeover. The acquiring company is able to negotiate a bank loan based on the target company's assets and then to go into the marketplace to make a cash tender offer. For example, CIT Financial left itself wide open in April 1979 when it sold off a banking subsidiary for $425 million. At that point CIT had cash balances equal to $20 per share for shares which had a market value in the $30–$40 range. RCA later bought the company for $65 per share.

While a takeover bid may not appeal to management, it may be enticing to stockholders, as previously indicated. Herein lies the basic problem. The bidding may get so high that stockholders demand action. The desire of management to maintain the status quo can come into conflict with the objective of stockholder wealth maximization.

## Premium Offers and Stock Price Movements

Until the latest merger wave, the average premium paid over market value in a merger or acquisition was of the magnitude of 20–25 per-

**Table 20–11**
**Tender offer bid premiums**

| Bidding Premium | Percent of Bids 1982 | Percent of Bids 1983 |
|---|---|---|
| 100% + | (2) | (8) |
| 90–99% | (1) | (1) |
| 80–89 | (3) | (5) |
| 70–79 | (6) | (3) |
| 60–69 | (3) | (5) |
| 50–59 | (9) | (6) |
| 40–49 | (10) | (11) |
| 30–39 | (17) | (11) |
| 20–29 | (15) | (21) |
| 10–19 | (17) | (15) |
| 0– 9 | (17) | (14) |
| Total | (100) | (100) |

Source: *Mergers and Acquisitions*, Spring 1984.

cent.[14] In the merger movement of the late 1970s and the 1980s, the average premium appears to have been closer to 50–60 percent.[15] Table 20–11 shows the tender-offer bid premiums for 1982 and 1983. In 1983, 8 percent of the major tender offers were for over 100 percent of the acquired firm's value.

The high premiums of the late 1970s and the 1980s may be related to market values for securities in general. To the extent that replacement value exceeds market value, a high premium over market value may be justified. Also, the companies acquired in the latest merger movement have tended to be of unusually high quality and thus have commanded a high premium. Alcon Labs, Coca Cola Bottling of Los Angeles, and Conoco are examples of thriving companies that demanded a high premium. The motivation of the acquiring company in making the purchase was often not to turn around a poor perfor-

[14]William A. Alberts and Joel E. Segall, *The Corporate Merger* (Chicago: University of Chicago Press, 1966), pp. 117–18. Also George D. McCarthy, *Acquisitions and Mergers* (New York: Ronald, 1963), pp. 92–102.

[15]"The Takeover Target's Defender," *Business Week*, March 16, 1977, p. 160. Also Henry Oppenheimer and Stanley Block, "An Examination of the Characteristics Associated with Merger Activity during the 1975–78 Period," Financial Management Association Meetings, 1980. Also selected issues of *Mergers and Acquisitions* (1981–85).

mance, but to take advantage of the superior market or product position of the acquired company.

Many of the acquisition candidates represented some of the most interesting stock market performers of the decade. Often the daily volume leaders and outstanding price movers were acquisition candidates. Researchers have found that potential acquirees have superior price performance on a risk-adjusted basis.[16] It is not surprising that a company which is offered a large premium over its current market value has a major upside movement. The only problem for the investor is that much of this activity may take place before the public announcement of the merger offer. If a firm is selling at $25 per share when informal negotiations begin, it may be $34 by the time an announced offer of $40 is made. Still, there are good profits to be made if the merger goes through.

A group of investors who specialize in merger situations came into high visibility in the late 1970s and the 1980s. Known as ARBS (arbitrageurs), their strategy is to purchase the stock of the acquisition candidate in the hope of being bought out at the tender offer price. In the prior example, they would accumulate stock at between $34 and $38 in the hope of selling out at $40. The ARBS often become the allies of acquiring companies because their profits (and their avoidance of losses) are dependent on the merger's actual completion.

In a stock-for-stock exchange, an arbitrageur may attempt to protect his profit position by buying the stock of the acquisition candidate and, at the same time, short-selling the stock of the acquirer. A short sell is a current sale of stock that is not owned, with the intention of acquiring the stock in the future to close out the position. The arbitrageur buys the acquiree's stock at $34 and simultaneously short-sells the acquiring company's stock at $40. When the merger has been consummated, he will trade the acquiree's stock for a share of the acquiring company's stock and use the stock to cover his $40 short position. Thus his sell price is preestablished at $40, and his buy price at $34. Even if the acquiring company's stock goes up or *down* from

[16]Gershon Mandelker, "Risk and Return: The Case of Merging Firms," *Journal of Financial Economics* 1 (December 1974), pp. 303–35. Mandelker found the merger effect beginning to influence the acquiree's stock seven months before consummation of the merger, with the cumulative average residual (excess returns) moving positively at that point.

**Table 20–12**
**Stock movement of potential acquirees**

| Acquirer—Potential Acquiree | Preannouncement | One Day after Announcement | One Day after Cancellation |
|---|---|---|---|
| Mead Corp.—Occidental Petroleum . . . . | 20⅜ | 33¼ | 23¼ |
| Olin Corp.—Celanese . . . . . | 16 | 23¾ | 16¾ |
| Chicago Rivet—MITE . . . . . | 20¾ | 28⅛ | 20¾ |

$40 after the merger has been announced, his sell price and profit spread have been established.

The only problem with this strategy or of any merger-related investment strategy is that the merger may be called off. In that case the merger candidate's stock, which shot up from $25 to $34, may fall back to $25, and the Johnny-come-lately investor would lose $9 per share.[17] In Table 20–12, we consider the case of three canceled mergers of the late 1970s.

Of course, if a new suitor comes along shortly after cancellation (or, in fact, causes the original cancellation), the price may quickly rebound. Such was the case when Gulf Oil canceled its plans to acquire Cities Service in 1982 and Occidental Petroleum stepped in to provide an acceptable offer.

All this information on price movement patterns has significance to corporate financial management, which must understand and react to the motivations of investors. For example, once the ARBS have established their investment position, these arbitrageurs will do everything possible to see that the merger goes through. This, at a minimum, will include voting all their shares in favor of a merger. On a more active basis, it may encompass a strategy of influencing other large stockholders, and it could ultimately include an attempt to discredit the management of a target company in the eyes of shareholders.

## Two-Step Buy-Out

Another merger ploy that has been undertaken in the recent merger movement is the two-step buy-out. Under this plan the acquiring com-

[17] Clearly, the arbitrageur would also not have new stock of the acquiring company to cover his short position since there would be no exchange of shares.

pany attempts to gain control by offering a very high cash price for 51 percent of the shares outstanding. At the same time, they announce a second, lower price that will be paid, either in cash, stock, or bonds, at a subsequent point in time. As an example, an acquiring company may offer stockholders of a takeover target company a $70 cash offer that can be executed in the next 20 days (for 51 percent of the shares outstanding). Subsequent to that time period, the selling stockholders will receive $57.50 in preferred stock for each share.

This buy-out procedure accomplishes two purposes. First of all, it provides a strong inducement to stockholders to quickly react to the offer. Those who delay must accept a lower price. Secondly, it allows the acquiring company to pay a lower total price than if a single offer is made. In the example above, a single offer may have been made for $68 a share. Assume 1 million shares are outstanding. The single offer has a total price tag of $68,000,000, while the two-step offer would have called for only $63,875,000.

| | |
|---|---|
| *Single offer* | |
| 1,000,000 shares at $68 = | $68,000,000 |
| *Two-step offer* | |
| 510,000 shares (51%) at $70 = | $35,700,000 |
| 490,000 shares (49%) at $57.50 = | 28,175,000 |
| | $63,875,000 |

An example of a two-step buy-out was the Mobil Oil attempt to acquire 51 percent of Marathon Oil shares at a price of $126 in cash, with a subsequent offer to buy the rest of the shares for $90 face value Mobil debentures. In this case, Marathon Oil decided to sell out to U.S. Steel, which also made a two-step offer of $125 in cash or $100 in notes to later subscribers. Incidentally, before the bidding began, Marathon Oil was selling for $60 a share.

The SEC has continued to keep a close eye on the two-step buy-out. Government regulators fear that smaller stockholders may not be sophisticated enough to compete with arbitrageurs or institutional investors in rapidly tendering shares to ensure receipt of the higher price. The SEC has emphasized the need for a pro rata processing of stockholder orders, in which each stockholder receives an equal percentage of shares tendered.

## Holding Companies

The holding company achieved its greatest popularity in the early part of the 20th century, and it is still in evidence today in a number of industries, particularly in public utilities. A holding company is one that has control over one or more other firms. In order to establish voting control, the holding company may own less than a majority interest but is able to determine policy as a result of widely spread minority interests among the other stockholders.

The primary advantage of the holding company is that it affords unusual opportunities for leverage. Assume that Giant Holding Corporation has the investment interests in Companies A, B, and C that are shown in Table 20–13. All numbers are assumed to represent millions of dollars. Also assume that Giant Holding Corporation has effective voting control of the three companies because of the widely dispersed interests of these companies' other owners. It owns 20 percent of the equity of Company A, as indicated by Giant Holding Corporation's balance sheet holding of $10 million in Company A (an asset) and Company A's common stock equity account of $50 million. In the case of Company B, the ratio is 37.5 percent ($15 million/$40 million), while for Company C it is 25 percent ($20 million/$80 million). Through these interlocking positions, Giant Holding Corporation controls $420 million in assets (the combined assets of the three companies). Note that it is doing this with only $20 million of common stock equity in its own firm. Its equity to "assets controlled" ratio is 4.8 percent ($20 million/$420 million). If we really want to get creative, we can assume that another holding company has control of Giant Holding Corporation with only a small investment in it, thus creating additional levels of ownership.

The holding company device also benefits from the isolation of the "legal" risks of the firms. Theoretically, if Company C loses money, this will not *legally* affect the other firms, because Company C is a separate legal entity with separate shareholders.

### Drawbacks

The drawbacks are those inherent in any pyramiding arrangement.[18] Although Companies A, B, and C are separate legal entities, and one

[18] There are also many serious legal questions associated with holding companies.

**Table 20–13**
**Assets, liabilities, and stockholders' equity of Giant Holding Corporation and related companies (in $ millions)**

GIANT HOLDING CORPORATION

| *Assets* | | *Liabilities and Stockholders' Equity* | |
|---|---|---|---|
| Common stockholdings | | | |
| Company A | $10 | Long-term debt | $15 |
| Company B | 15 | Preferred stock | 10 |
| Company C | 20 | Common stock equity | 20 |
| | $45 | | $45 |

COMPANY A

| *Assets* | | *Liabilities and Stockholders' Equity* | |
|---|---|---|---|
| Current assets | $ 50 | Current liabilities | $ 20 |
| Plant and equipment | 50 | Long-term debt | 30 |
| | $100 | Common stock equity | 50 |
| | | | $100 |

COMPANY B

| *Assets* | | *Liabilities and Stockholders' Equity* | |
|---|---|---|---|
| Current assets | $ 60 | Current liabilities | $ 10 |
| Plant and equipment | 60 | Long-term debt | 70 |
| | $120 | Common stock equity | 40 |
| | | | $120 |

COMPANY C

| *Assets* | | *Liabilities and Stockholders' Equity* | |
|---|---|---|---|
| Current assets | $ 80 | Current liabilities | $ 20 |
| Plant and equipment | 120 | Long-term debt | 100 |
| | $200 | Common stock equity | 80 |
| | | | $200 |

cannot force the bankruptcy of another, as has been implied, there can be an indirect chain effect that is disastrous. For example, if Company A has a bad year, it may be unable to pay dividends to the holding company, which, in turn, may be unable to pay interest on the $15 million it has in long-term debt. The more complicated the arrangement, the more vulnerable the operation is to reversals.

The holding company also suffers from the problem of multiple taxation. For example, Company A must pay taxes on its profits and then declare dividends to the holding company which are also partially taxable. Although there is an 85 percent exemption on dividends paid to another corporation, the 15 percent additional tax bite is still significant,[19] particularly when one considers that the stockholders of the holding company will have to pay a third tax on the dividends declared to them.

The administrative problems and procedures of a holding company are also worthy of note. With multiple managements, boards of directors, dividend policies, and reporting systems, the expenses are high and the opportunities for problems substantial.

## Summary

Corporations may seek external growth through mergers in order to achieve risk reduction, to improve access to the financial markets through increased size, or to obtain tax carry-forward benefits. A merger may also expand the marketing and management capabilities of the firm and allow for new-product development. While some mergers promise synergistic benefits (the 2 + 2 = 5 effect), this can be an elusive feature, with initial expectations exceeding the subsequent realities.

The cash purchase of another corporation takes on many of the characteristics of a classical capital budgeting decision. In a stock-for-stock exchange, there is often a trade-off between immediate gain or dilution in earnings per share and future growth. If a firm buys another firm with a P/E ratio lower than its own, there is an immediate increase in earnings per share, but the long-term earnings growth prospects must also be considered. The ultimate objective of a merger, as is true of any financial decision, is stockholder wealth maximization, and the immediate and delayed effects of the merger must be evaluated in this context.

The accounting considerations in a merger are also important. Where the purchase price exceeds the book value of the acquired firm (after postmerger asset value adjustments), goodwill may be created which must be written off directly against future earnings per share. In order to avoid goodwill creation, the merger may be treated as a pooling of interests rather than a purchase of assets if certain restrictive conditions

[19] Only if the holding company has an 80 percent or greater ownership interest can the second tax be avoided.

are met. For example, stock must be tendered rather than cash, debt, preferred stock, or other financial instruments.

In the merger wave of the late 1970s and the 1980s, the unsolicited tender offer for a target company gained in popularity. Offers were made at values well in excess of the current market price, and management of the target company became trapped in the dilemma of maintaining its current position versus agreeing to the wishes of the acquiring company, the arbitrageurs, and even the target company's own stockholders.

Finally, the holding company is viewed as a means of accumulating large asset control with a minimum equity investment through leveraging the investment. However, many tax, administrative, and legal problems are inherent in this form of organization.

## List of Terms

**merger**
**consolidation**
**portfolio effect**
**tax loss carry-forward**
**synergy**
**terms of exchange**
**market value maximization**
**pooling of interests**
**purchase of assets**
**goodwill**
**tender offer takeover**
**merger premium**
**merger arbitrageur**
**two-step buy-out**
**holding company**
**leveraged buy-out**

## Discussion Questions

1. Briefly discuss three significant features of the merger movement of the late 1970s and the 1980s.

2. Is risk reduction in the firm's portfolio of undertakings likely to be best achieved through horizontal integration, vertical integration, or conglomerate-type acquisitions?

3. If a firm wishes to achieve immediate appreciation in earnings per share as a result of a merger, how can this be best accomplished

in terms of exchange variables? What is a possible drawback to this approach in terms of long-range considerations?

4. What is the essential difference between a pooling of interests and a purchase of assets accounting treatment of a merger? Is goodwill amortization a tax-deductible expense?

5. If Ford Motor Company were to merge with American Motor Company, suggest three forms of synergy that might take place.

6. Generally a stockholder of the selling corporation will demand a higher price if cash consideration is tendered. Explain why this might be the case.

7. Explain how the weak stock market of the late 1970s served as an impetus to the merger wave of the late 1970s and 1980s.

8. It is possible for the postmerger P/E ratio to move in a direction opposite to that of the immediate postmerger earnings per share. Explain why this could happen.

9. Explain why unusually high premiums have been paid in the latest merger movement.

10. Suggest some ways in which firms have tried to avoid being part of a target takeover.

11. Why do management and stockholders often have divergent viewpoints about the desirability of a takeover?

12. How does a merger arbitrageur benefit from a possible merger? What is the danger in being a merger arbitrageur? Explain.

13. Compare the use of leverage in a holding company to the concept of operating and financial leverage explained in Chapter 5. What tax problems related to dividends does a holding company have?

14. What is the purpose(s) of the two-step buy-out from the viewpoint of the acquiring company?

## Problems

1. Assume the Arrow Corporation is considering the acquisition of Failure Unlimited. The latter has a $400,000 tax loss carry- forward. The projected earnings for Arrow Corporation are as follows:

| | 1987 | 1988 | 1989 | Total Value |
|---|---|---|---|---|
| Before-tax income . . . | $160,000 | $200,000 | $320,000 | $680,000 |
| Taxes (45%) . . . . . . . | 72,000 | 90,000 | 144,000 | 306,000 |
| Income available to stockholders . . . . | $ 88,000 | $110,000 | $176,000 | $374,000 |

*a.* How much will the total taxes of Arrow Corporation be reduced as a result of the tax loss carry-forward?

*b.* How much will the total income available to stockholders be for the three years if the acquisition takes place?

**2.** The McCoy Corporation desires to expand. It is considering a cash purchase of Hatfield Enterprises for $2,600,000. Hatfield has a $500,000 tax loss carry-forward that could be used immediately by the McCoy Corporation, which is paying taxes at the rate of 40 percent. Hatfield will provide $380,000 per year in cash flow (aftertax income plus depreciation) for the next 20 years. If the McCoy Corporation has a cost of capital of 14 percent, should the merger be undertaken?

**3.** Kemp's Supply Sidemolding is considering a cash acquisition of Roth Homebuilding for $2,200,000. Roth will provide the following pattern of cash inflows and synergistic benefits for the next 20 years. There is no tax loss carry-forward.

| | Years | | |
|---|---|---|---|
| | 1–5 | 6–15 | 16–20 |
| Cash inflow (aftertax) . . . . . . . . . | $220,000 | $240,000 | $280,000 |
| Synergistic benefits (aftertax) . . . . . | 20,000 | 22,000 | 40,000 |

The cost of capital for the acquiring firm is 12 percent. Should the merger be undertaken? (If you have any difficulty with delayed time value of money problems, consult Chapter 9.)

**4.** Ann Newberg helped start the Lovely Fragrance Company in 1951. At the time she purchased 100,000 shares of stock at $.10 per share. In 1986, she has the opportunity to sell her interest in the company to Holly Cosmetics for $50 cash per share. Her capital gains tax rate will be 20 percent.

*a.* If she sells out her interest, what will be the value for before-tax profit, capital gains taxes, and aftertax profit?

*b.* Assume, instead of cash, she accepts stock valued at $50 per share. She holds the stock for five years and then sells it for

$87.50 (the stock pays no cash dividends). What will be the value for before-tax profit, capital gains taxes, and aftertax profit?

*c*. Using a 10 percent discount rate, compare the aftertax profit figure in part *b* to part *a*. (That is, discount back the figure for five years.)

**5.** Hall Corporation is considering a two-step buy-out of Oates Inc. The latter firm has 1 million shares outstanding and its stock price is currently $30 per share. In the two-step buy-out, Hall will offer to buy 51 percent of Oates' shares outstanding for $58 in cash, and the balance in a second offer of 490,000 convertible preferred stock shares; each share of preferred stock would be valued at 45 percent over Oates' common stock value. Mr. Clark, a newcomer to the management team at Hall Corporation, suggests that only one offer for all of Oates' shares be made at $52.75 per share. Is the two-step buy-out or the single offer preferable in terms of minimizing cost?

**6.** A merger between Pica Corporation and Elite Corporation is under consideration. The financial information for these firms is as follows:

| | *Elite Corporation* | *Pica Corporation* |
|---|---|---|
| Total earnings | $300,000 | $600,000 |
| Number of shares of stock outstanding | 100,000 | 300,000 |
| Earnings per share | $3 | $2 |
| Price–earnings ratio | 8× | 12× |
| Market price per share | $24 | $24 |

*a*. On a share-for-share exchange basis, what will the postmerger earnings per share be?

*b*. If Pica Corporation pays a 25 percent premium over the market value of Elite Corporation, how many shares will be issued?

*c*. With the 25 percent premium, what will the postmerger earnings per share be? (Round to the nearest cent.)

*d*. With a 50 percent premium, how many shares will be issued and what will be the postmerger earnings per share?

*e*. With a 75 percent premium, how many shares will be issued and what will be the postmerger earnings per share?

*f*. Explain what has happend in parts *a*, *c*, *d*, and *e* in terms of relative P/E ratios and the earnings per share impact of the acquisition.

7. In the case of the Pica and Elite merger described in Problem 6, assume that a 100 percent premium will be paid, but that there is a 20 percent synergistic benefit to total earnings from the merger. Will the postmerger earnings go up or down, based on your calculations?

8. Median Corporation is considering a share-for-share exchange with Passive Corporation. The financial information for these firms is as follows:

| | *Passive Corporation* | *Median Corporation* |
|---|---|---|
| Total earnings | $10,000,000 | $15,000,000 |
| Number of shares of stock outstanding | 4,000,000 | 10,000,000 |
| Earnings per share | $2.50 | $1.50 |
| Price–earnings ratio | 4 × | 10 × |
| Market price per share | $10.00 | $15.00 |

Median Corporation has agreed to pay Passive Corporation a 20 percent premium over market value. Without the merger, Median Corporation will grow at a 12 percent rate for the next ten years. Passive Corporation is expected to grow by 2 percent per year.

*a.* Compute the postmerger earnings per share. (Round to the nearest cent.)

*b.* Compute the anticipated postmerger growth rate for the combined firms for the next 10 years. Weight the combined growth rate on the basis of relative earnings contributed to the merged firm.

*c.* Project earnings per share annually for the next 10 years for Median Corporation based on no merger and based on a merger with Passive Corporation.

9. As a second alternative, Median Corporation (in Problem 8) is also considering a merger with Dynamo Corporation. The financial information for these firms is as follows:

| | *Dynamo Corporation* | *Median Corporation* |
|---|---|---|
| Total earnings | $5,000,000 | $15,000,000 |
| Number of shares of stock outstanding | 2,500,000 | 10,000,000 |
| Earnings per share | $2.00 | $1.50 |
| Price–earnings ratio | 12× | 10× |
| Market price per share | $24.00 | $15.00 |

Median Corporation has agreed to pay Dynamo Corporation a 50 percent premium over market value. As previously stated, without the merger Median would grow at a 12 percent rate for the next 10 years. Dynamo Corporation is expected to grow at a 24 percent rate for the next 10 years.

*a.* Compute the postmerger earnings per share. (Round to the nearest cent.)

*b.* Compute the anticipated postmerger growth rate for the combined firms for the next 10 years.

*c.* Project earnings per share annually for the next 10 years for Median Corporation based on no merger (already computed) and based on a merger with Dynamo Corporation.

**10.** Based on the answers developed to Problems 8 and 9:

*a.* Briefly describe the characteristics of the Median Corporation merger with Passive Corporation in terms of initial dilution, break-even point, and impact after 10 years. Do the same for the Median Corporation–Dynamo Corporation merger. (No graphs are necessary.)

*b.* In the case of the merger between Median Corporation and Dynamo Corporation, assume the following possible immediate postmerger P/E ratios with the associated probabilities. Compute an expected value for the price of Median Corporation stock after the merger.

| P/E | Probability |
|---|---|
| 10 | .20 |
| 12 | .40 |
| 14 | .30 |
| 16 | .10 |

*c.* In regard to the Median Corporation–Dynamo Corporation merger, if the firms had wished to trade strictly on the basis of earnings per share, what would the exchange ratio be?

*d.* In regard to the Median Corporation–Dynamo Corporation merger, if 12 percent initial synergy were involved, what would the merger's break-even time period be? (That is, after how many years would earnings per share with and without merger be approximately equal?)

**11.** Assume the Shelton Corporation is considering the acquisition of Cook Inc. The expected earnings per share for the Shelton Corporation will be $3.00 with or without the merger. However, the standard deviation of the earnings will go from $1.89 to $1.20 with the merger because the two firms are negatively correlated.

*a.* Compute the coefficient of variation for the Shelton Corporation before and after the merger.
*b.* Discuss the possible impact on Shelton's postmerger P/E ratio, assuming that investors are risk averse.

**12.** General Meters is considering two mergers. The first is with Firm A in its own volatile industry, the auto speedometer industry, whereas the second is a merger with Firm B in an industry that moves in the opposite direction (and will tend to level out performance due to negative correlation).

*a.* Compute the mean, standard deviation, and coefficient of variation for both investments (consult Chapter 13 to review statistical concepts if necessary).

| *General Meters Merger with Firm A* | | *General Meters Merger with Firm B* | |
|---|---|---|---|
| *Possible Earnings ($ millions)* | *Probability* | *Possible Earnings ($ millions)* | Probability |
| $40 . . . . | .30 | $10 . . . . | .25 |
| 50 . . . . | .40 | 50 . . . . | .50 |
| 60 . . . . | .30 | 90 . . . . | .25 |

*b.* Assuming investors are risk averse, which alternative can be expected to bring the higher valuation?

**13.** The Heisman Corporation is considering the acquisition of the O'Brien Corporation. The book value of the O'Brien Corporation is $30 million, and the Heisman Corporation is willing to pay $80 million in cash and preferred stock. No upward adjustment of assets is anticipated. The Heisman Corporation has 2 million shares outstanding. A purchase of assets financial recording will be used, with a 40-year write-off of goodwill.

*a.* How much will the annual amortization be?
*b.* How much will the annual amortization be on a per share basis?
*c.* Is any tax benefit involved?
*d.* Explain how the recording of goodwill could have been avoided.

**14.** Maxima Corporation, a holding company, has investments in three other firms.

ALPHA CORPORATION

| Assets | | Liabilities and Stockholders' Equity | |
|---|---|---|---|
| Current assets . . . . . . . | $ 80 | Current liabilities . . . . . . | $ 40 |
| Plant and equipment . . . . | 120 | Long-term debt . . . . . . . | 40 |
| | | Common stock equity . . . . | 120 |
| | $200 | | $200 |

BETA CORPORATION

| Assets | | Liabilities and Stockholders' Equity | |
|---|---|---|---|
| Current assets . . . . . . . | $100 | Current liabilities . . . . . . | $ 30 |
| Plant and equipment . . . . | 200 | Long-term debt . . . . . . . | 70 |
| | | Common stock equity . . . . | 200 |
| | $300 | | $300 |

DELTA CORPORATION

| Assets | | Liabilities and Stockholders' Equity | |
|---|---|---|---|
| Current assets . . . . . . . | $150 | Current liabilities . . . . . . | $ 90 |
| Plant and equipment . . . . | 150 | Long-term debt . . . . . . . | 110 |
| | | Common stock equity . . . . | 100 |
| | $300 | | $300 |

Maxima Corporation has voting control of the three other corporations, with the following investment interests in each: 25 percent of the equity in Alpha, 20 percent of the equity in Beta, and 10 percent of the equity in Delta. Maxima Corporation's long-term debt is equal to 30 percent of its assets; its preferred stock is equal to 20 percent; and its common stock is equal to 50 percent.

*a*. Fill in the table below for Maxima Corporation.

| Assets | | Liabilities and Stockholders' Equity | |
|---|---|---|---|
| Common stockholdings | | | |
| Alpha Corporation | ________ | Long-term debt | ________ |
| Beta Corporation | ________ | Preferred stock | ________ |
| Delta Corporation | ________ | Common stock equity | ________ |
| Total | ________ | Total | ________ |

*b.* Compute the percentage of Maxima Corporation's equity to the total holding company assets in the three corporations.

## Selected References

Alberts, William A., and Joel E. Segall. *The Corporate Merger.* Chicago: University of Chicago Press, 1966 and 1974.

Appleyard, A. R., and G. K. Yarrow. "The Relationship between Take-Over Activity and Share Valuation." *Journal of Finance* 30 (December 1975), pp. 1239–49.

Austin, Douglas V. "The Financial Management of Tender Offer Takeovers." *Financial Management* 3 (Spring 1974), pp. 37–43.

Block, Stanley B. "The Effects of Mergers and Acquisitions on the Market Value of Common Stock." *Southern Journal of Business* 4 (October 1969), pp. 189–95.

Bradley, James W., and Donald H. Korn. "Acquisition and Merger Trends Affecting the Portfolio Manager." *Financial Analysts Journal* 33 (November–December 1977), pp. 65–70.

Conn, Robert L., and Nielsen, James F. "An Empirical Test of the Larson-Gonedes Exchange Ratio Determination Model." *Journal of Finance* 32 (June 1977), pp. 749–59.

Cummin, Robert I. "Unfriendly Corporate Takeovers—Old Style." *Financial Analysts Journal* 85 (June–August 1982).

Dellenbarger, Lynn E. "A Study of Relative Common Stock Equity Values in Fifty Mergers of Listed Industrial Corporations, 1950–57." *Journal of Finance* 18 (September 1963), p. 565.

Dodd, Peter, and Richard Ruback. "Tender Offers and Stockholder Returns." *Journal of Financial Economics* 5 (December 1977), pp. 351–73.

Hogarty, T. "The Profitability of Corporate Mergers." *Journal of Business* 43 (July 1970), pp. 317–27.

Larson, Kermit D., and Nicholas J. Gonedes. "Business Combinations: An Exchange Ratio Determination Model." *Accounting Review* 44 (October 1969), pp. 720–28.

Lewellen, Wilber G. "A Pure Financial Rationale for Conglomerate Merger." *Journal of Finance* 26 (May 1971), pp. 521–37.

Mandelker, Gershon. "Risk and Return: the Case of Merging Firms." *Journal of Financial Economics* 1 (December 1974), pp. 303–35.

Melicher, Ronald W., and David F. Rush. "Evidence on the Acquisition Related Performance of Conglomerate Firms." *Journal of Finance* 29 (March 1974), pp. 141–49.

Merjos, Anna. "Costly Propositions—Some Big Mergers Have Lately Fallen Through." *Barron's,* May 14, 1979, pp. 9–13.

Modigliani, Franco, and Richard A. Cohn. "Inflation, Rational Valuation, and the Market." *Financial Analysts Journal* 35 (March–April 1979), pp. 24–44.

Oppenheimer, Henry, and Stanley Block. "An Examination of the Characteristics Associated with Merger Activity during the 1975–78 Period," Financial Management Association Meetings, 1980.

Reilly, Frank K. "What Determines the Ratio of Exchange in Corporate Mergers?" *Financial Analysts Journal* 18 (November–December 1962), pp. 47–50.

Scott, James H., Jr. "On the Theory of Conglomerate Mergers." *Journal of Finance* 32 (September 1977), pp. 1235–49.

Shrieves, Ronald E., and Mary M. Pashley. "Evidence of the Association between Mergers and Capital Structure." *Financial Management* 13 (Autumn, 1984), pp. 39–48.

Stevens, Donald L. "Financial Characteristics of Merged Firms: A Multivariate Analysis." *Journal of Financial and Quantitative Analysis* 8 (March, 1973), pp. 149–58.

# 21 International Financial Management

## Introduction

During the post–World War II era, advances in communications and transportation systems brought people everywhere closer together. In this shrinking world, it became easier to interact with others through trade, regardless of geographic origin, location, or nationality. The political systems that emerged from World War II also contributed to the establishment of trade relations between nations. Under the Marshall Plan, the United States helped the war-torn nations of Western Europe rebuild their economies. Western Europe, Canada, and Japan experienced sustainable growth under the economic leadership of the United States. As the economies of western nations grew in this manner, their trade relations were also strengthened. Concurrently, European nations formed the European Common Market in an effort to promote better trade relations among themselves. Technology and cap-

---

Material for this chapter was developed by Professor G. N. Naidu in conjunction with the authors.

ital also started to flow from the United States to the allied countries. Thus the United States became the dominant partner in the world economy. The U.S. dollar received worldwide acceptance, and the members of the international trading community started using it as reserve currency.

Today, the world economy is more integrated than ever, and nations are dependent on one another for many valuable and scarce resources. Just as the United States is dependent on Saudi Arabia for part of its oil, the Saudis are dependent on the United States for computers, aircraft, and military hardware. Even an arch rival of the United States like the USSR has been dependent on the United States and Canada for agricultural commodities and high technology goods for many years. This growing interdependence necessitates the development of sound international business relations, which, in turn, will enhance the prospects for future international cooperation and understanding. It is virtually impossible for any country to isolate itself from the impact of international developments in an integrated world economy.

The significance of international business operations becomes more apparent if we look at the size of foreign sales relative to the domestic sales for major American corporations. Table 21–1 shows that in such companies as Colgate-Palmolive, Exxon, Gillette, and Mobil, foreign sales account for over 50 percent of total sales. Some of the nation's giant banks such as Citicorp and J. P. Morgan also derive more than 50 percent of their earnings from foreign sources.

Just as foreign operations affect the performance of American business firms, developments in international financial markets also affect our lifestyles. If you have been vacationing in Acapulco every winter, you might have been pleasantly surprised in 1985 that it didn't cost you as much as it had in 1984. The primary reason was the precipitous drop in the value of the Mexican peso against the U.S. dollar. For a similar reason, Disney World didn't attract as many British tourists in 1985 as it had in 1982. The situation, however, was reversed in 1986, when the dollar dropped sharply against many currencies. Thus the fluctuations in currency values affect many of us in one way or another.

This chapter deals with the international dimensions of corporate finance. We believe that this chapter provides a basis for understanding the complexities of international financial decisions. Such an understanding is important whether you work for a multinational manufac-

**Table 21–1**
**Selected U.S. multinational firms and their foreign operations**

| | Foreign Sales (percent of total sales) | Foreign Operating Profit (percent of total operating profit) | Foreign Assets (percent of total assets) |
|---|---|---|---|
| Avon Products | 37.4% | 53.2% | 27.1% |
| BankAmerica | 41.3 | 42.8 | 36.6 |
| Bankers Trust of New York | 55.4 | 58.3 | 54.8 |
| Burroughs | 40.4 | 72.2 | 34.1 |
| Chase Manhattan | 55.4 | 26.4 | 49.2 |
| Citicorp | 50.1 | 51.2 | 53.7 |
| Coca-Cola | 38.0 | 55.6 | 55.3 |
| Colgate-Palmolive | 52.3 | 48.1 | 38.4 |
| Dow Chemical | 53.6 | 55.3 | 45.9 |
| Exxon | 69.4 | 55.4 | 43.0 |
| Gillette | 51.8 | 54.0 | 45.5 |
| Goodyear | 30.7 | 26.9 | 34.6 |
| IBM | 40.4 | 39.4 | 36.1 |
| ITT | 37.4 | 76.9 | 28.8 |
| J. P. Morgan | 58.0 | 53.7 | 49.4 |
| Mobil | 55.9 | 78.1 | 41.2 |
| Pfizer | 44.2 | 36.1 | 36.9 |
| Texaco | 50.1 | 46.1 | 30.1 |
| Warner-Lambert | 39.7 | 58.3 | 28.2 |

Source: "The 100 Largest U.S. Multinationals," *Forbes*, July 29, 1985, pp. 186–88.

turing firm, a large commercial bank, a major brokerage firm, or any firm involved in international transactions.

International business operations, by their very nature, are complex, risky, and require special understanding. Many major U.S. banks have had to learn the lessons of international finance through painful experience. In the worldwide recession of 1981–83, many less developed, third world countries found difficulty in repaying their debt obligations as their exports dropped. The ingenuity of world financial institutions was challenged (and continue to be challenged) to avoid disaster.

In the following section of this chapter a description of the international business firm and its environment is presented. Then foreign exchange rates and the variables influencing foreign currency values are explained, and strategies dealing with foreign exchange risk are examined. The foreign investment decision is then illustrated through an example, and finally, international financing sources, including the Eurodollar market, the Eurobond market, and foreign equity markets, are discussed.

## The Multinational Corporation: Nature and Environment

The focus of international financial management has been the multinational corporation (MNC). One might ask, just what is a multinational corporation? Some definitions of a multinational corporation require that a minimum percentage (often 30 percent or more) of a firm's business activities be carried on outside its national borders. For our understanding, however, a firm doing business across its national borders is considered a multinational enterprise. There are several forms that multinational corporations can take. Four are briefly examined.

**Exporter** An MNC could produce a product domestically and export some of that production to one or more foreign markets. This is, perhaps, the least risky method—reaping the benefits of foreign demand without committing any long-term investment to that foreign country.

**Licensing agreement** A firm with exporting operations may get into trouble when a foreign government imposes or substantially raises an import tariff to a level at which the exporter cannot compete effectively with the local domestic manufacturers. The foreign government may even ban all imports into the country at times. When this happens, the exporting firm may grant a license to an independent local producer to use the firm's technology in return for a license fee or a royalty. In essence, then, the MNC will be exporting technology rather than the product to that foreign country.

**Joint venture** As an alternative to licensing, the MNC may establish a joint venture with a local foreign manufacturer. The legal, political, and economic environments around the globe are more conducive to the joint venture arrangement than any of the other modes of operations. Historical evidence also suggests that a joint venture with a local entrepreneur exposes the firm to the least amount of political risk. Consequently this position is preferred by most business firms and by foreign governments as well.

**Fully owned foreign subsidiary** Although the joint venture form is desirable for many reasons, it may be hard to find a willing and cooperative local entrepreneur with sufficient capital to participate. Under these conditions, the MNC may have to go it alone. For political reasons, however, a wholly owned foreign subsidiary is becoming more of a rarity in the mid-80s. The reader must keep in mind that whenever we mention a *foreign affiliate* in the ensuing discussion, it could be a joint venture or a fully owned subsidiary.

As the firm crosses its national borders, it faces an environment that is riskier and more complex than its domestic surroundings. Sometimes the social and political environment can be hostile. In spite of these difficult challenges, foreign affiliates often are more profitable than domestic businesses. A purely domestic firm faces several basic risks, such as the risk related to maintaining sales and market share, the financial risk of too much leverage, the risk of a poor equity market, and so on. In addition to these types of risks, the foreign affiliate is exposed to foreign-exchange risk and political risk. While the foreign affiliate experiences a larger amount of risk than a domestic firm, it actually lowers the portfolio risk of its parent corporation by stabilizing the combined operating cash flows for the MNC. This risk reduction occurs because foreign and domestic economies are less than perfectly correlated.

Foreign business operations are more complex because the host country's economy may be different from the domestic economy. The rate of inflation in many foreign countries is likely to be higher than in the United States. The rules of taxation are usually different. The structure and operation of financial markets and institutions also vary from country to country, as do financial policies and practices. The presence of a foreign affiliate benefits the host country's economy. Foreign affiliates have been a decisive factor in shaping the pattern of trade, investment, and the flow of technology between nations. They can have a significant positive impact on a host country's economic growth, employment, trade, and balance of payments. This positive contribution, however, is occasionally overshadowed by allegations of wrongdoing. For example, some host countries have charged that foreign affiliates subverted their governments and caused instability of their currencies in international money and foreign exchange markets. The less developed countries (LDCs) have, at times, alleged that foreign businesses exploit their labor with low wages. The multinational companies are also under constant criticism in their home countries where labor unions charge the MNCs with exporting jobs, capital, and technology to foreign nations while avoiding their fair share of taxes. In spite of all these criticisms, the multinational companies have managed to survive and prosper. The MNC is well positioned to take advantage of imperfections in the global markets. Furthermore, since current global resource distribution favors the MNC's survival and growth, it may be concluded that the multinational corporation is here to stay.

## Foreign Exchange Rates

Suppose you are planning to spend a semester in Paris studying the French culture. To put your plan into operation you will need French currency, that is, French francs (FF), so that you can pay for your expenses during your stay in France. How many French francs you can obtain for $1,000 will depend on the exchange rate at that time. The relationship between the values of two currencies is known as the exchange rate. The exchange rate between U.S. dollars and French francs is stated as dollars per francs or francs per dollar. For example, the quotation of $0.12 per franc is the same as FF8.33 per dollar. At this exchange rate you can purchase 8,330 French francs with $1,000. *The Wall Street Journal* publishes exchange rates of major foreign currencies each day. The names of some countries' currencies and their exchange rates relative to the U.S. dollar are shown in Table 21–2. This table shows dollars (fractions of dollars) that one can exchange for each unit of foreign currency ($/currency). As you may notice from this table, the exchange rates change over time. By comparing exchange rates in January 1982 with those of August 1985, you will observe that most currencies decreased in value relative to the dollar during that time. That is, the foreign currency would buy fewer dollars (fractions of dollars) in 1985 than in 1982. For example, the deutsche mark was the equivalent of .4462 dollars in January of 1982, but only .3506 dollars in August of 1985. By taking the reciprocal of these two values,

**Table 21–2**
**Selected currencies and exchange rates. Dollar (fractions of dollar) that one can exchange for each unit of foreign currency: $/currency**

| Country | Currency | Exchange Rate (U.S. dollars) January 4, 1982 | August 6, 1985 |
|---|---|---|---|
| Austria | Schilling | $0.0640 | $0.0497 |
| Belgium | Franc | 0.0262 | 0.0175 |
| Denmark | Krone | 0.1366 | 0.0945 |
| France | Franc | 0.1759 | 0.1151 |
| Germany | Deutsche mark | 0.4462 | 0.3506 |
| India | Rupee | 0.1102 | 0.0850 |
| Italy | Lira | 0.0008 | 0.0005 |
| Japan | Yen | 0.0046 | 0.0042 |
| Mexico | Peso | 0.0380 | 0.0029 |
| Netherlands | Guilder | 0.4067 | 0.3122 |
| Portugal | Escudo | 0.0154 | 0.0060 |
| South Africa | Rand | 1.0508 | 0.4500 |
| Spain | Peseta | 0.0104 | 0.0061 |
| Sweden | Krona | 0.1813 | 0.1188 |
| Switzerland | Franc | 0.5572 | 0.4235 |
| United Kingdom | Pound | 1.9260 | 1.3465 |

we could also say the dollar was worth 2.24 (1 ÷ 0.4462) deutsche marks in January of 1982 and 2.85 (1 ÷ 0.3506) deutsche marks in August of 1985. The U.S. dollar was weak against many foreign currencies during most of the 1970s and early 1980s, but in the mid-1980s, the U.S. dollar improved substantially against major currencies, as indicated in this example. Then in 1986, the dollar fell once again. No doubt the relationship will change many times during the 1980s.

## Factors Influencing Exchange Rates

The present international monetary system consists of a mixture of "freely" floating exchange rates and fixed rates. The currencies of the major trading partners of the United States are traded in free markets. In such a market the exchange rate between two currencies is determined by the supply of, and the demand for, those currencies. This activity, however, is subject to intervention by many countries' central banks. Factors that tend to increase the supply or decrease the demand schedule for a given currency will bring down the value of that currency in foreign exchange markets. Similarly, the factors that tend to decrease the supply or increase the demand for a currency will raise the value of that currency. Since fluctuations in currency values result in foreign exchange risk, the financial executive must understand the factors causing these changes in currency values. Although the value of a currency is determined by the aggregate supply and demand for that currency, this alone does not help our financial manager understand or predict the changes in exchange rates. Fundamental factors such as inflation, interest rates, balance of payments, and government policies are quite important in explaining both the short-term and long-term fluctuations of a currency value.

**Inflation** A parity between the purchasing powers of two currencies establishes the rate of exchange between the two currencies. Suppose it takes $1.00 to buy one dozen apples in New York and 2.50 deutsche marks to buy the same apples in Frankfurt, Germany. Then the rate of exchange between the U.S. dollar and deutsche mark is DM2.50/$1.00 or $0.40/DM. If prices of apples double in New York while the prices in Frankfurt remain the same, you know that the purchasing power of a dollar in New York will drop 50 percent. Consequently, you will be able to exchange $1.00 for only DM1.25 in foreign currency markets (or receive $.80 per DM). Currency exchange rates, therefore, tend to vary inversely with their respective purchasing powers in order to provide the same or similar purchasing power in each country. This is called the *purchasing power parity theory.* When the inflation rate differential between two countries changes, the exchange rate also adjusts to correspond to the relative purchasing powers of the countries.

**Interest rates** Another economic variable that has a significant influence on exchange rates is interest rates. As a student of finance, you should know that investment capital flows in the direction of higher yield for a given level of risk. This flow of short-term capital between money markets occurs because investors seek equilibrium through arbitrage buying and selling. If investors can earn 10 percent interest per year in the United States and 16 percent per year in Britain, they will prefer to invest in Britain, provided that the inflation rate and risk are the same in both countries. As investors buy British pounds with U.S. dollars, the value of the pound will appreciate relative to the dollar. At the same time, the increased demand for British securities also tends to reduce the interest rate differential between the United

Kingdom and the United States. Thus interest rates and exchange rates adjust until the foreign exchange market and the money market reach equilibrium. This interplay between interest rate differentials and exchange rates is called the *interest rate parity theory.*

**Balance of payments** The term *balance of payments* refers to a system of government accounts that catalogs the flow of economic transactions between the residents of one country and the residents of other countries. (The balance of payments statement for the United States is prepared by the U.S. Department of Commerce quarterly and annually.) It resembles the Funds Statement presented in Chapter 2, and keeps track of the country's exports and imports as well as the flow of capital and gifts. When a country sells (exports) more goods and services to foreign countries than it purchases (imports) from abroad, it will have a surplus in its balance of trade. Japan, for example, through its aggressive competition in world markets, exports more goods than it imports and has been enjoying a trade surplus for quite some time. Since the foreigners who buy Japanese goods are expected to pay their bills in yen, the demand for yen and, consequently, its value increase in foreign currency markets. On the other hand, continuous deficits in the balance of payments is expected to depress the value of a currency because such deficits would increase the supply of that currency relative to the demand.

**Government policies** A national government may, through its central bank, intervene in the foreign exchange market, buying and selling currencies as it sees fit to support the value of its currency relative to others. Sometimes a given country may deliberately pursue a policy of maintaining an undervalued currency in order to promote cheap exports. In communist countries the currency values are set by government decree. Even in some free market countries, the central banks fix the exchange rates, subject to periodic review and adjustment. At times, some nations affect the foreign exchange rate indirectly by restricting the flow of funds into and out of the country. Monetary and fiscal policies also affect the currency value in foreign exchange markets. For example, expansionary monetary policy and excessive government spending are primary causes of inflation, and continual use of such policies eventually reduces the value of the country's currency.

**Other factors** A pronounced and extended stock market rally in a country attracts investment capital from other countries, thus creating a huge demand by foreigners for that country's currency. This increased demand is expected to increase the value of that currency. Similarly, a significant drop in demand for a country's principal exports worldwide is expected to result in a corresponding decline in the value of its currency. The South African rand and British pound are two examples from recent history. A precipitous drop in gold prices and an apparent oil glut are cited as the reasons for the depreciation of these two currencies during the 1980–85 period. Political turmoil in a country often drives capital out of the country into stable countries. A mass exodus of capital, due to the fear of political risk, undermines the value of a country's currency in the foreign exchange market. Also, widespread labor strikes which may appear to weaken the nation's economy will have a depressing influence on its currency value.

Although a wide variety of factors that can influence exchange rates have been discussed, a few words of caution are in order. All of these variables will not necessarily influence all currencies to the same degree. Some factors may have an overriding influence on one currency's value, while their influence on another currency may be negligible at that point in time.

## Spot Rates and Forward Rates

When you look into a major financial newspaper (e.g., *The Wall Street Journal*), you will discover that two exchange rates exist simultaneously for most major currencies—the spot rate and the forward rate. The spot rate for a currency is the exchange rate at which the currency is traded for immediate delivery. For example, you walk into a local commercial bank and ask for French francs. The banker will indicate the rate at which the franc is selling, say FF9/$. If you like the rate, you buy 9,000 francs with $1,000 and walk out the door. This is a spot market transaction at the retail level. The trading of currencies for future delivery is called a forward market transaction. To illustrate, suppose IBM Corporation expects to receive FF 60 million from a French customer 30 days from now. It is not certain, however, what these francs will be worth in dollars 30 days from today. In order to eliminate this uncertainty, IBM calls a bank and offers to sell FF 60 million for U.S. dollars 30 days from now. In their negotiation, the two parties may agree on an exchange rate of FF 10/$. Since the exchange rate is established for future delivery, it is a forward rate. After 30 days, IBM delivers FF 60 million to the bank and receives $6 million. The difference between spot and forward exchange rates, expressed in dollars per unit of foreign currency, may be seen in the following values on August 6, 1985.

| *Rates* | *Deutsche Mark (DM)* (*$/DM*) | *British Pound (£)* (*$/£*) |
|---|---|---|
| Spot | $0.3506 | $1.3465 |
| 30-day forward | 0.3517 | 1.3421 |
| 90-day forward | 0.3536 | 1.3357 |
| 180-day forward | 0.3566 | 1.3282 |

The forward exchange rate of a currency is slightly different from the spot rate prevailing at that time. Since the forward rate deals with a future time, the expectations regarding the future value of that currency are reflected in the forward rate. Forward rates may be greater than the current spot rate (premium) or less than the current spot rate (discount). On August 6, 1985, forward rates on the deutsche mark were at a premium in relation to the spot rate, while the forward rates for the British pound were at a discount from the spot rate. This means that on that day, the participants in the foreign exchange market expected the deutsche mark to appreciate relative to the U.S. dollar in the future, and the British pound to depreciate against the dollar. The discount or premium is usually expressed as an annualized percentage deviation from the spot rate. The percentage discount or premium is computed with the following formula:

$$\text{Forward premium (or discount)} = \frac{\text{Forward rate} - \text{Spot rate}}{\text{Spot rate}} \times \frac{12}{\text{Length of forward contract (in months)}} \times 100 \qquad (21\text{–}1)$$

For example, on August 6, 1985, the 90-day forward contract in deutsche marks was selling at a 3.42 percent premium:

$$\left(\frac{0.3536 - 0.3506}{0.3506}\right) \times \frac{12}{3} \times 100 = 3.4227\%$$

while the 90-day forward contract in pounds was trading at 3.21 percent discount:

$$\left(\frac{1.3357 - 1.3465}{1.3465}\right) \times \frac{12}{3} \times 100 = 3.2083\%$$

Normally, the forward premium or discount is between 0.5 percent and 10 percent.

The spot and forward transactions are said to take place in the over-the-counter market. Foreign currency dealers (usually large commercial banks) and their customers (importers, exporters, investors, multinational firms, etc.) negotiate the exchange rate, the length of the forward contract, and the commission in a mutually agreeable fashion. Although the length of a typical forward contract may generally vary between one month and six months, contracts for longer maturities are not uncommon. The dealers, however, may require higher returns for longer contracts.

**Cross rates** Since all currencies are quoted against the U.S. dollar in *The Wall Street Journal*, sometimes it may be necessary to work out the cross rates for currencies other than the dollar. For example, on August 6, 1985, the French franc was selling for $0.1151 and the British pound was selling for $1.3465. The cross rate between the franc and the pound is 11.70 FF/L (pound). In determining this value, we show that one dollar will buy 8.688 francs (1 ÷ 0.1151) and a pound is equal to 1.3465 dollars. Thus 8.688 French francs per *dollar* times 1.3465 *dollars* per pound equals 11.70 French francs per pound.

## Managing Foreign Exchange Risk

When the parties associated with a commercial transaction are located in the same country, the transaction is denominated in a single currency. International transactions inevitably involve more than one currency (because the parties are domiciled residents of different countries). Since most foreign currency values fluctuate from time to time, the monetary value of an international transaction measured in either the seller's currency or the buyer's currency is likely to change when payment is delayed. As a result, the seller may receive less revenue than expected or the buyer may have to pay more than the expected amount for the merchandise. Thus the term *foreign exchange risk* refers to the possibility of a drop in revenue or an increase in cost in an international transaction due to a change in foreign exchange rates. Importers, exporters, investors, and multinational firms are all exposed to this foreign exchange risk.

The international monetary system has undergone a significant change over the last 10 years. The free trading, Western nations basically went from a fixed exchange rate system to a "freely" floating rate system. For the most part, the new system proved its agility and resilience during the most turbulent years of oil price hikes and hyperinflation of the last decade. The free market exchange rates responded and adjusted well to these adverse conditions. Consequently, the exchange rates fluctuated over a much wider range than before. The increased volatility of exchange markets forced many multinational firms, importers, and exporters to pay more attention to the function of foreign exchange risk management.

The foreign exchange risk of a multinational company is divided into three types of exposure. They are: accounting, or translation, exposure; transaction exposure; and economic exposure. An MNC's foreign assets and liabilities, which are denominated in foreign currency units, are exposed to losses and gains due to changing exchange rates. This is called accounting, or translation, exposure. The amount of loss or gain resulting from this form of exposure and the treatment of it in the parent company's books, depends on the accounting rules established by the parent company's government. In the United States, the rules are spelled out in Financial Accounting Standards Board *Statement No. 52* (FASB #52). Under FASB #52, all foreign currency denominated assets and liabilities are converted at the rate of exchange in effect on the date of balance sheet preparation. An unrealized translation gain or loss is held in an equity reserve account while the realized gain or loss is incorporated in the parent's consolidated income statement for that period. Thus FASB #52 reduces the impact of accounting exposure resulting from the translation of a foreign subsidiary's balance sheet on reported earnings of multinational firms.

However, foreign exchange gains and losses resulting from international transactions, which are known as transaction gains and losses, are reflected in the income statement for the current period. As a consequence of these transactional gains and losses, the volatility of reported earnings per share increases. Three different strategies can be used to minimize this transaction exposure.

1. Hedging in the forward exchange market.
2. Hedging in the money market.
3. Hedging in the currency futures market.

**Forward exchange market hedge** To see how the transaction exposure can be covered in forward markets, suppose Electricitie de France, an electric company in France, purchased a large generator from General Electric of the United States for FF 7.267 million on October 26, 1985, and GE was promised the payment in French francs in 90 days. Since GE is now exposed to exchange risk by agreeing to receive the payment in French francs in the future, it is up to GE to find a way to reduce this exposure. One simple method is to hedge the exposure in the forward exchange market. On October 26, 1985, to establish the forward cover, GE sells a forward contract to deliver the FF 7.267 million, 90 days from now in exchange for $1.376 million. On January 25, 1986, GE receives payment from Electricitie de France and delivers the FF 7.267 million to the bank that signed the contract. In return, the bank delivers $1.376 million to GE. Thus, through this international transaction, GE receives the same dollar amount it expected three months ago regardless of what happened to the value of French francs in the interim. In contrast, if the sale had been invoiced in U.S. dollars, Electricitie de France, not GE, would have been exposed to the exchange risk.

**Money market hedge** A second way to have eliminated transaction exposure in the previous example would have been to borrow money in French francs and then convert it to U.S. dollars immediately. When the accounts receivable from the sale is collected three months later, the loan is cleared with the proceeds. In this case, GE's strategy consists of the following steps. On October 26, 1985,

1. Borrow FF 7,055,000 (FF 7,267,000 / 1.03 = FF 7,055,000) at the rate of 12 percent per year for three months. You borrow less than the full amount of FF 7,267,000 in recognition of the fact that interest must be paid on the loan. Twelve percent interest for 90 days translates into 3 percent. Thus FF 7,267,000 is divided by 1.03 to arrive at the size of the loan prior to the interest payment.
2. Convert the French francs into the U.S. dollars in the spot market.

Then on January 25, 1986 (90 days later)

3. Receive the payment FF 7,267,000 from Electricitie de France.
4. Clear the loan with the proceeds received from Electricitie de France.

The money market hedge basically calls for matching the exposed asset (accounts receivable) with a liability (loan payable) in the same currency. Some firms prefer this money market hedge because of the early availability of funds possible with this method.

**Currency futures market hedge** Transaction exposure associated with a foreign currency can also be covered in the currency futures market. The International Monetary Market (IMM) of the Chicago Mercantile Exchange began trading in futures contracts in foreign currencies on May 16, 1972. Trading in currency futures contracts also made a debut on the London International Financial Futures Exchange (LIFFE) in September 1982. Other markets have also developed around the world. Just as futures contracts are traded in corn, wheat, hogs, and beans, foreign currency futures contracts are traded in these markets. Although the futures market and forward market are similar in concept, they differ in their operations. To illustrate the hedging process in the currency futures market, suppose that in June, the Chicago-based Continental Illinois National Bank considers lending 500,000 deutsche marks to a German subsidiary of a U.S. parent company for six months. It purchases the deutsche marks in the spot market, delivers them to the borrower, and simultaneously hedges its transaction exposure by selling December contracts in deutsche marks for the same amount. In December when the loan is cleared, the bank sells the deutsche marks in the spot market and buys back the December deutsche mark contracts. The transactions are illustrated as follows for the spot and futures market:

| *Date* | *Spot Market* | *Futures Market* |
|---|---|---|
| June 1 | Buys 500,000 deutsche marks (DM) at $0.3460/DM = $173,000 | Sells DM 500,000 for December delivery at $0.3450/DM = $172,500 |
| December 1 | Sells DM 500,000 at $0.3430/DM = $171,500<br>Loss = $1,500 | Buys DM 500,000 at $0.3430/DM = $171,500<br>Gain = $1,000 |

While the loan was outstanding, the deutsche mark dropped its value in relation to the U.S. dollar. Had the bank remained unhedged, it would have lost $1,500. By hedging in the futures market, the bank reduced the loss to only $500. A $1,000 gain in the futures market was used to cancel out all but $500 of the $1,500 loss in the spot market.

Hedging is not the only means companies have for protecting themselves against foreign exchange risk. Over the years, multinational companies have developed, for this purpose, elaborate foreign asset management programs which involve such strategies as switching cash and other current assets into strong currencies, while piling up debt and other liabilities in depreciating currencies. Companies also encourage the quick collection of bills in weak currencies by offering sizable discounts, while extending liberal credit in strong currencies.

## Foreign Investment Decisions

It is estimated from the *Directory of American Firms Operating in Foreign Countries* that there are more then 4,000 U.S. firms with one or more foreign affiliates. Direct investment abroad by U.S. firms is in excess of $200 billion. One might ask, what motivated the American firms to move their operations overseas? Several explanations are offered for the move to foreign soil. First, with the emergence of trading blocks like the common market in Europe, American firms feared that their goods might face import tariffs in those countries. To avoid such trade barriers, U.S. firms started manufacturing in foreign countries.

The second factor was the lower production costs overseas. Firms were motivated by the significantly lower wage costs prevailing in foreign countries. Consequently, firms in labor-intensive industries, such as textiles and electronics, moved some of their operations to countries where labor was cheap. Third, superior American technology gave U.S. firms an easy access to oil exploration, mining, and manufacturing in many developing nations. A fourth advantage relates to taxes. The U.S.-based multinational firms are able to postpone payment of U.S. taxes on income earned abroad until such income is actually repatriated (forwarded) to the parent company. This tax deferral provision can be used by an MNC to minimize its tax liability. Also, the corporate income tax rates elsewhere are often lower than in the United States. Some countries like Israel, Ireland, and South Africa offer special tax incentives for foreign firms that establish operations there. Although the benefits of lower taxes and lower wage costs, and the technological gap have gradually diminished in recent years, the average rate of return on U.S. investment abroad continues to be higher than the rate of return on U.S. domestic investments.

The decision to invest in a foreign country by a firm operating in an oligopolistic industry is also motivated by strategic considerations. When a competitor undertakes a direct foreign investment, other companies quickly follow with defensive investments in the same foreign country. Foreign investments undertaken by U.S. tire and rubber companies are classic examples of this competitive reaction. Wherever you find a Firestone subsidiary in a foreign country, you are likely to see a Goodyear affiliate also operating in that country.

Many academicians believe that international diversification of risks is also an important motivation for direct foreign investment. The basic premise of portfolio theory in finance is that an investor can reduce the risk level of a portfolio by combining those investments whose returns are less than perfectly positively correlated. In addition to domestic diversification, it is shown in Figure 21–1 that further reduction in investment risk can be achieved by diversifying across national boundaries. International stocks, in Figure 21–1, show a consistently lower percentage of risk compared to any given number of U.S. stocks in a portfolio. It is argued, however, that institutional and political constraints, language barriers, and lack of adequate information on foreign investments prevent investors from diversifying across

Figure 21–1
Risk reduction from international diversification

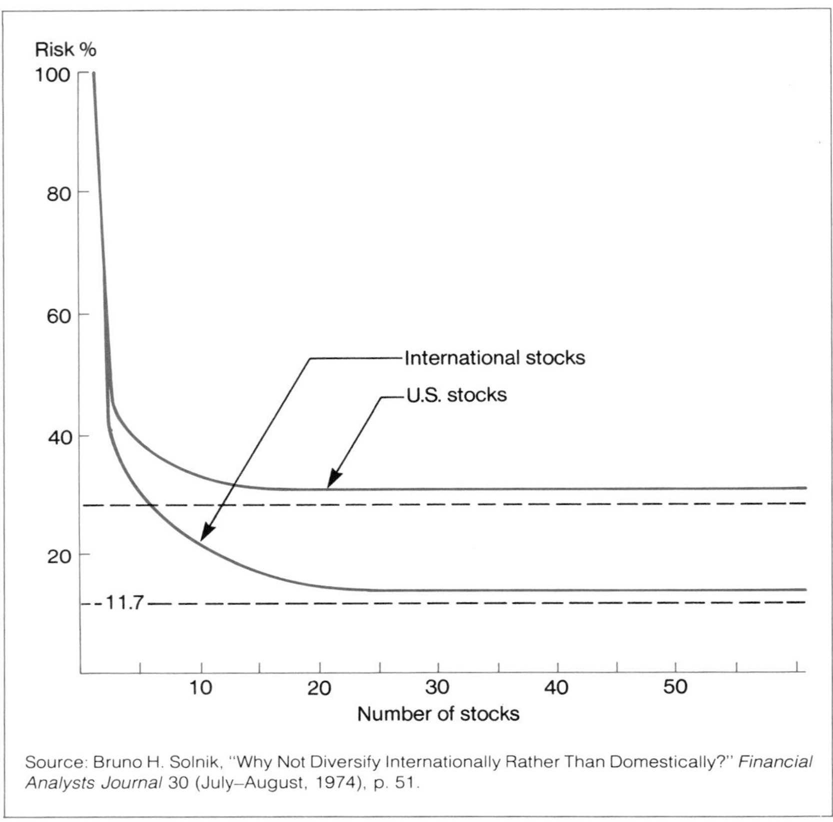


Source: Bruno H. Solnik, "Why Not Diversify Internationally Rather Than Domestically?" *Financial Analysts Journal* 30 (July–August, 1974), p. 51.

nations. Multinational firms, on the other hand, through their unique position around the world, derive the benefits of international diversification.[1]

While the U.S.-based firms took the lead in establishing overseas subsidiaries during the 1950s and 1960s, the European and Japanese firms have started this activity in the 1970s. The flow of foreign direct investment into the United States has proceeded at a rapid rate, par-

[1]This point is sometimes debated by those who suggest that multinationals are subject to the financial market conditions existing in their own country.

**Figure 21–2**
**Number of investments in the United States, by nationality of investors**

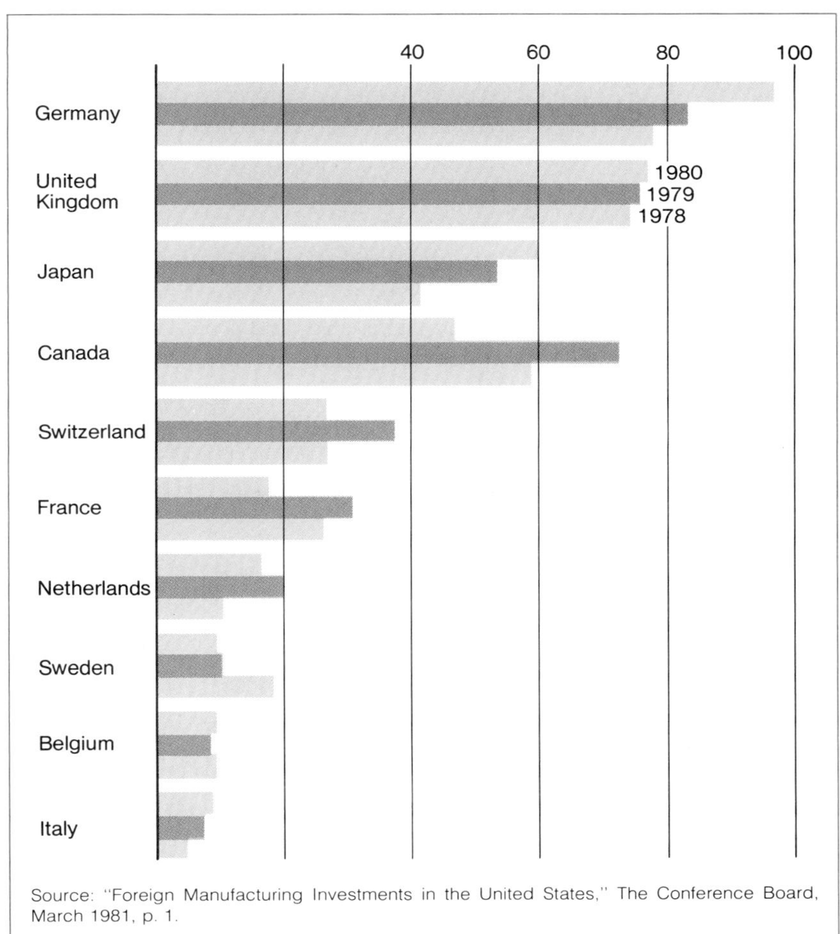


Source: "Foreign Manufacturing Investments in the United States," The Conference Board, March 1981, p. 1.

ticularly since 1975. Foreign investments in the United States are now well in excess of $50 billion. These investments employ over one million people. It is quite evident from these figures that the United States is becoming an attractive site for foreign investment. As shown in Figure 21–2, the graph showing investors by nationality, West Germany, the United Kingdom, Japan, and Canada are the major investors in the United States. In addition to the international diversification and strategic considerations, many other factors are responsible for this rapid inflow of foreign capital into the United States. Increased foreign labor costs in some countries and saturated overseas markets in others are partly responsible. In Japan, an acute shortage of land suitable for industrial development and a near total dependence on imported oil prompted some of their firms to locate in the United States. In Germany, a large number of paid holidays, restrictions limiting labor layoffs, and worker participation in management decision making caused many firms to look favorably at the United States. Political stability, large market size, and access to advanced technology are other primary motivating factors for firms to establish their operations in the United States.

## Analysis of Political Risk

Business firms tend to make direct investments in foreign countries for a relatively long period of time. Because of the time necessary to recover the initial investment, they do not intend to liquidate their investments quickly. The government may change hands several times during the foreign firm's tenure in that country, and when a new government takes over, it may not be as friendly or as cooperative as the previous administration. An unfriendly government can interfere with the foreign affiliates in many ways. It may impose foreign exchange restrictions, or the foreign ownership share may be limited to a set percentage of the total. Repatriation (transfer) of a subsidiary's profit to the parent company may be blocked, at least temporarily, and in the extreme case, the government may even expropriate (take over) the foreign subsidiary's assets. The multinational company may experience a sizable loss of income and/or property as a result of this political interference. Many well-known U.S. firms like Anaconda, ITT, and Occidental Petroleum have lost hundreds of millions of dollars in politically unstable countries. In the late 1970s and early 1980s, more than 60 percent of U.S. companies doing business abroad suffered some form of politically inflicted damage.[2] Therefore, anal-

[2]Ronald Alsop, "Foreign Ventures," *The Wall Street Journal*, March 30, 1981, p. 1.

ysis of foreign political risk is gaining more attention in multinational firms.

The best approach to protection against political risk is to conduct a thorough investigation of the country's political stability long before the firm makes any investment in that country. Companies have been using different methods for assessing political risk. Some firms hire consultants to provide them with a report of political risk analysis. Others form their own advisory committees (little state departments) consisting of top level managers from headquarters and foreign subsidiaries. After ascertaining the country's political risk level, the multinational firm can use one of the following strategies to guard against such risk:

1. One strategy is to establish a joint venture with a local entrepreneur. By bringing a local partner into the deal, the MNC not only limits its financial exposure but also minimizes antiforeign feelings.
2. Another risk management tactic is to enter into a joint venture, preferably with firms from other countries. For example, Chevron may pursue its oil production operation in Zaire in association with Royal Dutch Petroleum and Nigerian National Petroleum as partners. The foreign government will be more hesitant to antagonize a number of partner-firms of many nationalities at the same time.
3. When the perceived political risk level is high, insurance against such risks can be obtained in advance. Overseas Private Investment Corporation (OPIC), a federal government agency, sells insurance policies to qualified firms. This agency insures against losses due to inconvertibility into dollars of amounts invested in a foreign country. Policies are also available from OPIC to insure against expropriation, and against losses due to war or revolution. Many firms have made use of this service over the years. For example, Greenlaw, Inc., a Florida-based firm, insured its fruit-processing plant in the Dominican Republic through OPIC. Private insurance companies such as Lloyds of London, American International Group Inc., CIGNA, and others issue similar policies to cover political risk. Political-risk umbrella policies do not come cheaply. Coverage for projects in "fairly safe" countries can cost anywhere from 0.3 percent to 12 percent of the insured values per year. Needless to say, they are more expensive or unavailable in troubled countries.

OPIC's rates are lower than those of private insurers, and its policies extend for 20 years, compared to three years or less for private insurance policies.

## Cash Flow Analysis and the Foreign Investment Decision

Direct foreign investments are often relatively large in size. As we mentioned previously, these investments are exposed to some extraordinary risks such as foreign exchange fluctuations and political interference, which are nonexistent for domestic investments. Therefore, the final decision is often made at the board of directors level after considering the financial feasibility and the strategic importance of the proposed investment. Financial feasibility analysis for foreign investments is basically conducted in the same manner as it is for domestic capital budgets. Certain important differences exist, however, in the treatment of foreign tax credits, foreign exchange risk, and remittance of cash flows. To see how these are handled in foreign investment analysis, let us consider a hypothetical illustration.

Tex Systems Inc., a Texas-based manufacturer of word processing equipment, is considering the establishment of a manufacturing plant in Salaysia, a country in Southeast Asia. The Salaysian plant will be a wholly owned subsidiary of Tex Systems, and its estimated cost is 90 million ringgits (2 ringgits = $1). Based on the exchange rate between ringgits and dollars, the cost in dollars is $45 million. In addition to selling in the local Salaysian market, the proposed subsidiary is expected to export its word processors to the neighboring markets in Singapore, Hong Kong, and Thailand. Expected revenues and operating costs are as shown in Table 21–3. The country's investment climate, which reflects the foreign exchange and political risks, is rated BBB (considered fairly safe) by a leading Asian business journal. After considering the investment climate and the nature of the industry, Tex Systems has set a target rate of return of 20 percent for this foreign investment. Salaysia has a 25 percent corporate income tax rate, and has waived the withholding tax on dividends repatriated (forwarded) to the parent company. A dividend payment ratio of 100 percent is assumed for the foreign subsidiary. Tex Systems' marginal tax rate is

**Table 21–3**
**Cash flow analysis of a foreign investment**

| | Projected Cash Flows (million ringgits unless otherwise stated) | | | | | | |
|---|---|---|---|---|---|---|---|
| | Year 1 | Year 2 | Year 3 | Year 4 | Year 5 | Year 6 | |
| Revenues | 45.00 | 50.00 | 55.00 | 60.00 | 65.00 | 70.00 | |
| − Operating expenses | 28.00 | 30.00 | 30.00 | 32.00 | 35.00 | 35.00 | |
| − Depreciation | 10.00 | 10.00 | 10.00 | 10.00 | 10.00 | 10.00 | |
| Earnings before Salaysian taxes | 7.00 | 10.00 | 15.00 | 18.00 | 20.00 | 25.00 | |
| − Salaysian income tax (25%) | 1.75 | 2.50 | 3.75 | 4.50 | 5.00 | 6.25 | |
| Earnings after foreign income taxes | 5.25 | 7.50 | 11.25 | 13.50 | 15.00 | 18.75 | |
| = Dividends repatriated | 5.25 | 7.50 | 11.25 | 13.50 | 15.00 | 18.75 | |
| Gross U.S. Taxes (30% of foreign earnings before taxes) | 2.10 | 3.00 | 4.50 | 5.40 | 6.00 | 7.50 | |
| − Foreign tax credit | 1.75 | 2.50 | 3.75 | 4.50 | 5.00 | 6.25 | |
| Net U.S. taxes payable | 0.35 | 0.50 | 0.75 | 0.90 | 1.00 | 1.25 | |
| Aftertax dividend received by Tex Systems | 4.90 | 7.00 | 10.50 | 12.60 | 14.00 | 17.50 | |
| Exchange rate (ringgits/$) | 2.00 | 2.04 | 2.08 | 2.12 | 2.16 | 2.21 | |
| Aftertax dividend (U.S. $) | 2.45 | 3.43 | 5.05 | 5.94 | 6.48 | 7.92 | |
| $IF_{pv}$ (at 20%) | 0.833 | 0.694 | 0.579 | 0.482 | 0.402 | 0.335 | |
| PV of dividends ($) | 2.04 + | 2.38 + | 2.92 + | 2.86 + | 2.60 + | 2.65 = | $15.45 |

30 percent. It was agreed by Tex Systems and the Salaysian government that the subsidiary will be sold to a Salaysian entrepreneur after six years for an estimated 30 million ringgits. The plant will be depreciated over a period of six years using the staight-line method. The cash flows generated through depreciation cannot be remitted to the parent company until the subsidiary is sold to the local private entrepreneur six years from now. The Salaysian government requires the subsidiary to invest the depreciation-generated cash flows in local government bonds yielding an aftertax rate of 15 percent. The depreciation cash flows thus compounded and accumulated can be returned to Tex Systems when the project is terminated. Although the value of ringgits in the foreign exchange market has remained fairly stable for the past three years, the projected budget deficits and trade deficits of Salaysia may result in a gradual devaluation of ringgits against the U.S. dollar at the rate of 2 percent per year for the next six years.

Note the analysis in Table 21–3 is primarily done in terms of ringgits. Expenses (operating, depreciation, and Salaysian income taxes) are subtracted from revenues to arrive at earnings after foreign income taxes. These earnings are then repatriated (forwarded) to Tex Systems in the form of dividends. Dividends repatriated thus begin at 5.25 ringgits (in millions) in year one and increase to 18.75 ringgits in year six. The next item, gross U.S. taxes, refers to the unadjusted U.S. tax obligation. As specified, this is equal to 30 percent of foreign earnings before taxes (earnings before Salaysian taxes).[3] For example, gross U.S. taxes in the first year are equal to:

| | |
|---|---|
| Earnings before Salaysian taxes | $7.00 |
| 30% of foreign earnings before taxes | 30% |
| Gross U.S. taxes | $2.10 |

From gross U.S. taxes, Tex Systems may take a foreign tax credit equal to the amount of Salaysian income tax paid. Gross U.S. taxes minus this foreign tax credit are equal to net U.S. taxes payable. Finally, aftertax dividends received by Tex Systems are equal to dividends repatriated minus U.S. taxes payable. In the first year, the values are:

| | |
|---|---|
| Dividends repatriated | $5.25 |
| Net U.S. taxes payable | −0.35 |
| Aftertax dividends received by Tex Systems | $4.90 |

The figures for aftertax dividends received by Tex Systems are all stated in ringgits (the analysis up to this point has been in ringgits). These ringgits will now be converted into dollars. The initial exchange rate is 2.00 ringgits per dollar, and this will go up by 2 percent per year.[4] For the first year, 4.90 ringgits will be translated into 2.45 dollars. Since values are stated in millions, this will represent $2.45 million.

---

[3]If foreign earnings had not been repatriated, this tax obligation would not be due.

[4]The 2 percent appreciation means the dollar is equal to an increasing amount of ringgits each year. The dollar is appreciating relative to ringgits, and ringgits are depreciating relative to the dollar. Since Tex Systems earnings are in ringgits, they are being converted at a less desirable rate each year. Big Tex may eventually decide to hedge their foreign exchange risk exposure.

Aftertax dividends in U.S. dollars grow from $2.45 million in year one to $7.92 million in year six. The last two rows of Table 21–3 show the present value of these dividends at a 20 percent discount rate. The *total* present value of aftertax dividends received by Tex Systems adds up to $15.45 million. Repatriated dividends will be just one part of the cash flow. The second part consists of depreciation-generated cash flow accumulated and reinvested in Salaysian government bonds at 15 percent per year. The compound value of reinvested depreciation cash flows (10 million ringgits per year) is:

10 million ringgits × 8.754 = 87.54* million ringgits after six years

*Compound sum at 15 percent for six years (Appendix C at end of book).

These 87.54 million ringgits must now be translated into dollars and then discounted back to the present. Since the exchange rate is 2.21 ringgits per dollar in the sixth year (fourth line from the bottom in Table 21–3), the dollar equivalent of 87.54 million ringgits is:

87.54 million ringgits ÷ 2.21 = $39.61 million

The $39.61 million can now be discounted back to the present, by using the present value factor for six years at 20 percent (Appendix B).

$39.61 million
0.335 $IF_{pv}$
$13.27 million

The final benefit to be received is the 30 million ringgits when the plant is sold six years from now.[5] We first convert this to dollars and then take the present value.

30 million ringgits ÷ 2.21 = $13.57 million

The present value of $13.57 million after 6 years at 20 percent is:

$13.57 million
0.335 $IF_{pv}$
$ 4.55 million

The present value of all cash inflows in dollars is equal to:

| | |
|---|---|
| Present value of dividends | $15.45 million |
| Present value of repatriated accumulated depreciation | 13.27 |
| Present value of sales price for plant | 4.55 |
| Total present value of inflows | $33.27 million |

[5]Capital gains taxes are not a necessary consideration in foreign transactions of this nature.

The cost of the project was initially specified as 90 million ringgits, or $45 million. Thus we see the total present value of inflows in dollars is less than the cost, and the project has a negative net present value.

| | |
|---|---|
| Total present value of inflows . . . . . . . . | $ 33.27 million |
| Cost . . . . . . . . . . . . . . . . . . . . | 45.00 |
| Net present value . . . . . . . . . . . . . | $ − 11.73 million |

The project is not acceptable on the basis of net present value criteria. However, before such a recommendation is made to the board of directors, the financial analyst must reconsider the project and assess its strategic importance for the firm. One must debate whether or not the specific foreign project is consistent with the firm's over-all long-term goals. If the firm wants to use this foreign project as a base for its future marketing of small computers in this part of the world, then the negative net present value should not be the decisive factor in making the decision. As a next step, you need to consider any special circumstances of a nonroutine nature which may have led the firm to consider this foreign investment. For example, if Tex Systems' domestic market share is eroding, a new market penetration like the one under consideration may be crucial for the firm's future.[6]

## Financing International Business Operations

When the parties to an international transaction are well known to each other and the countries involved are politically stable, sales are generally made on credit, as is customary in domestic business operations. If the foreign importer is relatively new and/or the political environment is volatile, the possibility of nonpayment by the importer is worrisome for the exporter. In order to reduce the risk of nonpayment, an exporter may request that the importer furnish a letter of credit. The importer's bank normally issues the letter of credit in which

[6]The impact of the 20 percent discount rate should also not be overlooked. At discount rates commonly applied to conventional domestic investments (such as 10 percent), the project would be accepted based on net present value analysis.

the bank promises to subsequently pay out the money for the merchandise. For example, assume that Archer Daniels Midland (ADM) is negotiating with a South Korean trading company to export soybean meal. The two parties reach agreement on price, method of shipment, timing of shipment, destination point, etc. Once the basic terms of sale have been agreed to, the South Korean trading company (importer) applies for a letter of credit from its commercial bank in Seoul. The Korean bank, if it so desires, issues such a letter of credit, which specifies in detail all the steps that must be completed by the American exporter before payment is made. If ADM complies with all specifications in the letter of credit and submits to the Korean bank the proper documentation to prove that it has done so, the Korean bank guarantees the payment on the due date. On that date, the American firm is paid by the Korean bank, not by the buyer of the goods. Therefore, all the credit risk to the exporter is absorbed by the importer's bank, which is in a good position to evaluate the creditworthiness of the importing firm.

The exporter who requires cash payment or a letter of credit from foreign buyers of marginal credit standing is likely to lose orders to competitors. Instead of risking the loss of business, American firms can find an alternative way to reduce the risk of nonpayment by foreign customers. This alternative method consists of obtaining export credit insurance. The insurance policy provides assurance to the exporter that should the foreign customer default on payment, the insurance company will pay for the shipment. The Foreign Credit Insurance Association (FCIA), a private association of 60 U.S insurance firms, provides this kind of insurance to exporting firms.

## Funding of Transactions

Assistance in the funding of foreign transactions may take many forms.

**Export-Import Bank (Eximbank)** This agency of the U.S. government facilitates the financing of U.S. exports through its miscellaneous programs. In its direct loan program, the Eximbank lends money to foreign purchasers of U.S. goods such as aircraft, electrical equipment, heavy machinery, computers, and the like. The Eximbank also purchases eligible medium-term obligations of foreign buyers of U.S. goods at a discount from face value. In this discount program, private banks and other lenders are able to rediscount (sell at a lower price) promissory notes and drafts acquired from foreign customers of U.S. firms.

**Loans from the parent company or a sister affiliate** An apparent source of funds for a foreign affiliate is its parent company or its sister affiliates. In addition to contributing equity capital, the parent company often provides loans of varying maturities to its foreign affiliate. Although the simplest arrangement is a direct loan from the parent to the foreign subsidiary, such a loan is rarely extended because of foreign exchange risk, political risk, and tax treatment. Instead, the loans are often channeled through an intermediary to a foreign affiliate. *Parallel loans* and *fronting loans* are two examples of such indirect loan arrangements between a parent company and its foreign affiliate. A typical parallel loan arrangement is depicted in Figure 21–3.

In this illustration, an American firm wanting to lend funds to its Dutch affiliate locates a Dutch parent firm which wants to transfer funds to its U.S. affiliate. Avoiding the exchange markets entirely, the U.S. parent lends dollars to the Dutch affiliate in the United States, while the Dutch parent lends guilders to the American affiliate in the Netherlands. At maturity, the two loans would each be repaid to the original lender. Notice that neither loan carries any foreign exchange risk in this arrangement. In essence, both parent firms are providing indirect loans to their affiliates.

**Figure 21–3**
**A parallel loan arrangement**

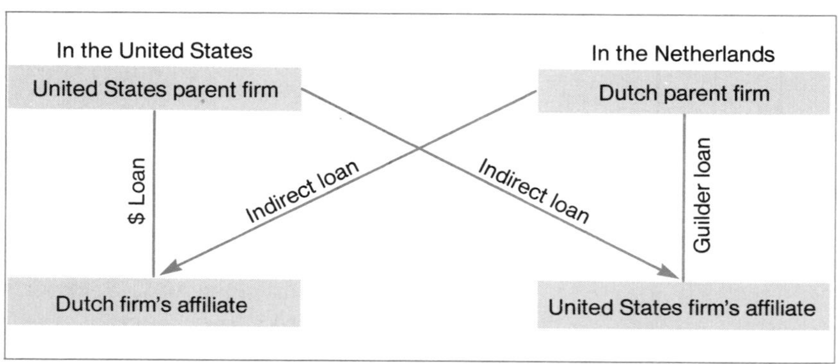

Figure 21–4
A fronting loan arrangement

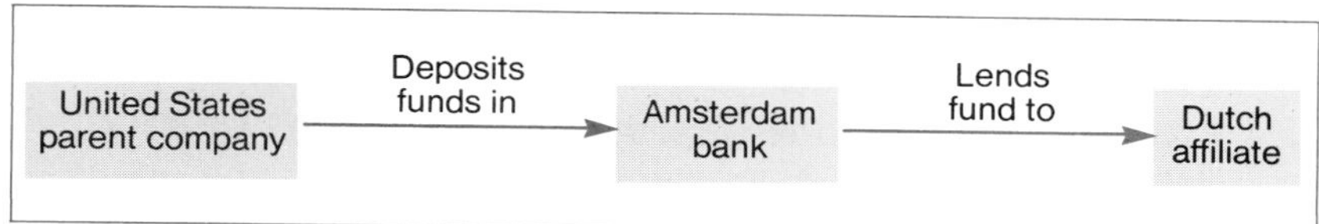


A fronting loan is simply a parent's loan to its foreign subsidiary channeled through a financial intermediary, usually a large international bank. A schematic of a fronting loan is shown in Figure 21–4.

In the example, the U.S. parent company deposits funds in an Amsterdam bank and that bank, in turn, lends the same amount to its affiliate in the Netherlands. In this manner, the bank fronts for the parent by extending a risk-free (fully collateralized) loan to the foreign affiliate. In the event of political turmoil, the foreign government is more likely to allow the American subsidiary to repay the loan to a large international bank than to allow the same affiliate to repay the loan to its parent company. Thus the parent company reduces its political risk substantially by using a fronting loan instead of transferring funds directly to its foreign affiliate.

Even though the parent company would prefer that its foreign subsidiary maintain its own financial arrangements, many banks are apprehensive about lending to a foreign affiliate without a parent guarantee. In fact, a large portion of bank lending to foreign affiliates is based on some sort of a guarantee by the parent firm. Usually because of its multinational reputation, the parent company has a better credit rating than its foreign affiliates. The lender advances funds on the basis of the parent's creditworthiness even though the affiliate is expected to pay back the loan. The terms of a parent guarantee may vary greatly, depending upon the closeness of the parent-affiliate ties, parent-lender relations, and the home country's legal jurisdiction.

**Eurodollar loans** The Eurodollar market is an important source of short-term loans for many multinational firms and their foreign affiliates.

Eurodollars are simply U.S. dollars deposited in European banks. A substantial portion of these deposits is held by European branches of U.S. commercial banks. About 85–90 percent of these deposits are in the form of straight term deposits with the banks for a specific maturity and at a fixed interest rate. The remaining 10–15 percent of these deposits represent negotiable certificates of deposit with maturities varying from one week to five years or longer. However, maturities of three months, six months, and one year are most common in this market.

Since the early 1960s, the Eurodollar market has become nearly a trillion-dollar market and has established itself as a significant part of world credit markets. The participants in these markets are diverse in character and are geographically widespread. Hundreds of corporations and banks, mostly from the United States, Canada, Western Europe, and Japan, are regular borrowers and depositors in this market.

U.S. firms have more than doubled their borrowings in the Eurodollar market during the early 1980s. The lower costs and greater credit availability of the Eurodollar market continue to attract borrowers. The lower borrowing costs in the Eurodollar market are often attributed to the smaller overhead costs for lending banks and the absence of a compensating balance requirement. The lending rate for borrowers in the Eurodollar market is based on the London Interbank Offered Rate (LIBOR), which is the interest rate for large deposits. Interest rates on loans are calculated by adding premiums to this basic rate. The size of this premium varies from 0.25 percent to 0.50 percent, depending on the customer, length of the loan period, size of the loan, etc. For example, Northern Indiana Public Service Company obtained a $75 million, three-year loan from Merrill Lynch International Bank in December 1980. The utility company offered to pay 0.375 points above LIBOR for the first two years and 0.50 points above for the final year of the loan. Over the years, borrowing in the Eurodollar market has been one eighth to seven eighths of a percentage point cheaper than borrowing at the U.S. prime interest rate. During the recent peak interest rate period in the United States, many cost-conscious domestic borrowers fled to the Eurodollar market. Having seen this trend, some U.S. banks began offering their customers the option of taking a LIBOR-based rate in lieu of the prime rate in order to stay competitive.

Lending in the Eurodollar market is almost exclusively done by commercial banks. Large Eurocurrency loans are often syndicated by a group of participating banks. The loan agreement is put together by a lead bank known as the manager, which is usually one of the largest U.S. or European banks. The manager charges the borrower a once-and-for-all fee or commission of 0.25 percent to 1 percent of the loan value. A portion of this fee is kept by the lead bank and the remainder is shared by all the participating banks. The aim of forming a syndicate, of course, is to diversify the risk, which would be too large for any single bank to handle by itself. Multicurrency loans and revolving credit arrangements can also be negotiated in the Eurocurrency market to suit borrowers needs.

**Eurobond market** When long-term funds are needed, borrowing in the Eurobond market is a viable alternative for leading multinational corporations. The Eurobond issues are sold simultaneously in several different national capital markets, but denominated in a currency different from that of the nation in which the bonds are issued. The most widely used currency in the Eurobond market is the U.S. dollar with almost 67 percent of all the issues denominated in that currency. The next currency in importance is the deutsche mark. Eurobond issues are underwritten by an international syndicate of banks and securities firms. Eurobonds of longer than seven years in maturity generally have a sinking fund provision.

Disclosure requirements in the Eurobond market are much less stringent than those required by the Securities and Exchange Commission (SEC) in the United States. Furthermore, the registration costs in the Eurobond market are lower than those charged in the United States. In addition, the Eurobond market offers tax flexibility for borrowers and investors alike. Since most Eurobonds are issued by a fully owned offshore finance subsidiary which is located in a tax-haven country such as Luxembourg, there are no withholding taxes on interest paid. Wealthy investors often buy Eurobonds through Swiss bank accounts so that their interest income can be kept anonymous. All these advantages of Eurobonds enable the borrowers to raise funds at a lower cost. Nevertheless, a caveat may be in order with respect to the effective cost of borrowing in the Eurobond market. When a multinational firm borrows by floating a foreign currency denominated debt issue on a long-term basis, it creates transaction exposure, a kind of foreign exchange risk. If the foreign currency appreciates in value during the bond's life, the cost of servicing the debt could be prohibitively high. Many U.S. multinational firms borrowed at an approximately 7 percent coupon interest by selling Eurobonds denominated in deutsche marks and Swiss francs in the late 1960s and early 1970s. Nevertheless, these U.S. firms experienced an average debt service cost of approximately 13 percent, which is almost twice as much as the coupon rate. This increased cost occurred because the U.S. dollar fell with respect to these currencies. Therefore, currency selection for denominating Eurobond issues must be made with extreme care and foresight. To lessen the impact of foreign exchange risk, some recently issued Eurobond issues were denominated in multicurrency units.

**International equity markets** The entire amount of equity capital comes from the parent company for a wholly owned foreign subsidiary, but a majority of foreign affiliates are not owned completely by their parent corporations. In fact, in countries like India and Malaysia, majority ownership of a foreign affiliate must be held by the local citizens. In some other countries, the parent corporations are allowed to own their affiliates completely in the initial stages, but they are required to relinquish partial ownership to local citizens after five or seven years. In order to avoid nationalistic reactions to wholly owned foreign subsidiaries, multinational firms such as Unilever Ltd., Schlumberger, General Motors, Ford Motor Company, and IBM sell shares to worldwide stockholders. It is also believed that widespread foreign ownership of the firm's common stock encourages the loyalty of foreign stockholders and employees toward the firm. Thus selling common stock to residents of foreign countries is not only an important financing strategy, but it is also a risk-minimizing strategy for many multinational corporations.

As you have learned in Chapter 14, a well-functioning secondary market is essential to entice investors into owning shares. To attract investors from all over the world, reputable multinational firms list their shares on major stock exchanges around the world. For instance, about 40 foreign companies are listed on the New York Stock Exchange, and the American Stock Exchange lists more than 70 foreign firms. Several hundred foreign issues are traded in the over-the-counter market. Even more foreign firms would sell stock issues in the United States and list on NYSE and AMEX were it not for the tough and costly disclosure rules in effect in this country and enforced by the Securities and Exchange Commission. Many foreign corporations such as Hoechst, Honda, Hitachi, Sony, Magnet Metals Ltd., DeBeers, and the like accommodate American investors by issuing American Depository Receipts (ADRs). All the American-owned shares of a foreign company are placed in trust in a New York bank. The bank, in turn, will issue its depository receipts to the American stockholders and will maintain a stockholder ledger on these receipts, thus enabling the holders of ADRs to sell or otherwise transfer them as easily as they transfer any American company shares. Most ADRs trade in the over-the-counter market, although a few are listed on the New York Stock Exchange. ADR prices tend to move parallel with the prices of the underlying securities in their home markets.

Looking elsewhere around the world, approximately 70 U.S. firms have listed their shares on the Toronto Stock Exchange and some 50 on the Montreal Exchange. Similarly, more than 100 U.S. firms have listed their shares on the London Stock Exchange. Approximately 160 foreign issues are listed on the Bourse de Paris, including 37 U.S. stocks. In addition, a number of foreign securities are traded on the French hors cote (OTC) market. Fully half the stocks listed on the Amsterdam stock exchange are foreign. To obtain exposure in an international financial community, listing securities on world stock exchanges is a step in the right direction for a multinational firm. This international exposure also brings an additional responsibility for the MNC to understand the preferences and needs of heterogeneous groups of investors of various nationalities. The MNC may have to print and circulate its annual financial statements in many languages. Some foreign investors are more risk averse than their counterparts in the United States, and prefer dividend income over less certain capital gains. Common stock ownership among individuals in countries like Japan and Norway is insignificant, with financial institutions holding substantial amounts of common stock issues. For example, only 5–10 percent of Japanese households own stock, while more than 70 percent have deposit accounts with commercial banks. Institutional practices around the globe also vary significantly when it comes to issuing new securities. Unlike the United States, European commercial banks play a dominant role in the securities business. They underwrite stock issues, manage portfolios, vote the stock they hold in trust accounts, and hold directorships on company boards. In Germany, the banks also run an over-the-counter market in many stocks.

**The International Finance Corporation** Whenever a multinational company has difficulty raising equity capital due to lack of adequate private risk capital in a foreign country, the firm may explore the possibility of selling partial ownership to the International Finance

Corporation (IFC). This is a unit of the World Bank Group. The International Finance Corporation was established in 1956 and it is owned by 119 member countries of the World Bank. Its objective is to further economic development by promoting private enterprises in these countries. The profitability of a project and its potential benefit to the host country's economy are the two criteria the IFC uses to decide whether or not to assist a venture. The IFC participates in private enterprise through buying equity shares of a business, providing long-term loans, or a combination of the two for up to 25 percent of the total capital. The IFC expects the other partners to assume managerial responsibility, and it does not exercise its voting rights as a stockholder. The IFC helps finance new ventures as well as the expansion of existing ones in a variety of industries. Once the venture is well established, the IFC sells its investment position to private investors in order to free up its capital.

## Some Unsettled Issues in International Finance

As firms become multinational in scope, the nature of their financial decisions also becomes more complex. A multinational firm has access to more sources of funds than a purely domestic corporation. Interest rates and market conditions vary between the alternate sources of funds, and corporate financial practices may differ significantly between countries. For example, the debt ratios in many foreign countries are higher than those used by U.S. firms. A foreign affiliate of an American firm faces a dilemma in its financing decision: Should it follow the parent firm's norm or that of the host country? Who must decide this? Will it be decided at the corporate headquarters in the United States or by the foreign affiliate? This is a matter of control over financial decisions. Dividend policy is another area of debate. Should the parent company dictate the dividends the foreign affiliate must distribute or should it be left completely to the discretion of the foreign affiliate? Foreign government regulations may also influence the decision. Questions like these do not have clear-cut answers. The complex environment in which the MNCs operate does not permit simple and clear-cut solutions. Obviously, each situation has to be evaluated individually, and specific guidelines for decision making must be established. Such coordination, it is to be hoped, will result in cohesive policies in the areas of working capital management, capital structure, and dividend decisions throughout the MNC network.

## Summary

When a domestic business firm crosses its national borders to do business in other countries, it enters a riskier and more complex environment. A multinational firm is exposed to foreign exchange risk and political risk in addition to the usual business and financial risks. In general, international business operations have been more profitable than domestic operations, and this higher profitability is one factor that motivates business firms to go overseas. International operations account for a significant proportion of the earnings for many American firms. U.S. multinational firms have played a major role in promoting economic development and international trade for several decades, and now foreign firms have started to invest huge amounts of capital in the United States.

International business transactions are denominated in foreign currencies. The rate at which one currency unit is converted into another is called the exchange rate. In today's global monetary system, the exchange rates of major currencies are fluctuating rather freely. These "freely" floating exchange rates expose multinational business firms to foreign exchange risk. To deal with this foreign currency exposure effectively, the financial executive of an MNC must understand foreign exchange rates and how they are determined. Foreign exchange rates are influenced by differences in inflation rates among countries, by differences in interest rates, by governmental policies, and by the expectations of the participants in the foreign exchange markets. The international financial manager can reduce the firm's foreign currency exposure by hedging in the forward exchange market, in the money markets, and in the currency futures market.

Multinational companies have made billions of dollars worth of direct investments in foreign countries over the years. Lower production costs overseas, tax deferral provisions, less foreign competition, and benefits of international diversification are some of the motivational factors behind the flow of direct investment between nations. Foreign direct investments are usually quite large in size and many of them are exposed to enormous political risk. Although discounted cash flow analysis is applied to screen the projects in the initial stages, strategic considerations and political risk are often the overriding factors in reaching the final decision. One of the most important differences between domestic and international investments is that the information on foreign investments is generally less complete and often less accurate. Therefore, analyzing a foreign investment proposal is more difficult than analyzing a domestic investment project.

Financing international trade and investment is another important area of international finance that one must understand in order to raise funds at the lowest cost possible. The multinational firm has access to both the domestic and foreign capital markets. The Export-Import Bank finances American exports to foreign countries. Borrowing in the Eurobond market may appear less expensive at times, but the effect of foreign exchange risk on debt-servicing cost must be weighed carefully before borrowing in these markets. Floating common stock in foreign capital markets is also a viable financing alternative for many multinational companies. The International Finance Corporation, which is a subsidiary of the World Bank, also provides debt capital and equity capital to qualified firms. These alternative sources of financing may significantly differ with respect to cost, terms, and conditions. Therefore, the financial executive must carefully locate and use the proper means to finance international business operations.

## List of Terms

**multinational corporation**
**balance of payments**
**expropriation**
**foreign exchange rate**
**foreign exchange risk**
**purchasing power parity theory**
**interest rate parity theory**
**currency futures contract**
**transaction exposure**
**translation exposure**
**repatriation of earnings**
**parallel loan**
**fronting loan**
**letter of credit**
**Export-Import Bank (Eximbank)**
**Foreign Credit Insurance Association (FCIA)**
**International Finance Corporation (IFC)**
**London Interbank Offered Rate (LIBOR)**
**Overseas Private Investment Corporation (OPIC)**
**American Depository Receipts (ADRs)**
**Eurodollars**
**Eurobonds**

## Discussion Questions

1. What risks does a foreign affiliate of a multinational firm face in today's business world?
2. What are some allegations that are sometimes made against foreign affiliates of multinational firms and against the multinational firms themselves?
3. List the factors that affect the value of a currency in foreign exchange markets.
4. Explain how exports and imports tend to influence the value of a currency.
5. Differentiate between the spot exchange rate and the forward exchange rate.
6. What is meant by translation exposure in terms of foreign exchange risk?
7. What factors influence a U.S. business firm to go overseas?
8. What procedure(s) would you recommend for a multinational company in studying exposure to political risk? What actual strategies can be used to guard against such risk?
9. What factors beyond the normal domestic analysis go into a financial feasibility study for a multinational firm?
10. What is a letter of credit?
11. Explain the functions of the following agencies:
    Overseas Private Investment Corporation (OPIC)
    Export-Import Bank (Eximbank)
    Foreign Credit Insurance Association (FCIA)
    International Finance Corporation (IFC)
12. What are the differences between a parallel loan and a fronting loan?
13. What is LIBOR? How does it compare to the U.S. prime rate?
14. What is the danger or concern in floating a Eurobond issue?

15. What are ADRs?

16. Comment on any dilemmas that multinational firms and their foreign affiliates may face in regard to debt ratio limits and dividend payouts.

## Problems

1. Using the foreign exchange rates for August 6, 1985, in Table 21–2, determine the number of U.S. dollars required to buy the following amounts of foreign currencies.

   *a.* 10,000 guilders.
   *b.* 2,000 deutsche marks.
   *c.* 100,000 yens.
   *d.* 5,000 Swiss francs.
   *e.* 20,000 kronas.

2. Obtain a recent copy of *The Wall Street Journal* and recalculate the currency exchanges of Problem 1. How do these figures compare to those obtained in the above problem? Has the dollar strengthened or weakened against these currencies?

3. *The Wall Street Journal* reported the following spot and forward rates for the Swiss franc ($/SF) as of August 6, 1985:

| | |
|---|---|
| Spot | $0.4235 |
| 30-day forward | 0.4250 |
| 90-day forward | 0.4256 |
| 180-day forward | 0.4280 |

   *a.* Was the Swiss franc selling at a discount or premium in the forward market on August 6, 1985?
   *b.* What was the 30-day forward premium (or discount)?
   *c.* What was the 90-day forward premium (or discount)?
   *d.* Suppose you executed a 90-day forward contract to exchange 100,000 Swiss francs into U.S. dollars. How many dollars would you get 90 days hence?
   *e.* Assume a Swiss bank entered into a 180-day forward contract with Citicorp to buy $100,000. How many francs will the Swiss bank deliver in six months to get the U.S. dollars?

4. Suppose a Danish krone is selling for $0.09739 and an Irish punt is selling for $1.0945. What is the exchange rate (cross rate) of the Danish krone to the Irish punt? That is, how many Danish krones are equal to an Irish punt?

5. Suppose a Netherland guilder is selling for $0.3122 and a Maltan lira is selling for $2.2099. What is the exchange rate (cross rate) of the Netherland guilder to the Maltan lira? That is, how many Netherland guilders are equal to a Maltan lira?

6. From the base price level of 100 in 1968, German and U.S. price levels in 1985 stood at 160 and 213, respectively. If the 1968 $/DM exchange rate was $0.30/DM, what should the exchange rate be in 1985? Suggestion: Using the purchasing power parity theory, adjust the exchange rate to compensate for inflation. That is, determine the relative rate of inflation between the United States and Germany and multiply this times $/DM of .30.

7. In Problem number 6, if the United States had somehow managed no inflation since 1968, what should the exchange rate be in 1985, using the purchasing power theory?

8. An investor in the United States bought a one-year Australian security valued at 142,860 Australian dollars. The U.S. dollar equivalent was $100,000. The Australian security earned 12 percent during the year, but the Australian dollar depreciated four cents against the U.S. dollar during the time period ($0.70/AD to $0.66/AD). After transferring the funds back to the United States, what was the investor's return on his $100,000? Determine the total ending value of the Australian investment in Australian dollars and then translate this value to U.S. dollars. Then compute the return on the $100,000 investment.

9. You are the vice president of finance for Exploratory Resources, headquartered in Houston, Texas. In January 1986, your firm's Canadian subsidiary obtained a six-month loan of one million Canadian dollars from a bank in Houston to finance the acquisition of a titanium mine in Quebec province. The loan will also be repaid in Canadian dollars. At the time of the loan, the spot exchange rate was U.S. $0.7366/Canadian dollar and the currency was selling

at a discount in the forward market. The June 1986 futures contract (face value = \$100,000 per contract) was quoted at U.S. \$0.7306.

*a*. Explain how the Houston bank could lose on this transaction.
*b*. How much is the bank expected to lose due to foreign exchange risk?
*c*. If there is a \$100 total brokerage commission per contract, would you still recommend that the bank hedge in the currency futures market?

**10.** The Livingston Corporation has a wholly owned foreign subsidiary in Jamaica. The subsidiary earns \$5 million per year before taxes in Jamaica. The foreign income tax rate is 20 percent. Livingston's subsidiary repatriates the entire aftertax profit in the form of dividends to the Livingston Corporation. The U.S. corporate tax rate is 40 percent of foreign earnings before taxes. Disregard any problems associated with exchange rates.

*a*. Complete the table below.

| | |
|---|---|
| Before-tax earnings | ________ |
| Foreign income tax @ 20% | ________ |
| Earnings after foreign income taxes | ________ |
| Dividends repatriated | ________ |
| Gross U.S. taxes @ 40% of foreign earnings before taxes | ________ |
| Foreign tax credit | ________ |
| Net U.S. taxes payable | ________ |
| Aftertax cash flow | ________ |

*b*. Now assume that there is a 10 percent withholding tax on dividends in Jamaica. Recompute the answer to part *a* by completing the following table.

| | |
|---|---|
| Before-tax earnings | ________ |
| Foreign income tax @ 20% | ________ |
| Earnings after foreign income taxes | ________ |
| Gross dividends distributed | ________ |
| Withholding tax @ 10% of dividends | ________ |
| Net dividends repatriated | ________ |
| Gross U.S. taxes at 40% of foreign earnings before taxes | ________ |
| Foreign tax credit (Foreign income tax + Withholding tax) | ________ |
| Net U.S. taxes payable | ________ |
| Aftertax cash flow | ________ |

**11.** The Office Automation Corporation is considering a foreign investment. The initial cash outlay will be $10 million. The current foreign exchange rate is 2 francs = $1. Thus the investment in foreign currency will be 20 million francs. The assets have a useful life of five years and no expected salvage value. The firm uses a straight-line method of depreciation. Sales are expected to be 20 million francs and operating cash expenses 10 million francs every year for five years. The foreign income tax rate is 25 percent. The foreign subsidiary will repatriate all aftertax profits to Office Automation in the form of dividends. Furthermore, the depreciation cash flows (equal to each year's depreciation) will be repatriated during the same year they accrue to the foreign subsidiary. The applicable cost of capital that reflects the riskiness of the cash flows is 16 percent. The U.S. tax rate is 40 percent of foreign earnings before taxes.

*a.* Should the Office Automation Corporation undertake the investment, if the foreign exchange rate is expected to remain constant during the five-year period?

*b.* Should the Office Automation undertake the investment, if the foreign exchange rate is expected to be as follows:

| | |
|---|---|
| Year 0 . . . . . . . . . | $1 = 2.0 francs |
| Year 1 . . . . . . . . . | $1 = 2.2 francs |
| Year 2 . . . . . . . . . | $1 = 2.4 francs |
| Year 3 . . . . . . . . . | $1 = 2.7 francs |
| Year 4 . . . . . . . . . | $1 = 2.9 francs |
| Year 5 . . . . . . . . . | $1 = 3.2 francs |

## Selected References

Aggarwal, Raj. "International Differences in Capital Structure Norms." *Management International Review* 21, no. 1 (1981), pp. 75–88.

Alsop, Ronald. "Foreign Ventures." *The Wall Street Journal* (March 30, 1981), p. 1.

Dufey, Gunter, and Ian Giddy. *The International Money Market*. Englewood Cliffs, N.J.: Prentice-Hall, 1978.

Eiteman, David, and Arthur Stonehill. *Multinational Business Finance*, 3d ed. Reading, Mass.: Addison-Wesley Publishing, 1982.

Errunza, Viharg. "Determinants of Financial Structure in the Central American Common Market." *Financial Management* 8 (Autumn 1979), pp. 72–77.

Folks, William R., Jr. "Decision Analysis for Exchange Risk Management." *Financial Management* 1 (Winter 1972), pp. 101–12.

"Foreign Manufacturing Investments in the United States." The Conference Board, March 1981, p. 1.

Gentry, James A; D. R. Mehta; S. K. Bhattacharya; R. Cobbaut; and J. Scaringella. "An International Study of Management Perceptions of the Working Capital Process." *Journal of International Business Studies* 10 (Spring–Summer 1979), pp. 28–38.

"The Hundred Largest U.S. Multinationals." *Forbes* (July 5, 1982), pp. 126–28.

Kolhagen, Steven W. "The Performance of Foreign Exchange Markets: 1971–1974." *Journal of International Business Studies* 6 (Fall 1975), pp. 33–39.

Lessard, Donald R. "World, National, and Industrial Factors in Equity Returns." *Journal of Finance* 29 (May 1974), pp. 379–91.

Naidu, G.N. "How to Reduce Transaction Exposure in International Lending." *The Journal of Commercial Bank Lending* 63 (June 1981), pp. 39–46.

———., and Tai Shin. "Effectiveness of Currency Futures Market in Hedging Foreign Exchange Risk." *Management International Review* 21, no. 4 (1981), pp. 5–16.

Ricks, David A., and R. A. Ajami. "Motives of Non-American Firms in Investing in the United States." *Journal of International Business Studies* 12 (Winter 1981), pp. 25–34.

Remmers, L.; A. Stonehill; R. Wright; and T. Beekhuisen. "Industry and Size as Debt Ratio Determinants in Manufacturing Internationally." *Financial Management* 3 (Summer 1974), pp. 24–32.

Rogalski, Richard, and Joseph Vinso. "Price Level Variations as Predictors of Flexible Exchange Rates." *Journal of International Business Studies* 8 (Summer–Spring 1977), pp. 71–81.

Rummel, R. J., and David A. Heenan. "How Multinationals Analyze Political Risk." *Harvard Business Review* 56 (January–February 1978), pp. 67–76.

Shapiro, Alan C. *Multinational Financial Management*. Boston: Allyn & Bacon, 1982.

Solnik, Bruno H. "Why Not Diversify Internationally Rather than Domestically?" *Financial Analysts Journal* 30 (July–August 1974), pp. 48–54.

Stanley, Marjorie T. "Capital Structure and Cost of Capital for the Multinational Firm." *Journal of International Business Studies* 12 (Spring–Summer 1981), pp. 103–20.

———., and Stanley Block. "Response by United States Financial Managers to Financial Accounting Standard No. 8." *Journal of International Business Studies* 9 (Fall 1978), pp. 89–99.

Summa, Donald. "Remittance by U.S.-Owned Foreign Corporations: Tax Considerations." *Columbia Journal of World Business* 10 (Summer 1975), pp. 40–45.

Weston, J. Fred, and Bart W. Sorge. *Guide to International Financial Management.* New York: McGraw-Hill, 1977.

# Appendixes

A Compound Sum of \$1, $IF_s$
B Present Value of \$1, $IF_{pv}$
C Compound Sum of an Annuity of \$1, $IF_{sa}$
D Present Value of an Annuity of \$1, $IF_{pva}$
E Tables of Squares and Square Roots

## Appendix A Compound sum of $1, $IF_s$ $S = P(1+i)^n$

| Period | Percent | | | | | | | | | | |
|---|---|---|---|---|---|---|---|---|---|---|---|
| | 1% | 2% | 3% | 4% | 5% | 6% | 7% | 8% | 9% | 10% | 11% |
| 1 | 1.010 | 1.020 | 1.030 | 1.040 | 1.050 | 1.060 | 1.070 | 1.080 | 1.090 | 1.100 | 1.110 |
| 2 | 1.020 | 1.040 | 1.061 | 1.082 | 1.103 | 1.124 | 1.145 | 1.166 | 1.188 | 1.210 | 1.232 |
| 3 | 1.030 | 1.061 | 1.093 | 1.125 | 1.158 | 1.191 | 1.225 | 1.260 | 1.295 | 1.331 | 1.368 |
| 4 | 1.041 | 1.082 | 1.126 | 1.170 | 1.216 | 1.262 | 1.311 | 1.360 | 1.412 | 1.464 | 1.518 |
| 5 | 1.051 | 1.104 | 1.159 | 1.217 | 1.276 | 1.338 | 1.403 | 1.469 | 1.539 | 1.611 | 1.685 |
| 6 | 1.062 | 1.126 | 1.194 | 1.265 | 1.340 | 1.419 | 1.501 | 1.587 | 1.677 | 1.772 | 1.870 |
| 7 | 1.072 | 1.149 | 1.230 | 1.316 | 1.407 | 1.504 | 1.606 | 1.714 | 1.828 | 1.949 | 2.076 |
| 8 | 1.083 | 1.172 | 1.267 | 1.369 | 1.477 | 1.594 | 1.718 | 1.851 | 1.993 | 2.144 | 2.305 |
| 9 | 1.094 | 1.195 | 1.305 | 1.423 | 1.551 | 1.689 | 1.838 | 1.999 | 2.172 | 2.358 | 2.558 |
| 10 | 1.105 | 1.219 | 1.344 | 1.480 | 1.629 | 1.791 | 1.967 | 2.159 | 2.367 | 2.594 | 2.839 |
| 11 | 1.116 | 1.243 | 1.384 | 1.539 | 1.710 | 1.898 | 2.105 | 2.332 | 2.580 | 2.853 | 3.152 |
| 12 | 1.127 | 1.268 | 1.426 | 1.601 | 1.796 | 2.012 | 2.252 | 2.518 | 2.813 | 3.138 | 3.498 |
| 13 | 1.138 | 1.294 | 1.469 | 1.665 | 1.886 | 2.133 | 2.410 | 2.720 | 3.066 | 3.452 | 3.883 |
| 14 | 1.149 | 1.319 | 1.513 | 1.732 | 1.980 | 2.261 | 2.579 | 2.937 | 3.342 | 3.797 | 4.310 |
| 15 | 1.161 | 1.346 | 1.558 | 1.801 | 2.079 | 2.397 | 2.759 | 3.172 | 3.642 | 4.177 | 4.785 |
| 16 | 1.173 | 1.373 | 1.605 | 1.873 | 2.183 | 2.540 | 2.952 | 3.426 | 3.970 | 4.595 | 5.311 |
| 17 | 1.184 | 1.400 | 1.653 | 1.948 | 2.292 | 2.693 | 3.159 | 3.700 | 4.328 | 5.054 | 5.895 |
| 18 | 1.196 | 1.428 | 1.702 | 2.206 | 2.407 | 2.854 | 3.380 | 3.996 | 4.717 | 5.560 | 6.544 |
| 19 | 1.208 | 1.457 | 1.754 | 2.107 | 2.527 | 3.026 | 3.617 | 4.316 | 5.142 | 6.116 | 7.263 |
| 20 | 1.220 | 1.486 | 1.806 | 2.191 | 2.653 | 3.207 | 3.870 | 4.661 | 5.604 | 6.727 | 8.062 |
| 25 | 1.282 | 1.641 | 2.094 | 2.666 | 3.386 | 4.292 | 5.427 | 6.848 | 8.623 | 10.835 | 13.585 |
| 30 | 1.348 | 1.811 | 2.427 | 3.243 | 4.322 | 5.743 | 7.612 | 10.063 | 13.268 | 17.449 | 22.892 |
| 40 | 1.489 | 2.208 | 3.262 | 4.801 | 7.040 | 10.286 | 14.974 | 21.725 | 31.409 | 45.259 | 65.001 |
| 50 | 1.645 | 2.692 | 4.384 | 7.107 | 11.467 | 18.420 | 29.457 | 46.902 | 74.358 | 117.39 | 184.57 |

**Appendix A (*concluded*) Compound sum of $1**

| Period | 12% | 13% | 14% | 15% | 16% | 17% | 18% | 19% | 20% | 25% | 30% |
|---|---|---|---|---|---|---|---|---|---|---|---|
| | *Percent* | | | | | | | | | | |
| 1 | 1.120 | 1.130 | 1.140 | 1.150 | 1.160 | 1.170 | 1.180 | 1.190 | 1.200 | 1.250 | 1.300 |
| 2 | 1.254 | 1.277 | 1.300 | 1.323 | 1.346 | 1.369 | 1.392 | 1.416 | 1.440 | 1.563 | 1.690 |
| 3 | 1.405 | 1.443 | 1.482 | 1.521 | 1.561 | 1.602 | 1.643 | 1.685 | 1.728 | 1.953 | 2.197 |
| 4 | 1.574 | 1.630 | 1.689 | 1.749 | 1.811 | 1.874 | 1.939 | 2.005 | 2.074 | 2.441 | 2.856 |
| 5 | 1.762 | 1.842 | 1.925 | 2.011 | 2.100 | 2.192 | 2.288 | 2.386 | 2.488 | 3.052 | 3.713 |
| 6 | 1.974 | 2.082 | 2.195 | 2.313 | 2.436 | 2.565 | 2.700 | 2.840 | 2.986 | 3.815 | 4.827 |
| 7 | 2.211 | 2.353 | 2.502 | 2.660 | 2.826 | 3.001 | 3.185 | 3.379 | 3.583 | 4.768 | 6.276 |
| 8 | 2.476 | 2.658 | 2.853 | 3.059 | 3.278 | 3.511 | 3.759 | 4.021 | 4.300 | 5.960 | 8.157 |
| 9 | 2.773 | 3.004 | 3.252 | 3.518 | 3.803 | 4.108 | 4.435 | 4.785 | 5.160 | 7.451 | 10.604 |
| 10 | 3.106 | 3.395 | 3.707 | 4.046 | 4.411 | 4.807 | 5.234 | 5.696 | 6.192 | 9.313 | 13.786 |
| 11 | 3.479 | 3.836 | 4.226 | 4.652 | 5.117 | 5.624 | 6.176 | 6.777 | 7.430 | 11.642 | 17.922 |
| 12 | 3.896 | 4.335 | 4.818 | 5.350 | 5.936 | 6.580 | 7.288 | 8.064 | 8.916 | 14.552 | 23.298 |
| 13 | 4.363 | 4.898 | 5.492 | 6.153 | 6.886 | 7.699 | 8.599 | 9.596 | 10.699 | 18.190 | 30.288 |
| 14 | 4.887 | 5.535 | 6.261 | 7.076 | 7.988 | 9.007 | 10.147 | 11.420 | 12.839 | 22.737 | 39.374 |
| 15 | 5.474 | 6.254 | 7.138 | 8.137 | 9.266 | 10.539 | 11.974 | 13.590 | 15.407 | 28.422 | 51.186 |
| 16 | 6.130 | 7.067 | 8.137 | 9.358 | 10.748 | 12.330 | 14.129 | 16.172 | 18.488 | 35.527 | 66.542 |
| 17 | 6.866 | 7.986 | 9.276 | 10.761 | 12.468 | 14.426 | 16.672 | 19.244 | 22.186 | 44.409 | 86.504 |
| 18 | 7.690 | 9.024 | 10.575 | 12.375 | 14.463 | 16.879 | 19.673 | 22.091 | 26.623 | 55.511 | 112.46 |
| 19 | 8.613 | 10.197 | 12.056 | 14.232 | 16.777 | 19.748 | 23.214 | 27.252 | 31.948 | 69.389 | 146.19 |
| 20 | 9.646 | 11.523 | 13.743 | 16.367 | 19.461 | 23.106 | 27.393 | 32.429 | 38.338 | 86.736 | 190.05 |
| 25 | 17.000 | 21.231 | 26.462 | 32.919 | 40.874 | 50.658 | 62.669 | 77.388 | 95.396 | 264.70 | 705.64 |
| 30 | 29.960 | 39.116 | 50.950 | 66.212 | 85.850 | 111.07 | 143.37 | 184.68 | 237.38 | 807.79 | 2,620.0 |
| 40 | 93.051 | 132.78 | 188.88 | 267.86 | 378.72 | 533.87 | 750.38 | 1,051.7 | 1,469.8 | 7,523.2 | 36,119. |
| 50 | 289.00 | 450.74 | 700.23 | 1,083.7 | 1,670.7 | 2,566.2 | 3,927.4 | 5,988.9 | 9,100.4 | 70,065. | 497,929. |

Source: Maurice Joy, *Introduction to Financial Management* (Homewood, Ill.: Richard D. Irwin, 1977).

## Appendix B Present value of \$1, $IF_{pv}$ $P = S\left[\frac{1}{(1+i)^n}\right]$

| Period | Percent | | | | | | | | | | | |
|---|---|---|---|---|---|---|---|---|---|---|---|---|
| | 1% | 2% | 3% | 4% | 5% | 6% | 7% | 8% | 9% | 10% | 11% | 12% |
| 1 | 0.990 | 0.980 | 0.971 | 0.962 | 0.952 | 0.943 | 0.935 | 0.926 | 0.917 | 0.909 | 0.901 | 0.893 |
| 2 | 0.980 | 0.961 | 0.943 | 0.925 | 0.907 | 0.890 | 0.873 | 0.857 | 0.842 | 0.826 | 0.812 | 0.797 |
| 3 | 0.971 | 0.942 | 0.915 | 0.889 | 0.864 | 0.840 | 0.816 | 0.794 | 0.772 | 0.751 | 0.731 | 0.712 |
| 4 | 0.961 | 0.924 | 0.885 | 0.855 | 0.823 | 0.792 | 0.763 | 0.735 | 0.708 | 0.683 | 0.659 | 0.636 |
| 5 | 0.951 | 0.906 | 0.863 | 0.822 | 0.784 | 0.747 | 0.713 | 0.681 | 0.650 | 0.621 | 0.593 | 0.567 |
| 6 | 0.942 | 0.888 | 0.837 | 0.790 | 0.746 | 0.705 | 0.666 | 0.630 | 0.596 | 0.564 | 0.535 | 0.507 |
| 7 | 0.933 | 0.871 | 0.813 | 0.760 | 0.711 | 0.665 | 0.623 | 0.583 | 0.547 | 0.513 | 0.482 | 0.452 |
| 8 | 0.923 | 0.853 | 0.789 | 0.731 | 0.677 | 0.627 | 0.582 | 0.540 | 0.502 | 0.467 | 0.434 | 0.404 |
| 9 | 0.914 | 0.837 | 0.766 | 0.703 | 0.645 | 0.592 | 0.544 | 0.500 | 0.460 | 0.424 | 0.391 | 0.361 |
| 10 | 0.905 | 0.820 | 0.744 | 0.676 | 0.614 | 0.558 | 0.508 | 0.463 | 0.422 | 0.386 | 0.352 | 0.322 |
| 11 | 0.896 | 0.804 | 0.722 | 0.650 | 0.585 | 0.527 | 0.475 | 0.429 | 0.388 | 0.350 | 0.317 | 0.287 |
| 12 | 0.887 | 0.788 | 0.701 | 0.625 | 0.557 | 0.497 | 0.444 | 0.397 | 0.356 | 0.319 | 0.286 | 0.257 |
| 13 | 0.879 | 0.773 | 0.681 | 0.601 | 0.530 | 0.469 | 0.415 | 0.368 | 0.326 | 0.290 | 0.258 | 0.229 |
| 14 | 0.870 | 0.758 | 0.661 | 0.577 | 0.505 | 0.442 | 0.388 | 0.340 | 0.299 | 0.263 | 0.232 | 0.205 |
| 15 | 0.861 | 0.743 | 0.642 | 0.555 | 0.481 | 0.417 | 0.362 | 0.315 | 0.275 | 0.239 | 0.209 | 0.183 |
| 16 | 0.853 | 0.728 | 0.623 | 0.534 | 0.458 | 0.394 | 0.339 | 0.292 | 0.252 | 0.218 | 0.188 | 0.163 |
| 17 | 0.844 | 0.714 | 0.605 | 0.513 | 0.436 | 0.371 | 0.317 | 0.270 | 0.231 | 0.198 | 0.170 | 0.146 |
| 18 | 0.836 | 0.700 | 0.587 | 0.494 | 0.416 | 0.350 | 0.296 | 0.250 | 0.212 | 0.180 | 0.153 | 0.130 |
| 19 | 0.828 | 0.686 | 0.570 | 0.475 | 0.396 | 0.331 | 0.277 | 0.232 | 0.194 | 0.164 | 0.138 | 0.116 |
| 20 | 0.820 | 0.673 | 0.554 | 0.456 | 0.377 | 0.312 | 0.258 | 0.215 | 0.178 | 0.149 | 0.124 | 0.104 |
| 25 | 0.780 | 0.610 | 0.478 | 0.375 | 0.295 | 0.233 | 0.184 | 0.146 | 0.116 | 0.092 | 0.074 | 0.059 |
| 30 | 0.742 | 0.552 | 0.412 | 0.308 | 0.231 | 0.174 | 0.131 | 0.099 | 0.075 | 0.057 | 0.044 | 0.033 |
| 40 | 0.672 | 0.453 | 0.307 | 0.208 | 0.142 | 0.097 | 0.067 | 0.046 | 0.032 | 0.022 | 0.015 | 0.011 |
| 50 | 0.608 | 0.372 | 0.228 | 0.141 | 0.087 | 0.054 | 0.034 | 0.021 | 0.013 | 0.009 | 0.005 | 0.003 |

**Appendix B (*concluded*) Present value of $1**

| Period | Percent | | | | | | | | | | | | |
|---|---|---|---|---|---|---|---|---|---|---|---|---|---|
| | *13%* | *14%* | *15%* | *16%* | *17%* | *18%* | *19%* | *20%* | *25%* | *30%* | *35%* | *40%* | *50%* |
| 1 | 0.885 | 0.877 | 0.870 | 0.862 | 0.855 | 0.847 | 0.840 | 0.833 | 0.800 | 0.769 | 0.741 | 0.714 | 0.667 |
| 2 | 0.783 | 0.769 | 0.756 | 0.743 | 0.731 | 0.718 | 0.706 | 0.694 | 0.640 | 0.592 | 0.549 | 0.510 | 0.444 |
| 3 | 0.693 | 0.675 | 0.658 | 0.641 | 0.624 | 0.609 | 0.593 | 0.579 | 0.512 | 0.455 | 0.406 | 0.364 | 0.296 |
| 4 | 0.613 | 0.592 | 0.572 | 0.552 | 0.534 | 0.515 | 0.499 | 0.482 | 0.410 | 0.350 | 0.301 | 0.260 | 0.198 |
| 5 | 0.543 | 0.519 | 0.497 | 0.476 | 0.456 | 0.437 | 0.419 | 0.402 | 0.320 | 0.269 | 0.223 | 0.186 | 0.132 |
| 6 | 0.480 | 0.456 | 0.432 | 0.410 | 0.390 | 0.370 | 0.352 | 0.335 | 0.262 | 0.207 | 0.165 | 0.133 | 0.088 |
| 7 | 0.425 | 0.400 | 0.376 | 0.354 | 0.333 | 0.314 | 0.296 | 0.279 | 0.210 | 0.159 | 0.122 | 0.095 | 0.059 |
| 8 | 0.376 | 0.351 | 0.327 | 0.305 | 0.285 | 0.266 | 0.249 | 0.233 | 0.168 | 0.123 | 0.091 | 0.068 | 0.039 |
| 9 | 0.333 | 0.300 | 0.284 | 0.263 | 0.243 | 0.225 | 0.209 | 0.194 | 0.134 | 0.094 | 0.067 | 0.048 | 0.026 |
| 10 | 0.295 | 0.270 | 0.247 | 0.227 | 0.208 | 0.191 | 0.176 | 0.162 | 0.107 | 0.073 | 0.050 | 0.035 | 0.017 |
| 11 | 0.261 | 0.237 | 0.215 | 0.195 | 0.178 | 0.162 | 0.148 | 0.135 | 0.086 | 0.056 | 0.037 | 0.025 | 0.012 |
| 12 | 0.231 | 0.208 | 0.187 | 0.168 | 0.152 | 0.137 | 0.124 | 0.112 | 0.069 | 0.043 | 0.027 | 0.018 | 0.008 |
| 13 | 0.204 | 0.182 | 0.163 | 0.145 | 0.130 | 0.116 | 0.104 | 0.093 | 0.055 | 0.033 | 0.020 | 0.013 | 0.005 |
| 14 | 0.181 | 0.160 | 0.141 | 0.125 | 0.111 | 0.099 | 0.088 | 0.078 | 0.044 | 0.025 | 0.015 | 0.009 | 0.003 |
| 15 | 0.160 | 0.140 | 0.123 | 0.108 | 0.095 | 0.084 | 0.074 | 0.065 | 0.035 | 0.020 | 0.011 | 0.006 | 0.002 |
| 16 | 0.141 | 0.123 | 0.107 | 0.093 | 0.081 | 0.071 | 0.062 | 0.054 | 0.028 | 0.015 | 0.008 | 0.005 | 0.002 |
| 17 | 0.125 | 0.108 | 0.093 | 0.080 | 0.069 | 0.060 | 0.052 | 0.045 | 0.023 | 0.012 | 0.006 | 0.003 | 0.001 |
| 18 | 0.111 | 0.095 | 0.081 | 0.069 | 0.059 | 0.051 | 0.044 | 0.038 | 0.018 | 0.009 | 0.005 | 0.002 | 0.001 |
| 19 | 0.098 | 0.083 | 0.070 | 0.060 | 0.051 | 0.043 | 0.037 | 0.031 | 0.014 | 0.007 | 0.003 | 0.002 | 0 |
| 20 | 0.087 | 0.073 | 0.061 | 0.051 | 0.043 | 0.037 | 0.031 | 0.026 | 0.012 | 0.005 | 0.002 | 0.001 | 0 |
| 25 | 0.047 | 0.038 | 0.030 | 0.024 | 0.020 | 0.016 | 0.013 | 0.010 | 0.004 | 0.001 | 0.001 | 0 | 0 |
| 30 | 0.026 | 0.020 | 0.015 | 0.012 | 0.009 | 0.007 | 0.005 | 0.004 | 0.001 | 0 | 0 | 0 | 0 |
| 40 | 0.008 | 0.005 | 0.004 | 0.003 | 0.002 | 0.001 | 0.001 | 0.001 | 0 | 0 | 0 | 0 | 0 |
| 50 | 0.002 | 0.001 | 0.001 | 0.001 | 0 | 0 | 0 | 0 | 0 | 0 | 0 | 0 | 0 |

Source: Maurice Joy, *Introduction to Financial Management* (Homewood, Ill.: Richard D. Irwin, 1977).

**Appendix C Compound sum of an annuity of $1, $IF_{sa}$ $S = R\left[\frac{(1+i)^n - 1}{i}\right]$**

| Period | Percent 1% | 2% | 3% | 4% | 5% | 6% | 7% | 8% | 9% | 10% | 11% |
|---|---|---|---|---|---|---|---|---|---|---|---|
| 1 | 1.000 | 1.000 | 1.000 | 1.000 | 1.000 | 1.000 | 1.000 | 1.000 | 1.000 | 1.000 | 1.000 |
| 2 | 2.010 | 2.020 | 2.030 | 2.040 | 2.050 | 2.060 | 2.070 | 2.080 | 2.090 | 2.100 | 2.110 |
| 3 | 3.030 | 3.060 | 3.091 | 3.122 | 3.153 | 3.184 | 3.215 | 3.246 | 3.278 | 3.310 | 3.342 |
| 4 | 4.060 | 4.122 | 4.184 | 4.246 | 4.310 | 4.375 | 4.440 | 4.506 | 4.573 | 4.641 | 4.710 |
| 5 | 5.101 | 5.204 | 5.309 | 5.416 | 5.526 | 5.637 | 5.751 | 5.867 | 5.985 | 6.105 | 6.228 |
| 6 | 6.152 | 6.308 | 6.468 | 6.633 | 6.802 | 6.975 | 7.153 | 7.336 | 7.523 | 7.716 | 7.913 |
| 7 | 7.214 | 7.434 | 7.662 | 7.898 | 8.142 | 8.394 | 8.654 | 8.923 | 9.200 | 9.487 | 9.783 |
| 8 | 8.286 | 8.583 | 8.892 | 9.214 | 9.549 | 9.897 | 10.260 | 10.637 | 11.028 | 11.436 | 11.859 |
| 9 | 9.369 | 9.755 | 10.159 | 10.583 | 11.027 | 11.491 | 11.978 | 12.488 | 13.021 | 13.579 | 14.164 |
| 10 | 10.462 | 10.950 | 11.464 | 12.006 | 12.578 | 13.181 | 13.816 | 14.487 | 15.193 | 15.937 | 16.722 |
| 11 | 11.567 | 12.169 | 12.808 | 13.486 | 14.207 | 14.972 | 15.784 | 16.645 | 17.560 | 18.531 | 19.561 |
| 12 | 12.683 | 13.412 | 14.192 | 15.026 | 15.917 | 16.870 | 17.888 | 18.977 | 20.141 | 21.384 | 22.713 |
| 13 | 13.809 | 14.680 | 15.618 | 16.627 | 17.713 | 18.882 | 20.141 | 21.495 | 22.953 | 24.523 | 26.212 |
| 14 | 14.947 | 15.974 | 17.086 | 18.292 | 19.599 | 21.015 | 22.550 | 24.215 | 26.019 | 27.975 | 30.095 |
| 15 | 16.097 | 17.293 | 18.599 | 20.024 | 21.579 | 23.276 | 25.129 | 27.152 | 29.361 | 31.772 | 34.405 |
| 16 | 17.258 | 18.639 | 20.157 | 21.825 | 23.657 | 25.673 | 27.888 | 30.324 | 33.003 | 35.950 | 39.190 |
| 17 | 18.430 | 20.012 | 21.762 | 23.698 | 25.840 | 20.213 | 30.840 | 33.750 | 36.974 | 40.545 | 44.501 |
| 18 | 19.615 | 21.412 | 23.414 | 25.645 | 28.132 | 30.906 | 33.999 | 37.450 | 41.301 | 45.599 | 50.396 |
| 19 | 20.811 | 22.841 | 25.117 | 27.671 | 30.539 | 33.760 | 37.379 | 41.446 | 46.018 | 51.159 | 56.939 |
| 20 | 22.019 | 24.297 | 26.870 | 29.778 | 33.066 | 36.786 | 40.995 | 45.762 | 51.160 | 57.275 | 64.203 |
| 25 | 28.243 | 32.030 | 36.459 | 41.646 | 47.727 | 54.865 | 63.249 | 73.106 | 84.701 | 98.347 | 114.41 |
| 30 | 34.785 | 40.588 | 47.575 | 56.085 | 66.439 | 79.058 | 94.461 | 113.28 | 136.31 | 164.49 | 199.02 |
| 40 | 48.886 | 60.402 | 75.401 | 95.026 | 120.80 | 154.76 | 199.64 | 259.06 | 337.89 | 442.59 | 581.83 |
| 50 | 64.463 | 84.579 | 112.80 | 152.67 | 209.35 | 290.34 | 406.53 | 573.77 | 815.08 | 1,163.9 | 1,668.8 |

**Appendix C (*concluded*) Compound sum of an annuity of $1**

| Period | 12% | 13% | 14% | 15% | 16% | 17% | 18% | 19% | 20% | 25% | 30% |
|---|---|---|---|---|---|---|---|---|---|---|---|
| | Percent | | | | | | | | | | |
| 1 | 1.000 | 1.000 | 1.000 | 1.000 | 1.000 | 1.000 | 1.000 | 1.000 | 1.000 | 1.000 | 1.000 |
| 2 | 2.120 | 2.130 | 2.140 | 2.150 | 2.160 | 2.170 | 2.180 | 2.190 | 2.200 | 2.250 | 2.300 |
| 3 | 3.374 | 3.407 | 3.440 | 3.473 | 3.506 | 3.539 | 3.572 | 3.606 | 3.640 | 3.813 | 3.990 |
| 4 | 4.779 | 4.850 | 4.921 | 4.993 | 5.066 | 5.141 | 5.215 | 5.291 | 5.368 | 5.766 | 6.187 |
| 5 | 6.353 | 6.480 | 6.610 | 6.742 | 6.877 | 7.014 | 7.154 | 7.297 | 7.442 | 8.207 | 9.043 |
| 6 | 8.115 | 8.323 | 8.536 | 8.754 | 8.977 | 9.207 | 9.442 | 0.683 | 9.930 | 11.259 | 12.756 |
| 7 | 10.089 | 10.405 | 10.730 | 11.067 | 11.414 | 11.772 | 12.142 | 12.523 | 12.916 | 15.073 | 17.583 |
| 8 | 12.300 | 12.757 | 13.233 | 13.727 | 14.240 | 14.773 | 15.327 | 15.902 | 16.499 | 19.842 | 23.858 |
| 9 | 14.776 | 15.416 | 16.085 | 16.786 | 17.519 | 18.285 | 19.086 | 19.923 | 20.799 | 25.802 | 32.015 |
| 10 | 17.549 | 18.420 | 19.337 | 20.304 | 21.321 | 22.393 | 23.521 | 24.701 | 25.959 | 33.253 | 42.619 |
| 11 | 20.655 | 21.814 | 23.045 | 24.349 | 25.733 | 27.200 | 28.755 | 30.404 | 32.150 | 42.566 | 56.405 |
| 12 | 24.133 | 25.650 | 27.271 | 29.002 | 30.850 | 32.824 | 34.931 | 37.180 | 39.581 | 54.208 | 74.327 |
| 13 | 28.029 | 29.985 | 32.089 | 34.352 | 36.786 | 39.404 | 42.219 | 45.244 | 48.497 | 68.760 | 97.625 |
| 14 | 32.393 | 34.883 | 37.581 | 40.505 | 43.672 | 47.103 | 50.818 | 54.841 | 59.196 | 86.949 | 127.91 |
| 15 | 37.280 | 40.417 | 43.842 | 47.580 | 51.660 | 56.110 | 60.965 | 66.261 | 72.035 | 109.69 | 167.29 |
| 16 | 42.753 | 46.672 | 50.980 | 55.717 | 60.925 | 66.649 | 72.939 | 79.850 | 87.442 | 138.11 | 218.47 |
| 17 | 48.884 | 53.739 | 59.118 | 65.075 | 71.673 | 78.979 | 87.068 | 96.022 | 105.93 | 173.64 | 285.01 |
| 18 | 55.750 | 61.725 | 68.394 | 75.836 | 84.141 | 93.406 | 103.74 | 115.27 | 128.12 | 218.05 | 371.52 |
| 19 | 63.440 | 70.749 | 78.969 | 88.212 | 98.603 | 110.29 | 123.41 | 138.17 | 154.74 | 273.56 | 483.97 |
| 20 | 72.052 | 80.947 | 91.025 | 102.44 | 115.38 | 130.03 | 146.63 | 165.42 | 186.69 | 342.95 | 630.17 |
| 25 | 133.33 | 155.62 | 181.87 | 212.79 | 249.21 | 292.11 | 342.60 | 402.04 | 471.98 | 1,054.8 | 2,348.80 |
| 30 | 241.33 | 293.20 | 356.79 | 434.75 | 530.31 | 647.44 | 790.95 | 966.7 | 1,181.9 | 3,227.2 | 8,730.0 |
| 40 | 767.09 | 1,013.7 | 1,342.0 | 1,779.1 | 2,360.8 | 3,134.5 | 4,163.21 | 5,529.8 | 7,343.9 | 30,089. | 120,393. |
| 50 | 2,400.0 | 3,459.5 | 4,994.5 | 7,217.7 | 10,436. | 15,090. | 21,813. | 31,515. | 45,497. | 280,256. | 165,976. |

Source: Maurice Joy, *Introduction to Financial Management* (Homewood, Ill.: Richard D. Irwin, 1977).

**Appendix D Present value of an annuity of $1, $IF_{pva}$** $A = R\left[\frac{1 - \frac{1}{(1+i)^n}}{i}\right]$

| Period | 1% | 2% | 3% | 4% | 5% | 6% | 7% | 8% | 9% | 10% | 11% | 12% |
|---|---|---|---|---|---|---|---|---|---|---|---|---|
| | | | | | | Percent | | | | | | |
| 1 | 0.990 | 0.980 | 0.971 | 0.962 | 0.952 | 0.943 | 0.935 | 0.926 | 0.917 | 0.909 | 0.901 | 0.893 |
| 2 | 1.970 | 1.942 | 1.913 | 1.886 | 1.859 | 1.833 | 1.808 | 1.783 | 1.759 | 1.736 | 1.713 | 1.690 |
| 3 | 2.941 | 2.884 | 2.829 | 2.775 | 2.723 | 2.673 | 2.624 | 2.577 | 2.531 | 2.487 | 2.444 | 2.402 |
| 4 | 3.902 | 3.808 | 3.717 | 3.630 | 3.546 | 3.465 | 3.387 | 3.312 | 3.240 | 3.170 | 3.102 | 3.037 |
| 5 | 4.853 | 4.713 | 4.580 | 4.452 | 4.329 | 4.212 | 4.100 | 3.993 | 3.890 | 3.791 | 3.696 | 3.605 |
| 6 | 5.795 | 5.601 | 5.417 | 5.242 | 5.076 | 4.917 | 4.767 | 4.623 | 4.486 | 4.355 | 4.231 | 4.111 |
| 7 | 6.728 | 6.472 | 6.230 | 6.002 | 5.786 | 5.582 | 5.389 | 5.206 | 5.033 | 4.868 | 4.712 | 4.564 |
| 8 | 7.652 | 7.325 | 7.020 | 6.733 | 6.463 | 6.210 | 5.971 | 5.747 | 5.535 | 5.335 | 5.146 | 4.968 |
| 9 | 8.566 | 8.162 | 7.786 | 7.435 | 7.108 | 6.802 | 6.515 | 6.247 | 5.995 | 5.759 | 5.537 | 5.328 |
| 10 | 9.471 | 8.983 | 8.530 | 8.111 | 7.722 | 7.360 | 7.024 | 6.710 | 6.418 | 6.145 | 5.889 | 5.650 |
| 11 | 10.368 | 9.787 | 9.253 | 8.760 | 8.306 | 7.887 | 7.499 | 7.139 | 6.805 | 6.495 | 6.207 | 5.938 |
| 12 | 11.255 | 10.575 | 9.954 | 9.385 | 8.863 | 8.384 | 7.943 | 7.536 | 7.161 | 6.814 | 6.492 | 6.194 |
| 13 | 12.134 | 11.348 | 10.635 | 9.986 | 9.394 | 8.853 | 8.358 | 7.904 | 7.487 | 7.103 | 6.750 | 6.424 |
| 14 | 13.004 | 12.106 | 11.296 | 10.563 | 9.899 | 9.295 | 8.745 | 8.244 | 7.786 | 7.367 | 6.982 | 6.628 |
| 15 | 13.865 | 12.849 | 11.939 | 11.118 | 10.380 | 9.712 | 9.108 | 8.559 | 8.061 | 7.606 | 7.191 | 6.811 |
| 16 | 14.718 | 13.578 | 12.561 | 11.652 | 10.838 | 10.106 | 9.447 | 8.851 | 8.313 | 7.824 | 7.379 | 6.974 |
| 17 | 15.562 | 14.292 | 13.166 | 12.166 | 11.274 | 10.477 | 9.763 | 9.122 | 8.544 | 8.022 | 7.549 | 7.102 |
| 18 | 16.398 | 14.992 | 13.754 | 12.659 | 11.690 | 10.828 | 10.059 | 9.372 | 8.756 | 8.201 | 7.702 | 7.250 |
| 19 | 17.226 | 15.678 | 14.324 | 13.134 | 12.085 | 11.158 | 10.336 | 9.604 | 8.950 | 8.365 | 7.839 | 7.366 |
| 20 | 18.046 | 16.351 | 14.877 | 13.590 | 12.462 | 11.470 | 10.594 | 9.818 | 9.129 | 8.514 | 7.963 | 7.469 |
| 25 | 22.023 | 19.523 | 17.413 | 15.622 | 14.094 | 12.783 | 11.654 | 10.675 | 9.823 | 9.077 | 8.422 | 7.843 |
| 30 | 25.808 | 22.396 | 19.600 | 17.292 | 15.372 | 13.765 | 12.409 | 11.258 | 10.274 | 9.427 | 8.694 | 8.055 |
| 40 | 32.835 | 27.355 | 23.115 | 19.793 | 17.159 | 15.046 | 13.332 | 11.925 | 10.757 | 9.779 | 8.951 | 8.244 |
| 50 | 39.196 | 31.424 | 25.730 | 21.482 | 18.256 | 15.762 | 13.801 | 12.233 | 10.962 | 9.915 | 9.042 | 8.304 |

**Appendix D (*concluded*) Present value of an annuity of $1**

| | Percent | | | | | | | | | | | | |
|---|---|---|---|---|---|---|---|---|---|---|---|---|---|
| Period | 13% | 14% | 15% | 16% | 17% | 18% | 19% | 20% | 25% | 30% | 35% | 40% | 50% |
| 1 | 0.885 | 0.877 | 0.870 | 0.862 | 0.855 | 0.847 | 0.840 | 0.833 | 0.800 | 0.769 | 0.741 | 0.714 | 0.667 |
| 2 | 1.668 | 1.647 | 1.626 | 1.605 | 1.585 | 1.566 | 1.547 | 1.528 | 1.440 | 1.361 | 1.289 | 1.224 | 1.111 |
| 3 | 2.361 | 2.322 | 2.283 | 2.246 | 2.210 | 2.174 | 2.140 | 2.106 | 1.952 | 1.816 | 1.696 | 1.589 | 1.407 |
| 4 | 2.974 | 2.914 | 2.855 | 2.798 | 2.743 | 2.690 | 2.639 | 2.589 | 2.362 | 2.166 | 1.997 | 1.849 | 1.605 |
| 5 | 3.517 | 3.433 | 3.352 | 3.274 | 3.199 | 3.127 | 3.058 | 2.991 | 2.689 | 2.436 | 2.220 | 2.035 | 1.737 |
| 6 | 3.998 | 3.889 | 3.784 | 3.685 | 3.589 | 3.498 | 3.410 | 3.326 | 2.951 | 2.643 | 2.385 | 2.168 | 1.824 |
| 7 | 4.423 | 4.288 | 4.160 | 4.039 | 3.922 | 3.812 | 3.706 | 3.605 | 3.161 | 2.802 | 2.508 | 2.263 | 1.883 |
| 8 | 4.799 | 4.639 | 4.487 | 4.344 | 4.207 | 4.078 | 3.954 | 3.837 | 3.329 | 2.925 | 2.598 | 2.331 | 1.922 |
| 9 | 5.132 | 4.946 | 4.772 | 4.607 | 4.451 | 4.303 | 4.163 | 4.031 | 3.463 | 3.019 | 2.665 | 2.379 | 1.948 |
| 10 | 5.426 | 5.216 | 5.019 | 4.833 | 4.659 | 4.494 | 4.339 | 4.192 | 3.571 | 3.092 | 2.715 | 2.414 | 1.965 |
| 11 | 5.687 | 5.453 | 5.234 | 5.029 | 4.836 | 4.656 | 4.486 | 4.327 | 3.656 | 3.147 | 2.752 | 2.438 | 1.977 |
| 12 | 5.918 | 5.660 | 5.421 | 5.197 | 4.988 | 4.793 | 4.611 | 4.439 | 3.725 | 3.190 | 2.779 | 2.456 | 1.985 |
| 13 | 6.122 | 5.842 | 5.583 | 5.342 | 5.118 | 4.910 | 4.715 | 4.533 | 3.780 | 3.223 | 2.799 | 2.469 | 1.990 |
| 14 | 6.302 | 6.002 | 5.724 | 5.468 | 5.229 | 5.008 | 4.802 | 4.611 | 3.824 | 3.249 | 2.814 | 2.478 | 1.993 |
| 15 | 6.462 | 6.142 | 5.847 | 5.575 | 5.324 | 5.092 | 4.876 | 4.675 | 3.859 | 3.268 | 2.825 | 2.484 | 1.995 |
| 16 | 6.604 | 6.265 | 5.954 | 5.668 | 5.405 | 5.162 | 4.938 | 4.730 | 3.887 | 3.283 | 2.834 | 2.489 | 1.997 |
| 17 | 6.729 | 6.373 | 6.047 | 5.749 | 5.475 | 5.222 | 4.988 | 4.775 | 3.910 | 3.295 | 2.840 | 2.492 | 1.998 |
| 18 | 6.840 | 6.467 | 6.128 | 5.818 | 5.534 | 5.273 | 5.033 | 4.812 | 3.928 | 3.304 | 2.844 | 2.494 | 1.999 |
| 19 | 6.938 | 6.550 | 6.198 | 5.877 | 5.584 | 5.316 | 5.070 | 4.843 | 3.942 | 3.311 | 2.848 | 2.496 | 1.999 |
| 20 | 7.025 | 6.623 | 6.259 | 5.929 | 5.628 | 5.353 | 5.101 | 4.870 | 3.954 | 3.316 | 2.850 | 2.497 | 1.999 |
| 25 | 7.330 | 6.873 | 6.464 | 6.097 | 5.766 | 5.467 | 5.195 | 4.948 | 3.985 | 3.329 | 2.856 | 2.499 | 2.000 |
| 30 | 7.496 | 7.003 | 6.566 | 6.177 | 5.829 | 5.517 | 5.235 | 4.979 | 3.995 | 3.332 | 2.857 | 2.500 | 2.000 |
| 40 | 7.634 | 7.105 | 6.642 | 6.233 | 5.871 | 5.548 | 5.258 | 4.997 | 3.999 | 3.333 | 2.857 | 2.500 | 2.000 |
| 50 | 7.675 | 7.133 | 6.661 | 6.246 | 5.880 | 5.554 | 5.262 | 4.999 | 4.000 | 3.333 | 2.857 | 2.500 | 2.000 |

Source: Maurice Joy, *Introduction to Financial Management* (Homewood, Ill.: Richard D. Irwin, 1977).

| $N$ | $N^2$ | $\sqrt{N}$ | $\sqrt{10N}$ | $N$ | $N^2$ | $\sqrt{N}$ | $\sqrt{10N}$ |
|---|---|---|---|---|---|---|---|
| | | | | 50 | 2 500 | 7.071 068 | 22.36068 |
| 1 | 1 | 1.000 000 | 3.162 278 | 51 | 2 601 | 7.141 428 | 22.58318 |
| 2 | 4 | 1.414 214 | 4.472 136 | 52 | 2 704 | 7.211 103 | 22.80351 |
| 3 | 9 | 1.732 051 | 5.477 226 | 53 | 2 809 | 7.280 110 | 23.02173 |
| 4 | 16 | 2.000 000 | 6.324 555 | 54 | 2 916 | 7.348 469 | 23.23790 |
| 5 | 25 | 2.236 068 | 7.071 068 | 55 | 3 025 | 7.416 198 | 23.45208 |
| 6 | 36 | 2.449 490 | 7.745 967 | 56 | 3 136 | 7.483 315 | 23.66432 |
| 7 | 49 | 2.645 751 | 8.366 600 | 57 | 3 249 | 7.549 834 | 23.87467 |
| 8 | 64 | 2.828 427 | 8.944 272 | 58 | 3 364 | 7.615 773 | 24.08319 |
| 9 | 81 | 3.000 000 | 9.486 833 | 59 | 3 481 | 7.681 146 | 24.28992 |
| 10 | 100 | 3.162 278 | 10.00000 | 60 | 3 600 | 7.745 967 | 24.49490 |
| 11 | 121 | 3.316 625 | 10.48809 | 61 | 3 721 | 7.810 250 | 24.69818 |
| 12 | 144 | 3.464 102 | 10.95445 | 62 | 3 844 | 7.874 008 | 24.89980 |
| 13 | 169 | 3.605 551 | 11.40175 | 63 | 3 969 | 7.937 254 | 25.09980 |
| 14 | 196 | 3.741 657 | 11.83216 | 64 | 4 096 | 8.000 000 | 25.29822 |
| 15 | 225 | 3.872 983 | 12.24745 | 65 | 4 225 | 8.062 258 | 25.49510 |
| 16 | 256 | 4.000 000 | 12.64911 | 66 | 4 356 | 8.124 038 | 25.69047 |
| 17 | 289 | 4.123 106 | 13.03840 | 67 | 4 489 | 8.185 353 | 25.88436 |
| 18 | 324 | 4.242 641 | 13.41641 | 68 | 4 624 | 8.246 211 | 26.07681 |
| 19 | 361 | 4.358 899 | 13.78405 | 69 | 4 761 | 8.306 824 | 26.26785 |
| 20 | 400 | 4.472 136 | 14.14214 | 70 | 4 900 | 8.366 600 | 26.45751 |
| 21 | 441 | 4.582 576 | 14.49138 | 71 | 5 041 | 8.426 150 | 26.64583 |
| 22 | 484 | 4.690 416 | 14.83240 | 72 | 5 184 | 8.485 281 | 26.83282 |
| 23 | 529 | 4.795 832 | 15.16575 | 73 | 5 329 | 8.544 004 | 27.01851 |
| 24 | 576 | 4.898 979 | 15.49193 | 74 | 5 476 | 8.602 325 | 27.20294 |
| 25 | 625 | 5.000 000 | 15.81139 | 75 | 5 625 | 8.660 254 | 27.38613 |
| 26 | 676 | 5.099 020 | 16.12452 | 76 | 5 776 | 8.717 798 | 27.56810 |
| 27 | 729 | 5.196 152 | 16.43168 | 77 | 5 929 | 8.774 964 | 27.74887 |
| 28 | 784 | 5.291 503 | 16.73320 | 78 | 6 084 | 8.831 761 | 27.92848 |
| 29 | 841 | 5.385 165 | 17.02939 | 79 | 6 241 | 8.888 194 | 28.10694 |
| 30 | 900 | 5.477 226 | 17.32051 | 80 | 6 400 | 8.944 272 | 28.28427 |
| 31 | 961 | 5.567 764 | 17.60682 | 81 | 6 561 | 9.000 000 | 28.46050 |
| 32 | 1 024 | 5.656 854 | 17.88854 | 82 | 6 724 | 9.055 385 | 28.63564 |
| 33 | 1 089 | 5.744 563 | 18.16590 | 83 | 6 889 | 9.110 434 | 28.80972 |
| 34 | 1 156 | 5.830 952 | 18.43909 | 84 | 7 056 | 9.165 151 | 28.98275 |
| 35 | 1 225 | 5.916 080 | 18.70829 | 85 | 7 225 | 9.219 544 | 29.15476 |
| 36 | 1 296 | 6.000 000 | 18.97367 | 86 | 7 396 | 9.273 618 | 29.32576 |
| 37 | 1 369 | 6.082 763 | 19.23538 | 87 | 7 569 | 9.327 379 | 29.49576 |
| 38 | 1 444 | 6.164 414 | 19.49359 | 88 | 7 744 | 9.380 832 | 29.66479 |
| 39 | 1 521 | 6.244 998 | 19.74842 | 89 | 7 921 | 9.433 981 | 29.83287 |
| 40 | 1 600 | 6.324 555 | 20.00000 | 90 | 8 100 | 9.486 833 | 30.00000 |
| 41 | 1 681 | 6.403 124 | 20.24846 | 91 | 8 281 | 9.539 392 | 30.16621 |
| 42 | 1 764 | 6.480 741 | 20.49390 | 92 | 8 464 | 9.591 663 | 30.33150 |
| 43 | 1 849 | 6.557 439 | 20.73644 | 93 | 8 649 | 9.643 651 | 30.49590 |
| 44 | 1 936 | 6.633 250 | 20.97618 | 94 | 8 836 | 9.695 360 | 30.65942 |
| 45 | 2 025 | 6.708 204 | 21.21320 | 95 | 9 025 | 9.746 794 | 30.82207 |
| 46 | 2 116 | 6.782 330 | 21.44761 | 96 | 9 216 | 9.797 959 | 30.98387 |
| 47 | 2 209 | 6.855 655 | 21.67948 | 97 | 9 409 | 9.848 858 | 31.14482 |
| 48 | 2 304 | 6.928 203 | 21.90890 | 98 | 9 604 | 9.899 495 | 31.30495 |
| 49 | 2 401 | 7.000 000 | 22.13594 | 99 | 9 801 | 9.949 874 | 31.46427 |
| 50 | 2 500 | 7.071 068 | 22.36068 | 100 | 10 000 | 10.00000 | 31.62278 |

| $N$ | $N^2$ | $\sqrt{N}$ | $\sqrt{10N}$ | $N$ | $N^2$ | $\sqrt{N}$ | $\sqrt{10N}$ |
|---|---|---|---|---|---|---|---|
| 100 | 10 000 | 10.00000 | 31.62278 | 150 | 22 500 | 12.24745 | 38.72983 |
| 101 | 10 201 | 10.04988 | 31.78050 | 151 | 22 801 | 12.28821 | 38.85872 |
| 102 | 10 404 | 10.09950 | 31.93744 | 152 | 23 104 | 12.32883 | 39.98718 |
| 103 | 10 609 | 10.14889 | 32.09361 | 153 | 23 409 | 12.36932 | 39.11521 |
| 104 | 10 816 | 10.19804 | 32.24903 | 154 | 23 716 | 12.40967 | 39.24283 |
| 105 | 11 025 | 10.24695 | 32.40370 | 155 | 24 025 | 12.44990 | 39.37004 |
| 106 | 11 236 | 10.29563 | 32.55764 | 156 | 24 336 | 12.45000 | 39.49684 |
| 107 | 11 449 | 10.34408 | 32.71085 | 157 | 24 649 | 12.52996 | 39.62323 |
| 108 | 11 664 | 10.39230 | 32.86335 | 158 | 24 964 | 12.56981 | 39.74921 |
| 109 | 11 881 | 10.44031 | 33.01515 | 159 | 25 281 | 12.60952 | 39.87480 |
| 110 | 12 100 | 10.48809 | 33.16625 | 160 | 25 600 | 12.64911 | 40.00000 |
| 111 | 12 321 | 10.53565 | 33.31666 | 161 | 25 921 | 12.68858 | 40.12481 |
| 112 | 12 544 | 10.58301 | 33.46640 | 162 | 26 244 | 12.72792 | 40.24922 |
| 113 | 12 769 | 10.63015 | 33.61547 | 163 | 26 569 | 12.76715 | 40.37326 |
| 114 | 12 996 | 10.67708 | 33.76389 | 164 | 26 896 | 12.80625 | 40.49691 |
| 115 | 13 225 | 10.72381 | 33.91165 | 165 | 27 225 | 12.84523 | 40.62019 |
| 116 | 13 456 | 10.77033 | 34.05877 | 166 | 27 556 | 12.88410 | 40.74310 |
| 117 | 13 689 | 10.81665 | 34.20526 | 167 | 27 889 | 12.92285 | 40.86563 |
| 118 | 13 924 | 10.86278 | 34.35113 | 168 | 28 224 | 12.96148 | 40.98780 |
| 119 | 14 161 | 10.90871 | 34.49638 | 169 | 28 561 | 13.00000 | 41.10961 |
| 120 | 14 400 | 10.95445 | 34.64102 | 170 | 28 900 | 13.03840 | 41.23106 |
| 121 | 14 641 | 11.00000 | 34.78505 | 171 | 29 241 | 13.07670 | 41.35215 |
| 122 | 14 884 | 11.04536 | 34.92850 | 172 | 29 584 | 13.11488 | 41.47288 |
| 123 | 15 129 | 11.09054 | 35.07136 | 173 | 29 929 | 13.15295 | 41.59327 |
| 124 | 15 376 | 11.13553 | 35.21363 | 174 | 30 276 | 13.19091 | 41.71331 |
| 125 | 15 625 | 11.18034 | 35.35534 | 175 | 30 625 | 13.22876 | 41.83300 |
| 126 | 15 876 | 11.22497 | 35.49648 | 176 | 30 976 | 13.26650 | 41.95235 |
| 127 | 16 129 | 11.26943 | 35.63706 | 177 | 31 329 | 13.30413 | 42.07137 |
| 128 | 16 384 | 11.31371 | 35.77709 | 178 | 31 684 | 13.34166 | 42.19005 |
| 129 | 16 641 | 11.35782 | 35.91657 | 179 | 32 041 | 13.37909 | 42.30839 |
| 130 | 16 900 | 11.40175 | 36.05551 | 180 | 32 400 | 13.41641 | 42.42641 |
| 131 | 17 161 | 11.44552 | 36.19392 | 181 | 32 761 | 13.45362 | 42.54409 |
| 132 | 17 424 | 11.48913 | 36.33180 | 182 | 33 124 | 13.49074 | 42.66146 |
| 133 | 17 689 | 11.53256 | 36.46917 | 183 | 33 489 | 13.52775 | 42.77850 |
| 134 | 17 956 | 11.57584 | 36.60601 | 184 | 33 856 | 13.56466 | 42.89522 |
| 135 | 18 225 | 11.61895 | 36.74235 | 185 | 34 225 | 13.60147 | 43.01163 |
| 136 | 18 496 | 11.66190 | 36.87818 | 186 | 34 596 | 13.63818 | 43.12772 |
| 137 | 18 769 | 11.70470 | 37.01351 | 187 | 34 969 | 13.67479 | 43.24350 |
| 138 | 19 044 | 11.74734 | 37.14835 | 188 | 35 344 | 13.71131 | 43.35897 |
| 139 | 19 321 | 11.78983 | 37.28270 | 189 | 35 721 | 13.74773 | 43.47413 |
| 140 | 19 600 | 11.83216 | 37.41657 | 190 | 36 100 | 13.78405 | 43.58899 |
| 141 | 19 881 | 11.87434 | 37.54997 | 191 | 36 481 | 13.82027 | 43.70355 |
| 142 | 20 164 | 11.91638 | 37.68289 | 192 | 36 864 | 13.85641 | 43.81780 |
| 143 | 20 449 | 11.95826 | 37.81534 | 193 | 37 249 | 13.89244 | 43.93177 |
| 144 | 20 736 | 12.00000 | 37.94733 | 194 | 37 636 | 13.92839 | 44.04543 |
| 145 | 21 025 | 12.04159 | 38.07887 | 195 | 38 025 | 13.96424 | 44.15880 |
| 146 | 21 316 | 12.08305 | 38.20995 | 196 | 38 416 | 14.00000 | 44.27189 |
| 147 | 21 609 | 12.12436 | 38.34058 | 197 | 38 809 | 14.03567 | 44.38468 |
| 148 | 21 904 | 12.16553 | 38.47077 | 198 | 39 204 | 14.07125 | 44.49719 |
| 149 | 22 201 | 12.20656 | 38.60052 | 199 | 39 601 | 14.10674 | 44.60942 |
| 150 | 22 500 | 12.24745 | 38.72983 | 200 | 40 000 | 14.14214 | 44.72136 |

| $N$ | $N^2$ | $\sqrt{N}$ | $\sqrt{10N}$ | $N$ | $N^2$ | $\sqrt{N}$ | $\sqrt{10N}$ |
|---|---|---|---|---|---|---|---|
| 200 | 40 000 | 14.14214 | 44.72136 | 250 | 62 500 | 15.81139 | 50.00000 |
| 201 | 40 401 | 14.17745 | 44.83302 | 251 | 63 001 | 15.84298 | 50.09990 |
| 202 | 40 804 | 14.21267 | 44.94441 | 252 | 63 504 | 15.87451 | 50.19960 |
| 203 | 41 209 | 14.24781 | 45.05552 | 253 | 64 009 | 15.90597 | 50.29911 |
| 204 | 41 616 | 14.28296 | 45.16636 | 254 | 64 516 | 15.93738 | 50.39841 |
| 205 | 42 025 | 14.31782 | 45.27693 | 255 | 65 025 | 15.96872 | 50.49752 |
| 206 | 42 436 | 14.35270 | 45.38722 | 256 | 65 536 | 16.00000 | 50.59644 |
| 207 | 42 849 | 14.38749 | 45.49725 | 257 | 66 049 | 16.03122 | 50.69517 |
| 208 | 43 264 | 14.42221 | 45.60702 | 258 | 66 564 | 16.06238 | 50.79370 |
| 209 | 43 681 | 14.45683 | 45.71652 | 259 | 67 081 | 16.09348 | 50.89204 |
| 210 | 44 100 | 14.49138 | 45.82576 | 260 | 67 600 | 16.12452 | 50.99020 |
| 211 | 44 521 | 14.52584 | 45.93474 | 261 | 68 121 | 16.15549 | 51.08816 |
| 212 | 44 944 | 14.56022 | 46.04346 | 262 | 68 644 | 16.18641 | 51.18594 |
| 213 | 45 369 | 14.59452 | 46.15192 | 263 | 69 169 | 16.21727 | 51.28353 |
| 214 | 45 796 | 14.62874 | 46.26013 | 264 | 69 696 | 16.24808 | 51.38093 |
| 215 | 46 225 | 14.66288 | 46.36809 | 265 | 70 225 | 16.27882 | 51.47815 |
| 216 | 46 656 | 14.69694 | 46.47580 | 266 | 70 756 | 16.30951 | 51.57519 |
| 217 | 47 089 | 14.73092 | 46.58326 | 267 | 71 289 | 16.34013 | 51.67204 |
| 218 | 47 524 | 14.76482 | 46.69047 | 268 | 71 824 | 16.37071 | 51.76872 |
| 219 | 47 961 | 14.79865 | 46.79744 | 269 | 72 361 | 16.40122 | 51.86521 |
| 220 | 48 400 | 14.83240 | 46.90415 | 270 | 72 900 | 16.43168 | 51.96152 |
| 221 | 48 841 | 14.86607 | 47.01064 | 271 | 73 441 | 16.46208 | 52.05766 |
| 222 | 49 284 | 14.89966 | 47.11688 | 272 | 73 984 | 16.49242 | 52.15362 |
| 223 | 49 729 | 14.93318 | 47.22288 | 273 | 74 529 | 16.52271 | 52.24940 |
| 224 | 50 176 | 14.96663 | 47.32864 | 274 | 75 076 | 16.55295 | 52.34501 |
| 225 | 50 625 | 15.00000 | 47.43416 | 275 | 75 625 | 16.58312 | 52.44044 |
| 226 | 51 076 | 15.03330 | 47.53946 | 276 | 76 176 | 16.61325 | 52.53570 |
| 227 | 51 529 | 15.06652 | 47.64452 | 277 | 76 729 | 16.64332 | 52.63079 |
| 228 | 51 984 | 15.09967 | 47.74935 | 278 | 77 284 | 16.67333 | 52.72571 |
| 229 | 52 441 | 15.13275 | 47.85394 | 279 | 77 841 | 16.70329 | 52.82045 |
| 230 | 52 900 | 15.16575 | 47.95832 | 280 | 78 400 | 16.73320 | 52.91503 |
| 231 | 53 361 | 15.19868 | 48.06246 | 281 | 78 961 | 16.76305 | 53.00943 |
| 232 | 53 824 | 15.23155 | 48.16638 | 282 | 79 524 | 16.79286 | 53.10367 |
| 233 | 54 289 | 15.26434 | 48.27007 | 283 | 80 089 | 16.82260 | 53.19774 |
| 234 | 54 756 | 15.29706 | 48.37355 | 284 | 80 656 | 16.85230 | 53.29165 |
| 235 | 55 225 | 15.32971 | 48.47680 | 285 | 81 225 | 16.88194 | 53.38539 |
| 236 | 55 696 | 15.36229 | 48.57983 | 286 | 81 796 | 16.91153 | 53.47897 |
| 237 | 56 169 | 15.39480 | 48.68265 | 287 | 82 369 | 16.94107 | 53.57238 |
| 238 | 56 644 | 15.42725 | 48.78524 | 288 | 82 944 | 16.97056 | 53.66563 |
| 239 | 57 121 | 15.45962 | 48.88763 | 289 | 83 521 | 17.00000 | 53.75872 |
| 240 | 57 600 | 15.49193 | 48.98979 | 290 | 84 100 | 17.02939 | 53.85165 |
| 241 | 58 081 | 15.52417 | 49.09175 | 291 | 84 681 | 17.05872 | 53.94442 |
| 242 | 58 564 | 15.55635 | 49.19350 | 292 | 85 264 | 17.08801 | 54.03702 |
| 243 | 59 049 | 15.58846 | 49.29503 | 293 | 85 849 | 17.11724 | 54.12947 |
| 244 | 59 536 | 15.62050 | 49.39636 | 294 | 86 436 | 17.14643 | 54.22177 |
| 245 | 60 025 | 15.65248 | 49.49747 | 295 | 87 025 | 17.17556 | 54.31390 |
| 246 | 60 516 | 15.68439 | 49.59839 | 296 | 87 616 | 17.20465 | 54.40588 |
| 247 | 61 009 | 15.71623 | 49.69909 | 297 | 88 209 | 17.23369 | 54.49771 |
| 248 | 61 504 | 15.74802 | 49.79960 | 298 | 88 804 | 17.26268 | 54.58938 |
| 249 | 62 001 | 15.77973 | 49.89990 | 299 | 89 401 | 17.29162 | 54.68089 |
| 250 | 62 500 | 15.81139 | 50.00000 | 300 | 90 000 | 17.32051 | 54.77226 |

| $N$ | $N^2$ | $\sqrt{N}$ | $\sqrt{10N}$ | $N$ | $N^2$ | $\sqrt{N}$ | $\sqrt{10N}$ |
|---|---|---|---|---|---|---|---|
| 300 | 90 000 | 17.32051 | 54.77226 | 350 | 122 500 | 18.70829 | 59.16080 |
| 301 | 90 601 | 17.34935 | 54.86347 | 351 | 123 201 | 18.73499 | 59.24525 |
| 302 | 91 204 | 17.37815 | 54.95453 | 352 | 123 904 | 18.76166 | 59.32959 |
| 303 | 91 809 | 17.40690 | 55.04544 | 353 | 124 609 | 18.78829 | 59.41380 |
| 304 | 92 416 | 17.43560 | 55.13620 | 354 | 125 316 | 18.81489 | 59.49790 |
| 305 | 93 025 | 17.46425 | 55.22681 | 355 | 126 025 | 18.84144 | 59.58188 |
| 306 | 93 636 | 17.49288 | 55.31727 | 356 | 126 736 | 18.86796 | 59.66574 |
| 307 | 94 249 | 17.52142 | 55.40758 | 357 | 127 449 | 18.89444 | 59.74948 |
| 308 | 94 864 | 17.54993 | 55.49775 | 358 | 128 164 | 18.92089 | 59.83310 |
| 309 | 95 481 | 17.57840 | 55.58777 | 359 | 128 881 | 18.94730 | 59.91661 |
| 310 | 96 100 | 17.60682 | 55.67764 | 360 | 129 600 | 18.97367 | 60.00000 |
| 311 | 96 721 | 17.63519 | 55.76737 | 361 | 130 321 | 19.00000 | 60.08328 |
| 312 | 97 344 | 17.66352 | 55.85696 | 362 | 131 044 | 19.02630 | 60.16644 |
| 313 | 97 969 | 17.69181 | 55.94640 | 363 | 131 769 | 19.05256 | 60.24948 |
| 314 | 98 596 | 17.72005 | 56.03670 | 364 | 132 496 | 19.07878 | 60.33241 |
| 315 | 99 225 | 17.74824 | 56.12486 | 365 | 133 225 | 19.10497 | 60.41523 |
| 316 | 99 856 | 17.77639 | 56.21388 | 366 | 133 956 | 19.13113 | 60.49793 |
| 317 | 100 489 | 17.80449 | 56.30275 | 367 | 134 689 | 19.15724 | 60.58052 |
| 318 | 101 124 | 17.83255 | 56.39149 | 368 | 135 424 | 19.18333 | 60.66300 |
| 319 | 101 761 | 17.86057 | 56.48008 | 369 | 136 161 | 19.20937 | 60.74537 |
| 320 | 102 400 | 17.88854 | 56.56854 | 370 | 136 900 | 19.23538 | 60.82763 |
| 321 | 103 041 | 17.91647 | 56.65686 | 371 | 137 641 | 19.26136 | 60.90977 |
| 322 | 103 684 | 17.94436 | 56.74504 | 372 | 138 384 | 19.28730 | 60.99180 |
| 323 | 104 329 | 17.97220 | 56.83309 | 373 | 139 129 | 19.31321 | 61.07373 |
| 324 | 104 976 | 18.00000 | 56.92100 | 374 | 139 876 | 19.33908 | 61.15554 |
| 325 | 105 625 | 18.02776 | 57.00877 | 375 | 140 625 | 19.36492 | 61.23724 |
| 326 | 106 276 | 18.05547 | 57.09641 | 376 | 141 376 | 19.39072 | 61.31884 |
| 327 | 106 929 | 18.08314 | 57.18391 | 377 | 142 129 | 19.41649 | 61.40033 |
| 328 | 107 584 | 18.11077 | 57.27128 | 378 | 142 884 | 19.44222 | 61.48170 |
| 329 | 108 241 | 18.13836 | 57.35852 | 379 | 143 641 | 19.46792 | 61.56298 |
| 330 | 108 900 | 18.16590 | 57.44563 | 380 | 144 000 | 19.49359 | 61.64414 |
| 331 | 109 561 | 18.19341 | 57.53260 | 381 | 145 161 | 19.51922 | 61.72520 |
| 332 | 110 224 | 18.22087 | 57.61944 | 382 | 145 924 | 19.54483 | 61.80615 |
| 333 | 110 889 | 18.24829 | 57.70615 | 383 | 146 689 | 19.57039 | 61.88699 |
| 334 | 111 556 | 18.27567 | 57.79273 | 384 | 147 456 | 19.59592 | 61.96773 |
| 335 | 112 225 | 18.30301 | 57. 87918 | 385 | 148 225 | 19.62142 | 62.04837 |
| 336 | 112 896 | 18.33030 | 57.96551 | 386 | 148 996 | 19.64688 | 62.12890 |
| 337 | 113 569 | 18.35756 | 58.05170 | 387 | 149 769 | 19.67232 | 62.20932 |
| 338 | 114 224 | 18.38478 | 57.13777 | 388 | 150 544 | 19.69772 | 62.28965 |
| 339 | 114 921 | 18.41195 | 58.22371 | 389 | 151 321 | 19.72308 | 62.36986 |
| 340 | 115 600 | 18.43909 | 58.30952 | 390 | 152 100 | 19.74842 | 62.44998 |
| 341 | 116 281 | 18.46619 | 58.39521 | 391 | 152 881 | 19.77372 | 62.52999 |
| 342 | 116 694 | 18.49324 | 58.48077 | 392 | 153 664 | 19.79899 | 62.60990 |
| 343 | 117 649 | 18.52026 | 58.56620 | 393 | 154 449 | 19.82423 | 62.68971 |
| 344 | 118 336 | 18.54724 | 58.65151 | 394 | 155 236 | 19.84943 | 62.76942 |
| 345 | 119 025 | 18.57418 | 58.73670 | 395 | 156 025 | 19.87461 | 62.84903 |
| 346 | 119 716 | 18.60108 | 58.82176 | 396 | 156 816 | 19.89975 | 62.92853 |
| 347 | 120 409 | 18.62794 | 58.90671 | 397 | 157 609 | 19.92486 | 63.00794 |
| 348 | 121 104 | 18.65476 | 58.99152 | 398 | 158 404 | 19.94994 | 63.08724 |
| 349 | 121 801 | 18.68154 | 59.07622 | 399 | 159 201 | 19.97498 | 63.16645 |
| 350 | 122 500 | 18.70829 | 59.16080 | 400 | 160 000 | 20.00000 | 63.24555 |

**Appendix E** (*continued*) **Tables of squares and square roots**

| $N$ | $N^2$ | $\sqrt{N}$ | $\sqrt{10N}$ | $N$ | $N^2$ | $\sqrt{N}$ | $\sqrt{10N}$ |
|---|---|---|---|---|---|---|---|
| 400 | 160 000 | 20.00000 | 63.24555 | 450 | 202 500 | 21.21320 | 67.08204 |
| 401 | 160 801 | 20.02498 | 63.32456 | 451 | 203 401 | 21.23676 | 67.15653 |
| 402 | 161 604 | 20.04994 | 63.40347 | 452 | 204 304 | 21.26029 | 67.23095 |
| 403 | 162 409 | 20.07486 | 63.48228 | 453 | 205 209 | 21.28380 | 67.30527 |
| 404 | 163 216 | 20.09975 | 63.56099 | 454 | 206 116 | 21.30728 | 67.37952 |
| 405 | 164 025 | 20.12461 | 63.63961 | 455 | 207 025 | 21.33073 | 67.45369 |
| 406 | 164 836 | 20.14944 | 63.71813 | 456 | 207 936 | 21.35416 | 67.52777 |
| 407 | 165 649 | 20.17424 | 63.79655 | 457 | 208 849 | 21.37756 | 67.60178 |
| 408 | 166 464 | 20.19901 | 63.87488 | 458 | 209 764 | 21.40093 | 67.67570 |
| 409 | 167 281 | 20.22375 | 63.95311 | 459 | 210 681 | 21.42429 | 67.74954 |
| 410 | 168 100 | 20.24846 | 64.03124 | 460 | 211 600 | 21.44761 | 67.82330 |
| 411 | 168 921 | 20.27313 | 64.10928 | 461 | 212 521 | 21.47091 | 67.89698 |
| 412 | 169 744 | 20.29778 | 64.18723 | 462 | 213 444 | 21.49419 | 67.97058 |
| 413 | 170 569 | 20.32240 | 64.26508 | 463 | 214 369 | 21.51743 | 68.04410 |
| 414 | 171 396 | 20.34699 | 64.34283 | 464 | 215 296 | 21.54066 | 68.11755 |
| 415 | 172 225 | 20.37155 | 64.42049 | 465 | 216 225 | 21.56386 | 68.19091 |
| 416 | 173 056 | 20.39608 | 64.49806 | 466 | 217 156 | 21.58703 | 68.26419 |
| 417 | 173 889 | 20.42058 | 64.57554 | 467 | 218 089 | 21.61018 | 68.33740 |
| 418 | 174 724 | 20.44505 | 64.65292 | 468 | 219 024 | 21.63331 | 68.41053 |
| 419 | 175 561 | 20.46949 | 64.73021 | 469 | 219 961 | 21.65641 | 68.48357 |
| 420 | 176 400 | 20.49390 | 64.80741 | 470 | 220 900 | 21.67948 | 68.55655 |
| 421 | 177 241 | 20.51828 | 64.88451 | 471 | 221 841 | 21.70253 | 68.62944 |
| 422 | 178 084 | 20.54264 | 64.96153 | 472 | 222 784 | 21.72556 | 68.70226 |
| 423 | 178 929 | 20.56696 | 65.03845 | 473 | 223 729 | 21.74856 | 68.77500 |
| 424 | 179 776 | 20.59126 | 65.11528 | 474 | 224 676 | 21.77154 | 68.84706 |
| 425 | 180 625 | 20.61553 | 65.19202 | 475 | 225 625 | 21.79449 | 68.92024 |
| 426 | 181 476 | 20.63977 | 65.26808 | 476 | 226 576 | 21.81742 | 68.99275 |
| 427 | 182 329 | 20.66398 | 65.34524 | 477 | 227 529 | 21.84033 | 69.06519 |
| 428 | 183 184 | 20.68816 | 65.42171 | 478 | 228 484 | 21.86321 | 69.13754 |
| 429 | 184 041 | 20.71232 | 65.49809 | 479 | 229 441 | 21.88607 | 69.20983 |
| 430 | 184 900 | 20.73644 | 65.57439 | 480 | 230 400 | 21.90800 | 69.28203 |
| 431 | 185 761 | 20.76054 | 65.65059 | 481 | 231 361 | 21.93171 | 69.35416 |
| 432 | 186 624 | 20.78461 | 65.72671 | 482 | 232 324 | 21.95450 | 69.42622 |
| 433 | 187 489 | 20.80865 | 65.80274 | 483 | 233 280 | 21.97726 | 69.50820 |
| 434 | 188 356 | 20.83267 | 65.87868 | 484 | 234 256 | 22.00000 | 69.57011 |
| 435 | 189 225 | 20.85665 | 65.95453 | 485 | 235 225 | 22.02272 | 69.64194 |
| 436 | 190 096 | 20.88061 | 66.03030 | 486 | 236 196 | 22.04541 | 69.71370 |
| 437 | 190 969 | 20.90454 | 66.10598 | 487 | 237 169 | 22.06808 | 69.78530 |
| 438 | 191 844 | 20.92845 | 66.18157 | 488 | 238 144 | 22.09072 | 69.85700 |
| 439 | 192 721 | 20.95233 | 66.25708 | 489 | 239 121 | 22.11334 | 69.92853 |
| 440 | 193 600 | 20.97618 | 66.33250 | 490 | 240 100 | 22.13594 | 70.00000 |
| 441 | 194 481 | 21.00000 | 66.40783 | 491 | 241 081 | 22.15852 | 70.07139 |
| 442 | 195 364 | 21.02380 | 66.48308 | 492 | 242 064 | 22.18107 | 70.14271 |
| 443 | 196 249 | 21.04757 | 66.55825 | 493 | 243 049 | 22.20360 | 70.21396 |
| 444 | 197 136 | 21.07131 | 66.63332 | 494 | 244 036 | 22.22611 | 70.28513 |
| 445 | 198 025 | 21.09502 | 66.70832 | 495 | 245 025 | 22.24860 | 70.35624 |
| 446 | 198 916 | 21.11871 | 66.78323 | 496 | 246 016 | 22.27106 | 70.42727 |
| 447 | 199 809 | 21.14237 | 66.85806 | 497 | 247 009 | 22.29350 | 70.49823 |
| 448 | 200 704 | 21.16601 | 66.93280 | 498 | 248 004 | 22.31519 | 70.56912 |
| 449 | 201 601 | 21.18962 | 67.00746 | 499 | 249 001 | 22.33831 | 70.63993 |
| 450 | 202 500 | 21.21320 | 67.08204 | 500 | 250 000 | 22.36068 | 70.71068 |

| $N$ | $N^2$ | $\sqrt{N}$ | $\sqrt{10N}$ | $N$ | $N^2$ | $\sqrt{N}$ | $\sqrt{10N}$ |
|---|---|---|---|---|---|---|---|
| 500 | 250 000 | 22.36068 | 70.71068 | 550 | 302 500 | 23.45208 | 74.16198 |
| 501 | 251 001 | 22.38303 | 70.78135 | 551 | 303 601 | 23.47339 | 74.22937 |
| 502 | 252 004 | 22.40536 | 70.85196 | 552 | 304 704 | 23.49468 | 74.29670 |
| 503 | 253 009 | 22.42766 | 70.92249 | 553 | 305 809 | 23.51595 | 74.36397 |
| 504 | 254 016 | 22.44994 | 70.99296 | 554 | 306 916 | 23.53720 | 74.43118 |
| 505 | 255 025 | 22.47221 | 71.06335 | 555 | 308 025 | 23.55844 | 74.49832 |
| 506 | 256 036 | 22.49444 | 71.13368 | 556 | 309 136 | 23.57965 | 74.56541 |
| 507 | 257 049 | 22.51666 | 71.20393 | 557 | 310 249 | 23.60085 | 74.63243 |
| 508 | 258 064 | 22.53886 | 71.27412 | 558 | 311 364 | 23.62202 | 74.69940 |
| 509 | 259 081 | 22.56103 | 71.34424 | 559 | 312 481 | 23.64318 | 74.76630 |
| 510 | 260 100 | 22.58318 | 71.41428 | 560 | 313 600 | 23.66432 | 74.83315 |
| 511 | 261 121 | 22.60531 | 71.48426 | 561 | 314 721 | 23.68544 | 74.89993 |
| 512 | 262 144 | 22.62742 | 71.55418 | 562 | 315 844 | 23.70654 | 74.96666 |
| 513 | 263 169 | 22.64950 | 71.62402 | 563 | 316 969 | 23.72762 | 75.03333 |
| 514 | 264 196 | 22.67157 | 71.69379 | 564 | 318 096 | 23.74686 | 75.09993 |
| 515 | 265 225 | 22.69361 | 71.76350 | 565 | 319 225 | 23.76973 | 75.16648 |
| 516 | 266 256 | 22.71563 | 71.83314 | 566 | 320 356 | 23.79075 | 75.23297 |
| 517 | 267 289 | 22.73763 | 71.90271 | 567 | 321 489 | 23.81176 | 75.29940 |
| 518 | 268 324 | 22.75961 | 71.97222 | 568 | 322 624 | 23.83275 | 75.36577 |
| 519 | 269 361 | 22.78157 | 72.04165 | 569 | 323 761 | 23.85372 | 75.43209 |
| 520 | 270 400 | 22.80351 | 72.11103 | 570 | 324 900 | 23.87467 | 75.49834 |
| 521 | 271 441 | 22.82542 | 72.18033 | 571 | 326 041 | 23.89561 | 75.56454 |
| 522 | 272 484 | 22.84732 | 72.24957 | 572 | 327 184 | 23.91652 | 75.63068 |
| 523 | 273 529 | 22.86919 | 72.31874 | 573 | 328 329 | 23.93742 | 75.69676 |
| 524 | 274 576 | 22.89105 | 72.38784 | 574 | 329 476 | 23.95830 | 75.76279 |
| 525 | 275 625 | 22.91288 | 72.45688 | 575 | 330 625 | 23.97916 | 75.82875 |
| 526 | 276 676 | 22.93469 | 72.52586 | 576 | 331 776 | 24.00000 | 75.89466 |
| 527 | 277 729 | 22.95648 | 72.59477 | 577 | 332 929 | 24.02082 | 75.96052 |
| 528 | 278 784 | 22.97825 | 72.66361 | 578 | 334 084 | 24.04163 | 76.02631 |
| 529 | 279 841 | 23.00000 | 72.73239 | 579 | 335 241 | 24.06242 | 76.09205 |
| 530 | 280 900 | 23.02173 | 72.80110 | 580 | 336 400 | 24.08319 | 76.15773 |
| 531 | 281 961 | 23.04344 | 72.86975 | 581 | 337 561 | 24.10394 | 76.22336 |
| 532 | 283 024 | 23.06513 | 72.93833 | 582 | 338 724 | 24.12468 | 76.28892 |
| 533 | 284 089 | 23.08679 | 73.00685 | 583 | 339 889 | 24.14539 | 76.35444 |
| 534 | 285 156 | 23.10844 | 73.07530 | 584 | 341 056 | 24.16609 | 76.41989 |
| 535 | 286 225 | 23.13007 | 73.14369 | 585 | 342 225 | 24.18677 | 76.48529 |
| 536 | 287 296 | 23.15167 | 73.21202 | 586 | 343 396 | 24.20744 | 76.55064 |
| 537 | 288 369 | 23.17326 | 73.28028 | 587 | 344 569 | 24.22808 | 76.61593 |
| 538 | 289 444 | 23.19483 | 73.34848 | 588 | 345 744 | 24.24871 | 76.68116 |
| 539 | 290 521 | 23.21637 | 73.41662 | 589 | 346 921 | 24.26932 | 76.74634 |
| 540 | 291 600 | 23.23790 | 73.48469 | 590 | 348 100 | 24.28992 | 76.81146 |
| 541 | 292 681 | 23.25941 | 73.55270 | 591 | 349 281 | 24.31049 | 76.87652 |
| 542 | 293 764 | 23.28089 | 73.62056 | 592 | 350 464 | 24.33105 | 76.94154 |
| 543 | 294 849 | 23.30236 | 73.68853 | 593 | 351 649 | 24.35159 | 77.00649 |
| 544 | 295 936 | 23.32381 | 73.75636 | 594 | 352 836 | 24.37212 | 77.07140 |
| 545 | 297 025 | 23.34524 | 73.82412 | 595 | 354 025 | 24.39262 | 77.13624 |
| 546 | 298 116 | 23.36664 | 73.89181 | 596 | 355 216 | 24.41311 | 77.20104 |
| 547 | 299 209 | 23.38803 | 73.95945 | 597 | 356 409 | 24.43358 | 77.26578 |
| 548 | 300 304 | 23.40940 | 74.02702 | 598 | 357 604 | 24.45404 | 77.33046 |
| 549 | 301 401 | 23.43075 | 74.09453 | 599 | 358 801 | 24.47448 | 77.39509 |
| 550 | 302 500 | 23.45208 | 74.16198 | 600 | 360 000 | 24.49490 | 77.45967 |

| $N$ | $N^2$ | $\sqrt{N}$ | $\sqrt{10N}$ | $N$ | $N^2$ | $\sqrt{N}$ | $\sqrt{10N}$ |
|---|---|---|---|---|---|---|---|
| 600 | 360 000 | 24.49490 | 77.45967 | 650 | 422 500 | 25.49510 | 80.62258 |
| 601 | 361 201 | 24.51530 | 77.52419 | 651 | 423 801 | 25.51470 | 80.68457 |
| 602 | 362 404 | 24.53569 | 77.58868 | 652 | 425 409 | 25.53240 | 80.80130 |
| 603 | 363 609 | 24.55606 | 77.65307 | 653 | 426 409 | 25.55386 | 80.80842 |
| 604 | 364 816 | 24.57641 | 77.71744 | 654 | 427 716 | 25.57342 | 80.87027 |
| 605 | 366 025 | 24.59675 | 77.78175 | 655 | 429 025 | 25.59297 | 80.93207 |
| 606 | 367 736 | 24.61707 | 77.84600 | 656 | 430 336 | 25.61250 | 80.99383 |
| 607 | 368 449 | 24.63737 | 77.91020 | 657 | 431 649 | 25.63201 | 81.05554 |
| 608 | 369 664 | 24.65766 | 77.97435 | 658 | 432 964 | 25.65151 | 81.11720 |
| 609 | 370 881 | 24.67793 | 78.03845 | 659 | 434 281 | 25.67100 | 81.17881 |
| 610 | 372 100 | 24.69818 | 78.10250 | 660 | 435 600 | 25.69047 | 81.24038 |
| 611 | 373 321 | 24.71841 | 78.16649 | 661 | 436 921 | 25.70992 | 81.30191 |
| 612 | 374 544 | 24.73863 | 78.23043 | 662 | 438 244 | 25.72936 | 81.36338 |
| 613 | 375 769 | 24.75884 | 78.29432 | 663 | 439 569 | 25.74879 | 81.42481 |
| 614 | 376 996 | 24.77902 | 78.35815 | 664 | 440 896 | 25.76820 | 81.48620 |
| 615 | 378 225 | 24.79919 | 78.42194 | 665 | 442 225 | 25.78759 | 81.54753 |
| 616 | 379 456 | 24.81935 | 78.48567 | 666 | 443 556 | 25.80698 | 81.60882 |
| 617 | 380 689 | 24.83948 | 78.54935 | 667 | 444 889 | 25.82634 | 81.67007 |
| 618 | 381 924 | 24.85961 | 78.61298 | 668 | 446 224 | 25.84570 | 81.73127 |
| 619 | 383 161 | 24.87971 | 78.67655 | 669 | 447 561 | 25.86503 | 81.79242 |
| 620 | 384 400 | 24.89980 | 78.74008 | 670 | 448 900 | 25.88436 | 81.85353 |
| 621 | 385 641 | 24.91987 | 78.80355 | 671 | 450 241 | 25.90367 | 81.91459 |
| 622 | 386 884 | 24.93993 | 78.86698 | 672 | 451 584 | 25.92296 | 81.97561 |
| 623 | 388 129 | 24.95997 | 78.93035 | 673 | 452 929 | 25.94224 | 82.03658 |
| 624 | 389 376 | 24.97999 | 78.99367 | 674 | 454 276 | 25.96151 | 82.09750 |
| 625 | 390 625 | 25.00000 | 79.05694 | 675 | 455 625 | 25.98076 | 82.15838 |
| 626 | 391 876 | 25.01999 | 79.12016 | 676 | 456 976 | 26.00000 | 82.21922 |
| 627 | 393 129 | 25.03997 | 79.18333 | 677 | 458 329 | 26.01922 | 82.28001 |
| 628 | 394 384 | 25.05993 | 79.24645 | 678 | 459 684 | 26.03843 | 82.34076 |
| 629 | 395 641 | 25.07987 | 79.30952 | 679 | 461 041 | 26.05763 | 82.40146 |
| 630 | 396 900 | 25.09980 | 79.37254 | 680 | 462 400 | 26.07681 | 82.46211 |
| 631 | 398 161 | 25.11971 | 79.43551 | 681 | 463 761 | 26.09598 | 82.52272 |
| 632 | 399 424 | 25.13961 | 79.49843 | 682 | 465 124 | 26.11513 | 82.58329 |
| 633 | 400 689 | 25.15949 | 79.56130 | 683 | 466 489 | 26.13427 | 82.64381 |
| 634 | 401 956 | 25.17936 | 79.62412 | 684 | 467 856 | 26.15339 | 82.70429 |
| 635 | 403 225 | 25.19921 | 79.68689 | 685 | 469 225 | 26.17250 | 82.76473 |
| 636 | 404 496 | 25.21904 | 79.74961 | 686 | 470 596 | 26.19160 | 82.82512 |
| 637 | 405 769 | 25.23886 | 79.81228 | 687 | 471 969 | 26.21068 | 82.88546 |
| 638 | 407 044 | 25.25866 | 79.87490 | 688 | 473 344 | 26.22975 | 82.94577 |
| 639 | 408 321 | 25.27845 | 79.93748 | 689 | 474 721 | 26.24881 | 83.00602 |
| 640 | 409 600 | 25.29822 | 80.00000 | 690 | 476 100 | 26.26785 | 83.06624 |
| 641 | 410 881 | 25.31798 | 80.06248 | 691 | 477 481 | 26.28688 | 83.12641 |
| 642 | 412 164 | 25.33772 | 80.12490 | 692 | 478 864 | 26.30589 | 83.18654 |
| 643 | 413 449 | 25.35744 | 80.18728 | 693 | 480 249 | 26.32489 | 83.24662 |
| 644 | 414 736 | 25.37716 | 80.24961 | 694 | 481 636 | 26.34388 | 83.30666 |
| 645 | 416 025 | 25.39685 | 80.31189 | 695 | 483 025 | 26.36285 | 83.36666 |
| 646 | 417 316 | 25.41653 | 80.37413 | 696 | 484 416 | 26.38181 | 83.42661 |
| 647 | 418 609 | 25.43619 | 80.43631 | 697 | 485 809 | 26.40076 | 83.48653 |
| 648 | 419 904 | 25.45584 | 80.49845 | 698 | 487 204 | 26.41969 | 83.54639 |
| 649 | 421 201 | 25.47548 | 80.56054 | 699 | 488 601 | 26.43861 | 83.60622 |
| 650 | 422 500 | 25.49510 | 80.62258 | 700 | 490 000 | 26.45751 | 83.66600 |

| $N$ | $N^2$ | $\sqrt{N}$ | $\sqrt{10N}$ | $N$ | $N^2$ | $\sqrt{N}$ | $\sqrt{10N}$ |
|---|---|---|---|---|---|---|---|
| 700 | 490 000 | 26.45751 | 83.66600 | 750 | 562 500 | 27.38613 | 86.60254 |
| 701 | 491 401 | 26.47640 | 83.72574 | 751 | 564 001 | 27.40438 | 86.66026 |
| 702 | 492 804 | 26.49528 | 83.78544 | 752 | 565 504 | 27.42262 | 86.71793 |
| 703 | 494 209 | 26.51415 | 83.84510 | 753 | 567 009 | 27.44085 | 86.77557 |
| 704 | 495 616 | 26.53300 | 83.90471 | 754 | 568 516 | 27.45906 | 86.83317 |
| 705 | 497 025 | 26.55184 | 83.96428 | 755 | 570 025 | 27.47726 | 86.89074 |
| 706 | 498 436 | 26.57066 | 84.02381 | 756 | 571 536 | 27.49545 | 86.94826 |
| 707 | 499 849 | 26.58947 | 84.08329 | 757 | 573 049 | 27.51363 | 87.00575 |
| 708 | 501 264 | 26.60827 | 84.14274 | 758 | 574 564 | 27.53180 | 87.06320 |
| 709 | 502 681 | 26.62705 | 84.20214 | 759 | 576 081 | 27.54995 | 87.12061 |
| 710 | 504 100 | 26.64583 | 84.26150 | 760 | 577 600 | 27.56810 | 87.17798 |
| 711 | 505 521 | 26.66458 | 84.32082 | 761 | 579 121 | 27.58623 | 87.23531 |
| 712 | 506 944 | 26.68333 | 84.38009 | 762 | 580 644 | 27.60435 | 87.29261 |
| 713 | 508 369 | 26.70206 | 84.43933 | 763 | 582 169 | 27.62245 | 87.34987 |
| 714 | 509 796 | 26.72078 | 84.49852 | 764 | 583 696 | 27.64055 | 87.40709 |
| 715 | 511 225 | 26.73948 | 84.55767 | 765 | 585 225 | 27.65863 | 87.46428 |
| 716 | 512 656 | 26.75818 | 84.61578 | 766 | 586 756 | 27.67671 | 87.52143 |
| 717 | 514 089 | 26.77686 | 84.67585 | 767 | 588 289 | 27.69476 | 87.57854 |
| 718 | 515 524 | 26.79552 | 84.73488 | 768 | 589 824 | 27.71281 | 87.63561 |
| 719 | 516 961 | 26.81418 | 84.79387 | 769 | 591 361 | 27.73085 | 87.69265 |
| 720 | 518 400 | 26.83282 | 84.85281 | 770 | 592 900 | 27.74887 | 87.74964 |
| 721 | 519 841 | 26.85144 | 84.91172 | 771 | 594 441 | 27.76689 | 87.80661 |
| 722 | 521 284 | 26.87006 | 84.97058 | 772 | 595 984 | 27.78489 | 87.86353 |
| 723 | 522 729 | 26.88866 | 85.02941 | 773 | 597 529 | 27.80288 | 87.92042 |
| 724 | 524 176 | 26.90725 | 85.08819 | 774 | 599 076 | 27.82086 | 87.97727 |
| 725 | 525 625 | 26.92582 | 85.14693 | 775 | 600 625 | 27.83882 | 88.03408 |
| 726 | 527 076 | 26.94439 | 85.20563 | 776 | 602 176 | 27.85678 | 88.09086 |
| 727 | 528 529 | 26.96294 | 85.26429 | 777 | 603 729 | 27.87472 | 88.14760 |
| 728 | 529 984 | 26.98148 | 85.32294 | 778 | 605 284 | 27.89265 | 88.20431 |
| 729 | 531 411 | 27.00000 | 85.38150 | 779 | 606 841 | 27.91057 | 88.26098 |
| 730 | 532 900 | 27.01851 | 85.44004 | 780 | 608 400 | 27.92848 | 88.31761 |
| 731 | 534 361 | 27.03701 | 85.49854 | 781 | 609 961 | 27.94638 | 88.37420 |
| 732 | 535 824 | 27.05550 | 85.55700 | 782 | 611 524 | 27.96426 | 88.43076 |
| 733 | 537 289 | 27.07397 | 85.61542 | 783 | 613 089 | 27.98214 | 88.48729 |
| 734 | 538 756 | 27.09243 | 85.67380 | 784 | 614 656 | 28.00000 | 88.54377 |
| 735 | 540 225 | 27.11088 | 85.73214 | 785 | 616 225 | 28.01785 | 88.60023 |
| 736 | 541 696 | 27.12932 | 85.79044 | 786 | 617 796 | 28.03569 | 88.65664 |
| 737 | 543 169 | 27.14774 | 85.84870 | 787 | 619 369 | 28.05352 | 88.71302 |
| 738 | 544 644 | 27.16616 | 85.90693 | 788 | 620 944 | 28.07134 | 88.76936 |
| 739 | 546 121 | 27.18455 | 85.96511 | 789 | 622 521 | 28.08914 | 88.82567 |
| 740 | 547 600 | 27.20294 | 86.02325 | 790 | 624 100 | 28.10694 | 88.88194 |
| 741 | 549 081 | 27.22132 | 86.08136 | 791 | 625 681 | 28.12472 | 88.93818 |
| 742 | 550 564 | 27.23968 | 86.13942 | 792 | 627 264 | 28.14249 | 88.99438 |
| 743 | 552 049 | 27.25803 | 86.20745 | 793 | 628 849 | 28.16026 | 89.05055 |
| 744 | 553 536 | 27.27636 | 86.25543 | 794 | 630 436 | 28.17801 | 89.10668 |
| 745 | 555 025 | 27.29469 | 86.31338 | 795 | 632 025 | 28.19574 | 89.16277 |
| 746 | 556 516 | 27.31300 | 86.37129 | 796 | 633 616 | 28.21347 | 89.21883 |
| 747 | 558 009 | 27.33130 | 86.42916 | 797 | 635 209 | 28.23119 | 89.27486 |
| 748 | 559 504 | 27.34959 | 86.48609 | 798 | 636 804 | 28.24889 | 89.33085 |
| 749 | 561 001 | 27.36786 | 86.54479 | 799 | 638 401 | 28.26659 | 89.38680 |
| 750 | 562 500 | 27.38613 | 86.60254 | 800 | 640 000 | 28.28427 | 89.44272 |

| $N$ | $N^2$ | $\sqrt{N}$ | $\sqrt{10N}$ | $N$ | $N^2$ | $\sqrt{N}$ | $\sqrt{10N}$ |
|---|---|---|---|---|---|---|---|
| 800 | 640 000 | 28.28427 | 89.44272 | 850 | 722 500 | 29.15476 | 92.19544 |
| 801 | 641 601 | 28.30194 | 89.49860 | 851 | 724 201 | 29.17190 | 92.24966 |
| 802 | 643 204 | 28.31960 | 89.55445 | 852 | 725 904 | 29.18904 | 92.30385 |
| 803 | 644 809 | 28.33725 | 89.61027 | 853 | 727 609 | 29.20616 | 92.35800 |
| 804 | 646 416 | 28.35489 | 89.66605 | 854 | 729 316 | 29.22328 | 92.41212 |
| 805 | 648 025 | 28.37252 | 89.72179 | 855 | 731 025 | 29.24038 | 92.46621 |
| 806 | 649 636 | 28.39014 | 89.77750 | 856 | 732 736 | 29.25748 | 92.52027 |
| 807 | 651 249 | 28.40775 | 89.83318 | 857 | 734 449 | 29.27456 | 92.57429 |
| 808 | 652 864 | 28.42534 | 89.88882 | 858 | 736 164 | 29.29164 | 92.62829 |
| 809 | 654 481 | 28.44293 | 89.94443 | 859 | 737 881 | 29.30870 | 92.68225 |
| 810 | 656 100 | 28.46050 | 90.00000 | 860 | 739 600 | 29.32576 | 92.73618 |
| 811 | 657 721 | 28.47806 | 90.05554 | 861 | 741 321 | 29.34280 | 92.79009 |
| 812 | 659 344 | 28.49561 | 90.11104 | 862 | 743 044 | 29.35984 | 92.84396 |
| 813 | 660 969 | 28.51315 | 90.16651 | 863 | 744 769 | 29.37686 | 92.89779 |
| 814 | 662 596 | 28.53069 | 90.22195 | 864 | 746 496 | 29.39388 | 92.95160 |
| 815 | 664 225 | 28.54820 | 90.27735 | 865 | 748 225 | 29.41088 | 93.00538 |
| 816 | 665 856 | 28.56571 | 90.33272 | 866 | 749 956 | 29.42788 | 93.05912 |
| 817 | 667 489 | 28.58321 | 90.38805 | 867 | 751 689 | 29.44486 | 93.11283 |
| 818 | 669 124 | 28.60070 | 90.44335 | 868 | 753 424 | 29.46184 | 93.16652 |
| 819 | 670 761 | 28.61818 | 90.49862 | 869 | 755 161 | 29.47881 | 93.22017 |
| 820 | 672 400 | 28.63564 | 90.55385 | 870 | 756 900 | 29.49576 | 93.27379 |
| 821 | 674 041 | 28.65310 | 90.60905 | 871 | 758 641 | 29.51271 | 93.32738 |
| 822 | 675 684 | 28.67054 | 90.66422 | 872 | 760 384 | 29.52965 | 93.38094 |
| 823 | 677 329 | 28.68798 | 90.71935 | 873 | 762 129 | 29.54657 | 93.43447 |
| 824 | 678 976 | 28.70540 | 90.77445 | 874 | 763 876 | 29.56349 | 93.48797 |
| 825 | 680 625 | 28.72281 | 90.82951 | 875 | 765 625 | 29.58040 | 93.54143 |
| 826 | 682 276 | 28.74022 | 90.88454 | 876 | 767 376 | 29.59730 | 93.59487 |
| 827 | 683 929 | 28.75761 | 90.93954 | 877 | 769 129 | 29.61419 | 93.64828 |
| 828 | 685 584 | 28.77499 | 90.99451 | 878 | 770 884 | 29.63106 | 93.70165 |
| 829 | 687 241 | 28.79236 | 91.04944 | 879 | 772 641 | 29.64793 | 93.75500 |
| 830 | 688 900 | 28.80972 | 91.10434 | 880 | 774 400 | 29.66479 | 93.80832 |
| 831 | 690 561 | 28.82707 | 91.15920 | 881 | 776 161 | 29.68164 | 93.86160 |
| 832 | 692 224 | 28.84441 | 91.21403 | 882 | 777 924 | 29.69848 | 93.91486 |
| 833 | 693 889 | 28.86174 | 91.26883 | 883 | 779 689 | 29.71532 | 93.96808 |
| 834 | 695 556 | 28.87906 | 91.32360 | 884 | 781 456 | 29.73214 | 94.02027 |
| 835 | 697 225 | 28.89637 | 91.37833 | 885 | 783 225 | 29.74895 | 94.07444 |
| 836 | 698 896 | 28.91366 | 91.43304 | 886 | 784 996 | 29.76575 | 94.12757 |
| 837 | 700 569 | 28.93095 | 91.48770 | 887 | 786 769 | 29.78255 | 94.10868 |
| 838 | 702 244 | 28.94823 | 91.54234 | 888 | 788 544 | 29.79933 | 94.23375 |
| 839 | 703 921 | 28.96550 | 91.59694 | 889 | 790 321 | 29.81610 | 94.28680 |
| 840 | 705 600 | 28.98275 | 91.65151 | 890 | 792 100 | 29.83287 | 94.33981 |
| 841 | 707 281 | 29.00000 | 91.70605 | 891 | 793 881 | 29.84962 | 94.39280 |
| 842 | 708 964 | 29.01724 | 91.76056 | 892 | 795 664 | 29.86637 | 94.44575 |
| 843 | 710 649 | 29.03446 | 91.81503 | 893 | 797 449 | 29.88311 | 94.49868 |
| 844 | 712 336 | 29.05168 | 91.86947 | 894 | 799 236 | 29.89983 | 94.55157 |
| 845 | 714 025 | 29.06888 | 91.92388 | 895 | 801 025 | 29.91655 | 94.60444 |
| 846 | 715 716 | 29.08608 | 91.97826 | 896 | 802 816 | 29.93326 | 94.65728 |
| 847 | 717 409 | 29.10326 | 92.03260 | 897 | 804 609 | 29.94996 | 94.71008 |
| 848 | 719 104 | 29.12044 | 92.08692 | 898 | 806 404 | 29.96665 | 94.76286 |
| 849 | 720 801 | 29.13760 | 92.14120 | 899 | 808 201 | 29.98333 | 94.81561 |
| 850 | 722 500 | 29.15476 | 92.19544 | 900 | 810 000 | 30.00000 | 94.86833 |

Appendix E (*concluded*) **Tables of squares and square roots**

| $N$ | $N^2$ | $\sqrt{N}$ | $\sqrt{10N}$ | $N$ | $N^2$ | $\sqrt{N}$ | $\sqrt{10N}$ |
|---|---|---|---|---|---|---|---|
| 900 | 810 000 | 30.00000 | 94.86833 | 950 | 902 500 | 30.82207 | 97.46794 |
| 901 | 811 801 | 30.01666 | 94.92102 | 951 | 904 401 | 30.83829 | 97.51923 |
| 902 | 813 604 | 30.03331 | 94.97368 | 952 | 906 304 | 30.85450 | 97.57049 |
| 903 | 815 409 | 30.04996 | 95.02631 | 953 | 908 209 | 30.87070 | 97.62172 |
| 904 | 817 216 | 30.06659 | 95.07891 | 954 | 910.116 | 30.88689 | 97.67292 |
| 905 | 819 025 | 30.08322 | 95.13149 | 955 | 912 025 | 30.90307 | 97.72410 |
| 906 | 820 836 | 30.09938 | 95.18403 | 956 | 913 936 | 30.91925 | 97.77525 |
| 907 | 822 649 | 30.11644 | 95.23655 | 957 | 915 849 | 30.93542 | 97.82638 |
| 908 | 824 464 | 30.13304 | 95.28903 | 958 | 917 764 | 30.95158 | 97.87747 |
| 909 | 826 281 | 30.14963 | 95.34149 | 959 | 919 681 | 30.96773 | 97.92855 |
| 910 | 828 100 | 30.16621 | 95.39392 | 960 | 921 600 | 30.98387 | 97.97959 |
| 911 | 829 921 | 30.18278 | 95.44632 | 961 | 923 521 | 31.00000 | 98.03061 |
| 912 | 831 744 | 30.19934 | 95.49869 | 962 | 925 444 | 31.01612 | 98.08160 |
| 913 | 833 569 | 30.21589 | 95.55103 | 963 | 927 369 | 31.03224 | 98.13256 |
| 914 | 835 396 | 30.23243 | 95.60335 | 964 | 929 296 | 31.04835 | 98.18350 |
| 915 | 837 225 | 30.24897 | 95.65563 | 965 | 931 225 | 31.06445 | 98.23441 |
| 916 | 839 056 | 30.26549 | 95.70789 | 966 | 933 156 | 31.08054 | 98.28530 |
| 917 | 840 889 | 30.28201 | 95.76012 | 967 | 935 089 | 31.09662 | 98.33616 |
| 918 | 842 724 | 30.29851 | 95.81232 | 968 | 937 024 | 31.11270 | 98.38699 |
| 919 | 844 561 | 30.31501 | 95.86449 | 969 | 938 961 | 31.12876 | 98.43780 |
| 920 | 846 400 | 30.33150 | 95.91663 | 970 | 940 900 | 31.14482 | 98.48858 |
| 921 | 848 241 | 30.34798 | 95.96874 | 971 | 942 841 | 31.16087 | 98.53933 |
| 922 | 850 084 | 30.36445 | 96.02083 | 972 | 944 784 | 31.17691 | 98.59006 |
| 923 | 851 929 | 30.38092 | 96.07289 | 973 | 946 729 | 31.19295 | 98.64076 |
| 924 | 853 776 | 30.39735 | 96.12492 | 974 | 948 676 | 31.20897 | 98.69144 |
| 925 | 855 625 | 30.41381 | 96.17692 | 975 | 950 625 | 31.22499 | 98.74209 |
| 926 | 857 476 | 30.43025 | 96.22889 | 976 | 952 576 | 31.24100 | 98.79271 |
| 927 | 859 329 | 30.44667 | 96.28084 | 977 | 954 529 | 31.25700 | 98.84331 |
| 928 | 861 184 | 30.46309 | 96.33276 | 978 | 956 484 | 31.27299 | 98.89388 |
| 929 | 863 041 | 30.47950 | 96.38465 | 979 | 958 441 | 31.28898 | 98.94443 |
| 930 | 864 900 | 30.49590 | 96.43651 | 980 | 960 400 | 31.30495 | 98.99495 |
| 931 | 866 761 | 30.51229 | 96.48834 | 981 | 962 361 | 31.32092 | 99.04544 |
| 932 | 868 624 | 30.52868 | 96.54015 | 982 | 964 324 | 31.33688 | 99.09591 |
| 933 | 870 489 | 30.54505 | 96.59193 | 983 | 966 144 | 31.34021 | 99.10321 |
| 934 | 872 356 | 30.56141 | 96.64368 | 984 | 968 256 | 31.36877 | 99.19677 |
| 935 | 874 225 | 30.57777 | 96.69540 | 985 | 970 225 | 31.38471 | 99.24717 |
| 936 | 876 096 | 30.59412 | 96.74709 | 986 | 972 196 | 31.40064 | 99.29753 |
| 937 | 877 969 | 30.61046 | 96.79876 | 987 | 974 169 | 31.41656 | 99.34787 |
| 938 | 879 844 | 30.62679 | 96.85040 | 988 | 976 144 | 31.43247 | 99.39819 |
| 939 | 881 721 | 30.64311 | 96.90201 | 989 | 978 121 | 31.44837 | 99.44848 |
| 940 | 883 600 | 30.65942 | 96.95360 | 990 | 980 100 | 31.46427 | 99.49874 |
| 941 | 885 481 | 30.67572 | 97.00515 | 991 | 982 081 | 31.48015 | 99.54898 |
| 942 | 887 364 | 30.69202 | 97.05668 | 992 | 984 064 | 31.49603 | 99.54920 |
| 943 | 889 249 | 30.70831 | 97.10819 | 993 | 986 049 | 31.51190 | 99.64939 |
| 944 | 891 136 | 30.72458 | 97.15966 | 994 | 988 036 | 31.52777 | 99.69955 |
| 945 | 893 025 | 30.74085 | 97.21111 | 995 | 990 025 | 31.54362 | 99.74969 |
| 946 | 894 916 | 30.75711 | 97.26253 | 996 | 992 016 | 31.55947 | 99.79980 |
| 947 | 896 809 | 30.77337 | 97.31393 | 997 | 994 009 | 31.57531 | 99.84989 |
| 948 | 898 704 | 30.78961 | 97.36529 | 998 | 996 004 | 31.59114 | 99.89995 |
| 949 | 900 601 | 30.80584 | 97.41663 | 999 | 998 001 | 31.60696 | 99.94999 |
| 950 | 902 500 | 30.82207 | 97.46794 | 1000 | 1 000 000 | 31.62278 | 100.00000 |

Source: From *Statistics: A Fresh Approach* by Sanders et al. Copyright © 1976 by McGraw-Hill, Inc. Used with permission of McGraw-Hill Book Company.

# Glossary

## A

**Accelerated Cost Recovery System (ACRS)** A system that specifies the allowable depreciation recovery period for different types of assets. The normal recovery period is generally shorter than that allowed before the passage of the 1981 Economic Recovery Tax Act.

**aging of accounts receivable** Analyzing accounts by the amount of time they have been on the books.

**American Depository Receipts (ADR)** These receipts represent the ownership interest in a foreign company's common stock. The shares of the foreign company are put in trust in a New York bank. The bank, in turn, issues its depository receipts to the American stockholders of the foreign firm. Many ADRs are listed on the NYSE and many more are traded in the over-the-counter market.

**American Stock Exchange (AMEX)** The second largest organized security exchange in the United States.

**annuity** A series of consecutive payments or receipts of equal amount.

**asset-based public offerings** Public offerings backed by receivables as collateral. Essentially, a firm factors (sells) its receivables in the securities markets.

**asset utilization ratios** A group of ratios that measures the speed at which the firm is turning over or utilizing its assets. We measure inventory turnover, fixed asset turnover, total asset turnover, and the average time it takes to collect accounts receivable.

**assignment** The liquidation of assets without going through formal court procedures. In order to affect an assignment, creditors must agree on liquidation values and the relative priority of claims.

**automated clearinghouse (ACH)** An ACH transfers information between one financial institution and another and from account to account via computer tape. There are approximately 30 regional clearinghouses throughout the United States that claim the membership of over 10,000 financial institutions.

**average collection period** The average amount of time accounts receivable have been on the books. It may be computed by dividing accounts receivable by average daily credit sales.

## B

**balance of payments** The term refers to a system of government accounts that catalogs the flow of economic transactions between countries.

**balance sheet** A financial statement that indicates what assets the firm owns, and how those assets are financed in the form of liabilities or ownership interest.

**banker's acceptance** Short-term securities that frequently arise from foreign trade. The acceptance is a draft that is drawn on a bank for approval for future payment and is subsequently presented to the payer.

**bankruptcy** The market value of a firm's assets are less than its liabilities, and the firm has a negative net worth. The term is also used to describe in-court procedures associated with the reorganization or liquidation of a firm.

**bear market** A falling or lethargic stock market. The opposite of a bull market.

**beta** A measure of the volatility of returns on an individual stock relative to the market. Stocks with a beta of 1.0 are said to have risk equal to that of the market (equal volatility). Stocks with betas greater than 1.0 have more risk than the market, while those with betas of less than 1.0 have less risk than the market.

**blanket inventory liens** A secured borrowing arrangement in which the lender has a general claim against the inventory of the borrower.

**bond ratings** Bonds are rated according to risk by Standard & Poor's and Moody's Investor Service. A bond that is rated Aaa by Moody's has the lowest risk, while a bond with a C rating has the highest risk. Coupon rates are greatly influenced by a corporation's bond rating.

**book value** (See net worth.)

**break-even analysis** A numerical and graphical technique that is used to determine at what point the firm will break even (revenue = cost). To compute the break-even point, we divide fixed costs by price minus variable cost per unit.

**brokers** Members of organized stock exchanges who have the ability to buy and sell securities on the floor of their respective exchanges. Brokers act as agents between buyers and sellers.

**bull market** A rising stock market. There are many complicated interpretations of this term, usually centering on the length of time that the market should be rising in order to meet the criteria for classification as a bull market. For our purposes a bull market exists when stock prices are strong and rising and investors are optimistic about future market performance.

## C

**call feature** Used for bonds and some preferred stock. A call allows the corporation to retire securities before maturity by forcing the bondholders to sell bonds back to it at a set price. The call provisions are included in the bond indenture.

**call premium** The premium paid by a corporation to call in a bond issue before the maturity date.

**capital** Sources of long-term financing that are available to the business firm.

**capital asset pricing model** A model that relates the risk-return trade-offs of individual assets to market returns. A security is presumed to receive a risk-free rate of return plus a premium for risk.

**capital gains taxes** Taxes on gains from holding assets. Long-term capital gains taxes apply to assets held for at least a year. The individual may exclude 60 percent of the gain from taxation and pay only the ordinary income tax rate on the remaining 40 percent.

**capital lease** A long-term, noncancelable lease that has many of the characteristics of debt. Under FASB *Statement No. 13*, the lease obligation must be shown directly on the balance sheet.

**capital markets** Competitive markets for equity securities or debt securities with maturities of more than one year. The best examples of capital market securities are common stock, bonds, and preferred stock.

**capital rationing** Occurs when a corporation has more dollars of capital budgeting projects with positive net present values than it has money to invest in them. Therefore, some projects that should be accepted are excluded because financial capital is rationed.

**carrying costs** The cost to hold an asset, usually inventory. For inventory, carrying costs include such items as interest, warehousing costs, insurance, and material-handling expenses.

**cash budget** A series of monthly or quarterly budgets that indicate cash receipts, cash payments, and the borrowing requirements for meeting financial requirements. It is constructed from the pro forma income statement and other supportive schedules.

**cash flow** A value equal to income after taxes plus noncash expenses. In capital budgeting decisions, the usual noncash expense is depreciation.

**certificates of deposit** A certificate offered by banks, savings and loans, and other financial institutions for the deposit of funds at a given interest rate over a specified time period.

**clientele effect** The effect of investor preferences for dividends or capital gains. Investors tend to purchase securities that meet their needs.

**coefficient of correlation** The degree of associated movement between two or more variables. Variables that move in the same direction are said to be positively correlated, while negatively correlated variables move in opposite directions.

**coefficient of variation** A measure of risk determination that is computed by dividing the standard deviation for a series of numbers by the expected value. Generally, the larger the coefficient of variation, the greater the risk.

**combined leverage** The total or combined impact of operating and financial leverage.

**commercial paper** An unsecured promissory note that large corporations issue to investors. The minimum amount is usually $25,000.

**common equity** The common stock or ownership capital of the firm. Common equity may be supplied through retained earnings or the sale of new common stock.

**common stock equivalent** Warrants, options, and any convertible securities that pay less than two thirds of the average Aa bond yield at the time of issue.

**common stockholder** Holders of common stock are the owners of the company. Common stockholders elect the members of the board of directors, who in turn help select the top management.

**compensating balances** A bank requirement that business customers maintain a minimum average balance. The required amount is usually computed as a percentage of customer loans outstanding or as a percentage of the future loans to which the bank has committed itself.

**composition** An out-of-court settlement in which creditors agree to accept a fractional settlement on their original claim.

**compound sum** The future value of a single amount or an annuity when compounded at a given interest rate for a specified time period.

**conglomerate** A corporation that is made up of many diverse, often unrelated divisions. This form of organization is thought to reduce risk, but may create problems of coordination.

**consolidation** The combination of two or more firms, generally of equal size and market power, to form an entirely new entity.

**constant dollar accounting** One of two methods of inflation-adjusted accounting that have been approved by the Financial Accounting Standards Board. Financial statements are adjusted to present prices, using the consumer price index. This is shown as supplemental information in the firm's annual report.

**consumer price index** An economic indicator published monthly by the U.S. Commerce Department. It measures the rate of inflation for consumer goods.

**contribution margin** The contribution to fixed costs from each unit of sales. The margin may be computed as price minus variable cost per unit.

**conversion premium** The market price of a convertible bond or preferred stock minus the security's conversion value.

**conversion price** The conversion ratio divided into the par value. The price of the common stock at which the security is convertible. An investor would usually not convert the security into common stock unless the market price were greater than the conversion price.

**conversion ratio** The number of shares of common stock an investor will receive if he exchanges a convertible bond or convertible preferred stock for common stock.

**conversion value** The conversion ratio multiplied by the market price per share of common stock.

**convertible security** A security that may be traded into the company for a different form or type of security. Convertible securities are usually bonds or preferred stock that may be exchanged for common stock.

**corporate stock repurchase** A corporation may repurchase its shares in the market as an alternative to paying a cash dividend. Earnings per share will go up, and if the price–earnings ratio remains the same, the stockholder will receive the same dollar benefit as through a cash dividend. Furthermore, the increase in stock price is a capital gain, whereas the cash dividend would be taxed as ordinary income. A corporation may also justify the repurchase of its stock because it is at a very low price or to maintain constant demand for the shares. Reacquired shares may be used for employee options or as part of a tender offer in a merger or acquisition. Firms may also reacquire part of their shares as a protective device against being taken over as a merger candidate.

**corporation** A form of ownership in which a separate, legal entity is created. A corporation may sue or be sued, engage in contracts and acquire property. It has a continual life and is not dependent on any one stockholder for maintaining its legal existence. A corporation is owned by stockholders who enjoy the privilege of limited liability. There is, however, the potential for double taxation in the corporate form of organization: the first time at the corporate level in the form of profits, and again at the stockholder level in the form of dividends.

**cost-benefit analysis** A study of the incremental costs and benefits that can be derived from a given course of action.

**cost of capital** The cost of alternative sources of financing to the firm. (See also weighted average cost of capital.)

**cost of goods sold** The cost specifically associated with units sold during the time period under study.

**coupon rate** The actual interest rate on the bond, usually payable in semiannual installments. The coupon rate normally stays constant during the life of the bond and indicates what the bondholder's annual dollar income will be.

**credit terms** The repayment provisions that are part of a credit arrangement. An example would be a 2/10, net 30 arrangement in which the customer may deduct 2 percent from the invoice price if payment takes place in the first ten days. Otherwise the full amount is due.

**cumulative preferred stock** If dividends from one period are not paid to the preferred stockholders, they are said to be in arrears and are then added to the next period's dividends. When dividends on preferred stock are in arrears, no dividends can legally be paid to the common stockholders. The cumulative dividend feature is very beneficial to preferred stockholders since it assures them that they will receive all dividends due before common stockholders can get any dividends.

**cumulative voting** Allows shareholders more than one vote per share. They are allowed to multiply their total shares by the number of directors being elected to determine their total number of votes. This system enables minority shareholders to elect directors even though they do not have 51 percent of the vote.

**currency futures contract** A futures contract that may be used for hedging or speculation in foreign exchange.

**current cost accounting** One of two methods of inflation-adjusted accounting approved by the Financial Accounting Standards Board in 1979. Financial statements are adjusted to the present, using current cost data rather than an index. This is shown as supplemental information in the firm's annual report.

**current yield** The yearly dollar interest payment divided by the current market price.

## D

**dealers** Participants in the market who transact security trades over-the-counter from their own inventory of stocks and bonds. They are often referred to as market makers since they stand ready to buy and sell their securities at quoted prices.

**debenture** A long-term unsecured corporate bond. Debentures are usually issued by large, prestigious firms having excellent credit ratings in the financial community.

**debt utilization ratios** A group of ratios that indicates to what extent debt is being used and the prudence with which it is being managed. Calculations include debt to total assets, times interest earned, and fixed charge coverage.

**decision tree** A tabular or graphical analysis that lays out the sequence of decisions that are to be made and highlights the differences between choices. The presentation resembles branches on a tree.

**declaration date** The day on which the board of directors officially states that a dividend will be paid.

**deferred annuity** An annuity that will not begin until some time period in the future.

**degree of combined leverage** A measure of the total combined effect of operating and financial leverage on earnings per share. The percentage change in earnings per share is divided by the percentage change in sales at a given level of operation. Other algebraic statements are also used, such as Formula 5–7 and footnote 3 in Chapter 5.

**degree of financial leverage** A measure of the impact of debt on the earnings capability of the firm. The percentage change in earnings per share is divided by the percentage change in earnings before interest and taxes at a given level of operation. Other algebraic statements are also used, such as Formula 5–5.

**degree of operating leverage** A measure of the impact of fixed costs on the operating earnings of the firm. The percentage change in operating income is divided by the percentage change in volume at a given level of operation. Other algebraic statements are also used, such as Formula 5–3 and footnote 2 in Chapter 5.

**dilution of earnings** This occurs when additional shares of stock are sold without creating an immediate increase in income. The result is a decline in earnings per share until earnings can be generated from the funds raised.

**discount rate** The interest rate at which future sums or annuities are discounted back to the present.

**discounted loan** A loan in which the calculated interest payment is subtracted or discounted in advance. Because this lowers the amount of available funds, the effective interest rate is increased.

**disinflation** A leveling off or slow down of price increases.

**dividend information content** This theory of dividends assumes that dividends provide information about the financial health and economic expectations of the company. If this is true, corporations must actively manage their dividends to provide the market with information.

**dividend payment date** The day on which a stockholder of record will receive his or her dividend.

**dividend payout** The percentage of dividends to earnings after taxes. It can be computed by dividing dividends per share by earnings per share.

**dividend record date** Stockholders owning the stock on the holder-of-record date are entitled to receive a dividend. In order to be listed as an owner on the corporate books, the investor must have bought the stock before it went ex-dividend.

**dividend reinvestment plans** Plans that provide the investor with an opportunity to buy additional shares of stock with the cash dividends paid by the company.

**dividend valuation model** A model for determining the value of a share of stock by taking the present value of an expected stream of future dividends.

**dividend yield** Dividends per share divided by market price per share. Dividend yield indicates the percentage return that a stockholder will receive on dividends alone.

**dual trading** Exists when one security, such as General Motors common stock, is traded on more than one stock exchange. This practice is quite common between NYSE-listed companies and regional exchanges.

**Dun & Bradstreet** A credit-rating agency that publishes information on over 3 million business establishments through its *Reference Book*.

**Du Pont System of Ratio Analysis** An analysis of profitability that breaks down return on assets between the profit margin and asset turnover. The second, or modified, version shows how return on assets is translated into return on equity through the amount of debt that the firm has. Actually return on assets is divided by (1 − debt/assets) to arrive at return on equity.

## E

**earnings per share** The earnings available to common stockholders divided by the number of common stock shares outstanding.

**economic indicators** Hundreds of indicators exist. Each is a specialized series of data. The data are analyzed for their relationship to economic activity, and the indicator is classified as either a lagging indicator, a leading indicator, or a coincident indicator of economic activity.

**economic ordering quantity (EOQ)** The most efficient ordering quantity for the firm. The EOQ will allow the firm to minimize the total ordering and carrying costs associated with inventory.

**efficient frontier** A line drawn through the optimum point selections in a risk–return trade-off diagram. Each point represents the best possible trade-off between risk and return (the highest return at a given risk level or the lowest risk at a given return level).

**efficient market hypothesis** Hypothesis which suggests that markets adjust very quickly to new information and that it is very difficult for investors to select portfolios of securities that outperform the market. The efficient market hypothesis may be stated in many different forms as indicated in Chapter 14.

**electronic funds transfer** A system in which funds are moved between computer terminals without the use of written checks.

**Employment Act of 1946** An act which specifies the four goals that the Federal Reserve Board should strive to achieve: economic growth, stable prices, high employment, and a balance of trade.

**Eurobonds** Bonds payable or denominated in the borrower's currency, but sold outside the country of the borrower, usually by an international syndicate.

**Eurodollar loan** A loan from a foreign bank denominated in dollars.

**Eurodollars** U.S. dollars held on deposit by foreign banks and loaned out by those banks to anyone seeking dollars.

**ex-dividend date** Four business days before the holder-of-record date. On the ex-dividend date the purchase of the stock no longer carries with it the right to receive the dividend previously declared.

**expectations theory of interest rates** This theory explains the shape of the term structure relative to expectations for future short-term interest rates. It is thought that long-term rates are an average of the expected short-term rates. Therefore, an upward-sloping yield curve would indicate that short-term rates will rise.

**expected value** A representative value from a probability distribution arrived at by multiplying each outcome by the associated probability and summing up the values.

**Export-Import Bank (Eximbank)** An agency of the United States government that facilitates the financing of United States exports through its miscellaneous programs. In its direct loan program, the Eximbank lends money to foreign purchasers of U.S. products—such as aircraft, electrical equipment, heavy machinery, computers, and the like. The Eximbank also purchases eligible medium-term obligations of foreign buyers of U.S. goods at a discount from face value. In this discount program, private banks and other lenders are able to rediscount (sell at a lower price) promissory notes and drafts acquired from foreign customers of U.S. firms.

**expropriation** The action of a country in taking away or modifying the property rights of a corporation or individual.

**ex-rights** The situation in which the purchase of common stock during a rights offering no longer includes rights to purchase additional shares of common stock.

**extension** An out-of-court settlement in which creditors agree to allow the firm more time to meet its financial obligations. A new repayment schedule will be developed, subject to the acceptance of creditors.

**external corporate funds** Corporate financing raised through sources outside of the firm. Bonds, common stock, and preferred stock fall in this category.

**external reorganization** A reorganization under the formal bankruptcy laws in which a merger partner is found for the distressed firm. Ideally, the firm should be merged with a strong firm in its own industry, although this is not always possible.

F

**factoring receivables** Selling accounts receivable to a finance company or a bank.

**federal budget deficit** Government expenditures are greater than government tax revenues, and the government must borrow to balance revenues and expenditures. These deficits act as an economic stimulus.

**federal budget surplus** Government tax receipts are greater than government expenditures. A rarity during the last 20 years. These surpluses have a dampening effect on the economy.

**federally sponsored agency securities** Securities issued by federal agencies such as the Federal Land Bank and Federal Home Loan Banks.

**Federal National Mortgage Association** A government agency that provides a secondary market in mortgages.

**Federal Reserve discount rate** The rate of interest that the Fed charges on loans to the banking system. A monetary tool for management of the money supply.

**field warehousing** An inventory financing arrangement in which collateralized inventory is stored on the premises of the borrower but is controlled by an independent warehousing company.

**FIFO** A system of writing off inventory into cost of goods sold in which the items purchased first are written off first. Referred to as first-in, first-out.

**Financial Accounting Standards Board** A privately supported rule-making body for the accounting profession.

**financial capital** Common stock, preferred stock, bonds, and retained earnings. Financial capital appears on the corporate balance sheet under long-term liabilities and equity.

**financial disclosure** Presentation of financial information to the investment community.

**financial futures market** A market that allows for the trading of financial instruments related to a future point in time. A purchase or sale takes place in the present, with a reversal necessitated in the future to close out the position. If a purchase (sale) takes place initially, then a sale (purchase) will be necessary in the future. The market provides for futures contracts in Treasury bonds, Treasury bills, certificates of deposits, GNMA certificates, and many other instruments. Financial futures contracts may be executed on the Chicago Board of Trade, the Chicago Mercantile Exchange, the New York Futures Exchange, and other exchanges.

**financial intermediary** A financial institution such as a bank or a life insurance company that directs other people's money into such investments as government and corporate securities.

**financial lease** A long-term noncancelable lease. The financial lease has all the characteristics of long-term debt except that the lease payments are a combination of interest expense and amortization of the cost of the asset.

**financial leverage** A measure of the amount of debt used in the capital structure of the firm.

**financial sweetener** Usually refers to equity options, such as warrants or conversion privileges, attached to a debt security. The sweetener lowers the interest cost to the corporation.

**fiscal policy** The tax policies of the federal government and the spending associated with its tax revenues.

**fixed costs** Costs that remain relatively constant regardless of the volume of operations. Examples are rent, depreciation, property taxes, and executive salaries.

**float** The difference between the corporation's recorded cash balance on its books and the amount credited to the corporation by the bank.

**floating rate bond** The interest payment on the bond changes with market conditions rather than the price of the bond.

**floating rate preferred stock** The quarterly dividend on the preferred stock changes with market conditions. The market price is considerably less volatile than it is with regular preferred stock.

**floor price** Usually equal to the pure bond value. A convertible bond will not sell at less than its pure bond value even when its conversion value is below the pure bond value.

**flotation cost** The distribution cost of selling securities to the public. The cost includes the underwriter's spread and any associated fees.

**forced conversion** Occurs when a company calls a convertible security that has a conversion value greater than the call price. Investors will take the higher of the two values and convert the security to common stock rather than take a lower cash call price.

**Foreign Credit Insurance Association (FCIA)** An agency established by a group of 60 U.S. insurance companies. It sells credit export insurance to interested exporters. The FCIA promises to pay for the exported merchandise if the foreign importer defaults on payment.

**foreign exchange rate** The relationship between the value of two or more currencies. For example, the exchange rate between U.S. dollars and French francs is stated as dollars per francs or francs per dollar.

**foreign exchange risk** A form of risk that refers to the possibility of experiencing a drop in revenue or an increase in cost in an international transaction due to a change in foreign exchange rates. Importers, exporters, investors, and multinational firms alike are exposed to this risk.

**founders' stock** Stock owned by the original founders of a company. It often carries special voting rights that allow the founders to maintain voting privileges in excess of their proportionate ownership.

**fourth market** A market of stocks and bonds in which there is direct dealing between financial institutions, such as investment bankers, insurance companies, pension funds, and mutual funds.

**fronting loan** A parent company's loan to a foreign subsidiary is channeled through a financial intermediary, usually a large international bank. The bank fronts for the parent in extending the loan to the foreign affiliate.

**fully diluted earnings per share** Equals adjusted earnings after taxes divided by shares outstanding, plus common stock equivalents, plus all convertible securities.

**futures contract** A contract to buy or sell a commodity at some specified price in the future.

G

**going private** The process by which all publicly owned shares of common stock are repurchased or retired, thereby eliminating listing fees, annual reports, and other expenses involved with publicly owned companies.

**golden parachute** Highly attractive termination payments made to current management in the event of a takeover of the company.

**goodwill** An intangible asset that reflects value above that generally recognized in the tangible assets of the firm.

H

**hedging** To engage in a transaction that partially or fully reduces a prior risk exposure by taking a position that is the opposite of your initial position. As an example, you buy some copper now but also engage in a contract to sell copper in the future at a set price.

**historical cost accounting** The traditional method of accounting in which financial statements are developed based on original cost minus depreciation.

**holding company** A company that has voting control of one or more other companies. It often has less than a 50 percent interest in each of these other companies.

**hurdle rate** The minimum acceptable rate of return in a capital budgeting decision.

**income statement** A financial statement that measures the profitability of the firm over a period of time. All expenses are subtracted from sales to arrive at net income.

**indenture** A legal contract between the borrower and the lender that covers every detail regarding a bond issue.

**indexing** An adjustment for inflation incorporated into the operation of an economy. Indexing may be used to revalue assets on the balance sheet and to automatically adjust wages, tax deductions, interest payments, and a wide variety of other categories to account for inflation.

**inflation** The phenomenon of price increase with the passage of time.

**inflation premium** A premium to compensate the investor for the eroding effect of inflation on the value of the dollar. In the 1980s the inflation premium has been 3 to 4 percent. In the late 1970s it was in excess of 10 percent.

**installment loan** A borrowing arrangement in which a series of equal payments are used to pay off the loan.

**interest factor (*IF*)** The tabular value to insert into the various formulas. It is based on the number of periods ($n$) and the interest rate ($i$).

**interest rate parity theory** A theory based on the interplay between interest rate differentials and exchange rates. If one country has a higher interest rate than another country after adjustments for inflation, interest rates and foreign exchange rates will adjust until the foreign exchange rates and money market rates reach equilibrium (are properly balanced between the two countries).

**internal corporate funds** Funds generated through the operations of the firm. The principal sources are retained earnings and cash flow added back from depreciation and other noncash deductions.

**internal rate of return (IRR)** A discounted cash flow method for evaluating capital budgeting projects. The IRR is a discount rate which makes the present value of the cash inflows equal to the present value of the cash outflows.

**internal reorganization** A reorganization under the formal bankruptcy laws. New management may be brought in and a redesign of the capital structure may be implemented.

**international diversification** Achieving diversification through many different foreign investments that are influenced by a variety of factors.

**International Finance Corporation (IFC)** An affiliate of the World Bank established with the sole purpose of providing partial seed capital for private ventures around the world. Whenever a multinational company has difficulty raising equity capital due to lack of adequate private risk capital, the firm may explore the possibility of selling equity or debt (totaling up to 25 percent) to the International Finance Corporation.

**inventory profits** Profits generated as a result of an inflationary economy in which old inventory is sold at large profits because of increasing prices. This is particularly prevalent under FIFO accounting.

**inverted yield curve** A downward-sloping yield curve. Short-term rates are higher than long-term rates.

**investment banker** A financial organization that specializes in selling primary offerings of securities. Investment bankers can also perform other financial functions, such as advising clients, negotiating mergers and takeovers, and selling secondary offerings.

**investment tax credit (ITC)** A percentage of the purchase price that may be deducted directly from tax obligations. Under the 1981 Economic Recovery Tax Act, a three-year recovery life asset is entitled to a 6 percent ITC. An asset with a life of five years or greater is entitled to an ITC of 10 percent.

L

**leading indicators** The most commonly followed series of economic indicators (a series of the 12 leading indicators). These are used to help forecast economic activity.

**lease** A contractual arrangement between the owner of equipment (lessor) and the user of equipment (lessee) which calls for the lessee to pay the lessor an established lease payment. There are two kinds of leases, financial leases and operating leases.

**letter of credit** A credit letter normally issued by the importer's bank in which the bank promises to pay out the money for the merchandise when delivered.

**level production** Equal monthly production used to smooth out production schedules and employ manpower and equipment more efficiently and at a lower cost.

**leverage** The use of fixed-charge items with the intent of magnifying the potential returns to the firm.

**leveraged buy-out** Existing management or an outsider makes an offer to "go private" by retiring all the shares of the company. The buying group borrows the necessary money, using the assets of the acquired firm as collateral. The buying group then repurchases all the shares and expects to retire the debt over time with the cash flow from operations or the sale of corporate assets.

**LIBOR** (See London Interbank Offered Rate.)

**life cycle curve** A curve illustrating the growth phases of a firm. The dividend policy most likely to be employed during each phase is often illustrated.

**LIFO** A system of writing off inventory into cost of goods sold in which the items purchased last are written off first. Referred to as last-in, first-out.

**limited partnership** A special form of partnership to limit liability for most of the partners. Under this arrangement, one or more partners are designated as general partners and have unlimited liability for the debts of the firm, while the other partners are designated as limited partners and are only liable for their initial contribution.

**liquidation** A procedure that may be carried out under the formal bankruptcy laws when an internal or external reorganization does not appear to be feasible, and it appears that the assets are worth more in liquidation than through a reorganization. Priority of claims becomes extremely important in a liquidation because it is unlikely that all parties will be fully satisfied in their demands.

**liquidity** The relative convertibility of short-term assets to cash. Thus, marketable securities are highly liquid assets, while inventory may not be.

**liquidity ratios** A group of ratios that allows one to measure the firm's ability to pay off short-term obligations as they come due. Primary attention is directed to the current ratio and the quick ratio.

**listing requirements** Financial standards that corporations must meet before their common stock can be traded on a stock exchange. Listing requirements are not standard, but are set by each exchange. The requirements for the NYSE are the most stringent.

**lockbox system** A procedure used to expedite cash inflows to a business. Customers are requested to forward their checks to a post-office box in their geographic region, and a local bank picks up the checks and processes them for rapid collection. Funds are then wired to the corporate home office for immediate use.

**London Interbank Offered Rate (LIBOR)** An interbank rate applicable for large deposits in the London market. It is a bench-mark rate just like the prime interest rate in the United States. Interest rates on Eurodollar loans are determined by adding premiums to this basic rate. Most often LIBOR is lower than the U.S. prime rate.

M

**majority voting** All directors must be elected by a vote of more than 50 percent. Minority shareholders are unable to achieve any representation on the board of directors.

**managing underwriter** An investment banker who is responsible for the pricing, prospectus development, and legal work involved in the sale of a new issue of securities.

**margin requirement** A rule that specifies the amount of cash or equity that must be deposited with a brokerage firm or bank, with the balance of funds eligible for borrowing. Margin is set by the Board of Governors of the Federal Reserve Board. For example, margin of 60 percent would mean that a $10,000 purchase would allow the buyer to borrow $4,000 toward the purchase.

**marginal corporate tax rate** The rate that applies to each new dollar of taxable income. For a corporation, the rate in 1986 is 15 percent on the first $25,000, 18 percent on the second $25,000, 30 percent on the third 25,000, 40 percent on the fourth $25,000, and 46 percent on all larger amounts.

**marginal cost of capital** The cost of the last dollar of funds raised. It is assumed that each dollar is financed in proportion to the firm's optimum capital structure.

**marginal principle of retained earnings** The corporation must be able to earn a higher return on its retained earnings than a stockholder would receive after paying taxes on the distributed dividends.

**market efficiency** Markets are considered to be efficient when (1) prices adjust rapidly to new information; (2) there is a continuous market in which each successive trade is made at a price close to the previous price (the faster the price responds to new information and the smaller the differences in price changes, the more efficient the market); and (3) the market can absorb large dollar amounts of securities without destabilizing the prices.

**market maker** (See dealers.)

**market risk premium** A premium over and above the risk-free rate. It is represented by the difference between the market return ($K_m$) and the risk-free rate ($R_f$), and it may be multiplied by the beta coefficient to determine additional risk-adjusted return on a security.

**market stabilization** Intervention in the secondary markets by an investment banker to stabilize the price of a new security offering during the offering period. The purpose of market stabilization is to provide an orderly market for the distribution of the new issue.

**market value maximization** The concept of maximizing the wealth of shareholders. This calls for a recognition not only of earnings per share but also how they will be valued in the marketplace.

**maturity date** The date on which the bond is retired and the principal (par value) is repaid to the lender.

**merger** The combination of two or more companies in which the resulting firms maintain the identity of the acquiring company.

**merger arbitrageur** A specialist in merger investments who attempts to capitalize on the difference between the value offered and the current market value of the acquisition candidate.

**merger premium** The part of a buy-out or exchange offer which represents a value over and above the market value of the acquired firm.

**minimum warrant value** The market value of the common stock minus the option price of the warrant multiplied by the number of shares of the common stock that each warrant entitles the holder to purchase.

**monetary policy** Management by the Federal Reserve Board of the money supply and the resultant interest rates.

**money market accounts** Accounts at banks, savings and loans, and credit unions in which the depositor receives competitive money market rates on a typical minimum deposit of $1,000. These accounts may generally have three deposits and three withdrawals per month, and are not meant to be transaction accounts, but a place to keep minimum and excess cash balances. These accounts are insured by various appropriate governmental agencies up to $100,000.

**money market funds** A fund in which investors may purchase shares for as little as $500 or $1,000. The fund then reinvests the proceeds in high-yielding $100,000 bank CDs, $25,000–$100,000 commercial paper, and other large-denomination, high-yielding securities. Investors receive their pro rata portion of the interest proceeds daily as a credit to their shares.

**money markets** Competitive markets for securities with maturities of one year or less. The best examples of money market instruments would be Treasury bills, commercial paper, and negotiable certificates of deposit.

**mortgage agreement** A loan which requires real property (plant and equipment) as collateral.

**multinational corporation** A firm doing business across its national borders is considered a multinational enterprise. Some definitions require a minimum percentage (often 30 percent or more) of a firm's business activities to be carried on outside its national borders.

**municipal securities** Securities issued by state and local government units. The income from these securities is exempt from federal income taxes.

**mutually exclusive** The selection of one choice precludes the selection of any competitive choice. For example, several machines can do an identical job in capital budgeting. If one machine is selected, the other machines will not be used.

## N

**National Market List** The list of the best-known and most widely traded securities in the over-the-counter market.

**national market system** A system mandated by the Securities Acts Amendments of 1975. The national market system that is envisioned will include computer processing and computerized competitive prices for all markets trading similar stocks. The exact form of the system is yet to be determined.

**net present value (NPV)** The NPV equals the present value of the cash inflows minus the present value of the cash outflows with the cost of capital used as a discount rate. This method is used to evaluate capital budgeting projects. If the NPV is positive, a project should be accepted.

**net present value profile** A graphical presentation of the potential net present values of a project at different discount rates. It is very helpful in comparing the characteristics of two or more investments.

**net trade credit** A measure of the relationship between the firm's accounts receivable and accounts payable. If accounts receivable exceed accounts payable, the firm is a net provider of trade credit; otherwise, it is a net user.

**net worth, or book value** Stockholders' equity minus preferred stock ownership. Basically, net worth is the common stockholders' interest as represented by common stock par value, capital paid in excess of par, and retained earnings. If you take all the assets of the firm and subtract its liabilities and preferred stock, you arrive at net worth.

**New York Stock Exchange (NYSE)** The largest organized security exchange in the United States. It also has the most stringent listing requirements.

**nominal GNP** GNP (gross national product) in current dollars without any adjustments for inflation.

**nominal yield** A return equal to the coupon rate.

**nonfinancial corporation** A firm not in the banking or financial services industry. The term would primarily apply to manufacturing, wholesaling, and retail firms.

**nonlinear break-even analysis** Break-even analysis based on the assumption that cost and revenue relationships to quantity may vary at different levels of operation. Most of our analysis is based on *linear* break-even analysis.

**normal recovery period** The depreciation recovery period (3, 5, 10, 15 years) under the Accelerated Cost Recovery System of the 1981 Economic Recovery Tax Act.

**normal yield curve** An upward-sloping yield curve. Long-term interest rates are higher than short-term rates.

## O

**open-market operations** The purchase and sale of government securities in the open market by the Federal Reserve Board for its own account. The most common method for managing the money supply.

**operating lease** A short-term, nonbinding obligation that is easily cancelable.

**operating leverage** A reflection of the extent to which fixed assets and fixed costs are utilized in the business firm.

**optimum capital structure** A capital structure that has the best possible mix of debt, preferred stock, and common equity. The optimum mix should provide the lowest possible cost of capital to the firm.

**Overseas Private Investment Corporation (OPIC)** A government agency that sells insurance policies to qualified firms. This agency insures against losses due to inconvertibility into dollars of amounts invested in a foreign country. Policies are also available from OPIC to insure against expropriation and against losses due to war or revolution.

**over-the-counter markets** Markets for securities (both bonds and stock) in which market makers, or dealers, transact purchases and sales of securities by trading from their own inventory of securities.

## P

**par value** Sometimes referred to as the face value or the principal value of the bond. Most bond issues have a par value of $1,000 per bond. Common and preferred stock may also have an assigned par value.

**parallel loan** A U.S. firm that wishes to lend funds to a foreign affiliate (such as a Dutch affiliate) locates a foreign parent firm (such as a Dutch parent firm) that wishes to loan money to a U.S. affiliate. Avoiding the foreign exchange markets entirely, the U.S. parent lends dollars to the Dutch affiliate in the United States, while the Dutch parent lends guilders to the American affiliate in the Netherlands. At maturity, the two loans would each be repaid to the original lender. Notice that neither loan carries any foreign exchange risk in this arrangement.

**participating preferred stock** A small number of preferred stock issues are participating with regard to corporate earnings. For such issues, once the common stock dividend equals the preferred stock dividend, the two classes of securities may share equally (or in some ratio) in additional dividend payments.

**partnership** A form of ownership in which two or more partners are involved. Like the sole proprietorship, a partnership arrangement carries unlimited liability for the owners. However, there is only single taxation for the partners, an advantage over the corporate form of ownership.

**payback** A value that indicates the time period required to recoup an initial investment. The payback does not include the time-value-of-money concept.

**percent-of-sales method** A method of determining future financial needs that is an alternative to the development of pro forma financial statements. We first determine the percentage relationship of various asset and liability accounts to sales, and then we show how that relationship changes as our volume of sales changes.

**permanent current assets** Current assets that will not be reduced or converted to cash within the normal operating cycle of the firm. Though from a strict accounting standpoint the assets should be removed from the current assets category, they generally are not.

**perpetuity** An investment without a maturity date.

**planning horizon** The length of time it takes to conceive, develop, and complete a project and to recover the cost of the project on a discounted cash flow basis.

**pledging receivables** Using accounts receivable as collateral for a loan. The firm usually may borrow 60 to 80 percent of the value of acceptable collateral.

**point-of-sales terminals** Computer terminals in retail stores that either allow digital input or use optical scanners. The terminals may be used for inventory control or other purposes.

**pooling of interests** A method of financial recording for mergers in which the financial statements of the firms are combined, subject to minor adjustments, and goodwill is *not* created.

**portfolio effect** The impact of a given investment on the overall risk–return composition of the firm. A firm must consider not only the individual investment characteristics of a project, but also how the project relates to the entire portfolio of undertakings.

**preemptive right** The right of current common stockholders to maintain their ownership percentage on new issues of common stock.

**preferred stock** A hybrid security combining some of the characteristics of common stock and debt. The dividends paid are not tax-deductible expenses for the corporation, as is true of the interest paid on debt.

**present value** The current or discounted value of a future sum or annuity. The value is discounted back at a given interest rate for a specified time period.

**price–earnings ratio** The multiplier applied to earnings per share to determine current value. The P/E ratio is influenced by the earnings and sales growth of the firm, the risk or volatility of its performance, the debt–equity structure, and other factors.

**primary earnings per share** Adjusted earnings after taxes divided by shares outstanding plus common stock equivalents.

**prime rate** The rate that the bank charges its most creditworthy customers.

**private placement** The sale of securities directly to a financial institution by a corporation. This eliminates the middleman and reduces the cost of issue to the corporation.

**profitability ratios** A group of ratios that indicates the return on sales, total assets, and invested capital. Specifically, we compute the profit margin (net income to sales), return on assets, and return on equity.

**pro forma balance sheet** A projection of future asset, liability, and stockholders' equity levels. Notes payable or cash is used as a plug or balancing figure for the statement.

**pro forma financial statements** A series of projected financial statements. Of major importance are the pro forma income statement, the pro forma balance sheet, and the cash budget.

**pro forma income statement** A projection of anticipated sales, expenses, and income.

**prospectus** A document that includes the important information that has been filed with the SEC through the registration statement. It contains the list of officers and directors, financial reports, potential users of funds, etc. It is for distribution to investors.

**public placement** The sale of securities to the public through the investment banker–underwriter process. Public placements must be registered with the Securities and Exchange Commission.

**public warehousing** An inventory financing arrangement in which inventory, used as collateral, is stored with and controlled by an independent warehousing company.

**purchase of assets** A method of financial recording for mergers in which the difference between the purchase price and the adjusted book value is recognized as goodwill and amortized over a maximum time period of 40 years.

**Purchasing power parity theory** A theory based on the interplay between inflation and exchange rates. A parity between the purchasing powers of two countries establishes the rate of exchange between the two currencies. Currency exchange rates, therefore, tend to vary inversely with their respective purchasing powers in order to provide the same or similar purchasing power.

**pure bond value** The value of the convertible bond if its present value is computed at a discount rate equal to interest rates on straight bonds of equal risk, without conversion privileges.

R

**real capital** Long-term productive assets (plant and equipment).

**real GNP** GNP (gross national product) in current dollars adjusted for inflation.

**real rate of return** The rate of return that an investor demands for giving up the current use of his or her funds on a noninflation-adjusted basis. It is payment for forgoing current consumption. Historically, the real rate of return demanded by investors has been of the magnitude of 2 to 3 percent. However, throughout the 1980s the real rate of return has been much higher; that is, 5 to 7 percent.

**refunding** The process of retiring an old bond issue before maturity and replacing it with a new issue. Refunding will occur when interest rates have fallen and new bonds may be sold at lower interest rates.

**regional stock exchanges** Organized exchanges outside of New York that list securities. Regional exchanges exist in San Francisco, Philadelphia, and a number of other U.S. cities.

**reinvestment assumption** An assumption must be made concerning the rate of return that can be earned on the cash flows generated by capital budgeting projects. The NPV method assumes the rate of reinvestment to be the cost of capital, while the IRR method assumes the rate to be the actual internal rate of return.

**repatriation of earnings** Returning earnings to the multinational parent company in the form of dividends.

**replacement cost** The cost of replacing the existing asset base at current prices as opposed to original cost.

**replacement cost accounting** Financial statements based on the present cost of replacing assets.

**required rate of return** That rate of return that investors demand from an investment (securities) to compensate them for the amount of risk involved.

**reserve requirements** The amount of funds that commercial banks must hold in reserve for each dollar of deposits. Reserve requirements are set by the Federal Reserve Board and are different for savings and checking accounts. Low reserve requirements are stimulating; high reserve requirements are restrictive.

**residual dividends** This theory of dividend payout states that a corporation will retain as much earnings as it may profitably invest. If any income is left after investments, it will pay dividends. This theory assumes that dividends are a passive decision variable.

**restructuring** Redeploying the asset and liability structure of the firm. This can be accomplished through repurchasing shares with cash or borrowed funds, acquiring other firms, or selling off unprofitable or unwanted divisions.

**rights offering** A sale of new common stock through a preemptive rights offering. Usually one right will be issued for every share held. A certain number of rights may be used to buy shares of common stock from the company at a set price that is lower than the market price.

**rights-on** The situation in which the purchase of a share of common stock includes a right attached to the stock.

**risk** A measure of uncertainty about the outcome from a given event. The greater the variability of possible outcomes, on both the high side and the low side, the greater the risk.

**risk-adjusted discount rate** A discount rate used in the capital budgeting process that has been adjusted upward or downward from the basic cost of capital to reflect the risk dimension of a given project.

**risk averse** An aversion or dislike for risk. In order to induce most people to take larger risks, there must be increased potential for return.

**risk-free rate of interest** Rate of return on an asset that carries no risk. U.S. Treasury bills are often used to represent this measure, although longer-term government securities have also proved appropriate in some studies.

**risk premium** A premium associated with the special risks of an investment. Of primary interest are two types of risk, business risk and financial risk. Business risk relates to the inability of the firm to maintain its competitive position and sustain stability and growth in earnings. Financial risk relates to the inability of the firm to meet its debt obligations as they come due. The risk premium will also differ (be greater or less) for different types of investments (bonds, stocks, etc.).

## S

**secondary offering** The sale of a large block of stock in a publicly traded company, usually by estates, foundations, or large individual stockholders. Secondary offerings must be registered with the SEC and will usually be distributed by investment bankers.

**secondary trading** The buying and selling of publicly owned securities in secondary markets such as the New York Stock Exchange and the over-the-counter markets.

**secured debt** A general category of debt which indicates that the loan was obtained by pledging assets as collateral. Secured debt has many forms and usually offers some protective features to a given class of bondholders.

**Securities Act of 1933** An act that is sometimes referred to as the truth in securities act because it requires detailed financial disclosures before securities may be sold to the public.

**Securities Acts Amendments of 1975** The major feature of this act was to mandate a national securities market. (See national market system.)

**Securities and Exchange Commission** The primary regulatory body for security offerings in the United States.

**Securities Exchange Act of 1934** Legislation that established the Securities and Exchange Commission (SEC) to supervise and regulate the securities markets.

**security market line** A line or equation that depicts the risk-related return of a security based on a risk-free rate plus a market premium related to the beta coefficient of the security.

**self-liquidating assets** Assets that are converted to cash within the normal operating cycle of the firm. An example is the purchase and sell-off of seasonal inventory.

**semiannual compounding** A compounding period of every six months. For example, a five-year investment in which interest is compounded semiannually would indicate an $n$ value equal to 10 and an $i$ value at one half the annual rate.

**semivariable costs** Costs that are partially fixed but still change somewhat as volume changes. Examples are utilities and "repairs and maintenance."

**serial bond** A bond issued by one company or municipality with a series of different maturity dates and interest rates that correspond to rates on competitive bonds with the same maturity and risk.

**shelf registration** A process which permits large companies to file one comprehensive registration statement (under SEC Rule 415), which outlines the firm's plans for future long-term financing. Then, when market conditions appear to be appropriate, the firm can issue the securities without further SEC approval.

**simulation** A method of dealing with uncertainty in which future outcomes are anticipated. The model may use random variables for inputs. By programming the computer to randomly select inputs from probability distributions, the outcomes generated by a simulation are distributed about a mean, and instead of generating one return or net present value, a range of outcomes with standard deviations is provided.

**sinking fund** A method for retiring bonds in an orderly process over the life of a bond. Each year or semiannually, a corporation sets aside a sum of money equal to a certain percentage of the total issue. These funds are then used by a trustee to purchase the bonds in the open market and retire them. This method will prevent the corporation from being forced to refund or raise a large amount of capital at maturity to retire the total bond issue.

**sole proprietorship** A form of organization that represents single-person ownership and offers the advantages of simplicity of decision making and low organizational and operating costs.

**sources and uses of funds statement** A statement of how changes in the balance sheet were financed over time. A source of funds is represented by an increase in stockholders' equity or liabilities as well as a decrease in assets. A use of funds is equated with a decrease in stockholders' equity or liabilities or an increase in assets.

**speculative warrant premium** The market price of the warrant minus the warrant's intrinsic value.

**spontaneous sources of funds** Funds arising through the normal course of business, such as accounts payable generated from the purchase of goods for resale.

**standard deviation** A measure of the spread or dispersion of a series of numbers around the expected value. The standard deviation tells us how well the expected value represents a series of values.

**step-up in conversion** A feature that is sometimes written into the contract which allows the conversion ratio to decline in steps over time. This feature encourages early conversion when the conversion value is greater than the call price.

**stock dividend** A dividend paid in stock rather than cash. A book transfer equal to the market value of the stock dividend is made from retained earnings to the capital stock and paid-in-capital accounts. The stock dividend may be symbolic of corporate growth, but it does not increase the total value of the stockholders' wealth.

**stock split** A divison of shares by a ratio set by the board of directors—2 for 1, 3 for 1, 3 for 2, and so on. Stock splits usually indicate that the company's stock has risen in price to a level that the directors feel limits the trading appeal of the stock. The par value is divided by the ratio set, and new shares are issued to the current stockholders of record to increase their shares to the stated level. For example, a two-for-one split would increase your holdings from one share to two shares.

**stockholders' equity** The total ownership position of preferred and common stockholders.

**stockholder wealth maximization** Maximizing the wealth of the firm's shareholders through achieving the highest possible value for the firm in the marketplace. It is the overriding objective of the firm and should influence all decisions.

**straight-line depreciation** A method of depreciation which takes the depreciable cost of an asset and divides it by the asset's useful life to determine the annual depreciation expense. Straight-line depreciation creates uniform depreciation expenses for each of the years in which an asset is depreciated.

**Subchapter S corporation** A special corporate form of ownership in which profit is taxed as direct income to the stockholders and thus is only taxed once as would be true of a partnership. The stockholders still receive all the organizational benefits of a corporation, including limited liability. The Subchapter S designation can only apply to corporations with up to 35 stockholders.

**subordinated debenture** An unsecured bond in which payment to the holder will take place only after designated senior debenture holders are satisfied.

**synergy** The recognition that the whole may be equal to more than the sum of the parts. The "2 + 2 = 5" effect.

## T

**tax loss carry-forward** A loss that can be carried forward for a number of years to offset future taxable income and perhaps be utilized by another firm in a merger or an acquisition.

**technical insolvency** A firm is unable to pay its bills as they come due.

**temporary current assets** Current assets that will be reduced or converted to cash within the normal operating cycle of the firm.

**tender offer takeover** An unfriendly acquisition which is not initially negotiated with the management of the target firm. A tender offer is usually made directly to the stockholders of the target firm.

**term loan** An intermediate-length loan in which credit is generally extended from one to seven years. The loan is usually repaid in monthly or quarterly installments over its life rather than the one single period.

**term structure of interest rates** The relationship between interest rates and maturities for securities of equal risk. Usually government securities are used for the term structure.

**terms of exchange** The buy-out ratio or terms of trade in a merger or an acquisition.

**third market** An over-the-counter market in listed securities. This market was created in the 1970s by traders who were attempting to buy and sell listed securities at lower commissions than could be obtained on the exchanges.

**tight money** A term to indicate time periods in which financing may be difficult to find and interest rates may be quite high by normal standards.

**trade credit** Credit provided by sellers or suppliers in the normal course of business.

**transaction exposure** Foreign exchange gains and losses resulting from *actual* international transactions. These may be hedged through the foreign exchange market, the money market, or the currency futures market.

**translation exposure** The foreign-located assets and liabilities of a multinational corporation, which are denominated in foreign currency units, and are exposed to losses and gains due to changing exchange rates. This is called accounting, or translation, exposure.

**Treasury bills** Short-term obligations of the federal government with maturities of up to one year.

**Treasury notes** Intermediate-term obligations of the federal government with maturities from three to five years.

**treasury stock** Corporate stock that has been reacquired by the corporation.

**trend analysis** An analysis of performance that is made over a number of years in order to ascertain significant patterns.

**trust receipt** An instrument acknowledging that the borrower holds the inventory and proceeds for sale in trust for the lender.

**two-step buy-out** An acquisition plan in which the acquiring company attempts to gain control by offering a very high cash price for 51 percent of the shares of the target company. At the same time the acquiring company announces a second lower price that will be paid, either in cash, stock or bonds, at a subsequent point in time.

U

**underwriting** The process of selling securities and, at the same time, assuring the seller a specified price. Underwriting is done by investment bankers and represents a form of risk taking.

**underwriting spread** The difference between the price that a selling corporation receives for an issue of securities and the price at which the issue is sold to the public. The spread is the fee that investment bankers and others receive for selling securities.

**underwriting syndicate** A group of investment bankers that is formed to share the risk of a security offering and also to facilitate the distribution of the securities.

**unsecured debt** A loan which requires no assets as collateral, but allows the bondholder a general claim against the corporation rather than a lien against specific assets.

## V

**variable costs** Costs that move directly with a change in volume. Examples are raw materials, factory labor, and sales commissions.

## W

**warrant** An option to buy securities at a set price for a given period of time. Warrants commonly have a life of one to five years or longer and a few are perpetual.

**warrant intrinsic value** (See minimum warrant value.)

**weighted average cost of capital** The computed cost of capital determined by multiplying the cost of each item in the optimal capital structure by its weighted representation in the overall capital structure and summing up the results.

**white knight** A firm that management calls upon to help it avoid an unwanted takeover offer. It is an invited suitor.

**working capital management** The financing and management of the current assets of the firm. The financial manager determines the mix between temporary and permanent "current assets" and the nature of the financing arrangement.

## Y

**yield** The interest rate that equates a future value or an annuity to a given present value.

**yield curve** A curve that shows interest rates at a specific point in time for all securities having equal risk but different maturity dates. Usually government securities are used to construct such curves. The yield curve is also referred to as the term structure of interest rates.

**yield to maturity** The required rate of return on a bond issue. It is the discount rate used in present-valuing future interest payments and the principal payment at maturity. It is used interchangeably with market rate of interest.

Z

**zero-coupon rate bond** A bond that is sold at a deep discount from face value. The return to the investor is the difference between the investor's cost and the face value received at the end of the life of the bond.

# Index

## A

## K–L

## Q–R

*This book has been set Compugraphic in 10.5 Plantin Roman, leaded 2.5 points. Part numbers are 84 point Helvetica Bold Outline and part titles are 30 point Helvetica Bold. Chapter numbers and titles are 36 and 24 point Helvetica Bold. The size of the type page is 26 by 46 picas.*